Readings in Western Civilization

ᘓ   **Vere dignum**

University of Chicago Readings in Western Civilization
John W. Boyer and Julius Kirshner, General Editors

1. **The Greek Polis**
   Edited by Arthur W. H. Adkins and Peter White

2. **Rome: Late Republic and Principate**
   Edited by Walter Emil Kaegi, Jr., and Peter White

3. **The Church in the Roman Empire**
   Edited by Karl F. Morrison

4. **Medieval Europe**
   Edited by Julius Kirshner and Karl F. Morrison

5. **The Renaissance**
   Edited by Eric Cochrane and Julius Kirshner

6. **Early Modern Europe: Crisis of Authority**
   Edited by Eric Cochrane, Charles M. Gray, and Mark A. Kishlansky

7. **The Old Regime and the French Revolution**
   Edited by Keith Michael Baker

8. **Nineteenth-Century Europe: Liberalism and Its Critics**
   Edited by Jan Goldstein and John W. Boyer

9. **Twentieth-Century Europe**
   Edited by John W. Boyer and Jan Goldstein

University of Chicago
Readings in Western Civilization

John W. Boyer and Julius Kirshner, General Editors

7
The Old Regime and the French Revolution

Edited by Keith Michael Baker

The University of Chicago Press

Chicago and London

Eric Cochrane, 1928–1985

ἀθάνατος μνήμη
Immortal memory

Keith Michael Baker is professor of history at Stanford
University.

The University of Chicago Press, Chicago 60637
The University of Chicago Press, Ltd., London
© 1987 by The University of Chicago
All rights reserved. Published 1987
Printed in the United States of America
96 95 94 93 92 91 90 89   5 4 3 2

Library of Congress Cataloging-in-Publication Data
Main entry under title:

University of Chicago readings in Western civilization.

Includes bibliographies and indexes.
Contents: 1. The Greek polis / edited by Arthur
W.H. Adkins and Peter White — 2. Rome : late republic
and principate / edited by Walter Emil Kaegi, Jr., and
Peter White — [etc.] — 7. The old regime and the
French Revolution / edited by Keith Michael Baker.
I. Boyer, John W.   II. Kirshner, Julius.   III. Title:
Readings in Western civilization.
CB245.U64 1987   909'.09821   85-16328
ISBN 0-226-06934-6 (v. 1)
ISBN 0-226-06935-4 (pbk. : v. 1)

ISBN 0-226-06949-4 (v. 7)
ISBN 0-226-06950-8 (pbk. : v. 7)

Contents

Series Editors' Foreword   ix

General Introduction   1

1. The Old Regime   13
   Social and Cultural Foundations   13
      1. Loyseau, *A Treatise on Orders*   13
      2. Bossuet, *Politics Derived from the Words of Holy Scripture*   31
   Absolute Monarchy on Trial   47
      3. A Royal Tongue-Lashing   47
      4. Remonstrance of the *Cour des Aides* (1775)   51
   Enlightenment and Reform   71
      5. Diderot, *The Definition of an Encyclopedia*   71
      6. Turgot, *On Foundations*   89
      7. Turgot, *Memorandum on Local Government*   97
      8. Protests of the Parlement of Paris (March, 1776)   118

2. From Reform to Revolution   124
   The Reform Crisis   124
      9. Proceedings of the Assembly of Notables (1787)   124
      10. Parlementary Opposition (April–May 1788)   135
   Calling the Estates General   143
      11. Order in Council Concerning the Convocation of the
          Estates General (5 July 1788)   143
      12. Sallier, *Recollections of a Parlementary Magistrate*   145
      13. Memorandum of the Princes of the Blood (December 1788)   151
      14. Sieyès, *What Is the Third Estate?*   154
      15. Regulations for the Convocation of the Estates General
          (24 January 1789)   180
   From Estates General to National Assembly   184
      16. Dispatches from Paris (April–July 1789)   184
      17. Deliberations at the Estates General (June 1789)   199

Abolition of the Feudal Regime   208
18. Peasant Grievances   208
19. Reports of Popular Unrest (July–September 1789)   217
20. Decrees of the National Assembly (10–11 August 1789)   226
21. The "October Days"   231
A National Constitution and Public Liberty   237
22. Declaration of the Rights of Man and of the Citizen   237
23. The Civil Constitution of the Clergy (12 July 1790)   239
24. Viefville des Essars, *On the Emancipation of the Negroes*
    (1790)   242
25. The Le Chapelier Law (14 June 1791)   247
26. The Constitution of 1791   249
27. Gouges, *Declaration of the Rights of Women*   261

3. Revolutionary Politics   269
The King's Flight and Popular Politics   269
28. The King's Declaration on leaving Paris (20 June 1791)   269
29. The Champ de Mars Massacre (17 July 1791)   272
30. National Assembly Debate on Clubs (20 September 1791)   278
The Fall of the Monarchy   286
31. Roland, *Letter to the King* (10 June 1792)   286
32. The Revolution of 10 August 1792   290
33. The "September Massacres"   296
The Convention Divided   302
34. The King's Trial   302
35. Purge by Insurrection (31 May–June 1793)   324
The Evolution of the Terror   330
36. Documents of the Sans-Culottes   330
37. Decree Establishing the *Levée en Masse* (23 August 1793)   340
38. "Make Terror the Order of the Day" (5 September 1793)   342
39. The Law of Suspects (17 September 1793)   353
40. Saint-Just, *Report to the Convention on Behalf of the
    Committee of Public Safety* (10 October 1793)   354
41. The Revolutionary Calendar   362
42. Robespierre, *Report on the Principles of Political Morality*
    (5 February 1794)   368
43. The Festival of the Supreme Being (8 June 1794)   384

4. After the Terror   392
44. Manifesto of the Directors (15 November 1795)   392
45. The Conspiracy of Equals (1796)   393
46. Bonaparte, *Letter to the Executive Directory* (15 July 1797)   404

47. The Coup d'Etat of 18 Brumaire 1799   405
48. Napoleonic Ideas   416

5. Reflections on the French Revolution   **428**
49. Burke, *Reflections on the Revolution in France*   428
50. Maistre, *Considerations on France*   445
51. Constant, *Ancient and Modern Liberty Compared*   452

Index   **463**

Series Editors' Foreword

This series is the result of almost four decades of teaching the History of Western Civilization course at the College of the University of Chicago. The course was founded in its present form in the late 1940s by a group of young historians at Chicago, including William H. McNeill, Christian Mackauer, and Sylvia Thrupp, and has been sustained during the past twenty-five years by the distinguished teaching of Eric Cochrane, Hanna H. Gray, Charles M. Gray, and Karl J. Weintraub. In the beginning it served as a counterpoint to the antihistorical and positivistic thrust of the general education curriculum in the social sciences in the Hutchins College. Western Civilization has since been incorporated as a year-long course into different parts of the College program, from the first to the last year. It now forms part of the general intercivilizational requirement for sophomores and juniors. It is still taught, as it has been almost constantly since its inception, in discussion groups ranging from twenty to thirty students.

Although both the readings and the instructors of the course have changed over the years, its purpose has remained the same. It seeks not to provide students with morsels of Western culture, nor to nourish their moral and aesthetic sensitivities, and much less to attract recruits for the history profession. Its purpose instead is to raise a whole set of complex conceptual questions regarding the nature of time and change and the intended and unintended consequences of human action and consciousness. Students in this course learn to analyze past events and ideas by rigorously examining a variety of texts. This is in contrast to parallel courses in the social sciences, which teach students to deploy synchronic and quantitative techniques in analyzing society, usually without reference to historical context or process.

Ours is a history course that aims not at imparting relevant facts or exotic ideas but at providing students with the critical tools by which to analyze texts produced in the distant or near past. It also serves a related purpose: to familiarize students with major epochs of that Western historical tradition to which most of them, albeit at times unknowingly, are heirs. The major curricular vehicle of the course is the *Readings in Western Civilization*, a nine-volume series of primary sources in translation, beginning with Periclean Athens and concluding with Europe in the twentieth century. The series is not meant to be a comprehensive survey of Western history. Rather, in each volume, we provide a large number of documents on specific themes in the belief that depth, not breadth, is the surest antidote to superficiality. The very extensiveness of the documentation in each volume allows for a variety of approaches to the same theme. At the same time the concentrated focus of individual volumes makes it possible for them to serve as source readings in more advanced and specialized courses.

Many people contributed to the publication of these volumes. The enthusiastic collaboration and labors of the members of the Western Civilization staff made it possible for these *Readings* to be published. We thank Barbara Boyer for providing superb editorial direction to the project and Mary Van Steenbergh for her dedication in creating beautifully text-edited manuscripts. Steven Wheatley's advice in procuring funding for this project was invaluable. Members of the University of Chicago Press have given their unstinting support and guidance. We also appreciate the confidence and support accorded by Donald N. Levine, the Dean of the College at the University of Chicago. Above all, we are deeply grateful for the extraordinary dedication, energy, and erudition which our late colleague and former chairperson of the course, Eric Cochrane, contributed to the *Readings in Western Civilization*.

We are grateful to the National Endowment for the Humanities for providing generous funding for the preparation and publication of the volumes.

John W. Boyer and Julius Kirshner

General Introduction

This volume brings together a selection of documents relating to a fundamental transformation in the history of Western civilization. The French Revolution swept away the traditional order in one of the oldest and most powerful monarchies of Europe, and changed the terms of social and political life in many others. Repudiating the accumulated weight of the past in order to inaugurate a new epoch in the relations among individuals and nations, the revolutionaries overturned thrones and altars, and abandoned inherited principles of order and hierarchy in favor of a radically new kind of politics. They claimed universal applicability for their doctrines as expressing the true nature of the rights of individual citizens, the absolute and enduring identity of the nation as a collective political entity, and the inalienability of national sovereignty as the essential principle of political right. Their new political logic transformed all aspects of French life—and spilled beyond French borders into much of the European continent—releasing social, political, and military energies hitherto unknown. It generated new forms of collective association, new processes of inclusion and exclusion, new forces of unity and division, new expressions of political solidarity, new institutions of social mobilization. It unfolded in a dramatic torrent of events, creating a script for modern revolutions which has continued to shape the meaning and understanding of political association, and to inspire efforts at social change, down to our own day.

From the very beginning, the Revolution astonished contemporaries and inspired them with varying degrees of exhilaration, suspicion, and terror. Within France and beyond, politicians and statesmen struggled to direct, control, or contain its unpredictable course, as it was impelled from monarchy to republic, from constitutionalism to revolutionary dictatorship, from representative government to the reign of Terror, from divided and imperiled democracy to military empire. Within France and beyond, philosophers and social theorists struggled to discover the deep-

1

est meaning of its radical doctrines and bloody events. Burke, Hegel, Condorcet, Constant, Bonald (to name but a few contemporaries), Comte, Marx and Tocqueville (among those who came later) found themselves driven by their impulse to understand and explain the French Revolution to formulate social theories and philosophies of history that have profoundly influenced modern consciousness. The history of the modern world—the history of liberalism and nationalism, conservatism and radicalism, socialism and democracy, revolution and reaction—remains, in many respects, the story of the assertion, repudiation, acceptance, contestation, extension and transformation of the principles of the French Revolution. For that reason, it continues to be one of the most thoroughly studied, and most constantly reinterpreted, of all human events.

Like its title, the basic approach of this volume is Tocquevillean.[1] This is to say, first, that political culture is its central theme (as was the case for Tocqueville's classic study) and that the documents it contains have been selected principally for their bearing on the nature, origins, and development of revolutionary political culture, and the implications of that political culture for the subsequent development of European consciousness. And it is to say, second, that the volume is organized around the basic problem posed by Tocqueville: the problem of understanding the French Revolution historically in relation to the social and political order which the revolutionaries simultaneously named and repudiated as the ancien régime.

The term ancien régime (or its English equivalent, Old Regime) now used by historians to designate the traditional social and political order that still existed in France, and in Europe more generally, in the eighteenth century, was itself born with the French Revolution. It was the phrase coined by the revolutionaries to describe the preceding order of things now swept away by the events and principles of 1789, and represented a way of saying that the act of revolution had introduced a break in time by repudiating the past as radically different from the present. This means that the Revolution defined the meaning of the Old Regime in the act of destroying it. But it also means that the Old Regime defined the meaning of the Revolution, whose principles were invented, and took on force and meaning, in opposition to it. If we are to comprehend the nature of the French Revolution, then, it is important to understand the nature of the Old Regime, the developments that placed its principles and practices in question, and the conflicts that accompanied the reforming efforts from which the Revolution was eventually to emerge. Only then

---

1. It may therefore be appropriate, in some courses, to accompany these documents with a reading of Tocqueville's *The Old Regime and the French Revolution.*

will it be possible to follow the process by which revolutionary ideology
was actually created in the course of the political struggles of 1788 and
1789, to recognize the tensions and contradictions implicit in that creation, and to identify the logic according to which they unfolded so dramatically in the course of revolutionary action.

The Old Regime

In accordance with these concerns, this volume has been divided into five
sections. The first, devoted to "The Old Regime," begins with two documents chosen to illustrate the basic assumptions underlying the traditional social and political order in France. Although the *Treatise on
Orders* by the jurist Loyseau was written in 1610, it retained its authority
until the very end of the Old Regime as one of the most systematic statements of the cultural principles of order and hierarchy upholding traditional French society, and of the conceptions of human life and social
value implicit in its differentiation into a multiplicity of orders and Estates. Read in conjunction with selections from Bossuet's celebrated
treatise on *Politics Derived from the Words of Holy Scripture,* the classic
exposition and defense of the principles of absolute monarchy as exemplified in the reign of Louis XIV, these excerpts from Loyseau's work
suggest the essential interconnection between two fundamental principles
of the Old Regime: the conception of social order as necessarily hierarchical, particularistic and corporative; and the idea of absolute monarchy
as the indispensable and divinely instituted form of rule in such a society.
    These abstract, relatively theoretical works by Loyseau and Bossuet
are followed by two documents chosen to illustrate aspects of the development of absolute monarchy as a form of government, and the institutional conflicts resulting from that development by the middle of the
eighteenth century. The first, the royal tongue-lashing delivered to the
magistrates of the Parlement (or high court) of Paris by Louis XV in
1766, is remarkable not only for its concise statement of the principles of
absolute authority, but for the daring and subversive doctrines it condemned in the assertions of the magistrates themselves. If this confrontation indicates that the practice of absolute monarchy itself was already at
issue between the monarch and the magistrates whose institutional function it was to uphold his authority as fount of justice, then a reading of
the *Remonstrance of the Cour des Aides* (1775) suggests some of the
reasons why. This document offers a kind of repertory of the grievances
which the older judicial institutions of the monarchy had directed against
the newer administrative apparatus of the absolute state in the preceding
decades. It provides a dramatic description of the increased centralization

accomplished in response to fiscal and military needs by the new administrative agents of the monarchy (the ministers at Versailles and the powerful intendants in the provinces) since the middle of the seventeenth century. It decries the disappearance of traditional forms of representation and local government, and the manner in which the demands of a complex and antiquated tax structure were being exacerbated by arbitrary practices and administrative secrecy. And it appeals to public opinion and the rights of nature in denouncing despotism and calling for responsible government grounded in representative institutions.

To understand the introduction of language such as this into French political debate, it is necessary to turn to the final set of documents in this first section, those dealing with the Enlightenment. The first of these is the article, "Encyclopedia," taken from the famous *Encyclopedia* edited by Diderot and d'Alembert between 1751 and 1765—the work that signalled the crystallization in France of the intellectual movement we know as the Enlightenment. As Diderot's article suggests, the Enlightenment took form as the work of an independent group of writers and thinkers who made the bold and undeniably subversive claim to exercise a public function to define the meaning of terms. In doing so, they not only arrogated to themselves an authority reserved by the absolute monarch, but they appealed (as Turgot's brief article on foundations clearly shows) to philosophical principles and conceptions of human existence that threatened the fundamental values of the corporate society of the Old Regime.[2]

It is one of the most revealing paradoxes of the last decades of the Old Regime that Turgot, whose article *On Foundations* epitomizes Enlightenment social thought in many aspects, became Louis XVI's most important minister (controller general, or finance minister) for two brief years between 1774 and 1776. The *Memorandum on Local Government* he ordered prepared for the monarch during this period (but never submitted) gives clear expression to the impulse of an enlightened minister to reconstitute government and society on rational, universal principles. The protests of the Parlement of Paris against some of his proposed edicts in 1776 leave little doubt as to the issues involved in such efforts at reform. Taken together, these two documents give a clear indication of the emerging tensions between the universalistic implications of the growth of absolute government on the one hand, and the particularistic assumptions underlying the traditional social order on the other.

---

2. These readings may, of course, be supplemented with other Enlightenment works readily available in inexpensive editions. Rousseau's political writings, for example, would be particularly appropriate, given the principal themes of this volume.

From Reform to Revolution

The revolution that was to resolve these tensions—and destroy the Old Regime in doing so—erupted during a constitutional crisis inaugurated by the government's efforts in 1787 to introduce tax reforms that could no longer be delayed. Thus the second section of this volume begins with two selections describing these reform efforts and the reactions to them. The first is drawn from the proceedings of the Assembly of Notables—a gathering of national and local dignitaries summoned by Louis XVI in 1787 to consider the need for fundamental changes in the fiscal and administrative system of the monarchy. The speech with which the controller general, Calonne, opened the assembly is dramatic in its denunciation of "abuses" and in its thoroughgoing proposals for reform, but it was met with distrust by the Notables. Their refusal to accept the government's reforms before they were assured of the introduction of responsible government led to Calonne's fall and to their own dismissal by his successor, Brienne. But when the latter turned to the Parlement of Paris to support his program, a new crisis occurred. As the second selection shows, parlementary protests against despotic government led to increasingly vigorous royal responses culminating in the May Edicts of 1788, which effectively suppressed the parlements' powers. In the widespread resistance that followed this coup d'état, the issue between liberty and despotism was clearly joined.

Demands for the convocation of the Estates General, the national assembly of the three Estates that had not met since 1614, lay at the heart of this particular conflict. But once the government agreed to call the Estates General, the nature of public debate was dramatically transformed: issues of equality and inequality came to cut across those of liberty and despotism. This development can be followed clearly in the next set of documents, devoted to the arguments over the calling of the Estates General as they unfolded in the autumn of 1788.

Initiated by the government's order of 5 July 1788, the debate took a radical turn after the Parlement of Paris declared (on 25 September) that the Estates General should meet according to the forms followed at its last meeting in 1614. The magistrates' motives for this declaration are suggested in the recollections of one of their number, Sallier, whose bitter attacks upon the new principal minister, Necker, suggest the intensity of the political maneuverings during this period, and the government's readiness to support and encourage the arguments of members of the Third Estate against adoption of the forms of 1614. For whatever their motives, the magistrates' declaration was widely portrayed as a defense of aristocratic, privileged interests. Pamphleteers for the Third Estate quickly responded with their own demands—for representatives drawn from their own ranks in numbers equal to those of the other two Estates combined (the "doubling of the Third Estate"), and for the elimination of the division of the Estates General into three separate bodies (the "vote by head" as opposed to the "vote by order"). These demands are articulated by Sieyès in *What is the Third Estate?*, a pamphlet justly celebrated for the brilliance with which it mobilized deep-seated resentments in support of these claims and demolished the conservative arguments against them (represented here by the *Memorandum of the Princes of the Blood*). But in studying *What is the Third Estate?*, it is important to recognize that this most famous of French Revolution pamphlets also went far beyond its ostensible demands on behalf of the Third Estate to assert a revolutionary conception of national sovereignty with radical political implications. No one recognized more clearly than Sieyès that, in debating the form of the Estates General as a national assembly, the French were in effect deciding the form and nature of the nation itself.

The extended argument over the forms of convocation of the Estates General came to a close when the government, introducing the "germs of democracy" within an absolute monarchy (as Sallier claimed), endorsed the doubling of the Third Estate and the principle of proportional representation (see the *Regulations for the Convocation of the Estates General* issued on 24 January 1789). But the government left undecided the crucial question of voting by head. The next set of documents ("From Estates General to National Assembly") shows the political process by which this issue was eventually decided when the Estates General finally met in May 1789: first as that body was transformed by the revolutionary action of the representatives of the Third Estate into a unitary assembly claiming the exercise of national sovereignty; and second, as the continued existence of the new National Assembly was secured by the popular uprising associated with the storming of the Bastille on 14 July.

The fall of the Bastille set off a chain reaction of events throughout France which forms the subject of the next set of documents ("Abolition of the Old Regime"). The events themselves are described in the reports of rural unrest that began to spread through a countryside in which economic crisis fed political discontent, frustrated expectations of reform kindled smoldering resentment against the privileged orders, and traditional fears, grievances, and patterns of popular protest were suddenly transmuted into insurrectionary action. Throughout the summer of 1789, peasants directed their fury against the châteaux and archives that were the symbols and instruments of seigneurial oppression. As markets and food supplies were disrupted, and fear of "brigands" serving the interests of the aristocracy swept through the countryside, townspeople organized and armed themselves for the defense of order.

Faced with this situation, the National Assembly was forced to take action. Although it had been successful in asserting its claim to represent the sovereign nation, the assembly's subsequent deliberations had been marked by uncertainty and division over the relation of privilege to the principles that should direct a new constitution. Now it was obliged to make good on its claim to express the national will by acting to restore order and safeguard property from further attack. But the assembly could not move to defend property without first deciding what property it was legitimate to defend. Fear of further disorder therefore forced it to decide the issue of rights and privileges. It did so in a dramatic evening session on 4 August 1789, an occasion that took on the emotional dimensions of a collective religious experience as speakers vied to denounce and abandon not only seigneurial privileges, but those of the nobility and clergy, of corporations, towns and provinces more generally. By the end of this momentous meeting—perhaps the most important single event of the whole Revolution—the entire particularistic structure of the Old Regime had in principle been swept away.

If the decrees that translated these actions into legislative form on 10–11 August tempered their immediacy somewhat, they nevertheless announced the assembly's determination to transform the entire social and political structure according to new principles. But full realization of this determination was to require yet another popular insurrection. Only after the "October Days," when a revolutionary crowd of women led a march upon Versailles which forced the king once again to accept the assembly's actions, did Louis XVI withdraw his opposition to this legislation.

By that time, however, the National Assembly had already agreed upon a *Declaration of the Rights of Man and of the Citizen* enunciating the principles that would underlie a "national constitution and public liberty." The remaining documents in this section illustrate some of the critical decisions subsequently taken by the assembly in the two years it took to translate the declaration's principles of natural rights and national sovereignty into a written constitution. The *Civil Constitution of the Clergy*, adopted on 12 July 1790, is important not only for the manner in which the assembly effectively nationalized the church order (by providing for its public support and for the democratic election of bishops and priests) but for its effects in driving those attached to traditional religious ways into increasingly overt counterrevolutionary activities. Viefville des Essars' pamphlet on the emancipation of blacks (1790) and Olympe de Gouges' *Declaration of the Rights of Women* (1791) illustrate the extent to which the assembly's legislation fell short of the promise of its universalistic principles. And the Le Chapelier Law (passed on 14 June 1791) shows the determination with which it sought to uphold its individualist principles by eliminating any vestige of corporatism from the new social and political order.

Finally, the selections from the French constitution eventually adopted in September 1791 provide the basic outlines of the new constitutional order. The Constitution of 1791 formally created a nation one and indivisible, exercising its sovereign will through a representative assembly. It transformed monarchical power into an administrative function limited in its powers, but endowed the king with a suspensive veto intended to check the exercise of legislative authority on the part of the representatives. It instituted citizenship as the fundamental status of individuals equal in their rights and obligations before the law, but separated the French into "active" and "passive" citizens according to a distinction that made property the criterion for participation in the actual conduct of public affairs by males (and whites). With its completion, many believed that the Revolution could be brought to a close. But the tensions and contradictions inherent in its basic provisions—between the idea of national sovereignty and the practice of representation; between the claims of legislative authority and the exercise of the suspensive veto; between the principle of equality among citizens and the introduction of the active/passive distinction among them—were to propel revolutionary politics in remarkable and unpredictable directions in the years that followed its acceptance. These developments form the subject of the third section of this volume, devoted to "Revolutionary Politics."

Revolutionary Politics

In fact, as the first set of documents in this section clearly shows, the tensions inherent in the new revolutionary politics had already become explicit in June 1791, before the new constitution was even adopted. In that month, Louis XVI made an abortive attempt to escape from Paris in order to rally counterrevolutionary forces to his support. The personal manifesto he left behind him included a bitter condemnation of the new forms of political conduct associated with the rise of the Jacobin clubs— the radical activism of revolutionary clubs and societies that was becoming an increasingly important feature of French political life during 1790 and 1791. Nor was the king alone in his distrust of the new politics: it was shared by many members of the National Assembly who saw popular radicalism as dangerous, not only because it threatened public order but because it infringed upon the assembly's authority and freedom to speak on behalf of the nation as a whole. The issue was joined when the assembly (fearing anarchy) opted to reinstate the recaptured king as soon as possible, while the more radical popular societies (fearing betrayal of the Revolution) responded with calls for his deposition. When, on 17 July

1791, demonstrators gathering at the Champ de Mars to petition for the king's replacement were fired upon by troops of the National Guard, a profound rift was opened within the revolutionary movement. Its nature and implications are well illustrated in the debate on the political role of clubs with which the Constituent Assembly concluded its existence in September 1791.

As the next set of documents (on "The Fall of the Monarchy") shows, this rift was to grow stronger during the life of the next national assembly. The new Legislative Assembly found itself consistently blocked by the royal veto in its efforts to take action against the counterrevolutionary activities of émigré nobles outside France, and those of refractory priests within. After the French declared war against the Hapsburg emperor on 20 April 1792, the conduct of the war became yet another source of division. Thus by the time that the minister of the interior, Roland, addressed his letter of resignation to the king in early June of that year, the issue of the royal veto had become the crucial question for the viability of the Constitution of 1791. As the threat of foreign invasion to suppress the Revolution became more acute, popular demonstrations calling for the king's removal became more pressing, and the assembly found itself more deeply divided between those who found the principal political threat in the king's behavior, and those who saw it in direct popular intervention. Incapable of decisive action to resolve this crisis, the representatives were obliged to accept a solution imposed upon them by the Parisian radical movement, acting in the name of direct popular sovereignty.

Thus when the revolutionary crowd marched upon the Tuileries palace on 10 August 1792, it not only overthrew the monarchy and effectively forced the elimination of the distinction between active and passive citizens, but it struck directly at the principle of representative government. Struggling vainly to reassert its authority against the insurrectionary popular government in the capital, the Legislative Assembly ended its days in the pall of the "September Massacres"—the slaughter of prisoners that occurred in Paris during the early days of September 1792, as fear of invasion drove revolutionary activists to vent their fury against counterrevolutionary suspects. The events of the summer of 1792 were to cast a long shadow over the deliberations of the National Convention which assembled at the end of September, introducing personal enmities and ideological divisions into its efforts to decide the king's fate and draw up a new republican constitution.

The bitterness of these personal enmities, and the depth of the ideological divisions associated with them, are dramatically revealed in the speeches over the trial of Louis XVI—speeches which mark one of the most profound turning points in the history of the French Revolution. For the issues in this debate went far beyond the mere question of the king's guilt. In fact, the most fundamental division arose not over *whether* the king was guilty, but over *which* king was guilty: the divine-right monarch of the Old Regime, or the constitutional monarch of 1791. On the answer to this question much depended: for if Louis Capet was to be regarded as a divine-right monarch (as Saint-Just and Robespierre insisted on behalf of the Jacobins) then he could not be tried as a citizen, nor was the Revolution over. Instead, Louis was to be killed as a vicious enemy by a people still seeking to cleanse itself of the stain of despotism; and a trial would do nothing but place in question the judgment already rendered by the direct action of the popular will on 10 August 1792. If, on the other hand, Louis Capet was to be regarded as a constitutional monarch (as Condorcet and the Girondins maintained), then a trial was necessary to vindicate the constitutional principles already established by the Revolution, thus bringing it to a close with a judicial demonstration that insurrection had given way to the rule of law. Indeed, at the limit (as Vergniaud argued) a referendum was also required to ensure that the representatives' judgment was consistent with the will of the people, formally expressed.

The trial of Louis XVI therefore raised fundamental questions about the nature and limits of the Revolution, as about the relationship between representation, insurrection, and popular sovereignty. It also deepened the distrust and hostility between the two leading factions within the Convention: the Girondins, who looked beyond Paris to the provinces for the authentic expression of popular sovereignty; and the Jacobins (or Montagnards) who turned for support to the revolutionary activism of the people of Paris. If the Girondins were successful in securing the king's trial, they nevertheless suffered a resounding defeat in their attempt to appeal his punishment to a decision by popular referendum. In the months that followed the execution of Louis XVI in January 1793—as economic unrest in the capital was exacerbated by news of a counterrevolutionary uprising in western France and military defeats to the north—they found themselves increasingly portrayed as a fractious minority preventing concerted action in defense of the Revolution. On 2 June, the Convention was forced by a new popular insurrection to order the arrest of twenty-nine Girondin deputies (see "Purge by Insurrection").

Their control of the assembly assured by this purge, the Montagnards lost no time in putting together a new republican constitution, quickly adopted by the Convention. Although it was ratified by popular vote in July, however, this Constitution of 1793 never went into effect. Instead, the Convention was driven by a series of political crises to create the emergency government generally referred to as the Terror. The evolution of this form of government is the subject of the last set of documents in this section.

The Terror, like earlier institutional expressions of revolutionary will, took shape as a result of a complex series of interactions between the deputies in the national assembly and the popular movement outside it. The mentality of the latter during this period is well illustrated by the documents of the sans-culottes—the preferred name of the revolutionary activists among the people of Paris. Passionate in their devotion to the Revolution, as in their hatred of all that seemed to stand in its way; convinced that the very bread upon which they depended was being hoarded by conspirators in league with the forces of counterrevolution within France and without; determined in their claim to the direct exercise of popular sovereignty, the sans-culottes pressed their demands upon the Convention throughout the summer and fall of 1793. Mass mobilization for national defense (the *Levée en Masse*), vigorous action against all those suspected of counterrevolutionary crimes or tendencies (the *Law of Suspects*), and the formal suspension of the constitution in favor of "revolutionary government" (see Saint-Just's speech of 10 October 1793) all derived in large measure from sans-culotte pressure to "make terror the order of the day." By the end of 1793, the Convention—led by its Committee of Public Safety, which now assumed the exercise of executive power—had created a centralized emergency government intended not only to institutionalize the use of terror against the enemies of the Revolution, but to monopolize that use on behalf of its friends. Thus sans-culotte extremism also fell victim to the Terror as the Committee of Public Safety, mobilizing the material and ideological resources of the nation to a degree hitherto unimaginable, forged the expression of a single, revolutionary will against internal and external enemies.

But the revolutionary dictatorship of the Terror went far beyond a mere response to emergency circumstances. On the contrary, it gave expression to profound political and moral imperatives lying at the heart of revolutionary ideology. Some indication of this may be found in the fact that, even as the government of the Terror was being improvised, the Convention was proceeding to institute a new, revolutionary calendar. Could there be a more powerful expression of the revolutionary will to efface the evil effects of the past and regenerate an entire people than such an effort to transform the symbolic dimensions of everyday life down to the very last second? Expressed in Robespierre's famous *Report on the Principles of Political Morality* and in the celebration of the Festival of the Supreme Being, this impulse to regeneration, this drive to create a world of virtue founded on natural principles, gave the Terror a moral purpose that was not to be abandoned when the counterrevolutionary armies were broken and the forces of foreign intervention driven back. Only with the fall of Robespierre, on the Ninth of Thermidor (27 July) 1794, did the dictatorship of the Terror come to a close.

After the Terror

It was to be another year, marked by anti-Terrorist purges and new acts of popular violence, before the stormy existence of the Convention finally ended with the adoption of a new republican constitution entrusting executive power to a five-man committee of directors. Neither royalist reactionaries nor radical republicans were prepared to accept the political and social stabilization that was the aim of the Directory, however, and its history added important new forms of action still fundamental to the modern repertory of revolution. In 1796, in a dramatic attempt to impose sans-culotte ideals, a group of conspirators led by Babeuf plotted a new kind of revolution that would overthrow the government by planned insurrection, using the apparatus of the centralized state to organize an egalitarian and communistic social order. Although this "Conspiracy of the Equals" was betrayed and suppressed, it was to exert a significant influence upon the imagination of many nineteenth-century socialists and revolutionaries.

The Directory, however, apparently had more to fear from the resurgence of royalism. When the 1797 elections resulted in a right-wing majority in the legislative councils, three of the directors purged the remaining two and expelled the royalist deputies in a military coup (the coup of 18 Fructidor) arranged with the support of the French commander in Italy, Napoleon Bonaparte. Two years later, with the coup d'état of 18 Brumaire 1799, Bonaparte acted to replace the weakened Directory. Not for the last time, a military coup claimed to bring revolution to a definitive close. The constitution announced on 25 December 1799, and accepted by the French people in a plebiscite the following February, combined revolutionary principles with the practice of authoritarian rule. Five years later, after another plebiscite, Napoleon was declared Emperor of the French and the imperial succession vested in members of his family. The final selection of Napoleonic documents indicates the zeal with which this son of the French Revolution resumed the tradition of absolute monarchy laid down by the Bourbons.

Reflections on the French Revolution

The volume concludes with selections suggesting the reorientation of European political and social thought that occurred as contemporaries struggled to comprehend the true nature and meaning of the extraordinary events of the French Revolution, to understand their implications for human action and association, and to grasp their consequences for the character of the state and the fabric of civil society.

1
The Old Regime

Social and Cultural Foundations

1. Loyseau, *A Treatise on Orders*

Charles Loyseau (1564–1627), eminent jurist and legal scholar, wrote a
series of treatises on French public law that gave powerful expression to
the impulse to consolidate social order in the wake of the Wars of Religion. Born near Paris, Loyseau followed his father into the legal profession. He served as a lawyer in the highest royal court, the Parlement of
Paris, and as judge in important local and seigneurial courts. First published in 1610, the *Traité des ordres et simples dignitez* is Loyseau's most
comprehensive theoretical work. His systematic account of the legal
forms and moral principles underlying the traditional social order remained authoritative until the very end of the Old Regime.

Foreword

It is necessary that there be order in all things, for their well being and for
their direction. The world itself is thus designated in Latin, on account of
the ornament and the grace of its admirable disposition. . . . Inanimate
creatures are all placed according to their high or low degree of perfection:
their times and seasons are certain, their properties regulated, their effects
assured. As for animate creatures, the celestial intelligences have their
hierarchical orders, which are immutable. And in regard to men, who are
ordered by God so that they may command the other animate creatures of

From *Les oeuvres de maistre Charles Loyseau* (Paris, 1666). Translation by Sheldon
Mossberg and William H. Sewell Jr., revised and expanded for this volume by the editor,
Keith Michael Baker.

this world here below, although their order is changeable and subject to vicissitude, on account of the particular liberty that God has given them for good and for evil, they nevertheless cannot exist without order.

Because we cannot live together in equality of condition, it is necessary that some command and others obey. Those who command have several orders, ranks, or degrees. Sovereign lords command all within their state, addressing their commands to the great; the great [address their commands] to the middling, the middling to the small, and the small to the people. And the people, who obey all of the others, are themselves separated into several orders and ranks, so that over each of them there are superiors responsible for the whole order before the magistrates, and the magistrates to the sovereigns. Thus by means of these multiple divisions and subdivisions, the several orders make up a general order, and the several Estates a state well ruled, in which there is a good harmony and consonance, and a correspondence and interconnectedness from the highest to the lowest, in such a way that through order a numberless variety is led to unity. . . .

How could a general of an army be quickly obeyed by all of his soldiers, if the army were not divided into regiments, the regiments into companies, the companies into squads; if the command of the general were not carried at once to the staff officers, by them to the captains, by the captains to the corporals, and by the corporals to the simple soldiers, the lowest soldier of the army thus being notified in a very short time? But the effect of order is yet more admirable in a state than in an army. For the army is compressed into a small place while the state ordinarily extends over a great country. The entire army lasts but a short time while the state endures almost forever. And that is the work of order. For the king is attended by his general officers, who send his mandates to the provincial magistrates, who send them to the city magistrates, who see that they are obeyed by the people.

Thus it is for those who command and also for the people, which obeys. Since the people is a body with several heads, it is divided by orders, Estates, or particular occupations. Some are dedicated particularly to the service of God, others to protecting the state by their arms, others to nourishing and maintaining it through peaceful occupations. These are our three orders or Estates General of France: the clergy, the nobility, and the Third Estate. But each one of these three orders is again subdivided into subordinate degrees, or subalternate orders, following the example of the celestial hierarchy. . . .

The degrees or subalternate orders of the clergy are sufficiently well-known. For in addition to the four minor orders and that of the tonsure, there are the sacred orders of subdeacon, deacon, priest, and bishop, to which may be added the order of cardinals and the various other orders of monks. The degrees of the nobility are the simple nobility, the high nobility, and the princes. Finally, as for the Third Estate, which is the largest, there are several orders: men of letters, financiers, merchants, artisans, husbandmen, and laborers. Most of these, however, are mere occupations rather than constituted orders.

Chapter I. Of Order in General

. . . The order to which this book is dedicated is a species of dignity, or honorable quality, which pertains to a number of persons in the same manner and under the same name. It does not in itself confer upon them any particular public power. But besides the rank that it gives them, it also brings a particular aptitude and capacity to attain either offices or *seigneuries*. . . . In French it is particularly called Estate, as being the dignity and the quality which is the most stable and the most inseparable from a man. . . . As for its definition, order may be defined as *dignity with aptitude for public power.*

For as I have said [elsewhere], there are three kinds of dignity: office, *seigneurie,* and order. They are related not only in terms of what they have in common, namely dignity, but also in terms of what makes them different, namely public power, in which they each participate differently. For office implies the exercise of public power, which is why I have defined it as *dignity with public function; seigneurie* implies ownership of public power, which is why I have defined it as *dignity with possession of public power;* and, finally, order implies only aptitude for public power, which is why I have defined it as *dignity with aptitude for public power.*

For example, membership in the order of the clergy does not in itself confer any public power, but it nevertheless renders those who are honored by it capable of benefices and ecclesiastical offices. Similarly, nobility is an order which is not in itself a public charge, but which gives its members a fitness for several high offices and *seigneuries* assigned to the nobility. Similarly, to be a doctor or licentiate in the law is not an office, but it is an order necessary to attain offices in the judiciary. Hence the office follows the order, and is conferred upon those who are of the order to which it is assigned. . . .

There is yet another well-marked difference between order and office, which is that office is something positive which can subsist without anyone filling it, and that it can pass from one person to the next without being lost or reduced to nothing. In brief, office seems to fall under the category of substance. Order, on the contrary, has nothing positive about it; it is not a substance which exists of itself but is a simple accident and comes under the category of quality. It is a simple quality, inseparable from the person and perishing with it, and in no way transmissible to another. . . .

For example, the offices of bailiff, lieutenant, and king's attorney continue to exist without anyone filling them; they do not perish when the officeholder dies or resigns, but simply change hands. But the quality of priest, or knight, or licentiate in the law is born and dies with the person, as it is the characteristic of the accident to die with its subject. And though after the death of a knight another be put in his place, it is not the same individual quality that is passed on to him, but another of the same kind. . . .

Thus, to pursue the nature of order in general, one must consider in the first place that, as order is more inherent and inseparable from the person than is office, forming the Estate of the person and imprinting upon the individual a perpetual character, more solemnity is ordinarily required to confer it than office, and more formality to take it away. . . .

In all times, however, those whom one has wished to admit to orders have been examined or otherwise had their capabilities tested. . . . We see that there are a great number of ceremonies for conferring all kinds of orders, whether ecclesiastical, sacred, or non-sacred, and for conferring religious orders (namely, the novitiate and the priesthood). To make knights, there are still other ceremonies which are completely different. And if there are no ceremonies to make princes and gentlemen, it is because these are irregular orders since they come from birth and not from any particular grant. In short, there are certain solemnities necessary to make licentiates and doctors, advocates and attorneys, and even masters of the trades.

Moreover, each order ordinarily has its particular mark, insignia, or visible ornament, which is solemnly displayed upon reception. . . .

As the ancient citizens of Rome had the toga, so now all of the clergy wear the long robe, which according to the ceremonial of the Roman Church . . . must be publicly vested on those receiving tonsure, which signifies entry into ecclesiastical orders. Because this mark of the long robe is common to ecclesiastics and men of letters, ecclesiastics (at least those belonging to sacred orders) bear as their particular mark the tonsured head. . . .

Besides this general mark, acolytes and other clerics of the four minor orders wear the surplice or the white robe. . . . Subdeacons have the phanon as the mark of their order, deacons have the stole, priests the chasuble, bishops the mitre, the staff, the gloves, and the ring; cardinals have the hat or bonnet and the scarlet robe. . . . Monks have a larger crown or tonsure than secular clerics. Thus Jesuits, who are half monks and half secular clergy, have a tonsure of medium size . . . and in addition each order of monks has its distinctive habit, not only from one order to another, but also from the novices to the fully professed members of the same order.

Among the nobility, simple gentlemen have their formal coats of arms, while knights have their spurs and gilded harnesses (at least that used to be their particular mark, but now only those have them who can afford them). The orders of knights have the gold chain or some other mark of their order. In addition, princes have the prince's cloak, which it is fitting that they should always wear.

Among commoners, doctors, licentiates, and bachelors have hoods of diverse sorts, according to the faculties to which they belong, as well as the long robe which they wear in common with ecclesiastics. Lawyers have the cornet, attorneys have only the long robe. . . .

Aside from these external ornaments, two other prerogatives of honor come from orders: title and rank. In regard to title, it is well-known that one may assume the title of one's order and add it to one's name, rather than the title of one's office. For order inheres more in the person than office. This is why the title of the order remains after one's resignation . . . while the title of the office is given up. Also, the title of the order must always be put immediately after one's name and before the title of the office, because the office is most often conferred in consequence of the order to which it is assigned, as has just been explained. . . .

As for rank, which is the prerogative of taking priority in sitting or marching, it is certain that orders produce it principally, even more so than do offices, as the very name of order denotes and signifies. . . .

In France, the three Estates have their order and rank one after the other, the ecclesiastical order being first, followed by the nobility, and the Third Estate last. This is true even though there are no statutes to this effect, because laws are scarcely made in matters simply of honor. But the ranks are willingly observed through honor, and certainly they are more honorable when they come from a voluntary respect. . . . For honor and love are two things so sublime and exalted that they cannot be commanded; nor can they be obtained with good grace by force; nor can any action assure them. If one thinks one possesses them by force, this is not love but fear and subjection, not honor but tyranny and oppression. . . . As love is necessary to the world, so are honor and rank; otherwise there would only be confusion among us. But it is necessary to earn both by merit, and maintain them by gentleness.

Thus since the ecclesiastical order is the first among us, it appears that even the least priest, even the lowest tonsured cleric, should take precedence over the greatest gentleman of the court (I refer here to private persons; those whose office gives them a particular rank are another matter) not because of his individual merit, but for the sake of his order and for that of God whose minister he is. . . . But because the ecclesiastical order is considered an exceptional and extraordinary order in the secular domain, our Redeemer having said that his realm is not of this world . . . it is commonly observed at present that those who enjoy some secular dignity do not wish to give place to priests unless they have an ecclesiastical dignity.

Similarly, I say that the least gentleman must take precedence over the richest and most honorable member of the Third Estate, speaking of course of private persons and when it is only a matter of rank among orders; but since the dignity of office is greater, and even enhances that of order in- asmuch as order is ordinarily required to hold office, it becomes a difficult issue when a commoner who holds office disputes precedence with a gentleman who does not. . . .

As for the power of orders, they ordinarily have none, their principal point of differentiation from offices being that they have no power of public administration. However, there are some orders that have a body and a par- ticular college, which sometimes have the privileges of making statutes and electing superior officers, who in turn have powers of correction over the whole body, as in the case of the craft guilds [*corps de métiers*]. . . .

It remains to speak of the loss or deprivation of order, which cannot properly be called "vacating" it because order, at least the individual quality of the person deprived of it, is completely lost and does not remain vacant, as an office or benefice does, to be transferred to another. This is why order is more difficult to lose than office, either by resignation or by forfeiture. In the case of death, which negates everything, there is no difference.

In regard to resignation, it is well-known that order is not resignable. A priest does not resign his order to another, neither does a knight, nor a li- centiate in the law, nor an advocate. . . . For an obvious example of how order is not lost by demission or resignation, consider that a bishop who resigns his bishopric still retains the episcopal order: he can in no way resign from it, nor otherwise separate it from his person. And lest it seem that this be a particular characteristic of sacred orders, it is shown [elsewhere] that those admitted to ennobling offices remain noble after re- signing their offices. . . .

As for deprivation by forfeiture, it is likewise neither as common nor as easy in the case of order as of office or benefice. . . . When a bishop is deprived of his bishopric, or a priest of his benefice, he is not however deprived of his order; when a gentleman is deprived of an office, he does not thereby lose his nobility; when a judge forfeits his office, he neverthe- less remains an advocate, licentiate in the law. . . .

In France, the order of knighthood is lost by infamy, because every stain is strictly contrary to it. . . . But as for other orders, whether eccle- siastical, noble, or of the Third Estate . . . they are not forfeited by infamy alone, nor even as a consequence of another punishment: it is necessary that one be formally sentenced to deprivation of order; and in the sacred orders of the Church an actual degrading is required in addition to formal deprivation. . . .

If, therefore, after a sentence prescribing deprivation of order, the ornaments of the condemned are sometimes publicly removed, this is done either to increase the shame of the sentence, or (more importantly) to avoid insult to the order when the condemned is executed. . . .

Chapter III. Of the Order of the Clergy

. . . In this Christian kingdom, we have bestowed on God's ministers the first rank of honor, rightly making the clergy (that is to say, the ecclesiastical order) the first of our three Estates of France. . . . In nearly all the states of Christendom the clergy are similarly constituted as a distinct order, as in France, which has always been more Christian and has honored the Church more than any other nation on earth. . . .

As in the case of each of the three orders or general Estates of France, there are among the clergy several degrees, or subalternate and partial orders subordinated one to another. While the clergy as a whole is generally divided into secular and regular orders, there are a number of secular and a number of regular orders. . . .

Let us begin by considering the secular orders. The tonsure is the entrance into all ecclesiastical orders, that which makes a man a cleric and distinguishes the clergy from the people by the shaving of the hair. . . . The tonsure is public evidence that one has dedicated oneself to God, renouncing and rejecting the extravagances of the body, notably the hair, which being an upper part of the human body has customarily been adorned and embellished by those in the world. . . .

Next come the four minor orders . . . porters, lectors, exorcists, and acolytes. Then come the three sacred orders of subdeacons, deacons, and priests. Above all these, there is the order of bishops, which is divided into bishops, archbishops, and primates or patriarchs. Finally, there is the order of cardinals which, while it differs from the other orders in having no particular consecration, yet is still more an order than an office. . . .

Unlike the secular orders of the clergy, which are distinguished by degree one above the other, the regular orders are completely different and separate from each other. In my opinion, they may be divided into five: hermits, monks, regular canons, mendicants, and the military orders.

I have put hermits first because they are the oldest. . . . In imitation of Saint John the Baptist, they took themselves into the desert to devote themselves more freely to a life of contemplation. . . . Hermits have never been bound to the three vows . . . Likewise, they have no fixed rule of life, but instead frame it more or less strictly for the purposes of their devotions, even quitting it entirely when they so wish. . . .

I call monks those who have a fixed rule of communal life. . . . The rule seems to have been introduced into Christianity in imitation of the Essenes, who were a very devout sect of Jews . . . and first practiced by Saint Anthony in Thebes, Saint Benedict in Italy, and Saint Basil in Greece. The latter was the first to bind monks to the three vows that we deem essential to our religion: obedience, chastity, and poverty. In short, we mean a resignation and renunciation, made for the honor of God, of the three kinds of goods with which men are endowed in this world: obedience concerning the soul, chastity concerning the body, and poverty concerning worldly goods. There are so many orders of monks, that is to say so many different rules, that it would be long and trying to discuss them all. . . .

Because monks were prevented from carrying out ecclesiastical functions outside their monasteries . . . Saint Augustine organized for the religious life the priests at his church in Hippo who were charged with the administration of sacraments and other ecclesiastical functions. He called them not monks but canons, that is to say subject to a certain rule of life that was a mixture of clerical status and the pure monastic existence. . . .

[The order of canons] was found so useful and so honorable that there was soon no cathedral without its canons. From this first institution, canons lived in the same way as the monastic orders, binding themselves to the three vows and even living a cloistered existence. . . . But little by little, their opulence led them to relax this austerity, to dispense with the poverty of sharing ecclesiastical goods, and thus with obedience, and thereby to convert their order into a benefice. Consequently, those who have remained committed to their initial institution and still observe the rule of Saint Augustine are named *regular canons,* to distinguish them from those who no longer observe their rule, and who are therefore called *secular canons.* . . .

Next come the orders of mendicants who, besides the vow of poverty (which affects monks only as individuals, since in common they may hold as many possessions as they may acquire) have vowed to beg: that is to say, to live on alms. . . . As a result, having vowed mendicity both individually and in common, their order is incapable of possessing any buildings.

Last among the regular orders are the military orders, either the Knights of Saint John of Jerusalem, whom we call the Hospitalers or the Knights of Malta, or the Teutonic Knights . . . or others of a similar kind. . . .

Chapter IV. Of the Order of the Nobility in General

Among the various plants and animals, nature itself has made this distinction: of a single species, some are gentle and domestic, while others are hardy and wild. These qualities are retained infallibly from their generation, so well, in fact, that the wild ones can never produce domestic ones nor the reverse. Likewise, it is natural that plants and beasts retain the characteristics of their semen because their vegetative or sensitive soul proceeds absolutely from a physical source (*a potestate materia,* as the philosophers say). But the rational soul of men, which comes directly from God who creates it when he sends it into the human body, does not have any natural participation in the qualities of the generative semen of the body to which it is joined.

This is why I am astonished to see how nearly all of the most noted philosophers and poets, ignoring this difference in souls, fancy that there are certain secret principles of virtue transferred from fathers to children by generation. Take, for example, the reasoning of Socrates, who concluded that as the most noble apples, grapes, or horses were the best, so it would be for men of the most noble race. And Aristotle (in the *Politics,* book 3, chapter 8) says that among all nations nobility is esteemed and honored because it is probable that he is excellent who is born of excellent parents. He therefore defines nobility . . . as virtue by birth. . . .

But this analogy [with the world of plants and animals] is false and misleading, for we often see that the children of good men are worthless and those of learned men ignorant. . . . If sometimes the good morals of children seem to conform to those of their fathers, this is not the result of generation, which contributes nothing to souls, but rather the result of education. In this respect, indeed, the children of good families have great advantages when it comes to virtue. This is true because of the careful instruction they receive and the continuous and weighty example of their fathers, and because of their obligation not to demean or belie their blood; and finally because of the respect and good reputation that the memory of their ancestors has gained them.

In any case, either because they are presumed to be the inheritors of paternal virtue, or because one wishes still to reward in them the merits of this virtue, those who have issued from good blood have been esteemed above others in all the nations of the world, and in all times. They have even been constituted as a separate order and been given a degree of honor which sets them apart from the great majority of the people. . . .

[In France] we have . . . that nobility which derives from ancient blood, and that which derives from dignities. The first has no beginning, the second has a beginning; the first is original, the second acquired. We tend to call the latter *nobility* and the former *generosity* or *gentility,* just as we commonly distinguish between noblemen and gentlemen.

To discover the origin of this gentility, or ancient and immemorial nobility, it is necessary to consider that as the Athenians and the Romans first divided their people into patricians and plebians, so from the first establishment of this monarchy, its people were divided into gentlemen and commoners, the one group destined to defend and maintain the state, either by counsel or force of arms, the other to nourish it by working the soil, engaging in commerce, or practising the crafts. This division has continued up to the present time. . . .

Alternatively, the nobility of France had its origin in the ancient mixture of the two peoples who came together in this kingdom, that is to say, the Gauls and the Franks who conquered and subdued them without attempting to exterminate or drive them away. But the Franks retained this prerogative over the Gauls, that they alone would hold public office, bear arms, and possess fiefs without having to contribute anything either to the lords of particular localities or to the sovereign for necessities of state. Instead, they were obliged only to fight in wars.

As for the conquered people, they were reduced to a condition of partial servitude. . . . In addition to being in this condition of partial servitude and being incapable of holding offices, bearing arms, or possessing fiefs, the people were also required to pay the *seigneur* a tribute or land tax, and occasionally to provide taxes for the unusual needs of the state. . . .

Now as the two races mixed and adapted to one another, this initially rigorous exclusion of commoners from holding offices, bearing arms, and possessing fiefs did not continue so strictly. But some vestiges of it still remain. In the case of offices, the principal ones, such as the crown, those in the king's household, and provincial governorships, may only be held by gentlemen. In the case of arms, commoners are not admitted into heavy cavalry regiments, and were not in earlier times allowed to hold important commissions in the infantry. In the case of fiefs, they are still ineligible to hold the principal fiefs and seigneuries, and as for simple fiefs, they must still pay the tax of *franc fief* for the right to hold them. But gentlemen have carefully guarded the liberty of exemption from any subsidies or obligations other than joining the king in war. . . .

Nevertheless . . . our ancient and immemorial nobility, whose beginnings are unknown, does not derive from right of nature, as does liberty, but rather from the ancient law and arrangement of the state. . . . Nobility is not simply a particular privilege, contrary to the common law, but has its origin in a public and general law and proceeds from means established to this effect long ago in each country. Accordingly, it is of much longer duration and is more firmly held than are simple privileges. This is a fundamental point, the basic for deciding an infinite number of questions that arise in this matter.

All this is true of that nobility ("gentility") which exceeds the memory of man. As for the nobility whose origins may be determined, in France it comes from ennoblement by the prince, who is ordained by God to distribute the substantial honors of this world. . . . The prince may ennoble in two ways: by means of a letter written expressly to this end, or by grant and investiture of offices and *seigneuries* that carry nobility with them, and in which the nobility that derives from dignity properly consists.

This ennoblement purges the blood and the posterity of the ennobled of all stain of commonness, raising him to the same quality and dignity as if his race had always been noble. . . . Nevertheless, because . . . this abolition of servitude or commonness is only an effacing of a mark that remains, it seems more of a fiction than a truth, since the prince cannot reduce being to nonbeing. . . .

Accordingly, in the common opinion, those ennobled either by royal letter or by the dignity of office are less esteemed than nobles by blood, although in fact they enjoy all the same privileges. . . . That is why in France we are so interested in hiding the origins of our nobility, so that we may reduce this type of nobility to that of the immemorial sort. . . .

We have three degrees of nobility in France: simple nobles, whom we call *gentlemen* and *esquires;* high nobles, whom we designate as *seigneurs* and *knights;* and those of the highest degree, whom we name *princes.* Each of these three degrees of nobility has its own effects. For simple nobility affects the blood and passes on to posterity in such a way that the older it is the more honorable it becomes. High nobility does not descend to posterity, at least in the same degree, but rather it is personal, being conferred upon the person for his particular merit, such as knighthood (which is a perfect order that perishes with the person), or by reason of his office or *seigneurie* (and in the latter case, it perpetually follows the office or *seigneurie*). Finally, princehood can come only from blood, but resides there in a manner opposite to that of simple nobility; for it is of a higher rank according to its recentness and its nearness to its source.

Chapter V. Of Simple Gentlemen

. . . The true rights of the nobility are as follows. First, as to power, it has been said in the first chapter that orders have no particular power, as offices have, but that they only produce an aptitude for offices, benefices, and *seigneuries*. This is confirmed above all in the order of the nobility, to which several of the latter are particularly assigned.

The offices assigned to the nobility are, first, all the principal offices and many of the subordinate offices in the king's household: namely, those of the Gentlemen of the Chamber, of the One Hundred Gentlemen, of Gentlemen Servants, of the Squires of the Stable, of the Gentlemen of the Royal Hunt and of the Falconry, and several others. . . . It is the same for all the principal military charges, from command of cavalry regiments to simple service in the heavy cavalry. . . . And as for infantry captaincies, gentlemen are also preferred; as, likewise, the edicts regulating nomination to the judicial offices maintain that gentlemen rather than commoners will be preferred.

As for benefices, although the ecclesiastical order is distinct from the order of the nobility, there are several cathedral churches, even several abbeys, where the dignities and even places as simple canons and monks are assigned to gentlemen. In general, however, gentlemen are favored in the Church by dispensations waiving requirements as to age, plurality of benefices, and even time of study required in order to become a doctor or a master.

Finally, in regard to *seigneuries,* it is claimed that all fiefs, since time immemorial, have been allotted to the nobility, and that commoners are today capable of receiving them only by dispensation, for which they pay the King the subsidy of *franc-fiefs* (which is to say, assigned to the free and gentlemen). However that may be, it is still true today that gentlemen alone are capable of holding either great or middling *seigneuries.* Thus the king's attorney, and even a higher *seigneur,* can constrain a commoner to give up a fief that has not been expressly invested in him by the king. . . .

So much for power. As for the honor pertaining to nobility, since it is the true effect of orders to produce honorable rank, as their name denotes, it is altogether reasonable that the nobility, which risks its life for the defense of the state, be honored by the people as its protector. Consequently, it is an established right among us that members of the order of the nobility outrank and take precedence over members of the Third Estate. There are only two exceptions to this rule, both of which concern offices with established rank. In the first place, those who are magistrates take precedence accordingly over gentlemen, as a result of the power of command which they have over them. Thus all those who reside within a magistrate's jurisdiction can be called his judicial subjects since he has the power of judging their goods, their honor and their life, as the case may be. In the second place, those who hold ennobling offices, such as the officeholders in the sovereign courts, the *secrétaires du roi,* and others of the same type, must always take precedence over simple gentlemen by blood, because in addition to being noble like the latter, they are also officers of the king; they thus have public power and an excellent function, which simple gentlemen do not.

As for other marks of honor, nobles have the right to call themselves Esquire and to bear coats of arms, even if they are men of the city and of the long robe, ennobled only by their offices. Moreover, all nobles (except those of the long robe) have the right to carry a sword as the ornament and sign of nobility, and in France they are even entitled to wear it in the king's own chambers. . . .

It is a matter of debate whether commoners are formally obliged to salute nobles, as the latter believe, even though the contrary is true. For . . . the salute is a recognition and obligation of subjection, which is formally owed only by subjects to those who command them, either by right of possession (as their *seigneurs*) or by the exercise of public function (as their magistrates). As a matter of honor and propriety, a salute is given to members of the high nobility, namely great lords and holders of high office, and all those entitled to call themselves knight; and from this same sense of propriety, we salute senior members of our families. But the most well-bred and cultivated among us salute all honorable persons, just as they salute family members of equal rank, and friends, as a matter of simple civility and courtliness. But these latter actions belong to the domain of manners, not law.

As for profits and pecuniary emoluments, it has been said above that there are none that pertain purely to orders as such. But the privileges of the nobility are yet very great. They include exemption from the *taille* and all other personal taxes levied for purposes of war.[1] It is certainly a very reasonable privilege that those who contribute their lives for the defense of the state be exempt from contributing their goods. For the same reason, gentlemen are exempt from lodging soldiers in their homes. . . . Gentlemen also have the privilege of hunting game in authorized places, seasons, and manners, a privilege which is justly denied to the common people for fear that it would lead them to abandon their ordinary employment to the public detriment. The hunt has also for good reason been limited to the nobility, so that nobles can maintain in peacetime an exercise resembling war. . . .

It is another privilege of gentlemen that when they commit a crime, they are not punished as rigorously as the common people. . . . This is true in terms of the severity of judgments and the nature of punishments (there are some punishments to which gentlemen are never condemned, such as hanging and flogging; on the contrary, common people are never decapitated . . .). It is also true that nobles receive grace and forgiveness from the prince more readily than do commoners. . . .

---

1. The *taille*, from which the nobility and clergy were exempt, was the basic direct tax of the Old Regime. Taxes are discussed more fully below, in document 4.

But there are two exceptions to this rule. The first consists in the fact that crimes repugnant to nobility, such as treason, larceny, perjury, or double-dealing are aggravated and made more serious by the dignity of the person committing them. . . . The second consists in the fact that corporal punishments inflicted on gentlemen are milder, but pecuniary punishments must be harsher. . . .

Activities leading to the forfeiture of nobility are those of the pleading attorney, clerk of the court, notary, sergeant, clerk, merchant, and artisan of all trades except glass-making. . . . What is at issue here is the fact that these activities are performed for profit. For rightly speaking, it is sordid profit that derogates from nobility, whose proper characteristic is living off rents or at least not selling its labor. On the other hand, the employments of judges, advocates, doctors, and professors of the liberal arts do not derogate from nobility, even when nobles live by means of these professions, because this kind of profit (which proceeds from the work of the mind not the hands) is honorary rather than mercenary.

Tilling the fields does not derogate from nobility, not because of its utility (as is commonly thought) but because nothing a gentleman does for himself, and without taking money from another, implies derogation. . . .

Chapter VI. Of the High Nobility

. . . Because the most perfect division is tripartite, I have most appropriately divided our nobility into simple, high and illustrious: meaning by simple nobility that which has not been raised by any other degree of honor; by high nobility that which is elevated and honored by some dignity, whether it be a knighthood, high office or *seigneurie;* and finally by illustrious nobility, that which derives from sovereign and illustrious blood, being connected by kinship with the sovereign prince, and capable of succeeding in turn to the sovereign power.

In order that this general division encompass all the degrees of nobility, which are far greater than three, it is necessary to subdivide the nobility of the higher degrees. We may divide the high nobility . . . into three: knights, great office-holders, and *seigneurs.* . . . But each of these refers in the end to the same kinds of dignity, claimed generally by all the high nobility. . . .

The order of knights is a quality of honor that kings and other sovereign princes attribute to those whom they wish to distinguish above other gentlemen as being more noble. They do this according to certain ceremonies designed to give the recipients greater distinction and prestige, ceremonies that the old tales have specified better than any good book. These consist of a vigil in church, followed by public and solemn prayers, after which the noble descends to his knees and is struck on the shoulder by the King with the flat of his sword . . . in the same way as slaves who were given their freedom in Rome were struck by the praetor with his rod . . . , as the bishop confers the order of tonsure, and as in conferring the degree of doctor in universities one gives a slap to the candidate as a last blow to be received as one enters into a quality henceforth exempt from them. . . .

Nobles of the other two degrees, simple gentlemen and princes, have their quality by nature, or at least from their birth, contrary to the rule common to other dignities. Knighthood, however, follows the common rule of orders in that no one is born a knight, but this order must be directly conferred upon the person. And even though princes rank above knights, princes are not true knights until they have received the order of knighthood. Even sons of kings are not born knights. . . .

Chapter VII. Of Princes

. . . The supreme degree of our nobility belongs to those we call *princes,* thereby bestowing upon them by honor and as a title of honorary dignity the name of Prince, which properly belongs to the sovereign alone. For *prince,* according to its true etymology, means the principal chief, he who has the sovereignty of the state; and this is what we mean when we speak simply of the prince.

This prince, who is the living image of God . . . is so august and so full of majesty that those who are born of him or who are related to him through the male line merit a particular respect and a rank above other subjects. So too this lieutenancy of God on earth, this absolute power over men that we call principality or sovereignty, is so perfectly excellent that any position approaching or offering hope of acceding to it must have great weight or effect. If the ancient emperors established honorary offices or dignities to be bestowed upon those who held no offices but deserved to do so, then our kings, with even greater reason, have been able to impart to their kin this honorary title of Prince, although they may not enjoy the true principality (which is sovereignty) but only the aptitude to attain it, directly or through their posterity, according to their degree of succession.

I speak notably of our kings, since no other kingdom in the world that I know has formed and established an order of princes similar in title and rank to that in France.

Chapter VIII. Of the Orders of the Third Estate

Inasmuch as order is a species of dignity, the Third Estate of France is not properly an order. For since it comprises all the rest of the people apart from the clergy and the nobility, this would imply that all the people of France without exception were in dignity. But inasmuch as order signifies a condition or occupation, or a distinct kind of person, the Third Estate is one of the three orders or general Estates of France. . . . In ancient Gaul, it was not taken into account or held in any respect or regard, as Caesar says in Book VI of *De Bello Gallico*. And following Caesar, M. Pasquier appropriately remarks in his *Livre des Recherches*[2] that during the first two dynasties of our kings there was no mention of the Third Estate, nor were the simple people called to the general assemblies held to reform the state: assemblies then called parlements, which we now call Estates General. These assemblies comprised only the prelates and the barons, that is to say the principal persons of the clergy and of the laity. . . . Pasquier adds that in the third dynasty our kings had adopted the custom of asking the common people for aid or subsidies for the necessities of war. In order to secure the people's consent (without which, at that time, no levy of funds could be raised) the kings henceforth summoned it to these assemblies which, for this reason, were called Estates General. This is why the common people is called the Third Estate . . . because it was added to the two others, which had been established a long time before. And this Third Estate of France enjoys much greater power and authority in our time than it did formerly, because nearly all of the officeholders of justice and finance belong to it, the nobility having scorned letters and embraced idleness. . . .

The term "Third Estate" is more comprehensive than that of "bourgeois," which comprises only the inhabitants of the towns, that in old French (and still today in German) are called *bourgs*. . . . Furthermore, the term "bourgeois" does not properly comprise all the inhabitants of the towns. For nobles, even if they make their home in the towns, do not qualify as bourgeois because the nobility is an order completely separate from the Third Estate, to which the bourgeoisie belongs. This is why the "bourgeois" is ordinarily opposed to the "noble," as when we say "*La Garde noble et bourgeoise.*" Moreover, base persons among the common people have no right to call themselves Bourgeois, since they have no share in the honors of the city nor any voice in the assemblies, in which rights bourgeoisie consists. . . .

What is more, properly speaking, bourgeois are not found in all towns but only in privileged towns, those which have the right to corporate and communal forms of government. For to be a citizen or bourgeois (as Plutarch defines it very well in his work on Solon) is to participate in the rights and privileges of a city; so that if the city has no communal government

---

2. Etienne Pasquier (1529–1615), lawyer and historian, was one of the most distinguished humanist scholars of sixteenth-century France. His *Recherches de la France* (which began to appear in 1560) sought to recover the early history of French institutions from the original documentary sources.

and corporate existence, neither officeholders nor privileges, it can have no bourgeois. . . .

In France, as in ancient Rome, there are several orders or degrees of the Third Estate . . . men of letters, financiers, those serving the courts, merchants, husbandmen, ministers of justice, and laborers. It is necessary to speak of each separately.

For the honor which is due to knowledge, I have put men of letters in the first rank. . . . Our men of letters are divided into four principal faculties, or branches of knowledge: theology, jurisprudence (under which are included civil and canon law), medicine, and the arts, which comprise grammar, rhetoric and philosophy. In each of these four faculties, there are three degrees: bachelor, licentiate, and doctor or master.

The bachelor . . . has completed his studies, and has been admitted to the course of the faculty leading to the doctorate or mastership. The licentiate has finished his course and completed all the required tasks and examinations, having been declared capable of obtaining the grade of doctor or master; that is why he enjoys nearly all the advantages of the doctor. Finally, the doctor has solemnly received the marks and signs of this dignity, and has obtained the power of publicly teaching others, and of conferring the same degree upon them, a power which the simple licentiate does not have. . . .

Another order or dignity of men of letters is that of advocate, which is conferred publicly by a magistrate, and can only be conferred upon those who already have the degree of doctor, or at least of licentiate, of civil or canon Law. . . .

In my opinion, financiers must rank after men of letters. . . . By financiers, I mean all those who undertake the handling of finances (that is to say the king's monies) whether they hold offices or not. For we are speaking here of orders, or rather of mere occupations, which are compatible with offices. It is true that in earlier times the tasks of finance were not offices, but simple commissions. . . . The majority of these were conferred by the people when it granted a levy to the king and named particular persons to allocate the levy equally, first among provinces . . . then among parishes . . . and finally among individual inhabitants of the parishes. . . . But since venality of offices has become customary, even the most minor financial operation has been made into an office. And because these offices ordinarily carry little honor or power, their remuneration is generally very high; added to which it is expected that, as those who pick peas keep a few in their hands, so those who handle finances keep their share—which they rarely forget to do. . . .

Next come practitioners or men of affairs . . . all those who, apart from judges and advocates, gain their living by the business and legal transactions of others. They are of two kinds: those of the long robe, namely clerks of the court, notaries, and attorneys . . . ; and those of the short robe, namely sergeants, trumpeters, appraisers, vendors, and others like them. . . .

After the principal practitioners . . . come the merchants, as much for the utility, indeed the public necessity, of commerce . . . as for their usual opulence, which brings them credit and respect. In addition to the latter, their ability to employ artisans and laborers brings them much power in the towns. Thus merchants are the last group among the people to receive honorable titles, to be called "honorable men" or "honest persons" and "bourgeois of the town." Titles such as these are attributed neither to husbandmen, nor to sergeants, nor to artisans, and still less to laborers, all of whom are reputed to be vile persons, as will shortly be explained. . . .

Husbandmen must, in my opinion, follow merchants and precede practitioners of the short robe . . . since in France rural life is the ordinary occupation of the nobility, while commerce brings derogation of nobility. It is true that by husbandmen I mean those ordinarily engaged in tilling for others as tenants, an exercise which is as strictly forbidden to the nobility as is commerce. But be that as it may, there is no life more innocent, no gain more in accord with nature than that of tilling the soil, which philosophers have preferred to all other vocations. In France, however, administrative policy has lowered them so much, even oppressed them, by taxes and by the tyranny of the gentlemen, that one is astonished that they can subsist, and that there are enough of them to provide nourishment for us all. Thus one sees that the majority prefer to be valets and carters for others, rather than masters and farmers in their own right.

In any case, today we consider common husbandmen and all other men of the village, whom we call peasants, as vile persons. . . .

The artisans, or tradesmen, are those who exercise the mechanical arts, which are so named to distinguish them from the liberal arts. This is because the mechanical arts were formerly practiced by serfs and slaves, and indeed we commonly call *mechanical* anything that is vile and abject. Nevertheless, because the mechanical arts demand considerable skill, masterships have been created in them, just as in the liberal arts. The statute requires a three-year apprenticeship under the same master (under penalty of beginning the apprenticeship again if one changes masters). Then one becomes a journeyman (in earlier times called a bachelor), that is to say an aspirant to the mastership. Finally, after three years as a journeyman working under a master, and having been found capable on the basis of public proof of adequate ability (in a piece of work called a *chef d'oeuvre*), one is received as a master. This is a very well-ordered arrangement, not only because no one is made a master who does not know his trade very well, but also because the masters thereby lack neither apprentices nor journeymen to help them in their work. . . .

Although artisans are properly mechanics and reputed to be vile persons, there are certain trades in which manufacture and commerce are combined. . . . Inasmuch as they participate in commerce, these trades are honorable, and those who exercise them are not numbered among the vile persons . . . but may be addressed as "honorable men" and "bourgeois" like other merchants. Apothecaries, goldsmiths, jewellers, haberdashers, wholesalers, drapers, hosiers, and others like them fall into this category, as one sees in the statutes.

On the other hand, there are trades which reside more in bodily strength than in the practice of commerce or in mental subtlety, and these are the most vile. . . .

For all the more reason, those engaged neither in manufacture nor commerce, and who gain their living only by the labor of their arms, whom we call *gens de bras,* or mercenaries, such as porters, masons' laborers, carters, and other day laborers, are the most vile of the common people. For there is no worse occupation than having none at all. Still, those who are occupied in gaining their living by the sweat of their brow, according to the commandment of God, are far better to be maintained than so many ablebodied beggars, with whom France is filled at present, because of excessive taxes. These latter cause needy persons to abandon everything, preferring to become vagabonds and tramps in order to live in idleness and carelessness at the expense of others, rather than to work continually without profit or to earn only to pay taxes. If this is not put in order quickly, there will be two unfortunate results of the immense proliferation of this rabble that is occurring daily: the fields will be left untended for lack of men willing to engage in this work; and travellers will no longer be safe on the roads, nor peasants in their homes.

2. Bossuet, *Politics Derived from the Words of Holy Scripture*

Jacques-Bénigne Bossuet (1627–1704) was a distinguished French churchman renowned for the eloquence of his preaching. In 1670, he was chosen by Louis XIV to serve as tutor to his son, the heir to the throne.

From Jacques-Bénigne Bossuet, *Politique tirée des propres paroles de l'Ecriture sainte*, in *Oeuvres choisies de Bossuet*, 5 vols. (Paris: Hachette, 1897–1901), vol. 2. Translated by Elizabeth D. McNeill with additions and revisions by the editor, Keith Michael Baker. Bossuet's biblical quotations are not always precise. We have followed the Douay-Rheims-Challoner translation of the Latin Vulgate used by Bossuet, modified where necessary to accord with Bossuet's text.

Bossuet wrote several works for the edification of his pupil, including this celebrated statement of the principles of royal absolutism (published post-humously in 1709).

Named bishop of Meaux in 1680, Bossuet became one of the great spokesmen for orthodoxy and unity in French religious life, upholding the authority of the Catholic church in France against the claims of Jan-senists and Protestants, on the one hand, and its independence against the threat of papal interference on the other.

Book 3: Wherein Begins the Explanation of the Nature and Properties of Royal Authority

ARTICLE 1. On distinguishing its essential characteristics.

Proposition 1. Royal authority has four essential characteristics or qualities.

First, royal authority is sacred; second, it is paternal; third, it is abso-lute; fourth, it is subordinated to reason. These will be explained in proper order in the following articles.

ARTICLE 2. Royal authority is sacred.

Proposition 1. God establishes kings as his ministers, and reigns through them over the people.

We have already seen that all power comes from God. As Saint Paul says, "The King is God's minister to thee, for good. But if thou do that which is evil, fear: for he beareth not the sword in vain. For he is God's minister: an avenger of evil actions" (Romans 13:4).

Princes serve therefore as ministers of God and as his lieutenants on earth. It is through them that he exercises his rule. "Do you think that you are able to withstand the Kingdom of the Lord, which he possesseth by the sons of David?" (II Chronicles 13:8). That is why we have shown that the royal throne is not that of a man but the throne of God himself: ". . . he hath chosen Solomon my son, to sit upon the throne of the Kingdom of the Lord over Israel" (I Chronicles 28:5). And again, "Solomon sat on the throne of the Lord. . ." (I Chronicles 29:23). And lest it should be consid-ered peculiar to the Israelites to have kings chosen by God, here is what Ecclesiasticus says: "Over every nation he set a ruler. And Israel was made the manifest portion of God" (Ecclesiasticus 17:14–15). He therefore rules over all nations and to them all he gives their kings, although he rules over Israel in a more clearly stated and distinctive fashion.

Proposition 2. The person of kings is sacred.

It is clear from the foregoing that kings' persons are sacred, and that any attack upon them is sacrilege. God causes kings to be anointed by his prophets with a holy anointing, as he does the priests and the altars. But even without the outward application of this anointment, kings are sacred because of their office; they are the representatives of the divine majesty, delegated by his providence to execute his commands. Thus God even calls Cyrus his anointed. "Thus saith the Lord to my anointed Cyrus, whose right hand I have taken hold of, to subdue all nations before him" (Isaiah 45:1).

The title of *christ* is given to kings, and throughout the Scripture one sees them called *christ*, or the Lord's anointed. With this venerable title, even the Prophets revere them, and regard them as associated with the sovereign empire of God, whose authority they wield over the people. "Speak of me before the Lord, and before his anointed, whether I have taken any man's ox or ass; whether I have taken a bribe at any man's hand; whether I have oppressed any man. And they said: thou hast not. And he said to them: the Lord and his anointed are witness this day, that you have no complaint to bring against me" (I Samuel 12:3–5). Samuel, after having judged the people with absolute power for twenty-one years on behalf of the Lord, thus accounts for his conduct before God and before Saul, whom he calls upon as witnesses, and by whose testimony he establishes his innocence.

One must guard kings as one would sacred things, and he who neglects thus to guard them is worthy of death. "As the Lord liveth, you are the sons of death," said David to Saul's captains, "you who have not kept your master, the Lord's anointed" (I Samuel 26:16). He who guards the life of a prince commits his own into God's keeping. David said to King Saul, "And as thy life hath been precious this day in my eyes, so let my life be precious in the eyes of the Lord, and let him deliver me from all peril" (I Samuel 26:24).

Twice God placed Saul in the hands of David; Saul did all he could to cause David's undoing; his men pressed David to rid himself of this unjust and impious prince; but the idea filled him with horror. "And he said to his men: The Lord be merciful unto me, that I may do no such thing as to lay my hand upon my master, the Lord's anointed" (I Samuel 24:7, 11; 26:23). Far from making any attack upon Saul, David was filled with fear at having cut off a piece of Saul's mantle, although he had only done it to show Saul how conscientiously he had spared his life. "David's heart struck him, because he had cut off the hem of Saul's robe" (I Samuel 24:6). So sacred did the king's person seem to David, and so afraid was he of violating, by the slightest irreverence, the respect that was Saul's due.

Proposition 3. The prince must be obeyed on principle, as a matter of religion and of conscience.

Saint Paul, having said that the prince is God's minister, concludes thus, "Wherefore be subject, of necessity: not only for fear of his wrath, but also for conscience' sake" (Romans 13:5). . . .

And again: "Servants, obey in all things your masters according to the flesh: not serving to the eye, as pleasing men; but in simplicity of heart; fearing God. Whatsoever you do, do it from the heart: as to the Lord, and not to men; knowing that you shall receive of the Lord the reward for your services. Serve Jesus Christ as your master" (Colossians 3:22–24). If the Apostle speaks thus of servitude, a state contrary to nature, what ought we to think about legitimate submission to princes who are magistrates, the protectors of public liberty? That is why Saint Peter said, "Be ye subject therefore for God's sake to the order that is established among men: whether it be to the king, as holding supreme power; or to governors as sent by him for the punishment of evildoers and for the praise of the good" (I Peter 2:13–14).

Even when kings and magistrates fail in this their duty, one must respect in them their office and their ministry. "Servants, be subject to your masters, not only to the good and gentle but also to the froward" (I Peter 2:18). There is therefore something religious about the respect rendered to a prince. Serving God and respecting kings are interconnected, and Saint Peter puts these two duties together: "Fear God. Honor the king" (I Peter 2:17).

Also, God endowed princes with a divine quality. "I have said: You are gods, and all of you are children of the most High" (Psalms 81:6). God Himself is made to speak thus by David.

From this it follows that the servants of God take their oaths upon the well-being and life of the king as though upon a divine and sacred thing. Uriah says to David, "By thy welfare and by the welfare of thy soul I will not do this thing" (II Samuel 11:11). Taken in the light of the Lord's commands, this holds true even if the king is an infidel: "By the health of Pharaoh, you shall not depart hence" (Genesis 42:15).

We ought to give heed here to the early Christians, and especially to Tertullian who speaks thus in the name of them all: "We swear, not by the genii of the Caesars, but by their life and their well being, which is more august than all the genii. Do you not know that genii are demons? But we, who see the emperors as the choice and the judgment of God, who gave them command over all nations, respect in them what God put there, and we hold it a solemn oath." And he says further, "What more can I say about our religion and our piety toward the emperor, whom we must respect as him whom our God hath chosen? I can say that the Caesar is more ours than yours, since it was our God who established him" (Tertullian, *Apology*, 32, 33).

It is therefore in the spirit of Christianity to respect kings with the sort of religion which Tertullian most aptly terms "the religion of the second majesty." This second majesty is but an outgrowth of the first, that is, of the divine majesty, which, for the good of human affairs, wished to cast some of its reflected brilliance upon kings.

Proposition 4. Kings must respect their power, and only use it for the public good.

Their power comes from on high, and as has been said, they must not think that they are the masters of this power, to use it as they please; but they must use it with fear and restraint as they should a thing coming to them from God, and for which God will demand an accounting. . . .

Kings must consequently tremble while using the power which the Lord gives them, and reflect upon how horrible a sacrilege it is to use for evil ends a power which comes from God. We have seen how kings are seated on the throne of God, grasping the sword which he himself put in their hand. How profane and how audacious of unjust kings, to sit upon the throne of God, giving orders contrary to the laws, and using the sword God gave them for doing violence and butchering his children!

Let kings therefore respect their might; for it is not theirs, but the might of the Lord, which must be used in a holy and religious manner. . . .

ARTICLE 3. Royal authority is paternal, and its true characteristic is goodness. . . .

Proposition 1. Goodness is a royal quality, and the true attribute of greatness.

"Because the Lord your God he is the God of gods, and the Lord of lords, a great God and mighty and terrible, who judgeth without regard to person nor taketh bribes. He doth judgment to the fatherless and the widow, loveth the stranger, and giveth him food and raiment" (Deuteronomy 10:17–18). Because God is great and complete in himself, he bends over backwards, as it were, to do good to men, in conformity with these words. "For according to his greatness, so also is his mercy" (Ecclesiasticus 2:23). He imbues kings with an image of his majesty in order to compel them to imitate his goodness. He raises them to a level where they no longer desire anything for themselves. We have heard David saying, "What can David add more to all this greatness, with which thou hast invested thy servant" (II Samuel 7:20; I Chronicles 17:18). And at the same time God told the kings that he gave them this greatness out of love for the people, "Because the Lord hath loved his people, therefore he hath made thee king over them" (II Chronicles 2:11). And again, "Blessed be the Lord thy God, whom thou hast pleased, and who hath set thee upon the throne of Israel: because the Lord hath loved Israel for ever, and hath appointed thee king, to do judgment and justice" (I Kings 10:9). That is why, in the passages where we read that the kingdom of David was imposed upon the people, the Hebrew and Greek read, *for* the people. This shows that the purpose of greatness is the good of the subjects. In fact, God, who created all men out of the same earth for a body, and equally placed his image and his likeness in all their souls, did not establish so many distinctions among men in order to have on one hand the haughty and on the other slaves and wretches. He raised up the great only for them to protect the common people; he only gave his power to kings in order to procure the public welfare, and for them to be the support of the common people.

Proposition 2. The prince is born not for himself but for the public.

This is a sequel to the preceding proposition. God confirms this truth with the example of Moses. . . .

If only princes could understand that their true glory lies in not existing for themselves, and that the public welfare which they bring about is a sufficiently worthy recompense on earth, while awaiting the eternal blessings that God reserves for them!

Proposition 3. The prince must look after the needs of the people.

The Lord said to David, "Thou shalt feed my people Israel, and be their shepherd" (II Samuel 5:2). . . .

It is a royal prerogative to minister to the needs of the people. Whoever else undertakes this function, to the prejudice of the prince, infringes upon royalty; that is why royalty is established; and the obligation to care for the people is the foundation upon which rest all the rights which sovereigns have over their subjects. That is why, in cases of great need, a people has the right of appeal to its prince. "And when all the land of Egypt was famished, the people cried to Pharaoh for bread" (Genesis 41:55). . . .

Proposition 4. Among the people, the prince must provide most carefully for the poor.

For they have the greatest need of him who is, through his office, the father and the protector of all. That is why the care of widows and orphans was entrusted by God principally to judges and magistrates. . . .

Book 4: Continuation of the Characteristics of Royalty

ARTICLE 1. Royal authority is absolute.

In order to make this term odious and unbearable, there are many who affect to confuse absolute government with arbitrary government. But in reality no two things are more distinct, as we will demonstrate when we speak of justice.

Proposition 1. The prince does not have to justify himself to anyone for what he commands.

"Observe the commandments that issue from the king's mouth, and keep the oath that thou hast taken to him. Be not hasty to depart from his face, and do not continue in an evil work. For he will do all that pleaseth him. And his word is full of power. Neither can any man say to him: why dost thou so? He that obeyeth shall find no evil" (Ecclesiastes 8:2–5). Without this absolute authority, the prince can neither do good nor repress evil; his power must be such that no one can hope to escape him; and as a matter of fact, the sole defense of individuals against the public power must be their innocence. This doctrine conforms to what Saint Paul said: "Wilt thou then not be afraid of the power? Do that which is good" (Romans 13:3).

Proposition 2. When the prince has judged, there is no other judgment.

Sovereigns' judgments are attributed to God himself. . . .

Princes are Gods and participate in some fashion in divine power. "I have said: You are gods, and all of you are children of the most High" (Psalms 81:6). Only God can review their judgments and their persons. "God hath stood in the congregation of gods: and being in the midst of them he judgeth gods" (Psalms 81:1).

That is why Saint Gregory, bishop of Tours, said to King Chilperic at a church council, "We speak to you; but you listen to us only if you wish to. If you do not wish to, who will condemn you, if not he who has said that he is justice itself?" It therefore follows that whoever does not wish to obey the king cannot appeal to another tribunal, but is irrevocably condemned to death as the enemy of the public peace and of human society. "He that will be proud, and refuse to obey the commandment of the priest and the decree of the judge: that man shall die, and thou shalt take away the evil from among thee" (Deuteronomy 17:12). And again, "He that shall refuse to obey all thy commands, let him die" (Joshua 1:18). Thus spake the people to Joshua.

The prince can correct himself when he finds he has done wrong, but against his authority there can be no remedy except by his authority. That is why a prince must be very careful what he orders. . . .

Proposition 3. There is no coactive force against the prince.

Coactive force is the power to compel the execution of legitimate orders. Legitimate command belongs only to the prince; to him alone also belongs coactive force. This is also why Saint Paul gave the sword only to the prince. "But if thou do that which is evil, fear: for he beareth not the sword in vain" (Romans 13:4). In a state, only the prince is armed; otherwise everything is in confusion and the state collapses into anarchy.

Whoever makes himself a sovereign prince takes everything into his own hands, the supreme judicial authority as well as all the forces of the state. . . .

This is what may be called the royal law of the Jews, where all the powers of kings are excellently set forth. To the prince alone belongs the general care of the people: that is the first article and basis of all the others; to him belong public works; to him belong defense and offense; to him belong decrees and ordinances; to him belong honorific titles; there is no power which is not dependent on him, no assembly but by his authority. Thus for the good of the state, all its force is gathered into a single whole. For power to exist outside of this is to divide the state, to ruin the public peace, to create two masters, which is in contradiction to the word of the Gospel, "No man can serve two masters" (Matthew 6:24).

By virtue of his office, the prince is the father of his people; by his majesty he is above petty interests; more than this, all his majesty and his natural interest are directed toward the preservation of the people, since, in short, if there is no people, there is no longer a prince. There is therefore nothing better than to leave all the power of the state to him who has the greatest interest in its preservation and grandeur.

Proposition 4. Kings are not thereby freed from all laws. [Here follows a long quotation from Deuteronomy 17:16–20.]

One must observe that this law included not only the religion but also the law of the kingdom, to which the prince was subject as much as others, or more than others, through the righteousness of his will. This is what princes find so hard to understand. As Saint Ambrose said: "Where will you find a prince who believes that what is not good is not permitted; who holds himself bound by his own laws; who believes that a ruler ought not to permit himself to do what is contrary to justice? But authority does not destroy the obligations of justice; on the contrary, it is by observing the prescriptions of justice that authority avoids criminal behavior. And the king is not exempt from the laws; for if he sins, he destroys the laws by his example." Saint Ambrose adds, "Can he who judges others escape his own judgment? And ought he to do that which he himself condemns?" Hence a Roman emperor's excellent dictum, "It is worthy of the majesty of a ruler to recognize his submission to the laws."

Kings are therefore subject, like others, to the equity of the laws, both because they ought to be just, and because they owe it to the people to give an example by maintaining justice; but they are not subject to the penalties of the law. In the language of theology, they are subject to the laws not as a coactive force but as a directive force.

Proposition 5. The people must remain peaceable under the authority of the king. . . .

Proposition 6. The people must fear the prince; but the prince need only fear to do evil. . . .

Fear is a necessary bridle for the people, because of their presumptuousness and their natural intractability. Therefore it is necessary for the people to fear the prince; but should the prince fear the people, then all is lost. . . .

Book 5: Fourth and Last Characteristic of Royal Authority

ARTICLE 1. Royal authority is subject to reason.

Proposition 1. Government is a work of reason and of intelligence.

"And now, O ye kings, understand: receive instruction, you that judge the earth" (Psalms 2:10). All men are formed for understanding, but especially you in whom is placed the trust of an entire great nation; who must be the soul and the intelligence of a state; and in whom must be found the primary reason for all its actions. The less you have to give reasons to others, the more you must have reason and intelligence yourself. The opposite of acting through reason is acting through passion or caprice. To act in a temper, as Saul did against David, being either pushed by jealousy or possessed by black melancholy, leads to all sorts of irregularities, inconstancies, inequalities, vagaries, injustices, and dizzinesses in one's conduct. . . .

Proposition 2. True firmness is the result of intelligence. . . .

Proposition 3. The wisdom of the prince makes the people happy. . . .

ARTICLE 4. Consequences of the foregoing doctrine; of majesty and its attributes.

Proposition 1. On the nature of majesty.

By majesty, I do not mean that pomp which surrounds kings, or that show of brilliance which dazzles the vulgar. This is but the reflection of majesty, and not majesty itself.

Majesty is the image of the glory of God in the prince. God is infinite; God is all. The prince, in his capacity as a prince, is not considered an individual man: he is a public person, the whole state is in him, the will of the whole people is contained within his own. As all perfection and all virtue are united in God, so is the entire power of individual persons united in the person of the prince. What greatness it is for a single man to hold such power!

God's power makes itself felt in an instant from one end of the world to the other. Royal power acts simultaneously throughout the realm. It keeps the whole realm in its proper state, just as God does for the whole world. Let God withhold his hand, and the world would collapse again into nothingness; let authority cease in the realm, and everything would be in confusion.

Consider the prince in his cabinet. Thence orders go out coordinating the actions of magistrates and captains, citizens and soldiers, provinces and armies on land and sea. He is the image of God, who sits on his throne in the highest heavens, governing the movements of the whole of nature. . . .

Book 6: The Duties of Subjects to the Prince

ARTICLE 1. On the service owed to the prince.

Proposition 1. One owes to the prince the same services one owes one's country.

There can be no doubt of this, once we have seen that the whole state is in the person of the prince. In him lies power, in him rests the will of the whole people. To him alone is it given to make all things conspire together for the public good. The service which one owes to the prince and that which one owes to the state must be made to coincide, as being inseparable.

Proposition 2. It is necessary to serve the state in the manner in which the prince understands such service.

For we have seen that in the prince lies the reason which guides the state. Those who think to serve the state otherwise than by serving the prince and by obeying him arrogate to themselves part of the royal authority; they trouble the public peace and the relationship of all to their chief. Such were the children of Sarviah, who, by a false zeal, wished to kill those whom David had pardoned. "What have I to do with you, children of Sarviah? You are a Satan this day to me" (II Samuel 19:22). The prince sees from further off and from higher up, and one must believe that he sees better. One must obey without murmur, since murmuring implies an inclination to sedition.

The prince knows the whole secret and sequence of affairs. To fail to obey his orders even for a moment is to put everything in jeopardy. . . .

Proposition 3. Only public enemies make a separation between the interest of the prince and the interest of the state. . . .

ARTICLE 2. The obedience due to the prince. . . .

Proposition 6. Subjects ought not to oppose the violence of princes except by respectful remonstrances, without mutiny and without murmurs, and with prayers for their conversion.

When God wished to deliver the Israelites from the tyranny of Pharaoh, he did not allow them to proceed with violent measures against that king, whose inhumanity toward them was unheard of. They respectfully asked for permission to leave Egypt and go into the desert to sacrifice to God. We have seen that princes ought to listen even to individual persons. How much more should they listen to a people that respectfully makes known its just complaints through proper channels! Pharaoh, hardened and tyrannical though he was, nonetheless listened to the Israelites. He heard Moses and Aaron. And he received "the officers of the children of Israel, who came and cried unto Pharaoh, saying: Why dealest thou so with thy servants?" (Exodus 5:15).

It is therefore permissible for an oppressed people to appeal to the prince through his magistrates and legitimate channels: but this must always be done respectfully. Remonstrances full of bitterness and grumbling are the beginning of sedition, which ought not to be tolerated. Thus the Israelites grumbled against Moses and never made a peaceable remonstrance to him. Moses never ceased to listen to them, to assuage them, to pray for them; and he gave a memorable example of the good will which princes owe their people. But God, to establish order, soundly punished the seditious ones. . . .

Book 7: The Special Duties of Royalty

ARTICLE 1. A general view of the duties of the prince.

Subjects have been taught their obligations. We have given princes a preliminary conception of theirs. It is necessary now to proceed to more detailed consideration; and to avoid any omission, let us make a precise enumeration of these duties.

The end of government is the good and the preservation of the state. To preserve it, first one must maintain therein a good constitution. Second, one must make good use of the resources with which it has been endowed. Third, one must save it from the dangers and difficulties that threaten it. In this same way is the human body preserved, by maintaining therein a good constitution; by taking advantage of the means by which the feebleness of human existence may be supported; by providing suitable remedies for the ills and afflictions that may attack the human frame.

The good constitution of the body of the state consists in two things, namely religion and justice: these are the internal and constitutive principles of states. By the former, God is given his due, and by the latter, men are given that which is fitting and proper to them. The resources essential to royalty and necessary for government are arms, counsel, wealth or finances (under which category we shall consider commerce and taxes). . . .

ARTICLE 2. On religion, understood as the good of nations and of civil society. . . .

Proposition 4. Since the true religion is founded on certain principles, it makes the constitution of states more stable and more secure.

It is true that false religions, insofar as they possess an element of goodness and truth in recognizing the obligation to respect a divinity to which human existence is subject, may entirely suffice to uphold the constitution of states. Nevertheless, they always leave in human consciences a residue of uncertainty and doubt, preventing the attainment of a perfect stability. . . . There is nothing enduring in false religions. They consist only in a zeal that is blind, seditious, turbulent, prejudiced, ignorant, confused, and without order and reason, as is shown by the disordered and tumultuous assembly of the Ephesians and their demented clamors in favor of their great Diana (Acts 19:24, 28, 34). This is far from the good order and sound stability which constitutes states, but it is the inevitable result of error. A solid foundation for states must therefore be sought in truth, which is the mother of peace; and truth is only to be found in the true religion.

ARTICLE 3. The true religion is made known by visible signs. . . .

Proposition 9. The prince ought to use his authority to destroy false religions in his state.

Thus Asa, Hezekiah and Josiah ground into powder the idols which their people adored. . . .

Proposition 10. A king may use force against the adherents of false religion; but gentleness is preferable.

"The king is God's minister. He beareth not the sword in vain. Whomsoever doeth evil must fear him as the avenger of evil actions" (Romans 13:4). He is the protector of the public peace, which rests on religion; and he must uphold his throne of which religion is the basis, as we have seen. Those who would not allow the prince to use force in matters of religion, because religion ought to be free, have fallen into impious error. Otherwise it would be necessary to permit idolatry, Mohammedanism, Judaism, all false religions, blasphemy and even atheism among all subjects and throughout the state; and the greatest crimes would be the least punished.

It is, however, only in an extremity that it is necessary to use force, especially the last resort, death. . . .

Book 8: Continuation of the Special Duties of Royalty—Of Justice

ARTICLE 1. Justice is founded on religion.

Proposition 1. God is the judge of judges, and presides over all judgments.

"God hath stood in the congregation of gods: and being in the midst of them he judgeth gods" (Psalms 81:1). These gods whom God judges are kings and the judges assembled under their authority to exercise their justice. He calls them gods, because in the language of Holy Scripture the name *God* means *judge:* thus the authority to judge is participation in God's sovereign justice, with which he has invested the kings of the earth. . . .

Proposition 4. Under a just God, there is no purely arbitrary power.

Under a just God, there is no power whose nature it is to be entirely unconstrained by natural, divine, or human law. There is, at least, no power on earth not subject to divine justice. All judges, even those most sovereign, whom God accordingly calls gods, are examined and corrected by a greater judge. . . .

ARTICLE 2. Of the government that is called arbitrary.

Proposition 1. There is a form of government among men that is called arbitrary, but that does not exist among us, in perfectly civilized states.

Four conditions are characteristic of such governments. First, the subject peoples are born slaves, which is to say that they are truly serfs; there are no free persons among them. Second, there is no property; all wealth belongs to the prince, and there is no right of succession from father to son. Third, the prince has the right to dispose at will, not only of his subjects' property but of their life, just as in the case of slaves. Fourth, and finally, there is no law but the prince's will.

This is what is called arbitrary power. I do not wish to examine whether it is lawful or unlawful. There are peoples and great empires that content themselves with it; and it is not for us to trouble them as to their form of government. It is enough to say that it is barbarous and hateful. These four conditions are very far from our own customs and manners; this arbitrary government does not exist among us.

It is one thing for the government to be absolute, and quite another for it to be arbitrary. It is absolute in terms of constraint, there being no power capable of compelling the sovereign, who in this sense remains independent of all human authority. But it does not follow from this that the government is arbitrary, because in addition to the fact that everything is subject to divine judgment (which also applies to the form of government just called arbitrary) empires have laws which by right nullify anything that is done contrary to them; it is always open to reverse such actions on another occasion, or at another time. In consequence, each individual remains in legitimate possession of his goods, since no one can believe that he will be able to hold securely anything that is contrary to the laws, whose vigilance and action against injustice and aggression are immortal. . . . And this is what one calls legitimate government, which is by its nature opposed to arbitrary government.

We deal here only with the first two conditions of what is called arbitrary power, as we have just defined them. For the last two seem so contrary to humanity and to society that they are all too clearly opposed to legitimate government. . . .

Book 9: The Resources of Royalty—
Arms, Wealth or Finances, and Counsel

ARTICLE 1. Of war and its just grounds, both general and particular.

Proposition 1. God makes princes warriors.

Therefore David says: "Blessed be the Lord my God, who giveth force to my arms for the fight, and teacheth my hands to war" (Psalms 143:1).

Proposition 2. God expressly commanded the Israelites to make war.

He ordered his people to make war on certain nations. . . .

Proposition 4. God wished to chastise these peoples [enemies of the Israelites] and to punish their impiety.

These were abominable nations, devoted from the beginning to all sorts of idolatry, injustice and impiety; a cursed race, among whom vice was ingrained by their corrupt customs. . . .

Proposition 6. God does not wish established inhabitants to be dispossessed of their lands, nor blood relationships to be disregarded. . . .

Proposition 7. There are other just grounds for waging war: acts of hostility, refusal of just and peaceful transit, violation of the law of nations by acts against ambassadors. . . .

ARTICLE 2. Unjust motives for war.

Proposition 1. First unjust motive: ambitious conquest. . . .

Proposition 2. Those who love war and wage war in order to satisfy their ambition are the declared enemies of God. . . .

Proposition 3. The character of ambitious conquerors, as portrayed in Holy Scriptures. . . .

[The prototype: Nebuchadnezzar.]

Here we see the first trait of an unjust conqueror. He had no sooner subdued a powerful enemy than he thought that everything belonged to him and that there was no people he could not oppress; and if anyone refused the yoke, his pride was aroused. He did not speak of attack; he believed himself to have a legitimate right over everyone. Because he was the strongest, he did not think himself an aggressor; and he claimed as mere defense his plan to invade the lands of free peoples. Since it was rebellion to safeguard liberty against his ambition, he spoke only of vengeance; and the wars he undertook appeared to him as just punishments for rebels.

He went further. Not content with invading so many countries which by no right belonged to him, he thought nothing would be worthy of his greatness except to become master of the whole universe. . . .

Proposition 4. While God seems to bestow everything on such conquerors, he actually prepares harsh punishment for them. . . .

Proposition 5. Second unjust motive for war: pillage. . . .

If wars of pillage were permitted, there would be no peaceful kingdom or province. . . .

Proposition 6. Third unjust motive: jealousy. . . .

Proposition 7. Fourth unjust motive: glory and the delights of victory. . . .

There is nothing more enticing than military glory. It often determines human affairs at a single blow, and seems to have a sort of universal power to force events. This is why glory tempts the kings of the earth so strongly. But we shall see how vain it is. . . .

Tenth and Last Book: The Resources of Royalty, Continued— Wealth, Counsel, the Difficulties and Temptations which Accompany Royalty and the Remedies which must be Applied

ARTICLE 1. Of wealth or finances: Commerce and taxes.

Proposition 1. There are expenditures which are necessary, and others which are for splendor and dignity. . . .

One may count, among necessary expenditures, all those required for war, such as fortifications, arsenals, and munitions, which have been mentioned before. The expenditures for magnificence and dignity are not less necessary, in their own way, to sustain majesty in the eyes of the people and of foreigners.

It would be an infinite task to recount the magnificence of Solomon. . . . And the Holy Bible does not disdain going into all this detail, because it served, in that time of peace, to make the power of so great a king felt and admired at home and abroad. . . .

God forbade ostentation inspired by vanity, and the foolish puffing up of a heart drunk with wealth, but he nevertheless wished the courts of kings to shine with magnificence, in order to impress upon the people an attitude of respect.

And even today, at the coronation of kings, as we have already seen, the Church makes this prayer: "May the glorious dignity and the majesty of the palace dazzle the eyes of all beholders with the great splendor of royal power, so that the light shall shine forth on all sides like a star." All these are words chosen to express the magnificence of a royal court which is demanded by God as a necessary support for royalty.

Proposition 2. A flourishing state is rich in gold and silver, and this is one of the fruits of a long period of peace.

Gold so abounded during the reign of Solomon that "silver was counted as nothing, and it was as plentiful (so to speak) as stones, and cedars as common as sycamores which grow (unwanted) in the plains" (I Kings 10:27). The Holy Bible points out that such wealth is the fruit of long peace, in order to make princes love that peace which produces such great things.

Proposition 3. The first source of such wealth is commerce and navigation. . . .

Proposition 4. The second source of wealth: the prince's domain. . . .

Proposition 5. The third source of wealth: tribute imposed upon vanquished kings and nations, which the Bible calls presents. . . .

Proposition 6. The fourth source of wealth: taxes paid by the people.

In every state the people contributes to the public expenditures, that is to say, to its own preservation; and the part of its property which it gives assures enjoyment of the remainder in liberty and security. . . .

Proposition 7. The prince ought to moderate taxes, in order not to overburden the people.

"And he that strongly squeezeth the paps to bring out milk, straineth out butter: and he that violently bloweth his nose bringeth out blood: and he that oppresseth men provoketh revolts and seditions" (Proverbs 30:33). This was Solomon's rule. . . .

Proposition 10. . . . Definition of true wealth.

From the passages which we have quoted, we must conclude that true riches are those we have called natural because they supply the true necessities of nature. The fertility of the soil and of animals is an indubitable source of true wealth; gold and silver come only secondarily to facilitate exchange.

Therefore it is necessary, following the example of the great kings whom we have cited, to take particular care to cultivate the soil, to maintain the pastures, and to raise animals skillfully. . . . A prince who attends to these things makes his people happy and his state flourishing.

Proposition 11. The true wealth of a kingdom is its men.

It is delightful to see, under good kings, the incredible multitude of people reflected in the astonishing size of their armies. On the contrary, it is shameful that Ahab and the depopulated kingdom of Israel camped with their armies "like two little herds of goats," while the opposing Syrian army covered the face of the earth. In the enumeration of the riches of Solomon, there is nothing more pleasing than the words, "Judah and Israel were innumerable, as the sand of the sea" (I Kings 4:20). The height of felicity and wealth consists in this, that this multitude of people "ate and drank of the fruit of its labors, each under his vine and under his fig tree, and was joyful" (I Kings 4:20, 25). Joy makes the body healthy and vigorous and improves the simple meal taken with the family, far from the fear of any enemy, while blessing the prince who loves peace as the author of so great a wellbeing. Even though such a prince finds himself compelled to go to war, he has no reason to fear it except out of a sense of justice and kindliness. A sad and languishing people loses courage and is good for nothing; the earth itself shows the carelessness with which it is worked; and families are small and forlorn.

Proposition 12. Sure means of increasing the population.

The sure means is to improve the people's lot. Under a wise prince, idleness is odious and ought not to be allowed to enjoy its unjust peace. Idleness corrupts good habits and encourages mischief. It also produces beggars, another race that ought to be banished from a well-run kingdom, as we are reminded by the law: "And there shall be no poor nor beggar among you" (Deuteronomy 15:4). One should not include beggars among the citizens, because they are a charge upon the state, they and their children. To suppress begging one must find a way to relieve poverty. Above all it is necessary to take care of marriages, to make the raising of children easy and pleasant, and to oppose illicit unions. The faithfulness, sanctity and happiness of marriage is a public interest and a source of happiness for the state.

Absolute Monarchy on Trial

3. A Royal Tongue-Lashing (Excerpts from the Official Transcript of the "Session of the Scourging," 3 March 1766)

The Parlement of Paris was the foremost of thirteen regional high courts in France, composed of magistrates who held purchasable offices conferring nobility. As law courts, the parlements gave force of law to royal edicts by registering them and applying them in judicial decisions. As guardians of the laws, they also had the right (and the responsibility) to submit remonstrances counseling the king concerning the legality of the edicts sent them for registration. The king, in turn, had the power to overrule parlementary objections, insisting on the registration of edicts in a special session known as a *lit de justice*.

Theoretically, a *lit de justice* brought the legislative process to an end. But in practice the parlements could continue opposition to royal policies of which they disapproved—falling back, in the last resort, on such tactics as the judicial strike (to which the crown could respond by the tactic of exiling the parlementary magistrates from the seat of their jurisdiction). Thus the legal and judicial functions of the parlements could be translated into a political challenge to the royal authority. In the 1750s and 1760s, conflict between the crown and the parlements became particularly acute, with the various parlements drawing together in a common movement of opposition under the leadership of the Parlement of Paris. This common action, among bodies that were strictly speaking quite separate, was justified in terms of an argument known as the *doctrine des classes:* the claim that the separate parlements were individual parts (or *classes*) of a single body, representative of the whole nation. Louis XV excoriated this doctrine in a special session of the Paris parlement on 3 March 1766, known as the *séance de la flagellation* ("session

From John Rothney, ed., *The Brittany Affair and the Crisis of the Ancien Regime*, pp. 175–78. © 1969 by Oxford University Press, Inc. Reprinted by permission.

of the scourging"). The king's speech is a remarkably concise statement
of the traditional claims of royal absolutism.

This day, after the report on several cases, the king's guards having seized
control of the doors, the court, informed that the king was coming to parlement, deputized messieurs . . . to go and receive him, who . . . met the
said lord king at the foot of the steps, opposite the Sainte-Chapelle, and
accompanied him. . . .

When the king had been elevated to his high place, had seated himself
and put on his hat, he said, "I wish the present session to be an exceptional
one. Monsieur the President, have the chambers assemble." The President,
having put on his hat, said, "Go to the Tournelle, to the Chambers, and
send for the Courts of Requests of the Palace." When all these gentlemen
had entered, taken their ordained places, and sat down, the king removed
his hat, and, having put it on again, said:

"Gentlemen, I have come in person to reply to your remonstrances.
Monsieur de Saint-Florentin, have this answer read by one of you."

Whereupon the Count de Saint-Florentin, having approached the king
and knelt, took from the hands of H. M. the reply, and, having resumed his
place, had it handed to Joly de Fleury, named above, who read it as follows:

"What has happened in my parlements of Pau and Rennes is no concern
of my other parlements; I have acted with regard to these two courts as my
authority required, and I owe an explanation to nobody.

"I would have no other answer to give to the numerous remonstrances
made to me on this subject, if their combination, the impropriety of their
style, the rashness of the most erroneous principles, and the pretension of
the new expressions which characterize them had not revealed the pernicious consequences of that idea of unity which I have already prohibited,
and which people wish to establish as a principle at the same moment in
which they dare to put it into practice.

"I shall not tolerate in my kingdom the formation of an association
which would cause the natural bond of similar duties and common responsibilities to degenerate into a confederation for resistance, nor the introduction into the monarchy of an imaginary body which could only upset its
harmony. The magistracy does not form a body, nor a separate order in the
three orders of the kingdom; the magistrates are my officers, responsible
for carrying out my truly royal duty of rendering justice to my subjects, a
function which attaches them to my person and which will always render
them praiseworthy in my eyes. I recognize the importance of their services;
it is an illusion, which can only tend to shake confidence by a series of
false alarms, to imagine that a plan has been drawn up to annihilate the

magistracy, or to claim that it has enemies close to the throne. Its real, its only enemies are those within it who persuade it to speak a language opposed to its principles; who lead it to claim that all the parlements together are but one and the same body, distributed in several classes; that this body, necessarily indivisible, is the essence and basis of the monarchy; that it is the seat, the tribunal, the spokesman of the nation; that it is the protector and the essential depositary of the nation's liberties, interests, and rights; that it is responsible to the nation for this trust and that it would be criminal to abandon it; that it is responsible, in all concerns of the public welfare, not only to the king, but also to the nation; that it is a judge between the king and his people; that as a reciprocal guardian, it maintains the balance of government, repressing equally the excesses of liberty and the abuses of authority; that the parlements co-operate with the sovereign power in the establishment of laws; that they can sometimes on their own authority free themselves from a registered law and legally regard it as nonexistent; that they must oppose an insurmountable barrier to decisions which they attribute to arbitrary authority, and which they call illegal acts, as well as to orders which they claim to be surprises, and that, if a conflict of authority arises, it is their duty to abandon their functions and to resign from their offices, even if their resignations are not accepted.

To try to make principles of such pernicious novelties is to injure the magistracy, to deny its institutional position, to betray its interests and to disregard the fundamental laws of the state; as if anyone could forget that the sovereign power resides in my person only, that sovereign power of which the natural characteristics are the spirit of consultation, justice, and reason; that my courts derive their existence and their authority from me alone; that the plenitude of that authority, which they only exercise in my name, always remains with me, and that it can never be employed against me; that to me alone belongs legislative power without subordination and undivided; that it is by my authority alone that the officers of my courts proceed, not to the formation, but to the registration, the publication, the execution of the law, and that it is permitted for them to remonstrate only within the limits of the duty of good and useful councilors; that public order in its entirety emanates from me, and that the rights and interests of the nation, which some dare to regard as a separate body from the monarch, are necessarily united with my rights and interests, and repose only in my hands.

"I am convinced that the officers of my courts will never lose sight of these sacred and immutable maxims, which are engraved on the hearts of all faithful subjects, and that they will disavow these extraneous ideas, that spirit of independence and these errors, the consequences of which they could not envisage without terror.

"Remonstrances will always be received favorably when they reflect only the moderation proper to the magistrate and to truth, when their secrecy keeps them decent and useful, and when this method [of remonstrance] so wisely established is not made a travesty of libelous utterances, in which submission to my will is presented as a crime and the accomplishment of the duties I have ordered as a subject for condemnation; in which it is supposed that the whole nation is groaning at seeing its rights, its liberty, its security on the point of perishing under a terrible power, and in which it is announced that the bonds of obedience may soon be broken. But if, after I have examined these remonstrances, and, knowing the case, I have maintained my will, my courts should persevere in their refusal to submit instead of registering at the very express command of the king (an expression chosen to reflect the duty of obedience), if they undertook to annul on their own authority laws solemnly registered, and if, finally, when my authority has been compelled to be employed to its full extent, they dared still in some fashion to battle against it, by decrees of prohibition, by suspensive opposition or by irregular methods such as ceasing their service or resigning, then confusion and anarchy would take the place of legitimate order, and the scandalous spectacle of an open contradiction to my sovereign power would reduce me to the unhappy necessity of using all the power which I have received from God in order to preserve my peoples from the terrible consequences of such enterprises.

"Let the officers of my courts, then, weigh carefully what my good will deigns once again to recall to their attention; let them, in obedience only to their own sentiments, dismiss all prospects of association, all new ideas and all these expressions invented to give credit to the most false and dangerous conceptions; let them, in their decrees and remonstrances, keep within the limits of reason and of the respect which is due me; let them keep their deliberations secret and let them consider how indecent it is and how unworthy of their character to broadcast invective against the members of my council to whom I have given my orders and who have shown themselves so worthy of my confidence. I shall not permit the slightest infraction of the principles set forth in this response. I would expect to find these principles obeyed in my Parlement of Paris, even if they should be disregarded in the others; let it never forget what it has so often done to maintain these principles in all their purity, and that the court of Paris should be an example to the other courts of the kingdom. . . ."

4. Remonstrance of the *Cour des aides* (6 May 1775)

The Paris *Cour des aides* was the court of appeals in the Paris region for matters pertaining to taxation. Like the parlements, it was composed of office-holding magistrates of noble rank. Together with the parlements, whose opposition to the administrative policies of the monarchy it generally shared, it was suppressed by chancellor Maupeou in 1771, when the government of Louis XV decided to take radical measures to reassert absolute royal authority. This "Maupeou revolution," as it was quickly called, threw France into a profound constitutional crisis only brought to an end by the accession of Louis XVI in 1774.

Eager to begin his reign on a note of harmony and concern for the public welfare, Louis XVI replaced Maupeou and restored the sovereign courts. One of the first actions of the Paris *Cour des aides,* once reinstated, was to draw up the following indictment of the fiscal policies of the crown, which offers a summation of the criticisms levelled at the administrative practices of the monarchy by the magistrates in the preceding two decades. Not surprisingly, the remonstrance was not well received by Louis XVI, who insisted on the dangers of "increasing the animosity of taxpayers against those whose ministry is necessary for the levying of taxes." To prevent publication, the magistrates were ordered to hand over the original draft, removing from the registers of their court "a document fit to perpetuate the memory of evils that the king would like to be forgotten." These precautions notwithstanding, a printed version of the remonstrance soon began to circulate.

The remonstrance was written by the First President of the *Cour des aides,* Chrétien-Guillaume de Lamoignon de Malesherbes, member of a distinguished noble family with a long tradition of legal service to the crown. An enlightened magistrate, the friend and supporter of Turgot, Malesherbes served briefly as minister on two occasions (1775–1776 and 1787–1788). He also undertook to defend Louis XVI when the king was tried before the revolutionary Convention. He was executed during the Terror, in 1794.

From *Mémoires pour servir à l'histoire du droit public en France, ou Recueil de ce qui s'est passé. . . à la Cour des Aides. . .* (Brussels, 1775). Translated for this volume by Keith Michael Baker and Anthea Waleson.

Sire:

Your *Cour des aides,* on its own behalf and that of the entire magistracy, has just protested against certain articles of the act reestablishing it. But an even more important duty remains: we must now plead the cause of the people before Your Majesty's tribunal. We must present a faithful picture of the taxes and dues levied in your kingdom, which are the object of the jurisdiction entrusted to us. We must make known to Your Majesty, as your reign begins, the real condition of this people—for the spectacle of a brilliant court will never remind you of it. Who knows, indeed, if the testimony of joy and affection Your Majesty received at your accession from all those able to approach your person may not lead you to form tragic misconceptions about the state of the rest of the nation? For these people were somewhat less miserable than those of the provinces and already happy in their expectations. This nation, Sire, has always shown its zeal and attachment for its masters by making the greatest efforts to maintain the splendor of their throne; but Your Majesty must at least be made aware of what these enormous contributions cost the unfortunate people. . . .

No consideration must stop us, Sire, when we have such important matters to present to Your Majesty. It is nonetheless with regret that we find ourselves obliged to recall those unfortunate times when the absence of ministers of justice and the silence of the laws gave free rein to the greed of financiers and the despotism of administrators. Your Majesty has brought an end to these public ills, and we would like their memory to be entirely effaced by this resounding act of your justice. . . . But there is an important truth, Sire, which we cannot avoid bringing to your attention without betraying our duty. The claim that it is necessary to affirm sovereign authority has served as a pretext for exactions which have been levied with impunity upon your subjects. A league has been formed between the enemies of the courts and those who make the people groan under the weight of arbitrary taxes. These latter lent their support to the destruction of the magistracy and their services in replacing it. The price of this terrible service was the sacrifice of the people to their greed. . . .

We would wish, Sire, that others besides ourselves could acquaint you with these disagreeable truths. Why is it not possible for Your Majesty to abandon today those fatal maxims of government, or rather that policy introduced a century ago by jealous ministers, which has reduced to silence all the orders of the state with the sole exception of the magistracy? Why is it not possible for the nation itself to articulate the interests dearest to it? Then, Sire, with what joy would we return to others the task of informing you of the excesses committed by this same ministry which wanted to destroy us! But since we alone still enjoy the ancient right of Frenchmen, the right of speaking to our kings and of protesting freely against infraction of the laws and of the national rights, we must not show our enemies a generosity which would make us guilty before the entire nation. . . .

France, and perhaps the whole of Europe, is burdened with the weight of taxes; the rivalry of the powers has led them into vying with each other to spend enormous sums which have made taxes necessary; and these taxes are doubled again as the result of an enormous national debt contracted during other reigns. Your Majesty must therefore remember that if your ancestors were covered with glory, that glory is still being paid for by the present generations. They won hearts through their liberality and they amazed Europe with their magnificence; but that magnificence and liberality created taxes and debts which still exist today. . . .

At your accession, all France proclaimed with its acclamations its love for the ruling dynasty. Yet stern duty, Sire, obliges us to tell you that those transports were also in part due to the opinion that has been formed of Your Majesty since your earliest childhood, and the hope that a wise economy would soon diminish the public burden.

But Sire, while this economy is demanded of you by the universal wishes of the entire nation, those who understand sovereign grandeur only in terms of luxury are always the ones who approach closest to the throne. While the wretches robbed of subsistence by harsh taxes are far from your sight, the objects of your benevolence and magnificence are always before your eyes. It has therefore been necessary to oppose to them the shocking, but not exaggerated, portrait of the condition of the people. May it always be before you, Sire! Had it been so for the kings who preceded you, Your Majesty would today be able to follow the dictates of your heart; when it was made known to you that the fiscal laws established in your kingdom are repugnant to humanity, you would not hesitate to revoke them, nor would you be prevented by the need to pay the state's debts, which is always the obstacle to reform of the most odious abuses. . . .

While it is not our function to present you with plans, Sire, and while we must above all avoid abandoning ourselves to uncertain systems, there is still a truth so important, so self-evident, so obviously appealing to Your Majesty that we feel obliged to put it before you. There would be a positive advantage for Your Majesty and an immense one for the people in simplifying the existing taxes and the laws assuring their collection. . . . Your tax farmers would save a great part of the cost of administration and smuggling would become more difficult, for nothing favors it so much as the complexity of the taxes and the obscurity of the regulations. And the people would gain the advantage of being less tormented by the investigations of the employees of the tax farms. . . . But until this work has been accomplished, until this new body of laws has been given to France, is there no other rein to be put upon the despotism of the tax farmers, based as it is upon the public's ignorance of the laws and of the administration of taxes? There is one, Sire, for you can order the Farmers General[1] to publish exact and detailed lists of the taxes to be raised, together with a short, clear, and methodical compendium of regulations which the public must observe and should therefore know. . . .

But we must warn Your Majesty that the tax farmers will only agree to this publication with reluctance, and their very reluctance will demonstrate its necessity. They do not wish the people to know its rights; they wish to keep it in blind submission to the General Farm. . . . But it is your duty, Sire, to procure this tool for your unhappy subjects. You owe them the support of the laws, which becomes illusory when the laws are not known to those who have the right to invoke them. . . .

The vexations occasioned by the collection of the farmed taxes have one justification: the necessity of procuring for Your Majesty the considerable revenue these taxes produce. But it would appear that there need be no such vexations in the case of the taxes levied directly upon the people. If the sum to be raised is fixed, as it should always be, it remains only to choose the form of collection that is most just, most simple, and least wasteful. Thus it is inexcusable to introduce into the levying of these taxes a despotism as useless as it is odious, and a form of administration which adds to the costs of collection that are always borne by the people. That, Sire, is what happens in the levying of all the direct taxes—the *taille,* the head tax (*capitation*), the twentieth (*vingtième*)[2]—and a part of these burdens are even felt in the various types of personal service demanded of the people, such as the militia and required labor service (*corvée*).[3]

But the discussion of these abuses necessarily leads us to much greater

1. The Company of Farmers General was a syndicate of financiers responsible for collecting the important indirect taxes of the Old Regime, such as the salt tax (*gabelle*), the tobacco tax, internal customs duties, tariffs, excises, and other miscellaneous duties. The tax farmers paid the government an annual sum for the privilege of collecting these taxes (thereby assuring regular government income) and made an immense profit on their investment. Given the complexity of the system of indirect taxes involved, they were required to employ a large bureaucracy, whose power was much resented by the populace at large.

2. These were the principal direct taxes at the end of the Old Regime. The oldest, the *taille,* was borne largely by the peasantry, since nobles and clergy were formally exempt, and the inhabitants of the towns were assessed more lightly. The *capitation* was a universal head-tax established in 1695: although it applied in principle to the privileged and non-privileged (but not to the clergy), inequitable assessment and collection greatly diminished its burden upon the nobility. The *vingtième* was a 5 percent income tax that was first introduced as an extraordinary tax in 1749 but soon became permanent; a second and even a third *vingtième* was added in subsequent years. This tax was imposed on all lay incomes, including those of the nobility. The clergy, while formally exempt from all direct taxes, voted an annual *don gratuit* ("free gift") which functioned as a tax in all but name.

3. The *corvée* consisted of unpaid labor service, in this case required for the construction

questions. The imposition of indirect taxes does not depend upon the form of government, but the apportionment of direct taxes is intimately connected with the constitution of the monarchy. The vices of this apportionment form part of a general administrative system which has long existed in your realm, and they can only be remedied by the reform of the entire system that Your Majesty may see fit to introduce.

We shall therefore examine the administration of each of the direct taxes in order that Your Majesty may observe the development of this disastrous system. But we must first consider its origin; we must make plain to Your Majesty its dominating principle and its consequences. You will perhaps be astonished, Sire, to see the extent to which the pretext of your authority has been abused and directed against that authority itself.

Allow us, Sire, to make use of the term *despotism,* odious as it is. Allow us to dispense with embarrassing circumlocutions when we have important truths to bring to your attention. The despotism against which we are protesting today is exercised, without your knowledge, by emissaries of the administration, persons absolutely unknown to Your Majesty. No, Sire, we are not about to offer Your Majesty useless and perhaps dangerous dissertations on the limits of your sovereign power. On the contrary, it is the right to appeal to that power which we are going to claim for all citizens. By *despotism* we refer only to that type of administration which tends to deprive your subjects of that right of appeal which is so precious to them, and which shields from your justice those who oppress the people.

The idea of despotism, or of absolute power, has not been the same in different times and among different peoples. One speaks often of a type of government called *oriental despotism:* not only does the sovereign enjoy absolute and unlimited power in this form of government, but each executor of his orders has boundless power. An intolerable tyranny is the necessary result. For there is an infinite difference between the power exercised by a master whose true interest is identified with his people's, and the force wielded by a subject intoxicated by power for which he was not destined, who amuses himself by aggravating its burden upon his equals. This sort of despotism, transmitted gradually to ministers of different ranks, reaches down to the lowliest citizen, so that there is no one in a great empire safe from it.

The vice of this government inheres both in its constitution and in its customs. It is in the constitution because the people subject to it have nei-

---

and maintenance of royal roads. It was imposed by royal administrators on those who paid the *taille* (i.e., the peasantry) in the local areas through which the roads passed. The royal *corvée* was imposed upon the peasantry in addition to the *corvée* often owed by the peasant to the local seigneur.

ther courts, nor bodies of law, nor representatives. Since there are no courts, authority is exercised by a single man. Since there are no fixed and positive laws, he who holds authority exercises it at his own discretion—which usually means according to his whim. Since there are no representatives of the people, the despot of a province can oppress it with impunity, against the will and without the knowledge of the sovereign.

Customs also contribute to this impunity because people subjected to this type of despotism are always prey to ignorance. No one reads, no news is relayed; the cries of the oppressed are not heard outside the region they inhabit. Thus the innocent victim does not have in his favor that recourse to public opinion which is such a powerful rein on the tyranny of subordinate officials.

Such is the unfortunate situation of these peoples that even the most just sovereign can only make the effects of his justice felt by those able to approach him directly, or in the few matters about which he himself can know. All that he can do for the rest of his subjects is to make as few mistakes as possible in choosing persons to exercise authority on his behalf, and to urge them to make the best choices they can for the subordinate positions. But whatever the sovereign does, the citizen of the lowest rank always trembles beneath the authority of a despot of the lowest rank, to whom he remains as fully subjected as the nobles to the sovereign himself.

It would seem that such a form of government cannot exist in nations which have laws, customs and enlightenment. Thus in civilized countries, even if the prince enjoys absolute power, the condition of the people ought to be very different. However absolute authority may be, justice can be rendered by the deliberation of courts bound by fixed laws. If judges depart from these laws, there is the possibility of appeal to higher courts and finally to the sovereign authority itself. All these appeals are possible because all the acts of authority are written, recorded, and deposited in the public registers, because there is no citizen who cannot find an enlightened defender, and because the public itself is the censor of the judges. Justice is not only rendered to individuals, but corporate bodies, communities, towns and entire provinces can also obtain it; and in order to be able to defend their rights, these latter should have assemblies and representatives.

Thus in a civilized country, even if it is subject to an absolute power, there ought to be no interest, either general or individual, which is not defended. All those entrusted with the exercise of sovereign power ought to be subject to three types of restraint: that of the laws, that of appeal to higher authority, and that of public opinion.

This distinction between the different types of absolute power is not new. The relevant definitions have often been given by jurists and authors, both ancient and modern, who have written about legislation. They are evident from what we read in the histories and accounts of different countries.

But we have been obliged to recapitulate them because we have a great truth to deduce from them. We must make clear to Your Majesty that the government which some would like to establish in France is the true despotism of uncivilized countries. In the most advanced country, in the century when manners and customs are most civilized, we are threatened with that form of government in which the sovereign cannot be enlightened, however sincerely he may desire it.

France, like the rest of western Europe, was once governed by feudal law; but each realm has experienced different transformations since that government was destroyed. There are nations which have been allowed to discuss their rights with the sovereign, and prerogatives have thereby been established. In others, absolute authority prevailed so quickly that none of the nation's rights were examined. This has resulted in at least one advantage for those countries: there is no pretext for destroying the intermediary bodies, or for infringing upon the natural liberty of all men to deliberate together regarding their common interests, and to appeal to the supreme power against the abuses of subordinate powers.

In France, the nation has always had a profound awareness of its rights and its liberty. Our traditional principles have more than once been recognized by our kings, who have gloried in being the sovereigns of a free people. Nonetheless, the articles of our freedom have never been drawn up, and the real power—that power of arms which, under the feudal government, was in the hands of the great nobles—has been totally concentrated in the royal power.

Thus when there have been great abuses of authority, the representatives of the nation have not been content to complain of bad administration. They have felt obliged to claim the nation's rights. They have spoken not only of justice, but of liberty. In response to their efforts the ministers, always quick to seize upon ways of shielding their administration from examination, have had the cleverness to render suspect both the protesting bodies and the protests themselves. To appeal to the king against his ministers has been regarded as an attack on his authority. The grievances of the Estates, the remonstrances of the magistrates, have been transformed into dangerous moves against which the government must protect itself. The most powerful kings of the earth have been persuaded that they must fear even the tears of a submissive people. And on this pretext, a government has been introduced into France which is more fatal than despotism and is worthy of oriental barbarism: the secret administration through which, under the eyes of a just sovereign and in the midst of an enlightened nation, injustice can show itself, nay more, flaunt itself openly. Entire branches of the administration are founded on systems of injustice, and no recourse is possible, either to the public or to superior authority.

This despotism of the administrators and, above all, this system of secrecy is what we must denounce to Your Majesty, for we would never have the temerity to discuss the other sacred rights of the throne. It is sufficient for us that, by reestablishing the magistracy, Your Majesty has disavowed the maxims of tyranny executed under a ministry now dismissed. We will follow Your Majesty's wishes in not stirring up questions which should never have been raised.

But it will not be an offense against *due subordination* to bring to your attention a series of infringements upon national liberty, upon the natural liberty of all men, which have made it impossible for you today to hear your subjects or to clarify the conduct of your administrators.

1. An attempt has been made to abolish the real representatives of the nation.

2. The protests of those representatives whom it has been impossible to destroy have been rendered illusory.

3. There is a desire to make such protests impossible. To achieve this end, two kinds of secrecy have been introduced. One seeks to conceal the operations of the administration from the eyes of the nation and from Your Majesty himself. The other hides the identity of the administrators from the public. This, Sire, is the outline of the system which we denounce to Your Majesty, and which we shall now describe more fully.

We declare that the first aim of this despotism is to do away with all the representatives of the nation. And if Your Majesty will carefully reflect on a series of indisputable facts, the demonstration of this truth will become clear.

The general assemblies of the nation have not been convoked for one hundred and sixty years, and for a long time before that they had become very infrequent—we might even venture to say almost useless, because what most required their presence, the establishment of taxes, was done without them.

Some provinces [called *pays d'Etats*] had their own assemblies or provincial Estates. Many have been deprived of this precious privilege and in the provinces where the assemblies of Estates still exist, their jurisdiction has been restricted within bounds which become narrower every day. It is not a rash assertion to say that there is a sort of continuous warfare in our provinces between the agents of arbitrary power and the representatives of the people, a war in which despotism makes new conquests every day.

The provinces which had no provincial Estates were called *pays d'élection*. Courts called *élections* actually existed there, composed of persons elected by the province itself; at least in the matter of apportioning taxes, they fulfilled some of the functions of the provincial Estates. These courts still exist under the name of *élections*, but the name is all that remains of their original purpose. Their officials are no longer really elected by the province and, insofar as they are, they have been made almost totally dependent upon the intendants for the exercise of the functions remaining to them. . . .

Each corporate body, each community of citizens, at least retained the right to administer its own affairs, a right which we will not say formed part of the original constitution of the realm, for it goes back even further than that. It is a natural right, the right of reason. Nonetheless, even this has been taken away from your subjects, and we do not fear to say that the administration has fallen in this matter into excesses which can only be called puerile.

Since powerful ministers have made it a political principle not to allow the national assembly to be called, we have come, step by step, to the point of declaring the deliberations of the inhabitants of a village void when they are not authorized by the intendant. If this community has to make an expenditure—no matter how small—it must obtain the consent of the intendant's subdelegate,[4] follow the plan he has chosen, employ the workers he favors, pay them as he decides. Similarly, if the community wishes to bring a lawsuit, its action must also be authorized by the intendant: the community's cause must be pleaded before this first tribunal before being brought into the courts of justice, and if the intendant's opinion goes against the inhabitants, or if their adversary can bring influence to bear upon him, the community is deprived of the ability to defend its rights.

These, Sire, are the means employed in the effort to stifle all municipal spirit in France, to extinguish, if possible, even the sentiment of citizenship. The whole nation has, so to speak, been declared incompetent and placed under tutelage.

The destruction of protesting bodies was a first step toward the destruction of the right to protest itself. We have not yet reached the point of an explicit prohibition of all appeals to the prince and all actions by the provinces, but Your Majesty knows that every petition invoking the interests of a province or of the entire nation is regarded as punishable outspokenness when it is signed by a single individual, and as the work of an illicit association when it is signed by several. It was, however, necessary to give the nation some apparent satisfaction when the Estates were no longer being called. Thus the kings announced that the courts of justice would take the place of the Estates and that the magistrates would be the representatives of the people.

4. The intendants were the principal agents of central royal administration in the French provinces. Established in the seventeenth century to superintend tax collection, they rapidly extended administrative control over a great range of financial, judicial, and economic matters. The intendancy was not a purchasable office: intendants were appointed for a specified time and subject to removal; they served, in effect, as the direct instruments of the king's will, as communicated to them by the ministers. Subdelegates were subordinate administrative officials, acting on the intendant's behalf in particular localities.

But after having given the magistrates this title in order to console the nation for the loss of its ancient and true representatives, every opportunity was taken to emphasize that the functions of the judges were limited to their own region and to matters of litigation. The same limits were placed upon the right of representation.

Thus all possible abuses could be committed in the administration without the king ever learning about it either from the representatives of the people (since in most provinces they no longer exist) or from the courts of justice (for they are set aside as incompetent as soon as they venture to speak of administrative matters) or from individuals who have been taught by examples of severity that it is a crime to invoke the justice of their sovereign.

Despite all these obstacles, public outcry—a type of protest which can never be totally extinguished—has always been feared by the administrators; and perhaps they have also been fearful that one day a king would, of his own accord, demand an account of the secrets of the administration. They therefore wished to make such an account impossible, or at least to ensure that one could only be rendered by the administrators themselves, without risk of any contradiction. This is the reason they have made such efforts to introduce clandestine administration everywhere. . . .

For example, it is acknowledged throughout Europe that nothing distinguished the last reign more than the construction of roads facilitating commerce and doubling the value of the realm's wealth. The government has believed until now that the forced labor tax (*corvée*) was necessary for this great work, yet the *corvée* is not authorized by any law of the realm. It seems that it should have been necessary to give this tax judicial sanction, and then it would have been possible to establish fixed and public rules for the allocation of labor that is often more oppressive for the people than the *taille* itself.

This is not the method that has been adopted. It is said that there was fear of the sensation that would be excited throughout the realm by a law which, in regulating the *corvée,* would appear to authorize it. Consequently, all the operations are carried out in secret and there has never even appeared a printed decree of the Royal Council concerning this exaction which has burdened the people for so long. Each province learns that the construction of a road has been ordered only when the work on it is begun; and if the choice of route is contrary to the best interests of the province, it is too late to oppose it. If the work is levied unjustly or too harshly, those who wish to complain have neither legal judges before whom to plead, nor fixed rules to oppose to the severity of the orders they have received, nor judicial means of proving the injustice that has been done them.

It is said that Your Majesty now wishes to mitigate the severity of the *corvée* or to substitute another sort of tax for it. Already grateful, the nation awaits these changes with confidence, and we dare to hope that the replacement for the *corvée* will not be infected with the same secrecy. We have nevertheless felt obliged to point out the abuses which infect the administration of this tax, since they are among the most shocking examples of the general system.

It is the same with the twentieth tax (*vingtième*) and in this case there is even less excuse for the abuse. For it can be said of the *corvée* that the speed necessary in the work does not permit waiting for the discussion of all individual injustices. But the *vingtième* is a tax which has been levied on the same properties every year for nearly forty years, almost without interruption. Is it believable that after these forty years the records of this tax are not yet entered in any register where individuals may consult them? . . . The greater part of the deceptions of the collectors of the *vingtième* are necessarily unknown and unpunished because of this secrecy. For example, when a collector betrays the interests of the treasury by sparing the taxpayer whom he wishes to favor (concealing his deception from the ministers by unjustly enlarging other quotas to make up the difference), those who have been injured cannot make this iniquity known because they could only do so through inspection of the entire roll, which is kept secret.

Your Majesty will see by this example that the sort of abuse favored by the secrecy of the rolls is precisely that which is most contrary to the interest of the king, to the interest of finance, to the fiscal interest. These are not the interests that administrators have protected in forbidding open access to the tax rolls; they have acted solely to shield their administration from investigation, and to insure impunity to their collectors.

And when all the precautions taken for this purpose prove to be insufficient, when the vexations become so obvious that there is no way of smoothing over them, it often happens that the guilty obtain immunity by way of the other sort of secrecy, which we have called secrecy of persons. This consists in the fact that most often one does not know and cannot discover who is responsible for each abuse of authority.

Immediate responsibility for the administration of your realm, Sire, is given by you to ministers aided by their clerks, and in certain branches to intendants of finance, again aided by their clerks. In the provinces, it is carried out by the intendants and their subdelegates. We will examine these different persons, commencing with the lowest rank, those in closest contact with the people.

An intendant's subdelegate is a man without rank and without legal power who has no right to sign any decree. Thus all those he executes are signed by the intendant. It is nevertheless known in the provinces that it is the subdelegate who decides upon many details into which the intendant himself cannot enter. If this subdelegate abuses his power, one can go only to the intendant. But how can we expect ordinary people to dare to seek such recourse when they see that the decree has been issued in the intendant's name, and that this superior magistrate will doubtless feel himself compromised and obliged to uphold it?

The relation between the subdelegate and the intendant in this respect is similar to that between the intendant and the minister, and between the minister and Your Majesty himself.

As often as possible, the intendant avoids making decisions in his own name. In all matters which might compromise him he takes the precaution of securing an Act of Council, or a letter of authorization from the minister. The individual from the province who wishes to appeal against the intendant's judgment and carry his grievances to the Council or the minister, has no recourse when he sees himself condemned in advance by a decision of the minister or an Act of Council. . . .

Finally, the minister himself has no rank in the realm, no direct authority. It is nevertheless in him that all power resides, because it is he who certifies Your Majesty's signature. He can do everything and be held responsible for nothing, because the authority of the name that he is permitted to use closes the lips of anyone who dares to complain.

Thus, just as the inhabitant of a village does not dare defend himself against the vexations of a subdelegate authorized by the decree of an intendant, we, inhabitants of the capital, we personally—magistrates entrusted by our office with bringing the truth to Your Majesty's ears—how many times have we seen ourselves charged with audacity for having protested against orders obtained by ministers from their unknowing king!

Let us dare to speak the entire truth to Your Majesty. Orders whose falseness was patently obvious have been put before us, and others in which the sacred royal name had demonstrably been prostituted in matters unworthy of the king's attention. When we have clearly revealed the petty passions of subordinates for which these orders were obtained—the petty vengeances, the petty patronage—have we not been told that it is lacking in respect for the King's Majesty to doubt that an order signed by the king was really issued by him? . . .

Furthermore, these same ministers have, during the last century, arrogated to themselves the management of so many matters of all kinds that they are unable even to handle them. Thus a new type of intermediary power has been established between your ministers and your other subjects, belonging neither to the provincial governors nor to the provincial intendants. This is the power of the clerks, persons absolutely unknown in the state, who nevertheless speak and write in the name of the ministers and consequently exercise a power as absolute and irresistible as theirs. Indeed, they are even more sheltered from all investigations because they are much less known.

Thus an individual without a patron, a provincial with no ties to the court, for example, can receive the harshest order without knowing by whom it was issued (so that he may obtain its revocation) nor the reasons for its issue (in order for him to present his defense). The order is signed by the king, but this obscure individual knows very well that the king has never heard his name. The king's signature is certified by a minister, but he also knows that he is not known to the ministers. He does not know whether the order has been obtained by the provincial intendant, or whether one of his enemies has gained access to the clerks of one or another level at Versailles, or if it is one of those blank orders which are sometimes given to different authorities in each province. He does not know and he remains in exile, perhaps even in chains. . . .

We certainly anticipate, Sire, that you will hear the accusation that we are attempting to introduce novelties into the administration. In fact, we are only tracing abuses to their source and proposing remedies long since abandoned—like that of having taxes of all kinds allocated by a local body in each province, or of admitting to this same body the representatives of the people who have been ignored for many centuries. Your Majesty should therefore clearly understand that if we are proposing measures that some call novelties, but which are really only the reestablishment of earlier rules, it is because the progress of despotism and the real innovations it is introducing every day make the reestablishment of true principles absolutely necessary.

This must not be concealed from you, Sire, because you wish to ensure the perpetual happiness of this nation which, at the moment of your accession, threw itself into your arms with such touching confidence. Your efforts must not be limited to the reformation of particular abuses; it is the entire system of administration that must be attacked. . . .

The taxes weigh upon the whole people, and their complexity is such that each province, each corporate body, each profession, is subject to some fiscal law which is particular to it and has personal grievances to reveal to Your Majesty. It is not right that a single minister should decide alone and uncontradicted on this multitude of questions, just as it is impossible that a single body of magistrates should interpret to Your Majesty this enormous number of different interests.

The most tangible proof we can offer of the sincerity of our zeal is to show Your Majesty how far, and in what cases, you must be on guard against the ministers and the other administrators. We shall also show Your Majesty how you may be saved from deception by listening to others beyond the magistrates who have for so long been the only ones in the kingdom to exercise the right of representation, and are sometimes inadequate to the entire fulfillment of that important function. . . .

It is certain that in many respects, and perhaps on the greatest number of subjects, the king's ministers merit his confidence more than anyone. For, generally speaking, everything that affects the glory of his reign also affects that of their ministry. Thus the sovereign cannot doubt that his ministers take the most sincere interest in his military success, in the maintenance of his authority within the realm, in the respect in which he is held by foreign powers.

But in other matters, the interest of the minister is not always that of the king. For example, when it is a question of enslaving the people to all the tools of the administration on the pretext of maintaining royal authority, or of extending this administration to cover the most minor matters, there is a great difference between these two interests. For it is not surprising that a subject who has become a minister should be delighted by the smallest details of power, that he should everywhere have friends to protect and enemies to persecute, that his pride should feed upon the obeisance that grows with the accumulation of powers. But a king is too great, too powerful, too far above his subjects to be moved by these petty passions, and he can only see his authority involved in objects worthy of him.

There is a third type of matter in which the ministers' interests not only diverge from the king's interest, but are absolutely contrary to it. This would include all those cases in which there is a question of introducing secret administration. For while it is always in the king's interest that the conduct of his ministers be clearly known, it is sometimes in the ministers' interest that their conduct remain hidden.

Finally, there are a large number of matters upon which, the interest of the king being contrary to that of the ministers, the people have the same interest as the king. But all the people of rank and importance in the state, all those who can approach the king or who can gain his attention, have the same interest as the ministers. And that, Sire, is what most merits your attention, and must be the object of your deepest reflections. For the combined interest of the ministers and all the powerful persons almost always prevails over that of the king and the people.

We have already demonstrated this in the case of the *vingtième* and the *capitation*. These two taxes, in relation to which the ministers and their subordinates have reserved to themselves the right to tax your subjects or modify their taxes arbitrarily and at will, give rise to a despotism odious to France and shameful for a free nation—a despotism contrary to the true interests of Your Majesty, and even to the fiscal interest which the despots constantly sacrifice to their own considerations. But this despotism is very useful to all men of importance because they are the ones who are always treated favorably by the ministers, by the intendants, by the other despots of this type.

It is the same with excessive expenditures. Proposals are constantly being made to restrict them and everyone applauds these reform proposals in theory. But when it comes to executing them, all the ministers, all those who control expenses refuse to do so, and they are supported by all the powers of the court and the capital because it is always these powerful personages who benefit from the ministers' favors.

Still another example is the abuse of the *lettres de cachet*[5] granted to individuals, which every powerful person in the realm thinks he has the right to obtain. And we magistrates, who regard ourselves as representatives of the people but who are also among those men of rank who have access to the ministers, must we not reproach ourselves with having never protested with sufficient energy against this type of abuse?

On all these subjects, Sire, there necessarily exist two parties in the realm. On one side are all those who have access to the king; on the other, the rest of the nation. A king who wants to be just must therefore draw his feelings from his own heart and his knowledge from that of the entire nation.

How then may a relationship between the king and the nation be established which will not be intercepted by all those surrounding a king? We must not hide it from you, Sire. The simplest and most natural means, the one most in accordance with the constitution of this monarchy, would be to listen to the assembled nation itself, or at least to allow assemblies in each province. No one should have the cowardice to tell you otherwise. No one should dare to leave you in ignorance of the fact that the unanimous wish of the nation is to obtain either the Estates General or at least the provincial Estates.

But we also know that for more than a century the jealousy of the ministers and perhaps that of the courtiers has constantly opposed these national assemblies. If France is ever so happy as to have Your Majesty one day decide in their favor, we foresee that difficulties of form will be raised. These difficulties will be easily surmounted when Your Majesty wishes it. They are not of the kind to constitute a real obstacle to the ardent entreaties of the people you love, though it is possible that they may delay for a time the reestablishment of the Estates it so passionately desires. In the mean-

---

5. *Lettres de cachet* were orders under the royal seal, usually commanding the arrest, imprisonment, or other punishment of particular individuals. In addition to their use by the government against those considered a threat to public order, *lettres de cachet* were often secured by private individuals for personal purposes—to discipline errant children, or even to settle private scores. Since they bypassed usual judicial procedures, *lettres de cachet* were frequently denounced at the end of the Old Regime as symbols of arbitrary power.

time, is there no other route by which the people's desires may reach a king who wishes to hear them?

We are not here speaking, Sire, in a language that is foreign to you. All Europe knew that it was Your Majesty's foremost wish on accession to the crown to facilitate the approach of all your subjects to the throne, and that you made it a rule to receive all petitions presented to you. But the secrecy of the administration constantly opposes the mutual desire of the king and the nation to communicate one with another and thwarts this first desire of a young king, one so precious for the people he must govern.

You receive petitions, Sire, from all your subjects. But great abuses can never be presented to you because a record of the government's operations nowhere exists. In order that Your Majesty may learn from the petitions you receive, administration must no longer remain hidden, and all the acts of authority executed in your name must be made known both to the public and to individuals who have the right to complain of them. It is also necessary that the reasons for these actions be published and that each act of authority bear the name of the person by whom it is issued, who must answer for any abuse of power on his part. Otherwise, petitions presented to the king have only a vague object and abuses of authority will always remain unknown and unpunished.

You receive petitions from all your subjects. But the latter are only permitted to appeal to your justice in their personal affairs, while corporate bodies, provinces, the state itself, remain without defenders. Until Your Majesty reestablishes the Estates, therefore, there should at least be deputies from each province, chosen by the province itself, to fulfill, for Your Majesty and your privy council, one of the functions which the attorneys general fill in the courts: that of setting out the interests of the public and above all of the province they represent. . . .

You receive petitions from all your subjects. But are you not aware, Sire, that the greatest number of your subjects, and particularly those who have the greatest need of your protection, are absolutely unable to implore it because they have neither the ability to draw up a memorandum themselves, nor the resources to have it done on their behalf, nor the connections necessary to have it presented before Your Majesty? And what are the resources of those who languish in prison, with every care taken to prevent their getting out, since it is known that the first use they would make of their liberty would be to implore your justice? The representatives of each province should therefore be specially authorized to appoint themselves the defenders of the poor, the weak, the oppressed, and above all the imprisoned, just as in the regular judicial system the attorneys general and advocates general are the natural defenders of the absent, the exiled, minors, in a word of those who cannot defend themselves.

You receive petitions from all your subjects. But there is an important truth, Sire, which we dare to reveal to you today because a year's experience is not enough to convince you of it. This is that the right of every individual to appeal to the sole person of the king is absolutely illusory, because it is impossible for Your Majesty alone to decide, with knowledge of all the facts, upon all the complaints and the often indiscreet requests of many millions of men.

Accordingly, the petitions must be referred back to the various departments. This means that each petition is sent to exactly that person against whom it is directed, for one does not have recourse to Your Majesty himself until one has exhausted all other possibilities and wants now to complain against the minister. But we have made clear that there are very important matters in which the entire ministry, and even those who surround your person, have an interest contrary to that of Your Majesty and of the nation.

Since what the entire nation knows should be communicated to Your Majesty, would it not be possible for the nation itself to examine all these petitions in the first instance, and for its voice to indicate those deserving Your Majesty's personal attention?

Here we must pause, Sire. We have dared to assert that the right of all subjects to appeal to the sole person of the king is useless and illusory, because this is an obvious truth of which Your Majesty himself is certainly convinced. But if we were to go so far as to propose that a public protest be allowed against abuses of the administration, would we not be charged with temerity? Would not all the enemies of public liberty, and especially those who have the privilege of speaking in your name, say that we wish to submit Your Majesty's own actions to public censure? Such an objection is calculated to impose the most respectful silence upon us. However, we ask your permission, Sire, to give you an account of what takes place before our eyes in the conduct of litigation.

A person who appears before a sovereign court has the right to have his arguments printed and published, and when he is appealing the sentence of a lower court the printed memoir stating his case is necessarily a critique of the judgment of that court. Similarly, individuals who appeal to Your Majesty against a decision of a sovereign court by demanding reversal, revision or otherwise, enjoy the same right. They print and publish memoirs signed by a lawyer attached to the Council or by individuals criticizing the decision of the sovereign court by which they believe themselves to have been wronged.

We recognize, Sire, that the publicity of these memoirs is not unanimously applauded. It is said that even the magistrates regard it as an abuse, maintaining that these statements should be used only for the instruction of the judges who must decide each case, and that the public should not be made the judge of the courts.

For our part, Sire, we have always believed and still believe ourselves answerable to Your Majesty and to the nation for the justice which we mete out to individuals. . . . Fundamentally, it is the essence of French justice to be administered publicly. All cases are naturally tried before a public audience, and when one calls the public to witness by means of printed memoirs this only adds to the public quality of the hearing. It may be objected that the profusion in which these memoirs are published is a novelty introduced only in recent years. But the charge of innovation is not a sufficient objection: there are useful novelties, and if we had rejected all innovation we would still be living under the empire of ignorance and barbarism. In any case, it is scarcely possible to regard this practice as a dangerous innovation. On the contrary, Sire, we see it as the reestablishment of the ancient judicial order of this realm, perhaps deriving from the original constitution of the monarchy. This observation will not be unworthy of your attention.

A very ancient monarchy has undergone transformations of many different kinds, particularly when it was founded during the centuries of ignorance and has survived into the most enlightened one. If one considers the history of the nation from this perspective, one sees that the progress of knowledge has produced an infinite difference between the customs and laws of different ages.

In the time of our first ancestors, all agreements between men were verbal and faith in the testimony of witnesses necessarily took the place of acts which no one would have known how to draw up. Similarly, there were only poorly drafted laws, often consisting in an uncertain tradition leaving everything to the interpretation of the judge.

The abuses of this arbitrary justice were enormous, and in all probability it was the very excess of this evil that led to the most simple and efficacious remedy: publicity. The kings themselves administered justice to the nation assembled in the Champ de Mars, with a vigor and authenticity unknown in modern times. Following their example, the great nobles of the state also administered justice, each in his own territory, in the presence of the people.

It must be realized that in this first age administration was not yet separated from the conduct of justice. Both were exercised by the king himself, aided by the expression of the public voice. These redoubtable monarchs even permitted people to complain publicly, in their presence, of the faults of their ministers. They did not fear the humble petitions of those who came to implore their aid, but they were determined to guard themselves against the seductions of those who interposed their precarious power between the king and the people.

In the following age, it became the practice to record the enactments that determined men's status and obligations, and there also emerged a corpus of written jurisprudence to be followed in giving judgments. This age, which could be called the age of writing, had great advantages over the one preceding it, for now the rights of citizens were founded upon established claims and one could hope to be judged not by men's fantasies but by the law itself.

However, the new judicial order had certain disadvantages unknown to previous centuries. There were fixed laws, but their study had become so complicated that only those who devoted themselves entirely to it could perform a judge's functions, or even understand their own affairs. A new order of citizens, the men of law, appeared in the nation. Some of them substituted for the great nobles of the state in rendering justice; others assumed the responsibility of arguing for the rights of individuals. And the nation, the greater part of which was still deep in ignorance, was obliged to place a blind confidence in them.

This was also the point at which justice ceased to be as public as it had been in earlier ages. It was still rendered publicly in hearings held within each tribunal, but when the details of a case required the examination of documents, the judges proceeded with that examination in closed session and the advantage of having the public witness the conduct of the judges was lost.

We note further that it was during this age that administration was separated from the conduct of justice. Lawsuits, and above all appeals, had so multiplied, and jurisprudence had become such a complex science, that it was no longer possible for justice to be rendered either by the king or by the great nobles. Kings entrusted this function to the magistrates, jurisconsults, and graduates in the law, but they reserved administration to themselves. And since the latter was exercised by letters from the prince, instead of the public proclamations of earlier days, everything was done in the secrecy of the cabinet.*

Finally there came a third age, which we shall call the age of printing. This is the period in which printing multiplied the advantages which writing had secured for men and eliminated its drawbacks. Since knowledge has been increased by printing, written laws are known today by everyone.

---

*It is worth noting that this second age was the period in which it was first thought possible to do without the Estates. Before that time, it was absolutely necessary for kings to assemble the nation in order that it might hear their wishes. Soon ministers found a way of making these assemblies more and more infrequent because it suited them to distance their administration from criticism. They then found it so agreeable to work in obscurity that they sought to thicken the veils with which they had covered themselves. This is what gave rise to that clandestine administration which has made so much progress since the time when the Estates General were last called. Thus the secrecy of administration began in the age of writing; and if it has made great progress during the age of printing, this is because appeal against the administration by means of public, printed memoirs is still not permitted. [Author's note.]

Anyone can understand his own affairs. The legal profession has lost the power it enjoyed as a consequence of other men's ignorance. Judges themselves may be judged by an informed public, and this judgment is much more severe and just when it is exercised through calm and reflective reading than when opinions are carried away in a tumultuous assembly.

The art of printing has thus given writing the same publicity that the spoken word possessed in the midst of the assemblies of the nation during the first age. But it has taken many centuries for the discovery of this art to have its full effect upon men. It has required that the entire nation gain the taste and habit of informing itself by reading. And it has required that enough men become skilled in the art of writing to lend their ministry to the entire public, taking the place of those gifted with natural eloquence, who made themselves heard by our forefathers on the Champ de Mars or in the public judicial hearings.

But the moment has arrived, Sire. Your subjects already enjoy its effects in the regular system of justice, since it has become customary to instruct the public and engage its interest by means of printed memoirs. Your Majesty could also confer this same privilege, this same advantage, upon those of your subjects who have grievances against the administration.

It would seem that an appeal to your Council or to your ministers against an intendant or a provincial governor could be as public as appeals to the sovereign courts against a lower court. After all, one may appeal directly to Your Majesty, by means of printed memoirs open to the public, against decisions made in your name by the superior courts—courts so long revered and made up of a great number of magistrates, in which decisions are reached only by a majority vote and after long discussion. Why could one not appeal with the same publicity against other acts of authority also committed in your name, acts which are only the work of a single man, decided upon in secret and with no preliminary discussion? . . .

France has the good fortune to have a master whose first desire was to be enlightened, and who has wanted to allow all his subjects to appeal to his personal justice against all abuses of authority. . . . We have reminded you of the example of those early kings who did not feel their authority threatened by the liberty they gave their subjects to implore their justice in the presence of the assembled nation. It is for you to judge, Sire, whether it will weaken your power to imitate in this matter the conduct of Charlemagne, that proud monarch who so greatly extended the prerogatives of his crown. By following his example you may again reign at the head of a nation whose entire body will be your council; and you will draw greater resources from it because you live in a much more enlightened century. . . .

Enlightenment and Reform

5. Diderot, *The Definition of an Encyclopedia*

The twenty-eight folio volumes of the *Encyclopédie, ou Dictionnaire raisonné des sciences, des arts et des métiers*—seventeen massive volumes of text accompanied by eleven volumes of plates—were published in Paris from 1751 to 1772. The work was originally intended by the publishers as a safe commercial venture involving the translation and revision of Ephraim Chambers' two-volume *Cyclopaedia* published in London in 1728. But when the general direction of the enterprise was entrusted to Denis Diderot (the son of a provincial cutler, at this time still trying not very successfully to scrape together a living in Paris as a translator and writer) and Jean le Rond d'Alembert (the illegitimate son of a noble, already established as a mathematician and member of the Royal Academy of Sciences in Paris) its scope was radically expanded. Diderot (1713–84) and d'Alembert (1717–83) envisaged the *Encyclopédie* as a monument to the enlightenment they saw stirring in Europe, a vast compendium which would bring together and systematize all knowledge worth reading, and an instrument of critical discussion and commonsense reasoning which would ultimately change society by changing "the common way of thinking." The hostile reception of the *Encyclopédie* among the conservative and orthodox made it the focal point of an increasingly bitter conflict of attitudes in the 1750s and 1760s.

ENCYCLOPEDIA, noun, feminine gender (*Philosophy*). This word signifies *unity of knowledge;* it is made up of the Greek prefix EN, *in,* and the nouns KYKLOS, *circle,* and PAIDEIA, *instruction, science, knowledge.* In truth, the aim of an *encyclopedia* is to collect all the knowledge that now lies scattered over the face of the earth, to make known its general structure to the men among whom we live, and to transmit it to those who will come after us, in order that the labors of past ages may be useful to the ages to come, that our grandsons, as they become better educated, may at the same time become more virtuous and more happy, and that we may not die without having deserved well of the human race. . . .

When one comes to reflect upon the vast subject matter of an encyclope-

Excerpt from Diderot, *Rameau's Nephew and Other Works*, translated by Jacques Barzun and Ralph H. Bowen, pp. 277–307. © 1956 by Jacques Barzun and Ralph H. Bowen. Reprinted by permission of Doubleday & Company, Inc.

dia, the one thing that can be perceived distinctly is that it cannot be the work of a single man. For how could one man, in the short space of his lifetime, hope to know and describe the universal system of nature and of art, seeing that the numerous and erudite society of academicians of *La Crusca* has taken forty years to compose its dictionary, and that the members of our French Academy worked sixty years on their *Dictionary* before publishing its first edition? Yet what is a linguistic dictionary, what is a compilation of the words of a language, assuming that it is executed as perfectly as possible? It is a very exact résumé of the articles to be included in a systematic encyclopedic dictionary.

But a single man, it may be said, can master all existing knowledge and can make such use as he desires of all the riches that other men have piled up. I cannot agree with this assumption. I am unable to believe that it is within the power of a single man to know all that can be known; to make use of all the knowledge that exists; to see all that is to be seen; to understand all that is comprehensible. Even if a systematic dictionary of the sciences and of the arts were to be nothing but a methodical collection of elementary principles, I should still want to know who is capable of discerning what is fundamental, and I should still ask who is the proper person to compose the elementary explanations; whether the description of the fundamental principles of a science or art should be a pupil's first attempt or the mature work of a master.

But to demonstrate, with the utmost degree of clarity, how difficult it is for one man ever to bring to completion a systematic dictionary of all knowledge, it is enough to emphasize only the difficulties that arise during the composition of a simple dictionary of words.

A general dictionary of words is a work in which one aims at establishing the meaning of the terms of a language, defining those which can be defined by giving a brief, accurate, clear, and precise enumeration of the qualities or ideas that are attached to them. The only good definitions are those which bring together the essential attributes of the thing to which the word refers. But does everyone have the talents required for knowing and explaining those attributes? Is the art of making good definitions so very common? Are we not all more or less in the same situation as children, who use, with extremely nice precision, an infinite number of words in place of which it would be absolutely impossible for them to substitute the true sets of qualities or ideas which the words stand for? How many unforeseen difficulties arise from this fact when we have occasion to establish the meaning of the most common expressions! We are continually discovering that the ones we least understand are also the ones that we use the most often. What is the cause of this strange phenomenon? It is that we are continually called upon to declare that a thing is *thus-and-so,* but almost never are we obliged to determine what it is *to be thus-and-so*. Our judgments most frequently refer to particular cases, and long habituation to the language and to social life suffices to guide us aright. We do nothing but repeat what we have heard all our lives. It is not at all the same thing when we seek to frame general theories that will embrace, without exception, a given number of particular cases. Nothing but the most profound meditations coupled with the most astonishing breadth of knowledge can lead us surely. I will clarify these principles by giving an example. We say—and no one ever makes a mistake on this point—of an infinite number of articles of all kinds that *they are luxuries;* but what is this *luxury* that we so infallibly attribute to so many things? This is the question which no one can satisfactorily answer with any degree of accuracy until after a discussion among all those who show the most discrimination in their use of the term *luxury*—a discussion which has never taken place and which is perhaps beyond the capacities of the persons concerned.

All terms must be defined, excepting only the radicals, that is to say, those which refer to simple sensations or to the most abstract general ideas. If any have been left out, the dictionary is incomplete. . . . And who will furnish an exact definition of the word *congruent* unless it be a geometrician? of the word *conjugation* unless it be a grammarian? of the word *azimuth* unless it be an astronomer? of the word *epic* unless it be a man of letters? of the word *exchange* unless it be a merchant? of the word *vice* unless it be a moralist? of the word *hypostasis* unless it be a theologian? of the word *metaphysics* unless it be a philosopher? of the word *gouge* unless it be a man well-versed in the manual arts? Whence I conclude that if the French Academy did not unite in its assemblies all the various kinds of human knowledge and the most diverse talents, it would be impossible for it not to overlook a large number of expressions which one would search for in vain in its *Dictionary;* or for it not to allow false, incomplete, absurd, or even ridiculous definitions to creep in. . . .

We shall have to conclude, then, that a good dictionary can never be brought to completion without the co-operation of a large number of men endowed with special talents, because definitions of words are in no way different from definitions of things, and because a thing cannot be well defined or described except by those who have made a long study of it. But if this is admitted, how much more would be required for the execution of a work which, far from being limited to the definition of words, aims at describing in detail all that pertains to things!

A systematic universal dictionary of the arts and sciences cannot, therefore, be the work of one man alone. I will go further and say that I do not believe it can be done by any of the learned or literary societies that now exist, taken singly or together.

The French Academy could furnish an encyclopedia only with what pertains to language and its usage; the Academy of Inscriptions and Belles-Lettres, only knowledge relating to ancient and modern profane history, to chronology, to geography, and to literature; the Sorbonne, only theology, sacred history, and superstitions; the Academy of Sciences, only mathematics, natural history, physics, chemistry, medicine, anatomy, and the like; the Academy of Surgery, only the art of the surgeon; that of Painting, only painting, sculpture, engraving, drawing, architecture, and related topics; the University, only that which we understand by the humanities, scholastic philosophy, jurisprudence, printing, and the like.

Run through the other societies that I may have omitted and you will find that each is occupied with a single field of knowledge—a field that is doubtless within the purview of an encyclopedia—but that each neglects an infinite number of other subjects that must be included. You will not find any single society that can provide you with that fund of general knowledge which you want. Better yet, lay them all under tribute, and you will discover how many things are still lacking; you will be obliged to have recourse to a large number of men of different sorts and conditions—men of genius to whom the gates of the academies are closed by reason of their low rank in the social scale. There are too many members of these learned companies if one's need is simply for human knowledge; there are not enough in all these societies if one is in search of a general science of man.

Without doubt it would be very useful to have all that one could obtain from each particular learned society; and the sum of what they could all provide would advance a universal dictionary a long way toward completion. There is, indeed, a task which, if undertaken, would render the academicians' labors even more directly subservient to the purpose of such a dictionary, and which the academies ought to be asked to do. I can conceive of two ways of cultivating the sciences: one is to increase the general fund of knowledge by making discoveries, and it is by this method that one comes to deserve the name of *inventor;* the other is to bring past discoveries together and reduce them to an ordered scheme so that more men may be enlightened and that each may contribute within the limits of his capacity to the intellectual progress of his age; we use the term *writers of texts* to apply to those who succeed in this second kind of enterprise, which is by no means an easy one. . . .

Having thought very seriously about the matter, I believe that the special task of an academician should be the advancement of the branch of learning to which he is attached. He should strive for immortality by writing books that would have nothing to do with the academy and would not form part of its collections, but would be published under his own name. The academy, for its part, should take as its task the assembling of all that is published on each subject. It should digest this information, clarify it, condense it, arrange it in an orderly way, and publish it in the form of treatises in which no topic would occupy more space than it deserves nor assume any importance except that which cannot be denied it. How many of the memoirs that now burden our collections would furnish not one single line to treatises of this kind!

An encyclopedia ought to make good the failure to execute such a project hitherto, and should encompass not only the fields already covered by the academies, but each and every branch of human knowledge. This is a work that cannot be completed except by a society of men of letters and skilled workmen, each working separately on his own part, but all bound together solely by their zeal for the best interests of the human race and a feeling of mutual good will.

I say, *a society of men of letters and of skilled workmen,* for it is necessary to assemble all sorts of abilities. I wish the members of this society to work separately because there is no existing society from which one could obtain all the knowledge one needs, and because if one wanted the work to be perpetually in the making, but never finished, the best way to secure that result would be to form a permanent society. For every society has its meetings; there are intervals between meetings; each meeting lasts for only a few hours; part of this time is wasted in disputes; and so the simplest problems consume entire months. . . .

I add: *men bound together by zeal for the best interests of the human race and by a feeling of mutual good will,* because these motives are the most worthy that can animate the souls of upright people and they are also the most lasting. One has an inward sense of self-approval for all that one does; one becomes enthusiastic, and one undertakes, out of regard for one's friends and colleagues, many a task that one would not attempt for any other consideration. I can certainly testify from my own experience that the success of such attempts is all the more assured. The *Encyclopedia* has brought together its materials in a very short time. It is no sordid self-interest that has assembled and spurred on the authors; rather they have seen their efforts seconded by the majority of the men of letters from whom they expected assistance, and the only annoyance they have suffered in the course of their work has been caused by persons who had not the talent necessary to contribute one single good page.

If the government were to meddle with a work of this sort it would never be finished. All that the authorities ought to do is encourage its completion. A monarch may, by a single word, cause a palace to rise up out of the grass; but a society of men of letters is not the same thing as a gang of laborers. An encyclopedia cannot be produced on order. It is a task that needs rather to be pursued with perseverance than to be begun with ardor.

An enterprise of this sort may on occasion be proposed in the course of a conversation at Court; but the interest which it arouses in such circles is never great enough to prevent its being forgotten amidst the tumult and confusion of an infinite number of more or less pressing affairs. Literary projects which great noblemen conceive are like the leaves that appear in the spring, grow dry in the autumn and fall in a heap in the depths of the forest, where the sustenance they give to a few sterile plants is all the effect they can be seen to produce. . . . Private individuals are eager to harvest the fruits of what they have sown; the government has none of this economic zeal. I do not know what reprehensible motive it is that leads people to deal less honestly with a prince than with his subjects. One assumes the lightest of obligations and then expects the most handsome rewards. Uncertainty as to whether the project will ever have any useful results fills the workmen with inconceivable indolence. To lend to all these disadvantages the greatest possible force, projects ordered by sovereigns are never conceived in terms of pure utility, but always in terms of the dignity of the sponsor; that is to say, the scale is as large as possible; obstacles are continually arising; men, special abilities, and time are needed in proportion to surmount them; and before the end is in sight, there is sure to intervene a change of ministers. . . . If the average life expectancy of an ordinary man is less than twenty years, that of a minister is less than ten. And not only are interruptions more frequent when it is a question of some literary project; they are also more damaging when the government is the sponsor than when the publishing enterprise is conducted by private individuals. In the event of shipwreck, the individual at least gathers up the debris of his undertaking and carefully preserves the materials that may be of service to him in a happier time; he hastens to salvage something from his investment. But the spirit of monarchy scorns this sort of prudence; men die, and the fruit of their toil disappears so completely that no one can discover what became of it.

The most important consideration, however, and one that lends added weight to the previous ones, is that an encyclopedia, like a dictionary, must be begun, carried forward and completed within a certain period of time. But sordid self-interest exerts itself to prolong any work that a king has commissioned. If one should devote to a universal and systematic dictionary all the long years that the vast scope of its subject matter seems to require, it would come about, thanks to the revolutionary changes which are scarcely less rapid in the arts and sciences than in language, that this dictionary would be a hundred years out of date, just as a dictionary of language which was composed slowly could end only by being a list of words used in the previous century. . . .

When one discusses the phenomena of nature, what more can one do than summarize as scrupulously as possible all their properties as they are known at the time of writing? But observation and experimental science unceasingly multiply both phenomena and data, and rational philosophy, by comparing and combining them, continually extends or narrows the range of our knowledge and consequently causes the meanings of accepted words to undergo change, renders their former definitions inaccurate, false, or incomplete, and even compels the introduction of new words.

But the circumstance that will give a superannuated appearance to the work and bring it the public's scorn will be above all the revolution that will occur in the minds of men and in the national character. Today, when philosophy is advancing with gigantic strides, when it is bringing under its sway all the matters that are its proper concern, when its tone is the dominant one, and when we are beginning to shake off the yoke of authority and tradition in order to hold fast to the laws of reason, there is scarcely a single elementary or dogmatic book which satisfies us entirely. We find that these works are put together out of the productions of a few men and are not founded upon the truths of nature. We dare to raise doubts about the infallibility of Aristotle and Plato, and the time has come when the works that still enjoy the highest reputation will begin to lose some of their great prestige or even fall into complete oblivion. Certain literary forms—for want of the vital realities and actual custom that once served them as models—will no longer possess an unchanging or even a reasonable poetic meaning and will be abandoned; while others that remain, and whose intrinsic value sustains them will take on an entirely new meaning. Such are the consequences of the progress of reason, an advance that will overthrow so many old idols and perhaps restore to their pedestals some statues that have been cast down. The latter will be those of the rare geniuses who were ahead of their own times. We have had, if one may thus express it, our contemporaries in the age of Louis XIV. . . .

In a systematic, universal dictionary, as in any work intended for the general education of mankind, you must begin by contemplating your subject in its most general aspects; you must know the state of mind of your nation, foresee the direction of its future development, hasten to anticipate its progress so that the march of events will not leave your book behind but will rather overtake it along the road; you must be prepared to work solely for the good of future generations because the moment of your own existence quickly passes away, and a great enterprise is not likely to be finished before the present generation ceases to exist. But if you would have your work remain fresh and useful for a long time to come—by virtue of its being far in advance of the national spirit, which marches steadily forward—you must shorten your labors by multiplying the number of your helpers, an expedient that is not, indeed, without its disadvantages, as I shall try to make plain hereafter.

Nevertheless, knowledge is not infinite, and cannot be universally diffused beyond a certain point. To be sure, no one knows just where this limit may be. Still less does anyone know to what heights the human race might have attained nor of what it might be capable, if it were in no way hampered in its progress. Revolutions are necessary; there have always been revolutions, and there always will be; the maximum interval between one revolution and another is a fixed quantity, and this is the only limit to what we can attain by our labors. For there is in every science a point beyond which it is virtually impossible to go. Whenever this point is reached, there will be created landmarks which will remain almost forever to astonish all mankind.

But if humanity is subject to certain limitations which set bounds to its strivings, how much narrower are the limits that circumscribe the efforts of individuals! The individual has but a certain quantity of energy both physical and intellectual. He enjoys but a short span of existence, he is constrained to alternate labor with repose; he has both instincts and bodily needs to satisfy, and he is prey to an infinite number of distractions. Whenever the negative elements in this equation add up to the smallest possible sum, or the positive elements add up to the largest possible sum, a man working alone in some branch of human knowledge will be able to carry it forward as far as it is capable of being carried by the efforts of one man. Add to the labors of this extraordinary individual those of another like him, and of still others, until you have filled up the whole interval of time between one scientific revolution and the revolution most remote from it in time, and you will be able to form some notion of the greatest perfection attainable by the whole human race—especially if you take for granted a certain number of accidental circumstances favorable to its labors, or which might have diminished its success had they been adverse.

But the general mass of men are not so made that they can either promote or understand this forward march of the human spirit. The highest level of enlightenment that this mass can achieve is strictly limited; hence it follows that there will always be literary achievements which will be above the capacities of the generality of men; there will be others which by degrees will fall short of that level; and there will be still others which will share both these fates.

No matter to what state of perfection an encyclopedia may be brought, it is clear from the very nature of such a work that it will necessarily be found among this third class of books. There are many things that are in daily use among the common people, things from which they draw their livelihood, and they are incessantly busy gaining a practical knowledge of these things. As many treatises as you like may be written about these matters and still there will always come a time when the practical man will know more about them than the writer of the book. There are other subjects about which the ordinary man will remain almost totally ignorant because the daily accretions to his fund of knowledge are too feeble and too slow ever to form any considerable sum of enlightenment, even if you suppose them to be uninterrupted.

Hence both the man of the people and the learned man will always have equally good reasons for desiring an encyclopedia and for seeking to learn from it.

The most glorious moment for a work of this sort would be that which might come immediately in the wake of some catastrophe so great as to suspend the progress of science, interrupt the labors of craftsmen, and plunge a portion of our hemisphere into darkness once again. What gratitude would not be lavished by the generation that came after this time of troubles upon those men who had discerned the approach of disaster from afar, who had taken measures to ward off its worst ravages by collecting in a safe place the knowledge of all past ages! In such a contingency—I may say it without being immodest because our *Encyclopedia* will perhaps never attain the perfection that would make it deserving of such honor—in such a contingency, men would speak, in the same breath in which they named this great work, of the monarch in whose reign it was undertaken, of the minister to whom it was dedicated, of the eminent men who promoted its execution, of the authors who devoted themselves to it, and of all the men of letters who lent their aid. The same voice that recalled these services would not fail to speak also of the sufferings that the authors were obliged to undergo, of the indignities that were heaped upon them; and the monument raised to their fame would have several faces where one would see in turn the honors accorded to their memory and the signs of posterity's reprobation for the names of their enemies. . . .

Both the real universe and the world of ideas have an infinite number of aspects by which they may be made comprehensible, and the number of possible systems of human knowledge is as large as the number of these points of view. The only system that would be free from all arbitrariness is, as I have said in our "Prospectus," the one that must have existed from all eternity in the mind of God. Hence the plan according to which one would begin with this eternal Being and then descend from Him to all the lesser beings that have emanated from His bosom in the course of time. This plan would resemble the astronomical hypothesis in which the scientist transports himself in imagination to the center of the sun so as to be able to calculate there the behavior of the heavenly bodies that surround him. It is a scheme that has both simplicity and grandeur, but one may discern in it a defect that would be serious in a work composed by men of science and addressed to all men in all ages to come. This is the fault of being too closely tied to our prevailing theology—a sublime science and one that is undoubtedly useful by reason of the knowledge that the Christian receives from it, but even more useful by reason of the sacrifices it demands and the rewards it promises.

As for a general system from which all that is arbitrary would be excluded—something we mortals can never hope to possess—it might not, perhaps, be so great an advantage to possess it. For what would be the difference between reading a book in which all the hidden springs of the universe were laid bare, and direct study of the universe itself? Virtually none: we shall never be capable of understanding more than a certain portion of this great book. To the extent that our impatience and our curiosity—which overmaster us and so often break up the course of our observations—disturb the orderly conduct of our reading, to that extent is our knowledge liable to become disjointed, as it now is. Losing the chain of inductive logic, and ceasing to perceive the connections between one step and those before and after, we would speedily come upon the same lacks and the same uncertainties. We are now busy trying to fill up the voids by means of the study of nature; we would still be busy trying to fill them up if we possessed and could meditate upon that huge book of which I have spoken; but the book would seem no more perfect to our eyes than would the universe itself, and the book would therefore be no less exposed to our presumptuous doubts and objections.

Since an absolutely perfect general plan would in no way supply the deficiencies arising from the weakness of our understanding, let us instead take hold of those things that are bound up with our human condition, being content to make our way upward from them toward some more general notions. The more elevated the point of view from which we approach our subject, the more territory it will reveal to us, the grander and more instructive will be the prospect we shall survey. It follows that the order must be simple, for there is rarely any grandeur without simplicity; it must be clear and easy to grasp, not a tortuous maze in which one goes astray and never sees anything beyond the point where one stands. No, it must rather be a vast, broad avenue extending far into the distance, intersected by other highways laid out with equal care, each leading by the easiest and shortest path to a remote but single goal.

Another consideration must be kept in view. I mean that if one banishes from the face of the earth the thinking and contemplating entity, man, then the sublime and moving spectacle of nature will be but a sad and silent scene; the universe will be hushed; darkness and silence will regain their sway. All will be changed into a vast solitude where unobserved phenomena take their course unseen and unheard. It is only the presence of men that makes the existence of other beings significant. What better plan, then, in writing the history of these beings, than to subordinate oneself to this consideration? Why should we not introduce man into our *Encyclopedia,* giving him the same place that he occupies in the universe? Why should we not make him the center of all that is? Is there, in all infinite space, any point of origin from which we could more advantageously draw the extended lines which we plan to produce to all the other points? With man at the center, how lively and pleasing will be the ensuing relations between man and other beings, between other beings and man!

For this reason we have decided to seek in man's principal faculties the main divisions within which our work will fall. Another method might be equally satisfactory, provided it did not put a cold, insensitive, silent being in the place of man. For man is the unique starting point, and the end to which everything must finally be related if one wishes to please, to instruct, to move to sympathy, even in the most arid matters and in the driest details. Take away my own existence and that of my fellow men and what does the rest of nature signify?

Although I believe that there is a point beyond which it is dangerous to add further material, I also think that one should not stop until one is very sure that this point has been reached. All the arts and sciences have their metaphysical principles, and this part is always abstract, elevated and difficult. None the less this part must be the main concern of a philosophical dictionary; and one must admit, too, that no matter how much remains to be done in this field, there will still be phenomena that cannot be explained. . . . It happens inevitably that the man of letters, the savant, and the craftsman sometimes walk in darkness. If they make some small amount of progress it is due to pure chance; they reach their goal like a lost traveler who has followed the right path without knowing it. Thus it is of the highest importance to give a clear explanation of the metaphysical basis of phenomena, or of their first, most general principles.

By this means the rest will be made more luminous and more certain in the reader's mind. Then all those alleged mysteries, for which some sciences are so much blamed—and which other scientists so often dwell upon in order to excuse their own obscurities—will vanish in the course of a sound metaphysical discussion like the phantoms of the night at the approach of day. The arts, their path well-lighted from the very first step, will advance rapidly and safely, and always by the shortest way. One must therefore make the most serious attempt to explain the reasons that lie at the roots of things, when these exist. One must assign causes when they are known, indicate effects when these are certain, resolve difficulties by the direct application of fundamental principles, demonstrate truths, expose errors, skillfully discredit prejudices, teach men to doubt and to wait, dissipate ignorance and put a just value on the different kinds of human knowledge, distinguish the true from the false, the true from the probable, the probable from the miraculous and the incredible, the common event from the extraordinary, the certain fact from the doubtful one, and the latter from those that are absurd and contrary to the laws of nature, understand the general course of natural events and take each thing only for what it is, and—consequently—inspire in men a taste for science, an abhorrence of lies, a hatred of vice and a love of virtue; for whatever does not have happiness and virtue as its final goal is worth nothing.

A thing that I consider intolerable is that one should lean upon some ancient writer's authority in questions that require only the use of reason. In what way is the truth changed by an attempt to bolster it with the name of some man who is in no wise infallible? Above all, let us have no quoting of poetry, for this is sure to seem feeble and poor in the midst of a philosophical discussion: let us rather consign these fragile ornaments to the articles dealing with literature. In that context I approve of them, on condition that they are tastefully used, or made to serve as examples to illustrate forcefully the point being made—either some defect that one wishes to correct or some especially felicitous bit that is singled out for praise.

In scientific writings it is the logical connection of ideas or of phenomena that directs our progress step by step as we advance; the subject is developed either by becoming more general or by descending to particulars depending upon our choice of method. The same will hold true of the general form of the articles in the *Encyclopedia,* but with the difference that in our dictionary we shall, thanks to the co-ordination of articles, enjoy advantages which one can scarcely hope to find in a scientific treatise, save at the expense of some sacrifice in quality. The use of *cross references,* the most important part of our encyclopedic scheme, will provide us with these opportunities.

I have in mind two sorts of cross reference—one concerned with words and the other with things. Cross references to things clarify the subject; they indicate its close connections with other subjects that touch it directly as well as its more remote connections with still other matters that might otherwise be thought irrelevant; and they suggest common elements and analogous principles. They also put added stress on elements of internal consistency within groups of facts, they elaborate upon the connections that each special branch of knowledge has with its parent tree, and they give to the whole *Encyclopedia* that unity so favorable to the establishment of truth and to its propagation. Moreover, whenever the occasion demands, they will also lend themselves to a contrasting purpose—they will confront one theory with a contrary one, they will show how some principles conflict with others, they will attack, undermine and secretly overthrow certain ridiculous opinions which no one would dare to oppose openly. When the author is impartial, they will always have the double function of confirming and of confuting, of disturbing and of reconciling.

There should be great scope for ingenuity and an infinite advantage for the authors in this latter sort of cross reference. From them the work as a whole should acquire an inner force and a secret efficacy, the silent results of which will necessarily be felt with the passage of time. Each time, for instance, that a national prejudice seems to merit respect, it will be necessary, in the article specially devoted to it, to discuss it respectfully and to surround it with all its panoply of probability and attractiveness; but by giving cross references to articles where solid principles serve as the foundation for diametrically opposed truths, we shall be able to throw down the whole edifice of mud and scatter the idle heap of dust. This method of putting men on the right path works very promptly upon good minds, and it operates unfailingly, without the least undesirable effect, secretly and unobtrusively, upon all minds. This is the way to lead people, by a series of tacit deductions, to the most daring conclusions. If these cross references, which now confirm and now refute, are carried out artistically according to a plan carefully conceived in advance, they will give the *Encyclopedia* what every good dictionary ought to have—the power to change men's common way of thinking.

Finally, there is a kind of cross reference—it can refer either to words or to things—which I should like to call satirical or epigrammatic. Such, for example, is the one to be found in one of our articles where, at the end of a pompous eulogy, one reads: "See CAPUCHON." The comic word, "capuchon" [monk's hood], together with what the reader will find under the heading "CAPUCHON," can easily lead him to suspect that the pompous eulogy was meant ironically, and that it is wise to read the article with the utmost precaution and with attention to the careful weighing of every word.

I should not like altogether to do without this kind of reference; it is often very useful. One can aim it secretly against certain ridiculous customs in the same way that the philosophical reference is directed against certain prejudices. It frequently affords a delicate and amusing way to pay back an insult without even seeming to put oneself on the defensive, and it offers an excellent means of snatching off the masks from the faces of certain grave personages.

We have had occasion to learn in the course of our editorial labors that our *Encyclopedia* is a work that could only be attempted in a philosophical century; that this age has indeed dawned; and that posterity, while raising to immortality the names of those who will bring man's knowledge to perfection in the future, will perhaps not disdain to remember our own names. We have felt ourselves spurred on by the ever so agreeable and consoling idea that men may speak to one another about us, too, when we shall have ceased to exist; we have been encouraged by hearing from the mouths of a few of our contemporaries a certain seductive murmur that gives us some hint of what may be said of us by those happy and enlightened men in whose interests we have sacrificed ourselves, whom we esteem and whom we love, even though they have not yet been born. We have sensed within ourselves a growing spirit of emulation which has moved us to sacrifice the better part of ourselves and which has ravished away into the void the few hours of our lives of which we are genuinely proud. Indeed, man reveals himself to his contemporaries and is seen by them for what he is: an odd mixture of sublime talents and shameful weakness. But our failings follow our mortal remains into the tomb and disappear with them forever; the same earth covers them both, and there remains only the eternally lasting evidence of our talents enshrined in the monuments we raise to ourselves, or in the memorials that we owe to public gratitude and respect—honors which a proper awareness of our own deserts enables us to enjoy in antici-pation, an enjoyment that is as pure, as great, and as substantial as any other pleasure, and in which there is nothing imaginary except, perhaps, the title deeds on which we base our pretensions. Our own claims are con-signed to posterity in the pages of this work, and in the future they will be judged.

I have said that it could only belong to a philosophical age to attempt an *Encyclopedia;* and I say so because a work such as this demands more in-tellectual courage than is commonly to be found in ages of pusillanimous taste. All things must be examined, all must be winnowed and sifted with-out exception and without sparing anyone's sensibilities. One must dare to see, as we are beginning to do, that the history of literary forms is much the same as that of the first codification of law or the earliest foundation of cities—all owe their origin to some accident, to some odd circumstance, sometimes to a flight of human genius; and those who come after the first inventors are for the most part no more than their slaves. Achievements that ought to have been regarded only as first steps came blindly to be taken for the highest possible degree of development, and so, instead of advancing a branch of art toward perfection, these first triumphs only served to retard its growth by reducing all other artists to the condition of servile imitators. As soon as a name was given to some composition of a particular kind everyone was obliged to model all his productions rigorously after that model, which was perhaps only a sketch. If, from time to time, there ap-peared men of bold and original genius who, weary under the prevailing yoke, dared to shake it off, to strike out in a new direction away from the beaten path, and to give birth to some work of art to which the conven-tional labels and the prescribed rules were not exactly applicable, they fell into oblivion and remained for a long time forgotten.

Now, in our own age, we must trample mercilessly upon all these an-cient puerilities, overturn the barriers that reason never erected, give back to the arts and sciences the liberty that is so precious to them. . . . The world has long awaited a reasoning age, an age when the rules would be sought no longer in the classical authors but in nature, when men would come to sense the false and the true that are mingled in so many of the arbitrary philosophies of art, whatever field one works in. (I take the term *philosophy of art* in its most general meaning, that of a system of accepted rules to which it is claimed that one must conform in order to succeed.)

But the world has waited so long for this age to dawn that I have often thought how fortunate a nation would be if it never produced a man of exceptional ability under whose aegis an art still in its infancy makes its first too-rapid and too-ambitious steps forward, thereby interrupting its natural, imperceptible rhythm of development. . . . When the arts and sciences advance by imperceptible degrees, one man will not differ enough from another man to inspire the latter with awe, to lay the foundations of a new style or to form the national taste. Consequently, nature and reason are safeguarded in all their rights. Should these have been lost, they are on the point of being recovered; we shall go on to show how important it is to be able to recognize and to seize upon such a moment.

As long as the centuries continue to unfold, the number of books will grow continually, and one can predict that a time will come when it will be almost as difficult to learn anything from books as from the direct study of the whole universe. It will be almost as convenient to search for some bit of truth concealed in nature as it will be to find it hidden away in an immense multitude of bound volumes. When that time comes, a project, until then neglected because the need for it was not felt, will have to be undertaken.

If you will reflect on the state of literary production in those ages before the introduction of printing, you will form a mental picture of a small number of gifted men who are occupied with composing manuscripts and a very numerous body of workmen who are busy transcribing them. If you look ahead to a future age, and consider the state of literature after the printing press, which never rests, has filled huge buildings with books, you will find again a twofold division of labor. Some will not do very much reading, but will instead devote themselves to investigations which will be new, or which they will believe to be new (for if we are even now ignorant of a part of what is contained in so many volumes published in all sorts of languages, they will know still less of what is contained in those same books, augmented as they will be by a hundred—a thousand—times as many more). The others, day laborers incapable of producing anything of their own, will be busy night and day leafing through these books, taking out of them the fragments they consider worthy of being collected and preserved. Has not this prediction already begun to be fulfilled? And are not several of our literary men already engaged in reducing all big books to little ones, among which there are still to be found many that are superfluous? Let us assume that their extracts have been competently made, and that these have been arranged in alphabetical order and published in an orderly series of volumes by men of intelligence—you have an *encyclopedia!*

Thus we have now undertaken, in the interests of learning and for the sake of the human race, a task to which our grandsons would have had to devote themselves; but we have done so under more favorable circumstances, before a superabundance of books should have accumulated to make its execution extremely laborious.

Because it is at least as important to make men better as it is to make them less ignorant, I should not be at all displeased if someone were to make a collection of all the most striking instances of virtuous behavior. These would have to be carefully verified, and then they could be arranged under various headings which they would illuminate and make vivid. Why should we be so concerned to preserve the history of men's thoughts to the neglect of the history of their good deeds? Is not the latter history the more useful? Is it not the latter that does the most honor to the human race? I have no wish to see evil deeds preserved; it would be better if they had never taken place. Men have no need of bad examples, nor has human nature any need of being further cried down. It should not be necessary to make any mention of discreditable actions except when these have been followed—not by the loss of the evildoer's life and worldly goods, which is all too often the sad consequence of virtuous behavior—but by a more fitting punishment of the wicked man: I want him to be wretched and despised as he contemplates the splendid rewards he has gained by his crimes. . . .

Whoever assumes responsibility for writing the part of a future encyclopedia devoted to the mechanical arts will never be able to perform his task to his own satisfaction or to that of others unless he has made a profound study of natural history (especially of mineralogy), unless he is expert in things mechanical, unless he is well-versed in theoretical as well as experimental physics, and unless he has made an extensive study of chemistry.

As a naturalist he will recognize at a glance the materials employed by craftsmen and artisans, materials which they generally claim are endowed with all sorts of mysterious properties.

As a chemist he will be fully conversant with the properties of these materials, and the reasons for a multitude of operations will be known to him. He will smell out secret recipes and the workmen will not be able to pull the wool over his eyes, for he will perceive in an instant the absurdity of their lies. He will grasp the whole nature of a process, no motion of the hand will escape him, for he will easily distinguish a meaningless flourish from an essential precaution. Everything he writes on the raw materials used in industry will be clear, authoritative, and instructive. Suggestions as to the means of perfecting the materials now in use, the possibility of recovering lost processes, and the ways of discovering new ones will present themselves abundantly to his mind.

Physics will make him master of an infinite number of phenomena which continue to be a source of lifelong astonishment to the simple workman.

With some knowledge of mechanics and geometry he will arrive without difficulty at a true and exact calculation of forces. He will need only to acquire experimental knowledge to moderate the rigor of his mathematical hypotheses. This quality of moderation is one that especially distinguishes the great master craftsmen from the ordinary workman, particularly when it is a question of constructing delicate machines. The workman never seems able to acquire a just idea of this principle of moderation unless he has in fact learned to practice it, and once he has formed wrong notions about it there is almost no chance of putting him straight.

Armed with these scientific attainments, our author will begin by drawing up a plan of classification according to which the various branches of industry will be attached to the natural substances which they transform. This will always be a workable plan, for the history of the arts and crafts is nothing but the history of nature put to use.

Then he will sketch out for each workman a rough memorandum whose outlines are to be filled in. He will require each one to discuss the materials he uses, the places from which he procures these, the prices he pays for them, the tools he uses, the products he makes, and the whole series of operations he performs.

He will compare the memoranda furnished by craftsmen with his own original sketch; he will confer with them; he will make them supply orally any details they may have omitted and explain whatever they may have left obscure.

However bad these memoranda may be, when written in good faith they will always be found to contain an infinite number of things which the most intelligent of men would never have perceived unaided, would never even have suspected, and hence could never have asked about. Indeed, he will wish to know still more, but these matters will be part of the trade secrets which workmen never reveal to anyone. I myself have found by experience that people who continually busy themselves with something are equally disposed to believe either that everyone knows these things which they are at no pains to hide, or that no one else knows anything about the things they are trying to keep secret. The result is that they are always ready to mistake any person who questions them either for a transcendent genius or for an idiot.

During the time when the workmen are filling out their questionnaires, the author may busy himself with correcting the articles which our *Encyclopedia* will have handed down to him. It will not take long to see that, despite all the pains we have been to, a few gross errors have slipped in, and that there are whole articles in which there is not a shadow of common sense; but he will learn from his own experience to be grateful to us for those parts that are well done and to forgive us for those that are poor. Above all, once he has made the rounds of the workshops over a certain period of time, money in hand, and once he has been made to pay dearly for the most ridiculous fabrications, he will know what sort of people these artisans are—especially here in Paris, where fear of the tax collector keeps them in a perpetual state of mistrust, and where they regard every man who questions them at all closely either as a spy for the farmers-general or as a rival craftsman who wants to set up shop. It seems to me that one might avoid these annoyances by seeking in the provinces all the information about the industrial arts that can be found there—the inquirer would be known for what he is; he would be talking to people who would not be suspicious of his motives, money is more valuable there, and time is not so precious. All of which makes me think that one would obtain information more easily and at less expense, and that the information itself would be more reliable.

One must indicate the origin of each art and follow its progress step by step whenever these steps are known; or, if they are not, then conjecture and hypothetical history must be substituted for the historical reality. One can be sure that in such cases, the imagined story will often be more instructive than the truth could possibly be.

But it is not the same with the origin and progress of an art or trade as it is with the origin and progress of a science. Learned men discuss things with each other, they write, they call attention to their discoveries, they contradict one another and are contradicted. These disputes make the facts plain and establish dates. Craftsmen, by contrast, live isolated, obscure, unknown lives; everything they do is done to serve their own interests; they almost never do anything just for the sake of glory. There have been inventions that have stayed for whole centuries in the closely guarded custody of single families; they are handed down from father to son; they undergo improvements or they degenerate without anyone's knowing to whom or to what time their discovery is to be assigned. . . .

There are trades where the craftsmen are so secretive that the shortest way of gaining the necessary information would be to bind oneself out to some master as an apprentice or to have this done by some trustworthy person. There would be few secrets that one would fail to ferret out by this method; all would have to be divulged without any exception.

I know that this desire for an end to secrecy is not shared by everyone. There are narrow minds, ill-formed souls, who are indifferent to the fate of the human race, and who are so completely absorbed in their own little group that they can see nothing beyond the boundaries of its special interests. These men insist that they deserve the title of good citizens, and I will allow it to them provided they will permit me to call them *bad men*. To listen to them talk, one would say that a well-executed encyclopedia, a general history of the industrial arts, should only take the form of a huge manuscript that would be carefully locked up in the King's library, hidden away from all other eyes but his, a state document and not a popular book. What is the good of divulging the knowledge a nation possesses, its private affairs, its inventions, its industrial processes, its resources, its trade secrets, its enlightenment, its arts, and all its wisdom! Is it not to these things that it partly owes its superiority over the rival nations that surround it? This is what they say; but this is what one might add: would it not be a fine thing if, instead of enlightening the foreigner, we could spread darkness over him or even plunge all the rest of the world into barbarism? People who argue thus do not realize that they occupy only a single point on our globe and that they will endure only an instant. To this point and to this instant they would sacrifice the happiness of future ages and that of the whole human race.

They know as well as anyone that the average duration of empires is less than two thousand years, and that in a briefer period of time, perhaps, the name *Frenchman*—a name that will endure forever in history—will be sought after in vain on the surface of the earth. Such considerations do not appreciably broaden the views of such persons; it seems that the word *humanity* is for them a word without meaning. Even so, they should be consistent! Yet in the very next breath they deliver tirades against the impenetrability of the Egyptian sanctuaries; they deplore the loss of the knowledge of the ancients; they are full of blame for the silence or negligence of ancient authors who have omitted something essential, or who speak so cryptically of many important subjects; and these critics do not see that they are demanding of the writers of earlier ages something they call a crime when a present-day writer does it, that they are blaming others for doing what they think it honorable to do. These "good citizens" are the most dangerous enemies that we have had in our capacity as editors. . . .

6. Turgot, *On Foundations*

Anne-Robert-Jacques Turgot, baron de l'Aulne, was born in 1727 of an ancient noble family with a tradition of public service. After training for the church (a not uncommon career for younger sons), he entered the magistracy as one of the *maîtres de requêtes* (masters of requests), the

From *Oeuvres de Turgot*, edited by Gustave Schelle, 5 vols. (Paris: Alcan, 1913–1923), vol. 1, pp. 584–93. Translated for this volume by the editor, Keith Michael Baker.

body of officials from whom royal intendants were customarily drawn. Appointed intendant of the generality of Limoges in 1761, Turgot became the model of an enlightened, reforming administrator. In 1774, with the accession of Louis XVI, he was named controller general. Some of the reforms he envisaged in that position are the subject of later documents in this volume.

As a young magistrate in the 1750s, Turgot became acquainted with the ideas for economic reform then current among enlightened officials, as well as the more theoretical formulations being developed by the physiocrats. The articles on philosophy and political economy he contributed anonymously to the *Encyclopédie* suggest the nature and impact of the thinking within this enlightened milieu. None was more radical in its implications for the Old Regime than the following, which was published in 1757.

FOUNDATION, noun, feminine gender (Politics and Natural Right). A very natural metaphor extends the words "to found," "founding," "foundation," to any enduring and permanent establishment, since the term "establishment" is itself based on the same metaphor.

One speaks in this sense of the "foundation" of an empire or republic. But in this article we will not consider institutions on this scale: what we could say about them relates to the first principles of political right, to the first creation of governments among men.

One also speaks of "founding" a sect, or of "founding" an academy, a college, a hospital, a convent, the giving of masses, prizes, public games, etc. In this sense, "to found" means to assign a fund or a sum of money to be used in perpetuity to fulfill the purpose the founder had in view, whether that purpose concerns divine worship, or public utility, or the mere vanity of the founder—which is often the only true motive, even when the two others serve to veil it. . . .

Our intention in this article is limited to examining the utility of *foundations* in general, as they relate to the public good, or rather to demonstrating their disadvantages. May the following considerations serve, together with the philosophic spirit of the age, to discourage new foundations and destroy what remains of superstitious respect for the old ones!

1. A *founder* is a man who desires to extend the effect of his own will for eternity. But even if we grant him the purest motives, are there not many reasons to question his enlightenment? Is it not very easy to do harm in wishing to do good? To foresee with certainty that an establishment will produce the promised effect, rather than one entirely contrary; to discern, behind the illusion of a near and apparent good, the real evils which a long

series of unseen causes will bring; to know society's real afflictions and trace them back to their causes; to distinguish remedies from palliatives; to safeguard oneself against the glamour of a seductive project; to subject a plan to severe and tranquil examination when it appears bathed in the glory cast upon it by the praises of a blind public and our own enthusiasm: all this would demand the effort of the most profound genius, and the political sciences may not yet be advanced enough to permit even that effort to succeed.

Foundations often aid a few individuals against an evil when its cause is general, and sometimes the very remedy applied to the effect increases the influence of the cause. We have a striking example of this sort of ineptitude in the establishment of houses of asylum for repentant women. In order to obtain entrance, it is necessary to offer proof of a debauched life. Clearly, this precaution was devised to prevent the *foundation* from being diverted to other objects; but doesn't that prove in itself that debauchery is not to be combatted by establishments such as these, which bear no relation to its true causes? What I have said of debauchery is also true of poverty. The poor have incontestable claims on the abundance of the rich; humanity and religion alike make it our duty to relieve the misfortunes of our fellow creatures. In fulfillment of these indispensable duties, charitable establishments have proliferated in the Christian world to relieve necessities of every kind, vast numbers of the poor are gathered together in hospitals, or fed by daily distributions at convent gates. With what result? With the result that misery is most common and most widespread in precisely the countries where these charitable resources are most abundantly available, as in Spain and some parts of Italy. The reason is very simple, and a thousand travellers have observed it. To provide free subsistence for a large number of men is to subsidize idleness and all the disorders deriving from it, making the condition of the loafer preferable to that of the man who works. As a consequence, the state is deprived because of the diminution of the total amount of labor and of the produce of the land, a large part of which is necessarily left uncultivated. This gives rise to frequent scarcities, an increase of misery, and depopulation. The race of industrious citizens is replaced by a vile populace, composed of wandering beggars, engaged in every sort of crime.

To understand the abuse of these misdirected alms, imagine a state so well administered that it had no poor (something certainly possible in a state with colonies to people). An institution offering free assistance to a certain number of men would soon create some poor, since it would give an interest to that number of men to become poor by abandoning their occupations. The result would be a loss in the labor and wealth of the state, an increase in the weight of the public burdens borne by the industrious, and a growth of all the disorders we see in the present state of society. Thus the purest virtues can deceive those who surrender themselves without precaution to every idea that may be inspired by them. But if these pious and worthy plans contradict the hopes that were conceived for them, what must we think of those *foundations* (undoubtedly the most numerous) whose only purpose and true object is the satisfaction of a frivolous vanity? I do not fear to say that, if the advantages and the disadvantages of all the existing foundations in Europe were compared, perhaps not one would be found to withstand the scrutiny of an enlightened policy.

2. But whatever the utility of a *foundation,* it bears within itself an irremediable defect deriving from its very nature—the impossibility of maintaining its function. Founders grossly deceive themselves if they imagine that their zeal can be communicated, down through the ages, to persons responsible for perpetuating its effects. There is no body that has not in the long run lost the sense of its original purpose. There is no sentiment that does not become weakened by mere habit, and by familiarity with the very objects that excite it. What confused emotions of horror, sadness, tenderness towards humanity, pity for the misery of those who suffer, are not experienced by the man who enters a hospital ward for the first time! But let him open his eyes and look around. In this very place, amidst this concentration of human miseries, those responsible for relieving them walk about inattentive and unconcerned. Routinely and without interest, they go from invalid to invalid, distributing the food and the remedies prescribed, sometimes with a deadly lack of concern. They abandon themselves to heedless conversation, and sometimes to the silliest and most cheerful ideas. Vanity, envy, hatred, all the passions reign there as they do elsewhere; and the groans, the shrill cries of pain, do not divert them from pursuit of their goals any more than the murmur of a stream interrupts an animated conversation.

If these are the effects of habit in relation to those objects most capable of moving the human heart, then no enthusiasm can be constantly sustained. And without enthusiasm, how can those responsible for a foundation fulfill its purpose continuously and faithfully? What interest will they have to counterbalance idleness, that affliction of human nature which tends constantly to reduce us to inaction? The very precautions taken by the founder to assure them a constant revenue relieves them from any pressure to deserve it. What if the founder has provided for the appointment of superintendents or inspectors to ensure that the conditions of the foundation are fulfilled? It will be the same with these inspectors as for others established to uphold any rule whatsoever. If the obstacle to maintenance of the rules comes from idleness, the same idleness on their part will prevent them from exposing it; if the abuse proceeds from pecuniary interest, they will readily share in the profit. Supervisors themselves must therefore be supervised, and where does this ridiculous progress stop? . . .

Thus almost all ancient foundations have degenerated from their original institution. New ones, established in the same spirit as the first, have been created either according to the same plan, or to a different one. These have degenerated in their turn, only to be replaced in the same manner. Measures are ordinarily so well taken by the founders to protect their establishments from the threat of change from the outside that it generally turns out to be easier—and it is certainly more prestigious—to found new establishments than to reform the old. But as a result of this doubling and tripling of foundations, the number of useless mouths in society, and the sum of wealth withheld from general circulation, are continually increased.

Some foundations—those endowed with money or fixed revenues—cease to fulfill their purpose for a different reason, simply as a result of the lapse of time. For, as everyone knows, every kind of fixed revenue has in the long run lost almost all its value [as a result of long-term monetary changes]. . . . This would present no great problem if the foundations so affected were entirely destroyed. But the structure of the foundation nevertheless continues to exist; only its purpose is abandoned. If, for example, the revenues of a hospital decline, the beds for the sick will be eliminated and one will make do with providing for the support of the chaplains.

3. Suppose, however, that a foundation has initially been created for a purpose of undeniable utility, that sufficient precautions have been taken to prevent its degeneration through idleness and negligence, that the nature of its endowment protects it from long-term changes in public wealth. Even so, the very immutability which the founders have sought to confer upon their creation is still a great problem, because time brings new revolutions which will sweep away whatever utility the foundation might initially have possessed, and may even make its continued existence harmful. Society does not always have the same needs. The nature and distribution of property, the divisions between the different orders of the people, opinions, manners, the general occupations of the nation or of its different sections, the climate itself, the illnesses and other accidents of human life—all these undergo continual variation. New needs arise, others cease to be felt. The proportion of those remaining changes daily; and as they diminish or disappear, so does the utility of the foundations designed to address them. The Crusades gave rise to innumerable foundations whose utility ceased with these wars. Without speaking of the military religious orders, Europe is still covered with leper hospitals, even though leprosy has long since disappeared here. The majority of foundations far outlive their utility. First, there are always men who profit from them, and therefore have an interest in maintaining them. Second, even when we become convinced of their

inutility, we take a long time before we decide to destroy them, to determine the measures or the formalities necessary to knock down structures that have held firm for many centuries (and are often attached to buildings one fears to disturb), or agree upon the use or distribution to be made of their remains. Third, because it takes a long time before we are convinced of their inutility, foundations have sometimes become positively harmful before they have even been suspected of being useless.

4. I have said nothing of the splendor of the buildings and of the pomp connected with some of the great foundations. In some cases, it would be an exaggeration to estimate their utility at one percent of what they cost.

5. Woe to me if my object in presenting these considerations were to fix man's attentions solely on his own self-interest, and to render him insensitive to the sufferings or the welfare of his fellow-beings, to extinguish in him the spirit of a citizen, and to substitute an indolent and base prudence for the noble passion of being useful to mankind! I want humanity, and the passion for the public good, to procure for men the same benefits as the vanity of founders—but more surely, more completely, at less cost, and without the disadvantages of which I have complained.

Among the different needs of society which enduring establishments or foundations have been intended to fulfill, let us distinguish two kinds. The first belong to society as a whole, and are simply the result of the interests of each of its parts, such as the general needs of humanity, sustenance for everyone, the good manners and education of children for all families. . . . It does not require much reflection to be convinced that social needs of this first kind are not such that they can be fulfilled by foundations, or by any other gratuitous means, and that, in this respect, the general good must be the result of the efforts of each individual in his own interest. Every able-bodied man ought to procure his subsistence by his work, because if he were fed without working, it would be at the cost of those who do work. The state's obligation to all its members is to destroy the obstacles which would impede them in their industry, or trouble them in the enjoyment of the fruits of that industry. As long as these obstacles exist, benefits to individuals will not diminish the general poverty, because the cause will remain untouched.

Similarly, every family owes its children an education, and has an immediate interest in providing for that education; the general improvement of education can arise only from the efforts of each family in particular. If you amuse yourself in endowing masters and scholarships in colleges, their utility will be felt only by a small number of individuals, favored by chance, who may not even possess the necessary talents to profit from them. For the nation as a whole, this will be but a drop of water cast into a vast sea, and you will have achieved very small results at very great expense. Furthermore, should one accustom people to ask for everything, receive everything, and owe nothing to themselves? This sort of begging, which spreads among all conditions of men, degrades a people and substitutes a spirit of lowness and intrigue for all the lofty passions.

Do men have a powerful interest in the good you wish to procure for them? Leave them free to attain it [*laissez-les faire*]: this is the great, the only principle. Do they appear to you to be less passionately motivated towards it than you would like? Increase their interest. If you wish to improve education, propose prizes for the emulation of parents and children; but let these prizes be offered to whoever can merit them, at least within each order of citizens. Let employments and positions of all kinds become the reward for merit and the assured outcome of work, and you will see emulation take fire immediately in the heart of every family. Your nation will soon be raised above itself; you will have enlightened its spirit; you will have given it character; you will have done great things—and it will not even have cost you as much as founding a single college.

The other class of public needs which foundations have been intended to serve may be regarded as accidental and limited to particular places and times—those entering less into the system of general administration, but requiring particular relief measures. It might be a question of relieving the hardships of a food shortage or an epidemic; of providing for the support of some old people or orphans, or for the care of abandoned children; of undertaking or maintaining public works to improve the amenity or the salubrity of a town; of improving agriculture or some of the backward arts in a locality; of rewarding the services rendered by a citizen to his town, or of attracting to it men celebrated for their talents. Public establishments and foundations are far from being the best means of securing all these benefits as fully as possible. Free use of a community's revenues; a contribution by all its members in the case of pressing and general need; a free association and voluntary subscriptions of some generous citizens, when the need is less urgent and less generally felt: these are the effective means of fulfilling all kinds of really useful projects.

In addition, this method has the inestimable advantage over foundations, that it is subject to no great abuse. Since the contribution of each individual is entirely voluntary, it is impossible for the funds to be diverted from their destination. If they were, their source would soon dry up. No money is lost in useless expenses, in luxury, or in building. It is a partnership of the same kind as in business, with the difference that its only object is the public good; and since the funds are used only under the scrutiny of the shareholders, these latter are in a position to see that they are used in the most advantageous manner. Resources are not made eternal for needs that are temporary; assistance is given only to that part of society which is suffering, to that branch of commerce which is languishing. If the need ceases, the generosity ceases, and its course is directed to other needs. There is never a doubling or tripling effect [as in the case of foundations], because the generosity of the public benefactors is determined only by the acknowledged, actual utility.

In short, this method withdraws no funds from general circulation; lands are not irrevocably taken over by idle hands, and their productivity under the hands of an active proprietor is limited only by their potential fertility. Let it not be said that these ideas are chimerical! England, Scotland, Ireland are full of such associations, and have for many years experienced their happy effects. What occurs in England can also occur in France; for, whatever one says, the English do not have the exclusive right of being citizens. We already have examples of such associations in some provinces, which proves that they are possible. I shall cite the particular case of the city of Bayeux, whose inhabitants have joined together to banish begging entirely from their town, and have succeeded in providing work for all able-bodied beggars, as well as alms for those unfit to work. This fine example deserves to be held up for all our towns to emulate. Nothing would be easier, if we really had the will, than to direct towards objects of certain and general utility the aspirations and tastes of a nation as sensitive to honor as our own, and as ready to yield to all the stimuli the government is able and willing to give.

6. These reflections should make us applaud the wise restrictions which the king, by his edict of 1749, has placed upon the liberty to create new foundations. Let us add that they should leave no doubt regarding the incontestable right—possessed first by the government in the civil domain, and next by the government and the Church in the domain of religion— to dispose of old foundations, to divert their funds to new objects, or, better still, to suppress them altogether. Public utility is the supreme law. It should not be weighed against any superstitious respect for the so-called *intention of the founder*—as if ignorant and short-sighted individuals had the right to chain to their capricious wills the generations yet unborn—nor against the fear of infringing upon the pretended rights of certain corporate bodies—as if particular corporate bodies had any rights in relationship to the state. Citizens have rights, and rights to be held sacred, even by the body of society—they exist independently of society, they are its necessary elements; they enter into society only to place themselves, with all their rights, under the protection of these same laws which assure their property and their liberty. But particular corporate bodies [*corps particuliers*] do not exist of themselves, or for themselves; they have been formed for society, and they must cease to exist immediately after they cease to be useful.

Let us conclude that no work of man is made for immortality. And since *foundations,* constantly multiplied by vanity, would in the long run absorb all resources and all private properties, in the end we have to be able to destroy them. If a tombstone had been erected for everyone who ever lived, it would have been necessary, in order to find land to cultivate, to over-throw these sterile monuments and to turn over the ashes of the dead to nourish the living.

7. Turgot, *Memorandum on Local Government*

In 1774, on the accession of Louis XVI, Turgot was named controller general. In this position, he became responsible for royal finances, and hence for administrative policies relating to taxation, the economy, and local government. With his recent experience as an intendant in mind, Turgot directed his secretary (the economist, Dupont de Nemours) to draft a long memorandum diagnosing the problems of provincial admin-istration and outlining the plans for national regeneration the controller general intended to submit to the king. Although this *Mémoire sur les municipalités* was written in 1775, Turgot fell from power before it could be presented to Louis XVI. But its arguments exercised a powerful in-fluence on administrative thinking in the remaining years of the Old Regime.

Sire:

To discover whether it is expedient to establish municipalities in those cantons of France where they do not exist, whether it is necessary to im-prove or change those already in existence, and how to constitute those it is deemed necessary to create, does not involve going back to the origin of municipal administrations, giving an historical account of the vicissitudes they have undergone, or even analyzing in great detail the diverse forms they exhibit today. It has been much too frequent a practice, in deciding what must be done in serious matters, to revert to the examination and ex-ample of what our ancestors did in times of ignorance and barbarism. This method serves only to lead justice astray in the multiplicity of facts pre-sented as precedents; and it tends to make princes disgusted with their most important functions, by persuading them that it is necessary to be pro-digiously learned in order to discharge these functions with success and

From *Oeuvres de Turgot*, edited by Gustave Schelle, 5 vols. (Paris: Alcan, 1913–1923), vol. 4, pp. 568–628. Translated for this volume by Keith Michael Baker and Anthea Waleson.

glory. However, it is really only necessary to understand thoroughly and to weigh carefully the rights and interests of men. These rights and interests are not very numerous, so that the science which comprises them, based upon the principles of justice that each of us bears in our heart, and on the intimate conviction of our own sensations, has a very great degree of certainty and yet is not at all extensive. It does not require the effort of long study, nor is it beyond the capabilities of any man of good will.

The rights of men gathered together in society are not founded on their history, but on their nature. There can be no grounds for perpetuating institutions created without reason. The kings who have been Your Majesty's predecessors pronounced the laws they judged fitting in the circumstances in which they found themselves. Sometimes they were mistaken. Often they were misled by the ignorance of their time. Even more often, they were constrained in their ability to act by very powerful particular interests which they did not believe themselves strong enough to overcome, and with which they preferred to compromise. There is nothing in their actions to oblige Your Majesty not to change the ordinances they established, or the institutions to which they lent their authority, once you have determined that this change is just, useful and possible.

Those among your subjects who are most accustomed to protesting would not dare deny Your Majesty a legislative power to reform these abuses as extensive as that of the princes who created them or left them in existence. The greatest power of all is the pure and enlightened conscience of those to whom providence has granted authority, the proven desire to achieve the good of all.

Your Majesty can thus regard himself as an absolute legislator and count on your good nation for the execution of your orders.

This nation is numerous. That it obey is not everything. It is necessary to make sure of being able to command it effectively. In order to succeed in this, it would first seem necessary to know, in fairly great detail, the nation's situation, its needs, its capabilities. This knowledge would doubtless be more useful than historical accounts of past positions. But it is also something that in the present state of affairs Your Majesty cannot hope to obtain, something that your ministers cannot promise themselves, that the provincial intendants are scarcely in a better position to acquire, and that even the subdelegates named by them can attain only very imperfectly for the small area entrusted to their care. From this situation there results an infinity of abuses in establishing the basis and distribution of the tax burden, as in the methods of raising taxes and in local administration. These are the abuses that excite the most unrest and which, since they weigh most heavily on the poorest classes of the people, effectively contribute the most to their misery. The only solution is to devise a form of administration according to which most of the things to be done are carried out well enough automatically, without the need for Your Majesty or your principal servants to know any but a small number of particular facts, or to concern themselves with them in any other way than by the general protection that you owe your subjects.

The search for this form of administration is the object of this memorandum.

The cause of the evil, Sire, stems from the fact that your nation has no constitution. It is a society composed of different orders badly united, and of a people among whose members there are but very few social ties. In consequence, each individual is occupied only with his own particular, exclusive interest; and almost no one bothers to fulfill his duties or to know his relationship to others. As a result, there is a perpetual war of claims and counterclaims which reason and mutual understanding have never regulated, in which Your Majesty is obliged to decide everything personally or through your agents. Everyone insists on your special orders to contribute to the public good, to respect the goods of others, sometimes even to make use of his own goods. You are forced to decree on everything, in most cases by particular acts of will, whereas you could govern like God by general laws if the various parts composing your realm had a regular organization and clearly established relationship.

Your realm is made up of provinces. These provinces are composed of cantons or districts which (depending on the province) are called *bailliages, élections, vigueries,* or some other such name. These districts are made up of a certain number of towns and villages, which are in turn inhabited by families. To them belong the lands which yield products, provide for the livelihood of the inhabitants, and furnish the revenues from which salaries are paid to those without land and taxes are levied to meet public expenditures. The families, finally, are composed of individuals, who have many duties to fulfill towards one another and towards society, duties justified in terms of the benefits they have received, and which they continue to receive daily.

But individuals are educated poorly regarding their duties within the family and not at all regarding those which link them to the state.

Families themselves scarcely know that they depend on this state, of which they form a part: they have no idea of the nature of their relationship to it. They consider the levying of the taxes required for the maintenance of public order as nothing but the law of the strongest; and they see no other reason to obey than their powerlessness to resist. As a result, everyone seeks to cheat the authorities and to pass social obligations on to his neighbors. Incomes are concealed and can only be discovered very imperfectly by a kind of inquisition which would lead one to say that Your Majesty is at war with your people. And in this type of war which, were it only apparent, would always be destructive and deadly, no one has an interest in taking the government's part, and anyone who did so would be regarded with hostility. There is no public spirit because there is no known and visible common interest. The villages and towns, whose members are thus disunited, have no more links between them in the districts to which they belong. They are unable to get together on any of the public works that might be necessary for them. The same applies to the various divisions of the provinces, and to the provinces themselves in relation to the realm as a whole.

Some of these provinces do, however, have a kind of constitution, assemblies, a sort of public will; they are called *pays d'Etats*. But since these Estates are composed of orders with very diverse claims, and with interests that are very separate one from another and from that of the nation, they are still far from producing all the good to be desired for the provinces in which they form part of the administration.

These local half-benefits are perhaps an evil; provinces enjoying them are less sensitive to the necessity for reform. But Your Majesty can bring them to recognize that necessity by giving the other provinces, which have no constitution at all, a constitution better organized than that which at present makes the *pays d'Etats* so full of pride. It is by means of example, Sire, that they can be brought to desire that your power authorize them to change what is defective in their present form.

In order to dissipate this spirit of disunity, which vastly increases the work of your servants and of Your Majesty, and which necessarily and prodigiously diminishes your power; in order to substitute instead a spirit of order and union which would mobilize the forces and means of your nation for the common good, gathering them together in your hand and making them easy to direct, it would be necessary to conceive of a plan that would link individuals to their families, families to the village or town to which they belong, towns and villages to the district of which they form part, districts to their province, and provinces finally to the state. This plan would involve instruction that would be compelling, a common interest, deliberating about it and acting according to it.

In regard to these matters—so fitting to engage Your Majesty's benevolent spirit and love for true glory—I dare to propose several institutions whose advantages I shall explain as I outline the project for your consideration.

The Means of Preparing Individuals and Families to Enter Effectively into a Well-Constituted Society

The first and perhaps the most important of all the institutions which I would believe necessary, Sire—that which would seem to me the most fitting to immortalize Your Majesty's reign and which would have the greatest influence on the kingdom as a whole—would be the formation of a council on national instruction responsible for the direction of the academies, universities, and secondary and elementary schools.

The first bond of nations is custom; the first foundation of custom is the instruction received from childhood regarding all the duties of man in society. It is astonishing that this science is so little advanced. There are methods and institutions for training grammarians, mathematicians, doctors, painters. There are none for training citizens. There would be, if national instruction were directed by one of Your Majesty's councils, in the public interest and according to uniform principles.

There would be no need for this council to be very large, because it would be necessary for it to be united in spirit. In accordance with this spirit, it would commission textbooks systematically planned and written in such a way that one would lead to another, and that the study of the duties of the citizen, as member of a family and of the state, would be the basis for all other studies, which would be organized in relation to their usefulness to society.

This council would supervise the entire organization of education and it could render literary bodies useful for that purpose. The present efforts of these bodies tend only to create savants, poets, men of wit and taste; those unable to aspire to this goal are neglected and count for nothing. A new system of education, which can only be established by Your Majesty's entire authority, seconded by a well-chosen council, would lead to the formation, among all classes of society, of virtuous and useful men, just souls, pure hearts, and zealous citizens. Those among them who then wished to devote themselves particularly to sciences and letters, and were capable of doing so, would be diverted from frivolous matters by the importance of the first principles which they had received, and would approach their work in a more vigorous and determined spirit. Taste itself would improve, as would the national tone: it would become more serious and more elevated, but, above all, more concerned with virtuous things. This would be the fruit of the uniformity of patriotic attitudes that the council on instruction would disseminate in all the teaching given to youth.

There is at present only one type of instruction that has any uniformity: religious instruction. Even here, this uniformity is not complete. Textbooks vary from one diocese to another; the Paris catechism is not the same as the Montpellier catechism, and neither is identical to that of Besançon. This diversity of textbooks is unavoidable in an educational system that has several independent heads. The instruction organized by your council on instruction would not have that drawback. It would be all the more necessary in that religious instruction is limited to heavenly things. The proof that this instruction is not sufficient for the morality to be observed between citizens, and especially between different groups of citizens, lies in the multitude of issues arising every day in which Your Majesty sees one part of your subjects seeking to vex another by exclusive privileges; with the result that your Council is forced to quash these requests and proscribe as unjust the pretexts they invoke.

Your kingdom, Sire, is of this world. It is over the earthly conduct of your subjects, towards one another and towards the state, that Your Majesty is obliged to watch for the sake of your conscience and the welfare of your crown. I do not wish to place any obstacle in the way of that instruction which has a higher object, and which already has its rules and ministers completely established. Quite the contrary. Nevertheless, I do not believe I can propose anything more advantageous for your people, more conducive to the maintenance of peace and good order and to the encouragement of all useful works, more fitting to make your authority cherished and your person daily more dear to the hearts of your subjects, than to provide them all with an education which clearly shows them their obligations towards society and towards your power which protects it, the duties which these obligations impose upon them, and the interest they have in fulfilling these duties for the public good, as for their own. This moral and social instruction demands textbooks written expressly for the purpose, in open competition and with great care, and a schoolmaster in each parish who will teach them to the children, together with reading, writing, arithmetic, measurement, and the principles of mechanics.

More learned instruction, progressively embracing the knowledge necessary for the citizens whose position requires more extensive enlightenment, would be taught in the secondary schools. But it would follow the same principles, more fully developed according to the functions which the rank of the students fits them to fill in society.

If Your Majesty approves this plan, Sire, I shall submit for your consideration a special memorandum containing the relevant details. But I dare to assert that, ten years from now, your nation would be unrecognizable; and that, by virtue of its intelligence, its good customs, its enlightened zeal for your service and for that of the country, it would be infinitely superior to all other peoples past and present. Children who are now ten years old would then find themselves men of twenty, prepared for the state, attached to the country, submissive to authority—not from fear, but by reason—supportive of their fellow citizens, accustomed to knowing and respecting the justice which is the first foundation of societies.

Such men will act well within their families, and will doubtless raise families that will be easy to govern in the villages to which they belong. But it is not necessary to await the fruits of this good education in order already to involve presently existing families in public affairs and in the service of Your Majesty. There is nothing to prevent engaging these families, as they now are, in the formation of regular villages which would be more than a mere aggregation of houses and cabins, and of inhabitants no less passive than their dwellings. It could even be a very good means of making education even more profitable, and of stimulating emulation among fathers and students, to offer honest ambition an objective, and merit an occupation, in the part that distinguished subjects will naturally come to play in the management of the affairs of the locality in which their family resides.

What Naturally Constitutes Villages, and the Type of Municipal Administration Possible for Them

A village is essentially composed of a certain number of families possessing the houses which form it and the lands pertaining to it.

Ecclesiastical administration has produced territorial divisions in this regard that are clearly understood. There is no very significant inequality among parishes and the small number which could be regarded as too large are further subdivided by means of ancillary or succursal churches. These divisions were produced by the necessity of limiting parishes to an area within the capability of a curé to fulfill the functions of his ministry. The division by parish (or, if one prefers, by succursal) can thus be, and in practice already is, adopted for villages. Each one of these divisions has a known and determined territory, making possible a political administration as clear as the religious administration exercised there by the curé. And this political administration, relative to that territory, cannot be more easily carried out than by those who actually live there.

The matters for which this administration might be responsible are as follows:

1. Allocation of taxes;

2. Deliberation as to public works, local roads, and other roads especially necessary for the village;

3. Responsibility for the administration of the poor and poor relief;

4. Consideration of the relationship of the parish to other neighboring villages and to the major public works of the district, with the responsibility for presenting the wishes of the parish in this regard to the superior authority which can decide on the matter.

These are essential questions if the affairs of each village are to be well conducted. Yet they could not be adequately decided either by the present syndics, who have no authority, or by the subdelegates, each of whom has too great a number of villages under his jurisdiction to know them well in detail. The officials responsible for the collection of the *tailles* and the *vingtièmes,* besides the fact that their jurisdictions are also too large, are liable to be constantly deceived by false declarations and by the interest that everyone has in misleading them in tax matters. And they have neither the authority, nor the right, nor the interest, to concern themselves with the other questions.

Furthermore, these tax officials always represent the government as making demands, as being in an adversary role vis-à-vis each individual, whereas an administration set up in the very locality for the allocation of taxes would be on the side of its own fellow citizens. And if difficulties arose, the sovereign authority would only have to appear there as the judge and protector of all.

The necessity of forming this village administration, which can relieve your government of a function that the people regard as odious, Sire, and at the same time provide for the special needs of each locality, seems to me to be very clearly established simply by setting it forth.

But on what principles must this municipal village administration be constituted, and who should participate in it? This is a fundamental question which presents itself, a discussion of which I must place before Your Majesty.

First, it is clear that one should not send officials taken from another locality, to whom it would be necessary to grant appointments or privileges. This would be too considerable a burden for the villages, and could be a source of harassment, or at least of complaint. The responsibilities of village administration are more or less of the same nature as those which each individual assumes voluntarily in the conduct of his own affairs, which he would be very angry to see entrusted to a public official. Thus it seems obvious that only the inhabitants of the village itself, who have a direct interest in the matter and for whom its success is amply sufficient recompense, should be engaged in this administration.

But should all the inhabitants of the village play an equal part? This is a second question, which demands to be treated in rather more depth.

It would seem, at first glance, that each head of a household living in a village should have a voice, at least in choosing those to be involved in the affairs of the community. But assemblies that are too numerous are subject to considerable disadvantages, tumult and conflicts. It is difficult for reason to make itself heard within them. The poverty of the voters would make them easily corruptible and could lead to the buying of positions in a way that would debase the nation (which Your Majesty wishes, on the contrary, to elevate, improve and ennoble), thereby destroying all the benefits of the good education it is intended to introduce. These considerations aside, it becomes clear, considering the question more closely, that the only people who really belong to a parish or village are those who possess landed property. The others are day laborers, who have only a temporary domicile: they go to mow hay in one canton, reap wheat in another, harvest grapes in a third. Laborers from the Limousin come to build houses in Paris; those of the Auvergne sweep chimneys in Spain. Throughout the kingdom, it is from members of the landless class of the countryside that valets are drawn, that a large proportion of the armies are recruited, as well as the lesser artisans who carry their skills wherever they judge that employment will be most profitable to them—this often being outside the kingdom. These people have one habitation today, another tomorrow. They are at the service of the nation in general. They must everywhere enjoy the clemency of the laws, the protection of Your Majesty's authority, and the security which it provides; but they do not belong to any locality. In vain would one wish to attach them to any one place rather than another. As mobile as their legs, they will only ever stop where they find themselves best off. It is up to the property-owners of each canton to attract these workers in proportion to their need for them. The state itself has only a moral right over them, and an administrative authority. It does not have the physical power to hold them within its boundaries. . . .

It is not this way with landowners. They are tied to the land by their property; they cannot cease to take an interest in the canton in which it is situated. They can sell it, true. But only in ceasing to be property-owners do they cease to be interested in the affairs of the region, and then their interest passes to their successor. Consequently, the possession of the land not only produces crops and revenues that furnish the means to pay salaries to those who need them, placing a man in the class of the wage payers rather than in the class of the wage earners of society. But it is the land, moreover, which indelibly ties the proprietor to the state, constituting the true right of citizenship.

It seems then, Sire, that only those who possess landed property can legitimately be granted the exercise of this right, or the vote in the parish assemblies.

This point established, a new and very important question arises, namely to determine whether all landed proprietors should have a vote, and an equal one.

I believe that Your Majesty could decide this question according to several considerations.

The natural division of inheritances causes that which is hardly sufficient for a single family to be divided among five or six children, each of these shares being frequently subdivided further among five or six others.

These children and their families can then no longer live off the land. If possible, they rent out their little property (which is insufficient even for their most essential needs) and turn to crafts, to trades, to commerce, to domestic service, to all the means of earning a salary at the expense of landed proprietors. It is by their labor that these new heads of house-holds—disinherited, so to speak, by the land—manage to subsist. They belong principally to the salaried class. The class of landed proprietors to which they only cling by a few rods of land, often uncultivated and without value, can claim them only in very little part. It is not natural that such men should have a vote equal to that of proprietors with landed property worth fifty thousand livres a year. It is not natural that one can acquire a vote giving the right of suffrage, or, in other terms, the right of citizenship, by buying a little plot of land on which a citizen cannot subsist.

We have spoken above of the serious disadvantage of giving the right of suffrage to people of too little fortune. God forbid that I ever advise Your Majesty to open a door through which venality and corruption could pene-trate even into the countryside! A hundred doors would be necessary for it to leave the rest of the country.

I would therefore consider the man without property in land adequate for the subsistence of his family as ineligible to vote as a proprietor and head of a household. But this man, if he possesses any property what-soever, however insufficient to sustain his household, nevertheless has an interest of his own in the just distribution of taxes and in the proper admin-istration of services and public works in his canton—at least in proportion to his small landed property. He cannot be given a full vote, but neither can a vote be entirely denied him. He is not, so to speak, a whole citizen: he is a greater or lesser fraction of a citizen.

I would call a man who possesses landed property yielding sufficient revenue to maintain a family a whole citizen, a freeholder, a free citizen, because he is or could be head of a household when it pleased him. He is in law what the Romans called *paterfamilias*. He has a fixed hearth and loca-tion; he stays on the land and there makes place for a family. According to present prices of goods and services, that assumes at least 600 livres (or the value of about 30 setiers of wheat) in net income from landed property.

An individual who has only 300 livres of income is only a half-citizen, because if he has a family at least half of its subsistence will have to be derived from salary earned from crafts, trades, commerce, or some other kind of work. He who has only 100 livres is only one-sixth of a citizen.

I would therefore propose that Your Majesty give one citizen's vote only to each portion of 600 livres in income. Thus, in parish assemblies, an individual who enjoyed this income would speak for himself. But those whose income was lower than this would be obliged to join together to ex-ercise their right (for example, two individuals each with 300 livres in reve-nue, or four with 150, or six with 100, or twelve with 50) naming between them a deputy who would carry the vote of the others and represent alone the citizen and head of a household whose patrimony their collective income could form. This deputy alone would attend the parish assembly and exercise a citizen's vote there, as much in his own name as in that of his associates who had united their fractions of a vote to form his. Those who had chosen him would have the right neither to enter nor to vote in the general assembly, but only the right to choose him for the year in a small particular assembly of their own.

In these particular assemblies, each fractional citizen would join with those others who best suited him to form their citizen's vote by common accord. Each one would have the right to name the deputy entrusted with their vote in proportion to his fraction. Thus, for example, if a proprietor with 200 livres in income joined with one who had 50 écus, one who had 100 livres, and three who had 50, in order to form their citizen's vote and to name the deputy to be charged with it, the six of them would be counted as if they were twelve electors—each one of those with 50 livres counting for one, the one with 100 livres counting for two, the one with 50 écus for three, and the one with 200 livres for four—and the whole would be summed up in a single deputy.

The parish assemblies would then be neither too numerous, nor too tumultuous, nor absolutely unreasonable. A presently cumbersome community comprising a hundred families or more would often be reduced to five or six persons exercising a citizen's vote, very few on their own account and the majority as empowered by fractional citizens. Each of the latter, however, would be represented in proportion to his interest; and since the election of citizens charged with a vote would be renewed each year, one would be morally sure that the civic voice [of the fractional citizens] would be expressed by those most worthy and most acceptable to the others.

Thus it seems just that Your Majesty permit fractional citizens to meet together to decide on the exercise by one among them of the vote granted to a certain amount of income, so that each landed proprietor, however small his property, can take pride in having a slight influence in the deliberations which concern him, in proportion to their potential relationship to his income. By the same token, it would be equally equitable, and it would above all be useful, to permit those whose income could support several families of citizens—and who consequently occupy the place of several such families on the land—to divide their vote theoretically, or to possess as many votes as they own full citizens' portions. Thus the individual who received 1200 livres of income from the land in a parish would have two votes in its assembly, he who had 100 louis would have four votes, and so on.

This arrangement appears to be founded on justice, since an individual who has four times the income in landed property in a parish has four times as much to lose if the affairs of this parish go badly, and four times as much to gain if everything prospers there.

It is just that a rich man, who has property and interests in several parishes, can vote and act in the capacity of citizen in each one in proportion to the interest he has there. It is no more strange to see one man represent several citizens and fulfill their functions than it is to see the same man possess several seigneurial domains and act in each one of them, not in his own private name, but as the local lord. Your Majesty himself possesses several states under different titles: he is king of Navarre, dauphin of Viennois, count of Provence. Thus it is not repugnant to consider a man who has two shares of citizenship as two citizens, and he can in the same way have several shares in several parishes, without that in one parish giving or taking away anything from that in another. Allowing him to enjoy this prerogative is allowing him only that which the nature of his property confers upon him.

This arrangement would be useful in that it would most often put the plurality of decisive votes on the side of the best educated, thereby rendering the assemblies much more reasonable than if the ill-instructed and uneducated were to predominate.

The kinds of questions upon which the parish assemblies might deliberate are not those in which the rich can be the oppressors of the poor. On the contrary, they are those in which they both have a common interest.

But the greatest advantage which will strike Your Majesty in the arrangement distributing citizens' votes on the basis of wealth is that it would mobilize (for the good of the country and of your service) the vanity and ambition which lead an individual to want to be someone of note, and direct it against the avarice which wishes to avoid taxation. The very procedure according to which votes are distributed will provide the best possible criterion for the distribution of the tax burden, and the one least subject to dispute.

If votes are assigned to a certain amount of income, the claim for a vote, or some fraction of a vote, or several votes, will be the confession and declaration of the relevant income. It follows that, the proportions of fortunes being known, the tax assessment will be carried out along with the distribution of votes, by the inhabitants themselves, without any difficulty. Individuals wishing to enjoy the full extent of the votes belonging to their property will make faithful declarations. Since these declarations will be made before the parish as a whole, each of whose members knows very well the lands of the others and their usual yield, there is no possibility of their being incorrect. If greed brought someone to sacrifice his position by not claiming the number of votes belonging to him, the other citizens of the parish—who would have a very strong interest in watching for such things, for they could not tolerate this maneuver without accepting a redistribution among themselves of the burden that individual wished to avoid—would not fail to point out the error. "You are too honest, Monsieur," they would say to the miser; "your property is worth so much; exercise your votes." If a dispute arose on this point, it could be judged like any other case relating to taxes. But then it would be a case between the parish and the delinquent, in which none of the unpleasantness that could arise would redound to the government. . . .

Another considerable advantage that can and must be derived from municipal village assemblies is the simple and inexpensive construction of a general land register for the kingdom. Since each assembly, in order to regulate the distribution of its votes, would be obliged to record, in the minutes of that distribution, by what title each of its members exercised a vote, it would naturally create a description of the lands belonging and adjacent to the village. It would be no great trouble for the village assembly to do this, because each member knows his own lands and those of his neighbors very well. Within a few years, they can be induced to justify their titles to votes by land surveys and topographical maps, provisionally awarding to the community the lands unclaimed in anyone's survey or those in the parish exceeding the measurements that each has given of his property. Giving the parish this interest in verifying the declarations would further ensure their fidelity.

The simple functions to which the village municipalities will be more or less limited will not be beyond the capabilities of anyone in the locality he inhabits and where, at all times, his patrimony is found. They would not interfere with the exercise of Your Majesty's authority. On the contrary, they would contribute to making that authority precious to your people since they would add to the latter's happiness and (together with the public instruction which would daily have a more certain influence) make it evident to everyone that the increase in national wealth and happiness was due to Your Majesty's laws and actions.

The greatest and perhaps the only difficulty that might arise in the simple operations entrusted to the parish municipal assemblies, could stem from the differential nature of the taxes successively introduced in times when the utility of the most simple forms was not known, and when pretensions to rank, backed by a real power, forced the burden of the greatest share of the public charges on to the people, who only possess the smallest share of the lands and revenues. The nobility is exempt from the *taille* and related taxes. The clergy enjoys an additional exemption from the *capitation* and the *vingtièmes,* for which it substitutes a voluntary gift very far from being in the same proportion to its revenues. The result is that the sum total of taxation, which would not be too heavy a burden if it were equally distributed over all the incomes in the state, falls only upon a portion of these incomes. It consequently seems intolerable to a great number of taxpayers and, in fact, excessively reduces the resources which should remain in the hands of the proprietors among the people for the upkeep and amelioration of their domains. These pretensions, which greed has cloaked with the mantle of vanity, have been a principal factor in inducing the kings who have been Your Majesty's predecessors to establish a multitude of taxes of all kinds on all types of commerce and consumption. By these indirect taxes they have been able, in effect, to extract a tax contribution from the nobility and the clergy, who are forced in their expenditures to pay the various levies imposed on all the objects they wish to enjoy, and who lose much more again on the value of the commodities subject to these taxes which are produced on their lands. . . .

It is such a shameful and odious thing to pride oneself on one's dignity in refusing aid and service to the country—as if the greatest dignity did not belong to those who served it the best—that one should perhaps not blame those who, not daring to fight against the arrogant and greedy pretensions of the nobility and clergy, have instead contrived to circumvent them. However, the taxes on expenditures and items of consumption entail such harsh procedures, occasion the sheer waste of so many expenses in litigation, obstruct commerce to such an extent, and so greatly restrict agriculture—which can only prosper in proportion to the ease with which its products can be sold advantageously—that they destroy or prevent the creation of infinitely greater revenues than they produce for Your Majesty, or even for those responsible for their collection, either as tax farmers or otherwise. The nobility and the clergy, whose share of the payment of these taxes is the largest (since they have the greatest amount of land, the most substantial proportion of the harvests, the largest incomes) also pay the largest part of the false costs of all kinds that these forms of taxation necessitate. They suffer infinitely more from the resulting diminution of their incomes than they would have from a regular tax contribution proportional to their wealth, assuming that expenses, items of consumption, work, commerce, agriculture, had remained free and flourishing.

Without adding to the burden now carried by the nobility and the clergy, and even diminishing it by a small degree—but, above all, giving considerable tax relief to the people—it would be easy to introduce a less onerous and destructive procedure to replace the taxes from which the first two orders are not exempt: taxes which are by their very nature harmful to the whole nation, to Your Majesty's power, to the affection you have a right to expect from your subjects, to the peace, the tranquility, and the unity which must reign in your empire. This is probably one of the tasks that heaven, in its goodness, has reserved for you. It will perhaps be a goal to which you will subsequently aspire, to make your kingdom wealthy enough—and your treasury, moreover, rich enough—to be able to rescind the special taxes to which the people are now subject, in such a way that the superior orders will retain only honorable distinctions rather than fiscal exemptions. These latter debase those who claim them in the eyes of reason and patriotism; they debase those who are excluded from them in the eyes of prejudice and vanity; and they are onerous to all in diminishing the general wealth and restricting the means of restoring it, which up to now have been too heavily drawn from the laboring classes: those whose expenditures and labor support, and alone can increase, the wealth of their superiors in rank. . . .

Thus it could be established that there would be three ways of convoking the municipal parish assemblies: as a small assembly, to consider only the distribution of the taxes to which the Third Estate alone is subject; as an intermediate assembly, to consider those taxes borne by the nobility as well as the Third Estate; and as a large assembly, to consider matters and tax assessments common to all those with properties or revenues in the parish, whatever their Estate.

This is a complexity which can subsequently be simplified, but which the confusion of the present tax system, and the prejudices related to it, make almost inevitable at this initial stage. . . .

Towns and Urban Municipalities

All the towns already have a type of municipal administration: a town corporation, provosts, *marchands,* mayors, *échevins, syndics, jurats,* consuls, or some other type of municipal officials. But in one town these officials buy their offices; in another, they are nominated by Your Majesty; in another, a number of nominees are elected among whom Your Majesty then makes a choice; in another, election is sufficient. Similarly, in some towns these officials have a set term of office; in others, they serve for life; in still others, the position is hereditary. The only uniformity is a spirit of regulation taken from the constitution of the Greek and Roman cities, that, for good or ill, it was wished to imitate when the towns in France were released from the dominion of feudal lords and began to acquire some liberties and privileges. This spirit tends to isolate each town effectively from the rest of the state, making it a separate little republic entirely concerned with sacrificing the surrounding villages and countryside to its own interest (most often misunderstood). It acts as a tyrant towards its neighbors, and a hindrance to the commerce and laboring activity carried out within its walls.

You have many times been obliged, Sire, to curb this spirit of disorder and exclusivity which currently characterizes the towns and is fostered by their present administration. Your Majesty understands the necessity of replacing it with a spirit of union, peace and mutual aid. This would be a reason to reform all the present town municipalities, even if one did not establish the village municipalities. But I dare to advise you not to do one without the other. These two operations seem to me to be only branches of the same operation, and it is in thus embracing all the objects directly relating to the one and the other, managing them together according to the uniform principles that are the hallmark of a great plan, that Your Majesty will command opinions, master them, and make the elevation and beneficence of your views respected by your people and by foreign nations.

The first principle of town municipalities is the same as that for the countryside: no one involves himself except in that which concerns him, and in the administration of his property. The countryside is composed of lands which return an income, and the only people who solidly belong to the village communities are those who possess these lands. The towns are comprised of houses.

The only things that cannot be carried away are the houses and the land on which they are built. If the town prospers and its population increases, the rents on houses are high. If commerce does not flourish, if it is not good to live there, men and movable capital go elsewhere and rents fall, sometimes to the point that the upkeep of the houses becomes a burden and they are left to tumble down: their owners (the only ones in the town who cannot transport their wealth) are consequently ruined. If rents are high, land for construction acquires a high price. If houses are unoccupied, the value of the land diminishes, and is reduced to its potential productive capacity. Thus it is always to the owners of houses and land in the towns that the affairs of these towns particularly matter; they are the ones who should particularly form urban municipalities.

But in order to allocate their citizens' votes in such a way that they have a real parity with those of the citizens of the countryside (for it is neither just nor useful that the townsman be better treated than the countryman) the vote must not be given to 600 livres of income in house rents. The owner of a house rented at 600 livres is much less considerable in the state than the proprietor of a field rented for 600 francs. A house is a type of property without security. Each and every year, repairs eat away a greater and greater part of its value. At the end of a century, more or less, the house must be rebuilt in its entirety. The capital used for its initial construction, and that subsequently spent for upkeep, is lost. The risk of fire even makes this cycle generally shorter. The field, which does not require the same upkeep and is not subject to the same risks, maintains its value perpetually. It can only suffer those vicissitudes which affect the state as a whole. Its master is a citizen as long as the country lasts. The owner of houses in the towns is nothing but a town dweller. The proprietor of a field worth 600 livres in income can always—even in the greatest calamities which would cause him to lose those who cultivate the land for him—become a cultivator of his own domain, and by his own work support his citizen family. The house owner with no renters, reduced to living in the house himself, would die there with his family if he had no other income.

A house is not a productive property, it is an expensive commodity. . . .

Since there is always a ratio between the use of capital and incomes, it seems that one could, without straying far from the truth, assume that the property owners in towns have the ordinary return on the capital sum at which their land would be valued. Today that would mean giving the citizen vote in the towns to the owner of a plot of land worth 18,000 livres or roughly 900 setiers of wheat, which would be roughly equivalent to the proprietor with 600 livres in income (or thirty setiers of wheat) in the countryside.

Apart from the fact that this evaluation seems justified in terms of the impartial equality Your Majesty wishes to observe towards his urban and rural subjects, this manner of determining the citizen votes in the towns has a notable advantage: that of preventing the tumult that would be created by excessively numerous assemblies of proprietors. There are few owners of houses in the towns for whom the land on which their buildings are constructed is worth 18,000 livres. One would find barely forty such proprietors in Paris. As a result, almost all urban proprietors will be only fractional citizens, and there will be much smaller fractions of citizens in the towns than in the countryside. There would thus be many small assemblies of house owners who were fractional citizens (assemblies which could be composed of twenty-five, thirty, or forty proprietors) to name among them the citizen charged to exercise his own vote and those of the other fractional citizens completing it. Since each parish or district assembly would therefore summon, at most, only one citizen for every twenty-five houses, this assembly itself would not be too numerous; it would proceed without tumult; reason could be spoken there. For it is important, in every deliberation in which a large number of persons have interests and rights, to be able—without attacking the former or violating the latter—to rid oneself nevertheless of the chaos of the multitude. . . .

The Second Level of Municipalities, or *Elections*

The object of the general establishment of a good civic education, even for men of the lowest classes, given under the direction of a council instituted for this purpose, would be to tie them to their family and to teach them how to live well in general with their dear ones, with other families, and in the state.

The object of the village and urban municipalities where the citizen proprietors would vote in person, and where even the fractional citizens would participate through representatives chosen by them and sharing in their interest, would be to tie families to the place of residence that their property indicated.

The object of the higher municipalities (by *élections,* provinces, and so on), which can only be conducted by means of deputies, is to establish a chain by which the most remote regions can communicate with Your Majesty without fatiguing you, enlighten you without obstructing you, facilitate the execution of your orders, and further enhance respect for your authority by saving it from errors and making it beneficent all the more often.

Parish deputies cannot be sent to a provincial assembly: that would involve too much business and too many people. On the one hand, numerous assemblies are the death of all reason. On the other, the way to save the time and trouble of higher administrations, sparing them errors and injustices, is to assure them the power to regulate important matters effectively, to relieve them of consideration of any matter which lower administrations could properly decide. This must be the function of the municipal assemblies of the *élections.*

These assemblies would be composed of a deputy from each of the first-level municipalities included in their jurisdiction. Like the villages, the towns would send only one deputy each, because like the villages they each form but a single community. An exception could be made at most for the provincial capitals, allowing them two deputies, and (if one wished) for the city of Paris, to allow it four. In the last analysis, this multiplication of deputies for capital cities is of no advantage. But it would perhaps be difficult to deny them this distinction, which they would seek to justify in terms of the multitude of citizens encompassed within their walls. . . .

The Third Level of Municipalities, or Provincial Assemblies

A provincial assembly would be composed of deputies from the second-level municipal assemblies, or the *élections* and districts of the province. Their number would not be considerable and would never exceed about thirty. Like the assemblies of the districts, they would have two sessions. In the first, they would verify the state of the *élections* or districts or regions, and determine their rank according to the number of communities comprised within them and the number of citizen votes they contained. The statement brought by each deputy of the number of parishes forming the district he represented, and the number of citizen votes included in them, would regulate this necessary arrangement in a very natural way.

It would then be decided whether or not there were grounds for granting relief to the districts that might be claiming it with regard to natural disasters they had experienced. If the decision was affirmative, the amount to be paid for this relief or aid would be immediately allocated among the other districts.

From that, the assembly would turn to an examination of public works projects that might be in the province's interest to undertake on its own behalf. For this purpose, the proposals that deputies had to make for their districts would be heard. If the works were decided upon, the necessary arrangements for the provision of funds would be passed by majority vote. If they seemed of a kind to concern several provinces, an invitation to participate in them would be addressed to these other provinces. (This freedom can also be permitted, even within provinces, to the municipal assemblies of the *élections* and of the parishes, among themselves.) And if the works projects seemed important enough to affect the whole kingdom, the provincial assembly would decide the extent to which the province could contribute (as being the most directly concerned) and draw up instructions requesting the aid of all the other provinces, to be presented by the deputy it would name to the grand general municipality of the kingdom.

If the province had experienced some great disaster, such as an epizootic disease that had destroyed cattle, it could also make a request through its deputy for aid from other provinces. It would further charge him to carry a copy of its registers, and an abstract of the registers of the district assemblies, to the general municipality, the common center of all the municipalities of the kingdom.

These first meetings of the provincial assemblies could last three weeks, and the expenses of the deputies of the district assemblies attending them would be defrayed by their constituents.

After the general municipality had been held, the provincial assemblies would hold their second session in order to allocate among their districts the sums that had to be paid. This second session, prepared for by the work of the first, could last eight days.

The Grand, or Royal, Municipality, or General Municipality of the Kingdom

This establishment, Sire, would complete the institution of the municipalities. It would be the means by which all the corresponding threads from the most remote regions of your kingdom would be brought together without difficulty under the dominion of Your Majesty.

The general municipality would be made up of a deputy from each provincial assembly, who would be allowed an assistant to replace him in case of illness, and help him with his paperwork. The assistants could attend the assemblies as spectators, but they would not have the right to participate or vote (except in the case of the deputy's illness).

All Your Majesty's ministers, on the contrary, would sit and vote in this assembly. And Your Majesty could occasionally honor it with your presence, to attend its deliberations, or to declare your will.

It would be in this assembly that taxes would be allocated among the various provinces, and that expenses would be voted, either for large-scale public works, or for aid to disaster-stricken provinces, or to those provinces proposing undertakings that they were not wealthy enough to complete.

In relation to these various matters, Your Majesty would begin by announcing, or having your finance minister announce, the sums it was necessary to request from the provinces as a whole in order to discharge the expenses of the state. This declaration would include the cost of the public works you had found it fitting to order. The assembly would then be left perfectly free to decide, by majority vote, on such other public works as it found appropriate, and to grant needy provinces such aid or relief as it wished, on condition that the cost be allocated as a surcharge on the other taxes imposed on the rest of the kingdom. . . .

After the second year, once the state of the kingdom's revenues has been determined from the number of citizen votes and the distribution of taxes has a secure base, Your Majesty could turn over the matter of the *vingtièmes* to the municipal assemblies as a mark of confidence. This would be an opportunity to display benevolence to the first general assembly and to suppress an administration that is costly and necessarily faulty, even though it is presently directed by men of distinguished merit.

Nothing would then be easier than to have the assemblies themselves request the reforms that Your Majesty intended to introduce, getting these same assemblies to propose the replacement of all the onerous and vexing taxes you intended to suppress.

And if, by some impossible occurrence, the assemblies did not come to do this, Your Majesty would be no less the master to implement these reforms by an act of authority after having demonstrated their utility (which, in general, no one would deny), and to legislate regarding the necessary replacement taxes. For the municipal assemblies, from the first to the last, would only be municipal assemblies, and not assemblies of Estates. They could bring enlightenment, and by their very constitution they would bring enlightenment regarding the distribution of taxes and the particular needs of each locality; but they would have no authority to oppose the indispensable and courageous operations that the reform of your finances requires.

They would have all the advantages of assemblies of Estates with none of their drawbacks: neither the confusion, nor the intrigue, nor the corporate interest, nor the animosities and prejudices of one order against another.

Giving neither grounds nor opportunity for the expression of that which is troublesome in those divisions among the orders, leaving only those aspects which can be honorific for illustrious families or for occupations worthy of respect, and grouping citizens in relation to their real usefulness to the state and the indelible place they occupy on the land by virtue of their property, they would tend to make of the nation but a single body, perpetually animated by one sole objective, the public good and the preservation of the rights of each individual.

They would accustom the nobility and the clergy to a substitute tax replacing those from which they are not currently exempt, and would establish reliable rules for the allocation of this substitute tax.

By the enlightenment and equity that they would bring to tax allocation, in general, they would render the tax burden less onerous to the people, although the returns would be greater. As a result of that increase, they would provide the means to bring relief to the lowest classes, gradually suppressing the taxes paid only by the Third Estate, and even by the nobility, and finally establishing a single, uniform tax on all incomes.

Then perhaps it would be possible to accomplish what has appeared to be chimerical until now: to put the state in a perfect and visible community of interest with all proprietors, such that the ordinary public revenue, being a set proportion of individual revenues, would increase with them through the care of a good administration, or diminish as they would if the kingdom became badly governed.

But it would be very difficult for the latter to occur. The government would no longer be overburdened with details. It could devote itself to the general considerations of a wise legislation. All particular questions, those of the parishes and *élections,* and even of the provinces, would be automatically handled by those who would know them best, those who, deciding on their own affairs, would never have cause for complaint.

Furthermore, the kingdom would be perfectly known. Within a few years, a general account of the state of France could be drawn up for Your Majesty, by provinces, *élections* and parishes, in which the description of each locality would be accompanied by its topographical map. In this way, Sire, if a village was discussed in Your Majesty's presence, you could immediately see its location, know the roads or other public works being proposed for it, discover its wealthy individuals and the form and income of their estates.

The constant assemblies and opportunities to act as deputy would be the best school for youths already grown. They would accustom these youths to concern themselves with serious and useful matters, by exposing them to wise discussions regarding the means of observing equity among families and the means of administering the territory intelligently and profitably by implementing the public works best suited to improve it. General discussion of this question in each locality would make men judicious and greatly diminish bad customs.

The civic education provided by the council on instruction throughout the kingdom, and the rational textbooks that it would commission and oblige all instructors to teach, would contribute further to the development of an educated and virtuous people. They would sow in the hearts of children the principles of humanity, justice, benevolence, and love of state: principles finding their application as the children advanced in age, and in consequence growing constantly stronger. They would bring patriotism to that high degree of enthusiasm only seen before in some of the nations of the ancient world; and this enthusiasm would be wiser and more solid because it would be based on a greater real happiness.

Finally, at the end of several years, Your Majesty would have a new people, a people above all others. Instead of the cowardice, corruption, intrigue, and greed Your Majesty has found everywhere, there would be virtue, altruism, honor and zeal. It would be common to be a good man. Your kingdom, united in all its mutually supportive parts, would appear to have multiplied its strength tenfold, and would in fact have increased it considerably. It would embellish itself each day as a fertile garden. Europe would regard Your Majesty with admiration and respect, and your people would love you with heartfelt adoration. . . .

8. Protests of the Parlement of Paris (March, 1776)

As controller general, Turgot embarked upon a vigorous reform policy, aimed at stimulating the French economy by implementing liberal economic principles and reforming the system of taxation. In September 1774, the government abandoned its restrictions on the internal grain trade (with the prudent exception of Paris); but this measure coincided with a bad harvest, producing widespread misery and a chain reaction of bread riots (the "flour war") in April and May of the following year. His principles unshaken, Turgot took severe measures against the rioters, then continued with his plans for fundamental reform by presenting six edicts to the Parlement of Paris for registration in February 1776.

From *Remontrances du Parlement de Paris au XVIIIe siècle (1715–1788)*, edited by Jules Flammermont, 3 vols. (Paris: Imprimerie Nationale, 1888–1898), vol. 3, pp. 275–92, 344–54. Translated by Keith Michael Baker and Ellen Ross.

The parlement objected most strongly to two measures, which they attacked as undermining the essential principles of the traditional social order. One proposed the abolition of the forced labor tax of the *corvée* and its replacement by a money tax levied on landowners including the nobility. Another proposed the dissolution of the guilds and similar corporations restricting the freedom of trade and industry.

Under fire from the parlementary magistrates at the same time that his position was being undermined by ministerial and court intrigue, Turgot was dismissed from office in May 1776.

Remonstrance against the Edict Suppressing the *Corvée* (2–4 March 1776)

The desire to relieve the burdens of the people is too worthy of praise in a sovereign and conforms too much to the wishes of your parlement for the latter ever to conceive the thought of dissuading Your Majesty from such a noble and legitimate goal.

But when projects that hold out this pleasing prospect lead to real and aggravated injustices, and even imperil the constitution and the tranquility of the state, it is our faithful duty, without seeking to place obstacles in the way of your beneficence, to set the barrier of the law against the imprudent efforts being made to pledge Your Majesty to a course of action the dangers and stumbling-blocks of which have been concealed from you. . . .

Your parlement was aware that the edict substituting a universal, indefinite, and perpetual land tax for the *corvée*, under the guise of apparent relief of the people, could at first glance have seemed a beneficent act inspired by love of humanity. But at the same time, Sire, your parlement did not doubt that a more careful examination of the edict would reveal to Your Majesty that it represents a policy burdensome even for those whom you wish to help, and contrary to the sentiments of justice that animate you.

Justice, Sire, is the first duty of kings; without it, the rarest virtue can produce the most unfortunate effects. Justice determines the true value of royal actions, it stamps the reigns of kings with a most sacred character, and it consecrates their memory forever.

The first rule of justice is to preserve for every man what belongs to him. This is the fundamental rule of natural law, of the law of nations and of civil government, a rule that consists not only in maintaining the rights of property, but also in preserving rights attached to the person and those which derive from the prerogatives of birth and Estate.

It follows from this rule of law and equity that any system tending under the guise of humanity and benevolence to establish an equality of duties between men, and to destroy those distinctions necessary in a well-ordered monarchy, would soon lead to disorder (the inevitable result of absolute equality). The result would be the overthrow of civil society, the harmony of which is maintained only by that hierarchy of powers, authorities, pre-eminences, and distinctions which keeps each man in his place and protects all Estates from confusion.

This social order is not only essential to the practice of every sound government: it has its origin in divine law. The infinite and immutable wisdom in the plan of the universe established an unequal distribution of strength and character, necessarily resulting in inequality in the conditions of men within the civil order. Despite the efforts of the human mind, this law of the universe is maintained in every empire, upholding in its turn the order that preserves it.

What dangers will not arise, then, from a plan stemming from an unacceptable system of equality, the first effect of which is to mix all the orders of the state together by subjecting them to the uniform yoke of a land tax? . . .

By its constitution, the French monarchy is composed of several distinct and separate Estates. This differentiation of conditions and of persons is as old as the nation; it was born with our manners; it is the precious chain that links the sovereign with his subjects. "If persons were not distinguished according to Estate, there would be nothing but disorder and confusion," says one of our most enlightened authors. "Because we cannot live together in equality of condition, it is necessary that some command and others obey. . . . Sovereign lords command all within their state, addressing their commands to the great; the great to the middling, the middling to the small, and the small to the people." *

In the assemblage formed by these different orders, *all the people of your kingdom are your subjects,* all must contribute to the needs of the state. But the general order and harmony are upheld, even in the manner in which the various orders make their contribution. The personal service of the clergy is to fulfill all the functions relating to education and religious observance and to contribute to the relief of the unfortunate through its alms. The noble dedicates his blood to the defense of the state and assists the sovereign with his counsel. The last class of the nation, which cannot render such distinguished service to the state, fulfills its obligation through taxes, industry and physical labor.

Such, Sire, is the ancient rule of the duties and obligations of your subjects. Though all are equally faithful and obedient, their diverse conditions have never been confused and the nature of their service is based on their

*Loyseau, *Traité des ordres* [see document 1, above].

Estate. "The service of the nobles is noble, as they are; a noble is not re-quired to pay the *taille*, nor to perform the vile *corvée*, but must serve in war and do other noble acts." *

These institutions were not formed by chance, and time cannot change them. To abolish them, the whole French constitution would have to be overturned. . . .

In freeing from the *corvée* the least class of citizens, which has been subject to it until now, the edict transfers the burden to the two orders of the state who have never had to pay it. There is no longer any difference be-tween your subjects; the noble and the ecclesiastic become subject to the *corvée*, or, what is the same thing, they must all pay the tax that replaces the *corvée*.

This is not, Sire, a struggle between rich and poor, as some have tried to convince you. It is a question of Estate, and a most important one, since it is a matter of knowing whether all your subjects can and must be treated indiscriminately, whether differences in conditions, ranks, titles and pre-eminence must cease to be acknowledged among them. To subject nobles to a tax to redeem the *corvée*, contrary to the principle that only *those who pay the "taille" must perform "corvée,"* is to declare nobles subject to the *corvée* like commoners; and once this principle is established, nobles could be constrained to perform the personal *corvée* as soon as it were reestablished.

Thus noblemen, the descendants of those ancient knights who placed or preserved the crown on the head of Your Majesty's forefathers, those poor and virtuous lineages who have squandered their blood for so many cen-turies for the defense and extension of the monarchy, or who, with another kind of magnanimity, have neglected the care of their own fortune, often expending it entirely in their total dedication to the public good; those pure-blooded nobles whose revenues are limited to the modest yield of the lands inherited from their fathers, which they cultivate with their own hands and often without the help of any servants other than their children: these could be exposed to the humiliation of seeing themselves dragged off to the *corvée!*

Who could even assure the nobles that after being made subject to the *corvée* they would not subsequently lose their exemption from the *taille?* Would it be any less difficult to abolish the immense gulf that separates their condition from that of former serfs, than to eliminate the one that separates nobles from those who are free citizens even though they are commoners? Certainly not.

* [Antoine] Loisel [*Institutions coutumières, manuel de plusieurs et divers sentences et proverbes, tants anciens que modernes, du droit coutumier, et plus ordinaire de France* (1646)], Bk. IV, sec. 8.

Once the first barrier is broken, the second would be much easier to overthrow. Indeed, how could the nobility not foresee with fear this new attack on its rights, when it is already being announced and developed as a sequel to the first attack in the pamphlets now being circulated with so much fanfare?

We are fully convinced, Sire, that the ill-considered implications of these unjust projects have not been presented to Your Majesty in their full extent; for your wisdom and fairness would never have accepted them. But it is only too common among the partisans of novelty to unveil their system only by degrees, seeking to induce the government to take first steps that will imperceptibly commit it to a path whose destination they hide. In this way, a monarch devoted to the laws is led farther than he realizes or wishes—a monarch who has just sworn before the altar in a most solemn ceremony to be the support and protector of the laws, and who has declared his wish to reign only according to them. . . .

Thus, in reflecting on the law and the constitution of this state, Your Majesty will no longer doubt that this plan, against which your parlement protests only in fulfillment of its duty, clearly leads to the annihilation of the ancient liberties of the nobility and the clergy, to the confusion of Estates, and to the subversion of the constitutional principles of the monarchy.

Parlementary Argument against the Edict Suppressing the Guilds (Presented to the King at the *lit de justice* of 12 March 1776)

. . . Liberty is without doubt the principle of all actions; it is the spirit of each Estate; it is above all the life and prime mover of commerce. But, Sire, this expression so common today, which has been made to reverberate from one end of the kingdom to another, must not be understood to mean an unlimited liberty that knows no other law than its caprice, and admits no rules but those that it makes for itself. This kind of liberty is nothing more than a veritable independence which would soon be transformed into license, opening the door to every abuse. Liberty, this source of wealth, would then become a source of destruction, a cause of disorders, an occasion for fraud and plunder, and the inevitable result would be the total annihilation of the arts and of artisans, of confidence and of commerce. . . .

Your subjects, Sire, are divided into as many different bodies as there are different Estates in the kingdom. The clergy, the nobility, the sovereign courts and lower tribunals, the officers attached to these tribunals, the universities, the academies, the chartered companies for financial affairs, those for commercial affairs: in every part of the state there are bodies existing which can be regarded as links in a great chain, the first link of which is in the hands of Your Majesty as head and sovereign administrator of all that constitutes the body of the nation.

The very idea of destroying this precious chain should be appalling. The corporations of merchants and artisans form a necessary part of this indivisible whole which contributes to the general order of the entire realm. For this purpose, Sire, because independence is a defect in the political constitution and men are always tempted to abuse liberty, the law has instituted corporations, created guilds, and established regulations. The law has wished to prevent fraud of all kinds and to remedy all abuses; the law watches equally over the interest of the buyer and the seller; it maintains mutual confidence between the two; it is, so to speak, under the guarantee of the public trust that the merchant displays his merchandise before the eyes of the customer and the customer receives it with confidence from the hands of the merchant. The guilds can be considered so many small republics occupied solely with the general interest of all the members that compose them; and if it is true that the general interest results from the union of the interests of each particular individual, it is equally true that each member, in working for his own personal advantage, works necessarily, even without wishing to, for the true advantage of the whole community. To unloose the springs that move this multitude of different bodies, to annihilate the guilds, to abolish the regulations, in a word to disperse the members of all the corporations, is to destroy all the various means which commerce itself must desire for its own preservation. Every manufacturer, every skilled artisan, every worker will see himself as an isolated being, dependent on himself alone and free to indulge all the flights of an often disordered imagination. All subordination will be destroyed, there will be no more weights and measures, thirst for gain will dominate all the workshops; and since honesty is not always the surest way to fortune, the entire public, native and foreigner alike, will be the constant dupes of artful methods secretly prepared to blind and seduce them. And do not believe, Sire, that in our constant concern with the public welfare, we are yielding to foolish terrors. Our resolution to protest has been prompted by the most powerful arguments, and Your Majesty would have the right one day to accuse us of prevarication if we tried to hide them. The principal argument is the interest of commerce in general, not only in the capital but in the entire kingdom, not only in France but in all of Europe, in fact, in the entire world.

2
From Reform to Revolution

The Reform Crisis

9. Proceedings of the Assembly of Notables (1787)

In 1786, confronting the reality of an immense deficit in government finances, the controller general, Calonne, decided that drastic action was unavoidable. Bringing together many of the projects proposed by earlier reforming administrators, he won the king's approval for a comprehensive program with profound implications for the social and political order of the Old Regime. To secure a measure of support for his proposals, while avoiding immediate confrontation with the parlements, Calonne decided to submit them to an Assembly of Notables—a gathering of national and local dignitaries of a kind that had been called to advise the monarch on earlier occasions (most recently in 1626!).

After an initial presentation of the royal program on 22 February 1787, the Notables divided into committees to discuss a series of memoranda outlining specific reforms in greater detail. Their reactions to the most important of Calonne's proposals—the creation of provincial assemblies in the *pays d'élection,* and the institution of a uniform land tax to be paid in kind—were more critical than the minister had anticipated. While generally enthusiastic about the proposal for the creation of provincial assemblies, the Notables opposed the idea that these bodies be composed of representatives of landowners assembled without differentiation among

From *Archives parlementaires de 1781 à 1860, première série (1787 à 1799),* edited by M. J. Mavidal and M. E. Laurent, 2d ed., 82 vols. (Paris: Dupont, 1879–1913), vol. 1, pp. 189, 192–98, 219–21, 232–36. Translated for this volume by the editor, Keith Michael Baker.

the Estates. They rejected the proposed land tax on the grounds that it would be indefinite in amount and duration, and therefore contrary to the principle that taxation was granted only in specific amounts for specific needs. And they pressed for the right to examine the statement of accounts in order to verify the extent of the royal deficit. Unable to outmaneuver this opposition, Calonne was forced from office early in April 1787, and his position taken a month later by his leading opponent among the Notables, the archbishop of Toulouse, Loménie de Brienne.

Adopting a more conciliatory policy, Brienne allowed the Notables to examine the statements of account in order to verify the existence of the deficit. But having done so, the assembly pressed for a policy of financial retrenchment and fiscal responsibility, while proclaiming its lack of authority to approve new taxes. Rescuing as much as he could from Calonne's great project for national regeneration, Brienne dismissed the assembly on 25 May 1787.

Speech by the Controller General [Calonne], 22 February 1787

Gentlemen, my responsibility today is a particular honor, in that the views the king has charged me to explain have become entirely his own in consequence of the careful attention His Majesty has devoted to each one before their adoption.

The very decision to communicate them to you, and the entirely paternal words you have just heard from His Majesty, are doubtless enough to excite your firmest confidence. But it must be raised to a new height, and infused with the most passionate emotion, as you learn with what constant assiduity the king has dedicated himself to the long and demanding work that has been required: first, to examine all the accounts I have placed before him in order to explain every aspect of the true situation of our finances; and, second, to discuss each of the measures I have proposed to improve the finances and bring new order to them. . . .

It would seem an easy matter for a financial minister to provide an exact annual accounting of the ordinary revenues and expenses. One would expect him to be able to derive it from the statements of account submitted to him at the end of each year, and from the account submitted by him to the king in settling funds for the following year. . . . But the extraordinary number of disparate and variable parts that make up these accounts; the complexity of the budgetary practices; the confusion caused by local deductions against collections subject to greater or lesser delay; the complications caused by the transfer of amounts and allocations from one year to the next; the incalculable number of unforeseen causes that may affect the magnitude of expenses and receipts; and, finally, the almost inevitable mixture of outstanding, current, and future amounts, of anticipated credits and real balances: all these causes, taken together, make it extremely difficult to determine the figures relating to each year and thereby establish a precise statement of the ordinary annual budget.

Convinced that it is nevertheless of the greatest importance to secure such a statement, and that to give the king the fullest information in this respect is a strict duty of my office, one required by the principles of a monarch who loves the truth, I have done everything possible to place before him a general account of the finances that I can guarantee and prove to be exact. . . .

Of necessity, the king has found the results neither doubtful nor satisfactory. I must admit, for I have been careful to conceal nothing, that the annual deficit is very considerable. I have informed the king regarding its origin, its growth, and its causes.

The origin of the deficit is very old; it has existed in France for centuries. . . . Its growth became alarming under the last reign. The deficit exceeded 74 million [livres] when the abbé Terray was called to the administration of the finances, and it was still 40 million when he left. Thus the finances were already in great disorder when His Majesty ascended to the throne. They remained in much the same state until 1776, at which date the deficit was estimated at 37 million by the man who shortly thereafter assumed responsibility for the financial administration.[1]

Between that date and May 1781, the reestablishment of the navy and the requirements of war made it necessary to borrow 440 million. It is obvious that all the reforms and improvements made during this period, however one evaluates them, were far from yielding enough to compensate for the increased expense resulting from the interest on these loans, which must be reckoned at 9 percent or 10 percent . . . and therefore exceeded 40 million a year. Thus the deficit grew, as the actual accounts demonstrate.

It grew even more between May 1781 and November 1783, which is hardly surprising, because the borrowing during that period amounted to about 450 million. I have established that the deficit was 80 million at the end of 1783 . . . and new increases have occurred since then. The causes are too well known for the effects to be mysterious. The former may be explained by a single observation: at the end of 1776, the deficit was 37 million; between that date and 1786, a total of 1,250 million was borrowed. . . .

1. A reference to Jacques Necker, who served as director-general of finances (in effect, controller general) from 1776 to 1781. Necker's famous *Compte-rendu* of 1781, the first published accounting of the royal finances, was attacked by Calonne as misrepresenting the true state of the deficit.

It is impossible to leave the state in constant risk of the imminent danger to which it is exposed by a deficit such as the present one. It is impossible to continue to have recourse each year to palliatives and expedients that delay the crisis, but only at the cost of rendering it ultimately more disastrous. It is impossible to do any good, to follow any program of economy, to procure any of the relief a good king envisages for his people, as long as this disorder continues.

I have been obliged to say this to the king, unveiling this sad truth before him. It has received all his attention, and he is profoundly convinced of the necessity to use the most efficacious means to remedy the situation. But what might these means be? To continue borrowing would be to aggravate the evil and precipitate the ruin of the state. To increase taxes would be to heap new burdens upon a people the king wishes to relieve. To borrow even further against future income would be to continue what has already been done too much; prudence demands that the amount so borrowed be reduced each year. To economize is certainly necessary: His Majesty wishes it; he is doing it; he will do more and more of it. All possible reductions in expenses, even in the king's own household; all those to be achieved in the different departments without harming the strength of the state, have been ordered, and are already having their effect. But economy alone, no matter how rigorous, would be insufficient. It can only be considered a secondary measure. . . .

What then remains to fill this alarming gap and arrive at the desired point? What remains to make up what is lacking and ensure the restoration of the finances? ABUSES!

Yes, Gentlemen, abuses account for a wealth of riches that the state has the right to reclaim, and which must serve to restore order. Prohibiting abuses offers the sole means of providing for all needs. From the very depths of disorder there must gush forth an abundant spring that will fertilize all the parts of the monarchy. Abuses find their defenders in interest, prestige, wealth, and ancient prejudices that time seems to have respected. But what can this vain alliance do against the public good and the needs of the state?

The greatest abuse of all would be to attack only those abuses of lesser importance, those affecting only the weak (who would offer only weak resistance to their reform), those whose reform would produce no salutary benefit. The abuses that must today be abolished for the public good are the most important and most protected, those with the deepest roots and the broadest branches. They are the abuses that weigh heavily on the productive and laborious class; the abuses of pecuniary privileges, exceptions to the common law, and so many unjust exemptions that can only free one group of taxpayers at the cost of aggravating the lot of the others. They are the general inequality in the allocation of taxes, the enormous disproportion existing between the contributions of one province and another, and between the burdens imposed upon different subjects of the same monarch. They are the severity and arbitrariness with which the *taille* is collected; the fear, the harassments, the virtual dishonor imposed upon trade in primary products; the internal customs offices, and the tax barriers that estrange different parts of the realm one from another. They are the taxes discouraging industry, those whose collection require excessive costs and innumerable agents, those which seem to invite smuggling, and then sacrifice thousands of citizens a year. They are the wasting away of the royal domain and the uselessness of its feeble remains; the degradation of the crown forests, and the vices of their administration. In short, they are everything that distorts production, everything that weakens credit, everything that makes revenues insufficient, and all the superfluous expenditures that absorb them.

Why have so many abuses, subject to eternal censure, resisted up to the present moment the condemnation of public opinion and the attempts of administrators to reform them? Because partial operations have been preferred where general operations alone could succeed; because it has been thought possible to repress disorder without extirpating its source; because efforts have been made to improve the organization of the state without correcting its contradictions, without returning it to the principle of uniformity, which can alone eliminate all the complex difficulties and revivify the entire body of the monarchy.

The views which the king wishes to communicate to you are all directed at this goal. They form neither a [factitious] system nor a new invention. On the contrary, they are the digest—one might say the combination—of the projects of public utility conceived for many years by the most consummate statesmen, and often brought into perspective by the actual experience of government. Some of these projects have been attempted in part, and all seem to have received the support of the nation. But until now their full implementation has seemed impossible because of the difficulty of reconciling a host of local customs, of opposing claims, privileges, and interests.

When one considers how many successive acquisitions, how many incorporations of regions governed in different ways, have contributed to the present identity of the realm, one should not be surprised at the disparities in governmental practice, the multitude of heterogeneous forms, and the confusion of principles that bring disunity to all its parts. . . .

However, not until the monarchy had extended to the limits naturally destined for it, until it had reached its maturity, and until internal and external peace had been achieved by the wise moderation of its sovereign, was it possible to conceive of reforming the vicious elements in its constitution, and to work to render the general regime more uniform.

It was reserved for a young and virtuous king—a king with no other passion than to achieve the happiness of his adoring subjects—to undertake, after mature examination, and to execute, with an unshakeable will, what none of his predecessors could effect: the introduction of harmony and consistency into all parts of the body politic, the perfection of its organization, and the establishment, at last, of the foundations for an unalterable prosperity.

In order to achieve this goal, he has adopted the simplest and most natural idea, that of the unity of principles, which is the aim of justice and the source of good order. He has applied this idea to the matters most essential to the administration of his realm, and he has assured himself, after long meditation upon the consequences that must result, that they offer the double advantage of increasing its revenues and relieving the burdens upon its people.

This general conclusion led His Majesty to concern himself first with the different forms of administration existing in the various provinces of the realm in which there is no assembly of Estates. In order that the allocation of public contributions may cease to be unequal and arbitrary in these provinces, he has determined to entrust responsibility for them to the property owners themselves. He has therefore drawn from the first principles of the monarchy the uniform plan of a graduated series of deliberations, according to which the expression of the desires of the taxpayers and their observations regarding everything that affects them will be transmitted from parish assemblies to district assemblies, from district assemblies to provincial assemblies, and thence to the foot of the throne.

His Majesty then directed his particular attention to establishing the same principle of uniformity, and of proportional equality, in the administration of the land tax, which he regards as the base and necessarily the standard for all other taxes. He recognized . . . that the *vingtièmes,* instead of falling as they should on all the lands in the kingdom in exact proportion to their value and productivity, allowed for an infinite number of exceptions that were more tolerated than they were legal; that the *pays d'Etats* paid disproportionate amounts; that prestige and wealth brought partial exemption from this tax, while those less well-off endured its full severity . . . ; finally, that instead of providing the government with essential knowledge of the productivity of the realm, and of the comparative resources of each province, the results of this general tax served only to demonstrate the shocking inequality in their respective burdens, and yielded an amount far short of what its name announced.

His Majesty has decided that there is a means of remedying these problems in accordance with the rules of a strictly distributive justice; of returning the tax to its fundamental principle and bringing it up to its true value, while overtaxing no one and even granting the people some relief;

and of making all privileges irrelevant to its mode of collection. This would be to replace the *vingtièmes* with a general tax, applying to all the land in the realm, which would consist of a proportion of everything produced (in kind where possible, but otherwise in money) and allow no exception even in respect to the king's own demesne, nor any other distinctions than those resulting from differences in the quality of the soil and variations in the harvest.

Ecclesiastical properties would necessarily be included in this general apportionment, since, if it is to be just, it must include all lands, as does the protection of which it is the price. But in order that these properties not be overtaxed by continuing payment of the tithes levied to pay the debt of the clergy, the king, as sovereign protector of the churches of his realm, has resolved to provide for the reimbursement of this debt by granting the clergy the authorizations necessary to free themselves from it.

The same principle of justice, which allows no exception in respect of the land tax, has also persuaded His Majesty of the equity of exempting the first orders of his state—which possess honorific distinctions that he intends them to retain, and even wishes them to enjoy more fully in future—from any kind of personal tax. Consequently, they should no longer pay the *capitation,* the nature and very name of which seem incompatible with their Estate.

His Majesty wishes that the revenue from the land tax replacing the *vingtièmes* could have made it possible immediately to diminish the burden of the *taille* as much as he intends. He knows how heavily that tax and the arbitrariness of its collection weighs on the part of his people which suffers most. If he has decided in his wisdom to defer the full implementation of his benevolent views until the results of the new form of land tax are known, and the provincial assemblies have enlightened him as to the means of rectifying its apportionment, he wishes at least to correct its principal defects provisionally, and to permit his people to begin enjoying a reduction in the total amount of this tax.

Complete liberty of the grain trade, guaranteed on behalf of agriculture and property under the sole condition that the demands of the provinces will be respected when any of them believe temporary prohibition of exports is necessary, but with no relaxation of the useful and unobtrusive care with which the king's paternal solicitude watches over anything affecting his people's subsistence; abolition of the *corvée* in labor, and the conversion of this excessive requirement into a more justly apportioned money tax, administered in a way that guarantees use of its revenues for the purpose intended; free trade in internal markets, with customs offices pushed back to the frontiers, a single tariff established in accordance with the interests of commerce, the abolition of many taxes harmful to industry or too likely to cause vexations, alleviation of the burden of the salt tax [*gabelle*]. . . . these, Gentlemen, are so many salutary measures entering into the plan His Majesty wishes presented to you in detail, measures contributing to the goals of order and uniformity that are its basis. . . .

In considering this entire plan, you will recognize that it is so conducive to good order, so necessary for the reform of abuses, and so advantageous for the people, that its implementation—regarding which His Majesty wishes to consult you—would be undeniably desirable even if the financial situation did not absolutely require it. . . . Called by the king to the honorable task of collaborating in his benevolent plans, animated by the sentiment of the purest patriotism, which fuses in all French hearts with love of the sovereign and of honor, you will proceed to your examination thinking only of the general welfare of the nation, whose eyes are fixed upon you. You will continually bear in mind that it is a matter of the destiny of the state, and that ordinary means could neither achieve the good the king wishes to accomplish for it, nor preserve it from the ills he wishes to prevent.

The purpose of the observations you will present to His Majesty will be to assist and enhance the accomplishment of his intentions. They will be inspired by zeal, and mixed with the expressions of gratitude due to a monarch who adopts only those projects in which he sees relief for his people, who makes himself one with his subjects, who consults them, and who shows himself to them only as a father.

Let others recall that principle of our monarchy: "as the king wills, so wills the law" [*si veut le roi, si veut la loi*]. His Majesty's principle is: "as the people's happiness wills, so wills the king." . . .

Protest of the Third Committee (16 March 1787)

The bureau, under the presidency of His Grace, the duc d'Orléans . . . , considering that it owes the king and the nation an account of its true sentiments, believes that it must explain the disparity between the principles that have dictated its judgment and those embodied in the memoranda submitted to it. The bureau acknowledges that its principles are contrary to those in the memorandum on the establishment of provincial assemblies, which it considers unconstitutional and lacking in the powers necessary to make them useful; in that on the so-called land tax to be collected in kind, which it considers indefinite, disproportionate, and wasteful; in that on the reimbursement of the debts of the clergy, which it considers to be contrary to the principles of property. The bureau believes itself obliged to declare further that it has not deliberated regarding any tax in money, collected or to be collected, established or to be established, under the name of

vingtièmes or any other name, because it desires first, before any deliberation, to see the accounts of revenues and expenditures, and plans and
projects announced by the controller general, and the measures of economy His Majesty proposes for the relief of his people. . . .

Protest of the Fourth Committee, 15 March 1787

. . . The bureau, under the presidency of His Grace the prince de
Condé, . . . [considers] in respect to the first memorandum, that the proposed composition of the provincial assemblies is opposed to the constitutive principles of the monarchy; in respect to the second memorandum, that the land tax in kind (which is its sole object) cannot be adopted;
and that the third, dealing with the liberation of the clergy [from its debt],
would occasion just alarm regarding property. . . .

Protest of the Fifth Committee, 9 March 1787

. . . The bureau considers that the establishment of provincial assemblies
would be useful, but that the plan proposed in the memorandum, in addition to its many defects, seems to depart from the French constitution in
that, by confusing the three orders, it destroys the hierarchy necessary for
the maintenance of royal authority and the existence of the monarchy. The
bureau proposes that these assemblies be given a form more analogous to
the constitution of the realm, and it begs His Majesty to invest them with
all the authority necessary to allocate taxes, to decide upon public works,
and to oversee and pay for their execution.

The bureau is of the opinion that levying taxes in kind is inadmissible,
because it is necessarily indefinite, disproportionate, unequal and wasteful;
that a tax levied in money must be apportioned among all the lands of the
realm, without exception and in proportion to their revenues; and that, to
enable the Notables to form a judgment regarding the necessity, the extent,
and the duration of a tax by comparing resources to needs, His Majesty
shall be asked to send them the accounts requested in their deliberation of 5
March. . . .

The bureau approves of reimbursement of the debts of the clergy, the
appropriateness of which is generally recognized; but holds that the two
measures proposed for this purpose . . . would endanger property, contravene the principles of distributive justice, and harm the general administration of the realm in some respects. . . .

The bureau is of the opinion that abolition of the *corvée* in labor is as
just as it is useful; and that all matters relating to the amount and apportionment of the [substitute] tax in money, as well as the responsibility to

decide upon, supervise, and pay for the resulting public works, be entrusted to the provincial assemblies. . . .

Speech by the Controller General [Brienne], 25 May 1787

Gentlemen, the king has ordered me to bring before you a brief statement of the result of your deliberations and a summary of the decisions His Majesty has taken in consequence of them. . . .

Troubles and dissensions (the ordinary result of civil wars), which the glorious reign of Henri IV could not entirely eliminate, obliged Louis XIII to transfer direct administrative responsibility to his Council, even down to the least detail. Thus, to recover the rights of authority, everything was made subject to its immediate control; it required more power to act, the less influence it had. The king does not believe that a regime dictated by circumstances ought to subsist when those circumstances have disappeared. He understands that the greater the force of authority, the greater its trust; that to restore a part of the administration to provincial assemblies would not enfeeble authority but enlighten it and make it more active.

Accordingly, His Majesty decided to establish such assemblies in every province of his realm which does not have its own Estates, and he believed that he should consult you regarding their creation and composition.

His Majesty has seen with satisfaction, as will his people with gratitude, that no personal sentiment or prejudice has influenced your deliberations. You have regarded the nation as one, understanding that none of the orders, corporate bodies, or particular associations composing it could have any interest other than the nation's. You have consequently abjured all distinctions in considering the matter of tax contributions: civil liberty, extended to every Estate, no longer permits those special taxes that are the unfortunate vestiges of servitude (whose payment they were). A better ordered government accordingly rejects all those pecuniary exemptions that were the consequence of these taxes. It is no longer permissible to think that he who receives least must pay most. . . .

The king is far from wishing to attack privileges and constituted forms. He knows that there are distinctions in a monarchy that it is important to preserve; that absolute equality is suitable only to states that are purely republican or purely despotic; that equality of taxation does not imply the confusion of ranks and conditions; that ancient forms are the safeguard of the constitution, and that when they are obliged to yield to the general utility, their traces must nevertheless be treated with respect.

These are the principles according to which the provincial assemblies will be established. The first two orders will preside and take precedence there, just as they always have in the national assemblies. . . .

Since a single interest must animate all three orders, one might believe that they should each have an equal number of representatives. The two first orders have preferred to be combined and united; thus the Third Estate, assured of possessing as many votes itself as the clergy and the nobility together, need never fear that particular interest will disturb the voting. Moreover, it is only just that so numerous and important a portion of His Majesty's subjects, one so deserving of royal protection, should receive compensation, in terms of the number of votes, for the influence that wealth, honors, and birth necessarily confer.

In accordance with the same principles, the king will order that votes be counted not by order but by head. The majority opinion, taken on the basis of order, does not always represent the real majority that alone truly expresses an assembly's wish. . . .

An enormous deficit was announced to you at the first session of this assembly. You have felt that, once the state's wound was known, it was necessary to probe its full extent; that the greatest misfortune for a powerful nation was to remain unenlightened as to the magnitude of the ills to be remedied; and that, if circumstances dictated extraordinary efforts, it should at least assure itself how far these efforts should extend and where they should stop.

The king has approved of your zeal. He has communicated to you all the available accounts, and after exhaustive examination you have certified, as far as it lay in your power to do so, the deficit whose reality it was necessary to establish. . . . If there are always resources to be found in any great fortune, how could there be none to hope for in a great realm? Order and economy are chief among them. You have suggested retrenchments and improvements to His Majesty, who anticipated you in announcing a number of economies that he had ordered; he has since made known that he will bring them up to at least 40 million. You must not be astonished that these economies have not yet been realized; abuses introduced gradually and imperceptibly cannot be reformed in a moment. . . . To remedy disorder in haste would be a kind of disorder itself. Already the queen has sought, and ordered others to seek, all the retrenchments possible in her household; already the princes, the king's brothers, are proposing to return to the royal treasury a part of the sums they receive from it; already the king has ordered his ministers and every paymaster to prepare all the economies possible in each part of the administration. . . .

These, Gentlemen, are the assurances you must take back to your fellow citizens. And if some of them impatiently ask what has been accomplished by this long and celebrated assembly, you will tell them with confidence that the nation there received from its sovereign a new life and existence in the provincial assemblies; that equality of taxation, suppression of the *corvée* in labor, liberty of the grain trade, were there established by the wish of the nation; that customs duties, salt taxes, and many onerous taxes were there destroyed or considerably moderated. You will tell them that the public debt is solidly assured; that balance will be established between revenues and expenses; that the latter will be constantly reduced, and the former made proportionate to real needs. You will add that all this will cost them sacrifices; but these sacrifices will be carefully considered, they will fall principally upon the wealthy, and they will endure only as long as the necessity for them. Finally, you will tell them that these hopes have been given to you by the king himself, that they have been guaranteed by the measures he has taken and communicated to you. . . .

10. Parlementary Opposition (April–May 1788)

Unable to secure the consent of the Assembly of Notables to his policies, Brienne turned to the Parlement of Paris, where the pattern of confrontation was repeated. The parlement registered edicts establishing freedom of the grain trade, abolishing the *corvée*, and instituting provincial assemblies; but it countered proposals for the land tax with a demand to verify the accounts and a declaration that only the Estates General could consent to indefinite taxation. When it refused to approve financial edicts, it was exiled in mid-August, 1787. It returned to Paris in September, willing to accept a compromise according to which a government loan would be approved in exchange for a promise that the Estates General would be called within five years.

This bargain was to be formalized in a special parlementary session on 19 November 1787 attended by the king. But fundamental disagreement arose when the king declared the loan edicts approved without first having the magistrates' votes counted. When the duc d'Orléans protested that this procedure was illegal, he was exiled by *lettre de cachet* and other leading magistrates were imprisoned. Parlementary protests against these actions continued until 13 April 1788, when the court decided to present strongly worded remonstrances upholding its claims to participate formally in the act of legislation. The king responded on 17 April with a declaration of his legislative sovereignty. Recognizing that extreme measures were being planned against it, the parlement countered on 3 May with a solemn declaration of the fundamental laws of the kingdom and new remonstrances denouncing the threat of royal despotism.

From *Archives parlementaires de 1781 à 1860, première série (1787 à 1799)*, edited by M. J. Mavidal and M. E. Laurent, 2d ed., 82 vols. (Paris: Dupont, 1879–1913), vol. 1, pp. 281, 283–88, 294. Translated for this volume by D. Carroll Joynes and Keith Michael Baker.

The government's response to the parlementary declaration of fundamental laws was dramatic. In a *lit de justice* held on 8 May, the king
announced his intention to reorganize the judiciary. The legislation known
as the May Edicts transferred responsibility for registration of proposed
laws, and the right to remonstrate against them, from the several parlements to a plenary court established for the entire realm. At the same
time, authority to hear many cases on appeal was transferred to reorganized lower courts in each locality. In effect, the parlements were stripped
of their powers.

Remonstrances of the Parlement (13 April)

. . . The king's sole will does not comprise the law; the simple expression
of that will does not constitute a nationally accepted procedure. To be binding, this expression of will must be made public according to legal forms
which require that it be freely verified. Such, Sire, is the French constitution, which was born with the monarchy itself.

Under the first dynasty, the king had his court, as he does now, while the
people had their [assemblies on the] Champ de Mars. The people consented to or requested a law, the king presented it or granted it, and this law
obtained or consented to by the people was confirmed by the king's court.

The votes of the people, the votes of the court, were freely cast. Knowledge of the spirit of the Franks, their laws, and their history is enough to
dispel any doubts on the matter.

The same liberty endured under the second dynasty. "The law," one ca-
pitulary says, "is made by the consent of the people and the constitution of
the king." The king's constitution, drafted in the royal court—the *placité
général*—received there its final form, and was inserted among the capitu-
laries. The legislation of Worms, dated 803, is one such precious monument that escaped the ravages of time, and one that clearly defined the
rights of the king, the people, and the *placité général:* the right of the king
to introduce or draw up the law; of the people to ask for or consent to the
law; and of the *placité général* to approve it and maintain it.

The king's court was composed of great nobles, bishops and senators.
All the laws of the first two dynasties testify to this. Hincmar identifies
them in his famous "letter on the composition of the palace." Kings called
the members of the court their loyal followers, their adjutants, their collab-
orators, the administrators of the public weal. Their own titles, the national
customs, laws, history, and the declarations of the kings themselves attest
to their right to vote in the presence of the king.

This right did not change under the third dynasty. The king's court surrounded the throne when Hugh Capet was installed upon it. It is difficult to

believe that this monarch could even dream of depriving his court of its right to vote with the king. History, on the contrary, teaches us that Hugh Capet and his successors quite wisely took advantage of this venerable right to retrieve important rights and large landholdings which the crown, during a period of weakness, had lost to wars, usurpations and concessions.

The king's court was thus described variously as the "court of the king," "the court of France," "royal court," "council," "grand council," "parlement," and "full parlement," according to the nature of the matters being considered and the character of the assemblies. Proof of this resides in the most solemn ordinances and the most memorable decrees. Some historians also add the name "baronage," which Louis XI is known to have used.

From Hugh Capet to Philip of Valois, the common legislative practice was for the king to come to his parlement, where the law was drawn up in his presence; sometimes, however, the parlement drew up the law in the absence of the king, who then gave his consent; on other occasions, the king gave the parlement a law upon which to deliberate. . . . During the reign of Philip of Valois, the custom was to address the laws directly to the parlement.

Even a brief look at the early registers of the parlement is enough to prove that, before and during the reign of Philip of Valois, it freely deliberated both on legislation and at judicial trials, sometimes in the presence of the king, and sometimes in his absence. . . .

It is true, Sire, that your parlement is Your Majesty's council; but it is your public council, your legal council, not your personal council [*counseil du cabinet*].

Members of the personal council are admitted and excluded as the king sees fit. At the legal council, the king can neither include nor exclude anyone.

In the personal council, the prince's choice is not subject to examination, to the taking of an oath, or to formal acceptance. In the legal council, the indelible status of an officer of the sovereign is endowed only after examination, the swearing of an oath, and a freely granted acceptance.

The personal council enjoys the king's confidence, whereas the legal council has the confidence of both the king and the law.

Finally, in his personal council, the king makes a decree. Hence the expressions "the king in his council" . . . "Seen by His Majesty, the king being in his council." In the public council, however, the king announces the decree. "Louis, by the Grace of God" . . . "Seen by the court" . . . "Our said court has ordered and now orders." If Your Majesty deigns to reflect on the differences in these formulas, which are as old as decrees themselves, you will recognize that the former indicate consultation, whereas the latter are proof of joint deliberation.

May it please God that these principles never infringe upon the legislative authority of Your Majesty. The right to verify laws is not the same as the right to make them; but if the authority that makes the law could also supplant or hinder verification, rendering it either a ridiculous precaution or an empty formality, the will of an individual could replace the public will, and the state would fall under the hand of despotism. . . .

The King's Response (17 April)

I have read your remonstrances. I wanted to respond to them so authoritatively that you neither doubt my intentions nor allow yourself to dismiss what I say.

It was superfluous to talk to me about the law of registration and the liberty of voting. When I hold my parlement, it is to listen to the discussion of the law that I come to present, and to decide more knowledgeably about its registration. That is what I did on 19 November last.

I heard all the views expressed. It is necessary to summarize them only when I am not in attendance at your deliberations; a statement of the voting is then all that is needed to inform me of the results of your opinions. When I am present, I judge for myself.

If the majority in my courts forced my will, the monarchy would be no more than an aristocracy of magistrates. This would be as contrary to the rights and interests of the nation as to those of sovereign authority. It would indeed be a strange constitution that reduced the king's will to the equivalent of that of one of his officers, and forced the legislator to have as many wills as there were different deliberations in the various courts of justice in his kingdom.

I must protect the nation from such an eventuality.

Everything was legal in the session of 19 November. The deliberation was complete because all opinions were heard. The votes were not recounted, because I was present. A majority should not be formed when it must not prevail. An edict was passed because whenever I hold my parlement to deliberate upon a matter of administration or legislation, the only edict is that which I order pronounced.

I have therefore been obliged to condemn your declaration, and I forbid you to adopt similar ones in future. . . . How many useful laws, which daily form the basis for your judgments, does France not owe to the authority of its kings, who had them registered not only without concern for a majority vote, but even against such a vote, and despite the parlements' resistance!

These principles must govern your conduct. I will never permit the least violation of them.

Declaration of the Parlement (3 May)

. . . The court, with all chambers assembled and with the peers in attendance, warned by public awareness and a familiar enough concatenation of
circumstances of the dreadful blows that threaten the nation in attacking
the magistracy;

Considering that the ministers' plans for action against the magistracy
are prompted by the court's resistance to two disastrous taxes, by its ac-
knowledgment of its incompetence to decide upon tax matters, by its call
for the convocation of the Estates General, and by its arguments on behalf
of the individual liberty of citizens;

Considering that the only purpose of these actions must be to conceal
past extravagances, without having recourse to the Estates General if possible, by resorting to methods which the court could not witness without
opposing: for its duty obliges it to be constant and unwavering in upholding
the authority of the laws, the word of the king, the public faith, and the
loans secured by tax revenues, against any plan that might compromise the
rights and obligations of the nation;

Considering, finally, that the doctrine of "sole will," clearly expressed
in the abrupt responses foisted upon our lord the king, announces a fatal
plan formed by the ministers to destroy the very principles of the monarchy, and leaves the nation no other resource than a clear pronouncement by
the court of the maxims it is charged to protect, and the convictions it will
never cease to endorse:

Declares that France is a monarchy governed by a king according to the
laws. That of these laws, the number that are fundamental include and
sanction:

—the right of the reigning house to the throne, passed from male to
male in order of primogeniture, to the exclusion of women and their
descendants;

—the right of the nation to grant subsidies freely, through the agency of
the Estates General, regularly convoked and constituted;

—the customs and treaty rights of the provinces;

—the irremovability of magistrates;

—the right of the courts in each province to verify expressions of the
king's will, and to order their registration only if they conform to the constitutive laws of the province, and to the fundamental laws of the state;

—the right of each citizen not to be summoned, for any reason, before
any but his natural judges, which are those designated for him by the law;

—the right, without which all others are useless, never to be arrested,
by any order whatsoever, except to be put immediately into the hands of
competent judges.

This court protests against any attempt to attack the principles set forth above. It also declares *unanimously* that it can in no case deviate from them. These indisputable principles bind all members of the court and are contained in their oath of office. Consequently, no member of the court can or will authorize the slightest change in this regard, or participate in any body other than this very court, composed of the same persons and vested with the same rights. In the event that the court is dispersed by force, rendering it powerless to uphold the principles contained in this declaration, it declares this inviolable depository immediately entrusted to the hands of the king, his august family, the peers of the realm, the Estates General, and each of the orders (dispersed or assembled) that constitute the nation. . . .

Remonstrances of the Parlement (3 May)

Sire, Your Majesty's response of the 17th of this month is distressing, but the courage of your parlement has not been weakened. The excesses of despotism were the only resource of the enemies of the nation and the truth; they have not feared to use them, their success is the harbinger of greater ills. To prevent this if possible will be your parlement's most zealous goal until the very end. In keeping silent, it would betray Your Majesty's dearest interests by abandoning the kingdom to all the incursions of arbitrary power. Such, in effect, would be the consequence of the maxims foisted upon Your Majesty. If your ministers make them prevail, our kings will no longer be monarchs, but despots; they will no longer reign by law but by force, over slaves instead of subjects. . . .

No, Sire, no aristocracy in France, but no despotism either. Such is the constitution; such also the desire of your parlement, and the interest of Your Majesty.

Accept for a moment the maxims foisted on Your Majesty—that the sole will of the king determines the law in administrative and legislative matters—and let the consequences enlighten us as to the principles.

The heir to the crown is named by the law: the nation has its rights, as does the peerage; each province has its customs and its rights; each subject his natural judges; each citizen his belongings; if he is poor, he at least has his liberty.

We dare to ask what rights, what laws, could resist the pretensions declared by your ministers in Your Majesty's name? Your sole will would decide in legislative matters! Would it then be legally possible for such a will to dispose of the crown, choose a new heir, give away provinces belonging to the crown, deny the Estates General the right to consent to subsidies? Could it destroy the peerage, make the magistracy removable, change customary law, overturn the judicial order, assume the sole right to judge, or to choose the judges in matters both civil and criminal? Could it declare itself co-owner of the goods of its subjects, and master of their liberty?

The administration wants loans and new taxes. If the king's will alone is law, then the king could create loans and impose taxes at will.

What if it pleased the king, mistakenly, to suppress all the sovereign courts of his realm and create new ones, in order to reduce their jurisdiction to the administration of justice? What if it pleased him to transplant citizens, magistrates, families, or entire companies of magistrates from one province to another? What if it pleased him to erect, over the ruins of the original magistracy, a unitary body that made a show of liberty while serving as an instrument of servitude? What if, still worse, it pleased him to permit ministers to sow division among the magistrates, pitting one against the other, forcing them to choose between opprobrium and disgrace, distinguishing between those who would relinquish the right of verification and those who would strive to retain it? Then it would be necessary to leave one's home, renounce one's country, give up one's affections, tear oneself away from one's colleagues, violate one's oath, betray the state, and expose oneself to dishonor—or else submit to the blows of despotism—and all that on a mere word from the king's mouth! . . .

The right to consent freely to taxes does not make the Estates General an aristocracy of citizens; the right freely to verify the laws does not make the parlements an aristocracy of magistrates.

Aristocrats govern; but your parlement does not aspire to govern. In its judgments, it is always subject to the law; its will is nothing. It pronounces, but the law decides. . . .

Does it follow that your parlement is attempting to reduce the king's will to the equivalent of that of one of his officers? No, Sire; the parlement remains at the foot of the throne to support it and to enlighten it; this is the sum of its ambition. It claims its most important rights only in the most respectful way; this respect, however, is not incompatible with liberty.

If it is a question of a trial, the king has no will to exercise. The law is there; it must decide; he is the first judge. . . .

If it is a question of taxation, it is up to the nation to grant it. The liberty of the Estates General remains beyond any doubts.

If it is a question of a law, then it is up to the courts to verify it; but since the right to verify laws is not the right to make laws, the courts can neither force nor supplant the will of the king. Your parlement, Sire, has already asserted this, and will continue to do so as often as the king's ministers attempt to obscure this truth. . . .

To justify despotism, one vainly pretends to fear for the legislator. "Will there then be as many wills as there are courts in the kingdom?" your ministers object. The reply can be found in history and in the laws. A general oath—the Coronation Oath—links the whole of France to its sovereign. But the king does not reign over all the provinces according to the same title: in Normandy, Brittany, Guyenne, Languedoc, Provence; in Dauphiné, Alsace and Burgundy; in Franche-Comté; in the conquered provinces, and in those added to the kingdom, different conditions govern obedience. . . .

To be just, the king's will must therefore vary from province to province. It is restrained, not by the courts, but by principles. And happy the restraints that render legitimate power more stable. Each province asked for a parlement to defend its particular rights. And these rights are not chimerical, nor are the parlements empty institutions. Otherwise, the king could say to Brittany, "I am taking away your Estates"; to Guyenne, "I am abrogating your treaty rights"; to the people of Béarn, "I no longer intend to take an oath to you"; to the nation itself, "I wish to change the Coronation Oath"; to all the provinces, "your liberties are restraints upon the legislator, your parlements oblige his will to vary; I abolish your liberties and destroy your parlements. . . ." Then, it is certainly true, the king's will could be uniform. Oh Sire! That it should even be possible for the parlement to imagine such dangers! Would it be just, would it be prudent, would it even be possible for your ministers to have formed such plans? Certainly this is neither the intention of Your Majesty, nor in your interests.

For your parlement, Sire, these principles, or rather those of the state entrusted to it, are immutable; it is not in the parlement's power to alter its conduct. Sometimes magistrates are called to sacrifice themselves for the laws; but such is their honorable and perilous condition that they must cease to exist before the nation ceases to be free. . . .

The King's Speech at a *Lit de Justice* (8 May)

There is not a single act of misconduct in which my parlement has not indulged during the last year.

Not content to elevate the status of each of its members' opinions to that of my own royal will, the parlement has dared to argue that an unforced registration is necessary to confirm what I have already decided, even at the nation's request. The provincial parlements have permitted themselves the same pretensions, the same actions.

As a result, worthwhile and desirable laws are not generally executed; the most important operations languish; credit is affected; justice is interrupted or suspended; and public tranquillity could ultimately be disturbed.

I owe it to my people, to myself, and to my successors, to put a stop to such infractions. I could have put a stop to them; I wish rather to prevent their effects.

I have been forced to punish some magistrates, but acts of severity are repugnant to my generous nature, even when they are indispensable.

I do not want to destroy my parlements, but to bring them back to their duties and to their original form. I want to transform a moment of crisis into a period beneficial to my subjects; to begin the reformation of the judicial order by reforming the tribunals which are its necessary basis; to provide my subjects with justice that is more prompt and less costly; to restore to the nation the exercise of its legitimate rights, which must always be consonant with its talents and abilities.

Above all, however, I wish to instill in all parts of the monarchy that unity and integrity without which a great kingdom is weakened by the very number and extent of its provinces.

The order I wish to establish is not new. The parlement was unitary when Philip the Fair settled it permanently in Paris. A great state requires one king, one law, and one registration. It requires tribunals with moderately sized jurisdictions, charged with the task of hearing the great majority of cases. It requires parlements in which the most important cases will be heard. It requires a special court, a repository of the kingdom's laws, charged with the responsibility of their registration. And, finally, it requires that the Estates General be assembled, not just once but as often as the needs of the state demand.

Such is the restoration that my love for my subjects has inspired, and sanctions today, for their welfare. It will always be my only goal to make them happy.

Calling the Estates General

11. Order in Council Concerning the Convocation of the Estates General (5 July 1788)

Resistance to the May Edicts was widespread. Opposition by the provincial parlements was supported by increasingly radical protests from the clergy and nobility, and dramatic outbursts of popular disorder occurred in a number of parlementary cities. In this context, demands for the convocation of the Estates General became even more pressing. Brienne's response was to issue the following decree. It was certainly an effort to

From *Receuil de documents relatifs à la convocation des Etats Généraux de 1789*, edited by Armand Brette, 4 vols. (Paris: Imprimerie Nationale, 1894–1915), vol. 1, pp. 19–22. Translated for this volume by the editor, Keith Michael Baker.

play for time, and may well have been a device to foster division among the opposition to ministerial policies. But it also dramatized the genuine difficulties involved in calling an assembly that had not met for 175 years. In inviting public discussion of this issue, Brienne opened the floodgates to the torrent of books and pamphlets that reshaped French political consciousness in the remaining months of 1788.

His Majesty, when he announced last November his intention to call the Estates General of the realm, immediately ordered all the researches required to render their meeting proper and useful to his people.

The researches completed to date reveal that the minutes of earlier Estates General provide adequate information concerning the administration, sessions, and functions of these assemblies, but that they are less adequate regarding the procedures leading to their convocation. . . .

The last Estates called in 1614 were convoked by *bailliages;*[1] but it seems that this procedure was not followed in every province. Since then, great changes have occurred in the number and size of *bailliages*. Several provinces have also been added to France, and in their case nothing can therefore be determined on the basis of previous practice. Finally, no definite information is available regarding electoral procedures, or the number and status of the voters or those they elected.

However, His Majesty has recognized that if these preliminary issues were not decided before the convocation of the Estates General, the beneficial effects to be expected from their meeting could not be achieved; the choice of deputies could be subject to dispute; their number could be disproportionate to the wealth or population of the respective provinces; the rights of certain provinces or towns could be compromised; the influence of the different orders could be insufficiently balanced; and, finally, the number of deputies could be too large or too small—possibly causing trouble and confusion, or preventing the nation from being adequately represented.

His Majesty will constantly seek to conform to earlier practices; but when these cannot be ascertained, he does not wish to decide matters upon which the records are silent before asking the views of his subjects, so that the latter will have all the greater confidence in an assembly that will be truly national, both in its composition and in its results.

The king has consequently resolved to command that all possible researches relating to the above matters be carried out in the archives of each province. The results of these investigations should be submitted to the provincial Estates and to the provincial and district assemblies of each

---

1. *Bailliages*, or bailiwicks, were the traditional local jurdisdictions of the Old Regime.

province, which will make known their views to His Majesty in the memoranda or reports they are invited to forward to him. . . .

The king hopes thereby to secure for the nation the most correct and fitting meeting of the Estates; to prevent disputes that could unnecessarily prolong its duration; to establish the proportion and harmony that must be upheld in the composition of each of the three orders; to ensure that the assembly enjoys the confidence of the people, according to whose wish it will have been formed; and, finally, to make it what it should be, the assembly of a great family with a common father at its head. . . .

12. Sallier, *Recollections of a Parlementary Magistrate*

On 8 August 1788, his hand forced by the desperate need to restore government credit, Brienne announced that the Estates General would meet in May 1789. Shortly thereafter, and for the same reason, he was replaced as principal minister by Jacques Necker, the Swiss banker who had served as director-general of finances from 1776 to 1781. Ever popular with the financial community, Necker's political stock had risen dramatically as opposition to government policies had increased. Reappointed by a reluctant Louis XVI, his first move was to abandon the May Edicts, restore the parlements to their functions, and press on with plans to call the Estates General as soon as possible.

One of the first acts of the Parlement of Paris upon its return was to declare (on 25 September) that the Estates General should meet according to the forms and procedures followed in 1614. This pronouncement was immediately interpreted by members of the Third Estate as a defense of privileged interests: virtually overnight, the magistrates lost the enthusiastic popular support they had enjoyed in previous months. In these recollections, Guy-Marie Sallier, a magistrate in the Parlement of Paris, explains his colleagues' reasons for opting for the forms of 1614, and describes through their eyes the rapid transformation of the political situation that occurred in the last months of 1788. Although written with the benefit of hindsight, Sallier's recollections are particularly interesting for their interpretation of Necker's actions and motivations during this period.

From *Annales françoises* . . . *(1774–1789)*, 2d ed. (Paris, 1813), pp. 209, 211–17, 226–30, 234, 241–42, 265–68. Translated for this volume by D. Carroll Joynes and Keith Michael Baker.

The last ministry had had the imprudence to declare that there existed no firm rule for the convocation, the composition, and the constitution of the Estates General. . . . The parlement considered that all would be lost if there were no certainties regarding such an important issue; that it would even prove impossible to convene a true Estates General if the spirit of system and innovation could discredit invariable and prescribed forms of procedure. And although it was obliged to lose its popularity by declaring against democracy, it did not hesitate to fulfill its duty at this point by recalling the fundamental principles regarding the legitimate constitution of the Estates General. The last to be held, in 1614, appeared to it to be necessarily the model, since it was convoked according to perfectly regular and proper procedures. This was articulated in a judicial decision adopted almost unanimously at the proposal of Robert de Saint Vincent. From that moment, the seditious vowed an implacable war against it. . . .

In deciding the form of the Estates General, the parlement wanted to prevent the disorders that could arise from conflicting opinions. Necker also busied himself with efforts to combat this effort to establish peace. The decision of the council on July 5, 1788 had sown doubts. Necker, going beyond Loménie [de Brienne], drafted another in order to establish certain so-called facts, publication of which would agitate the Third Estate even further. He had the king declare that in previous convocations of the Estates General, the representation of the Third Estate had been illusory; that the elections had been concentrated in the kingdom's principal cities . . . and that the others had enjoyed virtually no representation; that the inhabitants of the countryside did not *appear* to have participated in the election of deputies; and that the elections had been carried out by town councils composed of magistrates who held royal offices acquired by purchase.

Even if these facts had been true, it would have been a great mistake to publish them; but they were false. Necker knew it, and proof of this was given to the parlement. With more justification, but with just as little prudence, Necker also criticized the elections of 1614 for the lack of proportionality in the representation of the various *baillages,* since some very small ones had enjoyed the same rights in this regard as the largest ones. This is the same tactic used by the opposition leaders in the English Parliament: when they want to stir up trouble among the various parties, they denounce this same fault in their constitution, draw attention to the unequal size, wealth, and population of their counties, and then cry out for parliamentary reform.

To eliminate these alleged defects, the Notables assembled in 1787 were called back. They were to deliberate regarding the most regular and appropriate manner of convoking the next Estates General. These Notables had voted for double representation of the Third Estate in the provincial assemblies; and Necker persuaded himself that they would be of the same mind regarding the Estates General. In the event that they should decide otherwise, he reserved the option of invoking against the authority of their counsel the complaints of those to whom he was offering new rights, and the multitude of democratic writings that was about to inundate France. It was with this in mind that the preamble to the decree [summoning the Notables to reconvene] concluded with the king's assurance that he attached great importance to "the general consensus of opinions and views. . . ."

Necker's firm resolution to support in any way possible the spirit of innovation spread by the Orléans party[1] derived neither from a clear and absolute disregard for his duties, nor from the feelings of hatred and vengeance that had animated his predecessors, but rather from a political system which had always been his fantasy. Scorning the French constitution, which he claimed did not exist because he could not see it written in a solemn legal agreement, he turned his gaze, his desires, and his hopes towards the English constitution. That was the goal toward which all his efforts were directed; he thought he would be able to achieve it by giving the Third Estate a preponderance in the Estates General that would, according to him, result in a representative body composed only of two chambers. . . .

If Necker revealed this idea only to his most intimate associates, it was because he clearly saw that the king was far from sharing such views. With no hope of prevailing in this respect over what he called the ancient prejudices of the French princes, he sought to achieve his goal by indirect means, and by manipulating the various parties. Blinded by a mad presumption, he did not see that all was lost when official royal pronouncements stated that France had neither a constitutional law nor established precedents. It never occurred to him that if an upstart who was not even French thought himself qualified—amidst all the tumultuous passions he had unleashed—to give France a new law, then any citizen endowed with an ardent imagination could, like him, have the idea of proposing its constitution, call upon popular opinion for support, boast of its extent, and then rely upon the impetuousness of his proselytes. But such was Necker's egotism that he felt sure that he could steer the ship of state on this raging sea, and never doubted that a word from his mouth would suffice to pacify the turbulent waves when he wanted.

1. The duc d'Orléans, Prince of the Blood, was well-known for his liberal views, which some suspected were motivated by a desire for the throne. Elected to the Estates General, he was one of the first nobles to support the demands of the Third Estate. His revolutionary career was to earn him the soubriquet, "Philip Equality."

But the Third Estate would not have responded to his appeal without even more direct incitement. . . . To bring them to make complaints that appeared to be in their own particular interest, it took nothing less than the guaranteed protection of the government, in addition to its insinuations and its intrigues. . . .

[Once Necker recognized] that he could no longer count on the Assembly of Notables to make democracy prevail in the Estates General, he tried, unsuccessfully, to get the parlement involved in his enterprise. Failing at this, he conceived the idea of using it indirectly for his purposes, by offering it the role of mediator. He called upon [Duval] d'Eprémesnil,[2] and deceived him with his clever arguments. "Frightful dissension abounds everywhere," he said. "Doubling of the Third Estate's representation in the Estates General is being demanded. If it is obtained by force, all will be lost. Voting by head will follow from this violent conquest, and an angered Third Estate will know no moderation. We do not want voting by head any more than you, but we believe it necessary to grant the simple doubling of the Third Estate to calm things down and restore a measure of good faith. Let us consent to this double representation, and we will thereby save an endangered constitution. It would perhaps be harmful, and it would certainly be dangerous, for the parlement to come out explicitly for voting by order. But there is no need to do so. It will be enough for the moment not to abandon the principle, not to appear to place it in doubt. That is all the circumstances require. At the same time, let us reassure the Third Estate in regard to its fear that the *taille* will be continued as a tax to which it alone is subject. In that way, we will have removed every pretext for alarm and restored a measure of good faith. . . ."

Full of this notion of pacification, d'Eprémesnil managed with great difficulty to get the parlement's support for it. . . . A parlementary declaration [of 5 December] recalled the troubles disturbing the state and the strategies being used to incite the people to sedition and reduce the whole of France to anarchy. It declared that the number of deputies for each order at the Estates General had neither been specified by law nor established by long-standing custom; accordingly, in this matter, the parlement could only rely upon the wisdom of the king to take such measures as were necessary to bring about changes indicated by reason, liberty, justice, and the general desire. The parlement added a plea to the king to remove all pretexts for agitation and unrest by announcing immediately his intention to suppress the *taille* and replace it with taxes shared equally among the three orders.

2. Jean-Jacques Duval d'Eprémesnil had been one of the most radical opponents of royal power among the magistrates of the Paris parlement. He was arrested in May 1788 and remained imprisoned for four months. Returning to Paris a popular hero, he sought to undo the damage of the parlement's declaration of 25 September by urging it to take a more liberal position on the doubling of the Third Estate.

These declarations, made in the hope of bringing about peace, were far from successful. Writers from the Third Estate seized upon everything in them that served their cause, without ceasing to preach discord and distrust. Necker imitated them; and when this declaration (which he later cited as one of the most solemn authorities) was presented to the king, he dictated these disdainful words in sole response: "I have no reply to my parlement's pleas."

However, the Assembly of Notables was in session. In his opening address, Necker sought indirectly to move it in the direction of the party he was protecting. But from its earliest sessions on, the assembly demonstrated an attitude completely opposed to his views. . . .

Deprived of the Notables' support, Necker engaged wholeheartedly in the plot that had been sketched out for him. Carefully devised petitions were again circulated to the principal cities, and they came back with signatures of the municipal bodies and the corporations of the Third Estate. Deputations carried them to the foot of the throne where they were always given a hearing, while anyone who wanted to express an opposing point of view was set aside or unfavorably received. . . .

On another side, there were the newspapers. They were still under government control, these newssheets which six months earlier had argued for absolute power and treated any mention of the idea of liberty as an act of rebellion. Now they sported more popular colors and talked of little else but the rights of the nation and its sovereignty.[3] While they poured out praise for the minister and those who shared his views, they began to insult the individuals and corporate bodies that manifested opposing views. The cafés, which up until then had been kept under strict police surveillance, and where it had been forbidden to voice any political opinion, suddenly became schools for the public in democracy and insurrection. There, orators succeeded one another without interruption to maintain a state of agitation and excite people's minds with discussions, discourses and readings. Judicial procedures were parodied in mock trials of all the works written in defense of the ancient constitution. They burned the memoranda of the princes and legal indictments of the excesses of license. The decisions of the supreme court, unenforced since the government had declared itself the protector of insurrection, were also exposed to ridicule—thus teaching all those tempted to defend public order and monarchical institutions that they would be paid back with outrages which would not only go unpunished, but would even be encouraged.

Gatherings known as "clubs" had been introduced into France in recent

3. Sallier's claim that the press was still under government control at this point is doubtless an exaggeration. What is striking is the government's willingness to tolerate—or inability to prevent—the torrent of political argument that poured forth in the last months of 1788.

years by those who planned revolution. They had been prohibited in 1787 at the beginning of the government's difficulties with the parlement. Necker, when he was recalled to the ministry, hastened to reestablish them, and he made them one of the principal centers of agitation. . . .

Jealous of his influence and greedy for public favor, Necker [in announcing the royal decision concerning the elections to the Estates General] then permitted himself an action which even the most powerful ministers before him had never dared to take. He wanted to share the royal prerogative in order to bask in the adoration of the popular party.

Until this time, royal decisions had always been announced by laws or orders of the Council. A preamble set forth the reasons for the decision. The minister drafted this preamble, but it appeared under the king's name because he alone had the right to speak to his people. Necker changed this procedure so that he could attach his name with great fanfare to the measure which introduced the seed of democracy into the French constitution. The statement of the king's decision, published [on 27 December] under the new title of *Result of the Council,* was brief and had no preamble, while Necker proclaimed his own personal opinion in the form of a report and placed his statement alongside that of his royal master.

In this act without precedent in the annals of the French monarchy, Necker, adding insolence to pride, seemed to strive to make it known that it was less by persuasion than by the sheer force of will that he imposed these resolutions upon the monarch. . . . Against the authority of the majority of the Assembly of Notables, he opposed that of a minority; against constitutional principles he upheld party clamors—which he called "the muted sound of Europe, favoring in its confusion, every idea of general equity." Nor did he deny that to attack the rights of the first two orders was to contravene the principles of French government and to destroy the spirit of the monarchy. . . .

He remarked further that the people is rash in its claims; that once their first demand was granted, a string of others could follow, leading imperceptibly to democracy. But he left these grave objections unrefuted, content to assert that the doubling of the Third Estate would have no unfortunate consequences. Then he repeated, like the authors of the insurrection, that the Third Estate was everything; that its wishes were those of the entire nation; that its cause was linked to generous sentiments, and would always find support in the conversations and writings of those who knew how to make themselves heard and read. He did not even hesitate to resurrect the question that remained constantly unanswered: what more does the Third Estate want, since its independence and equality are already assured, and if it is certain never again to see pecuniary privileges stacked against it?

His way of evading this objection was to assert that if the Third Estate did not need double representation in order to defend itself, this would still be appropriate so that the deliberations of the Estates General could be more effectively transmitted back to the provinces.

Finally, insulting with sarcasm those he had already sacrificed, he reproached the first two orders for conjuring up fictitious threats and abandoning themselves to chimerical alarms. Then he urged them instead to celebrate the doubling of the Third Estate, which would assure them an expression of esteem all the more glorious in that the acclamations they received would be repeated by a greater number of voices.

This document, which would have been an offense if it had come from a private individual, was a true crime against the state on the part of a minister. . . . Partisans of the revolution read it with rapture. Their club in Paris was lit up as if after a victory, and hope, changed to certainty, gathered force and audacity. . . .

13. Memorandum of the Princes of the Blood (December 1788)

As recounted by Sallier in the preceding document, Necker reconvened the Assembly of Notables in November 1788 to advise him on the issue of the procedures to be followed in the convocation of the Estates General. The Notables overwhelmingly rejected the demands of the Third Estate that its representatives be equal in number to those of the other two orders combined (the "doubling" of the Third Estate) and that the three orders deliberate and vote together in a single body (voting "by head" rather than "by order"). They did, however, declare themselves in favor of equal taxation.

The arguments and apprehensions that prevailed in the Assembly of Notables were vividly expressed in this memorandum to the king signed by five of the Princes of the Blood who had again presided over its internal committees. (Two of the princes, the duc d'Orléans and the comte de Provence, the king's brother, declined to sign.)

. . . Sire, the state is in peril. Your person is respected, the virtues of the monarch assure him of the nation's homage. But, Sire, a revolution is being

From John Hardman, *The French Revolution: The Fall of the Ancien Regime to the Thermidorian Reaction 1785–1795*, pp. 72–74. © 1982 by John Hardman. Reprinted by permission of St. Martin's Press, Inc., and of Edward Arnold (Publishers) Ltd., where it appeared originally in the series Documents of Modern History, under the general editorship of A. G. Dickens.

prepared in the principles of government; it is being accomplished through the turmoil in men's minds. Institutions which were considered sacred and which have enabled this monarchy to flourish for so many centuries have been put into question or even decried as unjust.

The writings which have appeared during the Assembly of Notables; the memoranda which have been submitted to the princely signatories, the demands formulated by various provinces, towns or *corps;* the subject matter and style of these demands and memoranda all herald, all prove that there is a deliberate plan of insubordination and of contempt for the laws of the state. Every author sets himself up as a legislator; eloquence or a facile pen—even devoid of study, knowledge or experience—seem sufficient authorization to regulate the constitution of empires. Whoever advances a bold proposition, whoever proposes to change the laws is assured of readers and sectaries.

So fast does this deplorable mania develop that opinions which a short while ago would have appeared most reprehensible today seem reasonable and just. . . . Who can say where the audacity of opinions will stop? The rights of the throne have been called into question; opinion is riven over the rights of the two orders of the state; soon the rights of property will be attacked; inequality of wealth will be represented as something which needs to be reformed; already it has been proposed that feudal dues be abolished as representing a system of oppression, a barbarous survival.

Derived from these new theories, from the intention to change rights and laws, is the claim advanced by several sections of the Third Estate that their order should have two votes in the Estates-General whilst each of the two leading orders continues to have but one.

The princely signatories will not repeat what has been developed by several committees [of the Notables], namely the injustice and danger of innovations in the composition of the Estates-General; the host of resultant claims; the ease with which, if votes were counted by head and not by order, the interests of the Third Estate—better defended by the existing arrangements—would be compromised by corrupting members of the Third Estate; the destruction of the equilibrium so wisely established between the three orders and of their mutual independence.

It has been demonstrated to Your Majesty how important it is to preserve the only method of convoking the Estates which is constitutional, the mode hallowed by law and custom: the distinction between the orders, the right to deliberate in separate chambers, equality of votes [between them]—these unchangeable foundations of the French monarchy. . . .

These principles have been developed and proved, it would seem, irrefutably.

It only remains for the princely signatories to add the expression of feelings inspired by their attachment to the state and to Your Majesty.

They cannot conceal their fears for the state should the claims of the Third Estate be successful and the dire consequences of the proposed revolution in the constitution of the Estates: they perceive a sad vista unfolding; they see each king altering the rights of the nation according to his personal inclinations: a superstitious king giving extra votes to the clergy; a martial king showering them on the nobility, his comrades-in-arms; the Third Estate, now obtaining a majority of votes, then being punished for its success by these changes; each order, depending on the period, the oppressor or the oppressed; the Constitution rotten or unstable; the nation perpetually divided and henceforth always weak and unhappy.

But there are yet more immediate misfortunes. In a kingdom where for so long civil dissensions have not existed it is painful to pronounce the word schism. However we must expect this if the rights of the first two orders suffer any change. In this case one of these orders—or both of them perhaps—could refuse to recognize the Estates-General and thereby avoid confirming their degradation by appearing before the Assembly.

At any rate, who can doubt that we shall see a large number of gentlemen challenging the legality of the Estates-General, issuing protests and having them registered in the *parlements,* even addressing them to the assembly of the Estates? Henceforth what is decided in this Assembly would no longer, in the eyes of a portion of the nation, have the force of national consensus; and imagine the hold on the people of protests tending to dispense them from paying taxes granted by the Estates! Thus this Assembly, so desired and so necessary, would be nothing but a source of troubles and disorder.

But even were Your Majesty not to experience any obstacles in carrying out his intentions, could his noble, just and tender spirit consent to the sacrifice and humiliation of this brave, ancient and respected nobility which has shed so much blood for king and country . . . ?

In speaking for the nobility, the Princes of your Blood are speaking for themselves. They cannot forget that they form part of the body of the nobility, from which they should not be distinguished; that their highest title is that of gentleman: Henri IV said this and they delight in repeating his noble sentiments.

Let the Third Estate, then, stop attacking the rights of the first two orders—rights which are no less ancient than the monarchy and should be as unalterable as its constitution. Let them content themselves with requesting the reduction of their share of taxation which may be too great. Then the first two orders, recognizing in the Third Estate citizens who are dear to them, will be able, out of the generosity of their hearts, to renounce any prerogatives which have a pecuniary value and consent to carry their full share of public taxation.

The princely signatories ask to set the example of all the sacrifices which can contribute to the good of the state and to cement the union of the orders composing it.

14. Sieyès, *What Is the Third Estate?*

Hundreds of pamphlets appeared in the course of the great public debate over the forms to be followed in the convocation of the Estates General. Few, if any, could match this one in rhetorical force or revolutionary logic. Written in the last months of 1788, and published at the very beginning of 1789, Sieyès's famous pamphlet focused the resentments and shaped the demands of the Third Estate during the period of elections to the Estates General, defined the political strategy followed by its representatives when the assembly finally opened in May 1789, and elaborated principles that were to become fundamental in the subsequent development of revolutionary ideology.

Emmanuel-Joseph Sieyès (1748–1836) was the son of a minor financial official whose search for advancement through a church career had brought him by 1788 to the position of vicar-general in the diocese of Chartres. So successful was his pamphlet that he was elected deputy of the Third Estate of Paris despite his clerical status. He played a leading role in the early period of the French Revolution, only to lose influence as revolutionary politics grew more radical. Surviving the Terror, he eventually played an important role in the coup d'état that brought Napoleon to power.

Sieyès revised *What Is the Third Estate?* twice in the early months of 1789, elaborating upon some of its arguments and sharpening its language in minor respects. The following selections are taken from a translation based on the third edition.

The plan of this book is fairly simple. We must ask ourselves three questions.
    1. What is the Third Estate? *Everything.*
    2. What has it been until now in the political order? *Nothing.*
    3. What does it want to be? *Something.*

We are going to see whether the answers are correct. . . . We shall next examine the measures that have been tried and those that must still be taken for the Third Estate really to become something. Thus, we shall state:

From Emmanuel Joseph Sieyès, *What is the Third Estate?*, translated by M. Blondel and edited by S. E. Finer (London: Phaidon Press Ltd., 1964), pp. 53–63, 65–69, 71–81, 83–88, 94–104, 119–20, 124–30, 132–40, 142–47, 152–55.

4. What the Ministers have attempted and what even the privileged orders propose to do for it.

5. What ought to have been done.

6. Finally, what remains to be done in order that the Third Estate should take its rightful place.

Chapter 1. The Third Estate Is a Complete Nation

What does a nation require to survive and prosper? It needs *private* activities and *public* services.

These private activities can all be comprised within four classes of persons:

1. Since land and water provide the basic materials for human needs, the first class, in logical order, includes all the families connected with work on the land.

2. Between the initial sale of goods and the moment when they reach the consumer or user, goods acquire an increased value of a more or less compound nature through the incorporation of varying amounts of labour. In this way human industry manages to improve the gifts of nature and the value of the raw material may be multiplied twice, or ten-fold, or a hundred-fold. Such are the activities of the second class of persons.

3. Between production and consumption, as also between the various stages of production, a variety of intermediary agents intervene, to help producers as well as consumers; these are the dealers and the merchants. Merchants continually compare needs according to place and time and estimate the profits to be obtained from warehousing and transportation; dealers undertake, in the final stage, to deliver the goods on the wholesale and retail markets. Such is the function of the third class of persons.

4. Besides these three classes of useful and industrious citizens who deal with *things* fit to be consumed or used, society also requires a vast number of special activities and of services *directly* useful or pleasant to the *person*. This fourth class embraces all sorts of occupations, from the most distinguished liberal and scientific professions to the lowest of menial tasks.

Such are the activities which support society. But who performs them? The Third Estate.

Public services can also, at present, be divided into four known categories, the army, the law, the Church and the bureaucracy. It needs no detailed analysis to show that the Third Estate everywhere constitutes nineteen-twentieths of them, except that it is loaded with all the really arduous work, all the tasks which the privileged order refuses to perform. Only the well-paid and honorific posts are filled by members of the privileged order. Are we to give them credit for this? We could do so only if the Third Estate was unable or unwilling to fill these posts. We know the answer. Nevertheless, the privileged have dared to preclude the Third Estate. "No matter how useful you are," they said, "no matter how able you are, you can go so far and no further. Honours are not for the like of you." The rare exceptions, noticeable as they are bound to be, are mere mockery, and the sort of language allowed on such occasions is an additional insult.

If this exclusion is a social crime, a veritable act of war against the Third Estate, can it be said at least to be useful to the commonwealth? Ah! Do we not understand the consequences of monopoly? While discouraging those it excludes, does it not destroy the skill of those it favours? Are we unaware that any work from which free competition is excluded will be performed less well and more expensively? . . .

It suffices to have made the point that the so-called usefulness of a privileged order to the public service is a fallacy; that, without help from this order, all the arduous tasks in the service are performed by the Third Estate; that without this order the higher posts could be infinitely better filled; that they ought to be the natural prize and reward of recognised ability and service; and that if the privileged have succeeded in usurping all well-paid and honorific posts, this is both a hateful iniquity towards the generality of citizens and an act of treason to the commonwealth.

Who is bold enough to maintain that the Third Estate does not contain within itself everything needful to constitute a complete nation? It is like a strong and robust man with one arm still in chains. If the privileged order were removed, the nation would not be something less but something more. What then is the Third Estate? All; but an "all" that is fettered and oppressed. What would it be without the privileged order? It would be all; but free and flourishing. Nothing will go well without the Third Estate; everything would go considerably better without the two others.

It is not enough to have shown that the privileged, far from being useful to the nation, can only weaken and injure it; we must prove further that the nobility is not part of our society at all; it may be a *burden* for the nation, but it cannot be part of it.

First, it is impossible to find what place to assign to the caste of nobles among all the elements of a nation. I know that there are many people, all too many, who, from infirmity, incapacity, incurable idleness or a collapse of morality, perform no functions at all in society. Exceptions and abuses always exist alongside the rule, and particularly in a large commonwealth. But all will agree that the fewer these abuses, the better organised a state is supposed to be. The most ill-organised state of all would be the one where not just isolated individuals but a complete class of citizens would glory in inactivity amidst the general movement and contrive to consume the best part of the product without having in any way helped to produce it. Such a class, surely, is foreign to the nation because of its *idleness*.

The nobility, however, is also a foreigner in our midst because of its *civil and political* prerogatives.

What is a nation? A body of associates living under *common* laws and represented by the same *legislative assembly*, etc.

Is it not obvious that the nobility possesses privileges and exemptions which it brazenly calls its rights and which stand distinct from the rights of the great body of citizens? Because of these special rights, the nobility does not belong to the common order, nor is it subjected to the common laws. Thus its private rights make it a people apart in the great nation. It is truly *imperium in imperio*.

As for its *political* rights, it also exercises these separately from the nation. It has its own representatives who are charged with no mandate from the People. Its deputies sit separately, and even if they sat in the same chamber as the deputies of ordinary citizens they would still constitute a different and separate representation. They are foreign to the nation first because of their origin, since they do not owe their powers to the People; and secondly because of their aim, since this consists in defending, not the general interest, but the private one.

The Third Estate then contains everything that pertains to the nation while nobody outside the Third Estate can be considered as part of the nation. What is the Third Estate? *Everything*.

Chapter 2. What Has the Third Estate Been Until Now? *Nothing*

We shall examine neither the condition of servitude in which the People has suffered for so long, nor that of constraint and humiliation in which it is still confined. Its status has changed in private law. It must change still further: the nation as a whole cannot be free, nor can any of its separate orders, unless the Third Estate is free. Freedom does not derive from privileges. It derives from the rights of citizens—and these rights belong to all.

If the aristocrats try to repress the People at the expense of that very freedom of which they prove themselves unworthy, the Third Estate will dare challenge their right. If they reply, "by the right of conquest," one must concede that this is to go back rather far. Yet the Third Estate need not fear examining the past. It will betake itself to the year preceding the "conquest"; and as it is nowadays too strong to be conquered it will certainly resist effectively. Why should it not repatriate to the Franconian forests all the families who wildly claim to descend from the race of the conquerors and to inherit their *rights of conquest?* . . .

Let us pursue our theme. By Third Estate is meant all the citizens who belong to the common order. Anybody who holds a legal privilege of any kind deserts the common order, stands as an exception to the common laws and, consequently, does not belong to the Third Estate. As we have already said, a nation is made one by virtue of common laws and common representation. It is indisputably only too true that in France a man who is protected only by the common laws is a nobody; whoever is totally unprivileged must submit to every form of contempt, insult and humiliation. To avoid being completely crushed, what must the unlucky non-privileged person do? He has to attach himself by all kinds of contemptible actions to some magnate; he prostitutes his principles and human dignity for the possibility of claiming, in his need, the protection of a *somebody*.

But we are less concerned in this book with the civil rights of the Third Estate than with its relationship to the constitution. Let us see what part it plays in the States-General.

Who have been its so-called "Representatives"? Men who have been raised to the nobility or have received temporary privileges. These bogus deputies have not even been always freely elected by the People. In the States-General sometimes, and in the Provincial Estates almost always, the representation of the People is considered as inherent in the holder of certain offices.

The old aristocracy detests new nobles; it allows nobles to sit as such only when they can prove, as the phrase goes, "four generations and a hundred years." Thus it relegates the other nobles to the order of the Third Estate to which, obviously, they no longer belong.

In law, however, all nobles are equal—those whose nobility dates from yesterday just as much as those who succeed for better or for worse in hiding their origins or their usurpation. In law all have the same privileges. Only *opinion* distinguishes between them. But if the Third Estate must endure a prejudice sanctioned by law, there is no reason why it should submit to a prejudice contrary to law.

Let them create as many noblemen as they like; it still remains certain that the moment any citizen is granted privileges against the common laws, he no longer forms part of the common order. His new interest is contrary to the general interest; he becomes incompetent to vote in the name of the People. . . .

Some occasionally express surprise at hearing complaints about a threefold "aristocracy composed of the army, the Church and the law." They insist that this is only a figure of speech; yet the phrase must be understood strictly. If the States-General is the interpreter of the general will, and correspondingly has the right to make laws, it is this capacity, without doubt, that makes it a true aristocracy: whereas the States-General as we know it at present is simply a *clerico-nobili-judicial* assembly.

Add to this appalling truth the fact that, in one way or another, all departments of the executive have also fallen into the hands of the caste that provides the Church, the law and the army. As a result of a spirit of brotherhood or *comradeship,* nobles always prefer each other to the rest of the nation. The usurpation is total; in every sense of the word, they reign.

If you consult history in order to verify whether the facts agree or disagree with my description, you will discover, as I did, that it is a great mistake to believe that France is a monarchy. With the exception of a few years under Louis XI and under Richelieu and a few moments under Louis XIV when it was plain despotism, you will believe you are reading the history of a *Palace* aristocracy. It is not the King who reigns; it is the Court. The Court has made and the Court has unmade; the Court has appointed ministers and the Court has dismissed them; the Court has created posts and the Court has filled them. . . . And what is the Court but the head of this vast aristocracy which overruns every part of France, which seizes on everything through its members, which exercises everywhere every essential function in the whole administration? So that in its complaints the People has grown used to distinguishing between the monarch and those who exercise power. It has always considered the King as so certainly misled and so defenceless in the midst of the active and all-powerful Court, that it has never thought of blaming him for all the wrongs done in his name.

Finally, is it not enough simply to open our eyes to what is occurring around us at this very moment? What do we see? The aristocracy on its own, fighting simultaneously against reason, justice, the People, the minister and the King. The end of this terrible battle is still undecided. Can it still be said that the aristocracy is only a chimera!

Let us sum up: to this very day, the Third Estate has never had genuine representatives in the States-General. Thus its political rights are null.

Chapter 3. What Does the Third Estate Want to Be? *Something*

It is wrong to judge the claims of the Third Estate from the isolated remarks of certain authors who are partially aware of the rights of man. The Third Estate is still very backward in this matter, not only by comparison with the insight of students of the social order, but also with that mass of common ideas which constitutes public opinion. The authentic requests of the Third Estate can only be adjudged through the formal demands which the great municipalities of the kingdom have addressed to the government. What do we see therein? That the People wants to become *something,* and in fact, the least thing possible. It wants to have (1) genuine representatives in the States-General, i.e. deputies *drawn from its own ranks* and competent to interpret its wishes and defend its interests. But what good would it do the Third Estate to participate in the States-General if the interest opposed to its own were to preponderate there? It would simply sanction by its presence the oppression of which it would be the everlasting victim. Therefore, it most certainly cannot come and vote in the States-General unless its influence there *is at least equal to that of the privileged orders.* So it asks for (2) a number of representatives equal to that of the other two orders taken together. However, this equality of representation would become entirely illusory if each chamber voted separately. The Third Estate, therefore, asks for (3) the votes to be counted *by heads and not by orders.* Such is the whole extent of the claims which appear to have so alarmed the privileged orders; and for this reason alone have these come round to believing that the reform of abuses has become indispensable.

The Third Estate's modest aim is to possess an equal influence in the States-General to that of the privileged orders. Once again, could it ask for less? And is it not clear that if its influence is less than equal, it cannot hope to come out of its political non-existence and become *something?*

However, the great pity of it all is that the three articles which constitute the claim of the Third Estate are not enough to give it the equal influence which it cannot effectively dispense with. To grant it no more than an equal number of representatives drawn from its own ranks will be useless: for the privileged orders will continue to exercise their dominating influence in the very sanctuary of the Third Estate. . . . The more one considers this matter, the more one perceives the inadequacy of the three claims of the Third Estate.

However, even as they stand, they have been violently attacked. Let us examine the pretexts for such spiteful hostility.

First Claim of the Third Estate: That the Representatives of the Third Estate Be Chosen Solely from among Citizens Who Really Belong to the Third Estate.

We have already explained that really to belong to the Third Estate, one must either be untainted by privileges of any sort, or else relinquish them immediately and completely.

Those lawyers who have attained nobility through a door which for unknown reasons they have decided to close behind them are determined to sit in the States-General. They tell themselves: "The nobility does not want us and we for our part do not want the Third Estate. If only we could form a separate order, it would be wonderful; however, we cannot. What are we to do? Our only chance is to maintain the old abuse by which the Third Estate elected nobles. By doing this, we shall fulfil our desires without lowering our pretensions." All new nobles, whatever their origin, hastened to repeat in the same spirit that the Third Estate must be allowed to elect noblemen. The old nobility, which claims to be the true one, has not the same stake in maintaining the old abuse; but it knows how to take things into account. It thought: "We shall put our sons in the *House of Commons,* so that it is altogether an excellent idea to charge us with representing the Third Estate."

Once one has made up one's mind, reasons for it, as we well know, are never wanting. "We must maintain the ancient *custom,*" people said. An excellent custom which, intended to provide representation for the Third Estate, has positively excluded it from representation until this very day! The Third Estate has political rights as it has civil rights; and it alone must be able to exercise both. What an idea—to *distinguish* between orders when it is to the advantage of the first two and the misfortune of the third, but to fuse them *together* as soon as it becomes useful to the first two and harmful to the nation! What a custom—by which the Church and the aristocracy can take over the chamber of the Third Estate! In all candour, would the privileged feel they were being represented if the Third Estate could invade the deputation of *their* orders? . . .

Another argument is that if electors are restricted in their choice they will not be completely free. I have two answers to this so-called difficulty. First, those who raise it are hypocrites, and I will prove it. Everyone knows how lords domineer over the peasants and others who live in the countryside; everyone knows the habitual and the potential tactics of their multifarious agents, including their law-officers. Hence any lord who cares to influence the primary election is generally sure to be sent as a deputy to the "*bailliage,*" where it only remains to select a candidate from among the lords themselves or from those who have earned their most intimate trust. Is it then to preserve the People's freedom that you establish the possibility of abusing and betraying its trust? It is appalling to hear the sacred name of freedom profaned as a disguise for designs which are most adverse to it. Certainly, electors must be given the utmost freedom, and this is precisely why it is necessary to exclude from their deputation all the privileged classes who are too fond of overbearing the People.

My second answer is direct. In no circumstances can any freedom or right be unlimited. In all countries, the law prescribes certain qualifications without which one can be neither an elector nor eligible for election. For example, the law must decide the age under which one is incompetent to represent one's fellow-citizens. Thus, rightly or wrongly, women are everywhere excluded from mandates of this kind. It is unquestionable that tramps and beggars cannot be charged with the political confidence of nations. Would a servant, or any person under the domination of a master, or a non-naturalised foreigner, be permitted to appear among the representatives of the nation? Political liberty, therefore, has its limits, just as civil liberty has. The only question to answer is whether the non-eligibility of members of the privileged orders, which the Third Estate is asking for, is as vital as the other non-eligibilities I have just mentioned. Comparison runs completely in favour of this proposition; for the interests of a beggar or a foreigner might not conflict with the interest of the Third Estate, whereas nobles and clerics are, by their very status, supporters of the privileges which they themselves enjoy. Therefore, the restriction requested by the Third Estate is the most important of all the restrictions which the law, in accordance with equity and the nature of things, must lay down for the choice of representatives. . . .

In accord with these principles, we must not permit men of the Third Estate who are under the exclusive domination of members of the first two orders to be given the trust of the Commons. It is clear that their dependency makes them untrustworthy; unless they are formally excluded, the lords will not fail to use the influence which they can no longer use for themselves in favour of the men whom they control. Above all, beware, I beg you, of the multifarious agents of feudalism. It is to the odious remnants of this barbaric system that we still owe the division of France, to her misfortune, into three mutually hostile orders. All would be lost if the lackeys of feudalism came to usurp the representation of the common order. Who does not know that servants are more harsh and bold to defend their masters' interests than the masters themselves? I know that this proscription covers many people since it concerns, in particular, all officers of feudal tribunals and the like, but, in this instance, we must be governed by the logic of the situation. . . .

Some people have supposed that they reinforce the difficulty of which we have just disposed by submitting that the Third Estate does not contain enough intelligent or courageous members and so forth competent to represent it, and that it has no option but to call on the leading figures of the aristocracy. . . . So ridiculous a statement deserves no answer. Look at the *available* classes in the Third Estate; and like everyone else I call "available" those classes where some sort of affluence enables men to receive a liberal education, to train their minds and to take an interest in public affairs. Such classes have no interest other than that of the rest of the People. Judge whether they do not contain enough citizens who are educated, honest and worthy in all respects to represent the nation properly.

But then, it is argued, what if a "*bailliage*" insists on giving the mandate of the Third Estate only to a nobleman or an ecclesiastic? What if it has trust in only such a man?

I have already stated that there can be no freedom without limits and that, of all the qualifications that could be imposed on eligibility, the qualification the Third Estate requested was the most necessary. But let us give a direct answer. Supposing that one "*bailliage*" is determined to prejudice its own interests, does it follow that it must be allowed to prejudice the interest of others? If I alone am affected by the steps taken by my agent, a man may be content with simply saying to me: "Hard luck; but why did you make such a bad choice?" But, in the case in point, the deputies of a district are not merely the representatives of the "*bailliage*" which nominated them, they are also called upon to represent the whole body of citizens, to vote for the whole kingdom. One must therefore have a common rule and such qualifications, which, although they may displease some people, will reassure the whole of the nation against the whim of a few electors.

Second Claim of the Third Estate: That Its Deputies Be Equal in Number to Those of the Two Privileged Orders

I cannot refrain from repeating once more that the timid inadequacy of this claim is an after-effect of times gone by. The towns of the kingdom have not given enough consideration to the progress of enlightenment or even of public opinion. They would have met with no greater difficulties by demanding two votes to one; but they might even have been hastily granted the very equality which some people are so loudly opposing today.

Furthermore, when we want to decide a question of this kind, we must not simply do what is only too common, and give our personal wish or our will or custom as valid reasons. It is necessary to argue from principles. Like civil rights, political rights derive from a person's capacity as a citizen. These legal rights are identical for every person, whether his property happens to be great or small. Any citizen who satisfies all the formal requirements for an elector has the right to be represented, and the extent of his representation cannot be a fraction of the extent of some other citizen's representation. The right to be represented is single and indivisible. All citizens enjoy it equally, just as they are all equally protected by the law which they have helped to make. How can one argue on the one hand, that the law is the expression of the general will, i.e. the majority, and on the other hand that ten individual wills can cancel out a thousand individual wills? Would one not thereby run the risk of permitting a minority to make the law? Which would obviously be contrary to the nature of things.

If these principles, certain though they may be, are too remote from common view, I will direct the reader's attention to a comparison which lies under his very nose. Is it not a fact that it seems fair to everybody that the huge "*bailliage*" of Poitou should send more representatives to the States-General than the small "*bailliage*" of Gex? Why is that? Because, it is stated, the population and the contribution of Poitou are far more important than those of Gex. Thus it is admitted that there are principles according to which it is possible to determine the proportion of representatives. Should we take taxation as a basis? Although we have no exact information as to the amount of taxes paid by each order, it is obvious that the Third Estate pays more than one-half of the total.

With respect to population, everybody knows that the third order enjoys a vast numerical superiority over the first two. I have no better knowledge than anybody else as to the exact proportion; but, like anybody else, I can estimate. . . .

[Sieyès's calculations produced an estimated total of 81,400 clerics—revised from 80,400 in the first edition—and 110,000 nobles.]

Therefore, in total, there are less than 200,000 privileged individuals of the first two orders. Compare their number with the 25 or 26 million inhabitants, and draw your own conclusions.

Now, to reach the same solution on a basis of different but equally indisputable principles, let us bear in mind that the privileged classes are to the great body of citizens what exceptions are to the law. Any society must be governed by common laws and submitted to a common order. If exceptions are to exist, at least they ought to be rare; and they must never have the same weight and influence on the commonwealth as the common rule. It is absurd to oppose the interest of the privileged classes to the grand interest of the mass of the nation as if they were capable of counterbalancing each other. (We will explain this point at greater length in Chapter 6.) When, a few years hence, we look back on all the obstacles raised to the over-modest claim of the Third Estate, we shall be amazed at the inadequacy of the arguments used against it, and even more at the brazen effrontery of those who were bold enough to dig them up.

The very persons who invoke the authority of facts against the Third Estate could, if they were honest, find in those facts the guide for their own conduct. The existence of a mere handful of loyal cities was enough to constitute, under Philip the Fair, a Chamber of Commons in the States-General.

Since that day, feudal servitude has disappeared and rural areas have provided a numerous population of *new citizens*. Towns have increased in number and size. Commerce and arts have, as it were, created new classes thronging with prosperous families of educated and civic-minded citizens. Why did not this two-fold increase, so much greater than the loyal cities' ancient contribution to the nation, encourage the same authority to create two new chambers in favour of the Third Estate? Justice and sound policy alike require it.

No one dares act so unreasonably in respect of another kind of increase that has occurred in France, viz. the new provinces which have become united with her since the last States-General met. Nobody would dare to claim that these new provinces should have no representatives of their own over and above those who were in the States-General in 1614. But do not manufactures and the arts create new riches, new taxes and a new population just as much as territory does? Since this form of increase is easily comparable to that of territory why on earth should one refuse to accord it representatives over and above the number allotted to the States-General in 1614?

But I am trying to reason with people who are moved only by self-interest. Let us present them with an argument that might touch them more closely. Is it proper for the nobility of today to retain the language and attitudes which were characteristic of it in the gothic centuries? And is it proper for the Third Estate, at the end of the eighteenth century, to languish in the sad and cowardly customs of ancient servitude? If the Third Estate learns how to know itself and respect itself, the others will indeed respect it too. Reflect that the former ratio between the orders has been altered simultaneously on both sides. The Third Estate, which had been reduced to nothing, has reacquired by its industry something of what had been seized from it by the offence of those in power. Instead of demanding that its rights be restored, it has consented to pay for them; they have not been given back but sold back. But, at last, in one way or the other, it can take possession of them. It must realize that today it represents a reality within the nation, whereas formerly it represented only a shadow; that, while this long transformation was taking place, the nobility has ceased to be a monstrous feudal power free to oppress as it willed; that now it is the nobility that is a shadow, and that this shadow is still trying to spread terror through a whole nation—but to no avail, unless our nation is willing to be thought the basest in the world.

Third and Last Claim of the Third Estate: That the States-General Vote, Not by Orders, but by Heads

One can regard this question from three points of view: as apprehended by the Third Estate; as relating to the interests of the privileged classes; and in terms of sound principles. As far as the first of these is concerned, it would be pointless to add anything to what we have already said; clearly, the Third Estate considers that this claim is the necessary consequence of the two others.

The privileged classes fear the third order's possession of an influence equal to their own, and so declare it unconstitutional. This behaviour is all the more striking as they have, until this moment, enjoyed a superiority of two against one without seeing anything unconstitutional in this unjust predominance. They feel passionately that they must retain a veto on everything that might conflict with their interests. I am not going to restate the arguments by which a score of writers have combated this pretension, and the argument of "the ancient procedures." I want to make one observation only. There are, beyond any doubt, abuses in France; these abuses are profitable to some persons: but they hardly ever benefit the Third Estate, and, on the contrary, it is to the Third Estate that they do most harm. Now I ask: in such circumstances is it possible to abolish any abuse so long as those who profit therefrom retain a veto? Justice would be powerless—everything would depend entirely upon the magnanimity of the privileged classes. Would this correspond to our idea of what constitutes social order?

If we now turn to considering this question apart from any individual interest, but according to the principles appropriate to illuminate it, i.e. the principles of the science of social order,[1] it strikes us in a new light. I maintain that it is impossible to accept the claim of the Third Estate or to defend the privileged classes without turning some sure and certain ideas upside down. Naturally, I do not accuse the loyal towns of the kingdom of intending this. They simply wanted to come closer to their rights by asking for at least an equilibrium between the two influences. Moreover, they have formulated some excellent truths, for it is obvious that one order's right of *veto* over the others is likely to bring everything to a standstill in a country where interests are so conflicting. It is quite certain that unless votes are counted by heads the true majority may be set aside, which would be the supreme difficulty, since it would render legislation null and void. Such truths are indisputable. But the true question is whether the orders, as now constituted, could unite to vote by heads? No, they could not. If one relies on true principle, they cannot vote *together* at all, either by heads or by orders. Whatever the proportion arranged between them, it cannot achieve the intended aim: viz. to bind all representatives together by a *single* common will. This statement doubtless calls for elaboration and for proof. Allow me to postpone these until Chapter 6. I do not want to upset the moderate-minded, who always fret in case the truth should make its appearance at the wrong moment. I must first make them admit that, simply because of the privileged classes and nobody else, conditions are now such that it is time to come to a decision, and to proclaim what is true and just in its full strength.

---

1. In the first edition, Sieyès used the term "social science." This is the earliest use of the term so far discovered.

Chapter 4. What the Government Has Attempted and What the Privileged Classes Propose on Behalf of the Third Estate

[In the first two sections of this chapter, Sieyès reviews the inadequacies of the government's efforts to institute provincial assemblies and the resistance to reform presented by the two Assemblies of Notables.]

3. Patriotic Writers of the First Two Orders

It is noteworthy that the cause of the Third Estate should have been defended more eagerly and forcibly by ecclesiastical and noble writers than by the non-privileged classes themselves.

In this torpidity of the Third Estate I see nothing but the habitual silence and fear which are common among the oppressed, and it provides additional proof of how real that oppression is. . . . When the nation achieves its freedom it will remember with gratitude the patriotic writers of the first two orders who were the first to abjure archaic errors and who preferred the principles of universal justice to the murderous conspiracies of corporate interest against the interest of the nation. Until those public honours are conferred upon them, may they be pleased to accept the homage of a citizen whose soul is consumed for his country and who worships all efforts which help her rise from the rubble of feudalism!

The first two orders are unquestionably interested in reinstating the third in its rights. But let us not dissimulate; the guarantee of public liberty lies only where real power lies. We can be free only with the People and by the People.

If a consideration of such magnitude is too much for the frivolity and narrow egotism of the majority of Frenchmen, these must at least be impressed by the changes in public opinion. Day by day, the influence of reason spreads further, increasingly necessitating the restitution of the rights that have been usurped. Sooner or later, every class will have to withdraw inside the boundaries of the social contract, the contract which concerns everyone, and binds all the associates one to the other. Will this result in reaping its countless advantages, or in sacrificing them to despotism? This is the real question. During the long night of feudal barbarism, it was possible to destroy the true relations between men, to turn all concepts upside down, and to corrupt all justice; but, as day dawns, so gothic absurdities must fly and the remnants of ancient ferocity collapse and disappear. This is quite certain. But shall we merely be substituting one evil for another, or will social order, in all its beauty, take the place of former chaos? Will the changes we are about to experience be the bitter fruit of a civil war, disastrous in all respects for the three orders and profitable only to ministerial

power; or will they be the natural, anticipated and well-controlled consequence of a simple and just outlook, of a happy cooperation favoured by
the weight of circumstances and sincerely promoted by all the classes
concerned?

4. Promise to Bear Taxes Equally

The Notables[2] have formally expressed the wish that all three orders should
bear similar taxes, but this was not what they were asked to advise upon.
They were asked how to convoke the States-General, not what should be
the subject of its deliberations. Therefore, we must look upon that wish
just as we do upon those expressed by the peers, the *Parlement* and, finally,
by so many private associations and individuals, all of whom hasten to
agree today that the richer must pay as much as the poorer.

We cannot dissemble: so novel a cooperation has frightened some of the
public. Undoubtedly, some have said, it is good and praiseworthy to pledge
oneself to submit loyally to a fair distribution of taxes once the law has so
decided. But (they ask) what is the origin of so novel a zeal, of so much
agreement, of so much haste on the part of the second order? Was it its
hope that by offering a voluntary surrender it could avoid the necessity for
making it a legal act of justice? Is its excessive zeal to anticipate the work
of the States-General aimed at making the latter unnecessary? I will not
accuse the nobility of having told the King: "Sire, you need the States-
General only to restore your finances: well! we offer to pay as much as the
Third Estate; see whether this surplus could not deliver you from an assembly which worries us even more than it does you." No, it is impossible to
take this view.

More likely, one suspects, the nobility is trying to hoodwink the Third
Estate at the price of a kind of anticipation of justice, in order to divert it
from its current demands and so distract it from its need to be *something* in
the States-General. The nobility seems to be saying to the Third Estate:
"What are you demanding? Do you want us to pay as much as you do? That
is just and we shall do so. But let things proceed as in the past when you
were nothing and we were everything and when it was so easy for us to pay
only as much as we chose." . . .

To this the Third Estate can retort: "It is high time that you, like us, bore
the burden of a tax which is far more useful to you than to us. You correctly
foresaw that this monstrous iniquity could not last any longer. If we are free
to give what we choose, we clearly cannot, must not, and will not give any
more than you. Having made up our minds on this, we are virtually un-
moved by these acts of renunciation which you keep vaunting as the rarest

2. The reference is to the second Assembly of Notables. See documents 12 and 13, above.

fruit of the *generosity* and the honour of the *French Knights*. Yes, you will pay; not out of generosity, however, but out of justice; not because you consent to do so, but because you have to. We expect you to submit to the common laws, not to offer a token of insulting pity for an order which you have treated mercilessly for so long. But it is for the States-General to discuss this matter; today's question is how to constitute it properly. If the Third Estate is not represented in the States-General, the voice of the nation will be mute in that assembly, and none of its acts will be valid. Even if you were to find ways of rectifying everything without our participation we will not allow anyone to dispose of us without our consent. A long and lamentable experience prevents us from believing in the soundness of the best of laws when this comes merely as *a gift of the strongest.*"

The privileged classes never tire of saying that once the orders renounce their financial exemptions all is equal between them. If all is equal, what have they to fear from the demands of the Third Estate? Do they imagine that it wants to damage itself by attacking a common interest? If all is equal, why then all the efforts to stop the Third Estate emerging from its political incapacity?

But, may I ask, where is the miraculous power that insures France against the possibility of any abuse of *any sort* simply because the nobility pays its fair share of a tax? Alternatively if abuses or disorders still persist, then how can all be equal between those who profit and those who suffer from them?

All is equal indeed! Was it in a spirit of equality . . . that the Third Estate was ignominiously excluded from all offices and posts of any distinction? Was it the spirit of equality that made the Third Estate pay excess taxes so as to create the enormous quantity of resources of every kind for the exclusive use of what is called the *poor nobility?*

In all dealings between a privileged man and a commoner, is it not certain that the latter has no redress against oppression, since if he is bold enough to take legal action he has to appeal to members of the privileged classes? They alone dispose of authority and is not their first reaction to regard the commoner's law-suit as insubordination?

Why are the police agents so terrified when they act against a man of the privileged classes, even when they catch him red-handed, while they maltreat a pauper who is merely a suspect?

For whose benefit are all the judicial privileges, attributions, evocations, letters-patent of suspension and the like, with which to discourage or ruin the contending party? Can the non-privileged Third Estate dispose of these?

Which class of citizens are most exposed to personal humiliations from tax agents and the petty officials of every branch of the bureaucracy? The members of the Third Estate—that is, of course, the real Third Estate, i.e. the Third Estate which enjoys no exemptions.[3]

Why do the privileged nearly always escape the penalty for the most horrible of crimes? And why is public order thus robbed of its most effective examples?

With what ridiculous and ferocious contempt do you dare to relegate the criminal of the first two orders to the third, in order, so you proclaim, to *degrade* him and, apparently, to render him, in such company, *liable* to be executed! What would you say if the legislator, before punishing some scoundrel of the Third Estate, proposed to rid his order of him by giving him letters-patent of nobility?

The law lays down different penalties for the privileged classes and for the non-privileged. It appears to take a fond interest in a noble criminal and to seek to honour him right up to the scaffold. To this abominable distinction which, fundamentally, only potential criminals could wish to retain, is linked, as we know, a sentence of attainder for the entire family of the wretch who is executed without benefit of privilege. The law is responsible for this atrocity; and you would refuse to change it! If the *duty* is the same for everybody, and if the *infraction* is the same, why should the *penalty* be different? Remember: as things now stand, whenever you punish a privileged man you honour him but punish the nation which has already suffered enough from his crime.

I put it to you: cast but the most superficial glance over society and still repeat that all will be equal from the moment the nobility renounces its financial exemptions! Some men are only sensitive about money; their senses are literally paralysed at anything connected with liberty, honour or equality before the law, in short by all social rights apart from money; they cannot conceive of people worrying about anything except one crown more or one crown less. But it is not for the vile that I am writing this book.

How justify the exclusive privilege of carrying arms, even in peacetime, irrespective of any military function and without wearing the uniform of that profession? If the privileged man arms himself to defend his life, his property and his honour, why is a man of the Third Estate any less interested in protecting his life and his property? Is he less sensitive about honour? Who would dare argue that the law is so much more vigilant on his behalf that it therefore *excuses* him from arming for self-defence?

If all is equal, why the voluminous collections of laws benefiting the nobility? Have you perchance discovered how to favour one order without

---

3. The following six paragraphs were added to the third edition—a good example of the way in which Sieyès' revisions sought to sharpen the sense of grievance among the Third Estate.

damaging the others? You know full well that this discriminatory legislation turns the nobility into a race apart, born to rule, and everybody else into a nation of helots, destined to serve. Yet you dare lie to your conscience and try to bemuse the nation by clamouring that "all is equal."

Finally, even those laws which you think are the most general and impartial are themselves accessory to the privileges. Look at the spirit in which they are drafted; trace out their consequences. For whom do they appear to be made? For the privileged classes. Against whom? Against the nation. . . .

And so the People is to be content and to forget about all this because the nobility (forsooth!) *agrees* to pay, like the People! Future generations are to close their eyes to the enlightenment of their day and settle down quietly to a state of oppression which the present generation can no longer endure! But let us leave this inexhaustible topic, it does nothing but rouse indignation.

All taxes peculiar to the Third Estate must be abolished. This is indubitable. What an odd country, where the citizens who profit most from the commonwealth contribute least to it! Where there are taxes which it is shameful to bear and which the legislator himself styles "degrading"! To think only in terms of wholesomeness, what kind of society is it where you *lose caste* if you work? Where to consume is honourable but to produce is vile? Where laborious occupations are called *base?* As if anything but vice could be base, and as if this baseness of vice, the only true one, could be found mostly among those who work! . . .

Chapter 5. What Ought to Have Been Done? Basic Principles

In every free nation, and every nation ought to be free, there is only one way of settling disputes about the constitution. One must not call upon Notables, but upon the nation itself. If we have no constitution, it must be made, and only the nation has the right to make it. If we do have a constitution, as some people obstinately maintain, and if, as they allege, it divides the National Assembly into three deputations of three orders of citizens, nobody can fail to notice, at all events, that one of these orders is protesting so vigorously that nothing can be done until its claim is decided. Now, who has the right to judge in such a matter? . . .

But who will tell us for what purpose and in whose interest a constitution could have been given to the *nation* itself? The nation is prior to everything. It is the source of everything. Its will is always legal; indeed it is the law itself. Prior to and above the nation, there is only *natural* law. If we want to formulate a clear idea of that sequence of *positive* laws which can emanate exclusively from the will of the nation, the first are the *constitu-*

tional laws. These are of two kinds: some determine the organisation and the functions of the *legislative* body; the others determine the organisation and the functions of the various *executive* bodies. These laws are called *fundamental,* not in the sense that they could become independent of the national will, but because the bodies to which they grant existence and means of actions cannot modify them. Neither aspect of the constitution is the creation of the constituted power, but of the constituent power. No type of delegated power can in any way alter the conditions of its delegation. In this sense, and in this sense alone, are constitutional laws *fundamental.* Those which establish the legislative body are *founded* by the national will before any constitution has been established; they form the first stage of the constitution. Those which establish the executive bodies must similarly be the *ad hoc* product of a representative will. Thus all the parts of a government are interrelated and, in the last analysis, depend on the nation. . . .

The power exercised by the government has substance only in so far as it is constitutional; it is legal only in so far as it is based on the prescribed laws. The national will, on the contrary, never needs anything but its own existence to be legal. It is the source of all legality.

Not only is the nation not subject to a constitution, but it *cannot* be and it *must not* be; which is tantamount to saying that it is not.

It *cannot* be. From whom indeed could it have received positive form? Is there a prior authority which could have told a multitude of individuals: "I put you together under such and such laws; you will form a nation on the conditions I prescribe." We are not speaking here of brigandage or domination, but of a legitimate, that is to say voluntary and free, association.

Can it be said that a nation, by a primary act of will which is completely untrammelled by any procedure, can bind itself to express its will thereafter only in certain determined ways? In the first place, a nation can neither alienate nor waive its right to will; and whatever its decisions, it cannot lose the right to alter them as soon as its interest requires. Secondly, with whom would this nation have entered into such a contract? I see how it can *bind* its members, its mandatories, and all those who belong to it; but can it in any sense impose on itself duties towards itself? What is a contract with oneself? Since both parties are the same will, they are obviously always able to free themselves from the purported engagement.

Even if it could, a nation *must* not subject itself to the shackles of a defined procedure. That would put it in danger of losing its liberty for ever, for tyranny, under the pretext of giving the People a constitution, would only need a momentary success to bind it so closely by procedural rules that it would lose the ability to express its own will, and, consequently, to shake off the yoke of despotism. We must conceive the nations of the world as being like men living outside society or "in a state of nature," as it is called. The exercise of their will is free and independent of any civil form. Existing only within the natural order, their will can take full effect provided it bears the *natural* characteristics of a will. The manner in which a nation exercises its will does not matter; the point is that it does exercise it; any procedure is adequate, and its will is always the supreme law. To imagine a legitimate society, we assumed that the purely natural *individual* will had enough moral power to form the association; how then can we refuse to recognise a similar power in the equally natural *common* will? A nation is always in a state of nature and, amidst so many dangers, it can never have too many possible methods of expressing its will. Let us not be afraid of repeating it: a nation is independent of any procedures; and no matter how it exercises its will, the mere fact of its doing so puts an end to positive law, because it is the source and the supreme master of positive law. . . .

In the light of these explanations, we can answer the question we asked ourselves. The component parts of what you believe to be the French constitution are quite obviously at loggerheads. Whose task is it to decide? It is the nation's, independent as it necessarily is of any positive forms. Even if the nation enjoyed regular States-General, this constituted body would be incompetent to decide on a dispute concerning its own constitution. It would be a *petitio principii,* a vicious circle. . . .

It is time now to come back to the title of this chapter. *What ought to have been done* amidst all the difficulties and disputes about the coming States-General? Should we have convened Notables? No. Should we have let the nation and its interests languish? No. Should we have exercised diplomacy upon the interested parties to persuade them all to compromise? No. We should have resorted to the extreme measure of calling an extraordinary representative body. It is the nation that ought to have been consulted.

Let us answer two questions which still remain. Where is the nation to be found? Whose function is it to consult the nation?

1. Where is the nation to be found? Where it is: in the 40,000 parishes which embrace the whole territory, all its inhabitants and every element of the commonwealth; indisputably, the nation lies there. A geographical division would have been chosen so that "*arrondissements*" of 20 to 30 parishes could easily form and elect first deputies. Along similar lines, "*arrondissements*" would have formed provinces; and the provinces would have sent to the capital authentic extraordinary representatives with special powers to decide upon the constitution of the States-General.

You object that this procedure would have entailed too much delay? Surely no more than the succession of expedients which have simply led to further confusion. Besides, it was not a question of saving time, but of adopting workable measures to achieve the aim. Had people been willing and able to stick to true principles, more could have been done for the nation in four months than the progress of enlightenment and public opinion, powerful none the less as I believe it to be, could do in half a century.

But, if the *majority* of the citizens had nominated extraordinary representatives, what would have happened, you may ask, to the distinction between the three orders? What would have become of privileges? They would have become what they deserve to be. The principles which I have just recited are certainties. Abandon the hope of having social order, or else accept these principles. The nation is always free to amend its constitution. Above all, it cannot absolve itself from the responsibility of giving certainty to a disputed constitution. Everybody agrees on that today; cannot you see, then, that the nation could not interfere if it were itself merely a participant in the dispute? A body subjected to constitutional forms cannot take any decision outside the scope of its constitution. It cannot give itself another one. It becomes null and void from the moment when it moves, speaks or acts in any other than the prescribed forms. Even if the States-General were already in session, it would therefore be incompetent to decide upon the constitution. Such a right belongs only to the nation which, we continue to reiterate, is independent of any procedure and any qualifications.

As is obvious, the privileged classes have good reasons for befogging the concepts and principles which relate to this matter. They are boldly prepared today to uphold the opposite of the views they were advocating six months ago. At that time there was a single outcry in France: we had no constitution and we asked for one to be made. Today, we not only have a constitution but, if we are to believe the privileged classes, one which contains two excellent and unchallengeable provisions. The first is the *division* of the citizens *into orders;* the second is the *equality of influence* of each order in the formation of the national will. We have already sufficiently proved that even if both these elements were indeed comprised in our constitution, the nation would always be free to change them. It remains to examine more particularly the nature of this *equality* of influence that they seek to attribute to each order in the formation of the national will. We shall see that such an idea is impossibly absurd and that no nation could possibly include anything of the kind in its constitution.

A political society cannot be anything but the whole body of the associates. A nation cannot decide not to be the nation, or to be so only in a certain fashion: for that would be saying that it is not the nation in any other fashion. Similarly, a nation cannot decree that its common will shall cease to be its common will. It is sad to have to state facts which may appear so simple as to be silly, until one thinks of the conclusions they entail. It follows that no nation has ever been able to decree that the rights inherent in the common will, i.e. in the majority, should pass into the hands of the minority. The common will cannot destroy itself. It cannot change the nature of things, nor arrange that the opinion of the minority shall be the opinion of the majority. Clearly such a regulation would not be a legal or a moral act: it would be lunacy.

Consequently if it be claimed that under the French constitution two hundred thousand individuals out of twenty-six million citizens constitute two-thirds of the common will, only one comment is possible: it is a claim that two and two make five.

The sole elements of the common will are individual wills. One can neither deny the greatest number the right to play their part, nor decide that these ten wills are equivalent to only one while another ten wills amount to thirty. These are contradictions in terms, pure absurdities.

If for the slightest moment one loses sight of this self-evident principle that the common will is the opinion of the majority and not of the minority, there is no point in carrying on the discussion. One might just as well decide that the will of a single man is to be called the majority and that we no longer need States-General or national will at all. For, if the will of a nobleman can be worth as much as ten wills, why should not the will of a minister be worth as much as a hundred? a million? twenty-six million? On the basis of this reasoning, all the national deputies may as well be sent home and every demand of the People suppressed.

Is it necessary to insist further on the logical deduction from these principles? It is a certainty that among the national representatives, whether ordinary or extraordinary, influence must be proportionate to the number of citizens who have the *right* to be represented. If it is to accomplish its task, the representative body must always be the substitute for the nation itself. It must partake of the same *nature,* the same *proportions* and the same *rules*.

To conclude: these principles are all self-consistent and prove: (a) only an extraordinary representative body can establish or amend the constitution; (b) this constituent representative body must be set up without regard to the distinction between orders. . . .

2. Whose function is it to consult the nation? If the constitution provides for a legislature, each of its component parts would have the right to consult the nation, just as litigants are always allowed to appeal to the courts; or, rather, because the interpreters of a will are obliged to consult with those who appointed them to seek explanations about their mandate or to give notice of circumstances requiring new powers. But for almost two centuries we have been without representatives—even assuming that we had them at that time. Since we have none, who is going to take their place vis-à-vis the nation? Who is going to inform the People of the need for extraordinary representatives? . . . Ask, rather: who has not such a right?

It is the sacred *duty* of all those who can do something about it. *A fortiori,* the executive is qualified to do it; for it is in a better position than private individuals to give notice to the whole nation, to designate the place of the assembly and to sweep aside all the obstructions of corporate interests. The Prince indubitably, in so far as he is the first citizen, has a greater interest than anyone else in convoking the People. He may not be competent to decide on the constitution, but it is impossible to say that he is incompetent to bring such a decision about.

So it is not difficult to answer the question, "what ought to have been done?". The nation ought to have been convened, so as to send to the capital extraordinary representatives with a special mandate to frame the constitution for the ordinary National Assembly. . . .

Why, it may be asked, do I linger so long over *what ought to have been done?* Is not the past over and done with? To this I reply: first, that the knowledge of what ought to have been done may help us to know what must be done. Secondly, it is never unimportant to expound the correct principles of one's topic, particularly when it is so new to most minds. And, finally, the truths expounded in this chapter may conduce to a better understanding of those in the one that follows.

Chapter 6. What Remains to Be Done.
Development of Certain Principles

Gone is the day when the three orders were moved by the single thought of defending themselves against ministerial despotism and were ready to unite against their common enemy. . . .

In vain will the Third Estate await restitution of its *political* rights and the plenitude of its *civil* rights from the consensus of the orders. The fear of seeing abuses reformed alarms the aristocrats more than the desire for liberty inspires them. Between liberty and a few odious privileges, they have chosen the latter. The soul of the privileged has become identified with the favours of servitude. They are afraid now of the States-General for which they were lately so ardent. Everything goes well with them. They have no complaints, except for the spirit of innovation. They no longer require anything: fear has provided a constitution for them.

The Third Estate must now see the direction in which both thought and action are moving, and realise that its sole hope lies in its own intelligence and courage. Reason and justice are on its side; the least it must do is to assure itself of their full support. No, it is too late to work for the conciliation of all parties. What sort of an agreement could one hope for between the energy of the oppressed and the rage of the oppressors? They have dared utter the word *secession*. With it they have threatened both King and People. Heavens! How fortunate it would be for the nation if so desirable a secession could be perpetuated! How easy it would be to do without the privileged! How difficult it will be to induce them to become citizens!

The aristocrats who led the attack did not realise that they were making an enormous blunder by drawing attention to certain questions. Among a people used to servitude, truth can be left to sleep; but if you attract the attention of the People, if you tell it to choose between truth and error, its mind clings to truth as naturally as healthy eyes turn towards the light. And, light, in morals, cannot spread to any extent without, willy-nilly, leading to equity. . . . The Third Estate must, moreover, recognise the danger that unless it improves its status it cannot simply remain as it is. The circumstances do not permit of this faint-hearted calculation. Not to go forwards is to go backwards. Unless you want to proscribe this mass of iniquitous and anti-social privileges, you must decide to recognise and justify them. Yet the blood boils at the mere thought that it is possible to give *legal recognition,* at the close of the eighteenth century, to the abominable fruits of abominable feudalism. . . .

While the aristocrats talk of their honour but pursue their self-interest, the Third Estate, i.e. the nation, will develop its virtue, for if corporate interest is egotism, national interest is virtue. It will suffer the nobles to nourish their expiring vanity on the pleasure of abusing the Third Estate with the most insulting words in the vocabulary of feudalism. The nobles will repeat such words as *commoners, peasants* and *villeins,* forgetting that these terms, no matter in what sense one means them, either do not describe the Third Estate as it is today or are common to the three orders; forgetting also that, when these words did make sense, ninety-nine per cent of their own number were unquestionably *commoners, peasants* and *villeins,* and that the others, necessarily, were brigands. In vain do the privileged classes close their eyes to the revolution which time and events have effected: it is real for all that. There was once a time when the Third Estate was in bondage and the nobility was everything. Now the Third Estate is everything and nobility is only a word. But under cover of this word, however, and based solely on the strength of false opinion, a new and intolerable aristocracy has established itself; and the People has every reason not to want any aristocrats.

In this situation, what remains to be done by the Third Estate if it wants to take possession of its political rights in a way that will serve the nation? There are two methods of achieving this aim.

By the first method the Third Estate must meet separately; it must not cooperate with either the nobility or the clergy and it must not vote with them either by *orders* or by *heads*. Mark the enormous discrepancy between the assembly of the Third Estate and those of the other two orders. The former represents twenty-five million people and deliberates over the interests of the nation. The other two, even if they join together, derive their powers from only about two hundred thousand individuals and consider nothing but their own privileges. It is alleged that the Third Estate cannot form the *States-General* by itself. So much the better! It will form a National Assembly. Such important advice must be justified by showing that it is firmly based on the very essence of sound principle.

I maintain that the deputies of the clergy and of the nobility have nothing in common with national representatives, that no alliance is possible between the three orders in the States-General and that they are not only unable to vote *in common*, but neither by *orders* nor by *heads*. . . . Each order is in fact a separate nation which is no more competent to interfere in the affairs of the other orders than the States-General of Holland or the Council of Venice are to vote in the debates of the English Parliament. . . .

It follows logically from this that it is perfectly pointless to try to determine the ratio or proportion in which each order should participate in the making of the general will. This will cannot be *one* as long as you retain three orders and three representations. At the very most, these three assemblies could meet together to pass the same resolution, just as three allied nations can express the same wish. But they will never be *one* nation, *one* representation, *one* common will. . . .

I pointed out earlier that the Third Estate had two methods of obtaining its rightful place in the political order. If the first, which I have just described, seems a little too abrupt; if it is felt that the public must have time to accustom itself to liberty; if it is believed that the most obvious national rights still need, if they are disputed by even the smallest number, some kind of legal pronouncement that, so to speak, establishes them and gives them a final sanction; I am willing to concur. Let us then appeal to the tribunal of the nation which is the only competent judge in any disputes about the constitution. This is the second method open to the Third Estate. . . .

Nobody can deny that in the coming States-General the Chamber of the Third Estate will be fully competent to convoke the kingdom in *extraordinary representation*. Therefore, it is preeminently the duty of the Third Estate to explain the falsity of France's constitution to the citizenry. It is its duty to expostulate that since the States-General is composed of several orders, it must necessarily be ill-organised and incapable of fulfilling its national tasks; at the same time it is its duty to demonstrate the need to provide an extraordinary deputation with special powers to determine, by clearly defined laws, the constitutional forms of the legislature.

Until then, the order of the Third Estate will suspend, not of course its preparatory proceedings, but the exercise of its actual power; it will take no definitive decisions; it will wait for the nation to pass judgement in the great contention between the three orders. Such a course, I admit, is the most straightforward, the most magnanimous, and, therefore, the best suited to the dignity of the Third Estate.

The Third Estate can therefore view itself in either of two ways. The first is to regard itself simply as *an order;* in that case, it agrees not to shake off completely the prejudices of archaic barbarism; it recognises two other orders in the state, without however attributing to them more influence than is compatible with the nature of things; and it shows all possible regard for them by consenting to doubt its own rights until the supreme arbiter has made its decision.

From the second point of view, the Third Estate is the *nation.* In this capacity, its representatives constitute the whole National Assembly and are seized of all its powers. As they alone are the trustees of the general will, they do not need to consult those who mandated them about a dispute that does not exist. If they have to ask for a constitution, it is with one accord; they are always ready to submit to the laws that the nation may please to give them, but they do not have to appeal to the nation on any problem arising out of the plurality of orders. For them, there is only one order, which is the same as saying that there is none; since for the nation there can be only the nation.

The appointment of an *extraordinary* deputation, or at least the granting of special powers, as explained above, to settle the great problem of the constitution ahead of everything else, is therefore the true means of ending the present dissension and avoiding possible disturbances within the nation. Even if these disturbances gave no cause for alarm such a step would still be necessary because, disturbance or no disturbance, we have to know where our political rights lie and take possession of them. This will be seen to be more pressing when we realise that political rights are the sole guarantee of our civil rights and our personal freedom. I invite the reader to think this over. . . .[4]

---

4. Sieyès' pamphlet does not end here. He goes on, in a remarkable discussion (inspired by Rousseau and anticipating many of the constitutional arguments of later months), to consider the principles according to which a truly national assembly would be organized so that "particular interests are bound to remain isolated, and the will of the majority always in accordance with the general good."

15. Regulations for the Convocation of the Estates General (24 January 1789)

After considerable debate and division in the Royal Council, Louis XVI decided in favor of Necker's recommendations regarding the convocation of the Estates General. The *Result of the Council of 27 December 1788* affirmed the principle of representation of the Third Estate in proportion to the population of the electoral districts (*bailliages* or *sénéchaussées*) and announced that the deputies of the Third Estate would equal those of the other two Estates combined. But it remained silent on the matter of whether the Estates General should deliberate in common, or vote by head rather than by order. As a result, these became the crucial issues as soon as the Estates General met in May 1789.

Selections from the regulations finally drawn up for the elections to the Estates General are printed below. In addition to explaining the electoral mechanics responsible for the eventual character of the first national assembly in France for almost two centuries, they also suggest the tension between traditional and democratic principles that remained to be resolved by that body.

The King, in addressing letters of convocation for the Estates General to the divers provinces subject to his dominion, has desired that all his subjects be summoned to co-operate in the election of the deputies who are to constitute that great and august assembly. His Majesty has desired that, from the extremities of the kingdom and from the most obscure settlements, every one be assured that his wishes and claims will reach Him; . . . His Majesty has recognized, then, with real satisfaction that, by means of the graduated assemblies ordered throughout France for the representation of the third estate, he would have a means of communicating with all the inhabitants of his kingdom, and that he could approximate their needs and wishes more surely and directly. His Majesty has further endeavored to realize that particular objective by summoning to the assemblies of the clergy all the good and useful pastors who are intimately occupied daily with the poverty and relief of the people, and who are more familiar with their misfortunes and misgivings. Nevertheless, the King has provided that at no time will parishes be deprived of the presence of their *curés* or of eccle-

Reprinted with permission of Macmillan Publishing Company from John Hall Stewart, ed., *A Documentary Survey of the French Revolution*, pp. 31–33, 36–39. © 1951 by Macmillan Publishing Company.

siastics capable of substituting for them; and to that end His Majesty has permitted *curés* without vicars to exercise their suffrage by proxy.

The King summons, without discrimination, all members of the nobility, landowners or otherwise, to the right of being elected as deputies of that order; it is by their personal qualities, by the virtues for which they are accountable to their ancestors, that they have always served the State and will serve it again, and the most estimable among them will always be the most worthy of representing them.

In regulating the order of convocations and the form of assemblies, the King has wished to observe previous usage as far as possible. His Majesty, guided by this principle, has preserved in all *bailliages* which sent deputies directly to the Estates General in 1614 this privilege consecrated by time, provided at least that they have not lost the attributes for which such distinction was granted; and in order to establish a uniform rule, His Majesty has extended the same prerogative to the few *bailliages* which have acquired similar attributes since the last Estates General.

As a result of such arrangement, some small *bailliages* will have more deputies than if the division were exactly proportionate to their population; but His Majesty has reduced the disadvantage of such inequality by assuring to other *bailliages* a deputation proportionate to their population and importance; and the only consequence of these new combinations will be a slight increase in the general number of deputies. Respect for previous usage, however, and the necessity of reconciling it with present circumstances without offending the principles of justice, have rendered the entire organization of the next Estates General and all the preliminary arrangements very difficult and frequently defective. Such inconvenience would not have existed had an entirely free course been followed, determined only by reason and equity; but His Majesty has believed it better to satisfy the wishes of his people by reserving to the assembly of the Estates General the task of remedying unavoidable inequalities and preparing a more adequate system.

His Majesty . . . expects . . . that the voice of conscience alone will be heard in the choice of deputies to the Estates General. His Majesty exhorts the electors to remember that men of wisdom merit the preference, and that, by a happy accord of morality and politics, it is rare in public and national affairs that the most honest men are not also the most able. His Majesty is persuaded that the confidence due an assembly which is representative of the entire nation will prevent anyone's giving the deputies any instruction aimed at impeding or disturbing the course of deliberations. He hopes that all his subjects will keep constantly in mind the inappreciable good which the Estates General can effect, and that such an important consideration will preclude their yielding prematurely to a spirit of misgiving.

. . . Finally, His Majesty, according to the usage observed by the kings his predecessors, has determined to reassemble the Estates General of the kingdom about him, not with a view to restricting the liberty of their deliberations in any way, but in order to preserve for them the character dearest to his heart, that of counsel and friend. Accordingly, His Majesty has ordered and does order as follows. . . .

[The early articles of the regulations specify procedures according to which the clergy and the nobility of each *bailliage* will meet in separate assemblies to draft their *cahiers* and elect their deputies.]

24. Within a week at the latest after the notification and publication of the letters of convocation, all inhabitants constituting the third estate of the cities, as well as those of boroughs, parishes, and rural communities which have separate tax rolls, shall be required to assemble, in the form hereinafter prescribed, for the purpose of drafting the *cahier*[1] of their complaints and grievances and electing deputies to take the said *cahier* to the place and on the day designated by the act of notification and summons they have received.

25. Parishes and communities, and boroughs, as well as cities not included in the statement annexed to the present regulation, shall gather at the usual place of assembly and before the judge thereof, or, in his absence, before any other public official; at which assembly all inhabitants constituting the third estate, native or naturalized Frenchmen, twenty-five years of age, domiciled and included in the tax rolls, shall have the right to be present in order to cooperate in drafting the *cahiers* and electing delegates.

26. In the cities designated in the statement annexed to the present regulation the inhabitants shall assemble first by corporation. The corporations of arts and crafts shall elect one delegate for 100 individuals or fewer present at the assembly, two for more than 100, three for more than 200, and so on. The corporations of liberal arts, those of merchants, shipowners, and in general all other citizens associated through pursuit of the same occupation and constituting assemblies or authorized bodies, shall elect two delegates for 100 individuals or fewer, four for more than 100, six for more than 200, and so on. . . .

27. Inhabitants constituting the third estate of the said cities, who are not included in any bodies, communities, or corporations, shall assemble at the city hall on the day indicated by the municipal officials, and shall

---

1. The *cahier* was the statement of instructions that electoral assemblies gave to their representatives. Traditionally, it contained a list of the grievances the voters wished their deputy to express on their behalf (hence it was frequently called a *cahier de doléances*). In 1789, several thousand *cahiers* were produced, expressing the views of assemblies at every level of the complex electoral system.

elect two delegates for 100 individuals or fewer present at the said assembly, four for more than 100, six for more than 200, and so on in the same proportion.

28. The delegates elected in these several special assemblies shall form at the city hall, under the presidency of the municipal officials, the assembly of the third estate of the city, in which assembly they shall draft the *cahier* of complaints and grievances of the said city and elect deputies to convey it to the place and on the day indicated to them.

29. With the exception of Paris, no city shall send special deputies to the Estates General, the large cities being compensated therefor either by the greater number of deputies granted to their *bailliage* or *sénéchaussée* in proportion to the population of the said cities, or by the influence they are in a position to exert over the choice of such deputies. . . .

31. The number of deputies elected by parishes and rural communities to convey their *cahiers* shall be in the proportion of two for 200 households or fewer, three for more than 200 households, four for more than 300 households, and so on. The cities shall send the number of deputies determined by the general statement appended to the present regulation; and the number of deputies for all who are not included therein shall be established at four. . . .

33. In principal *bailliages* or *sénéchaussées* to which delegates of the third estate of secondary *bailliages* or *sénéchaussées* are to be sent, the *baillis* or *sénéchaux*, or in their absence their lieutenants, shall be required to convoke, prior to the day designated for the general assembly, a preliminary assembly of the delegates of the third estate of the cities, boroughs, parishes, and communities of their jurisdiction, to reduce their *cahiers* to one and to elect one-fourth of their members to take the said *cahier* to the general assembly of the three estates of the *bailliage* or *sénéchaussée,* and to co-operate with the delegates of the other secondary *bailliages* in the reduction of all the *cahiers* of the said *bailliages* or *sénéchaussées* to one and in the election of the number of deputies to the Estates General specified by the King's letter.

The reduction to one-fourth ordered above in the said principal and secondary *bailliages* shall take place not according to the number of delegates present but according to the number of those who ought to have been present at the assembly, in order that the influence which every *bailliage* is to have on the drafting of *cahiers* and the electing of deputies to the Estates General, in proportion to its population and the number of its dependent communities, may not be diminished by the absence of delegates from the assembly.

34. The reduction to one-fourth of the delegates of cities and communities for the election of deputies to the Estates General, ordered by His

Majesty in the principal *bailliages* where the delegates from other secondary *bailliages* are to meet, has been ordered for two reasons: first, to prevent too numerous assemblies in such principal *bailliages;* second, to reduce the difficulty and expense of more and longer journeys of a great number of delegates. Since, however, the second motive is lacking in principal *bailliages* which have no secondary *bailliages,* His Majesty has ordered that in the said principal *bailliages* which have no secondary *bailliages* the election of deputies of the third estate to the Estates General shall be effected, immediately after the union of the *cahiers* of all the cities and communities, by all the delegates of the said cities and communities who are present, unless the number of the said delegates exceeds 200; in which case only, the said delegates shall be required to reduce themselves to the said number of 200 for the election of deputies to the Estates General.

From Estates General to National Assembly

16. Dispatches from Paris (April–July 1789)

During this period the British embassy in Paris sent regular dispatches to London, reporting on French domestic affairs. These letters provide a fascinating account (here much abridged) of the mood in Paris as the Estates General assembled, and of the crisis that subsequently unfolded.

(*30th April 1789.*) This City has for some days past been alarmed by a very serious tumult, which began about six o'Clock on Monday evening when a number of workmen employed by a considerable manufacturer of painted paper assembled in a riotous manner for the purpose of burning in Effigy their Master, whose name is Réveillon, of whom they had demanded an increase of wages on account of the advanced price of bread, and who, as they had been designedly made to believe, had declared in a public Assembly that 15 Sols a-day were wages sufficient for workmen to subsist on: however the appearance of some French and Swiss Guards deterred the mob from committing any material outrage at that time, but on the following morning (Tuesday) the rioters assembled again in much greater force, a

From *Despatches from Paris, 1784–1790*, 2 vols., edited by O. Browning (London: Royal Historical Society, Camden 3d Series, vols. 16, 19, 1909–1910), vol. 2, pp. 186–89, 191–96, 198–202, 210–11, 215–27, 238–48.

considerable number of them having furnished themselves with bludgeons, and thus paraded the Faubourg St. Antoine menacing everybody who should attempt to obstruct their proceedings; it happened that on that day there were Races in the Bois de Vincennes which drew together a large company of persons of rank and fashion, many of whom in their road thither through the Faubourg St. Antoine were prevented passing that way by the vast concourse of people who were collected and who insisted on their declaring themselves in favor of the Tiers-Etat: the Military was called out, and about 2 o'clock the Troops were under the necessity of firing upon the mob, by which some few of them were killed and several wounded: this however did not prevent the people from getting possession of the house of Mons. Henriot, a manufacturer of salt-petre, the friend and neighbour of M. Réveillon which they compleatly stripped of every article and having piled up all the effects in the Street set fire to and burned them before the door of the house; most of the persons employed on this business were either killed in the house by the soldiers or taken; the few who were fortunate to escape got away upon the tops of the buildings, which they unroofed, and severely wounded some of the Soldiers with the tiles etc., which they threw down upon them.

Reinforcements of troops were in the mean time continually arriving, both Cavalry and infantry, and there was occasional firing upon the mob from six o'clock in the evening 'till 10 o'Clock at night by which time the streets were entirely cleared and tranquility thereby obtained: some accounts say that from three to four hundred of the people were destroyed. Twelve of the rioters were taken into custody, two of whom were executed yesterday evening without any attempt being made to rescue them. . . .

No other motive than the dearness of bread has been assigned by the unhappy wretches who were engaged in these excesses, most of whom were intoxicated to a very great degree; though some are disposed to suspect that the friends and supporters of the Parliament have secretly fermented the disturbance.

Reinforcements of troops have arrived from the environs of this City, and orders have been sent for all the Regiments at a certain distance to approach near to the Capital. The scene of tumult has been confined to the Faubourg St. Antoine tho' some detached parties of vagabonds have paraded parts of the Faubourg St. Germain and laid several carriages under contributions, urging in their behalf the extreme dearness of bread, but it does not appear that they belonged to the principal Mob, nor did they commit any further excesses. Bread is getting dearer every day: a great quantity of flour was brought in from the Country yesterday, but that can be only as a temporary supply and unless Government finds some means of effectually preventing the scarcity that is apprehended, the distress of the people must necessarily become insupportable. . . .

(*7th May 1789.*) Nothing has happened to disturb the tranquility of this Capital since I had last the honor of writing to Your Grace; reinforcements of Troops continue to arrive daily, and the utmost attention is given to check the slightest appearance of commotion among the people. The number of unhappy victims who were killed by the Military on the day of the principal tumult was somewhat exaggerated at first, yet, according to what has been ascertained, it is believed that not less than 200 persons lost their lives upon that occasion. Disturbances in the neighbouring Villages increase, and are likely to become still more alarming, for the scarcity of corn is general throughout the Kingdom. . . .

On Saturday last the Members of the States-General had the honor of being presented to His Majesty; and on Monday Their Majesties and all the Royal Family, excepting their Majesties' Children, attended by the Members went in procession to the Parish Church of Versailles, where a Sermon, suitable to the solemn occasion, was preached by the Bishop of Nancy: a great concourse of people attended and gave repeated marks of loyalty and affection to Their Majesties, who about 2 o'clock returned to the Palace. . . .

On the following day (Tuesday) His Majesty opened the Assembly of the States-General. . . . His Majesty delived His Speech with great dignity though He was interrupted in the course of it by the repeated acclamation of *Vive le Roi* accompanied by clapping of hands. . . . M. Necker afterwards addressed His Majesty and the Assembly in a written speech, the whole of which lasted three hours, but M. Necker, after reading a part of it, found himself obliged, on account of hoarseness, the effect of a cold, to crave His Majesty's indulgence in permitting one of the Clerks to read the remainder. . . .

M. Necker declared the present annual Deficit to be no more than 56 Millions, and pointed out means of supplying it without any extraordinary burthens upon the people: he gave the States-General to understand that His Majesty had been graciously pleased to call them together more from a desire of fulfilling the promise He had made and of meeting the wishes of His people than from any exigencies of the State, and, if I did not misunderstand the expression, implied that, in case the present assembly of the Nation should manifest a disposition to act in opposition to His Majesty's principles, the King might be induced to dissolve the States-General and have recourse to those methods for supplying the Deficit which the Director General of the Finances engages to provide.

The Establishment of an East India Company, and of a National Bank, consolidating the national debt, and in short whatever may contribute towards securing a national credit, were the principal subjects of the Minister's speech, for which he claimed the sanction of the States-General. He also slightly touched upon the Slave-Trade, observing that an enlightened and distinguished Nation had already set the example of bringing the abuses of that commerce to a thorough investigation.

No mention was made of His Majesty's prerogatives, so as to raise an expectation that any of them would be abandoned. His Majesty only pledged himself to assemble the Nation periodically. . . .

(*14th May 1789.*) The attention of the public being wholly engrossed by the States-General, nothing that has not some relation to that Assembly is at present the subject of conversation: the affairs of the Nation are not at all advanced since last week owing to the differences subsisting between the Nobility and the Tiers-Etat; the former having gone through the business of verifying their qualifications *par ordre,* while the latter refused to adopt that mode and protest against it, resolving that the whole Body of the States-General ought to verify their qualifications indiscriminately by choosing Commissioners from each order in common for that purpose. The Clergy have hitherto avoided taking any part in this delicate question, though there is reason to think that the majority of that Body are inclined to support the pretensions of the Tiers-Etat, for a fifth part of the ecclesiastical Deputies is composed of the lower class of Canons and Curates. . . .

The confusion and disorder that have prevailed are scarcely to be imagined . . . the pretensions of the Tiers-Etat are very high, an instance of which manifested itself the other day when some of the members of that Body took offence at the Clergy and Nobility being styled the two first Orders, and pretended that they had no right to that distinction, observing that the only one which was due to them is the simple appellation of Clergy and Nobility, and that in no other light would they in future be acknowledged by the Tiers-Etat.

I have the honor to send your Grace the printed Speeches as they were delivered by the King, the Garde des Sceaux, and M. Necker at the opening of the States-General; that of M. Necker it is thought upon closer inspection does not appear so calculated in favor of the Tiers-Etat as was at first conceived, and many of that Order are said to be very clamorous against the Minister upon the occasion. The mode of voting is another grand question as yet undecided.

M. Necker has not appeared to give any bias on this point, but unless His Majesty shall interpose and has influence enough to obtain a greater degree of harmony than at present prevails, the question is likely to remain without being brought to an issue, and the King may find Himself obliged to have recourse to those resources which the Director General of Finances has pointed out in his Discourse, as being in His Majesty's power without laying additional burthens on His People. . . .

(*21st May 1789.*) The original question, the subject of controversy between the Clergy and Nobility on one part and the Tiers-Etat on the other, remains yet undecided . . . I know that the greatest animosity prevails, both individually and collectively between the Nobility and the Tiers-Etat; the dignified Clergy is rather inclined to support the former, but the numerous Body of Vicars and Curates who are much connected with the Tiers-Etat makes it difficult to foresee what line of conduct they may resolve upon: during this situation of things, Government is much embarrassed how to act. The Provincial Nobility in particular are very high-spirited and exceedingly jealous of certain privileges which they have hitherto enjoyed and which they consider as independent of the Crown, nor, it is supposed, would they hesitate to secede from the National Assembly rather than relinquish them: They are already much dissatisfied with the conduct of the Court Nobles, by which they find themselves abandoned upon a division relative to the verifications of their qualifications, 46 or 47 having consented to the proposals made by the Tiers Etat, 180 against them. . . . The Stocks have fallen since the meeting of the States-General and public credit will sink entirely unless some measures be taken for proceeding on business in a regular manner. . . .

(*4th June, 1789.*) . . . I have been informed that the Nobility came to a resolution yesterday not to sign the Minute of the proceedings during the conference held by the Deputies of the three Orders in presence of His Most Christian Majesty's confidential Servants, alleging in vindication of their refusal that they could not subscribe their names to any act which admits the appellation of *Commons* to the Representatives of the Tiers-Etat: this Resolution will infallibly produce much discontent and probably heighten the resentment which has already shewn itself between the second and third Orders of the State.

It is not easy to foresee how these difficulties will terminate, the Nobility having manifested their determination not to deliberate *par tête* [by head] even though the present point in dispute, viz:—that of verifying the returns, should be amicably adjusted, which is scarcely to be expected, nearly connected as it is with what will be the next question on which the Nobility have, as I before mentioned, declared their unalterable resolution: the Tiers-Etat on the other hand are equally determined to force the Nobility to accede to their terms, so that unless the King, supported by the Clergy, shall have influence sufficient to effect an accomodation between the contending parties, the dismission of the States-General appears to be inevitable. . . .

The Tiers-Etat meet regularly every day in the grand Assembly Hall and admit strangers to hear the Debates, from which much inconvenience has arisen and their deliberations much prolonged. I am told that the most extravagant and disrespectfull language against Government has been held, and that upon all such occasions the greatest approbation is expressed by the Audience by clapping of hands and other demonstrations of satisfaction; in short the encouragement is such as to have led some of the Speakers on to say things little short of treason.

The Nobility, as may be supposed, are roughly treated in these debates and their conduct does not escape being represented in the most odious light possible. The Clergy and the Nobility hold their meetings in separate Chambers and neither of them admit strangers to be present at their deliberations.

It has been suggested by some of the Members of the Tiers-Etat that if the majority of the Clergy consisting of Curates who are favorable to the principles of the Tiers-Etat, and the small number of the Nobility who profess themselves attached also to the same principles, would join the Deputies of the Tiers-Etat, in that case the business of the Nation might be proceeded on, since an Assembly of States-General would thus be formally and constitutionally formed, but it is not to be imagined that a high-spirited Nobility, jealous of its privileges, or that the dignified Clergy would quietly submit to a measure which, if permitted, would inevitably exclude them from any future share in the Government of the Kingdom: a system which, in the attempt to establish it, could not fail to produce a civil war.

It does not seem to be well ascertained what part M. Necker is now disposed to take: some time ago it was evidently his wish that the voting should be *par tête* on some particular questions as stated in his speech, but since he has discovered that the Nobility continue firm upon that important question and that they will by no means submit to a regulation which would leave them at the mercy of the Representatives of the people, he is, I suspect endeavoring to hit upon some medium that may satisfy both Orders. . . .

(*11th June, 1789.*) . . . There is as little prospect as ever of harmony between that Body [the Tiers-Etat] and the Nobility: indeed to such a pitch is the animosity arisen that there is scarcely any hope entertained of a reconciliation; it is therefore the intention of the Tiers-Etat to verify their powers and thus in the course of a few days to constitute themselves, after which they will consider themselves as representatives of the Nation, and qualified to act as such independent of the other Orders, whatever measures these last may take to counteract their proceedings; this determined and extraordinary resolution will, it may be presumed from the present complexion of affairs, be productive of infinite confusion and of insurmountable embarrassment to the Ministers, who nevertheless seem to be waiting for some decisive step of one or the other of the contending Parties, by which the conduct of Government may be regulated: this supineness in the Cabinet may however prove fatal to their plans, if they have formed any, and may reduce the King to a necessity, which He must wish to avoid if possible, that of having recourse to very violent measures to maintain His authority against the efforts manifestly exerted by the Tiers-Etat, to lessen it as much as may be in their power to do. The Nobility have conducted themselves towards His Majesty in a much more respectfull manner, in matters of form, than the Tiers-Etat, though both have shewn themselves over tenacious of their rights, considering the unreserved manner with which His Majesty has professed His readiness to make every reasonable sacrifice that may be necessary to the welfare and future prosperity of His Kingdom.

The Clergy seem to be pursuing the same line of conduct with which they set out and continue to temporize with a view perhaps of becoming sooner or later the arbitrators in the contest between the other two Orders.

I inclose for your Grace's perusal the address of the Tiers-Etat . . . It is worthy of remark that they style themselves *Les Communes* [The Commons], an appellation which His Majesty does not acknowledge and designedly addresses their Deputation comme *Réprésentans du Tiers-Etat* [Representatives of the Third Estate]. . . .

(*18th June, 1789.*) The Tiers-Etat finding that there remained no longer any hopes of conciliation between their Order and that of the Nobility resolved the latter end of last week upon proceeding in a regular way to verify the returns of its Deputies which was accordingly done and the whole completed on Monday last: in consequence of an invitation to the two first Orders on the part of the Tiers-Etat to assemble in common with them, a few of the lower Clergy appeared amongst them, but have since retired to their own Order. On Tuesday the Tiers-Etat passed a vote constituting themselves the Representatives of the Nation; in the course of the debate upon this occasion very violent language was held against the Clergy and the Nobility, and the Strangers who were present testified their approbation to such a degree, that those members who were known to be desirous of moderating the animosity that prevailed found it expedient to remove from their places to avoid the insults which seemed to threaten them. The Assembly on that day did not break up 'till past 12 o'clock at night.

They met again yesterday when the Resolutions (*Arrêté National*) herewith enclosed were passed by a very great majority, by which, as your Grace will perceive, that Body assume the title of *l'Assemblée Nationale*. . . .[1]

Matters are every day growing exceedingly critical yet the King's Authority is still paramount, but if His Majesty once gives His decided approbation of the proceedings, such as they have hitherto been, of the Tiers-Etat, it will be little short of laying His Crown at their feet. The two first

---

1. See the following document.

Orders, it may be expected would in case of so marked a preference to their detriment secede: if however His Majesty on the other hand should espouse the cause of the Clergy and Nobility the people, tenacious of the footing to which they find themselves already advanced, and encouraged by the further advantages they have in view, would, if one may judge by the present temper of the times, be ready to support their cause by force, in which case the contest might at the outset be strongly disputed, but the Army whose zeal and activity are derived wholly from the Nobility, must soon throw the balance into the King's hands. The Army last year was certainly lukewarm in the King's interest, but the disposition of both Officers and Men is much changed, and they have upon all the late occasions shewn themselves to be entirely devoted to the Royal authority.

The Duc d'Orleans made a motion yesterday for the Nobility to accede to the proposal made to them by the Tiers-Etat so far as to join that Body in the great Assembly-Room and to deliberate with them in common, but to vote only, *par Ordre* [by order]: the Motion being in itself quite nugatory, as tending to no salutary end, was rejected by a majority of upwards of 50 votes.

The Clergy have not lately done anything of consequence, but they seem to be of a somewhat less inflexible disposition than the Nobility, and many of the inferior Clergy want very little encouragement to act in conjunction with the Tiers-Etat.

It was agitated in the Assembly of the Nobles whether a Deputation should be sent to the King to entreat His Majesty to take the affairs of the Nation entirely into his own hands; this, after a very long debate, was rejected by a very considerable majority: though it appeared that their concurrence was withheld only by the necessity, that it was conceived there would be, of calling forth the assistance of the Army in case their proposal should be accepted, which it was supposed must inevitably occasion an immediate civil war. . . .

(*25th June, 1789.*) On Saturday His Majesty, finding that the Tiers-Etat persisted in their resolutions, sent an order to shut the doors of the House of Assembly, and an Officer's Guard was posted at the entrance with an express order to prevent all persons whomseover from entering: the printed accounts state very accurately the measures which were in consequence taken by the Tiers-Etat, headed by their President, and the Resolutions which were passed unanimously by them on the same day in a Tennis Court at Versailles. . . .[2]

Their Majesties returned to Versailles from Marly on Sunday last, induced no doubt by the critical situation of affairs to fix themselves at the

2. See the following document.

place of their usual residence, where they would be less exposed than at so retired a situation as Marly to any surprize or sudden insult from the populace in its present state of fermentation. The Peasants in the neighbourhood of the Court have committed great outrages in the King's Forests in defiance of the Game-Keepers who, for want of sufficient support from Government, do not dare to oppose them; some of the Keepers have already fallen victims to these depredators, and one was shockingly butchered a few evenings since by three poachers not a league from Versailles. . . .

On Tuesday morning (the 23rd Inst.) His Majesty attended by the Princes of the Blood (the Duc d'Orleans, who sat as Deputy, excepted) the Maréchals of France and the Peers of the Realm, opened the meeting with the speeches from the Throne, which, with His Majesty's declarations respecting His future intentions and a kind of recapitulation of the different Cahiers, Your Grace will receive herewith.[3] The King was received by the populace, both going and on His return with great acclamations: when His Majesty entered the House of Assembly He was much applauded by all the three Orders, but on His retiring only the Clergy and Nobility testified marks of satisfaction and loyalty.

The Tiers-Etat proceeded to deliberate and continued their debates notwithstanding repeated messages from the King requiring them to break up the Assembly: they not only confirmed all their former resolutions but passed others of a very violent tendency.

M. Camus and M. de Mirabeau were the principal leaders in these proceedings: in the evening of Tuesday the Nobility with their President the Duc de Luxembourg waited in a Body on Their Majesties and the Royal Family to express the sense they entertained of their obligations to His Majesty, for His declared intention of supporting their Rights, and the true principles of the Constitution: their example was not followed by either of the other two Orders.

On the following day (Wednesday) the three Orders assembled in their respective Chambers, when nearly two hundred of the inferiour Clergy quitted their own Body and joined the Tiers-Etat which must have materially strengthened that Order: the rest of the Clergy separated under no small degree of consternation. . . .

It is beyond a doubt that the greatest want of harmony exists in the Cabinet, and no stronger proof can be given of it than the absence of M. Necker on Tuesday last from the Séance Royale, all the rest of the Ministers being present. . . . This Minister's popularity was strongly marked on Tuesday last when the Populace assembled in great number before his house at Ver-

3. See the following document.

sailles where they played off a fire-work and carried at the end of a long pole a transparent paper lanthorn on which was written: *Vive Necker, le sauveur d'un Pays opprimé,*[4] expressing at the same time, by loud acclamations, their extreme anxiety that he should remain in Office: M. Necker desirous of preserving tranquility, went out to the people and prevailed upon them to disperse by repeatedly assuring them that His Majesty had not any intention of dismissing him from His service. . . .

Such is the distracted State of this Country at present: a few hours even may possibly decide everything: if the King (whose conduct throughout has been marked with the most unfeigned desire of contributing to the happiness of his People) gives way in this moment of contest, a complete Revolution will have been effected in this powerfull and extensive Kingdom without recourse being had to violence, but if His Majesty decided to support the principles He advanced no later than Tuesday, a civil war is, in my opinion, inevitable. . . .

The reports concerning the scarcity of corn in the neighbourhood of Paris have but too much foundation: the deficiency of this material article extends to the distance of 15 leagues round the City and is so severely felt that Administration has been obliged to supply the different great Markets, by sending corn from the Magazines of the *Ecole Militaire* originally intended for the consumption of the Capital: in regard to the other Provinces of the Kingdom there is no further apprehension, as they are sufficiently supplied 'till the ensuing harvest which has every appearance of being very plentifull.

P.S. I have this moment heard from Versailles that the Duc d'Orleans with 48 members of the Nobility went and joined the Tiers-Etat in the great Assembly-Room: this important event has been received out of doors with the greatest demonstrations of joy; the rest of the Nobility continued sitting.

It is impossible to foresee what measures the King will adopt in consequence of this event.

The French Guards have, in some few instances within these few days, shewn a great reluctance to act and some of the men have declared that if they should be called upon to quell any disturbance they will, if compelled to fire, take care not to do any mischief. The Archbishop of Paris was very ill-treated last night by the mob at Versailles: his coach was broke to pieces and his horses much bruised: if the Guards had not protected him he must himself have been inevitably destroyed.

The people now are disposed to any desperate act of violence in support

4. "Long live Necker, Savior of an Oppressed Country!"

of the *Assemblée Nationale*. I shall not fail to send Your Grace immediate intelligence of any momentous ocurrence during this critical state of affairs. . . .

(*28th June 1789.*) I lose no time in communicating to Your Grace the important occurrences of yesterday at Versailles, and the sudden change effected thereby in the Constitution of this Kingdom.

The greater part of the Clergy having already joined the Tiers-Etat it remained only to be seen whether or not the Nobility would follow the example of that Order, as well as of a certain number of their own Members, headed by the Duc d'Orleans.

The whole day of Friday was passed in deliberating upon this important question, and yesterday, in consequence of the final resolution, the remainder of the Clergy and the whole of the Nobility (excepting three, whose names I have not hitherto been able to learn) went and joined the Tiers-Etat forming by this means a regular National Assembly, which will be confirmed by the King in due form on Tuesday next.

Your Grace may easily imagine what was really the case, that nothing but the pressing urgency of the moment could have induced the Nobility to relinquish at once all further design of persevering in their original determination; but when it was seen that the King's personal safety was actually endangered, that was a motive for giving way which could not be resisted: the fermentation of the people, from the moment when the Tiers-Etat had so far gained their point as to bring over to their Body a part of the other two Orders, for the purpose of verifying their returns in common, became very alarming, added to which some of the Military joined in the popular cry, and the French Guards had even been wrought upon to bind themselves by oath not to support the King under the present circumstances: many of these paraded the capital in small bodies, openly boasting of the engagement they had entered into not to obey their Officers: it may well be conceived the effect this had on the populace who now became quite ungovernable at Versailles, as well as at Paris, insomuch that the King and the Royal Family were no longer secure from outrage even in the Palace: in this situation of things His Majesty, after consulting with the Presidents of the two first Orders on Friday evening, decided upon writing the Letter, which I have the honor of sending Your Grace herewith inclosed, and which was addressed to the Duc de Luxembourg, President of the Nobility, at that time assembled:[5] this Letter occasioned a very warm and interesting debate, and there is reason to think would not after all have produced the desired effect, had it not been followed by one from the Comte d'Artois

---

5. This letter asked the remaining deputies of the nobility and clergy to meet with the Third Estate.

whereby His Royal Highness earnestly entreats that Assembly to comply with the King's wishes, representing the extreme danger to which His Majesty's person would be exposed, if that Body continued any longer to persist in their refusal to join the Tiers-Etat. No sooner was this Letter read than most of the Members started from their seats and declared themselves ready to give every proof in their power of their zealous affection for His Majesty, and tender regard for the safety of his person; immediately after which they proceeded to join the rest of the Deputies in the Common-Hall.

As soon as this event was known out of doors the greatest demonstrations of joy were manifested by the people, who assembled in great numbers under the windows of Their Majesties, crying: *Vivent le Roi et la Reine.* The King and Queen appeared for some minutes at the balcony, and upon their retiring, the people went in the same manner to the several apartments of the Royal Family.

They afterwards proceeded to M. Necker's House, where they remained a considerable time testifying their approbation of that Minister's conduct. . . .

Nothing can equal the despondency of the Nobility upon this occasion, forced as they have been by an extraordinary and unexpected impulse to sacrifice in one moment every hope they had formed and the very principles from which they had resolved and flattered themselves that no consideration whatever should oblige them to depart. . . .

(*16th July, 1789.*) I wrote to Your Grace on the 12th Inst. by a messenger extraordinary to inform you of the removal of M. Necker from His Majesty's Councils: I have now to lay before Your Grace an account of the general revolt, with the extraordinary circumstances attending it, that has been the immediate consequence of that step. On Sunday evening a slight skirmish happened in the Place de Louis XV, in which two Dragoons were killed, and two wounded of the Duc de Choiseuil's Regiment: after which all the troops left the Capital, and the populace remained unmolested masters of everything: much to their credit however, uncontrouled as they now were, no material mischief was done; their whole attention being confined to the burning of some of the Barriers. Very early on Monday morning the Convent of St. Lazare was forced, in which, besides a considerable quantity of corn, were found arms and ammunition supposed to have been conveyed thither as a place of security, at different periods from the Arsenal: and now a general consternation was seen throughout the Town: all shops were shut; all public and private works at a stand still and scarcely a person to be seen in the Streets excepting the armed *Bourgeoisie,* a temporary police for the protection of private property, to replace the established one which no longer had any influence.

In the morning of Tuesday the Hospital of Invalids was summonsed to surrender and was taken possession of after a very slight resistance: all the cannon, small arms and amunition were immediately seized upon, and every one who chose to arm himself was supplied with what was necessary . . . in the evening a large detachment with two pieces of cannon went to the Bastille to demand the ammunition that was there, the *Gardes Bourgeoises* [Civic Guard] not being then sufficiently provided: a flag of truce was sent on before and was answered from within, notwithstanding which the governor (the Marquis de Launay) contrary to all precedent fired upon the people and killed several: this proceeding so enraged the populace that they rushed to the very gates with a determination to force their way through if possible: upon this the Governor agreed to let in a certain number of them on condition that they should not commit any violence: these terms being acceded to, a detachment of about 40 in number advanced and were admitted, but the draw-bridge was immediately drawn up again and the whole party instantly massacred: this breach of honor aggravated by so glaring an act of inhumanity excited a spirit of revenge and tumult such as might naturally be expected: the two pieces of cannon were immediately placed against the Gate and very soon made a breach which, with the disaffection that as is supposed prevailed within, produced a sudden surrender of that Fortress: M. de Launay, the principal gunner, the tailer, and two old invalids who had been noticed as being more active than the rest were seized and carried to the *Hôtel de Ville* [City Hall] where, after a very summary trial before the tribunal there, the inferior objects were put to death and M. de Launay had also his head cut off at the Place de Grève, but with circumstances of barbarity too shocking to relate. . . . In the course of the same evening the whole of the *Gardes Françoises* [French Guard] joined the Bourgeoisie with all their cannon, arms and ammunition: the Regiments that were encamped in the *Champ de Mars,* by an Order from Government left the ground at 2 o'Clock yesterday morning and fell back to Sêve, leaving all their camp equipage behind them; the magazines of powder and corn at the *Ecole Militaire* were immediately taken possession of and a *Garde Bourgeoise* appointed to protect them. Nothing could exceed the regularity and good order with which all this extraordinary business has been conducted: of this I have myself been a witness upon several occasions during the last three days as I have passed through the streets, nor had I at any moment reason to be alarmed for my personal safety. . . .

The general wish now is that the King would come to Paris and it was hoped yesterday that His Majesty would be induced to shew Himself here on this day, but it is said that He is prevented coming by indisposition: it is thought difficult to foresee what measures the people will have recourse to: the general idea however is that an armed Body of Citizens to the number of at least 50,000 will go to Versailles and forcibly bring their Sovereign to the Capital. The disposition of the people at this moment is so unfavorable to the Court that I should not be surprized if the States-General, by appearing to give too much credit to the King's professions, should lose the consideration in which they have hitherto been held by the Nation.

The Populace will not easily forgive the removal of M. Necker; for they seem determined to push their resentment to the utmost lengths: but God forbid that should be the case, since they have already got the upperhand, for who can trust to the moderation of an offended multitude?

The regularity and determined conduct of the populace upon the present occasion exceeds all belief and the execration of the Nobility is universal amongst the lower order of people. . . .

Everybody since Monday has appeared with a cockade in his hat: at first green ribbons were worn but that being the colour of the Comte d'Artois' livery, red and white in honor of the Duc d'Orleans, have been substituted.

Thus, My Lord, the greatest Revolution that we know anything of has been effected with, comparatively speaking, if the magnitude of the event is considered, the loss of very few lives: from this moment we may consider France as a free Country; the King a very limited Monarch, and the Nobility as reduced to a level with the rest of the Nation. . . .

The Marquis de la Fayette is named commander in chief of the *Milice Bourgeoise* [Civic Militia] and M. Bailly, late President of the States-General, is appointed Prèvôt des Marchands: these nominations are made by the people.[6]

At least 200 workmen are employed in pulling down the Bastille, but as it is a construction of uncommon strength, it will require some time to erase it entirely. . . .

(*17th July, 1789.*) In the course of last night a courier from Versailles announced the King's intention of coming to Paris this day and, to the great joy and satisfaction of this City, He arrived about half past 2 o'clock in the afternoon. . . .

His Majesty had no other escort than the *Milice Bourgeoise,* as Commander in chief of which the Marquis de la Fayette rode a little before the King's coach, accompanied by several of the principal tradesmen of Paris: the whole way from the entrance at the Barrier at Passy to the *Hôtel de Ville* was lined on each side with armed citizens: the most perfect tranquility and, I might almost say, silence was preserved 'till His Majesty

6. The *milice bourgeoise,* or Paris civic militia, was soon transformed by the marquis de Lafayette into the Paris National Guard, which he led until October 1791. The *prévôt des marchands* (provost of merchants) was the head of the traditional local government of Paris, which was swept away by the municipal revolution that followed the taking of the Bastille. Thus Jean-Sylvain Bailly in effect became the revolutionary mayor of Paris, a position he retained until November 1791.

reached the Place de Louis XV (for it was settled that He should pass that way, and through the Rue St. Honoré by the Palais Royal) where nothing was heard but *Vive la Nation! Vive Necker! vivent les Gardes Françoises* to whose defection the nation is indebted for the Revolution that has taken place. The King appeared much depressed at entering the Town. I do not understand that His Majesty performed any particular act at the *Hôtel de Ville,* and I am told that He certainly did not sign to any engagement. He said that He appeared there to gratify the wishes of the Citizens of Paris and to assure them of His readiness to do everything in His power to quiet their minds and restore tranquility to the City. I have not been able yet to procure accurate information of all that passed at the *Hôtel de Ville* during the time the King staid there, nor what was the form of His Majesty's reception: certain however it is that He appeared much more composed on His return and every mark of loyalty and affection, sufficiently testifying the satisfaction that was felt, was given by an astonishingly numerous and well-disciplined populace: I think I can venture to say that there were not fewer than 150,000 men bearing arms this day in Paris. His Majesty passed by the *Place de Louis XV* about 7 o'clock on His return and probably reached Versailles about nine.

Whoever, of those who were present when the King passed by in His way to the *Hôtel de Ville,* had the least personal regard for His Majesty, must have felt for His situation during the mournfull procession which appeared to be rather that of a captive than of a patriot King: many people entertained apprehensions for his safety, not knowing how far the intemperate zeal of an indignant mob might provoke a hasty vengeance. . . .

(*July 22nd 1789.*) The Revolution in the French Constitution and Government may now, I think, be looked upon as compleated, beyond all fears of any further attempts being made by the Court Party to defeat it. The entrance of the King into Paris was certainly one of the most humiliating steps that he could possibly take. He was actually led in triumph like a tame bear by the Deputies and the City Militia. The whole party, inimical to the rights of the people, are dispersed. The Count d'Artois and his whole family (except the Countess, who is much beloved) the Condés, Contis, Polignacs, Breteuils, Vaudreuils, etc. are all fled and people are talking of confiscating their estates. The news we have from the Provinces are much more favorable than could have been expected. Every where the people and the soldiers seem to have been animated with the same spirit. In Brittany, where the greatest apprehensions were entertained, not a drop of blood has been spilt. The soldiers refused to obey their officers, and many of them joined the people. Fifty thousand Bretons were in arms, ready to march to the assistance of the Parisians, and there is no doubt, that if the King had not come round, they would not have left a Nobleman's house standing thro' the whole Province.

There certainly never was an instance of so astonishing a Revolution operated almost without bloodshed, and without the people being led on by any leader, or by any party, but merely by the general diffusion of reason and philosophy. We shall soon be able to form a guess what is the nature of the constitution that is intended to be adopted in France. A Committee of 8 members is chosen to form a plan, which will afterwards be laid before the whole Assembly for its approbation. . . . From what is known of their ideas and principles it is thought the Executive Power will be left solely to the King, who will be deprived of all share in the Legislative Authority, which will be lodged in the National Assembly, formed into one Body, without distinction of Orders. The best French Politicians (contrary to the opinion of de Lolme)[7] look upon the division of the Legislative Authority in England as a great defect in our constitution, and the principal source of that system of corruption which takes place with us. . . .

17. Deliberations at the Estates General (June 1789)

The following selections (which should be read in conjunction with the narrative account of events contained in the preceding document) provide the texts of some of the most important declarations in the series of confrontations that transformed the Estates General into a unitary assembly claiming the exercise of national sovereignty.

Declaration of the Third Estate (17 June 1789)

The presiding member: I shall put to the vote the different motions relating to the manner in which the assembly must constitute itself. Yesterday, it was demanded that each member affix his signature to the decision; I dare to present some reflections to the assembly concerning this demand.

Instead of strengthening our resolution, signing could weaken it; for once a resolution is taken by the assembly, it is considered to have been

7. The Swiss writer, Jean-Louis Delolme, whose account of the nature of the English constitution, published in 1771, became the definitive work on the subject for the next half-century. Delolme argued for the superiority of representative government and the balance of powers (as exemplified in the English case) over the direct democracy and unitary sovereignty celebrated by Rousseau. His authority was to be invoked unsuccessfully by those revolutionary leaders who favored the introduction of an English-style constitution with legislative power divided between the monarch and a bicameral representative assembly.

From *Archives parlementaires de 1787 à 1860, première série (1787 à 1799)*, edited by M. J. Mavidal and M. E. Laurent, 2d ed., 82 vols. (Paris: Dupont 1879–1913), vol. 8, pp. 127, 138, 143–47. Translated for this volume by the editor, Keith Michael Baker.

adopted unanimously; whereas signing, if it is not universal, shows that the resolution has been adopted only partially. Moreover, signing could become a fatal germ of division among us, thereby introducing two parties into an assembly whose unity has until now been its greatest strength.

These reflections are approved by the assembly, and the proposal for signatures is dropped. . . .

The motion of M. the abbé Sieyès is passed by a majority of 491 votes to 90.

The assembly consequently adopts the following declaration:

"The assembly, deliberating after the verification of powers, recognizes that this assembly is already composed of representatives sent directly by at least ninety-six percent of the nation.

"So weighty a delegation should not remain inactive because of the absence of the deputies of a few *bailliages,* or of some classes of citizens; for those who have been summoned but remain absent cannot prevent those present from exercising the plenitude of their rights, especially when the exercise of those rights is an imperious and pressing duty.

"Moreover, since it belongs only to verified representatives to contribute to the formation of the national will, and since all the verified representatives must be in this assembly, it is also essential to conclude that it belongs to it, and to it alone, to interpret and set forth the general will of the nation; between the throne and this assembly, there can exist no *veto,* no negative power.

"The assembly therefore declares that the collective work of national restoration can and must be commenced without delay by the deputies present, and that they must pursue it without interruption and without obstacle.

"The title of *National Assembly* is the only appropriate one for the assembly in the present circumstances, whether because its members are the only legitimately and publicly known and verified representatives, or because they are sent directly by the near totality of the nation, or finally because, since representation is one and indivisible, no deputy, no matter from what order or class he is chosen, has the right to exercise his functions apart from the present assembly.

"The assembly will never lose hope of bringing together within its midst all the deputies absent today; it will not cease to summon them to fulfil the obligation imposed upon them, that of contributing to the meeting of the Estates General. It declares in advance that, whenever in the course of the session now beginning the absent deputies present themselves, it will hasten to receive them and to share with them, after their powers have been verified, the continuation of the great work that must effect the regeneration of France.

"The National Assembly orders that the reasons for the present decision be immediately set down for presentation to the king and to the nation."

The assembly votes an address to the king to inform him of the decision taken. Repeated cries of *Long Live the King* are then heard.

The Tennis Court Oath (20 June 1789)

. . . M. Mounier presents an opinion that is supported by MM. Target, Chapelier, Barnave. He points out how strange it is that the assembly hall of the Estates General should be occupied by armed men, that no other meeting place should be offered to the National Assembly, that its president should be notified only by letters from the marquis de Brézé [the Grand Master of Ceremonies] and the national representatives only by posted notices, that they should finally be obliged to assemble at the Tennis Court on the rue du Vieux-Versailles to avoid interrupting their work; and he argues that the representatives of the nation, having been attacked in their rights and dignity, and warned of the force of intrigue and determination behind the present attempts to push the king into taking disastrous measures, must bind themselves to the public safety and the interests of the country by a solemn oath.

This proposition is approved by unanimous applause.

Having deliberated, the assembly adopts the following resolution, on the motion of M. Target, by a unanimous vote minus one:

"The National Assembly, considering that since it has been called to decide the constitution of the realm, to achieve the regeneration of public order, and to maintain the true principles of the monarchy, nothing can prevent it from continuing its deliberations in whatever place it may be forced to establish itself, and that wherever indeed its members are assembled, there is the National Assembly;

"Resolves that all the members of this assembly shall immediately take a solemn oath never to separate, and to reassemble wherever the circumstances demand, until the constitution of the realm has been established and secured on solid foundations; and that, the said oath having been taken, all its members, each individually, shall confirm by their signature this unshakeable resolution."

The declaration having been read, the president asks, on his own behalf and on that of the secretaries, to take the oath first, which they immediately do; the assembly then takes the same oath between the hands of its president. . . .

The Royal Session (23 June 1789)

. . . The king enters the chamber, accompanied by the Princes of the Blood, the dukes and peers, and the captains of his bodyguard. Upon his arrival, the deputies rise and then sit again.

The king makes a speech declaring the purpose of the session. It is couched in these terms:

Gentlemen, I believed that I had done everything in my power for the good of my people when I resolved to assemble you, when I surmounted all the difficulties surrounding your convocation, when I anticipated the desires of the nation, so to speak, in declaring in advance what I wished to do for its happiness.

It seemed that you had only to complete my work—and the nation awaited with impatience the moment when it would enjoy the prosperity that would necessarily be secured by the combination of the beneficent views of its sovereign and the enlightened zeal of its representatives.

The Estates General have been in session for almost two months, and they have not yet been able to reach agreement regarding the preliminaries to their operations. A perfect understanding should have sprung from the sole love of country, yet a fatal division throws alarm into every mind. I wish to believe, and like to think, that the French have not changed. But to avoid reproaching any of you, I consider that the renewal of the Estates General after so long a period, the agitation preceding their meeting, the purpose of this convocation (which is so different from that which brought your ancestors together), the restrictions placed upon your powers, and several other circumstances, have necessarily led to opposing positions, debates, and exaggerated claims.

I owe it to the common good of the realm, I owe it to myself, to put an end to these fatal divisions. In this conviction, Gentlemen, I have assembled you once more before me. As the common father of my subjects, as the defender of the laws of my realm, I come to reiterate its true spirit, and to put an end to the harm that may have been inflicted upon it.

But, Gentlemen, after having clearly laid down the respective rights of the different orders, I expect from the patriotic zeal of the two first orders, from their loyalty to my person, from their knowledge of the urgent ills of the state, that in affairs regarding the general good they will be the first to propose a union of opinions and sentiments that I regard as necessary in the present crisis, and which must effect the salvation of the state.

One of the secretaries of state then reads the following declaration:

The King's Declaration Concerning the Present Session of the Estates General

1. The king wishes that the ancient distinction among the three orders of the state be preserved in its entirety, as being essential to the constitution of his realm; and that the deputies freely elected by each of the three orders, forming three chambers and deliberating by order—but able, with the sovereign's consent, to agree to deliberate together—may alone be considered as forming the body of representatives of the nation. Accordingly, the king declares null and void the decisions taken by the deputies of the order of the Third Estate on the seventeenth of this month, and any that may have ensued, as illegal and unconstitutional. . . .

3. The king quashes and annuls, as anti-constitutional, contrary to the letters of convocation, and opposed to the interests of the state, restrictions on the powers of the deputies to the Estates General which, by impeding their liberty, would prevent them from accepting forms of deliberation adopted separately, by order, or in common, by the independent decision of each of the three orders.[1]

4. If, contrary to the king's intentions, some deputies have rashly sworn not to deviate from a particular form of deliberation, His Majesty leaves it to their consciences to decide whether the arrangements he is about to establish depart from the letter or the spirit of the commitment they have made.

5. The king permits deputies who believe themselves restricted by their mandates to demand new powers from their constituents; but His Majesty enjoins them to remain at the Estates General in the meantime, so that they may take part in all deliberations regarding the pressing affairs of state and give their opinion on an advisory basis.

6. His Majesty declares that, in subsequent sessions of the Estates General, he will never permit *cahiers* or mandates to be considered imperative; they must be merely instructions entrusted to the conscience and the free opinion of the deputies chosen.

7. His Majesty, having exhorted the three orders, for the salvation of the state, to meet together during this session of the Estates General only, in

---

1. A reference to the "binding mandate" by which some deputies were restricted in their freedom to go beyond, or act against, the explicit instructions given them by their constituents. A traditional feature of the old Estates General, the binding mandate was customarily used by communities and corporations to protect their particular interests by preventing their deputies from yielding to excessive royal demands. In 1789, some deputies declared themselves bound by their mandate not to accept deliberation in common or voting by head. The National Assembly itself repudiated the notion of binding mandates as incompatible with national sovereignty, on 8 July 1789.

order to deliberate in common regarding matters of general utility, wishes to make known his intentions concerning their manner of proceeding.

8. Issues regarding the ancient and constitutional rights of the three orders, the form of future Estates General, feudal and seigneurial properties, the advantageous rights and honorific prerogatives of the two first orders, are expressly excluded from the matters that may be considered in common.

9. The particular consent of the clergy will be required for all decisions that might affect religion, ecclesiastical discipline, the organization of secular and religious orders and communities. . . .

11. If, to facilitate their union, the three orders wish the decisions they take in common to be adopted only by a two-thirds majority, His Majesty is disposed to authorize this procedure. . . .

15. Good order, decency, and freedom of deliberation require His Majesty to forbid, as he expressly does forbid, any person other than the members of the three orders comprising the Estates General to be present at their discussions, whether they be held separately or in common.

The king resumes his speech, as follows:

It is also my wish, Gentlemen, that the different benefits I am granting to my people be laid before you. This is not to constrain your zeal within the circle that I am about to describe, for I shall adopt with pleasure any other plans for the public good proposed by the Estates General. I can say without deceiving myself that a king has never done as much as I have for any nation; but what other nation than the French can have deserved better by its sentiments? I shall not fear, however, to make this explicit: those who, by raising exaggerated claims and unjustified difficulties, would delay further the effect of my paternal intentions, would render themselves unworthy to be considered Frenchmen.

Declaration of the King's Intentions[2]

1. No new tax will be established, no new one extended beyond the term fixed by law, without the consent of the representatives of the nation.

2. Newly established taxes, or old ones that are extended, will not exceed in duration the period ending with the next session of the Estates General.

3. Since loans can lead to the need to increase taxes, no loans will be

2. The following declaration represents, in effect, the final statement in the monarchy's long effort to reform itself, the limit beyond which it could (or would) not go. Additional clauses not printed here proposed abolition of the *corvée*, the *taille*, the *franc-fief*, and of personal serfdom or *mainmorte* (on these latter, see the two following documents); establishment of free trade and the freedom of the press; legal reform and the reform of the *gabelle* and other indirect taxes.

raised without the consent of the Estates General, except that in case of war or other national emergency, the sovereign shall have the right to borrow up to 100 million francs without delay. For it is the king's express intention never to allow the safety of his realm to become dependent on anyone.

4. The Estates General will carefully examine the state of the finances, and demand all the information appropriate to enlighten them fully in this matter.

5. A statement of revenues and expenditures will be made public each year, in a form proposed by the Estates General and approved by His Majesty. . . .

8. The representatives of a nation faithful to the laws of honor and probity will in no way undermine public trust, and the king expects them to secure and consolidate the confidence of the state's creditors in the most solemn manner.

9. Once the expressly declared readiness of the clergy and the nobility to renounce their financial privileges has been given effect by their deliberations, it is the king's intention that these deliberations receive royal sanction, and that privileges or distinctions in the payment of taxes no longer exist in any form. . . .

12. All properties without exception will continue to be respected, and His Majesty explicitly includes under this name tithes, *cens, rentes,* feudal and seigneurial rights and dues,[3] and generally all the advantageous or honorific rights and prerogatives attached to lands, or belonging to persons. . . .

14. It is His Majesty's intention to determine, upon the advice of the Estates General, which occupations and offices shall in future retain the privilege of conferring and transmitting nobility. Notwithstanding, His Majesty, by royal right, will grant letters of nobility to those subjects who show themselves worthy of this reward by services to the king and to the state. . . .

16. The Estates General will examine and present to His Majesty the most suitable means of reconciling liberty of the press with the respect due to the religion, morals, and honor of the citizens.

17. Provincial Estates will be established in the various provinces or generalities of the realm; they will be composed of two-tenths clergy, a part of which will necessarily be chosen from the episcopal order; three-tenths nobility; and five-tenths members of the Third Estate.

18. Members of the provincial Estates will be freely elected by the respective orders, and a certain amount of property will be necessary to vote or to be eligible for election. . . .

3. On the particular nature (and fate) of these obligations, see the two following documents.

19. The deputies to these [provincial] Estates will deliberate in common on all matters. . . .

22. In addition to the administrative matters for which the provincial assemblies will be responsible, the king will entrust them with the administration of hospitals, prisons, workhouses and foundling hospitals . . . and other matters which could more usefully be administered by the provinces.

35. His Majesty, having called the Estates General to join with him in considering the great objects of public utility, and everything that can contribute to the happiness of his people, most expressly declares that he wishes to preserve the army in its entirety and without the least impairment, as well as all the authority, control and power over the military that French monarchs have always enjoyed.

The king, before withdrawing, makes a third speech, as follows:

Gentlemen, you have just heard the result of my deliberations and plans; they conform to my lively desire to bring about the public good; and if, through some unpredictable stroke of fate, you were to abandon me in such a fine enterprise, I should accomplish my people's good alone, and I should consider myself alone their true representative. Knowing your *cahiers* and the perfect harmony existing between the most general desire of the nation and my beneficent intentions, I shall have all the confidence—and I shall proceed towards my goal with all the courage and firmness—so rare a harmony must inspire.

Bear in mind, Gentlemen, that none of your projects or decisions can have the force of law without my particular approval. I am therefore the natural guarantor of your respective rights; and all the orders of the state may rely upon my fairness and impartiality.

Any defiance on your part would be a great injustice. Until now, I alone have done everything for the happiness of my people, and it is perhaps rare that a sovereign's sole ambition should be to bring his subjects to agree in accepting his benefits.

Gentlemen, I order you to separate immediately and to return tomorrow morning, each to the chamber assigned to your order, in order to resume your deliberations. Accordingly, I order the Grand Master of Ceremonies to prepare the assembly halls.

After the king's departure, the deputies of the nobility and a part of those of the clergy withdraw; all the members of the National Assembly and a number of the clergy remain in their seats.

The comte de Mirabeau is the first to speak, as follows: I admit that what you have just heard could be the country's salvation if the gifts of despotism were not always dangerous. What is this humiliating dictatorship, this show of arms, this violation of the temple of the nation, to command you to be happy? Who gives this command? Your agent, Gentlemen, he who ought to receive commands from you—from us, who are invested with a political and inviolable priesthood; from us, to whom alone twenty-five million men look for an assured happiness, because it must be achieved by consent, given and received by all. But the liberty of your discussions is fettered, a military force surrounds the assembly. Where are the enemies of the nation? Is Cataline at our doors? I demand that, covering yourselves with your dignity and legislative power, you take refuge in your sacred vow, which does not permit us to separate until we have made the constitution.

Shortly thereafter, the *marquis de Brézé* approaches the president of the assembly, and says: Gentlemen, you have heard the king's intentions.

The comte de Mirabeau rises in indignation and replies as follows:

Yes, Sir, we have heard the intentions that have been suggested to the king; and you, who are incapable of representing him before the Estates General, you who have no standing here and no right to speak, are not in a position to remind us of his speech. However, to avoid all equivocation and delay, I declare that if you have been charged to make us leave this place, you must ask for authority to use force, for we shall leave our seats only by the power of bayonets.

With unanimous voice, the deputies cry: Such is the wish of the assembly.

The Grand Master of Ceremonies withdraws.

A dismal silence reigns in the assembly. . . .

The abbé Sieyès: Gentlemen, however stormy the circumstances appear, we always have a light to guide us. Let us ask ourselves what powers we exercise and what mission brings us here together from all parts of France. Are we only the agents and officers of the king? In that case, we must obey and withdraw. But if we are the delegates of the people, let us fulfil our mission freely and courageously.

Is there a single one of you who would wish to abjure the high trust invested in you and return to your constituents to say, "I am afraid; you have placed the destiny of France in hands that are too feeble; replace me with a man more worthy to represent you?"

We have sworn, Gentlemen, to reestablish the French people in its rights—and our oath will not be an empty one. The authority that has appointed you to this great undertaking, the authority to which alone you are responsible, and which will be fully capable of defending you, is certainly far from crying out to us, "Enough!" "Stop!" On the contrary, it propels us on, and demands a constitution of us. Who can make a constitution without us? Who can do it, if not we? Is there a power on earth that can deprive you of the right to represent your constituents?

(This speech is buried with applause.)

The vote is taken by sitting and standing, and the National Assembly unanimously declares that it persists in its previous decisions.

The comte de Mirabeau: Today I bless liberty for the fine fruits it brings to maturity in the National Assembly. Let us secure our work by declaring inviolable the persons of the deputies to the Estates General. To do so is not to show fear, but to act with prudence; it is a check upon the violent counsels that besiege the throne.

After a short debate, this motion is adopted by a majority of 493 to 34; and the assembly disperses after having adopted the following resolution:

"The National Assembly declares that the person of each deputy is inviolable; that any individual, corporate body, tribunal, court, or commission that dares, during or after the present session, to prosecute, pursue, arrest (or order arrested), detain (or order detained) any deputy, on account of any arguments, proposals, opinions, or speeches made by him at the Estates General (as well as any person who lends his authority to any of the said actions, no matter the source of the orders he receives) has committed infamy and treason towards the nation, and is guilty of a capital crime. The National Assembly orders that, in the aforementioned cases, it will take all measures necessary to pursue, prosecute, and punish all those who are the authors, instigators, or executors of these acts."

Abolition of the Feudal Regime

18. Peasant Grievances

The calling of the Estates General, and the experience of drawing up the traditional *cahiers de doléances*—the statements of grievances carried to that assembly by the deputies on behalf of their communities—encouraged widespread hopes for the reform of abuses. In the countryside, no practices were more bitterly resented than the levying of seigneurial dues, which had long brought peasant communities into conflict with their local lords. The following documents reveal the nature and bitterness of peasant grievances in some communities. The first was addressed to Necker in May 1789 by the unfortunate peasants of a backward frontier province. The second, drafted in August by a parish priest, not only describes the

From Patrick Kessel, *La nuit du 4 août 1789* (Paris: Arthaud, 1969), pp. 307–12; and *Les comités des droits féodaux et de législation et l'abolition du régime seigneurial (1789–1793)*, edited by P. Sagnac and P. Caron (Paris: Imprimerie Nationale, 1907), pp. 3–7. Translated for this volume by Caroline Ford and Keith Michael Baker.

burden of seigneurial dues upon the peasantry, but suggests some of the resentments that led representatives of the lower clergy to side with the Third Estate in the events leading to the creation of the National Assembly.

Letter of the Inhabitants of Montjoye-Vaufrey to Necker (May 1789)

Your Grace,

The unhappy inhabitants of the parishes of the seigneurie of Montjoye-Vaufrey in Upper Alsace have the honor of bringing to your attention a statement of their grievances regarding the arbitrary and vexatious burdens with which their seigneur, on the basis of his personal authority and without title, overwhelms them.

If Your Grace would deign to take account of all the revolting and inhumane injustices described in this statement, from your sense of fairness they dare to hope for reform.

Joseph Erard and Jean François Voysard, who have been sent to wait on Your Grace to appeal to your humanity and beneficence and to obtain a consoling decision, are staying at the Grand Malbourough at Versailles where they await Your Grace's orders.

Upper Alsace
Bailliage de Belfort
  To His Grace, Monsieur Necker
  Minister of Finances
Statement concerning the unjust, onerous and vexatious dues and other outrageous burdens which the undersigned inhabitants of the seigneurie of Montjoye-Vaufrey are made to endure by M. le comte de Montjoye-Vaufrey.

The seigneurie of Montjoye-Vaufrey is a small region bristling with almost inaccessible mountains and covered in large part by forests of beech and pine. The soil is naturally barren and only produces brambles and thornbushes. It is part of Upper Alsace and circumscribed by the diocese of Basle, thereby forming the kingdom's boundary.

In this region, which is almost savage because of its location, nearly a thousand individuals live miserably, crushed in thousands of ways by the seigneur of Montjoye, who imposes upon them the entire weight of the most inhumane and detestable feudal regime. The truth of these expressions will be found to be more than convincing when the rights that he claims to have over them, and the manner in which they are exercised, are detailed.

The Tithe of the Sixth Sheaf

The seigneur demands one of every six sheaves produced on the majority of the lands of the seigneurie; the other sheaves are left to the owner, who uses one and a half sheaves for seed because the soil *only yields four sheaves* for every sheaf planted. The remaining three and a half sheaves, which form the only return he draws from his sowing, are used for his own nourishment and to pay other seigneurial dues. These same fields which only yield four sheaves to one are very difficult to work; as a result, an owner who would have them cultivated by another person could hardly draw enough from them to pay taxes and to pay and feed his laborers. The only advantage derived from holding this land is the ability to occupy one-self in gaining a subsistence which consists, in this unfortunate region, of eating bread that is half barley and half oats, milk, and vegetables. In addition to this tithe, each person gives a measure of wheat to the parish priest. A small village called Montfurain, composed of ten heads of households, gives the seigneur twenty quarters of wheat and twenty of oats without knowing why.

The Right of *Mortmain*[1]

The seigneur claims that these lands are still subject to mortmain—the same lands on which he collects such an outrageous tithe. He exercises this right with so much inhumanity that the poor unfortunate owner cannot sell his land, even when reduced to an indigence meriting the greatest compassion. We have seen infirm persons possessing land, but forbidden to sell it by the seigneur, led by their charitable fellow-citizens from village to village to beg for alms. If the gardens, houses, and orchards were once exempt from this duty, today he takes everything in the case of death where there is no heir.

Corvées

It would seem that the owners of these same lands should be left to enjoy the product of their soil in peace, obliged as they are to submit to such an outrageous tithe and to the odious exercise of the right of mortmain. But far from it. In addition, this seigneur requires from them five days of work at his bidding. If he obliges them to perform this service in actual labor, he assigns the work when it pleases him, and it has often been the case that those subject to the *corvée* could not fulfill their tasks in a day; they were then obliged to continue their work the next day, but all of that was only

1. Lands subject to mortmain reverted to the lord in the event that their owner died without legitimate children.

counted as one day of work. If he does not require actual labor from them, someone who has two oxen is forced to pay him six livres, six sols, eight deniers.[2] Some people have preferred to endure this additional charge rather than to provide the actual labor. The laboring man who has no beast of burden performs the *corvée* with his own hands; or, if he wants to commute his work into money, he is forced to pay three livres fifteen sols, whereas before he would only have paid thirty-three sols. Poor beggars are not exempt. They are seen going from door to door asking for bread in order to go and work for the seigneur, because recently he refuses all food to those required to work at the *corvée*.

Taxes, Hens, the Sale of Wine, Residence Rights

For each *journal*[3] of land he takes eight deniers in taxes (*tailles*), three hens for each hearth, and the poor are no more exempt than the richest inhabitant. He collects a tenth of the wine sold in inns, whereas the king only takes a twentieth; he makes each person who moves to a new community pay a florin a year for this right. Outsiders are also subject to this payment.

Withholding Right

For approximately ten years he has assumed withholding right with respect to most of the land sold in the seigneurie; he sells this right to whomever he wants, and the heir is thus banished from this land; the rights of blood are held in just as much contempt as those of humanity.

Communal Forests

His greed leads him to appropriate all of the communal forests. He sells them for his own profit. This usurpation has already been manifested with respect to the communities of Montjoye, Monnoiront and Les Choseaux. He gives them to whomever he pleases. The distribution is never in proportion to the needs of the individual: he disposes of them as an absolute master. However, individuals pay royal taxes and even the subsidy, a tax in Alsace particularly related to forests.

2. Livres, sols, and deniers were the basic currency units of the Old Regime. A livre (pound) was worth 20 sols, or sous (shillings), and a sol was worth 12 deniers (pennies). Other units mentioned in these documents include the louis, a gold coin worth 24 livres; the écu, a silver coin worth 3 livres; and the liard, a copper coin worth 3 deniers. Pistole, the name of a Spanish gold coin, was often used in France to mean 10 livres; franc, originally the name of a French gold coin, was also used interchangeably with livre (and was officially substituted for it in the French Revolution).

3. A *journal* was a measure of land equivalent to the amount a ploughman could plough in a day.

Communal Pasturelands

One can make the same observations with regard to communal pasture-lands. The seigneur does not allow land to be cleared at all unless one agrees to plant and to give him a sixth of what is produced. Otherwise it is forbidden to touch the least beech or pine. Sometimes he takes possession of certain portions of these pasturelands, which suit his convenience; at other times he cedes them to different individuals.

Beating the Woods

Nothing better proves the slavery in which he holds these unfortunate people, and the odious use that he makes of his power, than his obliging them to cater to his whims. When it pleases him and also as often as it pleases him, he obliges them to beat the woods in order to satisfy his plea-sure for hunting; he exercises this right arbitrarily, just as he does all of the others. The farming man who is thus forced to wander through the woods for a whole day receives neither sustenance, nor a gratuity, nor payment. If he refuses to do this work, the seigneur has him condemned to pay a fine to compensate for the loss of his enjoyment. The judge never fails to rule in favor of the litigant. This much will happen to the richest farming man, if he refuses to leave his necessary and useful work in order to bring the dead game to the seigneur's château, whatever the distance from where it is found, and this supposed obligation is not remunerated at all. It passes for an indispensable right. . . .

It will undoubtedly be asked how such odious and revolting abuses could be introduced in the seigneurie of Montjoye. That will no longer seem surprising when one learns that these unhappy inhabitants have often tried to obtain some alleviation through legal actions. For more than a cen-tury, they have taken their seigneur to court in order to oblige him to produce the legal titles in the name of which he oppresses them. To thwart such just steps, the predecessors of the current seigneur had the deputies of the leading communities clapped in irons and imprisoned; charged with in-subordination, they were in custody at the seigneur's will. The current seig-neur has again outdone his predecessors. He has kept imprisoned . . . an entire family composed of six heads of household for two months, and has charged each fifteen gold louis. He has had several others imprisoned. These sorts of violence hold all of these unfortunate people in the most cruel fear and slavery. Each imprisonment has been until now the signal for the creation of a new due; it is in this very unusual manner that he has known how to perpetuate these different vexations and to create new ones.

In short, this seigneur would like to invade everything because he believes himself to be the master of everything. He calls himself master of everything we possess. This is what he contends to prove it: *"Your persons, women, and children belonged to my ancestors. They had the right of life and death over you. As a result, your goods, which are only an accessory of the person, belonged to them. The gentle laws ordained by Christianity have put an end to rights over life and death, but they have not at all forbidden their exercise over what was accessory."* These are the reasons expressed in a writ served on various communities of the seigneurie during a time in which he took action concerning a suit which his subjects had with him. In a word, he does what he likes. One suffers new exactions at any time without being able to defend oneself against them—to the extent that the inhabitants of this unfortunate land will soon be forced to abandon it if no one deigns to cast a compassionate glance upon them. He does whatever he wants. Justice is meted out in his château. His judge, his court clerk, his fiscal officer, are his devoted nominees; their views turn only on pleasing him. His will is law in matters relative to his interests.

The first moment they heard that the Estates General of the realm had been convoked, and that their king was asking for their pleas and grievances, [the inhabitants of Montjoye-Vaufrey] received this news as a herald of the reestablishment of their rights. They beg to contribute as much as they can to the general good of the realm. They want to sacrifice all to the glory of their king and to the good of their country. To enable them to do so, they hope that their seigneur will be circumscribed within fixed and immutable limits; and that he will be required at last to exhibit the legal titles so long demanded of him, which no means have yet been effective in making him produce.

In order to confirm the veracity of the above statement, the individuals named have signed the original of this document. . . . [99 signatures].

A Country Priest's View of Seigneurial Dues

Dear Sirs,

I believe that I owe it to my conscience, to my parishioners, and to a great number of individuals of the Third Estate of the realm to inform you of my observations regarding seigneurial dues and the manner in which they are exacted. All of the facts that I put forward are true; if my style lacks refinement, my intentions are pure and are directed toward alleviating the burdens of the poor and even those of the state. I have 1,200 francs in income; I willingly offer up half of it.

Sauveterre, 10 August 1789

Séguin, parish priest of Sauveterre (in the diocese of Agen)

A Parish Priest's Notes on the Dues Which
Seigneurs Call Seigneurial Dues

My aim is not to contest seigneurial revenue provided it is based on sound original titles and not on mere verifications, which bring with them a considerable increase in the amount due. I intend only to demonstrate the fraudulent way in which the revenue is collected and the burden of the absurd accessories to it called sequels. These sequels are in money, hens, wax, days of work, and custodial rights.

A sequel in money seems to me to be an unwarrantable increase in revenue. If I allow for the hens, I cannot overlook the fact that twice their value in money is demanded; I know of titles which require the tenant to pay a hen or ten liards; despite this clause fifteen or twenty sols are exacted for each hen. Wax seems to me to be another ridiculous due, especially in a region where there are no beehives. . . .

The Required Use of Baking Ovens This *banalité*[4] is as revolting as that of mills; for the honor of baking the remains of a sack of wheat in the seigneur's oven, it is necessary to pay fifteen or twenty sols or seven or eight pounds of bread; this due is worse than the rent [to which it is added]. . . .

Death Duties The seigneur dies; a double rent is necessary to buy mourning clothes for his son or heirs. The tenant [*emphytéote*][5] dies, and his death plunges his wife and children into misery; a double rent is necessary nevertheless. It follows that if the seigneur and the vassal depart from this world in the same year a triple rent is required; this additional burden seems intolerable to me. . . .

The Right of Verified Titles If vanity alone had invented and supported these new titles, and they were made at the seigneurs' expense, I would grant them willingly, especially if these new deeds did not entail an increase in rent. But it is quite the contrary. All of the costs of verified titles are passed on to tenants—the costs of land-surveyors, notaries, and so on. The surveyor appears on the seigneur's land; he shrewdly pays his court to the seigneur, and doing so means that he must find a way to increase rent; the surface of the land is therefore made to stretch, willy-nilly, under the surveyor's compass, just as if it were dough under a pastry-maker's rolling

4. A seigneur's right to require those under his jurisdiction to use his mill, baking-oven, or wine-press.

5. A tenant under emphyteusis held property from the lord under certain restricted conditions.

pin. I have seen a surveyor who dared to tell the seigneur that he found a tenant's land short; the surveyor was sent away and the operation stayed and still stays unfinished.

I know of a tract of land where the last verifications increased the rent by a sixth. I checked it against former leases; I notified the seigneur but to no avail. . . .

What I have just said is enough to prove that seigneurs have put, and keep, their vassals in conditions of servitude loathsome to the French name. But that is not all. Let us now come to the way in which rents are collected.

A bailiff is given this responsibility, or more often a tax-farmer. . . . This tax-farmer or bailiff has a notice placed in front of the church door, announcing that rent is to be delivered on such and such a day; some of those who owe rent come forward to pay their rent in grain or in money.

If the money is good enough, the wheat is not: a sieve is required, and the sieve reduces a sack by two thirds; these wretched people, however, have gathered the finest wheat to be found. The measure is plenty large, the manner of measuring too shrewd; and if one of these unfortunates wishes to complain, he is threatened, mistreated, and shamefully driven out of the seigneur's granary. He is given his receipt, which says "paid as above and *without prejudice*"—instead of saying "paid the balance of the rent for this year, wheat so much, rye so much, and so forth for the rest." This is a clever way of avoiding the verification of frauds. And with the words *without prejudice,* the tenant can never flatter himself that he has a final receipt.

I said that the measure is plenty large and the manner of measuring very shrewd. I have made several tax-farmers or bailiffs admit in conversation that every year their pile of rent is on the large side by several sacks. I know a seigneur who, curious to verify for himself the quantity or the number of sacks of wheat that the bailiff had already collected, had all the wheat measured in his presence; he found a surplus of 20-and-some-odd sacks. "You are a rogue," says this good seigneur to his bailiff, and throws him out immediately.

Let us not forget that those paying their rent in money never pay less than the wheat is worth.

We have said previously that some come forward to pay their rent in grain or money, but the majority do not come forward because most do not have wheat or money at the time. "Ha!" says the tax-farmer or bailiff, "this riffraff does not come forward; all the better, I will make them come." Then, without wasting a moment, this cruel agent of the seigneur has a subpoena printed; the process-server in the area is summoned; he is given fifty or sixty copies which he serves in a day, and as many the next day. An agreement is made between the tax-farmer and the sergeant that the latter will content himself, for his salary, with thirty or forty sols a day. However, each of those subpoenaed will pay thirty or forty sols sooner or later; by this shameful manoeuvre, this scoundrel of a tax-farmer steals fifty or sixty francs in several days with impunity. Let us not forget to say that all of this is done in the name of the seigneur, who instead of being the father of his vassals becomes a tyrant.

It is necessary to come now to the condemnations; the judge pronounces a hundred in a morning, if necessary, with an agreement again made between the tax-farmer and the judge according to which the latter will content himself with half of his fees. The judge makes this sacrifice in favor of the tax-farmer; and despite this sacrifice, which he should make in favor of those owing the fees, he still makes a tidy sum for his day's work.

It is necessary now to come to the seizures, to the confiscation of goods, to the sale of grain or other confiscated goods; the agreements between the tax-farmer or bailiff and the sergeant are roughly the same as those regarding the subpoenas. Let us point out here that these perfidious tax-farmers or bailiffs call all of these roguish activities "dancing at the end of a stick"; I leave it to my reader to decide if this tax-farmer or bailiff does not merit being attached to a long pole—I mean from on high!

The Seigneurs' Justice The judge is too often an ignorant man, and if he is not, his officers are. Agents who, in the countryside, are almost always illiterate and ignorant of the laws, judge three-fourths of the cases in the judge's absence. The judge, who holds a number of different judgeships and is consequently far from a number of his seats, cannot be in court every day; so his agents act as judges, making incorrect and faulty judgments and often increasing fees unnecessarily. Sometimes they consult a lawyer and hand the proceedings over to him; these costs are factored into the bill to be paid by the defendants, who become the dupes and victims of the ignorance of their judges. . . .

I must observe here that the vexations of which I complain displease me among all seigneurs, especially among ecclesiastical seigneurs and even more so among monastic seigneurs. For a monastic lord in France, a man who has made a vow of poverty, to assume the status of a seigneur, to enjoy five, ten, or twenty thousand francs in rent, to devour alone more than all of the inhabitants of a small town or of a large country parish, in truth, I say, this is an abuse, an injustice, a scandal without example.

A country priest, a poor wretch of a *congruiste*,[6] is denied a hundred

6. A *congruiste* was a parish priest receiving the *portion congrue,* a fixed annual salary paid to him by the legal recipient of the tithe in that parish. The *portion congrue* was often a very small sum, falling far short of the amount retained by the holder of the tithe.

pistoles, and ten or twenty thousand livres of rent are allowed to the monastic seigneur. Yet this priest preaches the gospel, well or badly; he inspires in his parishioners the fear of God and obedience to his king; he administers the sacraments, he visits the sick, he buries the dead, he sometimes comforts the poor, he consumes his income with his parishioners and his neighbors; in short, he is of some utility. But the monastic seigneur is today, at one and the same time, useless and detrimental to the state and to religion.

I do not want to harm anyone, but my Estate and my religion compel me to take the side of the wretched. I am a witness to their misfortunes and to their misery; I can and must ask that the deep wounds inflicted upon them be healed, and, the noble boldness of the gospel permitting me, I take the liberty to do so. Above all, I invite the high and rich clergy to set an example; this is the one and only means of seeing the end of these days of horror and calamity, the only way for religion to regain all its strength and all its rights.

19. Reports of Popular Unrest (July–September, 1789)

In the provinces, news of the Estates General was awaited against the background of a deepening subsistence crisis resulting from the bad harvest of 1788. Popular unrest, outbursts of violence against those engaged in the grain trade, and the fear of vagabonds forced to beg more and more aggressively, were all traditional elements in such a situation. But in July 1789, with reports of the dismissal of Necker and the storming of the Bastille, they took on a new political tone. In a wave of revolutionary action, peasants directed their fury against the châteaux and archival repositories that were the symbols and sources of seigneurial privileges, and townspeople followed the example of Paris in transforming municipal government and organizing a civic guard for the defense of order.

From the Register of the Municipal Government of Mamers (22–23 July)

Today, July 22, 1789, at the town hall, the municipal body held a meeting . . . at which . . . the mayor presented a letter addressed to the municipal officers by M. Desfontaines, director of the tax farm administration in the

From *French Revolution Documents*, edited by J. M. Roberts (New York: Barnes and Noble, 1966), vol. 1, pp. 135–38, 140–41, 143–45, 147–49. Translated for this volume by Caroline Ford and Keith Michael Baker.

city of Alençon, announcing that the residents of this town were taking it upon themselves to abandon payment of the taxes due to his administration, even though the National Assembly had decreed that existing taxes would continue to be collected until laws had been enacted to the contrary. The director demanded that the municipal body use its authority to uphold tax obligations; and he declared his confidence that, at this moment when its representatives were concerning themselves with the public good, the municipal body would support their views, and act to maintain the legal claims of the tax farm administration and guarantee the safety of its agents. . . .

The municipal officers . . . also attested that, according to word which has spread, vagabonds and vagrants were roaming about in various cantons of the realm and above all in our neighboring provinces, disturbing the peace and public tranquillity, and threatening public repositories, receiverships, and perhaps even the properties of individuals. They declared that, given the importance of preventing such incursions, the general body of the residents would be consulted regarding steps to be taken to provide for peace and public safety in every respect; a general assembly would accordingly be announced. . . .

Today, July 23, 1789, at two o'clock in the afternoon, the king's attorney attached to this town hall appeared in the hall of the royal bailiwick of the city of Mamers, the usual meeting place for general assemblies, before the mayor and other municipal officers of the city undersigned. . . . At this assembly were gathered a great number of the undersigned residents, who decided that in order to guarantee the peace and public tranquillity, companies of civic militia shall be formed, following the capital's example. To accomplish this, it was decided that all of the residents shall be inscribed (street by street) in a register to be kept at the town hall for this purpose by the municipal officers; that, after this operation, the city shall be divided into four or more districts according to the number of residents registered; that companies shall be formed from among the wealthiest citizens, those in a position to serve on a permanent basis; that in addition, companies shall also be formed from among the less well-off citizens, to serve with the first companies in case of emergency; that these different companies shall choose their commanding officers, as well as a commandant to be elected by all of the companies assembled together. . . .

2. That in accordance with the letter of the director of the tax farm administration, taxes shall continue to be collected as in the past. . . .

5. That the alarming events that occurred yesterday and today shall be made known to our lords, the deputies of the Estates General.

6. That our lords, the deputies of the Estates General, shall be complimented on the indefatigable zeal with which they have worked until now toward public regeneration and public happiness.

7. That the *curé* of Mamers and the serving priest shall be asked to sing a *The Te Deum* [*sic*] next Sunday, as thanksgiving for the meeting of the three orders of the Estates General.

8. That our lords of the Estates General shall be entreated to have orders issued so that the civic militia will be furnished with arms by those who are responsible for the weapons depot in Le Mans.

9. That with regard to the motion concerning the alleviation of the burdens of the unfortunate, the workers of the linen manufactory of this city, a committee shall be named to attend to it. . . .

10. That the city shall continue to be illuminated this evening as it was last night in order to further the increase of good order and public tranquillity.

Drawn up and decided in the church of St. Nicolas, owing to the magnitude of the number of residents, which was greater than the usual place of assembly could hold . . . and signed by all residents with the exception of those who declared they did not know how to sign.

Letter from the Mayor of Dunkirk to the Intendant of Flanders (25 July)

. . . Tempers are beginning to get inflamed, and there have been threats to pillage granaries, and even to burn some; three hundred men were supposed to assemble last night for that purpose, so we have undertaken to raise a civic guard. All the merchants and respectable folk of this city came to the town hall yesterday around noon to register for it. Arrangements were made after dinner and the patriots began to go out at nine o'clock in the evening. The number of persons of good will is increasing considerably. We hope to find a sufficient number of them to oppose those with evil intentions—whose number is great, because of all the strangers. We increased the civic guard this morning to three hundred men, because of today's market, where there would have been a commotion if we had not taken this precaution. We have taken all precautions necessary to satisfy the people. The amount of wheat brought to market will be twice what it was last time. The *coupe* [of wheat], which should be increased by forty sols because it was increased at Bergues, will, to the contrary be diminished by an écu. As a result, the *coupe,* which was at forty-two livres last Saturday, will be reduced today to thirty-nine livres. We will indemnify bakers against the loss that will cause them, by drawing up an account of how much is consumed in the week. We will lower the price of our wheat at market by six livres per *rasière.*[1] We hope, through these measures, to be

---

1. The *coupe* and the *rasière* were local measures of volume.

able to satisfy the people and restore peace. But tempers are very heated. The wearing of the *cocarde*[2] two days ago—following a *Te Deum* that some young people arranged to be sung yesterday, and to which all of the corporate bodies were invited—was the moment and the cause of the tumult which reigns at present. People got fired up at the cabaret. Seditious remarks, drunkenness, the dearness of bread exacerbated this unrest. Add to this the events in the neighboring towns, all instigated by a dozen disreputable characters who talk openly in seditious terms. One does not need more to stir up an entire city. If this day passes tranquilly, we can hope for calm; but so little is necessary to feed the smouldering fire. We have many people in this city who are just looking for a fight. I hope that we will succeed in restoring the peace; we are completely in agreement with the major in charge of the square. . . . All of the guards have been doubled, and the garrison is ready to take up its arms at the first signal. . . .

Disorders in Franche-Comté (from a letter of 29 July)

You know what has happened in Paris and how the city has been put on the defense. The sudden retirement of Necker has produced a general and woeful revolution in the whole realm. Our province is in a most bereft state and above all our land from which seigneurs . . . have been obliged to flee for their safety. Four parishes have marched, invaded the abbey, and driven out the monks and the provost . . . all of the furniture, mirrors, beds were stolen, and the silverware, and nothing is left; they stayed there drinking for four days and destroyed all the wines. With God's permission, they dared to break open the doors of the church, stole the sacred vessels, and destroyed everything in the church; such a disaster has [not] been seen for a long time. They were all armed with guns, pitchforks, hatchets. Also they went, the schoolmaster at the head, to the church. Four of them were killed, twenty-nine wounded, and twelve imprisoned. . . . This is not all. In Champagné you know there is a beautiful house. At night, when everything was quiet, our fellows went there, broke everything, ripped everything down, and did not leave a piece intact, all of the interior to the last block of stone. . . . They suggested going for the throat and tearing down all of the dependent farm houses numbering about forty. My son got up, went to try to put a stop to this nonsense, to make them see the consequences of what they were doing, and he managed to calm all of them with a great deal of difficulty. Today all is quiet, and imagine our fear. I am still quite ill as you might expect; the château of Sossi belonging to Madame de Baufermont is

---

2. Wearing of the revolutionary *cocarde*, a rosette of red, white, and blue, became a symbol of support for the Revolution after the fall of the Bastille.

completely demolished. The loss of furniture is estimated at forty thousand livres. The princess was obliged to escape to Remirmont. Finally, all the nobles have left. Quite a ferocious war has been waged against them. However, they must give up something of their privileges to the state, but all of that will end badly. . . .

A Complaint to the National Assembly (20 August)

. . . On the 29th of July 1789, a party of foreign brigands together with my vassals and those of Urighi, the parish neighboring mine, came, two hundred of them, to my château of Sassy, in the parish of Saint-Christophe, near Argentan, and after having broken open the locks of the chest containing my legal titles, they took a large part of them, together with registers that could have been necessary to me, and carried them away or burned them in the woods next to my château. My guard could not put up any resistance, being the only guardian on this land where I do not live. These wretched people had the tocsin rung in neighboring parishes in order to assemble in greater numbers. I am all the more unhappy about this loss because I never made my vassals feel the odious weight of antique feudalism, from which I am delighted they can be redeemed in the present circumstance; but who will ever be able to prove and establish the wrong that they have done to my properties? I appeal to your prudence in order that some means be settled upon by the National Assembly to give me back what I am losing. . . .

I will take no steps against those I know among these brigands, who, not content with burning my documents, have killed all my pigeons. But I count upon complete justice from the spirit of equity which governs you and which gives me the greatest confidence.

Comte de Germiny

Deposition of a Steward in Lower Maine (August)

Last Monday, July 30, an infinite number of persons, vassals of the seigneurie of Hauteville and others, went to the château of the seigneurie, armed with guns, skewers, pitchforks, pikes, and other weapons. Having come out of the château to meet them, he asked them what they wanted. A certain Loison, from the parish of Chavaigné, came forward first, with an arrogant air, and told him that above all things he must have some money that he had paid as a fine incurred for hunting, and a gun which had been taken from him. The witness having replied to these people that he could not hand over his master's money without his participation, they said boisterously, "we must have some money, we must have some." Seeing himself coerced by these brigands, he told them to enter the common room, that he was going to give them satisfaction. He gave them: eighty-one livres to the said Loison, eighteen to Mathurin Lechat, six to René Baron, nicknamed "Storm," two hundred to one called F. Desgentais, as he signed on his receipt. He took a receipt from each of these persons, copies of which he has submitted. . . . He gave still more money to other persons whom he did not know because of the commotion that reigned. . . .

At the end of the handout, a certain René Fortin . . . came forward and said that . . . [the seigneur's feudal lawyer] had made him pay twenty écus too much on a repurchase, and that he would be very pleased to get this money back. The witness having shown him again that he had no more money, the said Fortin replied that he would give them to him when he could, that he would trust him for it, and was willing to show him that he had paid too much. After this handout, they all asked with fury that the documents and titles of the seigneurie of Hauteville be handed over. As they were in the charter-room in the middle of the commotion, some wanted him to bring them out and others that they be read. In all of this agitation, he was pushed again and again and shaken violently by the collar. They also asked for maps of the seigneurie, which he brought with M. Pommerolle. Several said that he was playing around with them by bringing them pictures instead of the map. He took out everything, with the help of Huet, the clerk, and Valleé, a worker and the château's guardian. Having all gone out into the courtyard, they demanded with the greatest fury the register of landed property which should have weighed from sixty to one hundred pounds, according to them, and threatened to come back in a few days to burn down the château if the whole thing were not handed over. He heard a voice which said to him that he was going to be put into the fire, but that it would first be necessary to build one. Seeing himself threatened from all sides and even his life in danger, he asked as a favor that he be allowed to go into the garden to relieve himself, and having obtained permission for this with difficulty, he went into the garden and had the door opened by Robillard, a gardener, and escaped, running as fast as his legs would carry him into the woods, where he hid until around eight o'clock. As he fled, he heard a gunshot behind him which he is told was fired by someone called René Dubreil. . . .

Letter from the Steward of the Duc de Montmorency, at Montmartin (2 August)

Sir, in order not to disturb your tranquillity, I have been silent about the legitimate fears which have troubled me too long; but, at this moment, I would believe it imprudent to leave you in ignorance of them. Brigandage and pillage are occurring everywhere. The populace, attributing the dearness of grain to the seigneurs of the realm, is venting its fury against all that belongs to them. All manner of reasoning fails: this unbridled populace only listens to its own fury, and in the whole of our province vassals are in such a state of revolt that they are ready to commit the greatest excesses; finally, even in this parish, which is convinced that the b[aron] de B[reteuil] and his family are in the château, it is boldly declared that the château is going to be burned down. You must imagine, sir, that I take all possible care in such circumstances. Every night, my household and I sit up in the greatest secrecy in order not to reveal any hint of an uneasiness which could be prejudicial to us. Although I know very well there are persons who have similar sentiments, I feign ignorance and redouble my vigilance toward all. Another anxiety which tears at my heart is not knowing if our seigneurs are safe from the popular fury. If it is in your power, I beg you to send me word of it.

At the moment when I was going to end my letter, I learned . . . that approximately three hundred brigands from all parts, together with the marquise of Longaunay's vassals, have made off with the records of revenues and dues owed to the seigneurie and demolished its dovecote: they then gave her an acknowledgement of the seizure signed in the name of *The Nation*. Four days ago, the same group went into a château of the prince of Monaco four leagues from Thorigny, in order to seize the records there also; not having found them, they let loose their fury on the château's furniture and reduced it to dust. The collector and his family were lucky enough to escape.

The château of Thorigny is threatened and no one doubts that it is going to be pillaged. What must we do and become?

The poor of this parish are dying of hunger: I am going to help a bit in this terrible misery and try to stop it, distributing fifty écus or so.

Declaration of the First Consul of Cordes-Tolosannes (2 August)

Considering that sudden fear has spread throughout the whole region; that a considerable number of brigands are scattered throughout the countryside who threaten to burn everything; that this fact has even made itself felt in the present community, as two stacks of wheat have just been burned; that if the weather had not been calm, the abovementioned fire would have burned this village of Cordes since the two stacks were placed near houses; that it would be fitting to provide for the public safety: in consequence it would be suitable to establish civic guards, place them in positions to forbid entry to these kinds of people and to patrol during the night, watch over houses, stacks of wheat and hay, catch brigands who have been able to

penetrate this community, and see that the haystacks are put at a considerable distance from the two villages of Cordes and Lafitte and from the
houses of the jurisdiction, in order to prevent the conflagration that could
result from them.

A Lynching at Saint-Denis (2 August)

[From depositions made 25 September by relatives of the dead man.]

They declared and told us that on the second of August last at eight
o'clock in the evening a popular riot broke out in the city of Saint-Denis in
[the Ile de] France, incited by people with evil intentions, who as a pretext
demanded a reduction in the price of bread; that the people, prompted by
these scoundrels, and under the influence of drink for the most part . . .
flocked to the town square in numbers of about two hundred to three hundred persons; that in this mob there were many women. Twenty-five or
thirty made their way to the town hall and forced the municipal officers,
who only numbered three at the time . . . to lower the price of bread, and
to fix it at two sols a pound. These officers, under duress, found themselves
obliged to give way and ordered a city employee to go immediately to the
bakers and proclaim that bread was two sols a pound.

At this point, part of this unruly populace went to the house of the said
M. Chatelle, burst open and broke down all the doors, broke the furniture
in a room on the ground floor belonging to the said M. Hébert, one of the
court's witnesses. Not finding M. Chatelle anywhere, they left, taking various effects with them. M. Chatelle, apprised of what had happened at his
home, left the town hall, led by his son, one of the court's witnesses, who
made him withdraw to the house of M. Broisse, a merchant in the square;
and the younger M. Chatelle, believing him to be safe in this house, went
to the constabulary to ask for help. When the officer refused to come, because he said that he had been given no orders, he came immediately to the
Paris town hall. In the meantime, M. Broisse forced M. Chatelle senior to
leave his house. Not knowing where to find refuge, M. Chatelle went to the
house of the priest of his parish of Trois Patrons, who hid him in the tower,
since the priest of the parish of St. Michel had refused to receive him. The
brigands, learning that he was there, came to find him, kicked up a horrible
commotion in the church, and pulled him from his hiding place. He suc-
cumbed to their blows; he was stabbed fourteen times by knives or other
sharp instruments. His head was separated from his body, and they abandoned themselves to other excesses known to the whole city; it was a soldier from the Provence regiment who cut off his head.

The court's witnesses observed that they were informed by public rumor
that the principal authors of this murder were Fournier, a bar owner; the

two brothers Jaquet, watercress cutters; Alavais, a drummer and licensed porter at the market; the said Bouquet [a locksmith] and his wife, a seller; Doliget, a printer; a woman, Janot, poulteress, daughter of mother Marguerite, a dairywoman; the former beadle of Trois Patrons; Grandseigne, son of a woman called Jacob, a baker; Lainé, son of Lainé, a water-carrier; the said soldier of the Provence Regiment.

From the Register of the Municipality of Chaumont (20 September)

[Commissioners sent by the municipality to buy grain report that] we have made purchases of grain in a few parishes of the Bassigny, where our visit had been anticipated by your bakers, who had established a price that we found very high, but were nevertheless obliged to accept. . . .

We have learned that one of your bakers, bringing back wheat bought by him, was attacked in the village of Biesles by a considerable mob of residents; that his cart was stopped, despite an escort of two mounted men of the constabulary and six musketeers . . . who were not able to resist the fury of these seditious people. This circumstance obliged us to have the convoy escorted by those in our pay, with a force sufficient to avoid the risk of a delay . . . as the grain was intended for the provisioning of the next day's market, which was yesterday; we therefore required the assistance of two mounted men of the constabulary brigade of Montigny and twenty musketeers of the detachment currently stationed there; we asked for an escort of two mounted men of the constabulary brigade of this city and ten musketeers of the detachment here.

It is only with the strong protection of this escort that your grain has been able to pass through the village of Biesles; again it was not without excesses and violence on the part of the residents of this village, who cry loudly that they will not let any grain through. You understand, Sirs, that this necessary precaution has occasioned expenses which again add markedly to the price of this grain; but this seditous agitation on the part of the residents of Biesles merits the most serious consideration. . . . The excesses and violence they have indulged in deserve punishment; and it is dangerous if other parishes imitate their example, which would interrupt the flow of grain in this area. . . .

[The register continues:] Concerning this matter the assembly decided after discussion that a letter will be sent to the provost of the constabulary to beg him to give particular attention to the . . . excesses and violence committed by the inhabitants of Biesles, who have taken it upon themselves to sound the tocsin, to arm themselves with pitchforks, scythes, and staves, and to wound one of the aforementioned musketeers. And he will be implored to use all diligence to quell these assaults that will lead to nothing less than murders, and to the starvation of the city of Chaumont, and even of the whole region, because all of the districts surrounding the city get their grain in the Bassigny. . . .

20. Decrees of the National Assembly (10–11 August 1789)

The wave of peasant uprisings against seigneurial rights and dues obliged the National Assembly to take action to restore order and protect property. But to do this meant that the assembly had to confront the critical question of what was to be protected as property. Fear of further disorder therefore gave immediate urgency to the issue of privileges that had been dividing the representatives in their preliminary efforts to formulate a declaration of constitutional principles. It also seemed to offer those in favor of abolishing privileges an opportunity to press the issue to a resolution.

On the evening of 4 August 1789, the assembly met to consider a proposed decree to enforce existing laws in favor of "the sacred rights of property and personal security." In response, the Vicomte de Noailles, a liberal noble, demanded that the assembly respond to the just grievances of the peasantry by abolishing seigneurial dues. Then, in what began as a parliamentary maneuver but was rapidly transformed into a profoundly emotional collective experience, speaker after speaker came forward to denounce and abandon not only the seigneurial privileges attacked by the peasantry, but the rights of the nobility and the clergy, of provinces, towns and corporations—in short, the entire particularistic structure of the ancien régime. Witnesses spoke of the "effervescence" of a moment in which calculation of personal interest evaporated and "the assembly, moved to tears, abandoned itself entirely to the delirium of sacrifices."

Amazed at what had occurred in this dramatic session, the assembly devoted the following days to more sober afterthought, and to the formulation of a more restrained statement of the principles it had so enthusiastically endorsed. The decrees of 10–11 August were the result of these deliberations. Although the king withheld approval of the decree abolishing the feudal regime until after the disturbances of the "October Days" (and litigation regarding its detailed implementation took much longer to settle), the Night of the Fourth of August had nevertheless brought the National Assembly to decisive action in the formulation and

From *Archives parlementaires de 1787 à 1860, première série (1787 à 1799)*, edited by M. J. Mavidal and M. E. Laurent, 2d ed., 82 vols. (Paris: Dupont, 1879–1913), vol. 8, pp. 378, 397–98. Translated for this volume by the editor, Keith Michael Baker.

application of the fundamental principles of the Revolution, and in the assertion of the sovereign power it had claimed on behalf of the nation.

Decree of 10 August

The National Assembly, considering that the enemies of the nation, now that they have lost the hope of preventing public regeneration and the establishment of liberty through the violence of despotism, seem to have conceived the criminal plan of achieving the same end through disorder and anarchy; that among other means, they have spread false alarms in the different provinces of the realm at the same time, and almost on the same day, proclaiming nonexistent incursions and acts of brigandage in order to cause crimes and excesses that attack persons and property equally, and deserve the most severe punishment since they disturb the universal order of society; that these men have carried their audacity to the point of spreading false orders, and even false royal edicts, arming one part of the nation against another at the very moment that the National Assembly is enacting decrees most beneficial to the interests of the people;

Considering that, in the general unrest, the most sacred properties, and even the harvests, the only hope of the people in this time of dearth, have not been respected;

Considering, finally, that the unity of all forces, the influence of all powers, every means of action and the zeal of every good citizen, must combine to repress such disorders;

Decides and decrees:

That all the municipalities of the realm, in the towns and in the countryside, will be vigilant in maintaining public peace, and that, at their mere written request, the national militia, as well as the constabularies, will be aided by troops. . . .

That arrested persons will be turned over to the tribunals of justice, interrogated immediately, and put on trial; but judgment and execution will be suspended in the case of those charged with being the authors of false alarms and the instigators of pillage and violence against property or persons; copies of the details of interrogations and other procedures will nevertheless be sent directly to the National Assembly, so that, by investigating and comparing the evidence gathered from different parts of the realm, it may discover the origin of these disorders, and see to it that the leaders of these conspiracies be subjected to exemplary punishments that will effectively repress such criminal acts;

That all seditious gatherings, whether in the towns or in the countryside, even under the pretext of hunting, will be immediately dispersed by the national militia, the constabularies and the troops, on the mere written request of the municipalities;

That in the towns and rural municipalities, as well as in each district of the cities, a register will be compiled of disreputable persons, men without trade or occupation, and those with no fixed domicile; these persons are to be disarmed, and the national militia will keep particular watch over their conduct;

That all the national militia will take an oath, between the hands of their commandant, to serve faithfully and well for the maintenance of peace, the defense of the citizens, and against those who disturb public repose; and that all the troops, namely the officers of all ranks and the soldiers, will take an oath to the nation and to the king, the head of the nation, with the most august solemnity;

That the soldiers will swear, before their entire regiment assembled at arms, never to abandon their flag, to be faithful to the nation, the king, and the law, and never to deploy those under their orders against the citizens, except at the written request of the civil or municipal officers, this request always to be read before the assembled troops;

That the curés of the towns and villages will read the present decree to their parishioners assembled in church, and that they will use . . . the influence of their ministry to reestablish peace and public tranquillity. . . .

Decree of 11 August

1. The National Assembly entirely destroys the feudal regime. It decrees that, among rights and dues—whether they are feudal obligations or *cens* payments[1]—those deriving from mortmain (as applied to lands or persons) and from personal serfdom, and those which represent them, are abolished without compensation; all others are declared redeemable, and the price and manner of redemption will be determined by the National Assembly. Those of the aforesaid rights that are not abolished by this decree will, however, continue to be collected until reimbursement has been completed.

2. The exclusive right to maintain small and large dovecotes is abolished. Pigeons will be cooped up for periods determined by the communities, during which time they will be regarded as game, and everyone will have the right to kill them upon his own land.

3. The exclusive right of hunting and of maintaining unenclosed warrens is likewise abolished, and each proprietor has the right to destroy all kinds of game (or have it destroyed), but only on his own property, and

---

1. The *cens* was the annual tax or quit-rent owed to the lord by non-privileged persons on land attached to the *seigneurie*.

subject to compliance with such regulations as may be made relative to public safety.

All hunting captaincies, even the royal ones, and all hunting preserves, under whatever name, are likewise abolished; measures for this purpose will be compatible with the respect due to property and liberty, and to the preservation of the personal pleasures of the king.

The president [of the National Assembly] is charged to ask the king for the reprieve of those banished or sentenced to the galleys simply for hunting, for the release of prisoners presently detained, and for the suppression of current legal procedures in this respect.

4. All seigneurial courts are suppressed without compensation; nevertheless, officers of these courts will continue to perform their functions until the National Assembly has provided for the establishment of a new judicial system.

5. Tithes of every kind, and dues substituted for them, under whatever name they may be known and collected (even when compounded as a lump sum), whether possessed by regular and secular bodies of clergy, by holders of benefices, vestries, or all those holding right of mortmain (even by the Order of Malta and other religious military orders), including those tithes which have been ceded to laymen in exchange for payments to parish priests [*portions congrues*], are abolished; but with the proviso that other means will be instituted to support divine worship, provide for the livelihood of ministers, relieve the poor, repair and rebuild churches and presbyteries, and maintain all the establishments, seminaries, schools, colleges, hospitals, religious communities and other institutions currently supported by the allocation of tithes.

However, until this has been done, and until the former possessors receive funds replacing the tithes, the National Assembly orders that the aforesaid tithes will continue to be collected in accordance with the laws, and in the customary manner.

As for other tithes, whatever their nature, they will be redeemable in the manner to be determined by the assembly; and until a law has been enacted on this subject, the National Assembly orders that their collection will also be continued.

6. All perpetual rents on land, whether paid in money or in kind, whatever their nature and origin, and to whomsoever they are due—holders under mortmain, proprietors of estates, possessors of dependencies, or the Order of Malta—will be redeemable; *champarts*[2] of every kind, and under any name, will likewise be redeemable at rates to be determined by the

2. The *champart* was a portion of the harvest (or the equivalent in money) owed to the lord by non-privileged persons on land attached to the *seigneurie*.

assembly. It will be prohibited to establish any nonredeemable dues in future.

7. The sale of judicial and municipal offices is abolished from this moment. Justice will be rendered without charge. Nevertheless, those holding these offices will continue to perform their functions and to receive the income from their positions until the assembly has made provision for their reimbursement.

8. The incidental fees of country priests are suppressed and shall cease to be paid as soon as provision has been made for increasing payments to parish priests [portions congrues] and providing for the support of vicars; a law will also be enacted to make provision for priests in the towns.

9. Pecuniary privileges in matters of taxation, whether they pertain to land or personal status, are abolished forever. Taxes will be levied on all citizens and properties in the same manner and in the same form; and means will be considered to effect proportional payment of all taxes, even those assessed for the last six months of the current tax year.

10. Since a national constitution and public liberty are more advantageous to the provinces than the privileges which some of them have been enjoying, and which must necessarily be sacrificed for the intimate union of all parts of the realm, it is declared that all the particular privileges of provinces, principalities, regions, cantons, towns and communities, whether financial or of any other kind, are abolished forever, and will be absorbed into the law common to all Frenchmen.

11. Every citizen, without distinction of birth, is eligible for all ecclesiastical, civil, and military positions and dignities, and no useful profession will imply derogation.

12. In future, no payments for annates, or for any other purpose whatsoever, will be sent to the court of Rome, to the vice-legation at Avignon, or to the nuncio's residence at Lucerne. Diocesan clergy will address themselves to their bishop for all provision of benefices and dispensations, which will be granted without cost, any withholding of benefices, anticipated rights of succession, or monthly sharings being disregarded, since all the churches of France must enjoy the same liberty.

13. Rights to the income of vacant benefices, to the estates and personal possessions of deceased clergy, and to abandoned property, quitrents, Peter's pence, and other dues of the same kind established in favor of bishops, archdeacons, archpresbyters, chapters, curés, and all others, under any name whatsoever, are abolished, but fitting provision shall be made for the support of deaconries and presbyteries which are not sufficiently endowed.

14. In future, plurality of benefices will not be permitted if the incumbent's income from any benefice or benefices exceeds the sum of three

thousand livres. Nor will it be permitted to receive several pensions from benefices, or a pension and a benefice, if the income already obtained from such sources exceeds the like sum of three thousand livres.

15. Once an account of current pensions, gifts, and stipends has been presented to the National Assembly, it will act in concert with the king to suppress those that are excessive; with the proviso that in future a fixed amount will be placed at the king's disposal for this purpose.

16. The National Assembly decrees that, in commemoration of the great and important decisions which have just been taken for the welfare of France, a medal will be struck, and a *Te Deum* sung in thanksgiving, in all the parishes and churches of the realm.

17. The National Assembly solemnly proclaims King Louis XVI *The Restorer of French Liberty.*

18. The National Assembly will wait upon the king in a body, to present to His Majesty the decree which it has just passed, to pay him the homage of its most respectful gratitude, and to beseech him to permit a *Te Deum* to be chanted in his chapel, and to attend it himself.

Once the constitution has been completed, the National Assembly will turn immediately to drafting the laws necessary to elaborate the principles it has laid down in the present decree, which the deputies will immediately send, together with the decree of the 10th of this month, into all the provinces, there to be printed and proclaimed, even from the parish pulpits, and posted wherever necessary.

21. The October Days

While women regularly participated in the decisive revolutionary interventions of the Parisian crowd, and even formed their own revolutionary club in 1793, the events of the October Days are particularly associated with their action. In Paris, bread shortages had been continuing to cause unrest throughout the late summer of 1789. In Versailles, Louis XVI had been continuing to withhold consent to acts of the National Assembly, such as the abolition of the feudal regime and the Declaration of the Rights of Man (see the following document). With the news that the king had summoned additional troops, and that the revolutionary tricolor had

Deposition of Madelaine Glain from *Women in Revolutionary Paris, 1789–1795*, edited by Darline Gay Levy, Harriet Bronson Applewhite and Mary Durham Johnson (Champaign, Illinois: University of Illinois Press, 1979), pp. 47–48. © 1979 by the Board of Trustees of the University of Illinois. Other depositions from Philip Dawson, ed., *The French Revolution*, pp. 59–61, 66–67. © 1967 by Prentice-Hall, Inc., Englewood Cliffs, NJ 07632. Reprinted by permission of the publisher.

been insulted at a banquet welcoming them, concern for bread combined with political outrage to fuel a new popular insurrection.

On 5 October, a crowd of women that had appeared at the Paris city hall to demand action on bread supplies decided to march on Versailles and lay their grievances before the National Assembly. They were followed by growing numbers of demonstrators, and eventually by the troops of the National Guard (with their commander, Lafayette, reluctantly at their head). Arriving at Versailles, the first contingent of women crowded into the National Assembly, which responded to their demands by ordering its president to lead a delegation of the marchers to the palace— where the king promised action to supply bread. Later that evening, threatened by the impending arrival of a new wave of demonstrators with the National Guard, Louis XVI also agreed to accept the legislation that had been proposed to him by the National Assembly. But this concession was not enough to satisfy the revolutionary crowd, which invaded the palace early the following morning. To calm the situation, the king finally agreed to demands that he move to Paris. The royal family was escorted back to the capital that afternoon by an exultant mob, to be followed some days later by the National Assembly. Both were to act in future under the watchful eyes of the people of Paris.

The depositions printed below were presented to a committee of inquiry subsequently established by the Paris municipal government.

Deposition of Madelaine Glain

Madelaine Glain, forty-two years old, a *faiseuse de ménage,* wife of François Gaillard, an office clerk in the District de l'Oratoire with whom she lives on rue Froidmanteau, no. 40, testifies that, having been forced, as many women were, to follow the crowd that went to Versailles last Monday, October 5, and having arrived at Sèvres near the porcelain manufactory, [and] a gentleman with a black decoration having asked them where they were going, they answered that they were going to ask for bread at Versailles. This gentleman urged them to behave themselves, but a woman whom the declarant knew to be a prostitute and who since then has been living with Lagrement, a soft drink peddler on rue Bailleul, having said that she was going to Versailles to bring back the queen's head, was sharply reproached by the others. Having arrived at the streets leading to Versailles, this same woman stopped a mounted Royal Guardsman, to whom she delivered many insults, threatening him with a bad, rusty sword which she held open in her hand. This Royal Guardsman said that she was a wretch, and in order to [make her] release the bridle of his horse, which she was holding, he struck her a blow which inflicted an arm wound. Having come at last to the Château with the intention of informing His Majesty concerning the motives of their proceedings, she, the declarant, found herself locked in, that is to say, her skirts caught on two spikes of the gate, from which a Swiss guard released her. After that she went with the other women to the hall of the National Assembly, where they entered, many strong. Some of these women having asked for the four-pound loaf at eight *sols,* and for meat at the same price, she, the declarant, called for silence, and then she said that they were asking that they not be lacking bread, but not [that it be fixed] at the price these women were wanting to have it. She did not go with the deputation to the Château but returned with Sieur Maillard and two other women to the Hôtel-de-Ville in Paris to bring back the decrees they were given at the National Assembly. Monsieur the mayor and the representatives of the commune were satisfied and received them with joy. Then she, the declarant, was led by the National Guard to the District de l'Oratoire to convey this good news. She cannot give us any news concerning what happened at Versailles on the sixth, but she learned, without being able to say from whom, that someone named Nicolas, a model in the academy, who lived at the home of Poujet, rue Champfleuri, on that day, Tuesday, had cut off the heads of two Royal Guards who had been massacred by the people, and since then the above-mentioned Nicolas has not reappeared in the *quartier.*

Deposition of Jeanne Martin

Jeanne Martin, age 49, practical nurse, wife of Jean Lavarenne, porter in the d'Aligre town-house, with whom she resides, Rue Bailleul, parish of Saint-Germain-l'Auxerrois; upon oath . . .

Deposes that on Monday, October 5, last, in the morning, in the Louvre Passage near the Infanta garden, she was forced by about forty women to go with them to Versailles; they put a stick in her hand, threatening to mistreat her if she did not march; she remarked to them that she had not had breakfast and did not have a *sou* with her; they answered, "March, march, you won't lack anything." To avoid the ill treatment with which she was threatened, she followed these women; having arrived at the Tuileries and intending to pass through the garden, they encountered the Swiss guard named Frederick who refused to permit it. This gave rise to a brawl between the Swiss and Maillard, who was at their head; the deponent, seeing two swords drawn and fearing a misfortune, struck both swords a blow with the stick she had, which disarmed the combatants; a man armed with a bayonet wanted to fall upon this Swiss; a rather badly dressed woman, holding a rusty sword blade without a hilt, wanted to strike the Swiss a blow; the deponent and other women opposed this, and in the scuffle the deponent was wounded in the hand; they all passed through the Tuileries and continued toward Versailles, with other women who joined them at the Place Louis XV, on the Cour la Reine, and after the city gate; having arrived at Sèvres, near the porcelain factory, they encountered two gentlemen, one wearing a black ribbon, the other dressed in a green suit, who asked them, "Where are you going, ladies?" They replied, "We're going to Versailles, to ask the King for bread for ourselves, our husbands and our children, and for the provisioning of the capital." These individuals said, "Go ahead, behave yourselves, don't be insolent to anyone, and peace be with you." Then a woman whom the deponent does not know but who was armed with a sword said, "Yes, we're going to Versailles; we'll bring back the Queen's head on the end of a sword." The other women made her be silent. The deponent remarks that along the road she saw different couriers pass—among others, one whom the women wanted to stop and who escaped after having thrown into the river a portfolio he carried; they let pass freely another courier who belonged to the Duke of Orléans and who was leaving Passy to go to Versailles; along the road they saw other couriers.

When they arrived in Versailles, the Flanders regiment was under arms on the left of the palace, and the King's Guards were before the central gate; they presented themselves to enter the court but were prevented from doing so. A man dressed in the uniform of the National Guard of Paris, armed with a saber, crossed the ranks of the King's Guards, one of whom left ranks, ran at him, saber in hand, and hit him a blow which knocked his hat off; three other King's Guards likewise left the ranks, saber in hand, to run after the man in the direction of the barracks; then the deponent lost sight of them. The women, unable to get into the palace court, and the deponent went to the National Assembly; they still had Maillard at their head and about twenty women, of whom the deponent was one. They were brought in to the rail at the front of the National Assembly; they were received with great joy and affability and were seated on a bench; it was Maillard, alone at first, who spoke, asking for bread for them, their husbands, and their children, and the provisioning of the capital. Two members of the Assembly and nine women were appointed as a deputation to the King; only seven went, she was told. The deponent remained at the front rail of the Assembly.

The deputation did not come back from the King until ten o'clock. The King's response was read, then turned over to M. le vicomte de Mirabeau, from whom the deponent received it to turn it over to the said Maillard, who was to bring it back promptly to the city hall. The Assembly having recessed at about one o'clock in the morning, the deponent and many other women slept in the hall. She did not notice any man disguised as a woman, and nothing happened contrary to respectability and decency. At five o'clock in the morning, on Tuesday the 6th, the deponent and two other women whose names and residences she does not know left the hall and went to the Place d'Armes and then to the palace, where she saw the populace arrive in great numbers and climb on the gates in order to get into the palace, which was not opened. At that moment, several King's Guards inside the palace fired musket shots at the people; the deponent noticed and recognized three or four from their uniforms and shoulder belts. This discharge killed a citizen in the Marble Court. The Guard who had killed this citizen was seized by the populace, who took him to the Place d'Armes, where he lost his life. Another King's Guard stabbed a citizen in the arm with a dagger; he was cruelly wounded and carried to the infirmary. This Guard was instantly wounded by a hatchet blow which cut off half his face and then taken to the Place d'Armes, where he was killed beside the first one. A man from the faubourg Saint Antoine who had a long beard and was armed with a hatchet cut the heads off the said King's Guards. Several King's Guards, likewise threatened by the women, were saved by the grenadiers of the National Guard. The deponent helped to parry a lance, which struck her in the right arm and dangerously wounded her.

A short time afterward, M. de La Fayette announced that the King was going to appear; in fact, the King and the royal family appeared on the balcony. Then the people shouted: "Vive le Roi, vive la Nation, vive le Dauphin!" The deponent and a few other women shouted "Vive la Reine," but women of the common people hit them to make them be quiet. The King and the royal family retired from the balcony. The Queen placed herself at a little window, and while she was there, women of the common people spouted all kinds of insults, which the deponent will not repeat to us here. The people shouted: "Vive le Roi! Le Roi à Paris! Le Roi à Paris!" [The King to Paris!] His Majesty consented to go; more shouts of "Vive le Roi!" were heard. The Queen, accompanied by M. le marquis de La Fayette, appeared on the balcony, and the latter said: "The Queen is distressed at what she sees before her eyes; she has been deceived; she promises that she will be so no longer; she promises to love her people, to be attached to them as Jesus Christ is to His church." As a sign of approval the Queen, tears streaming, raised her hand twice. The King asked for mercy for his Guards, and the people repeated his words. The King's Guards shouted "Vive le Roi! Vive la Nation!" and threw their hats, shoulder belts and, a few, even their money out of the windows. The grenadiers of the National Guard put their caps on the King's Guards' heads and also shouted "Vive le Roi! Vive la Nation!" and at this moment the King declared that at noon he would leave for Paris. . . .

Deposition of Marie-Rose Barré

Marie-Rose Barré, age 20, unmarried, a lace-worker, residing at 61 Rue Meslay; upon oath . . .

Deposes that on October 5 last, at about eight o'clock in the morning, going to take back some work, she was stopped at the Pont Notre Dame by about a hundred women who told her that it was necessary for her to go with them to Versailles to ask for bread there. Not being able to resist this great number of women, she decided to go with them. At the hamlet at the Point-du-Jour, two young men, unknown to her, who were on foot and going their way, told them that they were running a great risk, that there were cannon mounted at the bridge at Saint Cloud. This did not prevent them from continuing on their way. At Sèvres they had some refreshments; then they continued on their way toward Versailles. The two young men of whom she spoke met them near Viroflay and told them that they had escaped at Saint-Cloud but that at Versailles they would be fired on. But they continued on their way. At Versailles they found the King's Guards lined up in three ranks before the palace. A gentleman dressed in the uniform of the King's Guards, who, she was told, was the duc de Guiche, came to ask them what they wanted of the King, recommending peaceful behavior on their part. They answered that they were coming to ask him for bread. This gentleman was absent for a few minutes and then returned to take four of them to introduce them to the King. The deponent was one of the four. Before taking them to the King, he led them to the comte d'Affry, who requested that they be introduced to His Majesty right away, which was done.

They spoke first to M. de Saint-Priest, and then to His Majesty, whom they asked for bread. His Majesty answered them that he was suffering at least as much as they were, to see them lacking it, and that so far as he was able he had taken care to prevent them from experiencing a dearth. Upon the King's response, they begged him to be so good as to arrange escorts for the flour transports intended for the provisioning of Paris, because according to what they had been told at the bridge in Sèvres by the two young men of whom she spoke earlier, only two wagons out of seventy intended for Paris actually arrived there. The King promised them to have the flour escorted and said that if it depended on him, they would have bread then and there. They took leave of His Majesty and were led, by a gentleman in a blue uniform with red piping, into the apartments and courts of the ranks of the Flanders regiment, to which they called out, "Vive Le Roi!" It was then about nine o'clock. After this, they retired into a house on Rue Satory and went to bed in a stable. She does not know the names and addresses of the three women introduced to the King with her. Tired from the trip, having a swollen foot, she did not go Tuesday to the palace or the Place d'Armes, knows nothing, as a witness, of what happened there, and came back to Paris between four and five o'clock in the afternoon of that day in a carriage.

She adds that a fortnight later a gentleman whom she heard called M. de Saint-Paul came to her place and asked her to go to a court commissioner to make a formal declaration of what M. de Saint-Priest told her on Monday, October 5, at Versailles, when she presented herself to speak to the King. As the deponent did not know a court commissioner, Saint-Paul suggested Maître Chenu. The deponent remarks that she was then living on Rue du Four at the corner of Rue des Ciseaux. . . . The commissioner . . . took her declaration . . . in which she sets forth that having heard it said, by the two young men mentioned above, that of seventy wagons of flour intended for Paris only two had arrived, she informed M. de Saint-Priest of this, and he answered that as the grain shortage was equally bad everywhere it was not surprising that the inhabitants of places where flour passed through stopped it for their supply. Besides, the threshing season had not yet arrived, which caused the provisions to be smaller than they should be. . . . She told the commissioner that the minister did not say to her what was being attributed to him by the public: "When you had only one king, you had bread; now that you have twelve hundred of them, go and ask them for it," that in fact she did not hear the minister say this. Which is all that the deponent said she knows . . . and she has signed. . . .

A National Constitution and Public Liberty

22. Declaration of the Rights of Man and of the Citizen

After the dramatic assertion of revolutionary principles on the Night of the Fourth of August, the National Assembly moved quite quickly to the formulation of a declaration of rights that was to serve as a preamble to the new national constitution. The final articles of the declaration were adopted on 26 August 1789.

From *Archives parlementaires de 1787 à 1860, première série (1787 à 1799)*, edited by M. J. Mavidal and M. E. Laurent, 2d ed., 82 vols. (Paris: Dupont, 1879–1913), vol. 9, pp. 236–37. Translated for this volume by the editor, Keith Michael Baker.

The representatives of the French people, constituted as the National Assembly, considering that ignorance, disregard, or contempt for the rights of man are the sole causes of public misfortunes and the corruption of governments, have resolved to set forth, in a solemn declaration, the natural, inalienable, and sacred rights of man, so that the constant presence of this declaration may ceaselessly remind all members of the social body of their rights and duties; so that the acts of the legislative power and those of the executive power may be the more respected, since it will be possible at each moment to compare them against the goal of every political institution; and so that the demands of the citizens, grounded henceforth on simple and incontestable principles, may always be directed to the maintenance of the constitution and to the welfare of all.

Consequently, the National Assembly recognizes and declares, in the presence and under the auspices of the Supreme Being, the following rights of man and the citizen:

Article 1. Men are born and remain free and equal in rights. Social distinctions can be based only on public utility.

Article 2. The aim of every political association is the preservation of the natural and imprescriptible rights of man. These rights are liberty, property, security, and resistance to oppression.

Article 3. The source of all sovereignty resides essentially in the nation. No body, no individual can exercise authority that does not explicitly proceed from it.

Article 4. Liberty consists in being able to do anything that does not injure another; thus the only limits upon each man's exercise of his natural rights are those that guarantee enjoyment of these same rights to the other members of society. These limits can be determined only by law.

Article 5. The law has the right to forbid only actions harmful to society. No action may be prevented that is not forbidden by law, and no one may be constrained to do what the law does not order.

Article 6. The law is the expression of the general will. All citizens have the right to participate personally, or through their representatives, in its formation. It must be the same for all, whether it protects or punishes. All citizens, being equal in its eyes, are equally admissible to all public dignities, positions, and employments, according to their ability, and on the basis of no other distinction than that of their virtues and talents.

Article 7. No man may be accused, arrested, or detained except in cases determined by the law and according to the forms it has prescribed. Those who solicit, expedite, execute, or effect the execution of arbitrary orders must be punished; but every citizen summoned or seized by virtue of the law must obey at once; he makes himself guilty by resistance.

Article 8. The law must lay down only those penalties that are strictly and evidently necessary, and no one may be punished except by virtue of a law established and promulgated prior to the offense, and legally applied.

Article 9. Every man is presumed innocent until he has been found guilty; if it is considered indispensable to arrest him, any severity not necessary to secure his person must be strictly repressed by law.

Article 10. No one must be disturbed because of his opinions, even in religious matters, provided their expression does not trouble the public order established by law.

Article 11. The free expression of thought and opinions is one of the most precious rights of man: thus every citizen may freely speak, write, and print, subject to accountability for abuse of this freedom in the cases determined by law.

Article 12. To guarantee the rights of man and the citizen requires a public force; this force is therefore instituted for the benefit of all, and not for the personal advantage of those to whom it is entrusted.

Article 13. A common tax is indispensable to maintain the public force and support the expenses of administration. It must be shared equally among all the citizens in proportion to their means.

Article 14. All citizens have the right to ascertain, personally or through their representatives, the necessity of the public tax, to consent to it freely, to know how it is spent, and to determine its amount, basis, mode of collection, and duration.

Article 15. Society has the right to demand that every public agent give an account of his administration.

Article 16. A society in which the guarantee of rights is not secured, or the separation of powers not clearly established, has no constitution.

Article 17. Property being an inviolable and sacred right, no one can be deprived of it, unless legally established public necessity obviously demands it, and upon condition of a just and prior indemnity.

23. The Civil Constitution of the Clergy (12 July 1790)

By its decree of 11 August 1789, the National Assembly undertook to abolish tithes and provide other means for the support of divine worship. Such action became all the more necessary after church property was nationalized in December 1789. The radical changes in church organization adopted by the assembly in July 1790—called a "civil constitution

Reprinted with permission of Macmillan Publishing Company from John Hall Stewart, ed., *A Documentary Survey of the French Revolution*, pp. 169, 171–76, 178, 180. © 1951 by Macmillan Publishing Company.

of the clergy" on the grounds that they affected the temporal existence of the French church, not its spiritual life—became one of the most divisive issues of the entire revolutionary period. Clerical opposition to the new ecclesiastical order took on counterrevolutionary dimensions when, at the end of 1790, the National Assembly required all clergy to take an oath accepting the Civil Constitution. A vast majority of the bishops and large numbers of lower clergy refused; their recalcitrance was further re-inforced when in the spring of 1791 Pope Pius VI finally condemned the new French church as heretical and threatened clergy who acquiesced in it with excommunication. Popular support for the nonjuring priests and widespread resentment at the revolutionary intrusion upon traditional practices were to play a fundamental role in the emergence of counter-revolutionary movements, particularly in such areas as the Vendée.

The National Assembly, having heard the report of its Ecclesiastical Committee, has decreed and does decree the following as constitutional articles.

Title I. Of Ecclesiastical Offices

1. Each and every department shall constitute a single diocese, and each and every diocese shall have the same extent and limits as the department. . . .

4. No church or parish of France, and no French citizen, may, under any circumstances or on any pretext whatsoever, acknowledge the authority of an ordinary bishop or archbishop whose see is established under the name of a foreign power, or that of its delegates residing in France or elsewhere; without prejudice, however, to the unity of faith and communion, which shall be maintained with the Visible Head of the Universal Church as here-inafter provided. . . .

15. In all cities and towns of not more than 6,000 inhabitants there shall be only one parish; other parishes shall be suppressed and united with the principal church.

16. In cities of more than 6,000 inhabitants every parish may include a greater number of parishioners, and as many parishes shall be preserved or established as the needs of the people and the localities require. . . .

20. All titles and offices, other than those mentioned in the present constitution, dignities, canonries, prebends, half prebends, chapels, chaplain-cies, in both cathedral and collegiate churches, and all regular and secular chapters of either sex, abbeys and priories, regular or *in commendam,* of either sex, and all other benefices and *prestimonies* in general, of whatever kind and under whatever denomination, are abolished and suppressed dat-

ing from the day of publication of the present decree, and similar ones may never be established. . . .

Title II. Of Appointment to Benefices

1. Dating from the day of publication of the present decree, appointments to bishoprics and cures are to be made by election only.

2. All elections shall be by ballot and by absolute majority of votes.

3. The election of bishops shall take place according to the form prescribed by, and by the electoral body designated in, the decree of 22 December, 1789, for the appointment of members of the departmental assembly. . . .

7. To be eligible for a bishopric, one must have performed for at least fifteen years the duties of ecclesiastical ministry in the diocese, in the capacity of *curé,* officiating minister or vicar, or as superior or directing vicar of the seminary. . . .

16. Not later than a month subsequent to his election, the bishop-elect shall present himself in person to his metropolitan bishop; and if elected to the metropolitan see, to the oldest bishop of the *arrondissement,* with the *procès-verbal* of the election and proclamation, and shall request him to grant canonical confirmation.

17. The metropolitan or the senior bishop shall have the right to examine the bishop-elect, in the presence of his council, concerning his doctrine and morals. If he considers him qualified, he shall give him canonical institution; if he believes it his duty to refuse, the reasons for such refusal shall be given in writing, signed by the metropolitan bishop and his council, reserving to the interested parties the right to appeal by writ of error as provided hereinafter.

18. The bishop from whom confirmation is requested may not exact of the bishop-elect any oath other than profession of the Catholic, Apostolic, and Roman religion.

19. The new bishop may not apply to the Pope for confirmation, but shall write to him as the Visible Head of the Universal Church, in testimony of the unity of faith and communion which he is to maintain therewith. . . .

21. Before the ceremony of consecration begins, the bishop-elect shall take a solemn oath, in the presence of the municipal officials, the people, and the clergy, to watch with care over the faithful of the diocese entrusted to him, to be faithful to the nation, to the law, and to the King, and to maintain with all his power the Constitution decreed by the National Assembly and accepted by the King. . . .

25. The election of *curés* shall be conducted according to the forms pre-

scribed by, and by the electors designated in, the decree of 22 December, 1789, for the election of members of the district administrative assembly. . . .

Title III. Of Salaries of Ministers of Religion

1. Ministers of religion, performing the primary and most important functions of society, and obliged to reside continuously in the place of service to which the confidence of the people has called them, shall be maintained by the nation. . . .

Title IV. Of the Law of Residence

1. The law of residence shall be strictly observed, and all who are invested with an ecclesiastical office or function shall be subject thereto without distinction or exception.

2. No bishop may absent himself from his diocese for more than fifteen consecutive days during any year, except in case of real necessity and with the consent of the directory of the department in which his see is located.

3. Likewise, *curés* and vicars may not absent themselves from the place of their duties beyond the term established above, except for serious reasons; and even in such cases the *curés* shall be required to obtain the consent of both their bishop and their district directory, the vicars that of their *curés*.

24. Viefville des Essars, *On the Emancipation of the Negroes* (1790)

The employment of African slaves as laborers on West Indian plantations was one of the institutions of the Old Regime most universally condemned by enlightened thinkers, whose denunciations led in 1788 to the founding of an abolitionist organization, the Society of the Friends of the Blacks. While its founders included such figures as Condorcet, Lafayette, and Brissot, the society nevertheless lacked the broad base of support enjoyed by antislavery groups created earlier in Britain and the United States, where liberal intellectuals joined force with pietist protestant movements.

When the creation of the National Assembly opened up the possibility for real action against slavery and the slave trade, the abolitionists sud-

From Jean-Louis Viefville des Essars, *Discours et projet de loi pour l'affranchissement des nègres ou l'adoucissement de leur régime, et réponse aux objections des colons* (Paris, n.d.). Translated by Ralph Austen. © 1977 by The University of Chicago.

denly found themselves opposed by such major interests as the colonial
planters of Guadaloupe, Martinique and Saint-Domingue (the largest and
most profitable sugar-growing colony of the late eighteenth century) and
commercial and manufacturing groups from various French ports and in-
land towns. As a result, the only steps taken during the first three years of
the Revolution were towards the granting of political rights to the free
"colored" (mulatto and black) inhabitants of the West Indies—and even
these measures were blocked by the white colonists. By late 1791, the
nonwhite populations of Saint-Domingue—both slave and free—had
taken matters into their own hands by rising up in massive and bloody
revolt.

The revolutionary assemblies thus lost their opportunity to manage
an orderly end to slavery. Armies subsequently dispatched to Saint-
Domingue failed to restore French control of what then became the independent state of Haiti. Although emancipation was declared by the Convention in 1794, this law was abrogated by Napoleon. Slavery did not
come to an effective end in the remainder of France's overseas possessions until 1848.

The following selection forms the conclusion to a pamphlet by a rela-
tively obscure deputy, Jean-Louis Viefville des Essars. His arguments
and cautious program for emancipation are typical of the Society of the
Friends of the Blacks; the objections he addresses are equally typical of
antiabolitionist publications of this period.

OBJECTION: The legislation of emancipation would bring about a general
revolution with disastrous results.

RESPONSE: It is conceivable that such fears might be realized if the
slaves received their liberation all at once; but the self-interest of those ob-
jecting leads them to exaggerate everything and to add anxiety to excess.
The period of sixteen years [in the above-proposed plan] for assuring the
progressive existence of freedmen greatly reduces the danger, or rather
leaves none at all.

OBJECTION: Emancipation would deprive the colonists of their property, which they have acquired and hold under the laws of the state.

RESPONSE: The colonists have no more right to the unjust property of
their fathers than do the nobility to the privileges which they have abandoned, along with so many other rights taken from them as detrimental to
society. The former have not enjoyed these for even two hundred years; the
latter have had them for a thousand.

OBJECTION: In order to carry out such a project, it would be necessary to have a general agreement, a solemn and universal treaty involving
all the maritime powers.

RESPONSE: It would be chimerical to think that such a benevolent union could be brought about; the policies of courts are guided by other principles.

OBJECTION: But, in carrying this out, all the sacrifice would be on the part of France; England would lose infinitely less, since her colonies are in a very different situation than ours, having less need of slaves.

RESPONSE: It is true that the English colonies are at a more advanced stage of their cultivation, and that the French colonies are not near this; except, however, Martinique and Guadaloupe, where there are fewer large landowners and where the holdings, being consequently more divided, are better cultivated. From this a striking truth emerges, that we can profitably increase the number of our slaves, and that the English cannot.

Thus our unimproved lands could be distributed in small lots to emancipated slaves who, with minimal loans, could make the best possible use of them and reimburse the government with no delay at all while enriching themselves.

Thenceforward they would be attached to the soil by right of possession, and there would be no need to fear an insurrection which would deprive them of their well-being. Having become landowners, their population would double; the exchange of imports and exports would follow the same progression to the advantage of the metropolis.

In truth, all of this is a matter of indifference to the colonists, who speak and calculate only for their own interests and do not wish to take into consideration anything which does not suit them.

OBJECTION: The slave who is bought in Africa has been condemned to death or some harsh penalty in his own country; he abandons it without regret. His passage to our colonies, which allows him to avoid punishment, cannot be a misfortune or matter of affliction for him.

RESPONSE: It is ridiculous to attempt to insinuate that the slaves whom we take from the coasts of Africa have all been condemned to death or to harsh penalties. Let us be honest; we incite the desires of these simple men by all sorts of ruses, by an array of objects which we dangle before their eyes, and which seduce their imaginations. Thus we force these unfortunates, who have nothing better to offer us, to wage constant wars against one another so as to have people to sell to us. The slave merchants admit that it is common for them to sell us even their own children when they have no other means of satisfying the passions which we have incited in them, passions of which they would still be innocent if they could have avoided the misfortune of knowing us.

OBJECTION: The products of our own soil do not cost less sweat than those of our colonies. The slave is thus no more unfortunate than are the working people of France. He is even much less so, since his master, having an interest in his preservation, treats him more humanely and gently. The slaves' living quarters are kept in the most exact order, with the most attentive care, the greatest concern for the sick, the disabled, women in childbirth, the aged and infants. The slaves here present an appearance of gaiety and satisfaction; far from dreading their masters, they cherish and respect them.

They have their own landholdings, which they cultivate; and the sale of their produce gives them a surplus which they take to the market in order to procure for themselves and their families luxury clothing, jewelry, and choice foodstuffs. You can see among them a standard of comfort, of luxury, for which you would look in vain among the people of the French provinces. The richest and most beautiful chintzes, the finest fabrics, the most expensive Indian handkerchiefs, hardly suffice for the Negro who is believed to be so miserable. On witnessing the way they give parties, and their highly expressive dances, you would believe yourself to be in the midst of a rich and free population.

RESPONSE: The products of our own soil cost sweat, it is true; but the man who makes it bear fruit is not torn apart by blows, nor is he dragged to the fields like the vilest of animals, with his body all bleeding from the marks of the whip which is ceaselessly used upon him.

Finally, he is free. In the midst of labor forced upon him by misery, his pains are softened by the thought of the objects most dear to his heart, his wife and his children, for whom he wins subsistence in return for those caresses which relieve his exhaustion at the end of the day.

Why, now, cannot the colonists be more consistent? If they confer upon their slaves all the gifts and benefits which they have so charmingly painted for us; if they are always surrounded by the love and the respect of these slaves, do they have anything to fear from restoring the latter to liberty? Only the unfortunate seek vengeance against the authors of their woes. . . . What is missing in these details of generosity and benevolence is the truth. Living quarters administered with this spirit of humanity and comfort are not common. We admit that there are some whose masters are more just and humane, and treat their slaves well. But these are isolated examples; the greatest number are unjust and barbarous. . . .

OBJECTION: The national production, in the form of raw or manufactured goods, which France ships to her colonies or employs in the Negro trade, reaches 70 million livres; and in return she receives 230 millions worth of colonial commodities. Of this she consumes 90 millions; the surplus, reaching 140 millions, is the basis of an immense foreign trade which provides a very advantageous annual balance, increases the stock of cash, and stimulates all branches of French industry. . . . The abolition of the Negro trade would mean the renunciation of our colonies; it would mean their abandonment to the English, who would not miss the opportunity to seize them; it would mean the loss of all the advantages which we draw from them, and those deriving from the employment of a thousand or twelve hundred ships which provide vital links for the activity of the French provinces, and maintain the activity of our navy, and our ports.

RESPONSE: The abolition of the slave trade and the progressive freedom of the blacks as proposed here in no way implies the necessity of renouncing our colonies, or the right of sovereignty itself. Nor does it imply the renunciation of the natural privilege of continuing, to the exclusion of other nations, the provisionment of food and clothing to those children who should never forget the sacrifices and pains they cost their mother country before attaining the strength to provide for their own subsistence, or the rivers of blood which she has shed in order to defend their childhood.

It is rather dangerous to say that the English will take over our possessions. That is a prognosis which it is easier to make than to execute. It will first be necessary for the English to fight us for these colonies, because we certainly have no intention of abandoning them without any defense.

OBJECTION: There will be no more shipping, etc.

RESPONSE: Shipping will change very little. It will stay the same as long as the inhabitants of the colonies are unable to feed themselves and it is necessary for us to use vessels to bring them flour, wine, oil, salt, and clothing. It would be too difficult to exclude us from commerce in our own commodities, which foreign shippers come to us to secure.

OBJECTION: The number of slaves in the French colonies is six or seven thousand and the average price is 3,000 livres each. Their emancipation would require indemnification for the colonists.

RESPONSE: The number of slaves is not in dispute, but the price is rather exaggerated. No doubt it results from the contrivances of interested persons who want to raise fears about the necessity of a reimbursement which, in strict terms, if we assume it would take place, could be reduced by five sixths.

First, all the elderly Negroes, those in poor health, and those born in the colonies, have either paid back more than the price of their initial purchase, or cost nothing.

As for those who would remain to be redeemed, if they were all given their liberty immediately (which no reasonable person has ever proposed) and we assume a full reimbursement, with no deduction for services rendered, here is what the price would be. . . .

From the preceding [calculations] we can conclude that the average price of blacks in all our colonies, assuming that the population of Saint-Domingue alone equals that of all our other possessions, cannot be more than 1,416 livres, 10 sous, in French money. Even this estimate seems rather high, since there is little doubt that the colonists themselves would not buy at such a price.

But according to the proposal which has been presented, there can be no question of reimbursement. In this proposal, the term of service is fixed at twenty years; after that period, the masters are required to feed their slaves without being able to force them to work.

The very last to receive their freedom, even if they arrived within six months of the day of the publication of the decree, will have served sixteen years. Thus, strictly speaking, all that will be due for this numerically small group will be four-twentieths of their value.

Now it is obvious that the interests of the colonists have exaggerated everything.

However this may be, it cannot be disguised that in the situation in which we find ourselves, overwhelmed by the present, anxious about the future, in a state of ferment, of insecurity, of alarming scarcity, the moment is not favorable for emancipating the Negroes and prohibiting the slave trade. Such measures would only increase the disorders and anxieties which already bear only too heavily upon our existence. It would appear infinitely more wise to wait for a period of calm, when matters are put back into motion and order reestablished. In consequence, the question must be postponed.

But during this period of waiting, and with the consoling thought that this happy era is not far off, let us at least take care to ease the fate of these unfortunates, to put them under a wise and gentle control, and to allow them to benefit from all the improvements which are possible within their status.

25. The Le Chapelier Law (14 June 1791)

During the spring of 1791, workers in Paris joined together to organize a series of strikes and to negotiate with their employers. Their actions were denounced in the National Assembly by a member of the committee responsible for drawing up the constitution, Isaac-René-Guy Le Chapelier, who introduced the following decree. In Le Chapelier's eyes, the workers were trying to reassert the guild spirit of the Old Regime, an expression of corporate interest incompatible with revolutionary principles of individual liberty and public good. Testament to the laissez-faire convictions

Reprinted with permission of Macmillan Publishing Company from John Hall Stewart, ed., *A Documentary Survey of the French Revolution*, pp. 165–66. © 1951 by Macmillan Publishing Company.

of the overwhelming majority of the representatives, the Le Chapelier Law also presaged the tensions between the assembly and the people of Paris that were to develop in subsequent months, as popular activism increased and workers' demands for a controlled economy took on greater political force. The law remained in effect in France until 1884.

---

1. Since the abolition of all kinds of corporations of citizens of the same occupation and profession is one of the fundamental bases of the French Constitution, re-establishment thereof under any pretext or form whatsoever is forbidden.

2. Citizens of the same occupation or profession, *entrepreneurs,* those who maintain open shop, workers, and journeymen of any craft whatsoever may not, when they are together, name either president, secretaries, or trustees, keep accounts, pass decrees or resolutions, or draft regulations concerning their alleged common interests.

3. All administrative or municipal bodies are forbidden to receive any address or petition in the name of an occupation or profession, or to make any response thereto; and they are enjoined to declare null whatever resolutions have been made in such manner, and to make certain that no effect or execution be given thereto.

4. If, contrary to the principles of liberty and the Constitution, some citizens associated in the same professions, arts, and crafts hold deliberations or make agreements among themselves tending to refuse by mutual consent or to grant only at a determined price the assistance of their industry or their labor, such deliberations and agreements, whether accompanied by oath or not, are declared unconstitutional, in contempt of liberty and the Declaration of the Rights of Man, and noneffective; administrative and municipal bodies shall be required so to declare them. The authors, leaders, and instigators who have provoked, drafted, or presided over them shall be cited before the police court, at the request of the communal attorney, each condemned to a fine of 500 *livres,* and suspended for a year from the enjoyment of all rights of active citizenship and from admittance to the primary assemblies.

5. All administrative and municipal bodies are forbidden, on penalty of their members' being responsible therefor in their own names, to employ, admit, or allow to be admitted to their professions, in any public works, those *entrepreneurs,* workers, or journeymen who have provoked or signed the said deliberations or conventions, unless, of their own accord, they have presented themselves to the registrar of the police court to retract or disavow them.

6. If the said deliberations or convocations, posted placards, or circular letters contain any threats against *entrepreneurs,* artisans, workers, or for-

eign day laborers working there, or against those who are satisfied with a lower wage, all authors instigators, and signatories of such acts or writings shall be punished with a fine of 1,000 *livres* each and imprisonment for three months.

7. Those who use threats or violence against workers who are utilizing the liberty granted to labor and to industry by the constitutional laws shall be subject to criminal prosecution, and shall be punished according to the rigor of the laws as disturbers of the public peace.

8. All assemblies composed of artisans, workers, journeymen, day laborers, or those incited by them against the free exercise of industry and labor appertaining to every kind of person and under all circumstances arranged by private contract, or against the action of police and the execution of judgments rendered in such connection, as well as against public bids and auctions of divers enterprises, shall be considered as seditious assemblies, and as such shall be dispersed by the depositaries of the public force, upon legal requisitions made thereupon, and shall be punished according to all the rigor of the laws concerning authors, instigators, and leaders of the said assemblies, and all those who have committed assaults and acts of violence.

26. The Constitution of 1791

The constitution upon which the National Assembly began work in the summer of 1789 was finally completed two years later. It defined the organization of the new polity, the status and conditions of citizenship, and the nature and limits of government powers. Many of its provisions summarized comprehensive laws on various matters adopted during this two-year period. The drafting process was virtually finished in June 1791, when Louis XVI attempted to flee Paris (see document 28). The provisions relating to royal abdication were consequently added during the summer of 1791, and the revised document was reluctantly accepted by the king on 13 September. Selections from the Constitution of 1791 are printed below.

The National Assembly, wishing to establish the French Constitution upon the principles it has just recognized and declared, abolishes irrevocably the institutions which were injurious to liberty and equality of rights.

Neither nobility, nor peerage, nor hereditary distinctions, nor distinc-

Reprinted with permission of Macmillan Publishing Company from John Hall Stewart, ed., *A Documentary Survey of the French Revolution*, pp. 231–41, 244–57, 259–61. © 1951 by Macmillan Publishing Company.

tions of orders, nor feudal regime, nor patrimonial courts, nor any titles, denominations, or prerogatives derived therefrom, nor any order of knighthood, nor any corporations or decorations requiring proofs of nobility or implying distinctions of birth, nor any superiority other than that of public functionaries in the performance of their duties any longer exists.

Neither venality nor inheritance of any public office any longer exists.

Neither privilege nor exception to the law common to all Frenchmen any longer exists for any part of the nation or for any individual.

Neither *jurandes* nor corporations of professions, arts, and crafts any longer exist.

The law no longer recognizes religious vows or any other obligation contrary to natural rights or the Constitution.

Title I: Fundamental Provisions Guaranteed by the Constitution

The Constitution guarantees as natural and civil rights:

1st, That all citizens are admissible to offices and employments, without other distinction than virtues and talents;

2nd, That all taxes shall be assessed equally upon all citizens, in proportion to their means;

3rd, That similar offences shall be punished with similar penalties, without any distinction of persons.

The Constitution guarantees likewise as natural and civil rights:

Liberty to every man to come and go without being subject to arrest or detention, except according to the forms determined by the Constitution;

Liberty to every man to speak, write, print, and publish his opinions without having his writings subject to any censorship or inspection before their publication, and to worship as he pleases;

Liberty to citizens to assemble peaceably and without arms in accordance with police regulations;

Liberty to address individually signed petitions to the constituted authorities.

The legislative power may not make any laws which infringe upon or obstruct the exercise of the natural and civil rights recorded in the present title and guaranteed by the Constitution; but, since liberty consists of being able to do only whatever is not injurious to the rights of others or to public security, the law may establish penalties for acts which, assailing either public security or the rights of others, might be injurious to society.

The Constitution guarantees the inviolability of property, or a just and previous indemnity for that of which a legally established public necessity requires the sacrifice.

Property reserved for the expenses of worship and for all services of public benefit belongs to the nation, and is at its disposal at all times.

The Constitution guarantees conveyances which have been or may be made according to the forms established by law.

Citizens have the right to elect or choose the ministers of their religions.

A general establishment for *public relief* shall be created and organized to raise foundlings, relieve the infirm poor, and furnish work for the able-bodied poor who have been unable to procure it for themselves.

Public instruction for all citizens, free of charge in those branches of education which are indispensable to all men, shall be constituted and organized, and the establishments thereof shall be apportioned gradually, in accordance with the division of the kingdom.

National festivals shall be instituted to preserve the memory of the French Revolution, to maintain fraternity among the citizens, and to bind them to the Constitution, the *Patrie,* and the laws.

A code of civil law common to the entire kingdom shall be drafted.

Title II: Of the Division of the Kingdom and of the Status of Citizens

1. The kingdom is one and indivisible; its territory is divided into eighty-three departments, every department into districts, every district into cantons.

2. The following are French citizens: Those born in France of a French father; those who, born in France of a foreign father, have established their residence in the kingdom; those who, born in a foreign country of a French father, have established themselves in France and have taken the civic oath; finally, those who, born in a foreign country and descended in any degree whatsoever from a French man or a French woman expatriated because of religion, come to reside in France and take the civic oath.

3. Those who, born outside the kingdom, of foreign parents, reside in France become French citizens after five years of continuous domicile in the kingdom if, in addition, they have acquired real estate, married a French woman, or founded an agricultural or commercial establishment, and if they have taken the civic oath.

4. The legislative power may, for important reasons, bestow naturalization upon a foreigner, without other qualifications than establishment of a domicile in France and taking of the civic oath therein.

5. The civic oath is: *I swear to be faithful to the nation, to the law, and to the King, and to maintain with all my power the Constitution of the kingdom, decreed by the National Constituent Assembly in the years 1789, 1790, and 1791.*

6. French citizenship is lost: 1st, by naturalization in a foreign country; 2nd, by condemnation to penalties which entail civic degradation, as long as the condemned person is not reinstated; 3rd, by a judgment of contempt of court, as long as the judgment is not rescinded; 4th, by affiliation with

any foreign order of knighthood, or with any foreign corporate body which implies either proofs of nobility or distinctions of birth, or which requires religious vows.

7. The law considers marriage only as a civil contract.

The legislative power shall establish for all inhabitants, without distinction, the method by which births, deaths, and marriages are to be declared, and it shall designate the public officials who are to receive and preserve the records therefor.

8. French citizens, considered with respect to local relations which derive from their association in cities and in certain *arrondissements* of rural territory, constitute the *communes*.

The legislative power may establish the extent of the *arrondissement* of every commune.

9. The citizens composing a commune have the right to elect at stated times, according to the forms determined by law, those among them who, under the title of *municipal officials,* are responsible for administering the immediate affairs of the commune.

Some functions relative to the general interest of the State may be delegated to the municipal officials.

10. The rules which municipal officials are required to follow in the performance of their municipal duties and of those delegated to them for the general welfare shall be established by law.

Title III: Of Public Powers

1. Sovereignty is one, indivisible, inalienable, and imprescriptible. It appertains to the nation; no section of the people nor any individual may assume the exercise thereof.

2. The nation, from which alone all powers emanate, may exercise such powers only by delegation.

The French Constitution is representative; the representatives are the legislative body and the King.

3. The legislative power is delegated to a National Assembly, composed of temporary representatives freely elected by the people, to be exercised by it, with the sanction of the King, in the manner hereinafter determined.

4. The government is monarchical; the executive power is delegated to the King, to be exercised, under his authority, by ministers and other responsible agents in the manner hereinafter determined.

5. The judicial power is delegated to judges who are elected at stated times by the people.

Chapter I: Of the National Legislative Assembly

1. The National Assembly constituting the legislative body is permanent and is composed of only one chamber.

2. It shall be formed every two years by new elections.

Every period of two years shall constitute a legislature.

3. The provisions of the preceding article shall not apply to the next legislative body, the powers of which shall cease on the last day of April, 1793.

4. Renewal of the legislative body shall take place without need of sanction.

5. The legislative body may not be dissolved by the King.

Section 1: Number of Representatives—Bases of Representation

1. The number of representatives in the legislative body is 745, in proportion to the eighty-three departments of which the kingdom is composed, and apart from those which might be granted to the colonies.

2. The representatives shall be allotted among the eighty-three departments according to the three proportions of territory, population, and direct tax.

3. Of the 745 representatives, 247 are allocated on the basis of territory.

Each and every department shall elect three of these, except the department of Paris, which shall elect only one.

4. Two hundred and forty-nine representatives are allocated on the basis of population.

The sum total of the active population of the kingdom is divided into 249 parts, and every department elects as many deputies as it possesses parts of the population.

5. Two hundred and forty-nine representatives are allocated on the basis of direct tax.

The sum total of the direct tax of the kingdom is likewise divided into 249 parts, and every department elects as many deputies as it pays parts of the tax.

Section 2: Primary Assemblies—Selection of the Electors

1. In order to constitute the National Legislative Assembly, the active citizens shall meet every two years in primary assemblies in the cities and cantons.

The primary assemblies shall be formed, without need of sanction, on the second Sunday in March, if they have not been convoked previously by the public functionaries determined by law.

2. In order to be an active citizen it is necessary: to have been born, or to become, a Frenchman; to be fully twenty-five years of age; to be

domiciled in the city or canton for the period determined by law; to pay, in any part of the kingdom whatsoever, a direct tax equal at least to the value of three days' labor, and to present the receipt therefor; not to be in a position of domesticity, that is to say, a servant for wages; to be inscribed upon the roll of the National Guard in the municipality of his domicile; to have taken the civic oath.

3. Every six years the legislative body shall establish the *minimum* and *maximum* of the value of a day's labor, and the departmental administrators shall effect the local determination thereof for every district.

4. No one may exercise the rights of active citizenship in more than one place or by proxy.

5. The following are excluded from the enjoyment of the rights of active citizenship: those who are under indictment; those who, having been proved by authentic evidence to be bankrupt or insolvent, do not produce a general release from their creditors.

6. The primary assemblies shall choose electors in proportion to the number of active citizens domiciled in the city or canton.

One elector shall be chosen for every hundred active citizens, present or not, at the assembly.

Two shall be chosen for from 151 to 250, and so on.

7. No one may be chosen as an elector if, in addition to the qualifications necessary for active citizenship, he does not fulfill the following requirements:

In cities of more than 6,000 inhabitants, that of being proprietor or usufructuary of a property assessed on the tax rolls at a revenue equal to the local value of 200 days' labor, or of being tenant of a dwelling assessed on said same rolls at a revenue equal to the value of 150 days' labor;

In cities of fewer than 6,000 inhabitants, that of being proprietor or usufructuary of a property assessed on the tax rolls at a revenue equal to the local value of 150 days' labor, or of being tenant of a dwelling assessed on said same rolls at a revenue equal to the value of 100 days' labor;

And in rural districts, that of being proprietor or usufructuary of a property assessed on the tax rolls at a revenue equal to the local value of 150 days' labor, or of being farmer or *métayer* of properties assessed on said same rolls at the value of 400 days' labor.

With regard to those who are at the same time proprietors or usufructuaries on the one hand, and tenants, farmers, or *métayers* on the other, their revenues from such divers titles shall be cumulated up to the rate necessary to establish their eligibility.

Section 3: Electoral Assemblies—Election of Representatives

1. The electors chosen in each and every department shall assemble to elect the number of representatives whose election is assigned to their de-

partment, and a number of substitutes equal to one-third of that of the representatives.

The electoral assemblies shall be formed, without need of sanction, the last Sunday in March, if they have not been convoked previously by the public functionaries determined by law.

2. The representatives and the substitutes shall be elected by absolute majority of votes, and they may be chosen only from among the active citizens of the department.

3. All active citizens, whatever their position, profession, or tax, may be elected representatives of the nation.

4. Ministers and other agents of the executive power who are revocable at will, commissioners of the National Treasury, collectors and receivers of direct taxes, supervisors of the collection and administration of indirect taxes and national domains, and those who, under any denomination whatsoever, are connected with the military and civil household of the King shall be obliged to choose between their offices and that of representative.

Administrators, subadministrators, municipal officials, and commandants of the National Guards likewise shall be required to make their choice.

5. The performance of judicial duties is incompatible with those of representative of the nation, throughout the entire duration of the legislature.

Judges shall be replaced by their substitutes, and the King shall provide, by warrants of commission, for the replacement of his Commissioners at the courts.

6. The members of the legislative body may be re-elected to the following legislature, but thenceforth they may be elected only after an interval of one legislature.

7. The representatives elected in the departments shall not be representatives of a particular department, but of the entire nation, and no mandate may be given them. . . .

Chapter II: Of Monarchy, the Regency, and the Ministers

Section 1: Monarchy and the King

1. Monarchy is indivisible, and is delegated hereditarily to the reigning family, from male to male, by order of primogeniture, to the perpetual exclusion of women and their descendants.

(Nothing is presumed concerning the effect of renunciations in the present reigning family.)

2. The person of the King is inviolable and sacred; his only title is *King of the French*.

3. There is no authority in France superior to that of the law; the King reigns only thereby, and only in the name of the law may he exact obedience.

4. On his accession to the throne, or as soon as he has attained his ma-

jority, the King, in the presence of the legislative body, shall take oath to the nation *to be faithful to the nation and to the law, to employ all the power delegated to him to maintain the Constitution decreed by the National Constituent Assembly in the years 1789, 1790, and 1791, and to have the laws executed.*

If the legislative body be not in session, the King shall have a proclamation published, in which said oath, and the promise to reiterate it as soon as the legislative body has assembled, shall be set forth.

5. If, one month after the invitation of the legislative body, the King has not taken said oath, or if, after having taken it, he retracts it, he shall be deemed to have abdicated the throne.

6. If the King places himself at the head of an army and directs the forces thereof against the nation, or if he does not, by a formal statement, oppose any such undertaking carried on in his name, he shall be deemed to have abdicated the throne.

7. If the King, having left the kingdom, does not return after invitation has been made by the legislative body, and within the period established by proclamation, which may not be less than two months, he shall be deemed to have abdicated the throne.

The period shall date from the day of publication of the proclamation of the legislative body in the place of its sessions; and the ministers shall be required, on their responsibility, to perform all acts of the executive power, exercise of which by the absent King shall be suspended.

8. After express or legal abdication, the King shall be classed as a citizen, and as such he may be accused and tried for acts subsequent to his abdication. . . .

10. The nation provides for the splendor of the throne by a civil list, the sum of which shall be determined by the legislative body at each change of reign, for the entire duration of the reign. . . .

12. Apart from the guard of honor furnished him by the citizen National Guard of the place of his residence, the King shall have a guard, paid out of the funds of the civil list; it may not exceed the number of 1,200 infantry and 600 cavalry.

The grades and rules of promotion therein shall be the same as in the troops of the line; but those who compose the King's guard shall progress through all grades among themselves exclusively, and may obtain none in the army of the line.

The King may choose the men of his guard only from among those who are at present on active service in the troops of the line, or from among citizens who have served for a year as National guards, provided they are resident in the kingdom and have previously taken the civic oath.

The King's guard may not be ordered or requisitioned for any other public service. . . .

Section 4: The Ministers

1. The choice and dismissal of ministers appertains solely to the King.

2. The members of the present National Assembly and of subsequent legislatures . . . may not be promoted to the ministry or receive any positions, gifts, pensions, stipends, or commissions from the executive power or its agents throughout the duration of their functions, or for two years after having ceased the performance thereof. . . .

4. No order of the King may be executed unless it has been signed by him and countersigned by the minister or administrator of the department [of government].

5. The ministers are responsible for all offences committed by them against national security and the Constitution; for every attack upon property and individual liberty; for all dissipation of revenues reserved for the expenses of their department.

6. In no case may an order of the King, verbal or written, exempt a minister from his responsibility.

7. Ministers are required to present to the legislative body annually, at the opening of the session, an estimate of the expenditures that are to be made in their department, to render account of the use of the sums intended therefor, and to indicate whatever abuses have appeared in the several branches of the government.

8. No minister, in office or out of office, may be prosecuted criminally because of his administration, without a decree of the legislative body.

Chapter III: Of the Exercise of the Legislative Power

Section 1: Powers and Functions of the National Legislative Assembly

1. The Constitution delegates to the legislative body exclusively the following powers and functions:

1st, Proposal and enactment of laws; the King may only invite the legislative body to take a matter under consideration;

2nd, Establishment of public expenditures;

3rd, Establishment of public taxes, and determination of the nature, quota, duration, and method of collection thereof;

4th, Assessment of the direct tax among the departments of the kingdom, supervision of the use of all public revenues, and having account rendered thereof;

5th, Ordering the creation or suppression of public offices;

6th, Determination of the title, weight, stamp, and denomination of monies;

7th, Permission or prohibition of the introduction of foreign troops upon French territory and of foreign naval forces into the ports of the kingdom;

8th, Legislation annually, upon the proposal of the King, concerning the number of men and vessels of which the land and naval forces are to be composed, the pay and number of persons of every rank, the rules for admission and promotion, the forms of enrollment and discharge, the formation of ship crews, the admission of foreign troops or naval forces into the service of France, and the stipend of troops in case of demobilization;

9th, Legislation concerning the administration and ordering the alienation of the national domains;

10th, Prosecution, before the National High Court, of the responsibility of ministers and of the principal agents of the executive power;

Accusation and prosecution, before said same court, of those charged with attacks upon and conspiracy against the general security of the State or against the Constitution;

11th, Establishment of laws according to which purely personal tokens of honor or decorations shall be granted to those rendering services to the State;

12th, The legislative body alone has the right to award public honors to the memory of great men.

2. War may be declared only by a decree of the legislative body, rendered upon the formal and requisite proposal of the King, and sanctioned by him.

In case of imminent or actual hostilities, or of an ally to be supported or a right to be maintained by force of arms, the King shall immediately notify the legislative body thereof and shall make known the causes therefor. If the legislative body is in recess, the King shall convoke it immediately.

If the legislative body decides that war is not to be made, the King shall take measures immediately to effect the cessation or prevention of hostilities, the ministers remaining responsible for delays.

If the legislative body finds that the hostilities commenced are a culpable aggression on the part of the ministers, or of any other agent of the executive power, the perpetrator of the aggression shall be prosecuted criminally.

Throughout the entire course of the war the legislative body may request the King to negotiate peace; and the King is required to comply with such request.

As soon as the war has ended, the legislative body shall establish the period within which the troops raised in excess of the peace footing shall be demobilized and the army reduced to its ordinary footing.

3. Ratification of treaties of peace, alliance, and commerce appertains to the legislative body; and no treaty shall be effective without such ratification.

4. The legislative body has the right to determine the place of its sessions, to continue them as long as it deems necessary, and to adjourn itself. If it is not assembled at the beginning of every reign, it shall be required to convene without delay.

It has the right of police in the place of its sessions and over the external precincts determined by it.

It has the right of discipline over its members; but it may not pronounce punishment more severe than censure, arrest for a week, or imprisonment for three days.

It has the right, for its security and for the maintenance of the respect due it, to dispose of the forces which, with its consent, are established in the city where it holds its sessions.

5. The executive power may not have any body of troops of the line pass or sojourn within a distance of 30,000 *toises* of the legislative body, except upon its requisition or with its authorization. . . .

Section 3: Royal Sanction

1. The decrees of the legislative body are presented to the King, who may refuse his consent thereto.

2. In case the King refuses his consent, such refusal shall be only suspensive.

When the two legislatures following the one in which the decree was introduced have again successively presented the same decree in the same terms, the King shall be deemed to have given his sanction.

3. The consent of the King to every decree is expressed by the following formula, signed by the King: *The King consents and will have executed.*

The suspensive refusal is expressed thus: *The King will examine.*

4. The King is required to express his consent to, or refusal of, every decree within two months of its presentation.

5. No decree to which the King has refused his consent may be presented to him again by the same legislature.

6. Decrees sanctioned by the King and those presented by three consecutive legislatures shall have the force of *law* and shall bear the name and title of *laws*.

7. Nevertheless, the following shall be executed as laws without being subject to sanction: acts of the legislative body concerning its constitution in deliberative assembly; its internal police, and that which it may exercise in the external precincts it has determined; verification of the powers of its members present; injunctions to absent members; convocation of tardy primary assemblies; exercise of constitutional police over administrators and municipal officials; questions of eligibility or of the validity of elections.

Likewise, neither acts relative to the responsibility of ministers nor decrees showing that there is cause for accusation are subject to sanction.

8. Decrees of the legislative body concerning the establishment, prorogation, and collection of the public taxes shall bear the name and the title of *laws*. They shall be promulgated and executed without being subject to sanction, except for provisions establishing penalties other than fines and pecuniary restraints. . . .

Section 4: Relations of the Legislative Body with the King
1. When the legislative body is definitively constituted, it shall send a deputation to the King to inform him of such fact. Every year the King may open the session and propose the matters which he believes ought to be taken under consideration during the course thereof; nevertheless, such formality need not be considered necessary for the functioning of the legislative body. . . .

10. The ministers of the King shall have *entrée* to the National Legislative Assembly; they shall have a designated place therein.

They shall be heard, whenever they request it, concerning matters relative to their administration, or when they are required to give elucidations.

Likewise, they shall be heard on matters not related to their administration when the National Assembly grants them permission to speak.

Chapter IV: Of the Exercise of the Executive Power

1. The supreme executive power resides exclusively in the hands of the King.

The King is the supreme head of the general administration of the kingdom; the task of supervising the maintenance of public order and tranquillity is entrusted to him.

The King is the supreme head of the army and navy.

The task of watching over the external security of the kingdom and of maintaining its rights and possessions is delegated to the King. . . .

Section 3: Foreign Relations

1. The King alone may maintain political relations abroad, conduct negotiations, make preparations for war in proportion to those of neighboring states, allocate land and sea forces as he deems advisable, and regulate the direction thereof in case of war.

2. Every declaration of war shall be made in these terms: *On the part of the King of the French, in the name of the Nation.*

3. Conclusion and signature, with all foreign powers, of all treaties of peace, alliance, and commerce, and other conventions that he deems necessary for the welfare of the State appertain to the King, subject to ratification by the legislative body.

Chapter V: Of the Judicial Power

1. Under no circumstances may the judicial power be employed by the legislative body or the King.

2. Justice shall be rendered gratuitously by judges elected at stated times by the people and instituted by letters patent of the King, who may not refuse them.

They may not be removed except for duly determined forfeiture, or suspended except by acknowledged indictment.

The public prosecutor shall be chosen by the people.

3. The courts may not interfere with the exercise of the legislative power, suspend the execution of laws, encroach upon administrative functions, or summon administrators before them for reasons connected with their duties.

4. No commission or other attributions and evocations than those determined by law may deprive citizens of the judges legally assigned to them.

5. The right of citizens to terminate their disputes definitively by means of arbitration may not be impaired by acts of the legislative power. . . .

Title V: Of Public Taxes

1. Public taxes shall be deliberated upon and established annually by the legislative body, and unless expressly renewed, they may be effective only until the last day of the following session.

2. Under no pretext may the funds necessary for the payment of the national debt and the civil list be refused or suspended.

The stipend of ministers of the Catholic religion, pensioned, maintained in office, elected, or appointed by virtue of decrees of the National Constituent Assembly, constitutes part of the national debt.

Under no circumstances may the legislative body charge the nation with the payment of the debts of any individual.

3. Detailed accounts of the expenditure of ministerial departments, signed and certified by the ministers or general managers, shall be rendered public by being printed at the beginning of the sessions of every legislature.

The same shall apply to statements of receipts from divers taxes and from all public revenues. . . .

Title VI: Of the Relations of the French Nation with Foreign Nations

The French nation renounces the undertaking of any war with a view of making conquests, and it will never use its forces against the liberty of any people. . . .

27. Gouges, *Declaration of the Rights of Woman* (1791)

Feminist demands, though they had roots in the Enlightenment and found vociferous expression in the early years of the Revolution, received little

From *Women in Revolutionary Paris, 1789–1795*, edited by Darline Gay Levy, Harriet Bronson Applewhite and Mary Durham Johnson (Champaign, Illinois: University of Illinois Press, 1979), pp. 89–96. © 1979 by the Board of Trustees of the University of Illinois.

attention from the Constituent Assembly. The constitution was drawn up without any serious consideration of the possibility of women's suffrage, and it gave no attention to such issues as legal equality within marriage, the right to divorce, and women's rights to property. Although subsequent revolutionary legislation was to strengthen the inheritance and property rights of women, confer greater equality within marriage, and give them parity under the divorce law, these gains were largely eliminated by the Napoleonic Code.

The following manifesto, with its claim for the rights of women, appeared shortly after the adoption of the Constitution of 1791. Its author, Marie-Olympe de Gouges (1748–93), was one of the most prominent feminist writers of the revolutionary period. Imprisoned for her Girondin sympathies in July 1793, she was executed in November of that year. At about the same time, as part of their effort to control the popular movement that had brought them to power, the Jacobins proceeded to suppress political activism among women by prohibiting revolutionary women's clubs.

The Rights of Woman

Man, are you capable of being just? It is a woman who poses the question; you will not deprive her of that right at least. Tell me, what gives you sovereign empire to oppress my sex? Your strength? Your talents? Observe the Creator in his wisdom; survey in all her grandeur that nature with whom you seem to want to be in harmony, and give me, if you dare, an example of this tyrannical empire. Go back to animals, consult the elements, study plants, finally glance at all the modifications of organic matter, and surrender to the evidence when I offer you the means; search, probe, and distinguish, if you can, the sexes in the administration of nature. Everywhere you will find them mingled; everywhere they cooperate in harmonious togetherness in this immortal masterpiece.

Man alone has raised his exceptional circumstances to a principle. Bizarre, blind, bloated with science and degenerated—in a century of enlightenment and wisdom—into the crassest ignorance, he wants to command as a despot a sex which is in full possession of its intellectual faculties; he pretends to enjoy the Revolution and to claim his rights to equality in order to say nothing more about it.

Declaration of the Rights of Woman and the Female Citizen

For the National Assembly to decree in its last sessions, or in those of the next legislature:

Preamble. Mothers, daughters, sisters [and] representatives of the nation demand to be constituted into a national assembly. Believing that ignorance, omission, or scorn for the rights of woman are the only causes of public misfortunes and of the corruption of governments, [the women] have resolved to set forth in a solemn declaration the natural, inalienable, and sacred rights of woman in order that this declaration, constantly exposed before all the members of the society, will ceaselessly remind them of their rights and duties; in order that the authoritative acts of women and the authoritative acts of men may be at any moment compared with and respectful of the purpose of all political institutions; and in order that citizens' demands, henceforth based on simple and incontestable principles, will always support the constitution, good morals, and the happiness of all.

Consequently, the sex that is as superior in beauty as it is in courage during the sufferings of maternity recognizes and declares in the presence and under the auspices of the Supreme Being, the following Rights of Woman and of Female Citizens.

Article 1. Woman is born free and lives equal to man in her rights. Social distinctions can be based only on the common utility.

Article 2. The purpose of any political association is the conservation of the natural and imprescriptible rights of woman and man; these rights are liberty, property, security, and especially resistance to oppression.

Article 3. The principle of all sovereignty rests essentially with the nation, which is nothing but the union of woman and man; no body and no individual can exercise any authority which does not come expressly from it [the nation].

Article 4. Liberty and justice consist of restoring all that belongs to others; thus, the only limits on the exercise of the natural rights of woman are perpetual male tyranny; these limits are to be reformed by the laws of nature and reason.

Article 5. Laws of nature and reason proscribe all acts harmful to society; everything which is not prohibited by these wise and divine laws cannot be prevented, and no one can be constrained to do what they do not command.

Article 6. The law must be the expression of the general will; all female and male citizens must contribute either personally or through their representatives to its formation; it must be the same for all: male and female citizens, being equal in the eyes of the law, must be equally admitted to all honors, positions, and public employment according to their capacity and without other distinctions besides those of their virtues and talents.

Article 7. No woman is an exception; she is accused, arrested, and detained in cases determined by law. Women, like men, obey this rigorous law.

Article 8. The law must establish only those penalties that are strictly and obviously necessary, and no one can be punished except by virtue of a law established and promulgated prior to the crime and legally applicable to women.

Article 9. Once any woman is declared guilty, complete rigor is [to be] exercised by the law.

Article 10. No one is to be disquieted for his very basic opinions; woman has the right to mount the scaffold; she must equally have the right to mount the rostrum, provided that her demonstrations do not disturb the legally established public order.

Article 11. The free communication of thoughts and opinions is one of the most precious rights of woman, since that liberty assures the recognition of children by their fathers. Any female citizen thus may say freely, I am the mother of a child which belongs to you, without being forced by a barbarous prejudice to hide the truth; [an exception may be made] to respond to the abuse of this liberty in cases determined by the law.

Article 12. The guarantee of the rights of woman and the female citizen implies a major benefit; this guarantee must be instituted for the advantage of all, and not for the particular benefit of those to whom it is entrusted.

Article 13. For the support of the public force and the expenses of administration, the contributions of woman and man are equal; she shares all the duties [*corvées*] and all the painful tasks; therefore, she must have the same share in the distribution of positions, employment, offices, honors, and jobs [*industrie*].

Article 14. Female and male citizens have the right to verify, either by themselves or through their representatives, the necessity of the public contribution. This can only apply to women if they are granted an equal share, not only of wealth, but also of public administration, and in the determination of the proportion, the base, the collection, and the duration of the tax.

Article 15. The collectivity of women, joined for tax purposes to the aggregate of men, has the right to demand an accounting of his administration from any public agent.

Article 16. No society has a constitution without the guarantee of rights and the separation of powers; the constitution is null if the majority of individuals comprising the nation have not cooperated in drafting it.

Article 17. Property belongs to both sexes whether united or separate; for each it is an inviolable and sacred right; no one can be deprived of it, since it is the true patrimony of nature, unless the legally determined public need obviously dictates it, and then only with a just and prior indemnity.

Postscript. Woman, wake up; the tocsin of reason is being heard throughout the whole universe; discover your rights. The powerful empire of nature is no longer surrounded by prejudice, fanaticism, superstition, and lies. The flame of truth has dispersed all the clouds of folly and usurpation. Enslaved man has multiplied his strength and needs recourse to yours to break his chains. Having become free, he has become unjust to his companion. Oh, women, women! When will you cease to be blind? What advantage have you received from the Revolution? A more pronounced scorn, a more marked disdain. In the centuries of corruption you ruled only over the weakness of men. The reclamation of your patrimony, based on the wise decrees of nature—what have you to dread from such a fine undertaking? The *bon mot* of the legislator of the marriage of Cana? Do you fear that our French legislators, correctors of that morality, long ensnared by political practices now out of date, will only say again to you: women, what is there in common between you and us? Everything, you will have to answer. If they persist in their weakness in putting this non sequitur in contradiction to their principles, courageously oppose the force of reason to the empty pretentions of superiority; unite yourselves beneath the standards of philosophy; deploy all the energy of your character, and you will soon see these haughty men, not groveling at your feet as servile adorers, but proud to share with you the treasures of the Supreme Being. Regardless of what barriers confront you, it is in your power to free yourselves; you have only to want to. Let us pass now to the shocking tableau of what you have been in society; and since national education is in question at this moment, let us see whether our wise legislators will think judiciously about the education of women.

Women have done more harm than good. Constraint and dissimulation have been their lot. What force had robbed them of, ruse returned to them; they had recourse to all the resources of their charms, and the most irreproachable person did not resist them. Poison and the sword were both subject to them; they commanded in crime as in fortune. The French government, especially, depended throughout the centuries on the nocturnal administration of women; the cabinet kept no secret from their indiscretion; ambassadorial post, command, ministry, presidency, pontificate, college of cardinals; finally, anything which characterizes the folly of men, profane and sacred, all have been subject to the cupidity and ambition of this sex, formerly contemptible and respected, and since the revolution, respectable and scorned.

In this sort of contradictory situation, what remarks could I not make! I have but a moment to make them, but this moment will fix the attention of the remotest posterity. Under the Old Regime, all was vicious, all was guilty; but could not the amelioration of conditions be perceived even in the substance of vices? A woman only had to be beautiful or amiable; when she possessed these two advantages, she saw a hundred fortunes at her feet. If she did not profit from them, she had a bizarre character or a rare philosophy which made her scorn wealth; then she was deemed to be like a crazy woman; the most indecent made herself respected with gold; commerce in women was a kind of industry in the first class [of society], which, henceforth, will have no more credit. If it still had it, the revolution would be lost, and under the new relationships we would always be corrupted; however, reason can always be deceived [into believing] that any other road to fortune is closed to the woman whom a man buys, like the slave on the African coasts. The difference is great; that is known. The slave is commanded by the master; but if the master gives her liberty without recompense, and at an age when the slave has lost all her charms, what will become of this unfortunate woman? The victim of scorn, even the doors of charity are closed to her; she is poor and old, they say; why did she not know how to make her fortune? Reason finds other examples that are even more touching. A young, inexperienced woman, seduced by a man whom she loves, will abandon her parents to follow him; the ingrate will leave her after a few years, and the older she has become with him, the more inhuman is his inconstancy; if she has children, he will likewise abandon them. If he is rich, he will consider himself excused from sharing his fortune with his noble victims. If some involvement binds him to his duties, he will deny them, trusting that the laws will support him. If he is married, any other obligation loses its rights. Then what laws remain to extirpate vice all the way to its root? The law of dividing wealth and public administration between men and women. It can easily be seen that one who is born into a rich family gains very much from such equal sharing. But the one born into a poor family with merit and virtue—what is her lot? Poverty and opprobrium. If she does not precisely excel in music or painting, she cannot be admitted to any public function when she has all the capacity for it. I do not want to give only a sketch of things; I will go more deeply into this in the new edition of all my political writings, with notes, which I propose to give to the public in a few days.

I take up my text again on the subject of morals. Marriage is the tomb of trust and love. The married woman can with impunity give bastards to her husband, and also give them the wealth which does not belong to them. The woman who is unmarried has only one feeble right; ancient and inhuman laws refuse to her for her children the right to the name and the wealth of their father; no new laws have been made in this matter. If it is considered a paradox and an impossibility on my part to try to give my sex an honorable and just consistency, I leave it to men to attain glory for dealing with this matter; but while we wait, the way can be prepared through national education, the restoration of morals, and conjugal conventions.

Form for a Social Contract between Man and Woman

We, _____ and _____, moved by our own will, unite ourselves for the duration of our lives, and for the duration of our mutual inclinations, under the following conditions: We intend and wish to make our wealth communal, meanwhile reserving to ourselves the right to divide it in favor of our children and of those toward whom we might have a particular inclination, mutually recognizing that our property belongs directly to our children, from whatever bed they come, and that all of them without distinction have the right to bear the name of the fathers and mothers who have acknowledged them, and we are charged to subscribe to the law which punishes the renunciation of one's own blood. We likewise obligate ourselves, in case of separation, to divide our wealth and to set aside in advance the portion the law indicates for our children, and in the event of a perfect union, the one who dies will divest himself of half his property in his children's favor, and if one dies childless, the survivor will inherit by right, unless the dying person has disposed of half the common property in favor of one whom he judged deserving.

That is approximately the formula for the marriage act I propose for execution. Upon reading this strange document, I see rising up against me the hypocrites, the prudes, the clergy, and the whole infernal sequence. But how it [my proposal] offers to the wise the moral means of achieving the perfection of a happy government! I am going to give in a few words the physical proof of it. The rich, childless Epicurean finds it very good to go to his poor neighbor to augment his family. When there is a law authorizing a poor man's wife to have a rich one adopt their children, the bonds of society will be strengthened and morals will be purer. This law will perhaps save the community's wealth and hold back the disorder which drives so many victims to the almshouses of shame, to a low station, and into degenerate human principles where nature has groaned for so long. May the detractors of wise philosophy then cease to cry out against primitive morals, or may they lose their point in the source of their citations.

Moreover, I would like a law which would assist widows and young girls deceived by the false promises of a man to whom they were attached; I would like, I say, this law to force an inconstant man to hold to his obligations or at least [to pay] an indemnity equal to his wealth. Again, I would like this law to be rigorous against women, at least those who have the effrontery to have recourse to a law which they themselves had violated by their misconduct, if proof of that were given. At the same time, as I showed in *Le Bonheur primitif de l'homme,* in 1788, prostitutes should be placed in designated quarters. It is not prostitutes who contribute the most to the depravity of morals, it is the women of society. In regenerating the latter, the former are changed. This link of fraternal union will first bring disorder, but in consequence it will produce at the end a perfect harmony.

I offer a foolproof way to elevate the soul of women; it is to join them to all the activities of man; if man persists in finding this way impractical, let him share his fortune with woman, not at his caprice, but by the wisdom of laws. Prejudice falls, morals are purified, and nature regains all her rights. Add to this the marriage of priests and the strengthening of the king on his throne, and the French government cannot fail.

It would be very necessary to say a few words on the troubles which are said to be caused by the decree in favor of colored men in our islands. There is where nature shudders with horror; there is where reason and humanity have still not touched callous souls; there, especially, is where division and discord stir up their inhabitants. It is not difficult to divine the instigators of these incendiary fermentations; they are even in the midst of the National Assembly; they ignite the fire in Europe which must inflame America. Colonists make a claim to reign as despots over the men whose fathers and brothers they are; and, disowning the rights of nature, they trace the source of [their rule] to the scantiest tint of their blood. These inhuman colonists say: our blood flows in their veins, but we will shed it all if necessary to glut our greed or our blind ambition. It is in these places nearest to nature where the father scorns the son; deaf to the cries of blood, they stifle all its attraction; what can be hoped from the resistance opposed to them? To constrain [blood] violently is to render it terrible; to leave [blood] still enchained is to direct all calamities towards America. A divine hand seems to spread liberty abroad throughout the realms of man; only the law has the right to curb this liberty if it degenerates into licence, but it must be equal for all; liberty must hold the National Assembly to its decree dictated by prudence and justice. May it act the same way for the state of France and render her as attentive to new abuses as she was to the ancient ones which each day become more dreadful. My opinion would be to reconcile the executive and legislative power, for it seems to me that the one is everything and the other is nothing—whence comes, unfortunately perhaps, the loss of the French Empire. I think that these two powers, like man and woman, should be united but equal in force and virtue to make a good household. . . .

3
Revolutionary Politics

The King's Flight and Popular Politics

28. The King's Declaration on Leaving Paris (20 June 1791)

As political divisions deepened in France, the idea that the king should escape from Paris, repudiate revolutionary excesses, and appeal to the crowned heads of Europe for support, became increasingly attractive to those who favored the reassertion of royal authority. On the night of 20–21 June 1791, in a plan concerted with general Bouillé, the army commander in eastern France, Louis XVI secretly left Paris and headed toward the frontier. He was apprehended at Varennes, not far from the border with the Austrian Netherlands, and forced to return to Paris. General Bouillé immediately emigrated, the first of a series of military commanders to abandon the Revolution in dramatic circumstances.

Louis left behind him a personal declaration summarizing his grievances against the Revolution and denouncing the provisions of the impending constitution as destroying all but the shadow of royal power. He also particularly condemned the new political activism represented by the Jacobin clubs.

From John Hardman, *The French Revolution: The Fall of the Ancien Regime to the Thermidorian Reaction 1785–1795*, pp. 124–25, 132–34. © 1982 by John Hardman. Reprinted by permission of St. Martin's Press, Inc., and of Edward Arnold (Publishers) Ltd., where it appeared originally in the series Documents of Modern History, under the general editorship of A. G. Dickens.

As long as the King could hope to see order and prosperity restored to the kingdom by the measures employed by the Assembly and by his residence near that Assembly in the capital, he counted as naught any personal sacrifices. Had this hope been fulfilled, he would not even have argued the nullity attaching to all his proceedings since the month of October 1789 on account of his total lack of freedom. But now, considering that the sole recompense for so many sacrifices is to behold the destruction of the monarchy, authority flouted, the sanctity of property violated, the safety of the citizen everywhere endangered, crime go unpunished, and total anarchy trample on the laws without the semblance of authority given him by the new constitution being sufficient to cure any of the ills afflicting the kingdom, the King, having solemnly protested against all acts emanating from him during his captivity, believes it right to lay before the eyes of Frenchmen and of the whole world the record of his conduct and that of the form of government which has been introduced into the kingdom. . . .

[Louis then summarizes the sacrifices he has been obliged to accept since 1789 and denounces the proposed constitution as weakening executive power to the point that effective government will be impossible.]

This form of government, so vicious in itself, has become even more so for the following reasons:

(1) The Assembly, by means of its committees, constantly oversteps the limits which it has itself prescribed. It meddles with matters relating exclusively to the internal administration of the kingdom and to the administration of justice and thus combines all the powers. . . .

(2) In nearly all the cities and even in several country towns and villages associations have been founded with the name of *Société des amis de la Constitution:*[1] in defiance of the laws, they do not permit the existence of any other clubs that are not affiliated to themselves, thus forming an immense corporation more dangerous than any of those which existed previously. Without authorization, nay in contempt of all the laws, they deliberate on all aspects of government, correspond with each other on all subjects, make and receive denunciations, and post up their resolutions. They have assumed such a preponderance that all the administrative and judicial bodies, without excepting the National Assembly itself, nearly always obey their orders.

The King does not think it would be possible to govern so large and important a kingdom as France by the means established by the National Assembly such as they exist at present. His Majesty, in giving his assent,

1. "Societies of Friends of the Constitution" was the formal title of the network of societies usually kown as the Jacobin clubs, so-called because the Parisian society met in the former cloister of the Jacobin order.

which he knew well he could not refuse, to all decrees without distinction was motivated by the desire to avoid all discussion which experience had taught him to be pointless to say the least. In addition he feared lest people think that he wanted to delay or abort the work of the National Assembly, in the success of which the nation took so lively an interest. He placed his confidence in the wise men of that Assembly who would recognize that it is easier to destroy a form of government than to reconstruct one on totally different principles. They had several times recognized the necessity, when speaking about the intended revision of the decrees, of imparting that force of action and coercion which every government needs. They also recognized the need to give this government and the laws which ought to assure everyone's prosperity and place in society enough consideration to induce all those citizens to return to the kingdom who had been compelled to expatriate themselves, out of discontent in some cases and in the majority fear for life and property.

However, the nearer the Assembly approached to the end of its labours, the more the wise men were seen to lose their influence together with a daily increase of clauses which could only make government difficult, even impossible and inspire distrust and contempt for it: the other regulations instead of shedding a salutary balm on the wounds that were still bleeding in several provinces, only increased anxiety and soured discontent. The mentality of the clubs dominated and pervaded everything: the thousands of calumnious and incendiary papers and pamphlets which circulated every day merely echoed the clubs and pushed the public in the direction they wanted to lead it. The National Assembly never dared check this licence, far removed from true liberty; it has lost its influence and even the force it would have needed to retrace its steps and change what it thought should be corrected. It can be seen from the dominant mentality in the clubs and the way in which they are seizing control of the new primary assemblies what can be expected of them and if one can detect any disposition on their part to go back on anything, it is in order to destroy the remains of the monarchy and set up a metaphysical and doctrinaire form of government which would not work.

Frenchmen, is that what you wanted when you sent your representatives to the National Assembly? Did you want anarchy and the despotism of the clubs to replace the monarchical form of government under which the nation has prospered for fourteen hundred years? Did you want to see your king heaped with insults and deprived of his liberty whilst he was exclusively occupied with establishing yours? . . .

29. The Champ de Mars Massacre (17 July 1791)

The king's distrust of the new political activism was shared by many members of the National Assembly, which in the spring of 1791 became the target of growing popular protests against the restrictions on political participation proposed for the new constitution. On 10 May, the assembly had passed a decree banning the collective petitions that were the chief political instrument of the clubs. The threat of disorder its leaders associated with popular politics was a principal reason for their unwillingness to risk any action that might lead to the formal deposition of Louis XVI after his flight to Varennes. Although the royal exercise of executive powers was suspended on 21 June, the assembly voted on 16 July that the king's suspension would continue until the monarch had accepted the new constitution—in effect an announcement that it would be only temporary.

Immediately after the king's flight was known, however, republican sentiments had burst forth from the more radical popular societies, such as the Cordeliers Club, to which women and passive citizens were admitted as well as active citizens. Late in the evening of 15 July an excited crowd of these popular activists appeared at the end of a meeting of the more influential (and restricted) Jacobin Club, which had so far been unable to agree on any course of action regarding the king. At the crowd's urging, a committee was appointed to draw up a petition demanding the king's deposition. Presented to the society the following morning, this petition was immediately repudiated by many of the more conservative Jacobins, who seceded and formed a new club, the Feuillants.

On the afternoon of 16 July, the Jacobin petition was brought for signature to the great parade ground of the Champ de Mars, where a patriotic altar had been erected to celebrate the anniversary of the fall of the Bastille. There, republicans among the demonstrators raised objections to it and demanded that it be referred back to the Jacobin Club for revisions. Instead of revising it, however, the Jacobins decided to withdraw it altogether, on the grounds that the National Assembly had now determined the issue of the king's fate and was demanding vigorous action to prevent collective petitions. A new petition was hastily improvised the following

From Albert Mathiez, *Le club des Jacobins pendant la crise de Varennes et le massacre du Champ de Mars* (Paris: Champion, 1910), pp. 45–47, 135–36; *Actes de la Commune de Paris pendant la Révolution*, edited by Sigismund Lacroix, 16 vols. (Paris: Cerf, Noblet, Quantin, 1894–1914), 2d series, vol. 5, p. 394; *Lettres de Mme Roland*, edited by Claude Perroud, 2 vols. (Paris: Imprimerie Nationale, 1900–1902), vol. 2, pp. 333–36. Translated for this volume by the editor, Keith Michael Baker.

day by the demonstrators at the Champ de Mars. They were adding their signatures to it by the thousands when Bailly (the mayor of Paris) and Lafayette (commander of the National Guard) appeared with a detachment of troops and ordered them to disperse. In the subsequent confusion, the troops fired upon the crowd, killing perhaps as many as fifty people.

Petitions from this period are printed below, together with a letter in which Mme Roland (wife of the future Girondin minister) described the events of the "Champ de Mars Massacre."

Petition of the Society of Friends of the Rights of Man and of the Citizen [Cordeliers Club] to the Representatives of the Nation (21 June 1791)

We were slaves in 1789, we believed ourselves free in 1790, we are free at the end of June 1791. Legislators! You had distributed the powers of the nation you represent; you had invested Louis XVI with an inordinate authority; you had consecrated tyranny in establishing him as irremovable, inviolable and hereditary king; you had hallowed the enslavement of the French in declaring that France was a monarchy.

Good citizens lamented and opinions clashed vehemently; but the law existed and we obeyed it, awaiting our salvation from the progress of enlightenment and philosophy.

It seemed that this alleged contract between a nation which gives everything and an individual who gives nothing had to be maintained, and until the time that Louis XVI had been an ungrateful traitor we believed that we could only blame ourselves for having ruined our own work.

But times have changed. This alleged convention between a people and its king no longer exists: Louis has abdicated the throne; from now on Louis is nothing to us, unless he become our enemy.

The Society of Friends of the Rights of Man considers that a nation must do everything, either itself or through removable officers chosen by it; it considers that no individual in the state should reasonably possess enough wealth and prerogatives to be able to corrupt the agents of the political administration; it considers that there should be no employment in the state that is not accessible to all the members of the state; it considers, finally, that the more important an employment, the shorter and more transitory should be its duration. Convinced of this truth, and of the greatness of these principles, it can no longer close its eyes to the fact that monarchy, above all hereditary monarchy, is incompatible with liberty. Such is its opinion, for which it stands accountable to all Frenchmen.

It anticipates that such a proposition will raise up a legion of contradictors; but didn't the Declaration of Rights itself encounter contradictions? Nevertheless, this question is important enough to merit a serious study on the part of the legislators. They have already botched the revolution once because of lingering deference for the phantom of monarchy; let us therefore act without fear and without terror, and try not to bring it back to life. . . .

Legislators, you have a great lesson before your eyes. Consider well that, after what has happened, it is impossible for you to inspire in the people any degree of confidence in a functionary called a king. We therefore call upon you, in the name of the *patrie,* to declare immediately that France is no longer a monarchy, that it is a republic—or at least to wait until all the departments, all the primary assemblies, have expressed their opinion on this important question, before you think of casting the fairest empire in the world for a second time into the chains and shackles of monarchism. The society has decided that the present petition shall be printed, posted, and then sent to the departments and patriotic societies of the French empire.

Petition of the Jacobin Club (16 July 1791)

The Frenchmen undersigned, members of the sovereign;

Considering that in matters affecting the safety of the people, it has the right to express its desire in order to enlighten and direct the representatives who have received its mandate; that there has never been a more important question than that concerning the king's desertion; that the decree passed on 15 July contains no provision regarding Louis XVI; that while obeying this decree, it is important to decide promptly the matter of this individual's fate; that this decision must be based on his conduct; that Louis XVI, after having accepted the duties of kingship and sworn to defend the constitution, has deserted the post entrusted to him, has protested against this constitution by a declaration written and signed by his own hand, has sought to paralyze the executive power by his flight and orders, and to overthrow the constitution by his complicity with the men today accused of attacking it; that his betrayal, his desertion, his protestation (to say nothing of all the other criminal acts preceding, accompanying, and following these) entail a formal abdication of the constitutional crown entrusted to him; that the National Assembly has judged him to this effect in taking over the executive authority, suspending the king's powers, and holding him under arrest; that new promises to observe the constitution on Louis XVI's part could not offer a sufficient guarantee to the nation against a new betrayal and a new conspiracy;

Considering, finally, that it would be as contrary to the majesty of the outraged nation as to its interests to entrust the reins of the empire to a perfidious, traitorous fugitive;

Formally and expressly demands that the National Assembly accept, in the nation's name, Louis XVI's abdication on 21 June of the crown delegated to him, and provide for his replacement by all constitutional means.

The undersigned declare that they will never recognize Louis XVI as their king, unless the majority of the nation expresses a desire contrary to that contained in the present petition.

Petition to the National Assembly, Drawn Up on the Altar of the *Patrie* (17 July 1791)

Representatives of the Nation, you are approaching the end of your labors. Soon your successors, all named by the people, would have been following in your footsteps without encountering the obstacles presented to you by the deputies of the two privileged orders, necessarily the enemies of every principle of blessed equality.

A great crime is committed. *Louis XVI flees.* He shamefully abandons his post; the empire is on the verge of anarchy. Citizens stop him at Varennes and he is brought back to Paris. The people of this capital urgently demand that you make no pronouncement regarding the culprit's fate without having heard the express desire of the eighty-two other departments.

You postpone action. A multitude of addresses reach the Assembly. All sections of the empire demand simultaneously that Louis be brought to trial. But you, Gentlemen, you have decided in advance that he is innocent and inviolable, in declaring by your decree of the 16th [of July] that the constitutional charter will be presented to him when the constitution is completed. Legislators! This was not the wish of the people—and we considered that your greatest glory, your very duty, consisted in being the organs of the public will. You have doubtless been moved to this decision, Gentlemen, by the legion of those refractory deputies who protested in advance against the entire constitution. But Gentlemen, representatives of a generous and trusting people, recall that these 290 protestors had no voice in the National Assembly; that the decree is therefore null in form and substance. It is null in substance, because it is contrary to the desire of the sovereign; it is null in form, because it was carried by 290 individuals without standing.[1]

These considerations, all these concerns for the general good, this

1. On 9 July 1791, 293 deputies—many of whom had protested earlier against provisions in the proposed constitution that infringed upon the principle of royal inviolability—de-

pressing desire to avoid the anarchy to which we would be exposed by a lack of harmony between the representatives and the represented, all these require us to demand, in the name of the whole of France, that you reconsider this decree, taking into account the fact that Louis XVI's crime is proven, that this king has abdicated. Accept his abdication, and convoke a new constituent body that will proceed in a truly national manner to the sentencing of the culprit—and more especially to his replacement and to the organization of a new executive power.

Letter of Mme Roland (17–18 July 1791)

[*17 July*] The situation is becoming more and more confused, and it is possible that we will be in the midst of a civil war here within a week. Yesterday evening, the Assembly decreed that Louis XVI would remain suspended until the completion of the constitution, which would then be presented to him with the simple choice of accepting or rejecting it. You can imagine the indignation provoked by such a comedy, and the discontents that are growing everywhere. . . . Yesterday, the petition proposed to the citizens by the Jacobins was read at the Champ de Mars. It contained only the demand that the eighty-three departments be consulted regarding the fate of Louis XVI and his replacement in a constitutional manner. This latter phrase alienated many people, who see it as implying the elevation of a child to the throne and the exercise of regency powers by some ambitious person; it was inserted by [Choderlos de] Laclos, who is devoted to the Orléans, and no one has been able to change it.[2]

Today another petition is going to be drawn up, to demand the calling of the next legislature. A hundred thousand people are expected at the Champ de Mars.

The dominant faction, fearing nothing but opinion and the Jacobins' influence upon it, has just set up another club at the Feuillants in order to balance this influence. Division is being stirred up in the National Guards; this is a violent situation and it is bound to lead to an explosive rupture. Unhappily, I don't yet see enough unity on the good side; there is no com-

---

nounced the suspension of Louis XVI and the assumption of the exercise of executive power by the National Assembly after the king's flight to Varennes. The group declared that they would not participate in the assembly's debates on any matter that did not directly relate to the interests of the king and the royal family, for whose defense alone they would remain in the assembly.

2. See the Petition of the Jacobin Club, above. The demand that Louis XVI be replaced "by all constitutional means" was widely interpreted as a device to give regency powers to the duc d'Orléans, whose political ambitions were supported by the novelist, Pierre Choderlos de Laclos.

mon conviction on all the points about which there should really be agreement. Beyond the simple fact of not wanting Louis XVI, and desiring a change of legislature, there is infinite disagreement regarding all subsequent issues.

Our Assembly has already pronounced on the first matter, and as for the second, it is clear that it does not want to disperse before the completion of the constitution, nor hasten that completion, nor allow its successors to be named in advance.

Once again, the tinder of insurrection and civil war is accumulating and piling up; fire will break out at the first instant. . . .

[*18 July*] Mourning and death are within our walls; tyranny is seated on a bloodstained throne; it holds out its iron scepter, and liberty no longer exists in Paris except for National Guards who want to slit their brothers' throats. Citizens had assembled at the Champ de Mars with the peaceable intention of hearing and signing a petition calling for the nomination of deputies to the next legislature. The municipal authorities had been notified according to the rules. All those assembled were without weapons or sticks; women carrying or leading children made up a great part of this gathering, held outside, around the altar of the *patrie,* in a place open on all sides, and in the confidence of the most sacred rights and the most righteous sentiments. Two men were found hiding inside the structure, which they had reached by lifting up some planks: they were busy beneath the part where the altar is erected, making holes here and there under the spectators' feet. They were apprehended and taken to municipal authorities nearby; they were carrying brandy and other liquor; when they refused to reveal what they had been planning, some angry men seized upon them and hanged them. A cannon was brought to the scene; three municipal officials arrived and found calm restored; they listened to the petition, acknowledged that it was reasonable, and said that they would sign it if they had no official capacity; they also declared that they would have the cannon withdrawn, which was done. All this occurred before three o'clock.

In the afternoon, many people added to the crowd by taking their walk to the Champ de Mars. Suddenly, a new contingent of artillery arrived, and ten cannon were placed in front of the Ecole Militaire; a company of troops appeared, with the red flag in their midst; no formal warning was given to the citizens seated on the altar and signing the petition; the three formal warnings prescribed by the law were omitted. The first volley, which should only have fired powder, was loaded with shot; five or six others followed; the cavalry charged the people fleeing, and the saber struck down those spared by the cannon. Thus was put to rout this peaceful gathering of honest men, assembled in good public faith. A general alert had been sounded throughout Paris, to spread alarm and make people believe there was an uprising. Companies of guards appeared in great numbers, all bristling with bayonets; the Jacobin Club was besieged and a small door surrounded by soldiers was left as the only way out; the Palais Royal was filled with armed men, brandishing their weapons, and presenting the bayonet to the smallest group. . . . Slander, organized from afar, poured forth in torrents: incendiary petitions were printed, purporting to be those of the assembled citizens; scurrilous pamphlets were similarly circulated under the name of Robespierre, and distorted accounts of what had occurred. Finally, the conspirators—for that is what one must now call the dominant faction of the National Assembly, meeting at the Feuillants—are going to write, or have already written, to all the affiliated societies to get them to separate from the Jacobins and join with them. This is the ultimate means they intend to use to dominate opinion, as they are here oppressing persons. . . .

30. National Assembly Debate on Clubs (20 September 1791)

The "Champ de Mars Massacre" inaugurated a brief period of political repression directed at the popular movement, and dramatized the growing tension between the claims of political activism and the desire of moderates to bring the Revolution to an orderly close. This issue was foremost in the minds of the representatives in the very last days of the Constituent Assembly, as they debated a proposal for a new decree limiting the political role of clubs. The decree was adopted, but never implemented.

[Le Chapelier, speaking on behalf of the constitutional committee:] . . . One duty remains to your former constitutional committee. That duty is imposed upon it by you, by its love for the public good, and by its desire to secure and propagate all the principles preserving the constitution that France has just received after two and a half years of travails and alarms.

We intend to speak of those societies formed by enthusiasm for liberty and owing their prompt establishment to it, those societies which, during a stormy period, produced the happy effect of rallying public opinion and providing common centers for its expression, showing the opposing minority the extent of the enormous majority that wanted the destruction of

From *Archives parlementaires de 1787 à 1860, première série (1787 à 1799)*, edited by M. J. Mavidal and M. E. Laurent, 2d ed., 82 vols. (Paris: Dupont, 1879–1913), vol. 31, pp. 617–23. Translated for this volume by the editor, Keith Michael Baker.

abuses, the overthrow of prejudices, and the establishment of a free constitution.

But like all spontaneous institutions formed according to the purest motives—but soon deviating from their goal as a result of a considerable change in circumstances and of various other causes—these popular societies have taken on a kind of political existence they ought not to have.

As long as the Revolution lasted, this state of affairs was almost always more useful than harmful. When a nation changes its form of government, every citizen is a magistrate; all deliberate, and must deliberate, regarding the public good; and everything that impels, everything that ensures, everything that accelerates a Revolution must be put to use. A momentary agitation must be sustained and even increased, so that the Revolution, leaving no doubt to those opposing it, encounters fewer obstacles and reaches its end more quickly.

But when the Revolution is ended and the constitution of the state is fixed, when all public powers have been delegated and all the authorities brought into existence by that constitution, then its proper functioning requires that everything be restored to the most perfect order. Nothing must hinder the action of the constituted authorities, deliberation and power must be located only where the constitution has placed them, and everyone must have enough respect for his own rights as a citizen and for the delegation of public responsibilities not to exceed the former, or ever violate the latter.

Too many services have been rendered to the polity by the Societies of Friends of the Constitution, too much patriotism animates them, for it to be necessary in general to do more than warn the citizens composing them of the dangers to which these societies can expose the state. They are dragged into illegal actions by men who cultivate them only to stir them up, who gain admission to them only to acquire a sort of existence, who speak at their meetings only to prepare their own intrigues and to usurp a scandalous celebrity which favors their schemes. . . .

All citizens are permitted to assemble peaceably. In a free country, when a constitution founded on the rights of man has created a true state to which all belong [patrie], an intense and profound sentiment attaches all the inhabitants to the polity: they need to concern themselves with it, and to speak about it. Far from extinguishing or containing this sacred fire, all social institutions must contribute to sustain it.

But against this general interest, this lively affection stimulated by the existence of a true state and the free enjoyment of the rights of the citizen, must be placed the principles of public order and representative government.

There are no powers except those constituted by the will of the people expressed by its representatives; there are no authorities except those delegated by it; there can be no action except that of its agents entrusted with public functions.

To preserve this principle in all its purity, the constitution has abolished all corporations, from one end of the state to another, and it henceforth recognizes only the social body and individuals.

As a necessary consequence, it has prohibited any petition or poster issued in the name of a collectivity—a decree loudly decried by those who would like to buttress their factious voice with the authority of a society, but one whose wisdom has been recognized by all men willing to meditate briefly on the nature of the government we have adopted.

Societies, peaceful gatherings of citizens, clubs, are invisible in the state. If they abandon the private status the constitution confers upon them, if they rise up against the constitution, destroying it instead of defending it, then this precious rallying cry—"Friends of the Constitution"—seems nothing but a cry of agitation destined to disturb the exercise of the legitimate authorities.

These societies, for the most part composed of worthy citizens, of true friends of the state and zealous defenders of the constitution, will easily understand us when we tell them that, if the Revolution has sometimes led them to external acts, the established constitution reproves such acts;

That it is impossible for these societies to have affiliations with a kind of head without likening themselves to the corporate bodies that have been abolished, or making themselves into a corporate body far more dangerous than the old ones, because it will extend its branches throughout the state. This union, this political correspondence, necessarily leads to two equally fatal results. The societies take on a public existence. And they foster divisions that every good citizen must seek to extinguish—those divisions which reappear instantaneously whenever, with the aid of bizarre and corporative affiliations, a kind of exclusive privilege of patriotism is established, producing accusations against citizens who are not sectaries, and hatreds against nonaffiliated societies;

That deputations, collective addresses, participation in public ceremonies, recommendations, certificates given to favored persons, praise and blame distributed among the citizens, are so many infractions of the constitutional law, or means of persecution that evil men lay hold of;

That journals recording their debates, the publication of their resolutions, the galleries set up for spectators in their meeting halls, are acts contrary to the constitution;

That they commit a very grave crime when they seek to influence administrative or judicial acts. Even the Revolution cannot excuse these orders summoning public officials to account for their conduct; these acts of violence undertaken to stop judicial proceedings against so-called patriots; that audacity which has forced a tribunal to designate seats in its courtroom for deputies of these clubs to watch over criminal proceedings and judgments; these dispatches of agents to various places, charged with missions that may only be conferred by the constituted authorities upon persons in public office.

It is necessary to cast a veil over all these actions. It is even necessary for us to repeat that their purpose and goal has often been to preserve our efforts and our work against the attacks of evildoers, and that in confounding the latters' maneuvers they hastened the establishment of liberty.

But now they would only be punishable offenses, a criminal attack on the authorities established by the constitution—and the friends of this constitution, those who have sworn on their arms to maintain it, have contracted the obligation to distinguish themselves only by the most profound respect for the constituted powers, and the most absolute repudiation of any idea of a political existence proscribed by the constitution.

The societies that were formed to disseminate and support its principles are only meeting places, only clubs of friends who are no longer anything more than citizens, guarding the constitution. They can instruct themselves, discuss, communicate their knowledge one to another; but their proceedings, their subordinate acts, must never exceed the confines of their meetings; no public character, no collective action must characterize them.

No one can contest these constitutional principles, yet we still see them violated. Collective petitions are forbidden, yet they are addressed to the constituent body itself, they are posted in the streets, and administrative officials and municipal authorities are worn out by them. What is the source of these contraventions, whose authors are the most faithful friends of the constitution? Let us not impute them to the societies whose intentions are pure, but to a few men who mislead them.

It is therefore necessary to arm all honest citizens with these truths whose authority must become even more imposing when they are announced by the constituent body. The constitution is entrusted to the concern and courage of all Frenchmen. Those who march under its honorable banner will not suffer the idea of being accused of ignoring or destroying it.

Everyone has sworn to support the constitution, everyone calls for order and the public peace, everyone wants the Revolution to be ended. From now on, these are the unequivocal signs of patriotism. The time of destruction is past; no abuses remain to be abolished, no prejudices to combat. From now on, we must embellish this edifice that has liberty and equality as its cornerstones; we must make the new order cherished even by those who have shown themselves to be its enemies; and we must regard as our most fearsome adversaries those men who seek to undermine the estab-

lished authorities, to dominate certain societies in order to make them take
an active role in the administration of public affairs, turning them into arbitrary censors, turbulent detractors, and perhaps even despotic subjugators
of public officials. . . .

Having spoken of constitutional principles and acts contravening them,
is there any need for us to say that the public existence of societies, their
affiliations, their journals, their collective petitions, their illegal influence,
are fit to alarm all peaceful citizens and estrange all those who wish to live
peacefully under the protection of the laws?

It is in the nature of things that societies that deliberate seek to acquire
some external influence; that perverse or ambitious men seek to dominate
them and use them as instruments of their ambition and vengeance. If the
acts of these societies become public, if they are transmitted through a network of affiliations and announced in their journals, a constituted authority
can be rapidly debased or discredited, a citizen rapidly defamed. There is
no one who can resist such slander. A person is accused, but by his enemy;
the accusation is too easily given an air of public spiritedness; it is applauded in the society, and sometimes adopted; all the affiliated societies
are informed, and the most honest of men and most conscientious of public
servants can be the victim of the skillful maneuver of a bad man. From a
moral and social point of view, as well as from a constitutional one, there
must therefore be neither affiliations among societies, nor journals reporting their debates.

Recognize that public order, the confidence and security of a host of
citizens, greatly depends on this. No one wants a master other than the law.
If the societies could hold sway, if they could dispose of an individual's
reputation, if as corporate bodies they had networks and agents from one
end of France to the other, then their members would be the only free
men—or rather the license of a few associated persons would destroy public liberty. Thus there must be neither affiliations among societies, nor
journals reporting their debates. . . .

[After Le Chapelier presented a draft decree providing penalties against the
political intervention of societies in the conduct of public affairs, the assembly proceeded to discussion of his proposals.]

M. Robespierre: Gentlemen, it is proposed that the assembly order the
printing and distribution of the report it has just heard. However, this report is full of ambiguity and expressions attacking the principles of the
constitution; the language of liberty and of the constitution has been
spoken in a manner calculated to destroy them, and to conceal personal
views and individual resentments under the guise of goodness, justice, and
the public interest. *(Applause from the galleries.)*

Numerous members: Order! Order!

M. Robespierre: The art of speaking in this way is by no means foreign to revolutions, and we have seen it deployed often enough in the course of our own to have learned how to detect and unmask it. For myself, I confess that if I have ever felt acutely the joy of reaching the end of our session, it has been in witnessing this final example of that art, in hearing the charges that have just been leveled at the societies which have assured the Revolution.

I would have thought that, on the eve of our replacement by a new legislature, we could have relied on the enlightenment and zeal of our successors . . . to take the most appropriate action.

I remind myself with confidence—and this reassures me against the manner in which it is proposed to finish our session—I remind myself with confidence and satisfaction that a very great number of those about to replace us come from the bosom of these societies. *(Applause on the extreme left and in the galleries.)* I know that the hope and confidence of the French nation rests with them; to them the nation seems to entrust the task of defending liberty against the progress of a Machiavellian system that threatens its future ruin. . . .

The constitution guarantees Frenchmen the right to assemble peacefully and without arms; it guarantees them free communication of their ideas; it guarantees them the right to act in any way that is not directly contrary to the laws of the state. In accordance with these principles, I ask how anyone dares to tell you that correspondence between one gathering of peaceful, unarmed men and other assemblies of the same kind can be prohibited by the principles of the constitution? . . . Is it not self-evident that he is the one who has attacked these principles, that he is violating them in the most open manner, and that he only puts them forward today in order to disguise all that is odious in the attack he wishes to permit himself against liberty? How, and with what effrontery, will you send orders to the departments claiming to persuade citizens that the Societies of Friends of the Constitution are forbidden to correspond and affiliate? Affiliation is nothing but the relation between one legitimate society and another, according to which they agree to correspond one with another on matters of public interest. How can there be anything unconstitutional about that? Or rather, let someone prove to me that the constitutional principles that I have outlined do not hallow these truths. . . .

M. Le Chapelier: I demand to reply to M. Robespierre, who knows not a word of the constitution. *(Enthusiastic applause.)*

M. Prieur: And I demand to reply to M. Le Chapelier, who knows too many. *(Applause in the galleries.)* . . .

M. Robespierre: Praise is lavished on the Societies of Friends of the

Constitution: but in truth, this is done only to acquire the right to denigrate them, and to make extremely vague allegations that are far from proven and absolutely slanderous. But it doesn't matter, because at least the good that cannot be denied has been said—which is nothing other than acknowledgement of the services rendered to liberty and to the nation since the beginning of the Revolution. It seems to me that this consideration alone would have dispensed the constitutional committee from hastening so quickly to shackle societies which have, by its own admission, been so useful. But, they say, we no longer need these societies because the Revolution is over; it is time to break the instrument that has served us so well. *(Applause from the galleries.)* . . .

The Revolution is finished: I would certainly like to join you in supposing this to be true, although I am not entirely clear what meaning you attach to this proposition I have heard repeated with such pomposity. But assuming this to be the case, is it less necessary to propagate the knowledge, the constitutional principles, and the public spirit without which the constitution cannot exist? Is it less useful to form assemblies in which citizens can concern themselves together, in the most effective manner, with these matters, the dearest interests of their country? Is there a more legitimate or more worthy concern for a free people? To say truly that the Revolution is finished requires that the constitution be firmly established, for its fall or overthrow would necessarily prolong the Revolution, which is nothing but the efforts of the nation to preserve or attain liberty. How then can one propose to render null and without influence the most powerful means of consolidating the constitution, that which the committee's spokesman has himself acknowledged to have been generally recognized as necessary until now?

Whence comes this strange eagerness to remove all the supports buttressing an edifice that is still not firmly in place? What is this system that seeks to plunge the nation into a profound negligence regarding the most sacred of all its interests; that wishes to deny citizens any kind of anxiety, when everything suggests that to remain anxious is not madness; that makes a crime out of the watchfulness that reason imposes even upon peoples who have enjoyed their liberty for centuries?

For my part, when I see that the fledgling constitution still has enemies within and without, that language and external signs have changed while actions remain the same, and that hearts could only have been changed by a miracle; when I see intrigue and duplicity sounding the alarm at the same time they sow troubles and discord, and the leaders of opposing factions fighting less for the cause of the Revolution than for access to the power to dominate in the monarch's name; when I see the exaggerated zeal with which they prescribe blind obedience while proscribing even the name of liberty, and the extraordinary means they use to kill public spirit by resuscitating prejudices, irresponsibility, and idolatry: when I see these things, I do not think that the Revolution is finished. . . .

If I must adopt another language, if I must stop protesting against the plans of the enemies of the state, if I must applaud my country's ruin, order what fate you will for me, make me perish before the loss of liberty *(mutterings and applause);* even so, there will remain men in France sincerely enough devoted to liberty, farsighted enough to detect the traps that are laid for us on all sides, and to prevent the traitors from ever enjoying the fruits of their efforts.

I know that, to prepare the success of the plans offered today for your discussion, care has been taken to proliferate criticisms, specious arguments, slanders, and all the petty means used by the petty men who are at once the shame and the scourge of revolutions. *(Applause in the galleries; laughter in the center.)* I know that they have rallied to their opinions all the knaves and fools in France. *(Renewed laughter.)* I know that these kinds of schemes give great pleasure to all those persons who want to prevaricate with impunity, because anyone who wants to be corrupted fears the surveillance of informed citizens, just as brigands fear the light revealing their crimes. Only virtue can unearth this kind of conspiracy against the patriotic societies. Destroy them, and you will have eliminated the most powerful restraint against corruption; you will have overthrown the last obstacle to its schemes. For the conspirators, the intriguers, the ambitious will know well how to assemble and to elude the law whose passage they have secured; they will know well how to rally under the auspices of despotism in order to reign in its name, and they will be liberated from the societies of free men who assemble peaceably and publicly under common titles, because it is necessary to oppose the surveillance of honest men against the forces of ambitious and corrupt intriguers. Then they will be able to tear the state apart with impunity to raise their personal ambition on the ruins of the nation. . . .

M. d'André: It has been claimed that one could have left to our successors the task of passing this decree. But I maintain that we would do well to end our session by passing it . . . because it will prove that the Revolution is finished and we wish to consolidate it; that it can only be consolidated by tranquillity and order; that without tranquillity and order, credit will be destroyed, and the well-to-do will be unwilling to remain in the realm. It will prove that we wish consequently to repudiate—just as we have repudiated those who would like to bring back the old regime—those who would like to replace the regime that has been destroyed with a new regime perhaps more destructive than the old one, because it would make us absolutely the prey of intriguers, of the ambitious, of those who would stoop to the level of the populace. . . .

This is why we must pass this decree, why we must be unswerving in support of our principles to the very last moment. This is why above all, in finishing our session, we must pass a decree which, without destroying the Societies of Friends of the Constitution, nevertheless returns them to their just limits, and teaches them that they cannot, under any pretext, involve themselves in government matters in an active manner, nor encroach upon the constituted authorities. . . .

The Fall of the Monarchy

31. Roland, *Letter to the King* (10 June 1792)

The Legislative Assembly—the new national assembly that began meeting in October 1791—found itself internally divided and progressively at odds with the king as three issues came to dominate its deliberations. The first issue concerned the increasing number of French émigrés, predominantly nobles, now organizing under the leadership of the royal princes to overthrow the Revolution from without. Decrees aimed at countering these activities and punishing émigrés by confiscation of their property were vetoed by Louis XVI. The second issue concerned nonjuring priests, whose refusal to accept the Civil Constitution of the Clergy (see document 23) was making them a powerful magnet for counterrevolutionary sentiment and a particular target of revolutionary fervor. The assembly's measures against these refractory priests were similarly vetoed by the king. The third issue concerned the conduct of the fateful war which the French declared against the Hapsburg emperor on 20 April 1792. News of initial French defeats stirred up renewed unrest in Paris and fostered suspicions that the monarch and his generals were working for the nation's defeat as a means of suppressing the Revolution. Popular demands for the establishment of an armed camp to defend the capital were accepted by the assembly. But, once again, Louis XVI opposed the relevant legislation.

Thus by early June 1792, when the minister of the interior, Jean-Marie Roland de la Platière, addressed this letter to the king, the question of the royal veto had become the crucial test of the viability of the Constitution of 1791. Allied with the left wing of the Legislative Assembly, whose tactic it now was to force the monarch into cooperation with the assembly by using the threat of further popular violence, Roland had been effec-

From *Archives parlementaires de 1787 à 1860, première série (1787 à 1799)*, edited by M. J. Mavidal and M. E. Laurent, 2d ed., 82 vols. (Paris: Dupont, 1879–1913), vol. 45, pp. 163–64. Translated for this volume by the editor, Keith Michael Baker.

tively imposed upon the king as a member of the so-called Girondin ministry appointed in March 1792. His letter precipitated his dismissal (with other "patriotic" ministers) on 13 June, and initiated the crisis that eventually led to the fall of the monarchy.

The present situation in France cannot long continue. It is a state of crisis reaching its highest peak of intensity. It is bound to end with an outburst that must necessarily concern Your Majesty as much as it affects the entire empire.

Honored by your confidence, and occupying a position in which I owe you the truth, I dare to present it to you in its entirety. You yourself have imposed this obligation upon me.

The French have given themselves a constitution. It has created malcontents and rebels. The majority of the nation wish to maintain it: having sworn to defend it at the cost of their blood, they have joyfully welcomed the war that offers them a great means of securing it. However, the minority, sustained by hope, have combined all their efforts to win the advantage. Hence this internal struggle against the laws, this anarchy which good citizens bemoan while those with evil intentions assiduously profit from it to slander the new regime. Hence this division that has spread everywhere, and is everywhere inflamed; for indifference is not to be found anywhere—one wants either the triumph or the alteration of the constitution, one acts either to support or to change it. I shall refrain from examining what the constitution is in itself, in order to concentrate on what the circumstances require. Taking as objective a stance as possible, I shall seek to discover what may be expected and what most appropriately favored.

Your Majesty enjoyed great prerogatives which you believed to belong to monarchy. Brought up with the idea of preserving them, you could not possibly see them taken away with pleasure. Desire to recover them was as natural as regret at seeing them abolished. These sentiments, which derive from the nature of the human heart, have necessarily entered into the calculations of the enemies of the Revolution. They have therefore counted on secret favor until circumstances might permit open support. These tendencies could not escape the attention of the nation itself, and necessarily made it distrustful.

Thus Your Majesty has been constantly faced with the alternative of yielding to your initial habits and personal predilections, or of making the sacrifices dictated by philosophy and demanded by necessity—with the alternative, consequently, of emboldening the rebels while disquieting the nation, or of allaying the nation's fears by uniting with it. Everything has its season, and that of uncertainty has finally arrived.

Can Your Majesty ally himself openly with those who want to change the constitution, or must he generously and unreservedly commmit himself to making it triumph? That is the real question which the present situation makes it unavoidable to resolve. As for the very metaphysical issue of whether the French are ready for liberty, that will not be discussed here. It is not a matter of deciding what we will have become in a century's time, but of seeing what the present generation is capable of.

What has happened amidst the unrest in which we have been living for the past four years? Privileges that weighed heavily upon the people have been abolished. Ideas of justice and equality have been spread universally and have penetrated everywhere. The idea of the rights of man has legitimated the perception of these rights, and their solemn recognition has become a sacred doctrine. Hatred of the nobility, long inspired by feudalism, and then exacerbated by the open opposition of the majority of the nobles to the constitution that destroyed it, has become deep-rooted.

During the first year of the Revolution, the people saw these nobles as persons odious for the oppressive privileges they had enjoyed—but persons whom it would have ceased to hate after the destruction of these privileges, if the nobles' subsequent conduct had not strengthened every possible reason for fearing and combating them as an irreconcilable enemy.

Attachment to the constitution has grown proportionately. Not only did the people owe clear benefits to it, but since those who had habitually imposed every burden upon them were striving so powerfully to destroy or modify it, they concluded that it was preparing the way for even greater ones.

The Declaration of the Rights of Man has become a political gospel, and the French Constitution a religion for which the people is ready to perish.

Thus zeal has already gone so far as to substitute for the law on some occasions; and when the latter was not repressive enough to contain disruptive elements, the citizens have taken it upon themselves to punish them.

This is why the property of émigrés has been exposed to the ravages inspired by vengeance, why so many departments have believed themselves obliged to deal harshly with priests who were proscribed by opinion, and would have become its victims.

In this clash of interests, feelings have grown passionate. Far from being a word that imagination has delighted in embellishing, the *patrie* is a being to which sacrifices have been made, to which people are becoming daily more attached as a result of the concern it causes. It is a being which has been created by great effort, which arises in the midst of anxieties, which is loved for what it costs as much as for the hopes it inspires. All the attacks upon it serve to inflame enthusiasm for it. To what pitch will this enthusiasm mount at the moment when the enemy forces gathered without join with conspirators within to inflict the most grievous blows? The state of agitation is extreme in all parts of the empire; there will be a terrible explosion unless a rationally warranted confidence in Your Majesty's intentions can finally calm it. But this confidence will not be established on the basis of protestations; it can no longer be founded on anything but facts.

It is obvious to the French nation that the constitution can function, and that the government will have all the force it requires, from the moment Your Majesty, fully committed to the triumph of this constitution, supports the legislative body with the full power of enforcement, eliminating every pretext for restlessness on the part of the people, and all hope for the malcontents.

For example, two important decrees have been passed, both vitally affecting public tranquillity and the safety of the state. The delay in sanctioning them inspires distrust which, if prolonged, will cause discontent; and I must tell you that, in the present state of agitation, discontent can lead to anything.

The time for drawing back is over, no means of temporizing even remain. The revolution is achieved in people's minds; it will be completed at the cost of blood, and will be cemented by that blood, unless wisdom prevents misfortunes that can still be avoided.

I know that it is possible to imagine doing and controlling everything by extreme measures. But once force had been deployed to constrain the assembly—once terror had been spread in Paris, and division and astonishment around it—the whole of France would rise up in indignation. Tearing itself apart in the horrors of civil war, it would develop that dreadful energy that is the mother of virtues and crimes, and always fatal to those who have provoked it.

The safety of the state and Your Majesty's happiness are intimately linked; no power is capable of severing them. Cruel anguish and certain calamities surround your throne, unless it is upheld by you on the basis of the constitution, and consolidated during the peace that its maintenance must finally bring us. Thus the state of peoples' minds, the course of things, political considerations, and Your Majesty's interests, make it an indispensable obligation to unite with the legislative body and to respond to the nation's desire. . . .

The conduct of priests in many places, and the pretexts fanaticism was furnishing to malcontents, prompted the passing of a wise law against these troublemakers. Let Your Majesty give it his sanction: public peace demands it, and the safety of the priests calls for it. If this law is not put into effect, the departments will be forced to substitute for it with violent measures, as they are doing everywhere; and the angered people will make up for its absence with excesses.

Our enemies' endeavors, the unrest that is occurring in the capital . . . , the situation of Paris and its proximity to the frontiers, have made clear the need for a camp nearby. This measure, the wisdom and urgency of which have struck all good minds, only awaits Your Majesty's sanction. Why is it necessary for delay to give such sanction an air of reluctance, when dispatch would merit gratitude?

The efforts directed against this measure by the general staff of the Paris National Guard have already created suspicion that it was acting on a higher initiative. The declamations of outraged demagogues are already arousing apprehensions regarding their relations with those who want to overthrow the constitution. Public opinion is already impugning Your Majesty's intentions. Still more delay, and the saddened people will believe it sees in its king the friend and accomplice of conspirators.

Good heavens above! Could it be that you have struck the powers of the earth with blindness? Will they never have counsels other than those which lead them to their ruin?

I know that the austere language of truth is rarely welcome near the throne. I also know that revolutions become necessary precisely because this language almost never makes itself heard there. Above all, I know that I must use it before Your Majesty, not only as a citizen obedient to the laws, but as a minister honored with your confidence, or charged with duties that imply it; and I know of nothing that can prevent me from fulfilling a duty of which I am aware. . . .

32. The Revolution of 10 August 1792

Roland's dismissal prompted renewed agitation in Paris. On 20 June 1792, a crowd of demonstrators forced their way into the royal residence at the Tuileries palace and confronted the king with their demands for an end to his veto on the measures against émigrés and refractory priests, and that establishing a military camp near the capital. Their action deepened the division in the Legislative Assembly between those who found the principal political threat in the king's behavior, and those who saw it in direct popular intervention. The fears of the latter group were aggravated when the assembly voted to overrule the veto on the establishment of an armed camp for the defense of Paris. Volunteers for this duty (they were called

From *Archives parlementaires de 1787 à 1860, première série (1787 à 1799)*, edited by M. J. Mavidal and M. E. Laurent, 2d ed., 82 vols. (Paris: Dupont, 1879–1913), vol. 47, pp. 69–71, 457–58, 475–76, 645–46. Translated for this volume by the editor, Keith Michael Baker.

fédérés) were drawn from the most zealous revolutionary activists throughout France. When they advanced on the capital, they not only brought their enthusiasm for the Revolution—the *Marseillaise,* the great revolutionary hymn that became the French national anthem, was the marching song of the contingent from Marseille—but renewed demands for the king's suspension.

Such demands became even more insistent at the end of July 1792, when Paris received the news of the Brunswick Manifesto—the Duke of Brunswick's declaration, as commander of the Austrian and Prussian armies, that he was invading France to suppress revolutionary disorder and restore monarchical authority. As calls for the king's suspension gave way to the cry for his immediate deposition, the divided assembly still found itself incapable of decisive action. And the more it dithered, the more its authority as a representative body was imperiled by threats of a new assertion of direct popular sovereignty. The people of Paris, its revolutionary manpower reinforced by the *fédérés* on the one hand, and directed by an insurrectional committee on the other, took decisive action on 10 August 1792. After a violent and bloody attack on the Tuileries palace that cost some 900 lives (most belonging to the king's Swiss Guards), the royal family took refuge with the Legislative Assembly, which was finally obliged to declare the king's suspension.

The documents below are printed as they were presented to the Legislative Assembly. The reactions described in parentheses are those heard in the assembly itself, as they appear in its minutes.

Address of a Deputation of *Fédérés* to the Legislative Assembly (23 July 1792)

Representatives elected by the people to defend and preserve its rights, listen again today to its cry of sorrow.

Weeks have passed since you declared the *patrie* in danger, and you show us no way of saving it. Is it possible that you are still ignorant of the cause of our ills, or do not yet know the remedies? Well then, legislators, we citizens of the eighty-three departments—we whom the sole love of liberty has brought together here, who take strength in the considered and vigorously pronounced opinion of all Frenchmen—we shall tell you the remedy. We say to you that the source of our ills lies in the abuse of authority committed by the head of the executive power; that it lies further in the general staffs of the army, in a great proportion of the departmental and district directories, and in the tribunals. (*Applause from the galleries.*) We shall say to you further, with all the candor of a free people standing ready to defend its rights, that it exists in part in your midst. (*Applause from the galleries.*)

Legislators, the danger is imminent and we can no longer close our eyes to it; the reign of truth must begin. We are courageous enough to come and tell you this. Have courage enough to hear it.

Deliberate immediately and without interruption regarding the sole means of remedying our ills. Suspend the executive power, as it was suspended last year; in so doing, you will sever the root of all our difficulties. We know that the constitution does not speak of deposition; but to declare the king deposed it is necessary to judge him, and in order to judge him it is necessary that he be provisionally suspended. Convoke the primary assemblies (*applause from the galleries*) so that you are in a position to know directly the wish of a majority of the people that the nation be called upon to consider the alleged constitutional articles relating to the executive power.

Legislators, there is not an hour, not a second, to lose. The evil is at its height. Spare your country a universal upheaval, use all the power entrusted to you, and save the *patrie* yourselves. Are you fearful of bringing down a terrible responsibility on your heads, or is it rather—what we cannot believe—that you want to give the nation a proof of powerlessness. Only one resource would remain to it, that of deploying all its force and crushing all its tyrants. (*Applause on the left, and in the galleries.*) All of us, both you and we, have sworn to live free or die in defending our rights. Well, we have just renewed that oath which makes despots tremble when it is pronounced by men who know how to feel passionately. Either we shall emerge free from this conflict, or the tomb of liberty will also be our own. (*Enthusiastic applause on the left and in the galleries.*)

Excerpt from the Registers of the Mauconseil Section (31 July 1792; read to the Legislative Assembly on 4 August 1792)[1]

The assembly, gathered in the number of more than 600 citizens, deliberating on the dangers of the *patrie*,

Considering that these dangers grow worse every day because of the notorious perfidy of the executive power and all its agents;

---

1. The forty-eight Paris sections were the basic political and administrative subdivisions of the municipality. During this period their assemblies became the principal centers of popular political activism. Repudiating the distinction between active and passive citizens and asserting the right to assemble at will, they epitomized the revolutionary impulse towards direct democracy and cherished the right of insurrection as the immediate expression of popular sovereignty.

Considering that the nation can emerge from the dangerous crisis in which it finds itself only by a great effort;

Considering that it is impossible to save liberty by means of the constitution. (*Mutterings on the right.*)

Considering in this regard that the Constitution cannot be recognized as the expression of the general will. (*Renewed mutterings on the right.*)

Considering that Louis XVI has lost the nation's confidence, that the constituted powers have no force apart from opinion, and that the expression of this opinion is accordingly a strict and sacred duty for all citizens;

Consequently declares to all its brothers, in the most formal and solemn manner, that it no longer recognizes Louis XVI as king of the French; that in renewing the oath so dear to its heart, to live and die free, and to be faithful to the nation, it renounces the remainder of its vows as a betrayal of the public faith;

Resolves accordingly that next Sunday 5 August, it will proceed in its entirety into the midst of the legislative body, to notify that body of the present declaration and demand whether it wishes at last to save the *patrie,* awaiting the response it receives before taking the final decision that will be its right. . . .

[Violent protests are heard. The reading of the address is interrupted while the Convention votes on whether it should be continued.]

Promising in advance that it will bury itself under the ruins of liberty rather than subscribe to the despotism of kings;

Further resolves, while regretting that it cannot extend this measure to all the sections of empire, that an address will be presented to the forty-seven other sections, and to all the communes of the department of Paris, inviting them to adhere to the present resolution and to join it on 5 August next, at 11 o'clock, to appear before the legislative body, for the purposes outlined in the present resolution. . . .

Address of the Mauconseil Section to all the Citizens of the Department of Paris (read to the Legislative Assembly on 4 August 1792)

The holiest duty, the most cherished law,
Is to forget the law to save the *patrie.*

Citizens of all the sections,

The national assembly deliberates, but the enemy is approaching, and soon Louis XVI is going to deliver our cities over to the bloodstained chains of the despots of Europe.

Citizens, rise up, and come with us to demand of the senate whether it believes itself capable or not of saving the *patrie;* without leaving the bar of the assembly, let us at last obtain the right to forget the law in order to save the *patrie*.

The citizens of the Mauconseil section have conceived the noble plan of recovering their rights, making liberty triumphant or burying themselves in its ruins, and this splendid example will doubtless be imitated by all the sections of the empire.

Let Paris again be the wonder of the universe and the dread of despotism.

A despicable tyrant has already played too long with our destinies. Let us be careful not to wait until his triumph is assured to punish him. Citizens, rise up, and remember that a tyrant never pardons.

Without distracting ourselves further in calculating his errors, crimes, and betrayals, let us strike at the fearsome colossus of despotism, let it fall, let it break into pieces, and let the sound of its fall turn tyrants pale from one end of the earth to the other.

Let us all unite to pronounce the deposition of this cruel king. Let us say with one voice: *Louis XVI is no longer king of the French.*

Opinion alone gives power to kings. Well then! Citizens, let us make use of opinion to bring him down, for opinion makes and unmakes kings.

Louis XVI is abandoned to the most shameful condemnation, all the parts of the empire repudiate him with indignation; but none of them has expressed its opinion adequately.

The Mauconseil section therefore declares to all parts of the sovereign that in presenting the general desire *it no longer recognizes Louis XVI as king of the French,* that it renounces as a betrayal of its faith the oath it has taken to be faithful to him.

Betrayal is virtue, when crime is promised.

Citizens, imitate our example, tyranny collapses and France is saved for ever.

[After indignant reactions from some deputies, the two addresses of the Mauconseil section were referred to the Commission of Twelve, a special committee created earlier by the assembly to consider emergency measures.]

Vergniaud, *Report to the National Assembly on behalf of the Special Commission of Twelve* (4 August 1792)

You have charged your commission to present an immediate report regarding the deliberation and resolution of the Mauconseil section and the manner according to which the people could exercise its sovereignty.

This latter question requires too profound and considered a discussion to be presented to you at this time. As for the deliberation of the Mauconseil section, the commission has concluded that it is important to propose a decree on the matter, because the love of liberty has so inflamed minds, and passions have reached such a degree of excitation, that it appears important to prevent its deviations. This is the proposed decree:

The National Assembly, considering that sovereignty belongs to the whole people and not to a section of it;

That there would no longer be either government or a constitution, and we would be condemned to all the disorders of anarchy and civil strife, if each isolated individual or section of the empire could decide that it was withdrawing from some part of its obligations that might displease it, and refuse obedience to that law or those constituted authorities that it no longer wished to recognize;

Considering that if an ardent love of liberty has alone determined the citizens of the Mauconseil section to take the resolution that it has sent to the other sections, it is nevertheless important to the social order to repress deviations which could have the most fatal consequences, declares a state of emergency;

The National Assembly, after having declared a state of emergency, quashes as unconstitutional the deliberations or resolutions of the Mauconseil section, invites all citizens to contain their zeal within the limits of the law, and to be on guard against the intrigues of those who seek, by violating it, to compromise the public tranquillity and liberty itself.

[After having decreed a state of emergency, the assembly adopted the proposed decree.]

Vergniaud, *Report to the National Assembly on behalf of the Special Commission of Twelve* (10 August 1792)

Gentlemen, I come in the name of the special commission to lay a severe measure before you. I shall present it, however, without further elaboration, relying on the grief with which you must be filled after the events that have occurred. Decide whether it is necessary:

The National Assembly, considering that the dangers of the *patrie* have reached their height;

That the most sacred duty of the legislative body is to use every means to save it;

That it is impossible to find effective means of doing so as long as action is not taken to eliminate the source of its ills;

Considering that these ills stem principally from the suspicions inspired by the conduct of the head of the executive power, in a war undertaken in his name against the constitution and the nation's independence;

That these suspicions have provoked among various parts of the empire a desire for the revocation of the authority delegated to Louis XVI;

Considering nevertheless that the legislative body must not extend its own authority by any act of usurpation, nor does it wish to do so;

That in the extraordinary situation in which it finds itself placed by events unforeseen by any law, it cannot reconcile the obligation of its unshakeable fidelity to the constitution with its firm resolution to bury itself under the ruins of the temple of liberty rather than let liberty perish; that in appealing to the sovereignty of the people, and at the same time taking the indispensable precautions to ensure that this appeal not be made illusory by treasonous acts, decrees the following:

1. The French people is invited to form a National Convention: the special commission will present a proposal tomorrow indicating the form and date of this convention.

2. The head of the executive power is provisionally suspended from his functions, until the National Convention pronounces upon the measures it believes necessary to assure the sovereignty of the people and the reign of liberty and equality. . . .

7. The king and his family will remain within the confines of the legislative body until calm is restored in Paris. . . .

9. Any public agent, soldier, noncommissioned officer, officer of any rank whatsoever, and general of the army who abandons his post during these days of alarm is declared infamous and a traitor to the *patrie*.

10. The department and municipality of Paris shall proceed immediately to the solemn proclamation of the present decree.

11. The present decree shall be sent by special couriers to the eighty-three departments, which will be responsible for its reaching the municipalities within their jurisdiction within twenty-four hours, there to be proclaimed with the same solemnity.

[The proposed decree was immediately adopted by the assembly.]

33. The "September Massacres"

After the revolution of 10 August, the Legislative Assembly found itself abandoned by a majority of its members, and desperately struggling to reassert some vestige of its authority against the insurrectionary Paris Commune—the municipal government asserting the popular will of the forty-eight sections. The two bodies fought bitterly over the issue of retri-

From *The Despatches of Earl Gower*, edited by O. Browning (Cambridge: Cambridge University Press, 1885), pp. 213–16, 219–21, 223-28.

bution, first toward the troops who had resisted the people's attack on the Tuileries palace, and then toward those accused of counterrevolutionary activities more generally. Although a special tribunal was created on 17 August, its justice seemed neither speedy nor sure enough to satisfy popular demands.

The situation in the capital became even more tense after the fall of Longwy to the Duke of Brunswick on 23 August. In the expectation that foreign armies would soon be at the city gates, the Commune prepared frantically for a siege: building fortifications, gathering arms, and filling the prisons with suspected counterrevolutionaries. On 2 September, news reached Paris that Verdun was falling to the foreign army. In the state of emergency that followed, panic and popular fury led to bloody massacres, as prisons were invaded and prisoners slaughtered in the name of revolutionary justice. In the five days of the "September Massacres," between 1,000 and 1,400 prisoners (roughly half the prison population) were killed in Paris. They included many common criminals, as well as counterrevolutionary suspects.

The following reports are taken from the dispatches sent to London by British diplomats.

[*27 August 1792*] . . . The situation of Paris is more quiet than could be expected after the late violent convulsion; and as the people are all armed and the Government extremely feeble, the present tranquillity of the town is a strong proof of how much pains must have been taken to instigate the multitude to the unwarrantable proceedings of the 20th of June and 10th of August. The Jacobins seem to have gone farther than they at first intended, and not to have foreseen that the mob, the instrument with which they overturned the old government, was likely soon to become formidable to themselves; the Assembly itself being now a good deal under the influence of the rabble; for though the six ministers form what is called a *conseil exécutif provisoire*, the real power is transferred to the Municipality and different sections of Paris. The Municipality has been entirely occupied since the 10th in collecting as much evidence and as many proofs as possible to inculpate the conduct of Their Most Christian Majesties. For this purpose every suspected house has been searched and seals put on all papers belonging to the emigrants or their relations; many hundred people connected with the court and the aristocracy have been thrown into prison, and two or three of the most obnoxious have been executed. . . .

It being contrary to the Constitution to try the Most Christian King, the fate of that unfortunate monarch will probably be left undecided by the present Assembly; but the people will take effectual care that nothing shall divert the attention of the new Legislature from concluding the great business of the King immediately after it meets. . . .

[*29 August 1792*] . . . An authentic account of the surrender of Longwy having appeared in the Bruxelles Gazette, which arrived here on Monday last, the event could of course be no longer kept secret, and your Lordship may judge of the impression it has made on the public mind, by the conduct of the National Assembly, who, immediately after receiving the intelligence, came to a Decree "que les dangers de la Patrie s'accroissent," [that the dangers of the *patrie* are increasing] and that 30,000 men be forthwith raised in Paris and its environs, to reinforce the army.

Some orders which were lately given by this Government for arms from England and Holland not having been executed, the scarcity, particularly of musquets, is so great, that yesterday evening the Minister of Justice, Mr. Danton, applied, in the name of the Executive Power, to the National Assembly for leave immediately to authorise the different Municipalities to search every private house through the kingdom and seize upon all arms, horses, waggons, and in general upon whatever property be judged in the present exigence useful to the public service. He prefaced his speech by stating the alarming situation of the country which called for the most vigorous exertions, and seemed to intimate that in his opinion the public danger was much greater than generally imagined. After a short discussion the proposition of the minister was agreed to and decreed.

Preparations are carrying on to fortify the hill of Montmartre which commands most of the town of Paris, and a camp is marked out extending from the Bois de Boulogne all round the north part of the town. . . .

[*31 August 1792*] I had the honour to mention in my last that the Assembly and the Municipality of Paris were at variance in consequence of the latter having arrogated to themselves more power than is allowed them by the constitution. . . . Yesterday evening the quarrel between them was brought to a sort of crisis by a vigorous determination and decree of the Assembly to break the commissaries of the Municipality and to order them to appear at the bar and answer for their conduct. This decree was no sooner announced to the public, than addresses were sent from most of the sections of Paris to the Municipality, expressing their approbation of the conduct of those who had incurred the displeasure of the legislature, swearing adherence to the municipal officers, and obedience to their commands. The Municipality thought proper however to obey the orders of the Assembly, and, attended by a great concourse of people, appeared this morning, with Mr Péthion at their head at the bar, where after reading a long justification of their conduct, they informed the Assembly, that as the Municipality enjoyed the confidence of the people, who had sanctioned all its proceedings by the more general approbation, they desired the Legislature to reflect whether it would not be more prudent in them to *reconsider* the decree passed yesterday. The President of the Assembly in his answer to them made use of the most conciliatory language, represented to them the fatal effects which must ensue from the continuation of any misunderstanding in the present moment, between the Legislature and the Municipality, and told them that the very existence of the country depended upon the unanimity of the different members of the Government. He promised, however, that their case should be taken into immediate consideration and exhorted them to obey whatever the Assembly in its wisdom might judge right. The affair has, I understand, been made up within these two hours, the Municipality has been persuaded to give way, in consequence of Mr Péthion having exerted all his influence to bring his fellow citizens to reason, and the sections are now proceeding to elect new commissaries according to the decree of the National Assembly. . . .

[*3 September 1792*] I had the honour to mention in my last letter that a courier arrived here yesterday afternoon with an account that the Prussians were some leagues on this side Verdun. Immediately on receiving this intelligence the National Assembly decreed that as universal an alarm as possible should be spread through the whole country in order that no time might be lost in preparing for the general defence; in consequence however of the fermentation excited in Paris by the sounding the Tocsin, firing the alarm guns and beating to arms, the people assembled in different parts of the town in a very tumultuous manner, and at about seven o'clock in the evening surrounded the church called l'Église des Carmes, where about 160 Priests *non sermentés,* and taken into custody since the 10th, were confined. These unfortunate people fell victims to the fury of the enraged populace and were massacred with circumstances of barbarity too shocking to describe. The mob went afterwards to the prison of the Abbaye, and having demanded of the jailors a list of the prisoners they put aside such as were confined only for debt, and pulled to pieces most of the others. The same cruelties were committed during the night and continue this morning in all the other prisons of the town. When they have satiated their vengeance, which is principally directed against the refractory Priests, and those who were concerned in the affair of the 10th, it is to be hoped the tumult will subside, but as the multitude are perfectly masters, everything is to be dreaded. The Assembly deputed some of its most popular and most eloquent members to endeavour to bring the people to reason and a sense of their duty. These gentlemen escaped being insulted but were not listened to. The Royal Family were all safe and well late last night. It is impossible to describe to your Lordship the confusion and consternation which at present prevails here. The Prussians are advancing rapidly, they have already cut off the communication between the armies of Messrs Luckner and Dumouriez; and intelligence is just arrived that a detachment of 2000 men lately sent from hence to reinforce Verdun is fallen into the enemy's hands. . . .

[*4 September 1792*] About one o'clock on Sunday fore-noon three signal guns were fired, the Tocsin was rung, and one of the Municipality on horse-back proclaimed in different parts of the city, that the enemy was at the gates, Verdun was besieged, and could only hold out a few days. The inhabitants were therefore ordered to assemble in their respective sections, and from thence to march to the Champ de Mars, where they were to select an army of sixty thousand men.

The first part of this proclamation was put in execution, but the second was totally neglected. . . . A party at the instigation of some one or other declared they would not quit Paris, as long as the prisons were filled with Traitors (for they called those so, that were confined in the different Prisons and Churches), who might in the absence of such a number of Citizens rise and not only effect the release of His Majesty, but make an entire counter-revolution. To prevent this, a large body of sans-culottes attended by a number of Marseillais and Brestois, the hired assassins of a Party, proceeded to the Church de Carmes, rue de Vaugirard, where amidst the acclamations of a savage mob they massacred a number of refractory Priests, all the Vicaires de Saint Sulpice, the directors of the Seminaries, and the Doctors of the Sorbonne, with the *ci-devant* Archbishop of Arles, and a number of others, exceeding in all one hundred and seventy, including those that had been confined there since the tenth. After this they proceeded to the Abbaye, where they massacred a vast number of prisoners, amongst whom were also many respectable characters. These executioners increasing in number, different detachments were sent to the Châtelet, the prison de la Force, de Ste Pélagie, and the prisons of the Conciergerie. At all these places a most horrid massacre took place, none were exempted but debtors, and many of these fell victims to the fury of the people. During this sad scene, the more humane, which were but few in number, hurried to the National Assembly to obtain their interference for stopping such melancholy outrages. They immediately decreed that six of their members should go and see if it was possible to prevent such cruelties. With difficulty these members arrived at the Abbaye; when there, one of them got upon a chair to harangue the people, but neither he nor the others could make themselves heard, and with some risk, they made their escape. Many of the Municipality attended at the different prisons, and endeavoured to quell the fury of the people, but all in vain; they therefore proposed to the mob a plan of establishing a kind of Court of justice in the prisons, for the immediate trial of the remaining offenders. They caught at this, and two of the Municipality with a detachment of the mob, about two on Monday morning, began this strange Court of justice. The gaoler's list was called for, those that were confined for forging assignats, or theft, with the unhappy people that were any way suspected to be concerned in the affair of the 10th, were in general massacred; this form took place in nearly all the prisons in Paris. But early on Monday morning a detachment with seven pieces of cannon went to attack the Bicêtre. It is reported that these wretches charged their cannon with small stones and such other things, and fired promiscuously among the prisoners. I cannot however vouch for this, they have however not finished their cruelties there yet, and it is now past six o'clock Tuesday evening. To be convinced of what I could not believe, I made a visit to the prison of the Abbaye about seven o'clock on Monday evening, for the slaughter had not ceased. This prison, which takes its name from an adjoining Abbaye, stands in a narrow street, which was at this time from a variety of lights, as light as day; a single file of men armed with swords, or piques, formed a lane of some length, commencing from the prison door. This body might consist of about fifty; these people were either Marseillais, Brestois, or the National Guards of Paris, and when I saw them seemed much fatigued with their horrid work. For beside the irregular massacre that continued till two o'clock on Monday morning, many of them delighted with their strange office continued their services when I left them, which was about nine on Monday evening.

Two of the Municipality were then in the prison with some of the mob distributing their justice. Those they found guilty were seemingly released, but only to be precipitated by the door on a number of piques, and then among the savage cries of *vive la nation,* to be hacked to pieces by those that had swords and were ready to receive them. After this their dead bodies were dragged by the arms or legs to the Abbaye, which is distant from the prison about two hundred yards; here they were laid up in heaps till carts could carry them away. The kennel was swimming with blood, and a bloody track was traced from the prison to the Abbaye door where they had dragged these unfortunate people.

I was fortunate enough to be present when five men were acquitted. Such a circumstance, a by-stander told me, had not happened in the operations of this horrid tribunal; and these inconsistent murderers seemed nearly as much pleased at the acquittal of a prisoner as they were at his condemnation. The Governor of the Invalides happened to be one of those I saw acquitted, the street rung with acclamations of joy, but the old man was so feeble with fear, and suspense, and so overcome with the caresses of his daughter, who was attending to know his fate, that they both sunk lifeless into the arms of some of the spectators, who carried them to the Hospital des Invalides. The same congratulations attended the others that were acquitted and the same those that were condemned. Nothing can exceed the inconsistency of these people. After the general massacre of Sunday night many of the dead bodies were laid on the Pont-neuf to be claimed, a person in the action of stealing a handkerchief from one of the corpses was hacked to pieces on the spot, by the same people who had been guilty of so much cruelty and injustice. . . .

The Convention Divided

34. The King's Trial

In bringing down the monarchy, the revolution of 10 August also swept away the distinction between active and passive citizens: the National Convention which assembled in September 1792 to decide the king's fate and draw up a new constitution was elected by virtually universal male suffrage. From the very beginning, however, the Convention's deliberations were colored by two other legacies. The events of the preceding weeks had sown bitter personal mistrust among the leaders it inherited from the Legislative Assembly, separating those (like Brissot and his associates) who had fought for the authority of the assembly from those (like Robespierre and his allies) who had sided with the forces of popular insurrection in the capital. These personal enmities—played out, in turn, against the background of a more general fear of Parisian radicalism among many of the new deputies to the Convention—fed the factional conflicts that developed between the Girondins and the Jacobins (or Montagnards, so-called because they sat on the "mountain," the seats high on the left in the Convention). By and large, the Girondins looked beyond the assembly to the provinces for the authentic expression of popular sovereignty, while the Jacobins looked for support from the revolutionary activists of the people of Paris. The resulting divisions soon came into play as the deputies took up the matter of judging the king.

The course of the trial, which raised fundamental questions about the nature and limits of the Revolution, went through several phases. It was first necessary to decide whether, and on what grounds, the king should

From *Regicide and Revolution, Speeches at the Trial of Louis XVI*, edited by Michael Waltzer (New York: Cambridge University Press, 1974), pp. 121–27, 131–40, 155–56, 175–76, 179, 181–83, 189–96, 198–204.

be tried at all. The Constitution of 1791 declared the conditions under which the king was considered to have abdicated, and allowed for his punishment as a citizen for crimes committed after his abdication, but it made no provision for punishment (other than enforced abdication) for acts a dethroned monarch had committed while still king. The Convention was therefore obliged to decide between three positions, each of which held fundamental implications for the nature of the Revolution. The first held that Louis XVI could not now be legally tried or punished as a citizen for his previous actions as a king (the position of the king's few defenders). The second held that it was legally possible and politically desirable that he be tried, and if necessary punished, as a citizen for these actions (the conclusion reached by the committee initially chosen by the Convention to study the matter, supported by the Girondins, and represented in the following selections by Condorcet). The third held that Louis could not be tried as a citizen, that kingship itself was a crime for which he had already been condemned on 10 August, and that it was morally and politically imperative that he be punished immediately (the argument of the Jacobins, here represented by Saint-Just and Robespierre).

On 3 December, accepting the Girondin argument, the Convention formally decided that Louis XVI should be tried, and that it was the competent body to judge him. However, as legal evidence of the king's guilt quickly became overwhelming (indeed, his guilt was never really in doubt) another issue came to the fore. This involved the Girondin proposal that the Convention's verdict be submitted to a vote of the people before it was executed. Justified by the Girondins as a legitimate implication of the principle of popular sovereignty, the proposal was denounced by the Jacobins as a transparent maneuver to save the king and destroy the Revolution. The growing hatred and passionate distrust between the two factions is well revealed in the speeches on this issue by Robespierre and Vergniaud.

In mid-January 1793, the Convention brought the king's trial to a close by voting on three issues. On the first roll call, 716 of the 745 deputies voted to declare the king guilty; the remaining representatives were absent. On the second, a majority voted 424 to 283 against submitting this verdict to ratification by the people, thereby supporting the Jacobin position and inflicting a serious defeat upon the Girondins. On the third, there were 361 votes for immediate execution of the death penalty and 360 against, an outcome that prompted an additional roll call on the issue of reprieve. On 20 January, the Convention rejected reprieve by a vote of 380 to 310. Louis XVI was guillotined the following day.

Saint-Just, 13 November 1792

I shall undertake, citizens, to prove that the king can be judged, that the opinion of Morisson which would respect inviolability and that of the committee which would have him judged as a citizen are equally false, and that the king ought to be judged according to principles foreign to both. . . .[1]

The single aim of the committee was to persuade you that the king should be judged as an ordinary citizen. And I say that the king should be judged as an enemy; that we must not so much judge him as combat him; that as he had no part in the contract which united the French people, the forms of judicial procedure here are not to be sought in positive law, but in the law of nations.

Failing to make these distinctions, the committee fell into forms without principles, forms which would lead to the king's impunity, which would make him too long our cynosure, or which would leave on his sentence a stain of unjust or excessive severity. I have often observed that mistaken measures of prudence, delays, and reflections were here truly imprudent; and after the measure which retards the time when we shall be given laws, the most baneful would be that which would cause us to temporize with the king. Some day, perhaps, men as far removed from our prejudices as we are from those of the Vandals, will be astounded at the barbarousness of an age in which to judge a tyrant might be thought impious, where the people, having a tyrant to judge, raised him to the rank of citizen before examining his crimes; and thought rather of what would be said about them than about the task in hand; and when they made of a guilty man, belonging to the lowest class of humanity, I mean the class of oppressors, a martyr to their pride.

Some day men will be astonished that in the eighteenth century humanity was less advanced than in the time of Caesar. Then, a tyrant was slain in the midst of the Senate, with no formality but thirty dagger blows, with no law but the liberty of Rome. And today, respectfully, we conduct a trial for a man who was the assassin of a people, taken *in flagrante,* his hand soaked with blood, his hand plunged in crime. . . .

Citizens, if the people of Rome, after six hundred years of virtue and of hatred for kings, if Great Britain, after the death of Cromwell, saw kings reborn despite their energy, what must not those good citizens among us fear, those who are friends of liberty, seeing the axe tremble in our hands, seeing a people, from the first day of its liberty, respect the memory of its

---

1. Saint-Just is referring here to the earlier speeches by C.-F.-G. Morrisson, who insisted that the king could not be tried, and J.-B. Maihle (spokesman for the Committee on Legislation) who argued the committee's conclusion in favor of a formal trial by the Convention.

chains! What sort of Republic can we create in the midst of private quarrels and common weakness?

Some men search for a law which would allow the punishment of the king. But in the form of government from which we come, he was indeed inviolable with respect to each citizen. Between the people as a whole and the king, I do not however recognize any natural bond. It may be that a nation, stipulating the clauses of the social contract, might cloak its magistrates with dignity so that rights would be respected and laws obeyed by everyone. But that dignity, being for the profit of the people, has no warrant against them; it is theirs to give and to take away and can shield no one from their judgment. The citizens are bound by the contract; the sovereign is not; else the prince would have no judge and would be a tyrant. Thus Louis' inviolability did not extend beyond his crime and insurrection, for, if his inviolability were found to continue, if his inviolability were so much as considered, the result would be, Citizens, that he could not have been deposed and that the people would have been accountable for his power to oppress them.

The social contract is between citizen and citizen,' not between citizen and government. A contract affects only those whom it binds. As a consequence, Louis, who was not bound, cannot be judged in civil law. The contract was so oppressive as to bind the people and not the king; such a contract was of necessity void, since nothing is legitimate which is not sanctioned by ethics and nature.

All these reasons should lead you to judge Louis, not as a citizen, but as a rebel. By what right, moreover, would he require us to judge him in civil law, on account of our obligation toward him, when it is clear that he himself betrayed the only obligation that he had undertaken towards us, that of our protection? Is this not the last act of a tyrant, to demand to be judged in conformity with the laws that he destroyed? And, Citizens, were we to grant him such a trial, that is, in conformity with the laws, that is, as a citizen, by that means he would try us, he would try the people itself.

For myself, I can see no mean: this man must reign or die. He will prove to you that all his acts were acts of state, to sustain an entrusted power; for in treating with him so, you cannot make him answer for his hidden malice: he will lose you in the vicious circle created of your very accusations.

Citizens, thus it is that the oppressed people, in the name of their will, secure themselves with indissoluble chains forged of their own pride, whereas ethics and utility should be the single rule of laws. Thus, pricing our errors too high, we play at combatting them, rather than marching forward to truth.

What judicial procedure, what investigation, would you undertake into the enterprises and the pernicious designs of the king? Having first recognized that he was not inviolable for the sovereign people, and then, having seen his crimes writ large with the blood of the people, having seen the blood of your defenders flow, so to speak, to your feet, even to this image of Brutus, let us respect the king no longer. He oppressed a free nation; he declared himself its enemy; he abused its laws; he must die to assure the tranquillity of the people, since to assure his own, he intended that the people be crushed. Did he not review the troops before combat? Did he not take flight rather than halt their fire? What steps did he take to quell the fury of the soldiers? The suggestion is made that you judge him as a citizen, whereas you recognize that he was not a citizen, and that, far from protecting the people, he had them sacrificed to himself.

I will say more: a Constitution accepted by a king did not bind citizens; they had, even before his crime, the right to proscribe him and to send him into exile. To judge a king as a citizen, that will astound a dispassionate posterity. To judge is to apply the law; law supposes a common share in justice; and what justice can be common to humanity and kings? What has Louis in common with the French people that they should treat him well after he betrayed them?

A man of great spirit might say, in another age, that a king should be accused, not for the crimes of his administration, but for the crime of having been king, as that is an usurpation which nothing on earth can justify. With whatever illusions, whatever conventions, monarchy cloaks itself, it remains an eternal crime against which every man has the right to rise and to arm himself. Monarchy is an outrage which even the blindness of an entire people cannot justify; that people, by the example it gave, is guilty before nature, and all men hold from nature the secret mission to destroy such domination wherever it may be found.

No man can reign innocently. The folly is all too evident. Every king is a rebel and an usurper. Do kings themselves treat otherwise those who seek to usurp their authority? . . .

We are told that the king should be judged by a tribunal, like other citizens . . . But tribunals are established only for members of the polity, and I cannot conceive by what lapse of the principles of our social institutions a tribunal could be judge between king and sovereign. How could a tribunal have the power to give us a master and to absolve him, and how could the general will be cited before a tribunal?

We will be told that the verdict is to be ratified by the nation, but if that is possible, why can the nation itself not pass judgment? If we did not feel the weakness of such ideas, whatever form of government we might adopt would find us slaves. The sovereign would never be in its place, nor the magistrate in his, and the people would be unshielded from oppression.

Citizens, the tribunal which ought to judge Louis is not a judiciary tribunal: it is a council; it is the people; it is you. And the laws which ought to guide us are those of the law of nations. It is you who must judge Louis, but you cannot be a court of law, a jury, and a prosecutor; a formal trial would be unjust; and the king, regarded as a citizen, could not be judged by the same men who accused him. Louis is an alien among us; he was not a citizen before his crime; he had no suffrage, he could not bear arms. Since his crime, he is still less a citizen, and by what abuse of justice would you make him a citizen to condemn him? As soon as a man is guilty, he leaves the polity. Quite the contrary, Louis would gain entry by his crime. I would say more: if you declare the king a citizen, he will slip from your grasp. What obligation of his would you allege in the present state of things?

Citizens, if you are eager that Europe admire the justice of your verdict, these are the principles which ought to determine it. Those which the legislative committee proposes are a monument of injustice. In such a trial, forms are a mockery; you will be judged according to your principles. I shall always contend that the spirit in which the king is judged is also the spirit in which the Republic will be established. The theory behind your verdict will be that of your public offices, and the measure of your philosophy in the verdict, will be the measure of your liberty in the Constitution. . . .

Louis was another Catiline: the murderer, like that Roman consul, would swear that he saved his country. Louis waged war against the people: he was conquered. He is a barbarian, an alien, a prisoner of war; you have seen his perfidious schemes; you have seen his army; the traitor was not king of the French, he was king of a band of conspirators. He raised secret troops, he had private magistrates, he regarded the citizens as his slaves. Secretly, he had proscribed all good men of courage. He is the murderer of the Bastille, of Nancy, of the Champ-de-Mars, of the Tournai, of the Tuileries; what enemy, what alien has done us more harm? Wisdom and discretion speak with one voice: let him be judged promptly. He is a kind of hostage, preserved by villains. They seek to move us to pity; soon they will buy our tears; they will do anything to touch us, to corrupt us. People! If the king is ever absolved, remember that we are no longer worthy of your confidence and that you may accuse us of perfidy.

Robespierre, 3 December 1792

Citizens, the Assembly has unwittingly been brought far from the true question. There is no trial to be conducted here. Louis is not an accused man. You are not judges. You are, and you can only be, statesmen and representatives of the nation. You do not have a verdict to give for or against a man, but a measure to take for the public safety, a precautionary act to execute for the nation. A deposed king in a Republic is good only for two things: either to trouble the tranquillity of the state and to undermine liberty, or to strengthen both. And I maintain that the character of the deliberations hitherto goes directly against this latter aim. In fact, what course of action is wanted to unite the new-born Republic? Is it not to engrave on the hearts of all eternal contempt for royalty, and to strike dumb all the partisans of the king? Thus, presenting his crime to the world as a problem, his case as the subject of the most serious discussion, the most religious and the most difficult which might occupy the representatives of the French people, placing an immeasurable distance between even the memory of what he was and the dignity of a citizen—therein lies the secret of making him once more dangerous to liberty.

Louis was king, and the Republic is founded. The great question with which you are occupied is settled by this argument: Louis has been deposed by his crimes. Louis denounced the French people as rebels; to punish them he called upon the arms of his fellow tyrants. Victory and the people have decided that he alone was a rebel. Therefore, Louis cannot be judged; he has already been condemned, else the Republic is not cleared of guilt. To propose a trial for Louis XVI of any sort whatever is to step backward toward royal and constitutional despotism. Such a proposal is counter-revolutionary since it would bring the revolution itself before the court. In fact, if Louis could yet be tried, he might be found innocent. Do I say "found"? he is presumed innocent until the verdict. If Louis is acquitted, where then is the revolution? If Louis is innocent, all defenders of liberty are slanderers. Rebels were friends of truth and defenders of oppressed innocence. All the proclamations of foreign powers were but legitimate responses to a faction which sought to rule. Even the imprisonment that Louis has suffered until now is an unjust vexation. The members of the Federation, the people of Paris, all the patriots of the French empire, are guilty, and this great trial pending before the tribunal of nature between crime and virtue, between liberty and tyranny, is at last decided in favor of crime and tyranny. . . .

When a nation has been forced to resort to its right of insurrection, it returns to the state of nature insofar as the tyrant is concerned. How could the tyrant invoke the social contract? he abolished it. The nation, if it deems proper, may preserve the contract still, as it concerns the relations between citizens; but the effect of tyranny and of insurrection is to break completely all bonds with the tyrant and to reestablish the state of war between tyrant and people. Tribunals and judiciary procedure are constituted only for the members of the polity.

It is too great a contradiction to suppose that the Constitution might preside over this new order of things. That would be to suppose that it could outlive itself. What laws replace it? those of nature, which is the basis of society itself. The salvation of the people, the right to punish the tyrant, and the right to depose him are all the same thing. The methods of procedure are the same. The trial of a tyrant is the insurrection; his sentence is the end of his power; his punishment, whatever the liberty of the people demands.

A people does not judge as does a court of law. It does not hand down sentences, it hurls down thunderbolts; it does not condemn kings, it plunges them into the abyss; such justice is as compelling as the justice of courts. If the people armed themselves against their oppressors for their own safety, how could they be forced to imperil themselves once more in punishing those same oppressors? . . .

The trial of Louis XVI! but what is this trial if not an appeal from the insurrection to some tribunal or some assembly? When a king has been destroyed by the people, who has the right to revive him so as to create a new pretext for riot and rebellion—and what other effects could such a system produce? By opening an arena to the champions of Louis XVI, you renew the dispute between despotism and liberty; you consecrate the right to blaspheme against the Republic and against the people. For the right to defend the former despot carries with it the right to say all that pertains to his cause. You reawaken all the factions; you animate and enliven a slumbering royalism. One could freely take a position for or against. What is more legitimate or more natural than to repeat everywhere the maxims which his defenders would be able to profess openly at the bar, and from your very rostrum? What manner of Republic is it, whose founders solicit everywhere its adversaries to attack it in its cradle? You see what rapid progress such a system has already made.

In the month of August last, all the partisans of the king were in hiding; whosoever had dared to undertake an apology for Louis XVI would have been punished as a traitor. Today, they raise their audacious heads without fear of punishment. Today, the most disparaged writers of the aristocracy once again confidently take up their envenomed pens or find successors who surpass them in shamelessness. Today, pamphlets which are the precursors of all crimes inundate the city in which you reside, the eighty-three departments, and make their way even to the portals of this sanctuary of liberty. Today, armed men who have come unbeknownst to you and in violation of the laws, have made the streets of this city echo with seditious cries demanding impunity for Louis XVI. Today, Paris encloses in its heart men gathered, you have been told, to snatch him from the justice of the nation. . . . We have seen one part of this Assembly proscribed by the other almost as soon as it was denounced by folly and perversity combined. The cause of the tyrant alone is so sacred that it cannot be discussed long enough or freely enough. And why should this astonish us? The two parts of this phenomenon stem from the same cause. Those who are interested in Louis or his like must thirst for the blood of patriotic deputies who ask for the second time that he be punished. They can forgive only those who have softened in his favor. Was the plan to enslave the people while slaughtering their defenders at any moment abandoned? And all those who proscribe them today, calling them anarchists and agitators, are they not themselves bound to foment the disorder which their perfidious system promises? If we are to believe them, the trial will last for several months at least, continuing until the coming spring when we can expect a general attack from the despots. And what a chance for the conspirators! what food for intrigue and the aristocracy! Thus all the partisans of tyranny can still hope for aid from their allies; foreign armies can encourage the audacity of counter-revolutionaries while foreign gold tempts the fidelity of the tribunal which is to pronounce on the fate of Louis. What! All the savage hordes of despotism prepare themselves once again to tear at the entrails of France in the name of Louis XVI! Louis still wars against us from the depths of his prison cell; and some doubt if he is guilty and can be treated as an enemy! I should like to believe that the Republic is not a vain word employed to amuse us; yet what other means might they use to reëstablish monarchy?

The Constitution is invoked in his favor. I have no intention of repeating here all the unanswerable arguments brought forth by those who have deigned to combat that sort of objection.

On that subject I shall say but a word for those yet unconvinced. The Constitution forbade all that you have done. If the king could be punished only by deposition, you cannot sentence him to that without a formal judicial proceeding. You have no right to keep him imprisoned. He has the right to seek his release and an award of damages. The Constitution condemns you. Go, throw yourself at the feet of Louis XVI and plead for clemency.

As for me, I should blush to discuss such constitutional logic-chopping more seriously. I relegate it to the schools, or the law courts, or better yet, to the closets of London, Vienna, and Berlin. I cannot treat further of a subject whose very deliberation, I am convinced, is scandalous. . . .

Representatives, what is important to the people, what is important to you, is that you fulfill the duties with which the people have entrusted you. The Republic has been proclaimed, but have you given it to us? You have not yet passed a single law which justifies that name. You have not yet reformed a single abuse of despotism. Remove but the name and we have tyranny still; and moreover, viler factions, more immoral charlatans, new stirrings of disorder and civil war. The Republic! And Louis still lives! And you still place the person of the king between us and liberty! Let us beware turning criminal by force of scruple; let us beware that in showing too much indulgence for the guilty man we join him in his guilt. . . .

Regretfully I speak this fatal truth—Louis must die because the nation must live. Among a peaceful people free and respected both within and without their country, it would be possible to listen to the counsel of generosity which you are given. But a people which is still struggling for its liberty after so much sacrifice and so many battles; a people among whom the laws are not yet inexorable save for the unfortunate; a people among whom the crimes of tyranny are a subject of dispute, such a people must wish to be avenged; and the generosity with which you are flattered would resemble more closely that of a troop of brigands dividing their spoils.

I propose to you an immediate legal action on the fate of Louis XVI. As for his wife, you will send her back to the tribunals, along with all the other people accused of the same crimes. His son will be kept in the Temple until peace and public liberty have a firmer hold among us. As for Louis, I ask that the National Convention declare him, from this moment on, a traitor to the French nation, a criminal toward humanity. I ask that for these reasons, he give an example to the world in the very place where, on the tenth of August, the martyrs of liberty gave their lives; and that this memorable event be consecrated by a monument destined to nourish in the hearts of all people a sense of their own rights and a horror of tyrants; and to nourish in the spirit of tyrants, a salutary terror of the justice of the people.

Condorcet, 3 December 1792

In a case where an entire nation has been wronged and is at once prosecutor and judge, it is the opinion of mankind, the opinion of posterity, to which that nation is accountable. It must be able to declare: all the general principles of jurisprudence recognized by enlightened men in all lands have been respected. It must be able to defy the blindest partiality to cite a violation of the slightest rule of equity; and when that nation judges a king, then kings themselves, in their inmost hearts, must feel moved to approve the judgment.

It is important to the happiness of mankind that the conduct of France towards the man it too long called its king should be the final step in curing other nations of whatever superstition in favor of monarchy may remain among them. Above all, we should beware lest we increase that superstition among those still ruled by it. All nations do not recognize the eternal truths, the unshakable foundation of the French Republic; and whereas our philosophers and our soldiers spread them to foreign nations; whereas tyranny trembles as much before our maxims as before our armies, we would be imprudent to surprise, to frighten perhaps, by the boldness of our actions, those whom we may cause to respect severe but impartial equity. Thus, it is to the laws of universal justice, common to all constitutions, unalterable in the midst of clashing opinions and the revolutions of empires, that we must submit our decisions. . . .

Louis XVI should be judged because the revolution which has led us to the establishment of the Republic had, as its principal cause, the treason of him to whom the Constitution had entrusted all our means of defense.

It is important to prove to Europe, by a juridical discussion which allows cross-examination, that these motives were not chimerical, that they were not a pretext ably seized upon by a small group of men who wished to change the form of the Constitution.

The rights of the nation, doubtless, would not be changed. Abolition of the monarchy, equally, would be legitimate; but it is important for the cause of liberty that its defenders cannot be accused of having misled the people in order to incite them to reassert their legitimate rights. It is important that the nation know if it was led to the moment when the convocation of a Convention became necessary by those who sought to enlighten or by those whose end was to deceive.

The accusers of Louis XVI have the right to demand that a solemn judgment be pronounced between them and him, and that national justice decide if they were rash in their accusations; if they were slanderers or worthy citizens; if they dreamed, imagined, or discovered a great conspiracy.

Finally, if you weigh all the opinions by which France is divided, its relations with other lands, its internal situation, does not all this indicate that the juridical examination of these deeds is necessary, not for public safety, but for the prompt and peaceful consolidation of France?

Are not these oft multiplied proofs of treason already assailed? Has not the neglect of some formalities already been adduced to sap the authenticity or the authority of documents upon which these proofs are founded? Only a formal investigation, permitting cross-examination, before judges who had no part in the discussions raised between Louis XVI and the defenders of the rights of the people, can destroy such objections, scorned today, yet objections which supported by the gold of kings could by accrediting slanders against the French Revolution delay among other peoples the progress of liberty.

In a word, you owe to yourselves, you owe to mankind, the first example of the impartial trial of a king. . . .

Saint-Just, 27 December 1792

. . . I have heard talk of an appeal to the people of the verdict which the people itself will pronounce through our mouth.

Citizens, if you permit an appeal to the people, you will be saying to them, "the guilt of your murderer is in doubt." Do you not see that such an appeal would tend to divide the people and the legislature, would tend to weaken representation, to restore monarchy, to destroy liberty? And if, through intrigue, your verdict should be altered, I ask you, gentlemen, if you would be left with any course but to renounce the Republic and to lead the tyrant back to his palace, for there is but a small step from indulgence to the triumph of the king and thence to the triumph of monarchy. Yet should the accusing people, the ravaged people, the oppressed people, be the judge? Did it not decline that office after the tenth of August? Nobler, more scrupulous, less cruel than those who would send the accused before them, the people desired that a council might pronounce his fate. That tribunal has already shown too much weakness, and that weakness has already softened public opinion. If the tyrant appeals to the people who accuse him, he does that which Charles I never dared. In a flourishing monarchy, it is not you who judge the king, for you are nothing by yourselves, but the people judges and speaks through you.

Citizens, winged crime will fly through the Empire and captivate the ear of the people. O you who are entrusted with public morality, do not abandon liberty. When a people has escaped from oppression the tyrant is judged. Tyrants will stop at nothing in their attempts to weaken the people by raising the spectre of excess. Humanity, in their mouths, is cruelty to the people; pardon, which they urge on you, is the death knell of liberty. Must the people itself pardon the tyrant? Does not the sovereign, like the supreme Being, find laws to govern its conduct in ethics and in eternal justice? And by what law has nature sanctioned these great crimes? Louis' supporters ask that the verdict be sent before the people; what else would one propose, wishing to save the king and knowing that votes can be bought with foreign gold? No more should you forget that a single vote, in the case of a tyrant, suffices to prevent his pardon.

That day will decide the fate of the Republic; its doom is fixed if the tyrant goes unpunished. The enemies of the commonweal reappear, they meet, they grow in hope; the forces of tyranny gather the fragments as a reptile renews a lost limb. All evil men are of the king's party. Who here then can join him? False pity is on the lips of some, anger on the lips of others; nothing is omitted which might frighten or corrupt our hearts. Be steadfast in your severity and assure yourself of the gratitude of the people in time to come. Do not heed the empty consideration and empty clamour by which the schemers seek to play upon the respect you have for the rights of the people, the better to destroy them and deceive you. You called for war on all the tyrants of the world, and you would have respect for your own! Are bloody laws enforced only against the oppressed, and is the oppressor to be spared? . . .

There have been strange misunderstandings over the principles and the character of this question. Louis wishes to be king; he wishes to speak as king even while he denies it. But a man unjustly placed above the law can present his judge only with his innocence or his guilt. Let Louis prove that he is innocent; that is his only title to challenge our actions. Innocence has no need to challenge its judges; it has nothing to fear. Let Louis explain how the papers you have seen may favor liberty, let him show his wounds, and let us judge the people.

Some will say that the Revolution is over, that we have nothing more to fear from the tyrant, and that henceforth the law would decree the death of a usurper. But, citizens, tyranny is like a reed which bends with the wind and which rises again. What do you call a Revolution? The fall of a throne, a few blows levied at a few abuses? The moral order is like the physical; abuses disappear for an instant, as the dew dries in the morning, and as it falls again with the night, so the abuses will reappear. The Revolution begins when the tyrant ends. . . .

Robespierre, 28 December 1792

. . . Citizens, let me call you back to the supreme interest of the nation: its safety. What is it that demands your attention to Louis? It is not thirst for a vengeance unworthy of the nation; it is the need to strengthen public liberty and tranquillity through the punishment of a tyrant. Any manner of judgment, any system of delays which compromises public tranquillity is in direct opposition to your aims. And it were better had you simply neglected to punish him than that his trial lay fuel upon our troubles and kindle civil war.

Each instant of delay brings us a new danger; all delays awaken guilty hopes and further embolden the enemies of liberty. They encourage dark defiance and cruel suspicions in the midst of this assembly. Citizens, the voice of the alarmed nation urges you to hasten the decision which is to reassure it. What scruple yet fetters your zeal? . . .

To delay your judgment, you have heard about the honor of the nation and the dignity of the Assembly. The honor of nations consists in being free and virtuous, in striking down tyrants and avenging reviled humanity. The glory of the National Convention consists in displaying a great character and sacrificing servile prejudices to the sublime principles of reason and philosophy. It consists in saving the nation and strengthening liberty by offering a great example before all the world. I can see its dignity reduced as we forget the vigor of republican maxims, as we are lost in a maze of useless and ridiculous chicanery, and as the speakers before this Assembly cause the nation to embark once again on the course of monarchy.

Posterity will admire or despise you according to the degree of vigor you show on this occasion; and that vigor will be the measure as well of the boldness or the pliancy with which the foreign despots treat you. It will be the wages of our servitude or of our liberty, of our prosperity or of our misery. Citizens, victory will decide if you are rebels or benefactors of humanity, and the greatness of your character will decide the victory.

Citizens, to betray the cause of the people and our own conscience, to deliver the nation to all the disorder which delay in such a trial must awaken, that is the only danger we have to fear. It is time to leap over the fatal obstacle which has so long barred our course. Then doubtless we will march together toward our common aim of public felicity; then the hateful passions which mutter too often in the sanctuary of liberty will yield to love of public welfare and to the holy emulation of the friends of the land; and all the plots of enemies of public order will be confounded. But how far we still are from this goal if that strange opinion which at first we could hardly have dared imagine, which then we suspected, was, finally, in fact proposed openly. As for me, from that moment, I saw the confirmation of all my suspicions and all my fears.

At first we seemed to be troubled by the consequences which delays in the progress of this affair might bring. Now we risk rendering it interminable. We feared the unrest which each moment of delay might bring, and here we are guaranteed the overthrow of the Republic. Why, of what matter is it that a fatal plot be hidden beneath a veil of prudence or even beneath the pretext of respect for the sovereignty of the people? Such was the art of all tyrants under the mask of patriotism, who have until now assassinated liberty and been the cause of all our ills. These are not sophistical declamations, but results which you must weigh.

Yes, I say openly that I no longer see the trial of the tyrant as anything but a means to bring us back to despotism by way of anarchy. Citizens, I call you to witness. The first time there was any discussion of the trial of Louis the Last in the National Convention called expressly to judge him, when you left your departments enflamed with the love of liberty, filled with that generous enthusiasm which the recent proofs of the confidence of a magnanimous people inspired in you, which no foreign influence had changed, nay, at first when the question of opening this affair arose, suppose someone had said to you: "You think that you will have done with the trial of the tyrant in a week, in two weeks, in three months; you are mistaken. It will not be you who will pronounce his sentence, who will judge him in the end. I hereby propose that you send this affair to the twenty or thirty thousand sections into which France is divided, so that they may all pronounce on this point; and you will adopt this proposal." You would have laughed at the assurance of a man making such a motion. You would have rejected such a motion as incendiary, designed to kindle civil war. What is there to say! We are assured that tempers have changed. Such is the influence of a plague-ridden atmosphere among many of our number, that the simplest and most natural ideas are often stifled by the most dangerous sophisms. . . .

Today, I admit, no one would have us absolve Louis. We are still too close to the tenth of August and the day when monarchy was abolished. But we are asked to adjourn the end of his trial at a time when foreign powers are about to descend upon us, and to allow him the resource of civil war. Today, no one would seek to declare him inviolable, but only to assure that he remains unpunished; they seek not to reëstablish him on the throne, but merely to await events. Today, Louis still has this advantage over the defenders of liberty, that they are pursued with more vigor than is he. No one can doubt that they are now slandered with more care and at more cost than in July of 1791. And, certainly, the Jacobins were not more disparaged in the Constituent Assembly then than they now are in this body. Then, we were the factious men; today, we are the agitators and the anarchists. Then, Lafayette and his accomplices neglected to have us murdered; we must hope for the same clemency from his successors. Those great friends of peace, those famous defenders of the law, have since been declared traitors. But we gain nothing from that, while their old friends, several members of the then majority, are here to avenge them by persecuting us. But there is a fact which no one has mentioned and which is nonetheless worthy of provoking your curiosity: after a preparatory pamphlet distributed according to the custom of all members, the speaker who proposed and elaborated with such art and feeling the system of taking the question of Louis to the primary assemblies, sprinkling his discourse with the usual declamations against patriotism, is precisely the same man who, in the Constituent Assembly, gave his voice to the dominant cabal to define the doctrine of absolute inviolability, and who vowed our proscription for having dared defend the principles of liberty . . . in a word, it is the same man who, and this must be said, two days after the massacre on the Champ-de-Mars, dared propose a decree which would have established a commission to judge, without appeal, as quickly as possible, the patriots who had escaped the assassins' swords. I do not know if, since then, the ardent friends of liberty who still today press for the condemnation of Louis have become monarchists, but I heartily doubt that the men of whom I speak have changed their principles. It has been demonstrated to my satisfaction that under only slightly different circumstances, the same passions and the same vices tend irresistibly toward the same end. Then, intrigue gave us an ephemeral and vicious constitution; today, intrigue prevents us from writing a new one and leads us toward the dissolution of the State. . . .

What is sure is that whatever the result of this fatal measure, it must be to the advantage of their views. To provoke civil war the resolution need not even be executed completely. They trust to the unrest which is created within us by this stormy and endless deliberation. Those who do not wish to see Louis fall beneath the sword of law will not be sorry to see him sacrificed by a popular disturbance: they will neglect nothing in their attempts to provoke one. . . .

Yes, doubtless there is a plot to degrade the Convention and perhaps to cause its dissolution as a result of this interminable question. This plot is not found among those who seek energetically the principles of liberty, not among the people who have sacrificed everything to it, not in the majority of the National Convention which seeks the good and the true, not even among those who are the dupes of intrigue and the blind instruments of foreign passions. This plot thrives among a score of rascals who hold the reins, among those who are silent about the greatest concerns of the nation, who abstain above all from announcing an opinion on the question of the last king, but whose silent and pernicious activity causes all the ills which trouble us and prepares all those who await us.

How can we escape this abyss if not by returning to our principles and to the source of our ills? What peace can exist between oppressed and oppressor? What concord can reign where even the freedom of the vote is not respected? Any violation of such freedom is an attempt on the nation; a representative of the people does not permit himself to be stripped of the right to defend the interests of the people; no power can take this right from him without taking his life as well.

Already those who sought to assure continued discord, to control the deliberations, conceived the idea of dividing the assembly into majority and minority, a new means to insult and silence those who were designated as the latter. I do not recognize majority and minority here. The majority is composed of the good citizens. It is permanent since it belongs to no party; at each free deliberation it is renewed, since it belongs to the public cause and to eternal reason. And when the Assembly recognizes an error, the fruit of surprise, of haste, or of intrigue (which sometimes happens), then the minority becomes the majority. The general will is not formed in secret conventicles or around the tables of ministers. The minority retains an inalienable right to make heard the voice of truth, or what it regards as such. Virtue is always in the minority on this earth.

Without this, would not the earth be peopled by tyrants and slaves? Hampden and Sidney were of the minority, for they died on the scaffold. Critias, Anitus, Caesar, Clodius, were all of the majority; but Socrates belonged to the minority, for he swallowed the hemlock. Cato was of the minority, for he tore out his bowels. I know many men here who will, if need

be, serve liberty in the manner of Sidney; and were there only fifty . . .
This thought alone must send a shiver through the base intriguers who wish
to corrupt or to mislead the majority. Until that time, I ask at least that
priority be given to the tyrant. Let us unite to save the nation and let the
deliberation assume at last a character more worthy of us and of the cause
which we defend. Let us at least banish the deplorable incidents which do
us dishonor. Let us not spend more time in self persecution than would be
needed to judge Louis, and let us know how to gauge the subject which
disquiets us. Everything seems to conspire against the public welfare. The
nature of our debates agitates and embitters public opinion, and unhappily,
that opinion reacts against us. The mistrust of the representatives seems to
grow with the citizens' alarms. A proposal which we ought to hear calmly,
irritates us; malevolence daily exaggerates, imagines, or creates tales
whose aim is to strengthen prejudice; and the smallest causes can lead us to
the most terrible effects. The mere expression, sometimes too animated, of
the feeling of the public, which should be easy to control, becomes the
pretext for the most dangerous measures and for propositions which most
threaten our principles.

People, spare us at least this disgrace; keep your applause for the day
when we have passed one law that is of use to humanity. Do you not see
that you give them pretexts to slander the sacred cause which we defend?
Rather than violate these firm rules, turn your backs on the spectacle of our
debates. Remember the ribbon which your hand but lately held as an insurmountable barrier around the fatal dwelling of our tyrant, then still on the
throne. Remember that order has been maintained thus far without bayonets, by the virtue of the people alone. Far from your eyes we will not
struggle the less for liberty. We alone must now defend your cause. When
the last of your defenders has perished, then avenge them if you wish, and
take on the charge of making liberty triumph.

Citizens, whoever you are, set up a watch around the Temple; arrest, if it
is necessary, perfidious malevolence, even deceived patriotism, and confound the plots of our enemies. Fateful place! was it not enough that the
despotism of the tyrant weighed so long on this immortal city? Must his
very safekeeping be a new calamity for it? Is the trial to be eternal, so as to
perpetuate the means of slandering the people who took him from the
throne?

I have proven that the proposal to submit the question of Louis to the
primary assemblies would lead to civil war. If I cannot contribute to the
salvation of my country, I wish at least to be recorded, at this moment, for
the attempts I have made to warn you of the calamities which threaten it. I
ask that the National Convention declare Louis guilty and worthy of death.

Vergniaud, 31 December 1792

. . . What is the sovereignty of the people of which we hear so much, and to which I should like to think our homage is not mere words, to which I am sure the National Convention, at least, renders sincere homage?

It is the power to make laws, rules, in a word, all the acts concerning the happiness of society. The people exercise this power either themselves or through their representatives. In the latter case, and it is the one in which we find ourselves, the decisions of the representatives are executed as laws. But why? Because they are presumed to be the expression of the general will. Their validity comes from this assumption alone. This assumption alone causes them to be respected.

As a result, the people retain the right, inherent in their sovereignty, to approve or improve. As a result, if their presumed will does not coincide with the general will, the people retain the right to manifest their wishes. As soon as such a wish is made known, it should supersede the presumed will, that is, the decision of the national representatives. To take this right from the people would be to take sovereignty from them, to transfer it, by a usurpation nothing short of criminal, to the hands of the representatives chosen by the people, to transform their representatives into kings or tyrants.

Your conduct has been in accord with these principles. But you have distinguished between the Constitution and purely legislative acts, whether statutory or for the protection of the general safety. Since the Constitution formed the basis of civil society, the contract which united the citizens, you thought, and quite rightly, that it should be presented for the formal acceptance of all the members of society. As for purely legislative acts, as they are necessarily very numerous, they vary according to time, place, and circumstances. It would be contrary to the nature of representative government to submit them for deliberation to the people who elected representatives precisely because the extent of their territory or other causes kept them from the direct exercise of their sovereignty. You thought also, and quite rightly, that a tacit ratification would suffice for such acts, that is, it would suffice to enforce them that there be no challenge from the people who retain at all times the right to manifest their wishes. Let me reduce these diverse propositions to a single one: any act emanating from the representatives of the people is an act of tyranny, a usurpation of sovereignty, if it is not submitted to the people for either formal or tacit ratification. Therefore, the judgment which you will pass on to Louis should undergo one of these two processes of ratification.

To reply that even after its execution your judgment will be subjected to tacit ratification is to insult the people with the greatest impudence. There is no silent ratification; silence can be regarded as approbation only when he who is silent has the means to make himself heard with effect. Now it is evident that if your judgment were executed, the people would be able to present only sterile and empty challenges. . . .

It has been claimed that there will be insurmountable difficulties in convoking the primary assemblies; that it would mean taking the plowman from his plow, the workman from his work, wearying the citizens, wearing out their strength in dissertations on legal formalities, on subtle chicaneries. Furthermore, it has been added, foreign powers would profit from this reduction of our forces and, while we were busied in these wretched discussions, would invade our territory for a second time. And if the true friends of liberty joined together to repulse them, they would have the sorrow, while fighting for their country, of fearing the resurrection of tyranny within it.

I will admit that in this very moving speech I found great appeal to our feelings; I still seek in it a reason which might persuade me.[2] Where, in fact, are these great difficulties? Is it the proposal to send to the primary assemblies Louis' written statement, all the evidence produced against him, and the judgment of the Convention, and to submit all to their examination in the same way that the judgment of a *sénéchal* was submitted to a *parlement?* This would be truly a political absurdity. Let us clarify our ideas and be still so as to listen to ourselves. We have two obligations to fulfill. The first, to give the people a means of expressing its desires concerning an important act by the national representatives; the second, to show them a simple means without disadvantages. . . .

Discord, intrigue, civil war—images of the greatest disasters have been placed before us. Discord! you thought perhaps that agitators exercised the same control in the departments which a shameful weakness permitted them to usurp in Paris; that is a very great error. It is true that these perverse men are to be found all over the Republic; faithful to their mission, they have used all means to excite disorder, but everywhere they have been repulsed with the same disdain. The people have done no more than tolerate these men of impure blood; they have granted the law the most remarkable respect. In the departments, the general will is obeyed; it is understood that public and private liberty are founded on that obedience. Each primary assembly will send the result of its polling to its district. Each district will send the tally of the ballots of its primary assemblies to the department, each department will send the tally of its districts to the National Convention which will announce the result of the general tally. And I swear by the love of Frenchmen for their country, by their devotion to the

2. A reference to the preceding speech by Robespierre.

cause of liberty, by their unshakable fidelity to the law, not a single voice will be raised in objection.

But intrigue! Intrigue will save the king. You would be made to believe that the majority of the nation is composed of intriguers, aristocrats, *feuillants,* moderates, in short, of the counter-revolutionary *honnêtes gens* of whom Lafayette spoke at this bar. And to give credence to such a black slander against the majority of the people who, in other circumstances are so basely flattered, mankind has been impudently defamed. The cry goes up: "Virtue has always been in the minority on this earth." Citizens, Catiline was a minority in the Roman Senate, and if that conspiring minority had prevailed, it would have meant the end of Rome, of the Senate, of liberty. Citizens! In the Constituent Assembly, at least until the revision, Cazalès and Maury were also a minority,[3] and if that minority, half from the nobility, half from the priesthood, had succeeded by its holy and noble insurrections in stifling the zeal of the majority, that would have been the end of the Revolution, and you would still today grovel at the feet of Louis, who retains of his former grandeur only remorse at having abused it. Citizens! Kings are in the minority on earth, and to enslave nations, they also say that virtue is in the minority. They say as well that the majority of the people is composed of intriguers upon whom silence must be imposed by terror, if the empires of the world are to be preserved from a general upheaval.

The majority of the nation composed of intriguers, aristocrats, *feuillants,* and so forth! Thus, according to those who voice an opinion which reflects so honorably on their country, I see that there is no one in the entire land who is truly pure, truly virtuous, truly devoted to the people and to liberty, but themselves and perhaps a hundred of their friends whom they will have the generosity to associate with their glory. Thus, so that they might found a government worthy of the principles they profess, I think it will be quite fitting to banish from French soil all those families whose *feuillantisme* is so perfidious, whose corruption so deep; to change France into a vast desert and, for its rapid regeneration and greater glory, to abandon it to their sublime conceptions.

Discord! Intrigue! Civil war! Yet you voted that the new Constitution, as well as the decree which abolished the monarchy, should be presented for the approval of the people. You did not fear intrigues or civil war; why so much assurance in one case, so much dread in the other? If you seriously fear that presenting the judgment of Louis for the ratification of the people

3. J.-A.-M. de Cazalès and J. S. Maury were among the right-wing deputies to the Constituent Assembly who had most consistently opposed its policies as too extreme. By this time, both had emigrated.

might produce civil war, why do you not fear this terrible result from the decree which establishes a republican government? . . .

We are accused! Certainly I am not surprised. There are men whose every breath is an imposture, as it is the nature of the serpent to exist only by the distillation of venom.

We are accused! Ah! had we but the insolent pride or the hypocritical ambition of our accusers! If, like them, we took pleasure in boasting of the little good we have done, we would tell with what courage we constantly fought against the tyranny of kings and against the still more dangerous tyranny of the brigands who, in the month of September, sought to found their power on the debris of the monarchy. We would tell of how we concurred, at least by our votes, with the decree which ended the aristocratic distinctions between active and inactive citizens and called all members of society to the equal exercise of sovereignty. We would tell, above all, that on the tenth of August we did not leave the chair except to come to the rostrum to propose the decree of suspension for Louis, while all those valiant sons of Brutus, so ready to slaughter disarmed tyrants, buried their terror in an underground chamber and there awaited the issue of the battle which liberty waged against despotism.

We are accused, we are denounced, as was done on the second of September before the assassins' steel. But we know that Tiberius Gracchus died by the hand of a misled people, whom he had always defended. His fate holds no terror for us; all our blood is at the disposal of the people; and in shedding it for them, we will have but one regret—not to have more to offer.

We are accused, if not of wishing to provoke civil war in the departments, at least of provoking disturbances in Paris, by upholding an opinion which displeases the true friends of liberty!

But why would an opinion provoke disturbances? Because these true friends of liberty threaten with death those citizens who are so unhappy as not to share their opinions. Is this proof of the freedom of the National Convention? There will be disturbances in Paris, and you announce them! I admire the sagacity of such a prophesy. Does it in fact seem very difficult, Citizens, to predict the burning of a house while one carries the torch which is to light the fire?

Yes, they want civil war, these men who make the assassination of friends of tyranny a precept and who, at the same time, designate as friends of tyranny those whom their hate wishes to sacrifice. They want civil war, these men who call for arms against the representatives of the nation and for insurrection against its laws. They want civil war, the men who demand the dissolution of the government, the abolition of the Convention. They demand the abolition of the Convention, the dissolution of the government, these men who put forth as a principle, not that anyone would seek to disavow it, that in a great Assembly a minority can sometimes know the truth while the majority is fallen into error; but also that it is the duty of the minority to make itself judge of the errors of the majority and to make its judgments legitimate by insurrections. Catiline should reign in the Senate; the private will should be substituted for the general will; that is, the will of a few insolent oppressors should be substituted for that of the people and tyranny for liberty. They want civil war, these men who teach maxims destructive of the entire social order in this assembly, in popular gatherings, in public squares; they want civil war, these men who accuse reason of perfidious *feuillantisme,* justice of dishonorable cowardice, and humanity, holy humanity, of conspiracy. Those who call traitor any citizen who has not reached the heights of brigandage and assassination; those, finally, who pervert all notions of morality and by speeches full of artifice and hypocritical flattery constantly push the people to the most deplorable excess.

Civil war for having proposed that homage be rendered to the sovereignty of the people! In your opinion then, is sovereignty of peoples a calamity for mankind? I understand you; you wish to reign.

On the day of the Champ-de-Mars your ambition was more modest. Then you composed and sought signatures for a petition whose object was to have the people consulted about the fate of Louis, then returning from Varennes. Your heart was not tormented by fear of discord; it cost you no pain to recognize the sovereignty of the people. Could it be that then they agreed with your plans, which now they might cross? Is there in fact any sovereignty for you but that of your passions? Madmen! Did you flatter yourselves that France broke the scepter of kings that it might again bend its neck, degraded beneath the yoke?

They have spoken of courage, of greatness of soul; it would be, they said, a sign of weakness not to have the judgment executed before consulting the will of the people. I recognize no greatness in a legislator but that of being true to his principles. I know that in a revolution one is often reduced to veiling the statue of law, but it seems to me that this maxim is being strangely abused.

When one seeks to make a revolution against tyranny, it is necessary to veil the statue of the law which consecrates or protects tyranny. But when you veil the statue of the law which consecrates the sovereignty of the people—you start a revolution which will turn to the tyrant's profit. . . .

In summary: Any act emanating from the representatives of the people is an attempt against their sovereign if it is not submitted for formal or tacit ratification. The people alone, who promised inviolability to Louis, can declare that they wish to make use of the right to punish, which formerly they had renounced. Powerful considerations should hold you to these principles; if you are faithful to them, you run no risk of reproach. If the people desire the death of Louis, they will command it; if, on the contrary, you take their power from them, you will incur at least the reproach of having strayed from your duty; and what a terrifying responsibility such a deviation will bring upon your heads! . . . I have no more to say.

35. Purge by Insurrection (31 May–2 June 1793)

After their defeat in the king's trial, the political tide began to run against the Girondins. A rapidly worsening economic situation brought renewed unrest in Paris, exacerbated in March by word of a counterrevolutionary uprising in the Vendée (western France) and of the defeat of French forces in Holland under General Dumouriez—who subsequently defected to the Austrians. News of these reverses triggered an abortive popular uprising in the capital (on 10 March) and escalating demands for the expulsion of Brissot and his associates from the Convention, where they were being effectively portrayed by their enemies as an embattled minority preventing concerted action in defense of the Revolution. During this period, the alliance between the Montagnards in the assembly and the political activists in the sections also became closer. In April, Marat called for insurrectionary action to purge the divided assembly of the "criminal representatives" who were impeding its action, and the call was taken up by the Parisian sections. The Girondins responded by demanding Marat's impeachment, only to see him triumphantly acquitted by the Revolutionary Tribunal.

In May, the Girondins secured the creation of a special commission of the Convention to investigate and forestall the possibility of a new popular insurrection. The activities of this Commission of Twelve only served to inflame the situation further. With the threat of popular action growing (and as the Convention's votes went first to the Montagnards, then to the Girondins, then back to the Montagnards again) the commission was first suppressed on 27 May, then reinstated on 28 May, and then suppressed again on 31 May—this time while the assembly was surrounded by a vast insurrectionary crowd. Finally, on 2 June, the Convention was forced by popular action to decree the arrest of twenty-nine Girondin deputies. Other arrests followed as the Girondins were effectively eliminated as a political force. Their control of the assembly assured by this purge, the

From *Archives parlementaires de 1787 à 1860, première série (1787 à 1799)*, edited by M. J. Mavidal and M. E. Laurent, 2d ed., 82 vols. (Paris: Dupont, 1879–1913), vol. 66, pp. 20–21, 208, 481–82. Translated for this volume by the editor, Keith Michael Baker.

Montagnards lost no time in putting together a new republican constitution, which was submitted to the Convention on 10 June and adopted ten days later. Ratified by popular vote in July, this Constitution of 1793 was superseded by the emergency government of the Terror before it went into effect.

Three documents follow. The first offers a justification of the insurrectionary purge presented to the Convention by a committee of the Paris Commune. The second presents a denunciation of the purge by the citizens of Rennes—one of many such addresses received by the Convention as provincial cities began to rise up in revolt against the revolutionary extremism for which Paris now stood. The third gives the text of a speech by Danton, praising the effects of the new revolution from the Montagnard point of view. The reactions of the Convention to these manifestos are given in parentheses.

___

Address of the Central Revolutionary Committee of the Paris Commune (presented to the Convention on 3 June 1793)

Legislators,

Experience has just demonstrated in a truly sublime manner that sooner or later justice will have its day. The astonishing revolution that has just occurred before your eyes is a great lesson for those who will follow you in the conduct of legislation.

You have seen the people of Paris bestir itself in its entirety to resist oppression and demand justice against those whose presence was inimical to your labors—those to whom, with good reason, it attributed all the Republic's misfortunes. Three times, the sickened and outraged people rushed to arms. It had given a number of its fellow citizens the right to use its power; they acted to deliver it from the traitors who were dividing it. The tocsin sounded, the alarm gun fired, not to signal the spilling of blood, but to announce the dangers to liberty and the mortal blows being leveled at it.

You have long known the causes of the events we remind you of here. You carried in your bosom the germ of the evil. You had observed it since its birth; you had not stopped its growth, at first believing that the mass of the body was healthy, but without anticipating that the smallest germ could soon infect the whole. Enlightened only too late by the results of this chronic malady, you almost despaired of curing it.

The people, whose happiness you must achieve, saw in the fatal and continual divisions poisoning your political existence sad evidence of your powerlessness to make it happy, as well as you; it therefore decided to do for you what you could not do for it.

It owes to a long sequence of misfortunes the advantage of being able to envisage them calmly and to know how to prevent them. It has seen the whole of Europe take up arms to reduce it to slavery, its blood shamefully squandered by perfidious generals, its external enemies becoming daily more bold and insolent. . . . It has seen civil war ignited in the center of the Republic; its internal enemies emboldened by new crimes, and openly plotting its ruin; the scourge of famine provoked against it; its cause and that of liberty uselessly defended by its faithful representatives; discord called forth from one end of France to the other. It has seen Paris denounced and slandered in the departments; the seduced departments arming themselves against Paris; the departments themselves divided, town against town, section against section, citizen against citizen.

The people was conscious of all these evils: it was time to remedy them. It was urgently necessary to give a great example. Well, the people of Paris has risen up and given that example. It has overthrown the monstrous colossus that was growing up beside the statue of liberty, and threatened to crush it.

To prevail, the people has only to show itself; its triumph has not been bloody. . . .

Legislators, you had been halted at the very beginning of your career. You have long made vain efforts to free yourselves of those men who were digging a bottomless abyss for you, as for us. This odious struggle is over. Finish now the immortal work of the republican constitution. If all that you have been able to do until now has appeared without force, yet the torrents that storms produce quickly dry up; durable laws are conceived and delivered only in a time of calm. A single bad law is a rotten seed that develops into an infinite succession of crimes and misfortunes. Let each of you, entirely devoted to the public good, henceforth direct all your efforts to a common center, and you will see the people applauding your labors; the cries of grief and indignation which have been striking your ears for so long will change into acclamations of joy, and you will hear all around you only the blessings of your fellow citizens.

Address of the Citizens of Rennes, Meeting in Primary Assembly (read to the Convention on 9 June)

The National Convention is no longer free *(mutterings)* and the audacity of the bloody oppressors who dominate it is so excessive that the representatives of twenty-six million people have never been able to acknowledge the debasement into which a handful of criminals have plunged them. . . . *(Enough!)* Too long have we kept these cruel truths within our hearts . . . *(Enough!)* and too long have we called upon you in the name of the *patrie* to renounce your scandalous dissensions, or to dissolve your assembly if you no longer believe yourselves capable of saving France. You have been deaf to the voice of administrators throughout France! The voice of the people has been raised, it sounds forth everywhere, it announces the general will through the organ of all the communes. The people asks what has been done by the representatives of a nation which awaited its salvation and glory from them. What spectacle do they present to an anxious and attentive Europe? They have offered the universe the hideous spectacle of passions in turmoil. These are not men peacefully considering the public good; this is a violent, factious party—we have thought of saying a conspiratorial one—imprinting upon the majority of the National Convention a sentiment of terror that crushes it and reduces it to absolute nullity.

On 10 March this faction tries to have slaughtered, in the very midst of the National Convention itself, those representatives whose enlightenment and integrity it had to fear. The shameful scheme miscarries. Shortly thereafter, it provokes the proscription of those its daggers had been unable to reach. A solemn decree repudiates this attempt and secures the triumph of virtue. A commission is created to pursue and unmask this conspiracy hatched against public liberty and national representation. It is already picking up the threads, and already some of the guilty are being arrested— the factious subjugate one part of the Paris sections and take over the other, dragging them to the Convention, from which they wrest a decree dissolving the commission. The next day, this decree is revoked. This makes them even bolder; the tocsin sounds, the alarm gun is heard everywhere; and if they fail on this day to consummate their horrible attack, this is because all of Paris has risen up, and the mass of the people is pure. But they persevere; and two days later, their designated victims are in their power.

Here hitherto unheard-of violations of every principle pile up. All the horror of the blackest plot unfolds. The most sacred rights of man and of the citizen are ignored; the majesty of the nation is insulted; liberty and public confidence are attacked in their inmost sanctuary. A plebicide is committed without example in the annals of the most hideous despotism that ever existed. The secrecy of letters entrusted to the Paris post is now but an empty word: they are opened and confiscated, or closed again with a new seal that indicates and openly announces the crime that has been committed. All communication is interrupted between Paris and the departments. Paris is isolated from the entire Republic, and in this state of revolt by a criminal faction against the unity and indivisibility of the Republic, in this appalling overthrow of all the laws, France doubts whether its representatives are still living.

What is the people's duty in this situation? It must rise up in its entirety and march to Paris—not to fight against it, as those perfidious administrators want so insidiously to convince people—but to unite with the thousands of brothers who are only awaiting its presence to repudiate oppression and restore to the national representation its dignity, integrity, and liberty.

This movement will be fearsome. Calculate all its effects; hasten to prevent them. Revoke the odious decree arresting our most incorruptible defenders *(mutterings);* restore them to the Republic. You will answer with your heads.

Danton, *Speech to the National Convention* (14 June 1793)

In giving France a republican constitution, we are reaching the moment of the true founding of French liberty. Political bodies, like physical ones, always seem threatened with impending destruction at the point of a great creation. We are surrounded by storms, the thunder growls. So! The work that will immortalize the French nation will emerge from the midst of these outbursts. Remember, citizens, what happened at the time of Lafayette's conspiracy.[1] We seemed then to be in the same position in which we find ourselves today. Recall the state of Paris at that time: patriots were everywhere oppressed and proscribed; we were threatened with the greatest misfortunes. Today we are in the same situation—it seems that there is nothing but peril for those who have created liberty. Lafayette and his faction were soon unmasked: today, the new enemies of the people have betrayed themselves, they have fled, they have changed their name and status, and taken false passports. *(Applause.)* This Brissot, the leader of the impious sect that has just been smothered, this man who boasted of his courage and his poverty in accusing me of being covered with gold, is now only a wretch who cannot escape the blade of the laws, and to whom the people has already done justice in arresting him as a conspirator.

It is said that the Paris insurrection is causing agitation in the departments. I declare in the face of the universe that these events will be the glory of this superb city. I proclaim in the face of France that without the cannon of 31 May, without the insurrection, the conspirators would have triumphed, they would be giving us laws. *(Applause is heard on several occasions in a great part of the assembly and in the galleries.)* Let the crime of this insurrection fall upon us. I myself called for it when I said

---

1. After the Champ de Mars Massacre (see document 29) Lafayette was identified increasingly as an enemy of Parisian popular activism. Charged with command of the revolutionary armies, he nevertheless returned to Paris briefly from the frontier during the agitation preceding 10 August 1792, in an abortive effort to impose order. His subsequent denunciations of the Revolution of 10 August were met by his dimissal from his command. He fled France on 17 August 1792.

that if there were a hundred men like me in the Convention, we would resist oppression and establish liberty on unshakeable foundations.

Recall that the agitation reigning in the departments is reported to have
appeared only after the events that occurred here. Well, there are documents proving that before 31 May the departments had been sent a circular
urging them to form a federation and band together.

(*Many voices:* "That's true!")

What remains to be done? To identify ourselves with the people of
Paris, with all the good citizens, and to give an account of what has occurred. . . . No, the inhabitants of Paris do not begrudge the liberty of any
representative of the people; they have taken the attitude that was appropriate to them; they have risen in insurrection. Do not let the addresses slandering Paris that are arriving from the departments appall you; they are the
work of a few intriguers, not of the citizens of the departments—remember that similar ones came in support of the tyrant. *(Applause.)* Paris is the
center where everything comes to a head; Paris will be the focal point that
receives all the rays of French patriotism, burning all its enemies with
them. I demand that you explain yourselves faithfully regarding the insurrection that has had such happy results. The people sees that these men
who have been accused of wanting to gorge themselves on the blood of the
people have done more for the people's happiness in a week than the Convention, tormented by intriguers, had been able to accomplish since it
came into existence. *(Applause.)* This is the result that must be presented
to the people of the departments, which is good and will applaud your wise
measures. The fleeing criminals have spread terrors wherever they went;
they have exaggerated and misrepresented everything. Once disabused, the
people will react more strongly, and take vengeance against those who have
misled it.

As to the question that concerns us, I believe that we must take general
measures for all the departments; twenty-four hours should be granted to
the administrators who might have been led astray, without however giving
any amnesty to the ringleaders. Patriots must fight in the departments and
the communes against administrators who are aristocrats—they must be
replaced by true republicans. Finally, I ask the Convention to declare that,
without the insurrection of 31 May, liberty would be no more. *(Applause.)*

Citizens, no weakness. Make this solemn declaration to the French
people; tell it that some still want the return of the nobles, that the criminal
horde has just proved that it did not want a constitution, that it must pronounce between the Mountain and this faction. Say to French citizens:
"Resume the enjoyment of your imprescriptible rights; rally around the
Convention; prepare yourselves to accept the constitution it is going to

present to you—this constitution which, as I have already said, is a battery of guns firing upon the enemies of liberty, to destroy them all. Prepare an armed force, but let it be against the rebels in the Vendée." *(Applause.)* Suppress the rebellion in this part of France, and you will have peace.

The people, informed about this latest period of the Revolution, will not allow itself to be caught unawares. Slanders will no longer be heard against a city which has created liberty, which will not perish with it, but will triumph with liberty and pass with it into immortality. *(Enthusiastic applause.)*

The Evolution of the Terror

36. Documents of the Sans-Culottes

The term *sans-culotte* literally means "without breeches." It refers to those who wore the trousers of the common people, rather than the "aristocratic" breeches of the well-to-do. During the French Revolution "sans-culotte" became the preferred label for political activists among the Parisian populace, whose revolutionary interventions again and again pushed the Revolution to the left. Entrenched in the sections and in the municipal government (*Commune*) of Paris, the sans-culottes provided the insurrectionary striking force that made possible the overthrow of the monarchy, the purging of the National Convention, and the establishment of the Terror. Many of the extreme measures adopted during the Terror—for example, the General Maximum, the Levée en Masse, the Law of Suspects, and the creation of revolutionary government—originated in their demands. The sans-culottes were a socially diverse collection of shopkeepers, clerks, master craftsmen, journeymen and laborers; but they were held together by an intense devotion to the Revolution, a passion for direct popular government, and a profound aversion to aristocrats and to the rich.

From *Die Sansculotten von Paris: Dokumenten zur Geschichte der Volksbewegung, 1793–1794*, edited by Walter Markov and Albert Soboul (Berlin: Akademie Verlag, 1957), pp. 2–7, 98–108, 176–79, 214–19. "Not A Moment to Lose" translated by D. Carroll Joynes; other selections translated by Keith Michael Baker and William H. Sewell Jr.

An Answer to the Impertinent Question: But What Is a Sans-Culotte? (April 1793)

A sans-culotte, you stuck-up bastards? He is a being who always goes on foot, who has no millions, as all of you wish to have, no castle, no valets to serve him, and who lives simply with his wife and children, if he has any, on the fourth or fifth floor.

He is useful, because he knows how to plow a field, to forge, to saw, to file, to roof a building, to make shoes and to spill out the last drop of his blood for the salvation of the Republic.

And because he works, you will not meet him at the *Caffé de Chartres*, nor at the gambling dens where men conspire over a game of dice, nor at the Theater of the Nation when *l'Ami des lois* is playing, nor at the Vaudeville Theater at the playing of *la Chaste Susanne*, nor in the reading rooms where for two sous, which are so precious, one is offered the garbage of Gorsas with the *Chronique* and the *patriote français*.

In the evening, he attends his section, not powdered, perfumed, and booted in the hope of catching the attention of the female citizens at the tribune, but to support good motions with all his force and to pulverize those which come from the abominable faction of the men of estate.

For the rest, a sans-culotte always has his saber with its sharp edge—to split the ears of all the evil-doers. Sometimes he goes about armed with his pike; but at the first sound of the drum, one sees him depart for the Vendée, for the Army of the Alps, or for the Army of the North. . . .

Definition of the Moderate, the Feuillant, the Aristocrat, in Short of the Class of Citizens upon Whom Should Fall the Forced Loan That Must Be Raised throughout the Republic (May 1793)

[The guardian angel of liberty and equality of the Republic one and indivisible. To the citizens composing the committee of petitions, Paris.]

The aristocrat is one who out of scorn or indifference has not enrolled in the registers of the National Guard and has not taken his Civil Oath. . . . One who by his conduct, his activities, his speeches, his writings, and his connections has given proofs of how bitterly he regrets the passing of the Old Regime, and disapproves of the Revolution in all its parts. One whose conduct leads us to presume that he would send money to the emigrés or join the enemy army. He only lacks the ability to do the one and the chance to do the other. One who has always despaired of the triumph of the Revolution. One who has announced grievous news known to be false. One who by a perverted economy leaves land uncultivated without wishing either to lease it out or to rent it to a sharecropper or to sell it at its just value. One who has not bought national lands when he had the chance and the ability. And above all one who has declared that he dare not buy them; and counsels against performing that act of civic duty. One who has not furnished work to laborers and journeymen when he had the ability and the chance, at a price which is progressive relative to costs of food. One who has not contributed to subscriptions for the volunteers, and above all one who has never given in proportion to his ability. One who by his aristocratic sentiments does not frequent priests who have taken the oath, and above all one who has counseled not to do so. One who has not improved the lot of indigent and patriotic humanity; having notoriously the ability. One who out of ill will does not wear a *cocarde* of three inches in circumference. One who has bought other than national clothing, and above all those who do not glory in the title and the hairstyle of the sans-culotte.

The guardian angel of the republic assures you that the definition is very exact and that the true patriot has done the opposite for the general good, it is to be hoped it will be put into execution. No land tax unless the indigent class of the people pays only two sous for every hundred livres of property of any kind instead of twenty-five, fifty, and eighty-five livres as all the aristocratic municipal officers make them pay, above all those of the Vendée.

The annihilation of paternal despotism in permitting children or citizens to enjoy maternal as well as paternal properties, but the aristocratic concubines who become mistresses or wives find that perfectly legitimate. [*sic*]

Vengeance! Vengeance!

Not a Moment to Lose, or Discourse by Citizen Lacroix to the Unity Section, at the Meeting of July 28, 1793

The Executive Council and the Committee on Public Safety have just entrusted me with an important mission in the southern departments. . . . Before leaving, I would like to submit to you some reflections on the truly alarming position of the republic.

I have already, a number of times, pointed to the means to save our nation quickly and conclusively, to put an end to this crisis which exhausts patriotism and daily diminishes its resources. They have not been implemented as the circumstances require; a few of them have been translated into decrees, it is true, but only partially, and it is only from the entire set of them that one could hope for a happy outcome.

Since the 10th of August [1792], the only date from which we can really speak of the welfare of the people, we have been dragged ignominiously from treason to treason; we have been tossed back and forth between mixed successes and frightful reverses. The fatal experience of the past—those daily conspiracies—did not cure us of our credulity. We have always waited until we were at the edge of the abyss before we thought about not falling in. Our enthusiasm for a few ephemeral and perfidious successes, and the confidence which followed, cost the lives of thousands of republicans, fattened thousands of bloodsuckers, and finally brought the republic close to its coffin.

An entire year has almost gone by since 10 August, and during this long interval, in a revolution as fast as our own, it would have been easy to manufacture at least a million muskets, and at least twenty thousand cannon, by establishing throughout the republic a great number of new arms manufacturers and cannon foundries. We did not lack iron ore, because our soil produces it in abundance; and two hundred thousand bells have been awaiting the foundry. This measure which I proposed more than two years ago, was not passed until the 23d of this month, but it should not be at the moment one begins to perceive the depth of the precipice that one starts to consider what one should have done. Prudence and the general interest compel us to take quickly the measures that will prevent us from going over the edge. There is perhaps still time. Not that I would want to argue that liberty could be extinguished. It is indestructible, because the revolution is made in mens' spirits. . . . But by promptly employing measures proportional to the gravity of the danger, we will avoid terrible bloodshed; and we will save resources, which are already exhausted. These two considerations should be compelling in the eyes of friends of the nation and of humanity.

Before outlining the remedy, we must understand the disease. Let us therefore glance quickly at both the interior and exterior situations of the republic. Within, the monster of civil war, swollen with the poisons of Roland and his factions, armed with seditious and destructive torches, and disguised under the name of federalism, lashes out at different points within the republic. It tries to pierce the Parisian heart with its parricidal dagger, because it knows that Paris is, by its situation, and by its interest in the public welfare, the heart of the political body, and that with the heart once pierced, the body would be in danger of perishing.

Marseille, Toulon, Lyon, Bordeaux, and Caen are prey to the fury of federalism. The ardent friends of the people are being slaughtered there in an atrocious manner. The counterrevolutionaries constantly spread dissension in the body politic, stirring up citizens and spreading consternation into the very bosom of families. A concerted system of hoarding spreads its ill effects to the farthest hamlet in the Republic, dries up the very springs of the population, and reduces men to fighting with animals for their very food.

On the one hand, the royalists offer the people the ghastly face of famine, on the other, the plague with which they are afflicted and with which they would like to contaminate us.

Our present ills also have their source in the perfidious inertia of some government agents, in the dearth of men of talent, honest and energetic, in the fatal credulousness of the people, which seems to watch without concern the rapid successes of the rebels in the Vendeé, and the approach of even more horrible disasters. On the other hand, one sees conspirators go unpunished, and as a consequence, conspiracies constantly reemerging. One sees a selfishness destructive of all virtues private and public, dissipation of funds and an almost general corruption of all public servants, a frightful surge of passions opposed to the public good. In a word, private interests are at war with the general interest.

Such is our domestic situation.

On our frontiers, there are eleven armies made up of brave republicans, among whom have crept a few cowards and a few mercenary brigands, some generals whose treason or ineptitude have, up to now, caused our failures, a swarm of entrepreneurs, greedy speculators, capable of swallowing in a day the entire public purse. There is a frightful disorder in every administration; an almost complete lack of provisions and armaments on many frontiers, a general and long-planned deployment of all the forces in Europe against us; the numerous minions of despots blockading France in some fashion, wishing to make it a vast prison. Our navy is immobile, our commerce destroyed. In the north, our enemies' success in taking Condé places Valenciennes in the gravest danger; in the Midi, Bellegarde has fallen. We witness the fury of kings against that liberty which, establishing itself in France, they fear would have a strong attraction; their very real plan to attack the Republic very soon and on all fronts, with forces superior to ours, which we will then be obliged to divide, and hence to weaken; an all-too-evident connivance between the enemies within and those outside. Such is the picture of our exterior situation. I hasten now to outline our resources.

First, it is a given that the internal ills stem, in large part, only from the ideas of public opinion. It is therefore time to purge it of the venom it has absorbed from Roland and his followers. For his opium den we must substitute without delay a true office for the formation of public spirit, comprised of courageous and energetic writers who have defended the rights of the people with equal courage and steadfastness. . . .

Food for the body is as important as food for the soul; one cannot operate without the other. Famine is one of the secrets tyrants use to subjugate peoples and it is certain that our enemies' scheme is to have us starve in the very midst of plenty. To accomplish this they will employ, if they can, hoarders, terror and popular agitations, which almost invariably lead to artificial scarcity. It is especially Paris that they want to starve, because they know that if this center and rallying point of republicanism can be subjugated, they will be able to dominate the other departments more easily. Paris must therefore be supplied by every imaginable means. We must establish an office of public assistance and subsistence and send republican agents to buy grain in the Beauce, the Ile de France, the Soissonnais and the Brie. And enough must be bought not for a month, but for a year—then the counterrevolutionary plot will be pretty much destroyed.

Given that the fruits of the earth are intended by nature to fulfill the needs of all its offspring, the people has the incontestable right to restrict, within reasonable limits, the greed of rich landowners and hoarders, and to fix the price of basic commodities.

If this measure is not quickly enacted, the greed of the speculators will grow in proportion to our own weakness, and the people will starve to death on the very soil it has tilled, and in the very shadow of immense stockpiles of food. The adoption of this measure will frustrate the projects of our enemies. It will revive abundance . . . and how could it not be revived in a land where the soil produces twice as much grain as is needed to feed the people? . . .

Everyone will agree that the next three months are the most critical for the revolution, because our enemies within and without want to make use of all the means they have so long prepared to subjugate us, and these measures are such that we cannot destroy them without a general and extraordinary deployment of all the moral and physical forces of the republic.

For this purpose, it seems indispensable to me to send into each department one or more agents [*commissaires*] chosen from the ranks of the most vigorous republicans. Their powers would be such that they would have the right to choose, from among patriots in the departments, other agents for the provinces where they would be known, so that there would not be a single hamlet in the republic that is not visited by a friend of the people, charged with putting all the resources of the nation to use.

These agents will form throughout the republic an indissoluble chain of patriotism and prompt communication, and of the proper means to preserve liberty. They would identify men fit for combat, and inventory grain, arms, wagons and all the other things necessary for the general defense; they would enlighten the people as to its own best interests, imbue it with republican vigor, carry out decrees of the Convention, organize new battalions, and bring together into a single mass, at the central point in each department, the scattered forces of the republic. . . . They would oversee the various administrations and public establishments, such as hospitals, arms manufacturers, cannon foundries, food stores, ammunition, clothing and equipment. In a word, they would be able to take all appropriate measures to assure the triumph of liberty, and would be ready to transmit to the people, in the same hour, the same moment, that revolutionary momentum necessary to preserve the Republic.

The perfidious inertia of some agents of the government having left us with a dearth of friends, we will be obliged to have recourse to violent and extraordinary means to arm those who go to fight our enemies, such as disarming all those who will not go, or halting the private work of wheelwrights, carpenters, and woodworkers, and forcing them to make gun stocks, gun carriages, caissons, and wagons. We must stop the labors of locksmiths, blacksmiths, toolmakers and all ironworkers, in order that they be engaged solely on the manufacture of cannon and other items. All citizens without work will be engaged at the cannon foundries, which will be established, if necessary, right in our [military] camps. All horses not directly used in agriculture or in the transport of essential commodities must be used, without exception, for the needs of the state. All citizens, male or female, whoever they are, must be available for work on those projects of public utility for which they are suited. No one can be idle at a moment which will determine the fate of the world.

These bold measures would still be fruitless, and could even turn to our disadvantage, if the Convention did not immediately decree that any noble, any foreigner, any priest, who holds a place in our armies, must withdraw within twenty-four hours of the publication of the decree, to be replaced by unswerving republicans nominated by the soldiers, with the exception of the commanding generals.

Our disastrous experience in the past only demonstrates the indispensable necessity of adopting this measure; if it had been accepted when I proposed it, at the time of Dumouriez's treason, Custines, Biron, Wimphen [sic], and all the other conspirators would not have betrayed us.[1] . . . And finally, the Republic would not be in such very great danger, even though the dangers of the country have grown constantly since the horrible conspiracy of Dumouriez.

The revolutionary army, the camp of forty thousand men near Paris which had been decreed, has not yet been formed. Who is to be accused of

---

1. Dumouriez, Custine, Biron, and Wimpffen were all generals of aristocratic birth entrusted with command of one or another of the revolutionary armies. Dumouriez, formerly foreign minister in the Girondin ministry of Spring 1792, commanded the Army of the North until April 1793, when (after plotting with the Austrians to restore the monarchy) he deserted to the enemy. His betrayal heightened the suspicions cast upon the noble generals upon whose military expertise revolutionary governments still relied. Increasingly at odds with civil authorities, Custine and Biron were arrested in July 1793; the former was executed in August, the latter in December. Wimpffen joined the "federalist revolts" in the summer of 1793, but successfully evaded execution after their defeat.

such gross negligence; is it the former Committee of Public Safety, is it the Executive Council? Now that the Committee of Public Safety is comprised of true republicans, we have grounds to hope that it will take bold measures, that it will establish not only a camp of 40,000 men, but camps in many departments. . . .

The 10th of August seems an appropriate occasion upon which to inaugurate this great plan. At the very hour when the alarm bell rang in the palace of the tyrant, when his throne was broken to pieces, let that be the hour when our alarm shall ring out. The call will be sounded throughout the Republic. Let the friends of the nation take up their arms and form many battalions. Let those without weapons drive the munition wagons. Let women carry the vital supplies, or knead bread. Let the signal for combat be given by our national song—a week of enthusiasm can do more for the *patrie* than eight years of combat.

Petition to the National Convention Concerning a Special Jury against Hoarders (29 September 1793)

A law which has earned you the expression of our gratitude at first struck with terror those men who speculate in public misery, by hoarding all types of goods necessary to subsistance; but although their crimes are evident, although their sudden fortunes mark them for the vengeance of the laws, they are nevertheless beginning to get over their fright; they see that the instrument of death remains suspended in air instead of falling on their heads; they know that the most salutary institution of judgment by juries nearly always puts their fate into the hands of their friends—enriched like them, with the substance of the poor, and who fear to provide a bad example against themselves.

It is time that your law and the nation stopped serving as their laughing-stock. We demand much more than has been done so far in this regard: that a special jury for hoarders be chosen outside the class of merchants, bankers, speculators and even the rich; and that its opinions be given out loud, as has been done for the counterrevolutionaries, so that the execution of the law may be enlightened by taking place before the eyes of all, so that it may be given over to those who have the greatest interest in cutting off the fortunes and the heads of those who wish to take away from the nation its elements of life; that is to say uniquely to the poor citizens, to veritable sans-culottes. Because finally the sans-culottes are much more numerous; and it is an evident verity that the Nation is sans-culottes and that the small number of those who have all the riches in their hands are not the nation; that they are nothing but Privileged Persons, who are reaching the end of their privilege.

And let there be no fear of partiality in the judgments of the less fortunate citizens. They are rich in virtue, we fear only their long habitude of pardoning; which they must get rid of if they wish to save themselves and eventually to enjoy the public happiness that will be your creation. . . .

The general assembly of the section of the Observatory adopted this petition in the sessions of the 29th September and 11th October of the year II of the Republic one and indivisible. . . .

Be it known by the minutes of the report of the commissioners charged with communicating said petition to the forty-seven other sections of the Commune of Paris, that thirty-six of those to which the petition was communicated have adhered to it unanimously, and have named commissioners to present it to the National Convention, as containing the expression of their just indignation against these perverse beings who make a cruel game of speculating in public misery.

Extract from the Register of Deliberations of the General Council of the Commune of Paris, 20th Day of the 1st Month, Year II of the French Republic (11 September 1793)

Distinguishing characteristics of suspected persons, to whom certificates of civic loyalty must be refused:

1. Those who, in assemblies of the people, arrest its energy by crafty discourses, turbulent cries and threats.

2. Those, more prudent, who speak mysteriously of the misfortunes of the republic, are full of pity for the lot of the people, and are always ready to spread bad news with an affected grief.

3. Those who have changed their conduct and language in line with events; who, silent concerning the crimes of royalists and federalists, declaim emphatically against the trifling faults of the patriots; who, in order to appear republicans, affect an austerity, a studied severity, and yield as soon as it is a question of a moderate or an aristocrat.

4. Those who pity the farmers and greedy merchants against whom the law is obliged to take measures.

5. Those who have the words *Liberty, Republic* and *Patrie* constantly on their lips, but who consort with former nobles, counterrevolutionary priests, aristocrats, feuillants, moderates, and show concern for their fate.

6. Those who have taken no active part in revolutionary matters and who, to exonerate themselves, make much of their payment of taxes, their patriotic gifts, their service in the National Guard, by proxy or otherwise, etc., etc.

7. Those who received the republican constitution [i.e. the Jacobin Constitution of 1793] with indifference and have given credence to false fears concerning its establishment and duration.

8. *Those who, having done nothing against liberty, have also done nothing for it.*

9. Those who do not attend the meetings of their sections and give as excuses that they don't know how to speak or that their occupation prevents them.

10. Those who speak with contempt of the constituted authorities, the symbols of the law, popular societies, defenders of liberty, etc., etc.

11. Those who have signed counterrevolutionary petitions or frequented antidemocratic societies and clubs.

12. The partisans of Lafayette, and the assassins who followed him to the Champ de Mars.

The general council, having heard the list of characteristics distinguishing suspects, approves its wording; and considering that it is of the greatest importance to the republic to establish on fixed foundations the grounds for rejection or adoption for office, orders the publication and communication of the distinguishing characteristics of suspects to the forty-eight sections and the popular societies.

Petition of the William Tell Section to the Convention, 22 Brumaire (12 November) 1793

REPRESENTATIVES OF THE PEOPLE,

You have just given a terrifying example,[2] made to astonish the universe and strike fear into the most guilty.

The William Tell Section congratulates you. It will congratulate you still more if you maintain fear and terror as the great order of the day, that fear and terror which are the two most powerful levers of revolutionaries.

Blood is necessary to punish so many liberticidal and nationicidal crimes; still more is necessary to prevent those that would follow.

It is from this moment only that the soul of Pelletier, Marat, Chalier and so many other glorious martyrs of liberty begin to find appeasement.

Representatives, the death of a handful of conspirators cannot sever all the threads of the most execrable plot ever conceived in the human heart; a hecatomb of traitors is necessary to bring healing to all the wounds of the fatherland, butchered by unnatural children.

The aristocracy has not renounced its twilight schemes. Its favorite nourishment is murder and carnage. The fall of twenty-one heads, that of the indecent Marie-Antoinette and of the beastly inhabitants of the infernal

---

2. The execution of Marie-Antoinette and twenty-one Girondin deputies, including Brissot, Vergniaud and Gensonné.

palace, has only kindled its fury, and perhaps at this very moment it is planning to overthrow the firmest column of liberty.

There are still more enemies, no less dangerous.

There are the foul public pillagers. Legislators, spare none of these vampires of the *patrie*. Scrutinize the scandalous fortunes that ceaselessly insult the public misery and close the tombs only when our internal enemies, the most perfidious of all, are swallowed up within them.

Representatives, the days of mercy are past. Let the avenging blade fall upon every guilty head, let no criminal be spared. A great people expects great measures from you.

Never forget the sublime words of the prophet, Marat: *Sacrifice 200,000 heads, and you will save 1,000,000.*

Representatives, you have decreed a day of rest in every ten. But remember well that the malevolent know no days of rest.

Let each of us be a committee of surveillance. The forty-eight sections of the greatest commune of the Republic will never abandon you. To triumph or perish with you, such is their vow. The William Tell Section here solemnly takes that vow and demands that the anniversary of the punishment of the twenty-one be called the day of expiation.

37. Decree Establishing the *Levée en Masse* (23 August 1793)

During the spring and summer of 1793, the allied armies of the European monarchies advanced against the French on all fronts. In response to this threat, the sans-culottes called for the mobilization of the population and all of its resources against the external enemy. Adopted by the Convention on 23 August 1793, this measure, so enthusiastically demanded by urban political activists, encountered considerable resistance in the countryside, and in turn prompted further demands for revolutionary terror. It has been estimated that the Levée en Masse armed 300,000 men, bringing the army of the Republic to about 800,000.

1. Henceforth, until the enemies have been driven from the territory of the Republic, the French people are in permanent requisition for army service.

The young men shall go to battle; the married men shall forge arms and transport provisions; the women shall make tents and clothes, and shall

Reprinted with permission of Macmillan Publishing Company from John Hall Stewart, ed., *A Documentary Survey of the French Revolution*, pp. 472–74. © 1951 by Macmillan Publishing Company.

serve in the hospitals; the children shall turn old linen into lint; the old men shall repair to the public places, to stimulate the courage of the warriors and preach the unity of the Republic and hatred of kings.

2. National buildings shall be converted into barracks; public places into armament workshops; the soil of cellars shall be washed in lye to extract saltpeter therefrom.

3. Arms of caliber shall be turned over exclusively to those who march against the enemy; the service of the interior shall be carried on with fowling pieces and sabers.

4. Saddle horses are called for to complete the cavalry corps; draught horses, other than those employed in agriculture, shall haul artillery and provisions.

5. The Committee of Public Safety[1] is charged with taking all measures necessary for establishing, without delay, a special manufacture of arms of all kinds, in harmony with the *élan* and the energy of the French people. Accordingly, it is authorized to constitute all establishments, manufactories, workshops, and factories deemed necessary for the execution of such works, as well as to requisition for such purpose, throughout the entire extent of the Republic, the artists and workmen who may contribute to their success. . . . The central establishment of said special manufacture shall be established at Paris.

6. The representatives of the people dispatched for the execution of the present law shall have similar authority in their respective *arrondissements,* acting in concert with the Committee of Public Safety; they are invested with the unlimited powers attributed to the representatives of the people with the armies.

7. No one may obtain a substitute in the service to which he is summoned. The public functionaries shall remain at their posts.

8. The levy shall be general. Unmarried citizens or childless widowers, from eighteen to twenty-five years, shall go first; they shall meet, without delay, at the chief town of their districts, where they shall practice manual exercise daily, while awaiting the hour of departure. . . .

11. The battalion organized in each district shall be united under a banner bearing the inscription: *The French people risen against tyrants.*

12. Such battalions shall be organized according to established decrees, and their pay shall be the same as that of the battalions at the frontiers.

13. In order to collect supplies in sufficient quantity, the farmers and

1. The Committee of Public Safety, first established on 6 April 1793, was a provisional committee created by the Convention to coordinate the urgent measures deemed necessary to save the Republic. Reelected by the Convention on a regular basis, its twelve members became the effective government of France during the Terror.

managers of national property shall deposit the produce of such property, in the form of grain, in the chief town of their respective districts.

14. Owners, farmers, and others possessing grain shall be required to pay, in kind, arrears of taxes, even the two-thirds of those of 1793, on the rolls which have served to effect the last payment. . . .

17. The Minister of War is responsible for taking all measures necessary for the prompt execution of the present decree. . . .

18. The present decree shall be conveyed to the departments by special messengers.

38. "Make Terror the Order of the Day" (5 September 1793)

The dramatic events of 5 September 1793 were decisive in the evolution of the Terror. During the summer of 1793, the "federalist revolts" in Lyon, Marseille, Toulon and elsewhere had been added to the uprising in the Vendée, and the attacks of foreign powers, as threats to the unity and existence of the Revolution. Incited by news that the rebellious port of Toulon had surrendered to the English rather than fall to republican armies, and fearful of famine—signs of which they attributed to counterrevolutionary plotting—the Parisian crowd again marched on the Convention. The demands presented on behalf of the people, first by a delegation of representatives from the sections and the Paris Commune, and then by a second delegation from the Jacobin Club, were typical of the revolutionary mentality of the sans-culottes. Insisting upon more vigorous action to control food prices, assure supplies, and punish those suspected of counterrevolutionary activities, they called for the creation of "revolutionary armies." These latter, which should not be confused with the military armies of the Republic, were to be armed bands of militant activists organized to terrorize the enemies of the Revolution and to enforce emergency measures in its defense.

In the wake of this new popular uprising, the Convention passed the Law of Suspects (on 17 Sepember 1793) and the General Maximum (29 September 1793), two of the basic acts of the Terror. Although it was also obliged to decree the establishment of revolutionary armies (on 9 September 1793), these shock troops of terrorism were the most powerful example of the threat to government authority represented by sans-culotte

From *Réimpression de l'ancien Moniteur*, 32 vols. (Paris, 1858–1863), vol. 17, pp. 580–83, 586, 591. Translated for this volume by Caroline Ford and Keith Michael Baker.

activism. Once the apparatus of the Terror was consolidated under the central direction of the Committee on Public Safety, they were suppressed.

Proceedings of the National Convention (5 September 1793)

The president [Robespierre] declares that a great number of Parisian citizens request permission to file into the chamber and to present a petition by delegation.

The delegation is introduced; the mayor and several municipal officers are at its head.

The mayor of Paris: "Citizen representatives, Paris has not yet been without the means of subsistence. But for six weeks the fear of shortages has been bringing crowds of citizens to the bakers' doors every night. This fear is based on the fact that Paris is now fed only from one daily delivery to the next. The lack of any reserve stocks stems from the fact that the laws governing provisioning are not executed; it is also the result of the selfishness and ill will of rich owners of grain and this evil is common to all the large cities. The people, tired of these machinations, comes to you to present its resolution. The commune's attorney is charged with reading the petition of the citizens of Paris to you."

Chaumette: "Citizen legislators, the citizens of Paris, weary of a situation that has too long been uncertain and wavering, want to settle their fate once and for all.

"The tyrants of Europe and the internal enemies of the state viciously persist in their hideous scheme to starve the French people in order to vanquish it, and to force it into the shameful act of bartering its liberty and sovereignty for a piece of bread—something which it will assuredly never do. (A unanimous *No! No!* is heard.)

"New seigneurs, no less cruel, no less greedy, no less insolent than the old, have risen up in the ruins of feudalism; they have leased or bought the properties of their former masters, and continue to follow the paths beaten by crime, to speculate on public misery, to stifle the resources of abundance, and to tyrannize the destroyers of tyranny.

"Another class, as greedy, as criminal as the first, has gained control of basic necessities; you have struck at them, but you have only dazed them; and they continue their plunder in the very shadow of the laws.

"You have passed wise laws, which promise happiness. But they are not executed because the power needed to execute them is lacking, and if you do not create it promptly, they run the risk of falling into decrepitude almost at birth.

"At this very moment, the enemies of the country raise their knives against it, knives already stained with its blood. You control the arts, the arts obey, and in republican hands metal changes into tyrannicidal weapons; but where are the arms that must apply these weapons to the traitors' breasts?

"Hidden internal enemies, with the word liberty on their lips, stem the flow of life. Despite your benevolent laws, they close granaries, and coolly engage in the heinous calculation of how much a famine, a riot, a massacre is worth to them. Your spirit breaks at the thought; you give the keys of the granaries and the infernal ledgers of these monsters back to administrators. But where is the strong arm that will vigorously turn the key that is fatal to traitors? Where is the proud and immovable being, unyielding to any kind of intrigue and corruption, who will tear up the pages of the book written with the blood of the people, and turn it immediately into a death sentence against those who are starving the people? *(Applause.)*

"Every day we learn of new betrayals, new crimes; every day we are disturbed by the discovery and the reappearance of new conspiracies; every day new disturbances trouble the republic and are ready to drag it into their stormy whirlwinds, hurling it into the bottomless abyss of centuries to come. But where is the powerful being whose terrible cry will reawaken sleeping justice—or rather justice paralyzed, stupefied by the clamor of factions—and force it at last to strike off criminal heads? Where is the powerful being who will crush all these reptiles who corrupt everything they touch, and whose venomous bites stir up our citizens, transforming their political assemblies into gladiatorial arenas where each passion, each interest, finds apologists and an army?

"It is time, legislators, to put a stop to the impious struggle that has lasted since 1789, between the children of the nation and those who have abandoned it. Your fate, and ours, is tied to an unchanging establishment of the republic. We must either destroy its enemies, or be destroyed by them. They have thrown down the gauntlet in the midst of the people, and the people is taking it up. They have stirred up agitation. They have sought to separate and divide the mass of the citizens, in order to crush the people and to avoid being crushed by it themselves. Today the mass of the people must destroy them without resources, by its own weight and will.

"And you, Mountain forever renowned in the pages of history, be the Sinai of Frenchmen! Cast with thunder and lightening the eternal decrees of justice and of the people's will! Steadfast amidst the storms conjured up by the aristocracy, stir yourselves and tremble at the people's voice. The pent-up love of the public good has seethed in your loins long enough; let it burst forth with fury! Sainted Mountain! Become a volcano whose burning lava destroys forever the hopes of the evil and sears the hearts in which the idea of royalty is still found.

"No more quarter, no more mercy for traitors. *(The unanimous cry, No! No! resounds throughout the chamber.)* If we do not forestall them, they will forestall us. Between them and us, let us throw up the barrier of eternity. *(Applause.)*

"Patriots from all departments, and the people of Paris in particular, have shown patience enough up to now. We have been playing; but the day of justice and anger has come. *(Applause.)*

"Legislators, the immense gathering of citizens who assembled yesterday and today in the Commune building, and in the square outside it, passed only one resolution, and a delegation brings it before you. It is, *Food, and to get it, force for the law.* In consequence, we are charged to demand the formation of the revolutionary army which you have already decreed, and which the intrigue and dread of the guilty have aborted. *(Unanimous applause breaks out several times.)* Let this army form its core in Paris immediately and without delay, and let it be enlarged, in every department through which it travels, by all men who want a republic one and indivisible. Let this army be followed by an incorruptible and formidable tribunal, and by the fatal instrument which at a single stroke severs both the conspiracies and the days of their authors; let it be charged with forcing avarice and cupidity to cough up the wealth of the land, inexhaustible wet nurse of all children; let it bear these words on its standards, and let this be the order of every moment: *Peace to men of good will, war on those who starve people, protection for the weak; war on tyrants, justice, and no oppression.* Finally, let this army be composed in such a way that it can leave forces sufficient enough to restrain evil-minded people in all cities.

"Legislators, you have declared France to be in a state of revolution until its independence is assured; this decree must not have been passed in vain. Hercules is ready, put the club in his strong arms again, and soon the land of liberty will be purged of all the brigands infesting it. The country will breathe again. The people's provisions will be assured.

"We expect to see the aristocracy renew its efforts in order to revoke its death sentence, or at least to obtain a reprieve; the most cunning and subtle objections are going to be made in every political assembly; provisions for this army, the dangers that it could pose for liberty, are going to be talked about; all of the hackneyed commonplaces will be repeated, and we will answer that as for its provisions, not a grain of wheat will be consumed in excess of what is consumed now; there will not be extra mouths to feed, but simply mouths to feed elsewhere. The dangers that it will present to liberty? This army will be composed of republicans, and if some audacious person dares to say 'my army,' he will immediately be put to death. As for other objections, there will be only one reply to make. The welfare of the people has been deferred for too long, it is time for its enemies to be defeated."

Lively applause breaks out in all parts of the room and the galleries, and lasts for several minutes.

The president, speaking to the delegation: "Liberty will outlive the intrigues and schemes of conspirators. The solicitude of the Convention reaches out to the ills of the people. Let good citizens unite, let them make a last effort: the land of liberty, sullied by the presence of its enemies, is going to be freed from them. Today their death sentence is pronounced, and tomorrow aristocracy will cease to exist.

"The Convention will take your demands into consideration; it welcomes you to participate in this session."

Chaumette: "I must add some observations to the petition that I just presented to you. Yesterday the General Council of the Commune, together with the class of the worthy poor who filled its meeting hall and the square outside the Commune building, attended to the means of providing for their most pressing needs. We have observed that the decrease in the deliveries of basic necessities contributes to growing fears of famine and to rising prices of these very supplies. We have realized that the majority of those who grow market vegetables are in league to starve Paris by stashing them away in their storehouses. We have seen a carefully thought-out plan to destroy, through starvation, the people who made the revolution. We have looked at the map of the outskirts of Paris, and we have seen lands that serve the purposes of luxury, gardens, and parks, not one of which provides for the common utility.

"We demand that all gardens that have become national lands subject to sale be usefully cultivated. We beg you to look finally at the immense garden of the Tuileries; republican eyes will rest with greater pleasure on this former domain of the crown when it produces basic necessities. Would it not be better to grow the plants which hospitals need there than to let statues, trees in the shape of *fleurs-de-lys,* and other objects that were the accessories of the luxury and the pride of kings, remain?"

The delegation is formally admitted to the session.

It is followed by an immense number of citizens, who present themselves at the bar and enter one by one to the sound of applause and to the cheering of the assembly and the galleries. They position themselves on the tiers at the right side. Soon the whole floor is covered with citizens, both men and women: the cry *Long Live the Republic!* is heard several times. Citizens are seen in the middle of the crowd carrying placards bearing these words: *War on tyrants, war on aristocrats, war on those who starve the people,* etc.

Moise-Bayle: "I am turning into a motion all the measures proposed in the petition of the citizens of Paris. . . ."

There is applause, and a general demand for a vote. Publication of the petition is decreed.

Raffron: "I demand that the Ministry of the Interior be ordered to take all necessary measures for the formation of the revolutionary army, beginning today."

Dussaulx: "I demand that the Champs Elysées be converted to useful cultivation, as well as the Tuileries."

Billaud-Varennes: "By taking advantage of the energy of the people, we will finally exterminate the enemies of the revolution. We will lack neither provisions nor plots of land to grow them; what is more important, and what we must hope for, is that all the evil-minded disappear from the face of the earth. At last it is time, as we observed at the Convention; it is time, and more than time, that we settle the fate of the revolution; and indeed we must congratulate ourselves, since the very misfortunes of the people exalt its energy, and put us in a position to exterminate our enemies. I also wish to turn the proposed measures into a motion; but they are not sufficient. The moment to act has come, the time for deliberation has passed. All your enemies must be put under arrest this very day. *(Applause.)* I heard it said again yesterday that three thousand inspired men did not exist in Paris. Well! Let us show these persons that the whole people is as inspired as we are, that it is ready to march against its enemies, and that from today liberty will be assured. . . . If revolutions drag on, it is because only half measures are ever taken. Let us leave it to feeble souls to worry about the results of the revolution. We who estimate everything, who see the grand vision of what it must produce for the happiness of the people, let us advance with bold step along the route we have set ourselves. Let us save the people: it will aid us; it wants liberty whatever the price. Let us crush the enemies of the revolution, and from this very day the government takes action, the laws are executed, the lot of the people is strengthened, liberty is saved.

"In short, I demand the most prompt arrest of all suspected persons. . . .

"With regard to the organization of the revolutionary army, I demand that the minister of war be required forthwith to present a plan for its organization, and that we refer it to the municipality to be put into effect starting today. I demand that this decree be sent by extraordinary messengers so that the same army may be formed in all the departments, and our enemies finally destroyed. . . ."

Danton: "I agree with other members, notably Billaud-Varennes *(ap-*

plause), that we need to know how to profit from the sublime fervor of the people which crowds in around us. I know that when the people puts its needs forward, when it offers to march against its enemies, no measures are necessary beyond those the people itself presents—for the national spirit has dictated them. I think it would be a good thing for the Committee [of Public Safety] to make its report, to devise and propose the means of execution; but I also see that there is no reason not to decree a revolutionary army this very instant *(applause).* If possible, let us enlarge these measures.

"You have just proclaimed to the whole of France that it is still in a real and active state of revolution. Well, this revolution must be consummated. Never be afraid of agitation that could tempt counterrevolutionaries in Paris. Undoubtedly, they would like to extinguish the flame of liberty where it burns most ardently; but the immense mass of true patriots, of sans-culottes who have crushed their enemies a hundred times, still exists; it is ready to move into action. Know how to lead it and it will again confound and foil all intrigues. A revolutionary army is not enough; be revolutionary yourselves. Reflect upon the fact that industrious men who live by the sweat of their brow cannot attend the sections; that it is only in the absence of true patriots that intrigue can take over the section meetings. Decree, therefore, that two large section-meetings be held each week, and that the man of the people who attends these political assemblies receive just remuneration for the time they take from his work. *(Applause.)*

"It is also good that you proclaim to all our enemies that we are determined to be continually and completely prepared for them. You have ordered thirty million [francs] to be put at the disposition of the minister of war for the manufacture of weapons; decree that these emergency manufactures will only cease when the nation has given a gun to each citizen. Let us declare the firm resolution of having as many guns and almost as many cannon as there are sans-culottes. *(Applause.)* Let it be the republic that puts a gun into the hands of the citizen, of the true patriot; let it say to him: 'The country entrusts you with this weapon for its defense; you will represent it every month, and when you are required to do so by the national authority.' Let a gun be the most sacred thing among us; let each of us lose his life rather than his gun. *(Applause)* I therefore demand that you decree at least 100 million [francs] for the manufacture of weapons of all kinds; for, if we had all had arms, we would all have marched. It is our need of weapons which enslaves us. The country in danger will never be short of citizens. *(Same applause.)*

"But punishments remain to be meted out, both to the internal enemies already imprisoned and to those you have yet to seize. The revolutionary tribunal must be divided into a large enough number of sections *(several voices: It's done!)* that every day an aristocrat, a criminal, may pay for his crimes with his head. *(Applause.)*

"I therefore demand that Billaud's proposition first be put to the vote;

2. That it similarly be decreed that the sections of Paris hold special assemblies on Sundays and Thursdays, and that each citizen participating in these meetings who wishes to claim payment to meet his needs receive it at the rate of forty sous for each assembly;

3. That it be decreed by the Convention that 100 million [francs] be put at the disposal of the minister of war for the manufacture of arms, and notably of guns; that these special manufactures receive every encouragement and support that is necessary, and that they conclude their work only when France has given a gun to each good citizen.

"Finally, I demand that a report be drawn up on the means of increasing the activity of the revolutionary tribunal to a great extent. Let the people see its enemies fall; let it see that the Convention attends to its needs. The people is great, and it offers remarkable proof of its greatness this very moment. For although it has suffered from famine that is artificially created and designed to make it turn to counterrevolution, it has recognized that it is suffering in its own cause, and under despotism it would have exterminated all governments. *(Applause.)*

"Such is the character of the French, enlightened by four years of revolution.

"Let tribute be paid to you, exalted people! You unite greatness with perseverance. You are obstinate in your desire for liberty. You fast for liberty, and you must attain it. We will march with you, your enemies will be routed; you will be free!"

Universal applause breaks out in all parts of the room simultaneously; cries of *Long Live the Republic!* are heard repeatedly. All the citizens who fill the hall and the galleries rise as if impelled by the same force; some raise their hands into the air; others shake their hats; the enthusiasm seems universal.

Danton's three motions are carried.

Cheering is heard again. The room resounds with cries of *Long Live the Republic!* . . . The president announces a delegation composed of representatives of the Parisian sections and of the Society of Jacobins, so-called. The delegation is introduced.

The spokesman: "We come before you to present an address of the Society of Friends of Liberty and Equality meeting at [the former convent of] the Jacobins, together with the representatives of the forty-eight sections.

"You who have received the people's mandate, the country's dangers are extreme and the remedies must be also. You have decreed that the French shall rise up as one to drive far from our borders the brigands who ravage our countryside. But the satellites of tyrants, the savage islanders, the tigers of the North who bring destruction upon us, are less to be feared than the traitors who stir us up from within, who divide us, who arm us one against another. Impunity has emboldened them. The people loses heart as it sees the most guilty escape the nation's vengeance; all the friends of liberty are indignant to see that the fomenters of federalism have not yet been punished for their crimes. In public places, republicans speak with indignation of Brissot's crimes, pronouncing his name with nothing but horror. We remember that this monster was spewed forth by England in 1789 to upset our revolution and to hinder its march.

"We demand that he be tried, as well as his accomplices. *(Applause.)*

"The people is indignant to see that privileges still exist in the republic. What about it! The Vergniauds, the Gensonnés and other criminals, stripped by their treasons of the dignity of the people's representatives, have a palace for a prison, while poor sans-culottes groan in dungeons under the daggers of federalists! . . . *(Applause.)*

"It is time that equality pass the scythe over every head. It is time to terrorize all conspirators. Well then! Legislators, make terror the order of the day. *(Enthusiastic applause.)* Let us be in a state of revolution, since counterrevolution is everywhere plotted by our enemies. *(Same applause.)* Let the blade of the law hang over all who are guilty!

"We demand that a revolutionary army be established, that it be divided into a number of sections, that each be followed by a fearsome tribunal, and by the terrible instrument executing the vengeance of the laws. We demand that this army and its tribunals continue their functions until the republic's soil is purged of traitors, down to the death of the last conspirator. *(Numerous outbursts of applause from citizens present at the session.)*

"Before doing anything else, banish this class burdened with crimes which still insolently occupies the highest positions in our armies, where they have only distinguished themselves by their betrayals since the beginning of the war. Nobles were always the irreconcilable enemies of equality and of the whole of humanity; to deprive them of all means of increasing the hordes of our enemies, we demand that they be imprisoned until peace is restored; this race thirsty for blood must henceforth see none flow but its own. The departed spirits of victims heaped up by betrayals demand a spectacular revenge, and the voice of the people imposes it upon you as law." *(Applause from many sides follows the reading of this address.)*

The president, speaking to the delegation: "Citizens, it is the people that has made the revolution; it is up to you in particular to assure the execution of the prompt measures that must save the *patrie*. You ask for the establishment of a revolutionary army; your wish is achieved. Already the Convention, heedful of everything that can intimidate and foil foreign powers and their agents, has decided that this army will soon be formed.

"Yes, courage and justice are the order of the day. All good citizens, instead of trembling, will bless the moment when the Convention took measures to secure the fate of the revolution at last. All Frenchmen will bless the society to which you belong, the society in whose name, together with that of the city of Paris, you come to ask for these imperative and definitive measures. All criminals will perish on the scaffold, the Convention has solemnly sworn it. Already it has taken steps to increase the activity of the revolutionary tribunal. Tomorrow it will busy itself with increasing the number of judges and juries.

"The Convention applauds your patriotism; it welcomes you to participate in the session."

The delegation is introduced and files past, to the sound of applause. . . . [Turbulent discussion continued until, late in the afternoon, a spokesman for the Committee of Public Safety appeared to address the assembly.]

Barère, in the name of the Committee of Public Safety: "For several days everything has seemed to point to a movement afoot in Paris. Intercepted letters, destined either for abroad or for aristocrats within the country, told of constant endeavors made by their agents to incite an immediate uprising in what they call the *big city.* Well! They will have this last uprising—*(enthusiastic applause)*—but it will be organized and carried out legally by a revolutionary army that will finally put into effect the mighty slogan we owe to the Commune of Paris: *'Make terror the order of the day.'* This is the way to make the royalists, the moderates, and the counter-revolutionary rabble that perturbs you disappear in an instant. The royalists want blood; well! they will have the blood of conspirators, of the Brissots, the Marie-Antoinettes. They want to stir up a movement, well! they are going to feel its effects. We are not speaking of illegal acts of vengeance; special tribunals are going to bring this about. You will not be shocked by the means that we present to you when you understand that these criminals are still conspiring in the recesses of their prisons, that they are the rallying points for our enemies. Brissot has said and written that before his head falls, those of part of the Convention would no longer exist, and that the Mountain would be destroyed. This is the way they seek to use terror to check you in your revolutionary march.

"The royalists want to upset the work of the revolution. Conspirators, the Convention will upset yours! *(Enthusiastic applause.)*

"They want to destroy the Mountain. Well! The Mountain will annihilate them!

"As early as tomorrow, the Committee will propose measures to create a revolutionary army of six thousand men in Paris, with twelve hundred gunners. *(Applause.)*

"Royalists cry out every day *to the one and indivisible republic*—they want to destroy it. They hoard basic necessities or obstruct markets—and they accuse the Convention of these acts. They speculate, and degrade the *assignats*—and they lay the blame on the Convention. They put the squeeze on the flow of provisions near Paris—and there they are inveighing against the Convention which takes steps every day to facilitate and accelerate new deliveries. Royalists surrender our ports to the English—and they have it said by traitors and published in the Midi that *the Convention wants to surrender the ports*. Royalists instigate agitation around Paris; they lead poor citizens astray or borrow their names and clothing—then they slander the sans-culottes and the Convention.

"What is required to put an end to so many crimes and conspiracies? A revolutionary army that sweeps away conspirators; an army that is organized in the same way as battalions of national guards, and can therefore be mustered today and mobilized tomorrow. We must have an army that carries out all the measures of public safety to be decreed by the Convention. We must have an army, not only for Paris, but wherever counterrevolutionary movements make themselves feared.

"For four years the aristocracy has sought, either with gold or with intrigue, by imaginary terrors or calumnies, to establish itself on the territory of this vast city that witnessed the birth of liberty. For four years, its soil has beaten them back. But the counterrevolutionaries have formed a ring around Paris. Under the pretext of spending the summer in the country, they have gone to live in the châteaux that arrogance and feudalism have erected. This is where the counterrevolutionaries gather, where symbols of royalty, the religious images of these alleged citizens, have been found. There these men, scattered among the villages, alarm the people, inciting them to draw up petitions concerning food supplies, whilst the harvest has been more than abundant everywhere.

"What a moment for them to have chosen to spread from one village to another these terrors that impede and delay the provisioning of Paris! Yesterday and today the mayor and minister of the interior declared to us that deliveries were declining.

"You had taken a wise measure providing that the Maximum would be the same in all departments. Well! This is the moment they have chosen to create agitation over food supplies. They wanted to surround this law with suspicion and fears at the very moment of its inception, because they knew it would be effective.

"So far, the Committee of Public Safety has been able to prepare only a fraction of the measures that it must propose to you.

"But you have already adopted some very good ones. The measure relative to the arrest of suspected persons has been prompted by the representatives of the sections and by the members of the excellent Society of Jacobins, who watch night and day over the public safety. The same patriots are busy drawing up others.

"We limit ourselves to proposing the raising of a revolutionary army, and a useful and urgent means of removing from Paris this enormous crowd of military men who have quit their posts or who are not on active duty."

39. The Law of Suspects (17 September 1793)

Action against persons suspected of revolutionary activity was one of the chief demands of the crowd that marched upon the Convention on 5 September 1793. Enacted in response to that demand, the Law of Suspects provided the principal legal basis for the Terror.

1. Immediately after the publication of the present decree, all suspected persons within the territory of the Republic and still at liberty shall be placed in custody.

2. The following are deemed suspected persons: 1st, those who, by their conduct, associations, talk, or writings have shown themselves partisans of tyranny or federalism and enemies of liberty; 2nd, those who are unable to justify, in the manner prescribed by the decree of 21 March last, their means of existence and the performance of their civic duties; 3rd, those to whom certificates of patriotism have been refused; 4th, public functionaries suspended or dismissed from their positions by the National Convention or by its commissioners, and not reinstated, especially those who have been or are to be dismissed by virtue of the decree of 14 August last; 5th, those former nobles, husbands, wives, fathers, mothers, sons or daughters, brothers or sisters, and agents of the *émigrés,* who have not steadily manifested their devotion to the Revolution; 6th, those who have emigrated during the interval between 1 July, 1789, and the publication of the decree of 30 March–8 April, 1792, even though they may have returned to France within the period established by said decree or prior thereto.

3. The Watch Committees[1] established according to the decree of 21 March last, or those substituted therefor, either by orders of the representatives of the people dispatched to the armies and the departments, or by virtue of particular decrees of the National Convention, are charged with

Reprinted with permission of Macmillan Publishing Company from John Hall Stewart, ed., *A Documentary Survey of the French Revolution,* pp. 477–79. © 1951 by Macmillan Publishing Company.

1. The Watch Committees (*comités de surveillance*) were initially spontaneous instruments of political vigilance formed by revolutionary activists at the local level. Their existence was regularized by the Convention on 21 March 1793. The Law of Suspects greatly expanded their legal powers.

drafting, each in its own *arrondissement,* a list of suspected persons, with issuing warrants of arrest against them, and with having seals placed on their papers. Commanders of the public force to whom such warrants are remitted shall be required to put them into effect immediately, under penalty of dismissal.

4. The members of the committee may order the arrest of any individual only if seven are present, and only by absolute majority of votes.

5. Individuals arrested as suspects shall be taken first to the jails of the place of their detention; in default of jails, they shall be kept under surveillance in their respective dwellings.

6. Within the following week, they shall be transferred to national buildings, which the departmental administrations shall be required to designate and to have prepared for such purpose immediately after the receipt of the present decree.

7. The prisoners may have their absolutely essential belongings brought into said buildings; they shall remain there under guard until the peace.

8. The expenses of custody shall be charged to the prisoners, and shall be divided among them equally: such custody shall be confided preferably to fathers of families and to the relatives of citizens who are at or may go to the frontiers. The salary therefor is established, for each man of the guard, at the value of one and one-half days of labor.

9. The Watch Committees shall dispatch to the Committee of General Security of the National Convention, without delay, the list of persons whom they have arrested, with the reasons for their arrest and with the papers they have seized in such connection.

10. If there is occasion, the civil and criminal courts may have detained, in custody, and dispatched to the jails above stated, those who are accused of offences with regard to which it has been declared that there was no occasion for indictment or who have been acquitted of charges brought against them.

40. Saint-Just, *Report to the Convention on Behalf of the Committee of Public Safety* (10 October 1793)

The youngest member of the Convention, Louis-Antoine Léon de Saint-Just was also one of its greatest orators and most zealous theorists of revolutionary government. Idealistic and authoritarian, he remained closely associated with Robespierre throughout the period of the Terror.

From *Réimpression de l'ancien Moniteur*, 32 vols. (Paris, 1858–1863), vol. 18, pp. 106–10. Translated for this volume by Caroline Ford and Keith Michael Baker.

As a result of this speech, the constitution passed (but never implemented) in the summer of 1793 was formally suspended in favor of revolutionary government, and executive power was centralized in the hands of the Committee of Public Safety. The committee's power was further consolidated by the decree of 4 December 1793, which purged local governments and placed them under the strict control of the Committee of Public Safety, abolished the "revolutionary armies," and curtailed unauthorized expressions of revolutionary activism.

Why is it necessary, after so many laws and so many measures, to call your attention again to government abuses in general, and to matters relating to the economy and the system of provisioning? Your wisdom and the just wrath of patriots have not yet vanquished the evil that everywhere contends with the people and the revolution: the laws are revolutionary, those who execute them are not.

It is time to proclaim a truth which should henceforth never be absent from the minds of those who govern: the republic will only be established when the sovereign will represses the monarchical minority, and rules over it by right of conquest.

You no longer have anything to discuss with the enemies of the new order of things, and liberty must conquer at whatever price.

Your Committee of Public Safety, which is in a position to see the entire range of public misfortunes, has determined their causes. It has found them in the weakness with which your decrees are being executed, in the wastefulness of the administration, in the lack of stability in the conduct of the state, in the variability of the passions that influence the government.

It has therefore resolved to set the state of things before you, and to present you with the means it believes appropriate to consolidate the revolution, to overthrow federalism, to relieve the people and to bring it abundance, to strengthen the armies, to cleanse the state of the conspiracies infesting it.

There is no prosperity to hope for as long as the last enemy of liberty breathes. You have to punish not only the traitors, but even those who are indifferent; you have to punish whoever is passive in the republic, and who does nothing for it. For, since the French people has manifested its will, all that is opposed to it is outside the sovereign; all that is outside the sovereign is the enemy.

If conspiracies had not disturbed this empire, if the country had not been a thousand times victim to indulgent laws, it would be nice to govern according to maxims of peace and natural justice. These maxims are accepted among the friends of liberty; but between the people and its enemies there is no longer anything in common but the sword. It is necessary to govern with iron those who cannot be governed by justice. It is necessary to oppress tyrants.

You have had energy; the public administration has lacked it. You have wanted thrift; public finance has not seconded your efforts. Everyone has pillaged the state. Generals have waged war against their armies. Those possessing goods and provisions, together with everything that was vicious in the monarchy, have joined in league against you and the people.

A people has only one dangerous enemy, and that is its government. Yours has constantly made war against you with impunity.

Our enemies have found no obstacles to their conspiracies. The agents chosen under the former ministry, partisans of the royalists, are the natural accomplices of every attempt to destroy the country. You have had few patriotic ministers; this is why all the chief leaders of the army and of the administration—strangers to the people, so to speak—have constantly gone over to serve the schemes of our enemies.

The people is sometimes mistaken, but it is mistaken less than individuals. The corps of generals is out of sympathy with the nation because it emanates neither from the nation's choice, nor from the choice of its representatives. It has less respect from the soldier, because it is less worthy of respect given the manner in which it has been chosen. Discipline suffers accordingly, and the corps of generals still remains monarchical in its nature.

It is possible that there is not a single military commander who is not secretly basing his fortune on betrayal in favor of kings.

One cannot identify military men too closely with the people and the country.

It is the same with the primary agents of government. Bad choice of government officials is the cause of our misfortunes. Positions have been bought, and they are not bought by worthy men. The schemers perpetuate themselves: a villain is driven out of one administration, and he enters another.

Government is therefore a perpetual conspiracy against the present order of things. Six ministers make appointments to government posts; they may be pure but they are solicited for positions; they choose blindly. Those immediately under them are solicited, and choose, in the same way; thus the government is a hierarchy of errors and outrages.

The ministers admit that they no longer find anything but inertia and carelessness beyond their immediate subordinates and those once removed.

It is possible for France's enemies to have your entire government occupied in three months by conspirators. Three get in, and they bring in six. If at this very moment one rigorously scrutinized the men who administer the state, out of 30,000 employed there would perhaps be very few to whom the people would give its confidence.

Citizens, all the enemies of the republic are in its government. In vain you waste your strength within these walls to make laws. In vain your committee, in vain several ministers aid your efforts. Everything conspires against them and you.

We have discovered that the agents administering hospitals have, for six months, furnished flour to the rebels in the Vendée.

The rich have become richer since the imposition of taxes particularly intended to favor the people. They have doubled their wealth; they have doubled their means of seduction.

Have no doubt that the wealthy contribute to the continuation of the war. They are the ones who are everywhere in competition with the state for its purchases. They place their funds in the hands of disloyal administrators, special government agents, messengers; the government is in league with them. You prosecute hoarders; you cannot prosecute those who appear to be buying for the armies.

Genius is necessary to make a prohibitive law which no abuse eludes; the thieves deprived of office put the funds they have stolen into the hands of those who succeed them.

The majority of men declared suspect have invested in provisioning. The government is the insurance company for every act of plunder and for all crimes.

Everything is bound together in the government; the evil in each part influences the whole. The waste in the public treasury has contributed to the rise in the price of provisions and to the success of conspiracies. This is how:

Three billion [francs], stolen by suppliers and agents of all kinds, today compete with the state in its purchases, with the people in the markets and at merchants' counters, with soldiers in their garrisons, with commerce abroad. These three billion ferment in the republic. They recruit for the enemy; they corrupt generals; they buy public posts; they bribe judges and magistrates, and make crime stronger than law. Those who have enriched themselves want to grow richer; and while he who desires the necessities of life is patient, he who desires what is superfluous is cruel. Hence the misfortunes of the people, whose virtue remains impotent against the activity of its enemies.

You have passed laws against hoarders; those who should apply the laws hoard themselves. . . .

Nobody is honest in the public administration. Patriotism is but lip service; each sacrifices all the others, and sacrifices nothing that is in his own interest. . . .

The bread that the rich give is bitter; it compromises liberty. Bread belongs by right to the people in a state wisely administered. . . .

The various laws you applied earlier to provisioning would have been good, had not men been bad.

When you passed the Law of the Maximum, the enemies of the people, who were richer than it was, bought at prices above the legal maximum.

The markets ceased to be supplied as a result of the avarice of those who sold: the price of foodstuffs fell, but they were scarce.

The agents of a great number of communes competed to buy; and as anxiety spread and fed upon itself, each commune wanted to build a stock of supplies, thereby bringing famine about in the act of guarding against it.

Fertile departments were inundated with buying agents; everything was bought in advance. Purchases were even made for the Duke of York; buying-agents with guineas were spotted.

The people, and agents charged with military provisioning, obliged to buy at the legal maximum, only found what shame of crime or self-interest had not dared to sell at a higher price.

Thus our enemies have taken advantage of our very laws and have twisted them in their favor. . . .

In the circumstances in which the republic finds itself, the constitution cannot be established. It would destroy itself. It would become the guarantee for crimes against liberty, because it would lack the force of violence necessary to restrain them. The current government is also too hampered.

You are too distant from all these criminal attacks. The sword of the laws must go everywhere and with the greatest rapidity; your arm must be present everywhere to stop crime.

You must prevent the independence of administrations, divide authority, identify it with the revolutionary movement and with you, and multiply it.

You must tighten all the bonds of responsibility, and control the power that is often terrible to patriots and indulgent to traitors. All duties toward the people are ignored. The insolence of the persons in office is unbearable; fortunes are quickly made.

It is impossible for the revolutionary laws to be executed if the government itself is not constituted in a revolutionary manner. You cannot hope for prosperity if you do not establish a government which, while gentle and moderate toward the people, will be terrible toward itself as a result of the intensity of its organization. This government must weigh on itself and not on the people. Every injustice on its part toward citizens, every betrayal, every act of indifference toward the country, every laxity to which it is subject, must be sovereignly repressed.

It is necessary to specify duties exactly, hedging in abuse with the sword, so that everything is free in the republic except those who conspire against it and who govern badly.

The conspiracies that have rent the republic for a year have made clear to us that the government has conspired unceasingly against the country; the eruption of the Vendée has grown without its progress being stopped. Lyon, Bordeaux, Toulon, Marseille have revolted, selling themselves to the enemy, without the government having done anything to prevent or stop this evil.

Today, now that the republic has twelve hundred thousand men to feed, rebels to subdue and the people to save; now that Europe must be shown decisively that it is beyond its power to reestablish monarchical authority among us, you must make the government fit to support you in your plans, appropriate to measures of the economy and public happiness.

You must make roads safe, promptly construct numerous vessels, fill the public treasury, restore abundance, supply Paris with provisions until the peace, as if it were in a state of siege. You must put everything in motion, rally the armies to the people and to the National Convention.

It is also important that the duties of the people's representatives attached to the armies be strictly prescribed. They must be the fathers and friends of the soldier. They must sleep under a tent, they must be present during military exercises, they must avoid intimacy with generals, so that the soldier has confidence in their justice and their impartiality when he approaches them. The soldier must find them ready to listen to him night and day. The representatives should eat alone. They should be frugal, remembering that they answer for the public safety and that the eternal destruction of kings is preferable to momentary indolence.

Those who make revolutions in the world, those who want to do good, must sleep only in the tomb.

The people's representatives in the military camps . . . must know the name of every soldier; they must pursue every injustice, every abuse, for great vices have been introduced into army discipline. Battalions of the Army of the Rhine have been seen begging on the march; a free people is humiliated by these indignities; they die of hunger, those who respected the booty of Belgium! . . .

Until today, we have lacked institutions and military laws appropriate to the system of the republic we are trying to found. During a time of innovation, everything that is not new is pernicious. The military art of monarchy no longer suits us; these are different men and different enemies. . . .

It is time to remedy so many abuses, if you want the republic to take hold. The government must not only be revolutionary against aristocracy. It must be revolutionary against all those who steal from the soldier, who deprave the army by their insolence, who by dissipating the public's wealth would reduce the people to slavery and the empire to its dissolution through misfortune. So many evils find their source in the corruption of some and the carelessness of others.

It is necessary during revolutions to combat the resistance of some to change, and the laziness of others in carrying it out; the superstition of some for the authority overthrown, and the ambition and hypocrisy of others. It is therefore certain that the new government establishes itself with difficulty, forming its plans only at great cost; for a long time it remains without clearly determined resolutions. Liberty has its infancy; one dares to govern neither with severity nor with weakness, because liberty comes from a salutary anarchy, and slavery returns with absolute order.

However, the enemy redoubles his efforts and activity. He makes war on us, not in the hope of conquering us militarily, but to weaken the government and prevent it from establishing itself. He does so to spill the blood of the defenders of liberty, and to diminish their number, so that after the death of all ardent men, terms will be reached with the cowards awaiting him. One hundred thousand patriots have perished during the past year; a terrible wound for liberty! Our enemy has only lost slaves; epidemics and wars strengthen the authority of kings.

It is therefore necessary for our government to recover from one side what it lost on the other. It must make it impossible for the enemies of liberty to jeopardize liberty as good people perish. We must make war prudently and spare our blood, for this is all that they are after—Europe is thirsty for it! You have 100,000 men in the tomb who no longer defend liberty.

The government is their assassin; they have been killed by the crime of some, the impotence and incompetence of others.

All those employed by the government are lazy; every man with a position does nothing himself and takes on secondary agents; these in turn have their own agents, and the republic falls prey to twenty thousand fools who corrupt it, who wage war against it, who bleed it dry.

You must cut down the number of agents everywhere so that the senior officials work and think.

The ministry is a world of paper. I don't know how Rome and Egypt governed without this resource; one thought a great deal, and wrote little. The sheer volume of the government's correspondence and orders is a sign of its inertia; government is impossible with too many words. Representatives of the people, generals, administrators, are surrounded by offices like former men of the palace; nothing is done, and expenditure is nonetheless enormous. Bureaucracy has replaced monarchism; the demon of writing makes war on us, and government stops.

There are few men at the head of our establishments whose vision is broad and sincere. Public service, as it is now conducted, is not a matter of virtue but of profession.

Everything has finally contributed to the misfortune of the people, to shortages, to aristocracy, to greed, to inertia, to thieves, to bad method.

The entire government must be reformed to stop the drive towards tyranny our enemies are striving to give it. When all abuses are corrected, the repression of every evil will bring good, and abundance will spring up again.

I have rapidly gone over the situation of the state, its needs and its misfortunes: it is for your wisdom to do the rest. All talents must combine to extend the views of the Committee of Public Safety. It has charged me to present the following measures to you.

The National Convention, approving the report of the Committee of Public Safety, decrees the following:

Of Government

1. The provisional government of France will be revolutionary until the peace.

2. The provisional executive council, ministers, generals, and constituted bodies are placed under the surveillance of the Committee of Public Safety, which will give a weekly account of their activities to the Convention.

3. Every security measure must be taken by the provisional executive council, with the authorization of the Committee [of Public Safety], which will give a weekly account of these measures to the Convention.

4. Revolutionary laws must be executed quickly. The government will correspond immediately and directly with the districts regarding security measures.

5. The generals-in-chief will be appointed by the Convention, on the recommendation of the Committee of Public Safety.

6. Since government inertia is the cause of setbacks, deadlines for the execution of laws and measures of public safety will be fixed; violation of the deadlines will be punished as a crime against liberty.

Provisioning

7. A chart of grain production in each district, drawn up by the Committee of Public Safety, will be printed and distributed to all the members of the Convention, to be acted upon without delay.

8. The needs of each department will be estimated and guaranteed; surpluses will be subject to requisition;

9. A chart of what is produced by the Republic will be addressed to the people's representatives, to the ministers of the navy and the interior, to the ministers of provisioning. They must requisition supplies in the *arrondissements* assigned to them. Paris will have a special arrondissement. . . .

Public Safety

12. The direction and use of the revolutionary army will be constantly regulated in such a way as to repress counterrevolutionaries. The Committee of Public Safety will present a plan for this.

13. The council will send garrisons to cities where counterrevolutionary movements appear. These garrisons will be paid and maintained by the rich of these cities until peace is restored.

Finance

14. A tribunal and board of auditors will be created. This tribunal and this jury will be appointed by the National Convention. It will be charged to proceed against all those who have managed public revenues since the revolution and to demand that they account for their fortunes. . . .

41. The Revolutionary Calendar

The idea of a secular, rational calendar to replace the Christian Gregorian calendar had surfaced before the French Revolution. But it was felt to be a necessity in a period that sought the revolutionary regeneration of mankind. On 22 September 1792, the date of the proclamation of the French Republic, the Convention ordered that a project for a new calendar be drawn up by its Committee on Public Instruction. The committee's report was presented on 20 September 1793 by its president, Charles-Gilbert Romme, and its proposals adopted on 5 October 1793. Romme proposed that the months, ten-day weeks (*décades*), and days simply be designated numerically; but after some discussion, a committee headed by the poet, Phillipe-François Fabre d'Eglantine, was charged with the task of finding appropriate names. Fabre d'Eglantine's proposals, which reflect the dechristianizing mentality inherent in the Terror, were presented and adopted on 24 October 1793. Other changes of name were incorporated into the definitive decree of 24 November 1793.

Although it became mandatory for public documents, the new calendar never took root in popular use and was abandoned during the Napoleonic period.

Romme, *Report on the Republican Era* (20 September 1793)

Citizens, I come to submit for your discussion a study of the calendar of the republican era. I do so on behalf of the Committee on Public Instruction, to which you entrusted its preparation.

You have undertaken one of the most important operations in the prog-

From *Procès-verbaux du Comité d'instruction publique de l'Assemblée législative*, edited by James Guillaume, 7 vols. (Paris: Imprimerie Nationale, 1891–1959), vol. 2, pp. 440–41, 582–84, 697–99, 701. Translated for this volume by Caroline Ford and Keith Michael Baker.

ress of the arts and of the human spirit, one which could only succeed in a time of revolution: to eliminate the diversity, incoherence, and imprecision in weights and measures that have constantly hindered commerce and industry, and to derive the unique and unvarying standard for all new measures from the size of the earth itself.

The arts and history, for which time is an element or a necessary instrument, also require new measures of duration which are similarly free from the errors that credulity and superstitious routine have transmitted from centuries of ignorance to us.

The common era began among an ignorant and credulous people, and in the midst of troubles that foreshadowed the impending fall of the Roman Empire. For eighteen centuries, it served to date the progress of fanaticism, the degradation of nations, the scandalous triumph of pride, vice and stupidity, the persecutions and debasements endured by virtue, talent, and philosophy at the hands of cruel despots or in their names.

Do we wish to see engraved on the same tables, sometimes by a debased, sometimes by a free and patriotic instrument, the celebrated crimes of kings and the execration to which they are condemned today, the religiously revered deceits perpetrated by a few priests, and the opprobrium which justly pursues the infamous and conniving confidants of the corruption and plunder of courts? No! The common era was the era of cruelty, lies, perfidy and slavery; it ended with royalty, the source of all our ills.

The Revolution has renewed the souls of Frenchmen; it educates them each day in republican virtues. Time opens a new book in history; and in its new march, as majestic and simple as equality, it must engrave with a new and vigorous instrument the annals of regenerated France.

Such is the spirit of your decree of 22 September 1792, which orders that, beginning with that day, all public acts be dated as from the first year of the Republic. It is the extension of this decree that I present to you today. . . .

1. The era of the French begins with the foundation of the Republic, which took place on 22 September 1792 of the common era, the day the sun reached the true autumnal equinox, entering the sign of Libra at nine o'clock, eighteen minutes, thirty seconds in the morning, as measured by the Paris Observatory.

2. The calendar of the common era is abolished for civil affairs.

3. The beginning of each year is fixed at midnight beginning the day when the true autumnal equinox falls, as measured by the Paris Observatory.

4. The first year of the French Republic began at midnight, 22 September 1792, and ended at midnight, 21–22 September 1793.

5. The second year began on 22 September 1793 at midnight. . . .

7. The year is divided into twelve equal months of thirty days each, followed by five days completing the ordinary year which belong to no month. They are called *complementary days.*[1]

8. Each month is divided into three equal parts of ten days each; these are called *décades,* and distinguished one from another as first, second, and third.

9. The months, days of the *décade,* and complementary days are designated by ordinal denominations: first, second, third etc., day of the *décade;* first, second, third, etc., complementary day.

10. In memory of the revolution which, after four years, has led France to a republican government, the leap period of four years is called the *Franciade.*

The intercalary day that must end this period is called the *Day of the Revolution.* This day follows the five complementary days.

11. The day, from midnight to midnight, is divided into ten parts, each of which is divided into ten others, and so on down to the smallest measurable units of duration.[2] This article will only be obligatory for public acts starting from the first month of the third year of the Republic.

12. The Committee on Public Instruction is charged with having the calendar printed in various formats, with a simple explanation of its principles and most frequent uses.

13. The new calendar, as well as the explanation, will be sent to administrative bodies, municipalities, tribunals, justices of the peace and all public officers, to teachers and professors, to the armies and popular societies. The provisional executive council will have it given to ministers, consuls, and other French agents in foreign countries.

14. All public acts are dated according to the new organization of the year.

15. Professors and teachers, mothers and fathers, and all those who direct the education of the children of the Republic, will hasten to explain the new calendar to them, in conformity with the explanation attached to it.

16. Every four years, or every *Franciade,* on the Day of the Revolution, republican games will be celebrated in memory of the French Revolution.

1. These days were subsequently named *Sansculottides* (or Days of the Sans-culottes) and designated for the celebration of Virtue, Genius, Work, Opinion, and Reward.

2. This decimal organization of hours, minutes and seconds required a decimal clock. Few were actually made, and this provision seems to have had little effect.

Fabre d'Eglantine, *Report on Behalf of the Commission to Draw up the Calendar, Day 3 of the 2d month of the 2d year of the French Republic* **(24 October 1793)**

The regeneration of the French people, the establishment of the Republic, have of necessity brought with them the reform of the common calendar. We could no longer count the years during which kings oppressed us as an era during which we had lived. The prejudices of the throne and the church, and the lies of each, sullied each page of the calendar we were using. You have reformed this calendar and substituted another, in which time is measured by more exact, symmetrical computations; this is not enough. Long usage of the Gregorian calendar has filled the memory of the people with a considerable number of images that it has long revered, and which today remain the source of its religious errors. It is therefore necessary to replace these visions of ignorance with the realities of reason, sacerdotal prestige with the truth of nature. We conceive nothing except through images: in the most abstract analysis, in the most metaphysical combination of ideas, our understanding only proceeds by means of images, our memory only rests and relies upon them. You must therefore apply them to your new calendar if you want the method and entire organization of this calendar to penetrate the understanding of the people easily, and to engrave itself rapidly in its memory.

This should not be your only goal. Inasmuch as it is in your power, you should let nothing penetrate the understanding of the people, with regard to institutions, that does not bear the full stamp of public utility. You must seize this fortunate opportunity to use the calendar, the most common and everyday book of all, to bring the French people back to agriculture. Agriculture is the political element of a people such as we—a people upon whom the earth, the sky, and nature look with so much love and affection.

What if at each moment of the year, the month, the *décade,* and the day, the glances and the thoughts of the citizen fell upon an agricultural image, a gift of nature, or an object of rural economy? You should be in no doubt that this would move the nation profoundly toward the agricultural system, and that each citizen would conceive a love for the real and actual gifts of nature he enjoys—you have evidence in the fact that for centuries the people conceived such a love for imaginary objects, alleged saints, which it did not see and which it knew even less. I will go further and say that priests only succeeded in giving substance to their idols by attributing to each one a direct influence over matters of tangible interest to the people: thus Saint John became the bestower of harvests, and Saint Mark the protector of the vine.

If arguments were required to demonstrate the irresistible power of images over human intelligence, I would not need to enter into metaphysical analyses. I would find adequate demonstration in the theory, doctrine, and practice of priests.

Take an example. Priests, whose universal and definitive goal is and always will be to subjugate the human species and enslave it under their dominion, instituted the practice of commemorating the dead. They did so to inspire disgust in us for earthly and worldly riches in order to enjoy them in greater abundance themselves; to make us dependent on them through the myth and imagery of purgatory. But you see here their skill in seizing upon the imagination of men and controlling it to suit their purposes. To act out this farce, they didn't choose a setting smiling with gaiety and freshness, which would have made us cherish life and its pleasures. They chose 2 November to lead us to the tombs of our fathers—a time when the disappearance of fine days, the presence of a sad, gray sky, the fading of the earth's colors and the falling of the leaves filled our soul with melancholy and sadness. Taking advantage of nature's farewells, they took possession of us in order to lead us through Advent and their numerous alleged holy days to all that they had insolently conjured up to be mystical for the predestined (in other words, for imbeciles) and terrifying for the sinner (in other words, for the clear-sighted).

Priests, these men who appeared to be the enemies of human passions and of the sweetest sentiments, wanted to turn them to their own advantage. They wanted the domestic restlessness of young lovers, the flirtatiousness of both sexes, the love of finery, vanity, ostentation, and the other affections of life's finest age, to bring youth back to religious slavery. It wasn't during winter that they lured youth into making a spectacle of itself. On the contrary, it was during the most beautiful days, the longest and most exciting of the year, that they held a profusion of triumphal and public ceremonies, called the *Fête-Dieu*. Into these ceremonies they cleverly introduced all that is most appealing in worldliness, luxury, and finery. Of course there were festivities celebrating the devotion of young girls, who on that day were less strictly watched; festivities in which the sexes were encouraged to mingle and to show themselves to one another, in which the flirtatious and vain could flaunt themselves and enjoy the finery necessary for their passions: they swallowed, with their pleasure, the poison of superstition.

Finally, the priests, acting as always to extend their domination, wanted to subjugate completely the majority of those working the land, in other words most of the people. They brought the passion of self-interest into play, acting upon the credulity of men through the use of the greatest images of all. It was not under a burning and unbearable sun that they called the people into the fields: the harvests are gathered then, and the hope of the laborer is fulfilled; the seduction would only have been partial. Instead, it was in the beautiful month of May, at the moment when the rising sun has not yet absorbed the dew and freshness of dawn, that the priests, enveloped in superstitious reverence, dragged whole tribes of credulous people into the fields. There, in the guise of the Rogation Days' services, their ministry interposed itself between us and the sky. After appearing in our eyes to unfold nature in its greatest beauty, after having shown us the earth in all its finery, they seemed to say to us, and said in effect: "It is we, the priests, who have made the countryside green again; it is we who impregnate these fields with such beautiful hope; it is through our mediation that your granaries will be filled. Believe us, respect us, obey us, enrich us. Otherwise, the hail and the thunder, which are at our command, will punish you for your incredulity, your obstinacy, and your disobedience." Then the tiller of the soil, struck by the beauty of the spectacle and the richness of the images, believed, fell silent, obeyed, and easily attributed the miracles of nature to the illusion of the priests.

Such was the skill exercised upon us by priests; such is the influence of images.

The Commission that you named to give the new calendar greater impact upon the mind and make it more accessible to memory has therefore concluded that it would fulfill this goal if it succeeded in striking the imagination by use of names and instructing it through the content and succession of images.

The first idea upon which we have based our proposal is to use the calendar to consecrate the agricultural system, and to lead the nation back to it, marking periods and fractions of the year with intelligible or visible signs taken from agriculture and the rural economy.

The more memory is presented with fixed points of reference, the more easily it operates. We have therefore developed the idea of giving each month of the year a characteristic name that would convey its characteristic temperature and the types of agricultural produce then in season, and at the same time suggest the type of season to which it belongs among the four composing the year.

This latter effect is achieved by four endings, each given to three consecutive months, which produce four different sounds indicating the seasons to which they apply. . . .

Thus the names of the months are:

AUTUMN	WINTER
Vendémiaire (Vintage)	Nivôse (Snow)
Brumaire (Fog)	Pluviôse (Rain)
Frimaire (Frost)	Ventôse (Wind)

SPRING	SUMMER
Germinal (Buds)	Messidor (Harvest)
Floréal (Flowers)	Thermidor (Heat)
Prairial (Meadow)	Fructidor (Fruit)

The effect of these names, as I have said, is such that by simply pronouncing the name of the month one will be perfectly aware of the nature and implications of the season, the temperature, and the state of vegetation. Thus on 1 Germinal, the ending of the word will effortlessly depict to the imagination that Spring is beginning; the construction and the image that the word presents will suggest that the elements are at work; the signification of the word, that seeds are developing.[3]

42. Robespierre, *Report on the Principles of Political Morality* (5 February 1794)

By the end of 1793, revolutionary government had in large part achieved its military goals. The rebellious "federalist" cities had been subjugated by republican armies, Toulon had been evacuated by the British, counter-revolutionary forces in the Vendée had been decisively defeated, and the armies of the European powers turned back. In this context, the policies of the Committee of Public Safety came under growing criticism in the ideological struggle between moderates like Danton, who thought the apparatus of the Terror should now be dismantled, and extremists like Hébert who asserted the sans-culotte program for social levelling and revolutionary activism. In this celebrated speech, presented to the Convention on behalf of the Committee of Public Safety, Maximilien Robespierre explained his own views regarding the nature and uses of terror. His report served as a prelude to the elimination of the two opposing factions: Hébert and his associates were executed on 24 March; Danton on 6 April.

3. Fabre d'Eglantine went on to propose that the fifth day of each *décade* celebrate a domesticated animal, and the tenth an agricultural instrument. He also proposed the naming of the *sansculottides* discussed in note 1.

From *The Ninth of Thermidor: The Fall of Robespierre*, edited by Richard T. Bienvenu, (Oxford: Oxford University Press, 1968), pp. 32–49.

17 Pluviôse, Year II [5 February 1794]

Citizen-representatives of the people.

Some time ago we set forth the principles of our foreign policy; today we come to expound the principles of our internal policy.

After having proceeded haphazardly for a long time, swept along by the movement of opposing factions, the representatives of the French people have finally demonstrated a character and a government. A sudden change in the nation's fortune announced to Europe the regeneration that had been effected in the national representation. But, up to the very moment when I am speaking, it must be agreed that we have been guided, amid such stormy circumstances, by the love of good and by the awareness of our country's needs rather than by an exact theory and by precise rules of conduct, which we did not have even leisure enough to lay out.

It is time to mark clearly the goal of the revolution, and the end we want to reach; it is time for us to take account both of the obstacles that still keep us from it, and of the means we ought to adopt to attain it: a simple and important idea which seems never to have been noticed. Eh! how could a lax and corrupt government have dared realize it? A king, a haughty senate, a Caesar, a Cromwell are obliged above all to cover their plans, to compromise with all the vices, to humor all the parties, to crush the party of the honest folk, to oppress or deceive the people, in order to reach the goal of their perfidious ambition. If we had not had a greater task to fulfill, if we had been concerned here only with the interests of a faction or of a new aristocracy, we could have believed, like certain writers still more ignorant than they are depraved, that the plan of the French revolution was written out in full in the books of Tacitus and Machiavelli, and we could have sought the duties of the people's representatives in the histories of Augustus, Tiberius, or Vespasian, or even in that of certain French legislators; because, except for a few nuances of perfidy or cruelty, all tyrants are alike.

For ourselves, we come to make the world privy to your political secrets, so that all our country's friends can rally to the voice of reason and the public interest; so that the French nation and its representatives will be respected in all the countries of the world where the knowledge of their real principles can penetrate; so that the intriguers who seek always to replace other intriguers will be judged by sure and easy rules.

We must take far-sighted precautions to return the destiny of liberty into the hands of the truth, which is eternal, rather than into those of men, who are transitory, so that if the government forgets the interests of the people, or if it lapses into the hands of corrupt individuals, according to the natural course of things, the light of recognized principles will illuminate their treachery, and so that every new faction will discover death in the mere thought of crime.

Happy the people who can arrive at that point! Because, whatever new outrages are prepared against them, what resources are presented by an order of things in which the public reason is the guarantee of liberty!

What is the goal toward which we are heading? The peaceful enjoyment of liberty and equality; the reign of that eternal justice whose laws have been inscribed, not in marble and stone, but in the hearts of all men, even in that of the slave who forgets them and in that of the tyrant who denies them.

We seek an order of things in which all the base and cruel passions are enchained, all the beneficient and generous passions are awakened by the laws; where ambition becomes the desire to merit glory and to serve our country; where distinctions are born only of equality itself; where the citizen is subject to the magistrate, the magistrate to the people, and the people to justice; where our country assures the well-being of each individual, and where each individual proudly enjoys our country's prosperity and glory; where every soul grows greater through the continual flow of republican sentiments, and by the need of deserving the esteem of a great people; where the arts are the adornments of the liberty which ennobles them and commerce the source of public wealth rather than solely the monstrous opulence of a few families.

In our land we want to substitute morality for egotism, integrity for formal codes of honor, principles for customs, a sense of duty for one of mere propriety, the rule of reason for the tyranny of fashion, scorn of vice for scorn of the unlucky, self-respect for insolence, grandeur of soul for vanity, love of glory for the love of money, good people in place of good society. We wish to substitute merit for intrigue, genius for wit, truth for glamor, the charm of happiness for sensuous boredom, the greatness of man for the pettiness of the great, a people who are magnanimous, powerful, and happy, in place of a kindly, frivolous, and miserable people—which is to say all the virtues and all the miracles of the republic in place of all the vices and all the absurdities of the monarchy.

We want, in a word, to fulfill nature's desires, accomplish the destiny of humanity, keep the promises of philosophy, absolve providence from the long reign of crime and tyranny. Let France, formerly illustrious among the enslaved lands, eclipsing the glory of all the free peoples who have existed, become the model for the nations, the terror of oppressors, the consolation of the oppressed, the ornament of the world—and let us, in sealing our work with our blood, see at least the early dawn of universal bliss—that is our ambition, that is our goal.

What kind of government can realize these wonders? Only a democratic or republican government—these two words are synonyms, despite the abuses in common speech, because an aristocracy is no closer than a monarchy to being a republic. Democracy is not a state in which the people, continually meeting, regulate for themselves all public affairs, still less is it a state in which a tiny fraction of the people, acting by isolated, hasty, and contradictory measures, decide the fate of the whole society. Such a government has never existed, and it could exist only to lead the people back into despotism.

Democracy is a state in which the sovereign people, guided by laws which are of their own making, do for themselves all that they can do well, and by their delegates do all that they cannot do for themselves.

It is therefore in the principles of democratic government that you should seek the rules of your political conduct.

But, in order to lay the foundations of democracy among us and to consolidate it, in order to arrive at the peaceful reign of constitutional laws, we must finish the war of liberty against tyranny and safely cross through the storms of the revolution: that is the goal of the revolutionary system which you have put in order. You should therefore still base your conduct upon the stormy circumstances in which the republic finds itself; and the plan of your administration should be the result of the spirit of revolutionary government, combined with the general principles of democracy.

Now, what is the fundamental principle of popular or democratic government, that is to say, the essential mainspring which sustains it and makes it move? It is virtue. I speak of the public virtue which worked so many wonders in Greece and Rome and which ought to produce even more astonishing things in republican France—that virtue which is nothing other than the love of the nation and its laws.

But as the essence of the republic or of democracy is equality, it follows that love of country necessarily embraces the love of equality.

It is still true that that sublime sentiment supposes the preference of public interest to all particular interests, whence it follows that love of country implies or produces all the virtues. There is no other force, for what are they but the strength of soul which makes men capable of these sacrifices? And how, for example, can the slave of avarice or ambition be made to sacrifice his idol for the good of the country?

Not only is virtue the soul of democracy, but virtue can only exist within that form of government. Under a monarchy I know of only one individual who can love his country—and who, for this, does not even need virtue— the monarch. The reason for this is that among all the people of his state, the monarch alone has a fatherland. Is he not the sovereign, at least in fact? Does he not stand in place of the people? And what is the fatherland if it is not the land where one is a citizen and a participant in the sovereign power?

As a consequence of the same principle, within aristocratic states the word *patrie* means nothing except to the patrician families who have invaded sovereignty.

It is only under a democracy that the state is the fatherland of all the individuals who compose it and can count as many active defenders of its cause as it has citizens. There lies the source of the superiority of free peoples above all others. If Athens and Sparta triumphed over the tyrants of Asia and the Swiss over the tyrants of Spain and Austria, one can seek no other cause.

But the French are the first people of the world who have established real democracy, by calling all men to equality and full rights of citizenship; and there, in my judgment, is the true reason why all the tyrants in league against the Republic will be vanquished.

There are important consequences to be drawn immediately from the principles we have just explained.

Since the soul of the Republic is virtue, equality, and since your goal is to found, to consolidate the Republic, it follows that the first rule of your political conduct ought to be to relate all your efforts to maintaining equality and developing virtue; because the first care of the legislator ought to be to fortify the principle of the government. Thus everything that tends to excite love of country, to purify morals, to elevate souls, to direct the passions of the human heart toward the public interest, ought to be adopted or established by you. Everything which tends to concentrate them in the abjection of selfishness, to awaken enjoyment for petty things and scorn for great ones, ought to be rejected or curbed by you. Within the scheme of the French revolution, that which is immoral is impolitic, that which is corrupting is counter-revolutionary. Weakness, vice, and prejudices are the road to royalty. Dragged too often, perhaps, by the weight of our former customs, as much as by the imperceptible bent of human frailty, toward false ideas and faint-hearted sentiments, we have less cause to guard ourselves against too much energy than against too much weakness. The greatest peril, perhaps, that we have to avoid is not that of zealous fervor, but rather of weariness in doing good works and of timidity in displaying our own courage. Maintain, then, the sacred power of the republican government, instead of letting it decline. I do not need to say that I have no wish here to justify any excess. The most sacred principles can indeed be abused. It is up to the wisdom of the government to pay heed to circumstances, to seize the right moments, to choose the proper means; because the manner of preparing great things is an essential part of the talent for performing them, just as wisdom is itself an element of virtue.

We do not intend to cast the French Republic in the Spartan mold; we wish to give it neither the austerity nor the corruption of a monastic cloister. We have come to present to you in all its purity the moral and political principle of popular government. Thus you have a compass which can guide you amid the storms of all the passions and the whirlwinds of intrigue which surround you. You have the touchstone by which you can test all your laws, all the proposals which are made to you. In comparing them unceasingly with that principle, you can from now on avoid the usual perils which threaten large assemblies, the danger of surprises and of hasty, incoherent, and contradictory measures. You can give to all your operations the cohesion, the unity, the wisdom and the dignity that ought to distinguish the representatives of the first people of the world.

The obvious consequences of the principle of democracy do not require detailed description; it is the simple and fruitful principle itself which deserves to be expounded.

Republican virtue can be considered as it relates to the people and as it relates to the government. It is necessary in both. When the government alone is deprived of it, there remains a resource in the virtue of the people; but when the people themselves are corrupt, liberty is already lost.

Happily virtue is natural to the people, despite aristocratic prejudices to the contrary. A nation is truly corrupt when, having gradually lost its character and its liberty, it passes from democracy to aristocracy or to monarchy; this is the death of the body politic through decrepitude. When after four hundred years of glory avarice finally drove from Sparta its morality together with the laws of Lycurgus, Agis died in vain trying to bring them back! Demosthenes thundered in vain against Philip of Macedon, Philip found more eloquent advocates than Demosthenes among the degenerate inhabitants of Athens. There was still as large a population in Athens as in the times of Miltiades and Aristides, but there were no longer any true Athenians. And what did it matter that Brutus killed a tyrant? Tyranny still lived in every heart, and Rome existed only in Brutus.

But, when, by prodigious efforts of courage and reason, a people breaks the chains of despotism in order to make of them trophies to liberty; when, by the force of its moral character, it leaves, as it were, the arms of death in order to recapture the vigor of youth; when it is in turn sensitive and proud, intrepid and docile—such a people can be stopped neither by impregnable ramparts nor by the countless armies of tyrants ranged against it; it halts only before the image of the law. If such a people does not move rapidly forward to the height of its destiny, it can only be the fault of those who govern it.

Moreover one could say, in a sense, that in order to love justice and equality the people have no need of a great degree of virtue; it suffices if they love themselves.

But the magistrate is obliged to sacrifice his interest to the interest of the people, and his pride in power to equality. The law must speak with authority especially to those who are its instruments. The government must weigh heavily upon its parts in order to hold them all in harmony. If there exists a representative body, a highest authority constituted by the people, it is up to it to inspect and ceaselessly control all the public functionaries. But who will curb the legislature itself, if not its own sense of virtue? The higher this source of public order is elevated in position, the purer it should be; the representative body must begin, then, by submitting all the private passions within it to the general passion for the public welfare. Fortunate are the representatives when their glory and even their interests, as much as their duties, attach them to the cause of liberty!

We deduce from all this a great truth—that the characteristic of popular government is to be trustful towards the people and severe towards itself.

Here the development of our theory would reach its limit, if you had only to steer the ship of the Republic through calm waters. But the tempest rages, and the state of the revolution in which you find yourself imposes upon you another task.

This great purity of the French revolution's fundamental elements, the very sublimity of its objective, is precisely what creates our strength and our weakness: our strength, because it gives us the victory of truth over deception and the rights of public interest over private interests; our weakness, because it rallies against us all men who are vicious, all those who in their hearts plan to despoil the people, and all those who have despoiled them and want impunity, and those who reject liberty as a personal calamity, and those who have embraced the revolution as a livelihood and the Republic as if it were an object of prey. Hence the defection of so many ambitious or greedy men who since the beginning have abandoned us along the way, because they had not begun the voyage in order to reach the same goal. One could say that the two contrary geniuses that have been depicted competing for control of the realm of nature, are fighting in this great epoch of human history to shape irrevocably the destiny of the world, and that France is the theater of this mighty struggle. Without, all the tyrants encircle you; within, all the friends of tyranny conspire—they will conspire until crime has been robbed of hope. We must smother the internal and external enemies of the Republic or perish with them. Now, in this situation, the first maxim of your policy ought to be to lead the people by reason and the people's enemies by terror.

If the mainspring of popular government in peacetime is virtue, amid revolution it is at the same time [both] virtue and *terror:* virtue, without which terror is fatal; terror, without which virtue is impotent. Terror is nothing but prompt, severe, inflexible justice; it is therefore an emanation of virtue. It is less a special principle than a consequence of the general principle of democracy applied to our country's most pressing needs.

It has been said that terror was the mainspring of despotic government. Does your government, then, resemble a despotism? Yes, as the sword which glitters in the hands of liberty's heroes resembles the one with which tyranny's lackeys are armed. Let the despot govern his brutalized subjects by terror; he is right to do this, as a despot. Subdue liberty's enemies by terror, and you will be right, as founders of the Republic. The government of the revolution is the despotism of liberty against tyranny. Is force made only to protect crime? And is it not to strike the heads of the proud that lightning is destined?

Nature imposes upon every physical and moral being the law of providing for its own preservation. Crime slaughters innocence in order to reign, and innocence in the hands of crime fights with all its strength.

Let tyranny reign for a single day, and on the morrow not one patriot will be left. How long will the despots' fury be called justice, and the people's justice barbarism or rebellion? How tender one is to the oppressors and how inexorable against the oppressed! And how natural—whoever has no hatred for crime cannot love virtue.

Yet one or the other must succumb. Indulgence for the royalists, some people cry out. Mercy for the scoundrels! No—mercy for innocence, mercy for the weak, mercy for the unfortunate, mercy for humanity!

Social protection is due only to peaceful citizens; there are no citizens in the Republic but the republicans. The royalists, the conspirators are, in its eyes, only strangers or, rather, enemies. Is not the terrible war, which liberty sustains against tyranny, indivisible? Are not the enemies within the allies of those without? The murderers who tear our country apart internally; the intriguers who purchase the consciences of the people's agents; the traitors who sell them; the mercenary libelers subsidized to dishonor the popular cause, to kill public virtue, to stir up the fires of civil discord, and to prepare political counter-revolution by means of moral counter-revolution—are all these men less to blame or less dangerous than the tyrants whom they serve? All those who interpose their parricidal gentleness to protect the wicked from the avenging blade of national justice are like those who would throw themselves between the tyrants' henchmen and our soldiers' bayonets. All the outbursts of their false sensitivity seem to me only longing sighs for England and Austria.

Well! For whom, then, would they be moved to pity? Would it be for two hundred thousand heroes, the elite of the nation, cut down by the iron of liberty's enemies or by the daggers of royalist or federalist assassins? No, those are only plebeians, patriots; in order to be entitled to their tender interest, one must be at least the widow of a general who has betrayed our country twenty times. To obtain their indulgence, one must almost prove that he has sacrificed ten thousand Frenchmen, as a Roman general, in order to obtain his triumph, was supposed to have killed, I believe, ten thousand enemies. They listen composedly to the recital of the horrors committed by the tyrants against the defenders of liberty—our women horribly mutilated, our children murdered at their mothers' breasts, our prisoners undergoing horrible torments for their moving, sublime heroism. The too slow punishment of a few monsters who have fattened on the purest blood of our country is termed by them a horrible butchery.

They suffer patiently the misery of generous citizens who have sacrificed their brothers, children, husbands to the finest of causes, while they lavish their most generous consolations upon conspirators' wives. It is accepted that such women can seduce justice with impunity, pleading (against liberty) the cause of their near relations and their accomplices. They have been made almost a privileged corporation, creditor and pensioner of the people.

With what simple good-heartedness are we still the dupes of words! How aristocracy and moderatism still govern us by the murderous maxims they have given us!

Aristocracy defends itself better by its intrigues than patriotism does by its services. Some people would like to govern revolutions by the quibbles of the law courts and treat conspiracies against the Republic like legal proceedings against private persons. Tyranny kills; liberty argues. And the code made by the conspirators themselves is the law by which they are judged.

When it is a matter of the national safety, the testimony of the whole world cannot compensate for the proof of actual witnesses, nor obviousness itself for documentary evidence.

Slowness of judgments is equal to impunity. Uncertainty of punishment encourages all the guilty. Yet there are complaints of the severity of justice, of the detention of enemies of the Republic. Examples are sought in the history of tyrants because our enemies do not wish to select them from the history of peoples nor derive them from the spirit of threatened liberty. In Rome, when the consul discovered a plot and simultaneously smothered it by putting to death the accomplices of Catiline, he was accused of having violated the legal forms. And by whom? By the ambitious Caesar, who wanted to swell his faction with the horde of conspirators, by Piso, Clodius, and all the evil citizens who themselves feared the virtue of a true Roman and the severity of the laws.

To punish the oppressors of humanity is clemency; to pardon them is barbarity. The rigor of tyrants has only rigor for a principle; the rigor of the republican government comes from charity.

Therefore, woe to those who would dare to turn against the people the terror which ought to be felt only by its enemies! Woe to those who, confusing the inevitable errors of civic conduct with the calculated errors of perfidy, or with conspirators' criminal attempts, leave the dangerous schemer to pursue the peaceful citizen! Perish the scoundrel who ventures to abuse the sacred name of liberty, or the redoubtable arms which liberty has entrusted to him, in order to bring mourning or death into patriots' hearts! This abuse has existed, one cannot doubt it. It has been exaggerated, no doubt, by the aristocracy. But if in all the Republic there existed only one virtuous man persecuted by the enemies of liberty, the government's duty would be to seek him out vigorously and give him a dazzling revenge.

But must one conclude from these persecutions, brought upon the patriots by the hypocritical zeal of the counter-revolutionaries, that one must give freedom to the counter-revolutionaries and renounce severity? These new crimes of the aristocracy only show the need for severity. What proves the audacity of our enemies, if not the weakness with which they have been pursued? That is due, in large part, to the slack doctrine that has been preached lately in order to reassure them. If you listen to those counsels, your enemies will reach their goal and will receive from your own hands the ultimate prize of their evil crimes.

How frivolous it would be to regard a few victories achieved by patriotism as the end of all our dangers. Glance over our true situation. You will become aware that vigilance and energy are more necessary for you than ever. An unresponding ill-will everywhere opposes the operations of the government. The inevitable influence of foreign courts is no less active for being more hidden, and no less baneful. One senses that crime, frightened, has only covered its tracks with greater skill.

The internal enemies of the French people are divided into two factions, like two corps of an army. They march under the banners of different colors and by diverse routes, but they march toward the same goal. That goal is the disruption of the popular government, the ruin of the Convention— which is to say, the triumph of tyranny. One of these two factions pushes us toward weakness, the other toward excess. The one wants to change liberty into a frenzied nymph, the other into a prostitute.

The minor intriguers, and often even some good but misled citizens, are ranged in one or the other of these parties. But the chiefs belong to the cause of royalty or aristocracy and always unite against the patriots. The rascals, even when they make war upon each other, hate each other much less than they detest the well-meaning folk. Our country is their prey; they fight each other in order to divide it. But they form a league against those who are defending it.

One group has been given the name of moderates. There is perhaps more wit than accuracy in the term *ultra-revolutionaries* by which the others have been called. That name, which cannot be applied in a single case to the men of good faith whose zeal and ignorance can carry them beyond the sound policy of the revolution, does not precisely characterize the perfidious men whom tyranny hires in order, by a false and deadly diligence, to compromise the sacred principles of our revolution.

The false revolutionary is even more often, perhaps, short of rather than in excess of the revolution. He is moderate; he is insanely patriotic, according to the circumstances. What he will think tomorrow is set for him today by the committees of Prussia, England, Austria, even by those of Muscovy. He opposes energetic measures and exaggerates their import when he has been unable to impede them. He is severe toward innocence but indulgent toward crime, accusing even the guilty who are not rich enough to purchase his silence nor important enough to merit his zeal, but carefully refraining from being compromised to the point of defending slandered courage; now and then discovering plots that have already been discovered, ripping the masks off traitors who are already unmasked and even decapitated, but extolling living and still influential traitors; always eager to embrace the opinion of the moment and not less alert never to enlighten it, and above all never to clash with it; always quick to adopt bold measures, provided they have many drawbacks; slandering those who speak only of the advantages, or better, adding all the amendments which can render the measures harmful; speaking the truth sparingly, and just so much as he must in order to acquire the right to lie with impunity; exuding good drop by drop and pouring out evil in torrents; full of fire for the grand resolutions which signify nothing; worse than indifferent to those which can honor the people's cause and save our country; giving much attention to the forms of patriotism; very much attached, like the devout whose enemy he declares himself to be, to formal observances—he would prefer to wear out a hundred red caps than to do one good deed.

What difference can you find between the false revolutionaries and your moderates? They are servants employed by the same master, or, if you wish, accomplices who feign a quarrel in order better to hide their crimes. Judge them not by the different words they use but by the identity of the results. He who attacks the National Convention by his senseless speeches, and he who deceives it in order to compromise it, are they not in agreement? He who, by unjust rigors forces patriotism to tremble for itself, invokes amnesty in favor of aristocracy and treason. Such a man, who was calling France to the conquest of the world, had no other goal than to call the tyrants to the conquest of France. The foreign hypocrite who for five years has been proclaiming Paris the capital of the globe only expresses, in another jargon, the anathemas of the vile federalists who dedicated Paris to destruction. To preach atheism is only a way of absolving superstition and accusing philosophy; and the war declared against divinity is only a diversion in royalty's favor.

What other method remains for combatting liberty? Will one, on the example of the first champions of the aristocracy, go about praising the delights of servitude and the benefits of the monarchy, the supernatural genius and the incomparable virtues of kings?

Will one go about proclaiming the vanity of the rights of man and the principles of eternal justice?

Will one go about exhuming the nobility and the clergy or calling for the imprescriptible rights of the high bourgeoisie to their double inheritance?

No. It is much more convenient to don the mask of patriotism in order to disfigure, by insolent parodies, the sublime drama of the revolution, in order to compromise the cause of liberty by a hypocritical moderation or by studied extravagance.

And so the aristocracy establishes itself in popular societies; counter-revolutionary pride hides its plots and its daggers beneath rags; fanaticism smashes its own altars; royalism sings victory hymns to the Republic; the nobility, overwhelmed with memories, tenderly embraces equality in order to smother it; tyranny, tainted with the blood of the defenders of liberty, scatters flowers on their tomb. If all hearts are not changed, how many countenances are masked! How many traitors meddle in our affairs only to ruin them!

Do you wish to test these people? Ask of them, in place of oaths and declamations, real services.

Is action needed? They orate. Is deliberation required? Then they clamor for action. Have the times become peaceful? They obstruct all useful change. Are times stormy? Then they speak of reforming everything, in order to throw everything into confusion. Do you want to keep sedition in check? Then they remind you of Caesar's clemency. Do you want to deliver patriots from persecution? Then they propose to you as a model the firmness of Brutus. They discover that so-and-so was a noble when he served the Republic; they no longer remember this as soon as he has betrayed it. Is peace appropriate? Then they display the rewards of victory. Has war become necessary? They praise the delights of peace. Must our territory be defended? They wish to go and punish the tyrants beyond the mountains and seas. Is it necessary to recapture our own fortresses? They want to take the churches by assault and ascend to heaven. They forget the Austrians in order to make war on the devout. Do we need the faithful support of our allies? They declaim against all the governments of the world and suggest that you put on trial the great Mogul himself. Do the people come to the capital to give thanks to the gods for their victories? They intone lugubrious chants over our previous reverses. Is it a matter of winning new victories? In our midst they sow hatreds, divisions, persecutions, and discouragement. Must we make the sovereignty of the people a reality and concentrate their strength by a strong, respected government? They discover that the principles of government injure popular sovereignty. Must we call for the rights of the people oppressed by the government? They talk only of respect for the laws and of obedience owed to constituted authority.

They have found an admirable expedient for promoting the efforts of the republican government: it is to disorganize it, to degrade it completely, to make war on the patriots who have joined in our successes.

Do you seek the means for provisioning your armies? Are you busy wresting from greed and fear the supplies of food that they have caused to be hidden away? They groan patriotically over the public misery and announce a famine. The desire to foresee evil is for them always a reason for magnifying it. In the north they have killed the hens and deprived us of eggs on the pretext that the hens eat grain. In the south it was a question of destroying the mulberry trees and the orange trees on the pretext that silk is a luxury article and oranges are superfluous.

You could never have imagined some of the excesses committed by hypocritical counter-revolutionaries in order to blight the cause of the revolution. Would you believe that in the regions where superstition has held the greatest sway, the counter-revolutionaries are not content with burdening religious observances under all the forms that could render them odious, but have spread terror among the people by sowing the rumor that all children under ten and all old men over seventy are going to be killed? This rumor was spread particularly through the former province of Brittany and in the *départements* of the Rhine and the Moselle. It is one of the crimes imputed to [Schneider] the former public prosecutor of the criminal court of Strasbourg. That man's tyrannical follies make everything that has been said of Caligula and Heliogabalus credible; one can scarcely believe it, despite the evidence. He pushed his delirium to the point of commandeering women for his own use—we are told that he even employed that method in selecting a wife. Whence came this sudden swarm of foreigners, priests, nobles, intriguers of all kinds, which at the same instant spread over the length and breadth of the Republic, seeking to execute, in the name of philosophy, a plan of counter-revolution which has only been stopped by the force of public reason? Execrable conception, worthy of the genius of foreign courts leagued against liberty, and of the corruption of all the internal enemies of the Republic!

Thus among the continual miracles worked by the virtue of a great people, intrigue still mingles the baseness of its criminal plots, baseness directed by the tyrants and quickly incorporated into their ridiculous manifestos, in order to keep the ignorant peoples in the mire of shame and the chains of servitude.

Eh! what effects do the heinous crimes of its enemies have upon liberty? Is the sun, veiled by a passing cloud, any less the star which animates nature? Does the impure scum on the beach make the Ocean any less mighty?

In deceitful hands all the remedies for our ills turn into poisons. Everything you can do, everything you can say, they will turn against you, even the truths which we come here to present this very day.

Thus, for example, after having disseminated everywhere the germs of civil war by a violent attack against religious prejudices, these individuals will seek to fortify fanaticism and aristocracy against the very measures, in favor of freedom of religion, that sound policy has prescribed to you. If you had left free play to the conspiracy, it would have produced, sooner or later, a terrible and universal reaction; but if you stop it, they will still seek to turn this to their account by urging that you protect the priests and the moderates. You must not even be surprised if the authors of this strategy are the very priests who have most boldly confessed that they were charlatans.

If the patriots, carried away by a pure but thoughtless zeal, have somewhere been made the dupes of their intrigues, they will throw all the blame upon the patriots; because the principal point of their Machiavellian doctrine is to ruin the Republic, by ruining the republicans, as one conquers a country by overthrowing the army which defends it. One can thereby appreciate one of their favorite principles, which is that one must count men as nothing—a maxim of royal origin, which means that one must abandon to them all the friends of liberty.

It is to be noticed that the destiny of men who seek only the public good is to be made the victims of those who seek to advance themselves, and this comes from two causes: first, that the intriguers attack using the vices of the old regime; second, that the patriots defend themselves only with the virtues of the new.

Such an internal situation ought to seem to you worthy of all your attention, above all if you reflect that at the same time you have the tyrants of Europe to combat, a million and two hundred thousand men under arms to maintain, and that the government is obliged continually to repair, with energy and vigilance, all the injuries which the innumerable multitude of our enemies has prepared for us during the course of five years.

What is the remedy for all these evils? We know no other than the development of that general motive force of the Republic—virtue.

Democracy perishes by two kinds of excess: either the aristocracy of those who govern, or else popular scorn for the authorities whom the people themselves have established, scorn which makes each clique, each individual take unto himself the public power and bring the people through excessive disorders, to annihilation or to the power of one man.

The double task of the moderates and the false revolutionaries is to toss us back and forth perpetually between these two perils.

But the people's representatives can avoid them both, because government is always the master at being just and wise; and, when it has that character, it is sure of the confidence of the people.

It is indeed true that the goal of all our enemies is to dissolve the Convention. It is true that the tyrant of Great Britain and his allies promise their parliament and subjects that they will deprive you of your energy and of the public confidence which you have merited; that is the first instruction for all their agents.

But it is a truth which ought to be regarded as commonplace in politics that a great body invested with the confidence of a great people can be lost only through its own failings. Your enemies know this; therefore do not doubt that they are applying themselves above all to awaken in your midst all the passions which can further their sinister designs.

What can they do against the national representation if they do not succeed in beguiling it into impolitic acts which can furnish the excuse for their criminal declamations? They are therefore necessarily obliged to desire two kinds of agents, those who seek to degrade it by their speeches, and those in its very bosom, who do their utmost to deceive it in order to compromise its glory and the interests of the Republic.

In order to attack this Convention with success, it was useful to begin civil war against the representatives in the *départements* which had justified your confidence, and against the Committee of Public Safety; and so they have been attacked by men who seemed to be fighting among themselves.

What better could they do than to paralyze the government of the Convention and to smash its mainsprings at the moment which is to decide the destiny of the Republic and of the tyrants?

Far from us is the idea that there yet exists in our midst a single man weakling enough to wish to serve the tyrants' cause! But farther from us still is the crime, for which we would not be pardoned, of deceiving the National Convention and betraying the French people by a culpable silence! For this is the good fortune of a free people, that truth, which is the scourge of despots, is always its strength and safety. Now it is true that there still exists a danger for our liberty, perhaps the only serious danger which remains for it to undergo. That danger is a plan which has existed for rallying all the enemies of the Republic by reviving the spirit of faction; for persecuting patriots, disheartening them, ruining the faithful agents of the republican government, rendering inadequate the most essential parts of our public service. Some have wished to deceive the Convention about men and about things; they have sought to put it on the wrong track about the causes of abuses which they have at the same time exaggerated, so as to make them irremediable; they have studiously filled it with false terrors, in order to lead it astray or paralyze it; they seek to divide it, above all to divide the representatives sent out to the *départements* and the Committee of Public Safety. They have sought to influence the former to contradict the measures of the central authority, in order to bring disorder and confusion; they have sought to embitter them upon their return, in order to make them the unknowing instruments of a cabal. The foreigners profit from all private passions, even from abused patriotism.

They first decided on going straight to their goal by slandering the Committee of Public Safety; they flattered themselves aloud that it would succumb under the weight of its laborious duties. Victory and the good fortune of the French people defended it. Since that time they have decided on praising it while paralyzing it and destroying the fruit of its labors. All those vague declamations against necessary agents of the Committee; all those plans for disorganization, disguised under the name of reforms, already rejected by the Convention, and reproduced today with a strange affectation; this eagerness to extol the intriguers whom the Committee of Public Safety was obliged to remove; this terror inspired in good citizens; this indulgence with which one flatters the conspirators—this entire scheme of imposture and intrigue, whose principal author is a man [Fabre d'Églantine] whom you have driven from your bosom, is directed against the National Convention and tends to give reality to the vows of all the enemies of France.

It is since the time when this scheme was made public and made real by public actions, that aristocracy and royalism have again begun to raise their insolent heads and patriotism has again been persecuted in a part of the Republic, that the national authority has experienced resistance of a sort which the intriguers had not lately displayed. Even if these indirect attacks had served only to divide the attention and energy of those who have to carry the immense burden which is your charge, and to distract them too often from the great measures of public safety, to occupy themselves with thwarting dangerous intrigues,—even so, they could still be considered as a division useful to our enemies.

But let us reassure ourselves. Here is the sanctuary of truth; here reside the founders of the Republic, the avengers of humanity and the destroyers of tyrants.

Here, to destroy an abuse it suffices to point out its existence. It suffices for us to appeal, in the name of our country, from counsels of self-love or from the weaknesses of individuals, to the virtue and the glory of the National Convention.

We are beginning a solemn debate upon all the objects of its anxiety, and everything that can influence the progress of the revolution. We adjure it not to permit any particular hidden interest to usurp ascendancy here over the general will of the assembly and the indestructible power of reason.

We will limit ourselves today to proposing that by your formal approval you sanction the moral and political truths upon which your internal administration and the stability of the Republic ought to be founded, as you have already sanctioned the principles of your conduct toward foreign peoples. Thereby you will rally all good citizens, you will take hope away from the conspirators; you will assure your progress, and you will confound the kings' intrigues and slanders; you will honor your cause and your character in the eyes of all peoples.

Give the French people this new gage of your zeal to protect patriotism, of your inflexible justice for the guilty, and of your devotion to the people's cause. Order that the principles of political morality which we just expounded will be proclaimed, in your name, within and without the Republic.

43. The Festival of the Supreme Being (8 June 1794)

Although not the first of the great revolutionary festivals, the Festival of the Supreme Being is the most famous, and the one most closely associated with Robespierre, whose ideas and political ascendancy it reflected. Having eliminated the moderate (Dantonist) and extremist (Hébertist) factions he attacked in his *Report on the Principles of Political Morality,* Robespierre moved to inaugurate the Reign of Virtue anticipated in that speech. In May, he proposed an entire cycle of revolutionary festivals, to begin with the Festival of the Supreme Being. This latter was intended to celebrate a new civil religion as opposed to Christianity as it was to the atheism of the extreme dechristianizers (whose earlier Cult of Reason Robespierre and his associates had repudiated). The ceremony was planned in great detail by the most outstanding painter of the revolutionary period, Jacques-Louis David. Robespierre presided over the entire affair as president of the Convention. In the following selection, his two speeches have been inserted at the appropriate points in the published instructions for the participants in the festival.

From *Procès-verbaux du Comité d'instruction publique de l'Assemblée législative,* edited by James Guillaume, 7 vols. (Paris: Imprimerie Nationale, 1891–1959), vol. 4, pp. 561–66; and *Réimpression de l'ancien Moniteur,* 32 vols. (Paris, 1858–1863), vol. 20, pp. 683–84. Translated for this volume by Caroline Ford and Keith Michael Baker.

Two days after the Festival of the Supreme Being, the Terror was intensified by the passage of a new law expanding the definition of suspected persons and relaxing the rules of evidence for the Revolutionary Tribunal. During this Great Terror, more than 1,300 persons were executed within six weeks. However, covert opposition to Robespierre was growing within the Convention and the revolutionary committees. He was overthrown by the Convention on 9 Thermidor (27 July 1794) and executed the following day.

At exactly five in the morning, a general call will be sounded in Paris.

All citizens, men and women, will be invited by this call immediately to adorn their houses with the cherished colors of liberty, either by hanging their flags once more, or by embellishing the houses with garlands of flowers and greenery.

They will then go to the seats of their respective sections to await the signal for departure.

All men will be unarmed, excepting youths fourteen to eighteen years old, who will be armed with sabers and with guns or pikes.

In each section, these youths will form a square battalion marching twelve across, in the middle of which will be placed the banners and flags of the armed force of each section, carried by those who are ordinarily entrusted with them.

Each male citizen and young boy will hold an oak branch in his hand.

All female citizens, mothers and girls, will be dressed in the colors of liberty. Mothers will hold bouquets of roses in their hands, and girls will carry baskets filled with flowers.

To stand on the mountain raised in the Champ de la Réunion, each section will choose ten old men, ten mothers, ten girls from fifteen to twenty years old, ten youths from fifteen to eighteen years old, and ten male children below the age of eight.

The ten mothers chosen by each section will be in white and wear a tricolored sash from right to left.

The ten girls will also be in white and will wear the sash like the mothers. The girls will have their hair braided with flowers.

The ten youths will be armed with swords. . . .

Citizens, male and female, will take care to provide themselves with oak branches, and with bouquets, garlands, and baskets of flowers, and to deck themselves in the colors of liberty.

At exactly eight in the morning a volley of artillery fired at the Pont Neuf will signal the moment to proceed to the National Garden.

Citizens will leave from their respective sections in two columns, each six abreast: the men and boys to the right, and the women, girls, and children below the age of eight, to the left.

The square battalion of youths will be placed between the two columns, at the center.

The sections will be invited to arrange themselves in such a way that the female column is not more numerous than the male column, to avoid disturbing the order so necessary to establish in a national festival. . . .

Upon arrival at the National Garden, the columns of men will assemble in the part of the garden on the side of the so-called Terrace of the Feuillants, the columns of women and children on the side of the river terrace, and the square battalions of youths in the great avenue in the center. . . .

When all the sections have arrived at the National Garden, a delegation will go to the Convention to announce that everything is prepared to celebrate the festival of the Divinity.

The National Convention will descend via the balcony of the Pavilion of Unity to the amphitheater adjoining that pavilion.

It will be preceded by a large body of musicians, who will place themselves on the two flights of the staircase.

The president, speaking from the rostrum, will explain to the people the reasons determining this solemn festival, and invite it to honor the Author of Nature.

[*Robespierre spoke as follows:*

The eternally happy day which the French people consecrates to the Supreme Being has finally arrived. Never has the world he created offered him a sight so worthy of his eyes. He has seen tyranny, crime, and deception reign on earth. At this moment, he sees an entire nation, at war with all the oppressors of the human race, suspend its heroic efforts in order to raise its thoughts and vows to the Great Being who gave it the mission to undertake these efforts and the strength to execute them.

Did not his immortal hand, by engraving in the hearts of men the code of justice and equality, write there the death sentence of tyrants? Did not his voice, at the very beginning of time, decree the republic, making liberty, good faith, and justice the order of the day for all centuries and for all peoples?

He did not create kings to devour the human species. Neither did he create priests to harness us like brute beasts to the carriages of kings, and to give the world the example of baseness, pride, perfidy, avarice, debauchery, and falsehood to the world. But he created the universe to celebrate his power; he created men to help and to love one another, and to attain happiness through the path of virtue.

He it is who placed remorse and terror in the breast of the triumphant oppressor, and peace and pride in the heart of the oppressed innocent; who forces the just to hate the wicked, and the wicked to respect the just. He it is who adorns the brow of beauty with modesty, to make it more beautiful; who makes the mother's heart beat with tenderness and joy; who bathes with delicious tears the eyes of the son pressed against his mother's breast. He it is who silences the most imperious and tenderest passions before the sublime love of country; who has covered nature with charms, riches, and majesty. Everything that is good is his work, or it is himself. Evil belongs to the depraved man who oppresses his fellow man, or who acquiesces in that oppression.

The Author of Nature linked all mortals together in an immense chain of love and happiness. Perish the tyrants who have dared to break it!

Frenchmen, Republicans, it is up to you to cleanse the earth they have sullied and to restore the justice they have banished from it. Liberty and virtue issued together from the breast of the Divinity. One cannot reside among men without the other.

Generous people, do you want to triumph over all your enemies? Practice justice and render to the Divinity the only form of worship worthy of him. People, let us surrender ourselves today, under his auspices, to the just ecstasy of pure joy. Tomorrow we shall again combat vices and tyrants; we will give the world an example of republican virtues: and that will honor the Divinity more.]

After this speech, a symphony will be played. At the same time, the president, armed with the Flame of Truth, will descend from the amphitheater and approach a monument raised on a circular basin, representing the monster, Atheism.

From the middle of this monument, which the president will set on fire, the figure of Wisdom will appear.

After this ceremony, the president will return to the rostrum and speak again to the people, who will answer him with songs and cries of joy.

[*Robespierre spoke again, as follows:*

He has returned to nothingness, this monster which the spirit of kings has spewed forth over France. Let all the crimes and ills of the world disappear with him. Armed in turn with the daggers of fanaticism and the poisons of atheism, kings still conspire to assassinate humanity. If they can no longer disfigure the Divinity with superstition in order to implicate him in their transgressions, they endeavor to banish him from the earth to reign alone with crime.

People, fear no more their sacrilegious conspiracies. They can no more tear the world from the breast of its author than the remorse from their own hearts. You who are wretched, hold up your woeful heads: you can again raise your eyes to the sky with impunity. Heroes of the country, your generous devotion is not a brilliant folly; the minions of tyranny may be able to assassinate you, but it is not in their power to annihilate you completely. Man, whoever you are, you can again think well of yourself. You can attach your transitory life to God himself and to immortality. Let nature thus regain all its magnificence, and wisdom all its empire. The Supreme Being is not destroyed.

It is wisdom, above all, that our guilty enemies want to drive from the Republic. To wisdom alone does it belong to consolidate the prosperity of empires; it is for her to guarantee the fruits of our courage. Let us therefore associate her with all our enterprises. Let us be serious and discreet in all our deliberations, as men who determine the interests of the whole world. Let us be ardent and obstinate in our anger against sworn tyrants, imperturbable in the heat of danger, patient in our work, terrible during setbacks, modest and vigilant in success. Let us be generous toward those who are good, compassionate toward the unfortunate, inexorable toward the wicked, just toward everyone. Let us not count on unalloyed prosperity, on triumph without obstacles, or on anything that depends upon the fortune or perversity of another. Let us depend only on our constancy and our virtue. Alone, but infallible guarantors of our independence, let us crush the ungodly union of kings still more by our force of character than by the force of our arms.

Frenchmen, you are fighting kings; you are therefore worthy to honor the Divinity. Being of beings, author of nature, the brutalized slave, the vile henchman of despotism, the perfidious and cruel aristocracy insult you by invoking you; but the defenders of liberty can abandon themselves with confidence to your paternal breast. Being of beings, we have no unjust prayers to offer you. You know the creatures issued from your hands; their needs escape your eyes no more than their most secret thoughts. Hatred of perfidy and of tyranny burns in our hearts, together with love of justice and love of country; our blood flows for the cause of humanity. This is our prayer, these are our sacrifices; this the devotion we offer you.]

A second rolling of drums will signal the moment to leave for the Champ de la Réunion. The march will be organized in the following order:

1. A detachment of cavalry, preceded by its trumpets;
2. A corps of firemen;
3. Gunners;
4. A group of one hundred drummers and pupils of the National Institute;
5. Twenty-four sections marching in two columns, each six abreast, men

on the right and women and children on the left, with the battalions of youths at the center of the two columns of their respective sections. In the middle of the twenty-four sections will march a band of musicians bound for the Army of the North;

6. The group of old men, mothers, children, girls, and youths armed with sabers, chosen to position themselves on the mountain raised in the Champ de la Réunion;

7. A troop of musicians, who will play patriotic tunes during the march;

8. The National Convention, surrounded by a tricolored sash carried by children decorated with violets, youths adorned with myrtle, men adorned with oak, and old men adorned with vine branches and olives.

Each representative will carry in his hand a bouquet of wheat stalks, flowers and fruits.

In the middle of the national representative body there will be a float, upon which will shine an ornament composed of the instruments of the arts and crafts and the products of French soil. This float will be drawn by eight healthy bulls, adorned with festoons and garlands.

9. A group of one hundred drummers;

10. Twenty-four sections marching in the same order as the first twenty-four, with the blind childrens' float in the middle. The blind children will perform a hymn to the Divinity, with words by Citizen Deschamps and music by Citizen Bruni;

11. A corps of cavalry closing the march. . . .

Having reached the Champ de la Réunion, the column of men will form to the right of the mountain, and the column of women to the left.

The first group of drummers will position themselves behind the mountain, on the river side, at a distance that will be indicated to them.

All the square battalions of youths will form a circle around the mountain.

The group of old men and youths will position itself on the mountain, to the right.

The group of girls and mothers, leading the seven- to ten-year-old children by the hand, will position themselves on the mountain, to the left.

The national representative body will occupy the highest part of the mountain, and the musicians will place themselves in the center.

The second group of drummers will remain in front of the mountain, on the *Ecole militaire* side, at a distance that will be indicated to them.

As soon as everyone is positioned in the order indicated above, the troop of musicians will play a hymn to the Divinity.

After this hymn a great symphony will be performed.

The symphony having ended, the old men and youths standing on the mountain will sing a first verse to the tune of the Marseillaise, and will swear together to lay down their arms only after having annihilated the enemies of the Republic.

Old Men and Youths

Powerful God, of an intrepid people
You defend the ramparts;
Victory has, with a swift flight,
Accompanied our banners (*twice*).
From the Alps to the Pyrenees
Kings have seen pride fall;
In the North, our fields are the coffin
Of their dismayed armies.

Chorus

Before laying down our triumphant swords,
Let us swear (*twice*) to annihilate crime and tyrants.

All the men spread throughout the Champ de la Réunion will repeat the refrain in chorus.

The mothers and girls positioned on the mountain will sing a second verse. The girls will promise only to marry citizens who have served the country; and the mothers will thank the Supreme Being for their fertility.

The Women

Listen to maidens and mothers,
Author of fertility!
Our husbands, our children, our brothers
Fight for liberty (*twice*).
And if some criminal hand
Puts an end to such beautiful destinies,
Their sons will come to their tombs
To avenge the paternal ashes.

Chorus

Before laying down your triumphant swords
Swear (*twice*) to annihilate crime and tyrants.

All the women throughout the Champ de la Réunion will repeat the refrain together.

The third and last verse will be sung by everyone on the mountain.

Men and Women

Warriors, offer courage;
Young women, offer flowers;
Mothers, old men, as your tribute

Offer your triumphant sons (*twice*).
Bless in this day of glory
The sword consecrated by their hands;
On this sword, avenger of humans,
The Eternal engraved victory.

Chorus

Before laying down our/your triumphant swords,
Let us swear (*twice*) to annihilate crime and tyrants.

Mothers will lift up the youngest of their children, presenting them in homage to the Author of Nature.

At the same time, girls will throw flowers in the air, and youths will draw their sabers, swearing to make their arms victorious everywhere. Old men, overjoyed, will put their hands on the youths' heads and give them paternal benediction.

The people as a whole will repeat the last refrain in chorus. . . .

After the last verse, a general discharge of artillery, symbol of the nation's vengeance, will be heard. All Frenchmen, joining their emotions in a fraternal embrace, will end the festival by making the air resound with the general cry: *Long Live the Republic!*

4
After the Terror

44. Manifesto of the Directors (5 November 1795)

In the reaction that followed Robespierre's fall, the apparatus of the Terror was dismantled and many of its leading partisans were eventually purged by the Convention or punished by acts of popular violence. After a new constitution was adopted in October 1795, the Convention finally came to an end. The new constitution relied upon the authority of a five-man Executive Directory to implement its goals, which are well described in the following document. However, neither royalist reactionaries nor radical republicans were prepared to accept the "stabilization" of 1795, and the period of the Directory was marked by unrest and conspiracies to seize political control.

Frenchmen, the Executive Directory has just been installed.

Resolved to maintain liberty or to perish, it is determined to consolidate the Republic and to give all dispatch and vigor to the Constitution.

Republicans, rely upon it, its destiny will never be separated from yours; inflexible justice and the strictest observance of laws will be its rule. To wage an active war on royalism, to revive patriotism, to repress all factions vigorously, to destroy all party spirit, to annihilate every desire for vengeance, to establish concord, to restore peace, to regenerate morals, to reopen the sources of production, to revive commerce and industry, to stifle speculation, to revivify the arts and sciences, to re-establish plenty and the public credit, to reinstate social order in place of the chaos which is inseparable from revolutions, finally, to obtain for the French Republic the

Reprinted with permission of Macmillan Publishing Company from John Hall Stewart, ed., *A Documentary Survey of the French Revolution*, pp. 655–656. © 1951 by Macmillan Publishing Company.

happiness and glory which it awaits—such is the task of your legislators and of the Executive Directory . . .

Wise laws, promptly and energetically enforced, will soon cause us to forget our prolonged sufferings.

But so many evils cannot be compensated for, so much good accomplished in a day. The French people are just and loyal; they will perceive that . . . we need time, calm, patience, and confidence proportionate to the efforts we have to make. Such confidence will not be betrayed if the people no longer allow themselves to be won over to the perfidious suggestions of royalists who are resuming their plots, of fanatics who are ceaselessly inflaming opinions, and of public leeches who are always taking advantage of our miseries.

It will not be betrayed if the people do not attribute to the new authorities the disorders occasioned by six years of revolution, which can be expiated only with time; it will not be betrayed if the people recall that, for more than three years, every time the enemies of the Republic . . . have aroused tempers and occasioned disturbances, . . . such agitations have served only to increase discredit, and to retard production and plenty, which only order and public tranquillity can produce.

Frenchmen, you will not shackle a newborn government . . . ; but you will support with wisdom the ever active efforts and the imperturbable progress of the Executive Directory towards the prompt establishment of public happiness; and soon, with the glorious title of Republicans, you will irrevocably assure national peace and prosperity.

45. The Conspiracy of Equals (1796)

A dramatic but unsuccessful attempt to overthrow the Directory was made in 1796 by a group of conspirators known as the "Society of Equals." Its leader was François-Noël Babeuf (1760–97), a poor feudal lawyer turned revolutionary who had adopted the nickname "Gracchus" to signal his demands for a redistribution of property. Before his imprisonment during the Terror, Babeuf had allied himself with the sans-culottes and served as a public functionary engaged in the provision of food supplies—an experience vital to his realization of the potential of a revolutionary administration to organize an egalitarian and communistic social order. After the fall of Robespierre, he began publishing a radical journal, the *Tribune*

From *Socialist Thought. A Documentary History*, edited by Albert Fried and Ronald Sanders (New York: Doubleday, 1964), pp. 56–70. © 1964 by Albert Fried and Ronald Sanders.

of the People, which supported the continuing demands of the sans-culottes for "bread and the Constitution of 1793." But when the Convention forcefully put down attempted sans-culotte uprisings in April and May 1795 (Germinal–Prairial, Year III), it became clear that the conditions that had made possible the great revolutionary *journées* no longer obtained. Imprisoned several times during this period, Babeuf concluded that revolutionary change could no longer be simply dictated from the streets: it required a concerted insurrectionary coup.

However, the plans for the Conspiracy of Equals were betrayed by an informer, and Babeuf was executed in 1797 after a dramatic trial. Some of his accomplices escaped with jail sentences, including Filippo Buonarroti who went on to write an account of the whole affair from which the following selections are taken. Buonarroti's work and subsequent political activity became the link between the ideas of men like Robespierre and Babeuf and those of many nineteenth-century socialists and revolutionaries.

Analysis of the Doctrine of Babeuf by the Babouvists (1796)

1. Nature has given every man an equal right to the enjoyment of all its goods.

2. The purpose of society is to defend this equality, which is often attacked in the state of nature by the wicked and the strong, and to increase, through universal cooperation, the common enjoyment of the goods of nature.

3. Nature has imposed upon everyone the obligation to work; no one has ever shirked this duty without having thereby committed a crime.

4. All work and the enjoyment of its fruits must be in common.

5. Oppression exists when one person exhausts himself through toil and still lacks everything, while another swims in abundance without doing any work at all.

6. No one has ever appropriated the fruits of the earth or of industry exclusively for himself without having thereby committed a crime.

7. In a true society, there must be neither rich nor poor.

8. Those rich men who are not willing to renounce their excess goods in favor of the indigent are enemies of the people.

9. No one may, by the accumulation of all the available means of education, deprive another of the instruction necessary for his well-being; instruction must be common to all.

10. The aim of the Revolution is to destroy inequality and re-establish the common welfare.

11. The Revolution is not finished, because the rich are absorbing all

goods and are exclusively in command, while the poor are toiling in a state of virtual slavery; they languish in misery and are nothing in the State.

12. The constitution of 1793 is the true law of Frenchmen, because the People have solemnly accepted it.

Babeuf's Defense (From the Trial at Vendôme, February–May 1797)

. . . After the 13th of Vendémiaire,[1] I observed that the majority of the people, tired of a Revolution whose every fluctuation and movement had only brought death, had been—one can only say—royalized. I saw that in Paris the simple and uninstructed multitude had actually been led by the enemies of the people into a cordial contempt for the Republic. This multitude, who are capable of judging things only by their sensations, had been easily persuaded to make a comparison that goes something like this: What were we under royal domination, what are we under the Republic? The answer was entirely to the detriment of the latter. It was then quite simple to conclude that the Republic was something detestable and that monarchy was better. And I was unable to see anything in the new constitutional structure or in the attitudes of the men whose task it was to run the machinery of government that would bring people to like this Republic any more than they did. I said to myself: the Republic is lost, barring some stroke of genius that could save it; surely monarchism will not hesitate to regain its hold upon us. I looked around me and saw many people who were defeated, even among those patriots, once so fervent and courageous, who had made so many successful efforts to strengthen Liberty. The sight of universal discouragement, of—if I can go so far as to say this—absolute *muzzling* all around; then the sight of disarmament, the complete stripping away of all the guarantees that the people had once been given against any unwarranted undertakings on the part of those who govern them; the recent imprint of irons that almost all energetic men bore on their flesh; and what seemed to me the almost complete conviction of many people who were not able to offer very good reasons for their attitude, that the Republic might really, after all, be something other than a blessing; these various causes had very nearly brought all spirits to a state of total resignation, and everyone seemed ready to bend under the yoke. I saw no one who might be disposed to revive the courageous mood of earlier days. And yet, I told myself, the same ferment of zeal and of love for all men still exists. There are perhaps still ways of keeping this Republic from being lost. Let every

---

1. 13 Vendémiaire, Year IV (5 October 1795), the date of an abortive right-wing insurrection aimed at preventing former members of the Convention from extending their control into the Directory.

man make an effort to summon back his strength; let every man do what he can. For my own part, I am going to do whatever I believe to be within my power.

I gave words to these feelings in my *Tribune of the People*. I said to everyone: Listen: Those among you who have apparently come around to feeling, as a result of a long series of public calamities, that the Republic is worthless and that the Monarchy might be preferable—you people are right, I swear it. I spelled it out in capital letters: WE WERE BETTER OFF UNDER THE KINGS THAN WE ARE UNDER THE REPUBLIC. But you must understand which Republic I mean by that. A Republic such as the one we see is totally worthless, without a doubt. But this, my friends, is not the true Republic. The true Republic is something that you do not yet even know about.

All right then, if you wish, I will try to tell you something about it, and I am almost certain that you will idolize it.

The Republic is not a word—not even several words—empty of meaning. The words *Liberty* and *Equality,* which have continuously resounded in your ears, cast a spell over you in the early days of the Revolution because you thought that they would signify something good for the People. Now they mean nothing to you at all, because you see that they are only vain articulations and ornaments of deceitful formulas. You must be made to learn that in spite of all this, they can and must signify a good that is precious for the greatest number.

The Revolution, I went on in my discourse to the people, need not be an act totally without results. So many torrents of blood were not spilled merely to make the lot of the people worse than it had been before. When a people makes a revolution, it is because the play of vicious institutions has pushed the best energies of a society to such an extreme that the majority of its useful members can no longer go on as before. It feels ill at ease in the situation that prevails, senses the need to change it, and strives to do so. And the society is right to do so, because the only reason it was instituted in the first place was to make all its members as happy as possible: *The purpose of society is the common welfare.*

It is this formula, comprised within the first article of the covenant of the Year I of the Republic, that I have always held to as my own, and I will continue to do so.

The aim of the revolution also is the well-being of the greatest number; therefore, if this goal has not been achieved, if the people have not found the better life that they were seeking, then the revolution is not over, even though those who want only to substitute their own rule for somebody else's say that it is over, as you would expect them to. If the revolution is really over, then it has been nothing but a great crime.

So I strove to make people understand what the nature of the *common welfare*, which is the aim of society, or of the *welfare of the greatest number*, which is the aim of the Revolution, might be.

I inquired into the reasons why at certain given periods the greatest number were not more fortunate. This inquiry led me to the following conclusion, which I dared to print in one of my first issues after the 13th of Vendémiaire:

"There are periods in which the ultimate effect of the cruel social order is that the whole of the society's wealth is concentrated in the hands of a few. Peace, the natural state of things when all men are happy, is necessarily threatened at a time like this. The masses can no longer exist; they are completely dispossessed, and encounter only pitiless hearts among the caste that is hoarding everything. Effects such as these determine what will be the eras of those great revolutions predicted in books, in which a general upheaval of the system of property is inevitable, and in which the revolt of the poor against the rich is driven by such necessity that nothing can vanquish it."

The plaintiffs have described, on page 78 of the supplement to their *Exposé*, a document that has as its title: *Analysis of the Doctrine of Babeuf*. There are a great many questions concerning it in various parts of the record of the trial, and it has been regarded as the *extreme* among all ideas of social upheaval. Therefore, it will be useful to examine this work in detail. . . .

When I was cross-examined during the trial, I declared that this document had not been drawn up by me, but, acknowledging that it was a fair analysis of the principles I had proclaimed, I approved it, and consented to its being printed and published. It was in effect a faithful summary of the doctrine that I had scattered throughout the various issues of my newspaper.

This doctrine appears to play the essential and fundamental role in a conspiracy. It figures in the accusation under the title, "Pillage of Property"; it is what terrifies the plaintiffs as they reproduce it in every odious form. They call it, successively, "agrarian law," "brigandage," "devastation," "disorganization," "dreadful system," "horrible upheaval," "subversion of the social order," "atrocious project," the sole result of which would necessarily be "the destruction of the human species; the reversion to the savage state, a life of roaming about in the woods, anyone who survived . . . the total abandonment of all culture, of all industry . . . nature left to her own resources . . . the strong setting up their superiority over the weak as the sole source of rights; men becoming, if this doctrine is accepted, more ferocious than brute animals, fighting furiously over every scrap of food that they come upon. . . ."

This is most certainly the crux of the accusation. The other points are only accessories or appendages to it. The ends justify the means. To reach a certain goal, one must vanquish everything that stands in the way. Now, as to the hypothesis of social change in question, whether one chooses to describe it, after the fashion of the plaintiffs, as subversive of the whole social order, or to characterize it, in chorus with the philosophers and the great legislators, as a sublime regeneration, it is indubitable that this change could not be brought about except by the overthrow of the established government and the suppression of everything in the way. These acts of upheaval and suppression would therefore be only the accessory, the necessary means for achieving the principal object, which is the establishment of what we and the philosophers call *the general or common welfare,* and what our accusers call *devastation and pillage.* It therefore stands proven as if mathematically, that the part of the accusation based upon my alleged resolve to found a system which has been appreciated in such greatly varying ways, is the principal and almost the sole part of the accusation, since the others are only branches emanating from it.

It follows from this, it seems to me, that we must necessarily examine the following questions: did I really preach such a system? If so, in what spirit did I preach it—in the form of mere speculation, or with the hope of conspiring to bring it about by force and in spite of the people? Has this system been genuinely proven bad and destructive? Has it never been preached by anyone but me? Was it not preached before me, and did anyone before this, including even the kings themselves, ever aspire to punish its foremost apostles?

Several of these questions will soon be resolved. The first in two words. I really did preach the system of the *common welfare;*—I mean by these words, *the welfare of all, the general welfare.* I said that the social code which established in its opening line that the welfare of men was *the sole purpose of society,* consecrated in this line the unassailable standard of all truth and of all justice. It entirely sums up the Law of Moses and the prophets. I defy anyone to maintain to me that men, when they form themselves into an association, can have any other purpose, any other desire, than the happiness of all. I defy anyone to argue that they would have consented to this union if they had been told that it would be made up of institutions that would soon place the burden of toil upon the greatest number, force them to sweat blood and die of hunger, in order that a handful of privileged citizens could be maintained in luxury and idleness. But meanwhile all this has come about, as if the eternal laws did not in any way proscribe it, and so I have the right, as I am a man, to reiterate my demand that we carry out the original compact, which, though tacitly conceived, I admit, was nevertheless written in ineffaceable letters into the fibre of every human heart. Yes, it is one voice that cries out to all: *the purpose of society is the common welfare.* This is the primitive contract; it needs no other terms to clarify its meaning; it covers everything, because all institutions must be made to flow from this source, and nothing can be allowed to degenerate from its standard.

As for the second question, I have preached the system of the welfare of all only as a simple philanthropic speculation, as a simple proposition to the people, depending entirely upon the condition of their acquiescence. One can see, then, how far I was from being able to realize such a scheme; for no man can, without deluding himself excessively, flatter himself that this acquiescence would be easy to obtain, and I can assure you that it is far easier to calculate all the obstacles that stand in the way of obtaining it, the endless opposition that would be encountered, and to judge all this insurmountable in advance.

In the course of my narration I will prove that I have done nothing to establish this system by force and in spite of the people.

In order to see if this system is really as bad, destructive and reprehensible as the plaintiffs make it out to be, citizen Jurors, you must weigh against their views some of the reasons that I offered in justification of it during the course of my propagandistic work. In addition to the *Analysis* already presented, which, as I have pointed out, I did not compose, but which I have nevertheless approved and adopted, I myself offered in one of my writings a *résumé* justifying this doctrine. I will present it to you faithfully, citizen Jurors. What I am about to give you is my frank and sincere confession. . . . Here then, presented with the utmost confidence, is the declaration that I believe I must make to you, expressed exactly as it was in my writings, concerning the purposes and the motives of men when they form themselves into a civil order.

"The lot of the individual" (I said in my *Tribune of the People,* No. 35, page 102), "did not have to worsen when he passed from the natural to the social state.

"By its origins, the land belongs to no one, and its fruits are for everyone.

"The institution of private property is a surprise that was foisted upon the mass of simple and honest souls. The laws of this institution must necessarily bring about the existence of fortunate and unfortunate, of masters and slaves.

"The law of *heredity* is supremely abusive. It produces poor men from the second generation on. The two children of a man who is sufficiently rich divide up his fortune equally. One of them has only one child, the other has a dozen. Each of these latter children then has only one-twelfth of the fortune of the first brother, and one-twenty-fourth of that of the grandfather. This portion is not sufficient to provide a living. Some of them are obliged to work for their rich first cousin; thus emerge masters and servants from among the grandchildren of the same man.

"The law of *alienation* is no less unjust. This man who is already the master of others descended from the same grandfather pays arbitrarily for the labor that they are obliged to do for him. This wage is still not enough to enable them to subsist; they are obliged to sell their meager portion of the inheritance to him upon whom they are now dependent. Thus they have been expropriated; if they leave any children, these poor waifs will have nothing but their wits to rely on.

"A third cause hastens the emergence of masters and servants, of the overly fortunate and the extremely unfortunate: it is the differences in wage and esteem that mere opinion attaches to the different forms of production and industry. A fantastic opinion of this sort leads people to attribute to the work-day of someone who makes a watch twenty times the value of that of someone who plows a field and grows wheat. The result is that the watch-maker is placed in a position whereby he acquires the patrimony of twenty plowmen; he has therefore expropriated it.

"These three roots of public misfortune, all the progeny of *property—heredity, alienation* and *the diversity of value that arbitrary opinion, as sole master, is able to assign to the various types of production and labor*—give rise to all the vices of society. They isolate all the members of society; they make of every household a little republic consecrated to a murderous inequality, which can do nothing but conspire against the large republic."

When I arrived at these conclusions, citizen Jurors, and found that I had to regard them as irrefutable truths, I was soon led to derive the following consequences from them:

"If the land does not belong to anyone; if its fruits are for all; if possession by a small number of men is the result of only a few institutions that abuse and violate the fundamental law, it follows that this possession by a few is an usurpation. It follows that, at all times, whatever an individual hoards of the land and its fruits beyond what he needs for his own nourishment has been stolen from society.

"All our civil institutions, our reciprocal transactions, are nothing but acts of perpetual brigandage, authorized by barbarous laws, under whose sway we are occupied only in tearing each other apart.

"Our society of swindlers brings all sorts of vice, crime and misfortune in the wake of its atrocious primordial conventions, against which good men ally themselves in a vain attempt to make war upon them. In this they cannot be victorious because they do not attack the evil at its roots, because their measures are only palliatives drawn from the reservoir of false ideas created by our organic depravity.

"It is clear, then, from all that has been said, that everything owned by those who have more than their individual due of society's goods, is theft and usurpation.

"It is therefore just to take it back from them.

"Even someone who could prove that he is capable, by the individual exertion of his own natural strength, of doing the work of four men, and so lay claim to the recompense of four, would be no less a conspirator against society, because he would be upsetting the equilibrium of things by this alone, and would thus be destroying the precious principle of equality.

"Wisdom imperiously demands of all the members of the association that they suppress such a man, that they pursue him as a scourge of society, that they at least reduce him to a state whereby he can do the work of only one man, so that he will be able to demand the recompense of only one man.

"It is only our species that has introduced this murderous folly of making distinctions in merit and value, and it is our species alone that knows misfortune and privation.

"There must exist no form of privation but the one that nature imposes upon everyone as a result of some unavoidable accident, in which case these privations must be borne by everyone and divided up equally among them.

"The products of industry and of genius also become the property of all, the domain of the entire association, from the very moment that the workers and the inventors have created them, because they are simply compensation for earlier discoveries made through genius and industry, from which the new inventors and workers have profited within the framework of social life, and which have helped them to make their discoveries.

"Since the knowledge acquired is the domain of everyone, it must therefore be equally distributed among everyone.

"A truth that has been impertinently contested by bad faith, by prejudice, by thoughtlessness, is the fact that this equal distribution of knowledge among everyone would make all men nearly equal in capacity and even in talent.

"Education is a monstrosity when it is unequal, when it is the exclusive patrimony of a portion of the association: because then it becomes, in the hands of this portion, an accumulation of machinery, an arsenal of all sorts of weapons that helps this portion of society to make war against the other, which is unarmed, and to succeed thereby in strangling it, deceiving it, stripping it bare, and shackling it down to the most shameful servitude.

"There are no truths more important that those that one philosopher has proclaimed in these terms: 'Declaim as much as you wish on the subject of the best form of government, you will still have done nothing at all so long as you have not destroyed the seeds of cupidity and ambition.'

"It is therefore necessary that the social institutions be such that they eradicate within every last individual the hope that he might ever become richer, more powerful, or more distinguished because of his talents, than any of his equals.

"To be more specific, it is necessary *to bind together everyone's lot;* to render the lot of each member of the association independent of chance, and of happy or unfavorable circumstance; *to assure to every man and to his posterity, no matter how numerous it may be, as much as they need, but no more than they need;* and to shut off from everybody all the possible paths by which they might obtain some part of the products of nature and of work that is more than their individual due.

"The sole means of arriving at this is to establish a *common administration;* to suppress private property; to place every man of talent in the line of work he knows best; to oblige him to deposit the fruit of his work in the common store, to establish a simple *administration of needs,* which, keeping a record of all individuals and all the things that are available to them, will distribute these available goods with the most scrupulous equality, and will see to it that they make their way into the home of every citizen.

"This form of government, proven by experience to be practicable, since it is the form applied to the 1,200,000 men of our twelve Armies (what is possible on a small scale is possible on a large scale as well), is the only one that could result in unqualified and unalterable universal welfare: *the common welfare, the aim of society.*

"This form of government," I continued, "will bring about the disappearance of all boundary lines, fences, walls, locks on doors, trials, thefts, and assassinations; of all crimes, tribunals, prisons, gibbets, and punishments; of the despair that causes all calamity; and of greed, jealousy, insatiability, pride, deception, and duplicity—in short, of all vices. Furthermore (and the point is certainly essential), it will put an end to the gnawing worm of perpetual inquietude, whether throughout society as a whole, or privately within each of us, about what tomorrow will bring, or at least what next year will bring, for our old age, for our children and for their children."

This, citizen Jurors, was the interpretation of the code of nature with which my mind was occupied. I believed that I could see everything written on the immortal pages of this code. I brought these pages to light and published them. Certainly it was because I loved my fellow man, and because I was persuaded that the social system which I conceived was the only one that could bring about his happiness, that I wanted so much to see him disposed to adopt it. But I did not imagine—it would have been a most illusory presumption—that I could have converted him to this idea: it would have taken no more than a moment's contemplation of the flood of passions now subjugating us in this era of corruption that we have come upon, to become convinced that the odds against the possibility of realizing such a project are more than a hundred to one. Even the most intrepid partisan of my system ought to be convinced of this.

All this, then, citizen Jurors, was, more than anything else, a consolation that my soul was seeking. Such is the natural and palpable inclination felt by every man who loves his fellows, who gives thought to the calamities of which they are the victims, who reflects that they themselves are often the cause of these afflictions, to examine in his imagination all the possible curative measures that could be taken. If he believes that he has found these remedies, then, in his powerlessness to realize them, he afflicts himself for the sake of those whom he is forced to leave to their suffering, and contents himself with the feeble compensation of tracing for them the outlines of the plan that he feels could end their woes for all time. This is what all our philosopher-legislators did, and I am at best only their disciple and emulator, when I am doing anything more than merely repeating, echoing, or interpreting them. Rousseau said: "I fully realize that one should not undertake the chimerical project of trying to form a society of honest men, but I nevertheless believed that I was obliged to speak the whole truth openly." When you condemn me, citizen Jurors, for all the maxims that I have just admitted stating, it is these great men whom you are putting on trial. They were my masters, my sources of inspiration—my doctrine is only theirs. From their lessons I have derived these maxims of "pillage," these principles that have been called "destructive." You are also accusing the monarchy of not having been quite as inquisitional as the government of our present Republic; you accuse them of not having prevented the corrupting books of a Mably, a Helvetius, a Diderot, or of a Jean Jacques Rousseau, from falling into my hands.[2] All those who govern should be considered responsible for the evils that they do not prevent. Philanthropists of today! It is above all to you that I address myself. It is because of these philosophical poisons that I am lost. Without them, I would perhaps have had your morality, your virtues. Like you, I would have detested brigandage and the overthrow of the existing social institutions above all things; I would have had the tenderest solicitude for the small number of powerful men of this world; I would have been pitiless toward the suffering multitude. But no, I will not repent of having been educated at the school of the celebrated men whom I have just named. I will not blaspheme against them, or become an apostate against their dogmas. If the axe must fall upon my neck, the lictor will find me ready. It is good to perish for the sake of virtue—

---

2. Babeuf's claim to trace his doctrine to particular philosophies of the Enlightenment was based, in part, on mistaken attribution of anonymous works he had read.

46. Bonaparte, *Letter to the Executive Directory* (15 July 1797)

When he wrote this letter from Milan, Napoleon Bonaparte was in command of a brilliantly successful French army in Italy. He had driven the Austrians from northern Italy, establishing the Cisalpine Republic and forcing the Austrians into negotiations. At the same time, he felt his successes and expansionist policies threatened (along with the Directory) by the strength of the royalists in the elections of March 1797. This threat was dispelled by the coup d'état of 18 Fructidor (4 September 1797). Aided by Bonaparte, who dispatched one of his generals with an army from Italy, three of the Directors purged the remaining two and ordered the unsatisfactory election results of the preceding spring quashed. The Treaty of Campo Formio, in which the Austrians recognized the French gains in Belgium and Italy and secretly agreed to French seizure of the left bank of the Rhine, was signed on 17 October 1797.

I enclose a copy of the letter I have received from General Clarke:[1] you will see from it that negotiations are still dragging on. There can be no doubt that the Emperor wants to see how events go in France, and that foreign influence counts for more than is generally supposed in all these machinations.

A great many Paris papers reach the army—especially the worst of them; but the result is quite contrary to what they intend. Indignation is rampant in the army. The men are asking angrily whether the only reward they are to expect, on their return home, for all their labours, and for their six years at the front, is the assassination which threatens every patriot. The situation gets worse every day, and I think that you, Citizen Directors, will soon have to take it in hand. . . . There is not a man here who would not sooner die sword in hand than be assassinated in some dark corner of Paris.

For my own part, I am used to sacrificing all my private interests; yet I cannot be insensible to the outrageous slanders circulated every day, and upon every oportunity, by some 80 journals, whilst there is not one that gives them the lie. I cannot be insensible to the treachery and the accumulation of outrages suggested in the motion printed by order of the Council

From *Napoleon Self-Revealed*, translated by J. M. Thompson, (Boston, Mass.: Houghton-Mifflin, 1934), pp. 38–39. Reprinted by permission of Basil Blackwell.

1. An intermediary in the peace negotiations with the Austrians.

of the Five Hundred. I see that the Clichy Club[2] would like to march over my body in order to destroy the Republic. Are there no Republicans left in France? After conquering Europe, are we to be reduced to searching for some corner of the earth in which to end our unhappy days?

One stroke, and you can save the Republic—save 200,000 lives, perhaps, which stand or fall with it, and make peace within 24 hours. Arrest the *émigrés*. Destroy the influence of foreigners. If this needs force, summon the armies. Break up the presses of the papers which are in English pay—they are more sanguinary than any Marat.

To return to myself: I cannot go on living in this clash of loyalties; if no remedy can be found to cure the country's ills, and to put an end to the rule of murder and to the influence of Louis XVIII, I must ask to be relieved of my command. . . .

47. The Coup d'Etat of 18 Brumaire 1799

Upon his return from Italy, Bonaparte was placed in command of an army preparing to invade England. Convinced that such an invasion was impracticable, he persuaded the Directory to strike indirectly by taking Egypt and threatening England's empire in India. Sailing from Toulon in May 1798, with 35,000 men and a corps of scientists, he took Cairo in July only to find himself stranded when Nelson destroyed his fleet in harbor at Abukir Bay (1 August 1798). After an unsuccessful Syrian campaign and further victories in Egypt, Bonaparte slipped back into France where the ineffective Directory found itself faced with disaffection at home and a new enemy coalition abroad. Allying himself with the directors Sieyès and Roger-Ducos, and aided by his brother Lucien (president of the Council of Five Hundred), Napoleon overthrew the Directory in the coup d'état of 18 Brumaire (9 November) 1799. The Constitution of 1799, establishing the Consulate, was proclaimed on 13 December 1799.

2. A royalist club that threatened to dominate the representative bodies of the Directory after the elections of 1797 gave the royalists imposing strength.

Reprinted with permission of Macmillan Publishing Company from John Hall Stewart, ed., *A Documentary History of the French Revolution*, pp. 763–65, 768–80. © 1951 by Macmillan Publishing Company. "Napoleon's Speech to the Council of Elders" and "Proclamation of the Consuls to the French People" from *Correspondance de Napoléon I*, 32 vols. (Paris: Imprimerie Impériale, 1858–1869), vol. 6, pp. 3–6, 8–9. Translated for this volume by the editor, Keith Michael Baker.

Bonaparte's Speech to the Council of Elders, 19 Brumaire, Year VIII (10 November 1799)

Citizen Representatives, the circumstances in which you find yourselves are no ordinary ones; you are on a volcano.

Permit me to speak to you with the frankness of a soldier and, in order to escape the trap which is set for you, suspend your judgment until I have finished what I have to say.

Yesterday, I was peacefully in Paris when you summoned me to notify me of the decree of transfer and charge me with its execution. I immediately assembled my comrades and we flew to your aid. Well! Today slanders are heaped upon me. There is talk of Caesar, of Cromwell, of military government. If I had wanted military government, would I have rushed to lend my support to the representative body of the nation?

Citizen Representatives, time is pressing; it is essential that you take prompt measures. The Republic no longer has a government. Four of the Directors have resigned; I have deemed it necessary to place the fifth under surveillance, by virtue of the power you have conferred upon me. The Council of Five Hundred is divided; only the Council of Elders remains. From it I hold my powers. Let it take action, let it speak: I am here to carry out its will. Let us save liberty! Let us save equality!

(*A cry:* And the constitution?)

The constitution! You have destroyed it yourselves. You violated it on 18 Fructidor; you violated it on 22 Floréal; you violated it on 30 Prairial. No one respects it any longer. I will speak openly. Since my return, I have not ceased to be surrounded by intrigue. Every faction hastened to embrace me. Men who insolently call themselves "the only patriots" came to tell me that the constitution must be set aside; to purify the Councils, they proposed to exclude men who are sincere friends of the *patrie*. This is their attachment to the constitution! I became fearful for the republic. I joined with my brothers in arms; and we have come to form our ranks around you. There is no time to lose; let the Council of Elders pronounce. I am not an intriguer; you know me; I believe I have given enough proofs of my devotion to my *patrie*. Those who speak to you of the constitution well know that, violated at every moment, mutilated at every page, the constitution no longer exists. The sovereignty of the people, liberty, equality, these sacred foundations of the constitution, still remain: they must be saved. If by constitution one means these sacred principles, all the rights belonging to the people, all those belonging to each citizen, my comrades and I are ready to shed our blood to defend them. But I will not prostitute the meaning of a constitutional act by applying the term to purely administrative regulations which offer the citizen no guarantee. As for what follows, I declare that once this is over I shall be nothing in the republic but the arm supporting what you have established.

Citizen Representatives, the Council of Five Hundred is divided; the factional leaders have brought this about. The men of Prairial, who wish to bring back to the soil of liberty the scaffolds and the horrible regime of the Terror, are surrounding themselves with their accomplices and preparing to carry out their frightful plans. Already the Council of Elders is being blamed for the measures it has taken and for placing its trust in me. For my part, I am not shaken. Should I tremble before conspirators, I whom the coalition could not destroy? If I am a traitor, may you all be Brutus. And as for you, my comrades who accompany me, you, brave grenadiers whom I see surrounding this place, may these bayonets with which we have triumphed together be turned immediately against my heart. But also, should any orator in foreign pay dare pronounce against your general the word "outlaw," let the thunder of war crush him instantly. Remember that I march accompanied by the god of war and the god of fortune.

I withdraw. . . . You will proceed to deliberate. Command, and I will carry out your orders.

(*Many voices:* Give names! Give names!)

Each had his ideas; each had his plans; each had his group and associates. Citizen Barras, Citizen Moulin had theirs. They made propositions to me.

(*Many voices:* The General Committee!)

There is no longer any need for the General Committee; the whole of France must learn what we wish to make known; we would be the most unworthy of men if we did not immediately take all the measures that can save liberty and equality.

Since my arrival, all the magistrates and officials with whom I have spoken have demonstrated to me their conviction that the constitution, so frequently violated and continually disregarded, is headed towards destruction; that it offers the French no guarantee because it lacks a firm basis. All the factions are convinced of this; all are ready to profit from the fall of the present government; all have come to me; all have wished to win me over to their side. I have felt it my duty to unite only with the Council of Elders, the first body of the republic. I repeat to you that you cannot act too promptly, if you wish to stop the movement which is going to kill liberty, perhaps in an instant.

Deliberate, Citizen Representatives, I have just told you truths that everyone has whispered to himself, but that someone must finally have the courage to say aloud. The means of saving the *patrie* are in your hands; if you hesitate to use them, if liberty perishes, you will answer for it before the universe, before posterity, before France and your families.

Bonaparte's Statement upon Becoming Consul, 19 Brumaire, Year VIII (10 November 1799)

On my return to Paris I found division among all authorities, and agreement upon only one point, namely, that the Constitution was half destroyed and was unable to save liberty.

All parties came to me, confided to me their designs, disclosed their secrets, and requested my support; I refused to be the man of a party.

The Council of Elders summoned me; I answered its appeal. A plan of general restoration had been devised by men whom the nation has been accustomed to regard as the defenders of liberty, equality, and property; this plan required an examination, calm, free, exempt from all influence and all fear. Accordingly, the Council of Elders resolved upon the removal of the Legislative Body to Saint-Cloud; it gave me the responsibility of disposing the force necessary for its independence. I believed it my duty to my fellow citizens, to the soldiers perishing in our armies, to the national glory acquired at the cost of their blood, to accept the command.

The Councils assembled at Saint-Cloud; republican troops guaranteed their security from without, but assassins created terror within. Several deputies of the Council of Five Hundred, armed with stilettos and firearms, circulated threats of death around them.

The plans which ought to have been developed were withheld, the majority disorganized, the boldest orators disconcerted, and the futility of every wise proposition was evident.

I took my indignation and grief to the Council of Elders. I besought it to assure the execution of its generous designs; I directed its attention to the evils of the *Patrie* . . . ; it concurred with me by new evidences of its steadfast will.

I presented myself at the Council of Five Hundred, alone, unarmed, my head uncovered, just as the Elders had received and applauded me; I came to remind the majority of its wishes, and to assure it of its power.

The stilettos which menaced the deputies were instantly raised against their liberator; twenty assassins threw themselves upon me and aimed at my breast. The grenadiers of the Legislative Body whom I had left at the door of the hall ran forward, placed themselves between the assassins and myself. One of these brave grenadiers had his clothes pierced by a stiletto. They bore me out.

At the same moment cries of "Outlaw" were raised against the defender of the law. It was the fierce cry of assassins against the power destined to repress them.

They crowded around the president, uttering threats, arms in their hands; they commanded him to outlaw me; I was informed of this; I ordered him to be rescued from their fury, and six grenadiers of the Legislative Body secured him. Immediately afterwards some grenadiers of the Legislative Body charged into the hall and cleared it.

The factions, intimidated, dispersed and fled. The majority, freed from their attacks, returned freely and peaceably into the meeting hall, listened to the proposals on behalf of public safety, deliberated, and prepared the salutary resolution which is to become the new and provisional law of the Republic.

Frenchmen, you will doubtless recognize in this conduct the zeal of a soldier of liberty, a citizen devoted to the Republic. Conservative, tutelary, and liberal ideas have been restored to their rights through the dispersal of the rebels who oppressed the Councils . . .

Proclamation to the French Nation, 21 Brumaire, Year VIII (12 November 1799)

The Constitution of the Year III was dying. It could neither guarantee your rights, nor assure its own existence. Repeated assaults were robbing it irreparably of the people's respect. Malevolent, greedy factions were dividing up the republic. France was finally approaching the last stage of a general disorganization.

Patriots have come together. All that could harm you has been set aside. All that could serve you, all that remained pure in the national representation has united under the banner of liberty.

Frenchmen, the Republic, strengthened and restored to that rank in Europe which it should never have lost, will see the realization of its citizens' hopes and the fulfillment of its glorious destiny.

Swear with us the oath we are taking to be faithful to the Republic, one and indivisible, founded on equality, liberty and the representative system.

The Consuls of the Republic
   Bonaparte.   Roger Ducos.   Sieyès

Constitution of the French Republic

Title 1. Of the Exercise of the Rights of Citizenship

1. The French Republic is one and indivisible.

Its European territory is divided into departments and communal *arrondissements*.

2. Every man fully twenty-one years of age, born and resident in France, who has had himself enrolled upon the civic register of his communal *arrondissement,* and has since lived for one year on the territory of the Republic, is a French citizen. . . .

7. The citizens of every communal *arrondissement* shall designate by vote those among them whom they believe to be most suited to administer public affairs. A list of trustworthy persons, containing the names of one-tenth of the number of citizens who have the right to co-operate therein, will result from such vote. The public functionaries of the *arrondissement* are to be selected from such first communal list.

8. Likewise the citizens included in the communal lists of a department shall designate one-tenth of their number. A second, or departmental, list, from which the public functionaries of the department are to be taken, will result from such vote.

9. Likewise the citizens named in the departmental list shall designate one-tenth of their number. A third list, comprising the citizens of the department who are eligible to national public office, will result from such vote.

14. . . . The lists of eligibles shall be constituted for the first time during the course of the Year IX.

Citizens selected for the initial formation of the established authorities shall constitute a necessary part of the first lists of eligibles.

Title 2. Of the Conservative Senate

15. The Conservative Senate shall be composed of eighty members, at least forty years of age, irremovable, and holding office for life.

16. Appointment to the position of senator shall be made by the Senate, which shall choose from among three candidates presented by the Legislative Body, the Tribunate, and the First Consul respectively. . . .

18. A senator shall always be ineligible for other public office.

19. All the lists drawn up in the departments by virtue of article 9 shall be directed to the Senate; they shall constitute the national list.

20. From said list the Senate shall choose the legislators, tribunes, consuls, judges of cassation, and commissioners of accounting.

21. It shall sustain or annul all acts referred to it as unconstitutional by the Tribunate or the Government; . . .

22. Revenues from certain national domains shall be set apart for the expenses of the Senate. The annual stipend of each of its members shall be drawn from said revenues, and shall equal one-twentieth of that of the First Consul.

23. The sessions of the Senate shall not be public.

24. Citizens *Sieyès* and *Roger Ducos,* retiring consuls, shall be appointed members of the Conservative Senate; they shall meet with the second and third Consuls appointed by the present Constitution. Said four citizens shall appoint the majority of the Senate, which then shall complete itself and shall proceed to the elections entrusted to it.

Title 3. Of the Legislative Power

25. New laws shall be promulgated only when the draft thereof has been proposed by the Government, communicated to the Tribunate, and decreed by the Legislative Body. . . .

27. The Tribunate shall be composed of one hundred members, at least twenty-five years of age; they shall be renewed annually by one-fifth, and shall be re-eligible indefinitely so long as they remain on the national list.

28. The Tribunate shall discuss drafts of laws; it shall vote the adoption or rejection thereof.

It shall send three orators, taken from its own membership, who shall set forth and defend before the Legislative Body its motives concerning each of said projects.

It shall refer the lists of eligibles and acts of the Legislative Body and the Government to the Senate on grounds of unconstitutionality alone.

29. It shall express its will concerning laws made or to be made, abuses to be corrected, and improvements to be undertaken in all branches of the public administration, but never upon civil or criminal matters brought before the courts.

The wishes it manifests by virtue of the present article shall have no necessary consequence, and may not oblige any constituted authority to deliberate. . . .

31. The Legislative Body shall be composed of three hundred members, at least thirty years of age; they shall be renewed annually by one-fifth.

It must always include at least one citizen from each and every department of the Republic. . . .

34. The Legislative Body shall make laws by secret ballot, and without any discussion on the part of its members, on the basis of drafts of laws argued before it by the orators of the Tribunate and the Government.

35. The sessions of the Tribunate and those of the Legislative Body shall be public; the number of spectators at either of them may not exceed two hundred.

36. The annual stipend of a tribune is 15,000 francs; that of a legislator, 10,000 francs.

37. Every decree of the Legislative Body shall be promulgated by the First Consul on the tenth day after its issuance, unless, within such period, recourse has been had to the Senate on grounds of unconstitutionality. Such recourse may not be had against promulgated laws. . . .

Title 4. Of the Government

39. The Government shall be entrusted to three Consuls, appointed for ten years and indefinitely re-eligible. . . .

The Constitution appoints as First Consul citizen *Bonaparte*, former provisional Consul; as Second Consul, citizen *Cambacérès*, former Minister of Justice; and as Third Consul, citizen *Lebrun*, former member of the commission of the Council of Elders.

40. The First Consul shall have special functions and prerogatives in which he may be replaced temporarily by one of his colleagues when necessary.

41. The First Consul shall promulgate laws; he shall appoint and dismiss at will the members of the Council of State, the ministers, the ambassadors and other external agents in chief, the officers of the army and navy, the members of the local administrations, and the commissioners of the Government at the courts. He shall appoint all criminal and civil judges, other than justices of the peace and judges of cassation, without power to remove them.

42. In other acts of the Government, the Second and Third Consuls shall have consultative voice; they shall sign the register of such acts in order to attest their presence, and if they wish they may record their opinions therein; after which the decision of the First Consul shall suffice.

43. The stipend of the First Consul shall be 500,000 francs in the Year VIII. That of each of the other two Consuls shall equal three-tenths of that of the First Consul.

44. The Government shall propose laws and make regulations necessary for assuring their execution.

45. The Government shall direct the receipts and expenditures of the State, in conformity with the annual law determining the amount thereof; it shall superintend the manufacture of monies, of which the law alone shall order the issuance and determine the denomination, weight, and standard.

46. If the Government is informed that some conspiracy is being plotted against the State, it may issue warrants of apprehension and arrest against the persons who are assumed to be the authors or accomplices thereof; but if they are not set at liberty or brought to trial within a period of ten days after their arrest, the minister who signed the warrant shall be deemed guilty of the crime of arbitrary imprisonment.

47. The Government shall provide for the internal security and the external defence of the State; . . .

49. The Government shall maintain external political relations, conduct negotiations, sign, have signed, and conclude all treaties. . . .

50. Declarations of war and treaties of peace, alliance, and commerce shall be proposed, discussed, decreed, and promulgated as are laws. . . .

51. The secret articles of a treaty may not be detrimental to the open articles.

52. Under the direction of the Consuls, a Council of State shall be charged with drafting projects of law and regulations for public adminis-

tration, and with solving difficulties which may arise in administrative matters. . . .

54. The ministers shall procure the execution of laws and regulations for public administration.

55. No act of the Government may have effect unless signed by a minister. . . .

57. The detailed accounts of the expenditures of each and every minister, signed and certified by same, shall be made public.

58. The Government may elect or retain as Councillors of State and as Ministers only those citizens whose names are registered on the national list. . . .

Title 5. Of the Courts

60. Each and every communal *arrondissement* shall have one or more justices of the peace, elected directly by the citizens for three years.

Their principal duty shall consist of conciliating parties whom they shall urge, in case of nonconciliation, to obtain judgment through arbitrators.

61. In civil matters there shall be courts of first instance and courts of appeal. . . .

62. In the case of crimes entailing corporal or ignominious penalties, a first jury shall admit or reject the indictment; if it be admitted, a second jury shall take cognizance of the facts, and the judges, forming a criminal court, shall apply the penalty. . . .

63. The duties of public prosecutor before a criminal court shall be performed by the commissioner of the Government.

64. Crimes not entailing corporal or ignominious penalties shall be tried by courts of correctional police, subject to appeal to the criminal courts.

65. For the entire Republic there shall be one Court of Cassation, to pronounce upon appeals in cassation from judgments in the last resort rendered by the courts, upon appeals for changes of venue on grounds of legitimate suspicion or for public security, and upon suits against an entire court.

66. The Court of Cassation shall not have cognizance of the grounds of suits; but it may quash judgments rendered upon proceedings in which forms have been violated, or which contain some express contravention of the law; and it shall refer the grounds of the suit to the court which has cognizance thereof. . . .

68. Judges, other than justices of the peace, shall hold office for life, . . .

Title 6. Of the Responsibility of Public Functionaries

69. The functions of the members of the Senate, the Legislative Body, and the Tribunate, and those of the Consuls and the Councillors of State entail no responsibility.

70. Personal offences entailing corporal or ignominious penalties, committed by a member of the Senate, the Tribunate, the Legislative Body, or the Council of State, shall be prosecuted before the ordinary courts, after a deliberation of the body to which the accused belongs has authorized such prosecution.

71. Ministers accused of private offences entailing corporal or ignominious penalties shall receive the same treatment as members of the Council of State.

72. The Ministers shall be responsible: 1st, for every act of the Government signed by them and declared unconstitutional by the Senate; 2nd, for nonexecution of laws and regulations for public administration; 3rd, for special orders given by them, if such orders are contrary to the Constitution, laws, or regulations.

73. In the case of the preceding article, the Tribunate shall denounce the Minister by an instrument upon which the Legislative Body shall deliberate in the usual forms, after having heard or summoned the accused. The Minister placed on trial by a decree of the Legislative Body shall be tried by a High Court, without appeal and without recourse to cassation.

The High Court shall be composed of judges and jurors. The judges shall be chosen by the Court of Cassation from its own membership, the jurors from the national list, . . .

Title 7. General Provisions

76. The house of every person dwelling upon French territory is an inviolable sanctuary.

During the night no one shall have the right to enter thereinto except in case of fire, flood, or a request from inside the house.

During the day it may be entered for a special purpose determined either by law or by an order issued by a public authority.

77. In order that the warrant ordering the arrest of a person may be executed, it is necessary: 1st, that it express explicitly the grounds for the arrest and the law in execution of which it has been ordered; 2nd, that it be issued by an official who is formally provided by law with such power; 3rd, that it be made known to the person arrested, and that he be provided with a copy thereof. . . .

80. The production of the imprisoned person may not be refused to his kinsmen and friends bearing an order from the civil official, who shall always be required to grant same unless the warden or jailer presents an order of the judge to hold the person *incommunicado.* . . .

82. All severities, other than those authorized by law, which are employed in arrests, imprisonments, or executions shall be crimes.

83. Every person shall have the right to address individual petitions to any constituted authority, and especially to the Tribunate. . . .

86. The French nation declares that pensions shall be granted to all soldiers wounded in the defence of the *Patrie,* as well as to the widows and children of soldiers who die on the field of battle or as a consequence of wounds. . . .

88. A National Institute shall be responsible for collecting discoveries and perfecting the arts and sciences.

89. A commission of national accounting shall regulate and verify the accounts of the receipts and expenditures of the Republic. Said commission shall be composed of seven members chosen by the Senate from the national list. . . .

91. The government of the French colonies shall be determined by special laws.

92. In case of armed revolt or disturbances threatening the security of the State, the law may suspend the authority of the Constitution wherever and for whatever length of time it determines.

Said suspension may be declared provisionally in such cases by an order of the Government when the Legislative Body is in recess, provided that said body be convoked as soon as possible by an article of said same order.

93. The French nation declares that under no circumstances will it permit the return of Frenchmen who, having abandoned their *Patrie* since 14 July, 1789, are not included in the exceptions provided by laws rendered against *émigrés;* it forbids any new exception in such connection.

The property of *émigrés* shall be acquired irrevocably for the benefit of the Republic. . . .

95. The present Constitution shall be presented subsequently for acceptance by the French people.

Proclamation of the Consuls to the French People, 24 Frimaire, Year VIII (15 December 1799)

Frenchmen!

A Constitution is presented to you.

It terminates the uncertainties which the provisional government introduced into external relations, into the internal and military situation of the Republic.

It places in the institutions which it establishes first magistrates whose devotion has appeared necessary for its success.

The Constitution is founded on the true principles of representative government, on the sacred rights of property, equality, and liberty.

The powers which it institutes will be strong and stable, as they must be in order to guarantee the rights of citizens and the interests of the State.

Citizens, the Revolution is established upon the principles which began it: It is ended.

48. Napoleonic Ideas

In 1804, after a plebiscite that declared the French nation overwhelmingly in favor of a change that would fuse revolutionary principles and monarchical authority, Napoleon was declared Emperor of the French and the imperial succession was vested in members of his family. The selections that follow (taken principally from his letters) suggest some of the conceptions of education, government, religion, social order, and his own world-historical significance that governed his conduct as emperor.

On Education

[February 16, 1805] . . . Perhaps the time will soon arrive for considering the question whether we ought not to form a corporation of teachers. If so, should this corporation or order be a religious association, whose members take a vow of chastity, renounce the world, and so on? There does not seem to be any connexion between the two ideas.

As things are, the educational personnel consists of Provisors, Censors, and Professors. A teaching corporation could be formed if all the Provisors, Censors, and Professors in the Empire were under one or more chiefs, like the Generals, Provincials, etc., of the Jesuits; and if it were the rule that no one could become a Provisor or Censor without first being a Professor, and no one a Professor in the higher classes who had not been so in the lower— if, in fact, there were regular stages of promotion in a teacher's career, such as to encourage rivalry, and to provide, at every time of life, not only enough to live on, but also something to look forward to. A man who has devoted himself to teaching ought not to marry until he has passed several stages in his career: marriage ought to be, for him as for other men, a distant goal that he cannot attain till he has secured an adequate position and income, by holding a post whose stipend enables him to support a family without abandoning his profession. If this were so, the conditions of the teaching profession would be the same as those of other civil careers.

There would be *esprit de corps* among teachers. The most distinguished members of the corporation could be taken under the Emperor's protection,

From *Napoleon Self-Revealed*, translated by J. M. Thompson (Boston, Mass.: Houghton-Mifflin, 1934), pp. 109–10, 119–23, 134–37, 148–49, 171–72, 274–75, 359–60. Reprinted by permission of Basil Blackwell. "Address to the Clergy of Milan" translated for this volume by the editor, Keith Michael Baker, from *Correspondance de Napoléon I*, 32 vols. (Paris: Imprimerie Impérial, 1858–1869), vol. 6, pp. 426–28.

and his patronage would raise them even higher in public esteem than the priests were, at a time when priesthood passed for a rank of nobility. Everyone knew how important the Jesuits were. It would not be long before the same prestige attached to the corporation of teachers, if people saw a man, whose education had begun in the *lycée,* picked out for his talents to be himself a teacher, promoted from stage to stage, and finding himself, before the end of his career, in the front ranks of state officials.

Of all political questions this is perhaps the most important. There will be no stability in the state until there is a body of teachers with fixed principles. Till children are taught whether they ought to be Republicans or Monarchists, Catholics or Unbelievers, and so on, there may indeed be a state, but it cannot become a nation. It will rest on vague uncertain foundations. It will be constantly exposed to changes and disorders.[1]

On Governing Italy

[To Prince Eugène,[2] Viceroy of Italy, 5 June 1805] By entrusting you with the government of Our Kingdom of Italy, We have given you proof of the respect your conduct has inspired in Us. But you are still at an age when one does not realise the perversity of men's hearts; I cannot therefore too strongly recommend to you prudence and circumspection. Our Italian subjects are more deceitful by nature than the citizens of France. The only way in which you can keep their respect, and serve their happiness, is by letting no one have your complete confidence, and by never telling anyone what you really think of the ministers and high officials of your court. Dissimulation, which comes naturally at a maturer age, has to be emphasised and inculcated at yours. If you ever find yourself speaking unnecessarily, and from the heart, say to yourself, "I have made a mistake," and don't do it again. Show respect for the nation you govern, and show it all the more as you discover less grounds for it. You will come to see in time that there is little difference between one nation and another. The aim of your administration is the happiness of my Italian peoples; and the first sacrifice you will have to make will be to fall in with certain of their customs which you detest. In any position but that of Viceroy of Italy you may boast of being a Frenchman: but here you must forget it, and count yourself a failure unless the Italians believe that you love them. They know there is no love without

1. These ideas were realized in 1806 by the establishment of the Imperial University, the centralized, hierarchical system of state education that has since remained a basic feature of French national life.

2. Napoleon took the crown of the Kingdom of Italy (formerly the reorganized Cisalpine Republic) in 1805 and appointed his stepson, Eugene Beauharnais, to rule as his viceroy.

respect. Learn their language; frequent their society; single them out for special attention at public functions; like what they like, and approve what they approve.

The less you talk, the better: you aren't well enough educated, and you haven't enough knowledge, to take part in informal debates. Learn to listen, and remember that silence is often as effective as a display of knowledge. Don't be ashamed to ask questions. Though a Viceroy, you are only 23; and however much people flatter you, in reality they all know your limitations, and honour you less for what they believe you to be than for what they hope that you will become.

Don't imitate me in every respect; you need more reserve.

Don't preside often over the State Council; you have too little experience to do so successfully—though I see no objection to your attending it, whilst an Assessor acts as president, from his ordinary seat. Your ignorance of Italian, and of legislation too, for that matter, is an excellent excuse for staying away. Anyhow, never make a speech there: they would listen to you, and would not answer you back; but they would see at once that you aren't competent to discuss business. So long as a prince holds his tongue, his power is incalculable; he should never talk, unless he knows he is the ablest man in the room.

Don't trust spies. They are more trouble than they are worth. There is never enough unrest at Milan to bother about, and I expect it is the same elsewhere. Your military police make sure of the army, and that is all you want.

The army is the one thing you can deal with personally, and from your own knowledge.

Work with your ministers twice a week—once with each of them separately, and once with them all together in Council. Half the battle will be won when your ministers and councillors realise that your only object in consulting them is to listen to reason, and to prevent yourself being taken by surprise.

At public functions, and at fêtes, whenever you have Frenchmen and foreigners together, arrange beforehand where they are to be, and what you are to do. It is better never to form a following; and you must take the greatest care not to expose yourself to any sort of affront. If anything of the kind occurs, don't stand it. Prince, ambassador, minister, general—whoever it may be, even if it is the Austrian or Russian ambassador, have him arrested on the spot. On the other hand, such incidents are always a nuisance; and what matters little in my case might have troublesome results in yours.

Nothing is so advisable as to treat the Italians well, and to get to know all their names and families. Don't show too much attention to foreigners: there is nothing to gain by it. An ambassador will never speak well of you, because it is his business to speak ill. Ministers of foreign countries are, in plain words, accredited spies. It is as well to keep them at arm's length. They always think better of those they seldom see than of their professed friends and benefactors.

There is only one man here at Milan who really matters—the Minister of Finance: he is a hard worker, and knows his job well.

Although they know I am behind you, I have no doubt they are trying to gauge your character. See that your orders are carried out, particularly in the army: never allow them to be disobeyed.

The public decree that I have signed defines the powers I am delegating to you. I am reserving for myself the most important of all—the power of directing your operations. Send me an account of your doings every day. It is only by degrees that you will come to understand how I look at everything.

Don't show my letters to a single soul, under any pretext whatsoever. It ought not to be known what I write to you, or even that I write at all. Keep one room to which no one is admitted—not even your private secretaries.

You will find M. Méjan useful, if he doesn't try to make money; and he won't do that if he knows that you are watching him, and that a single act of this kind will ruin him in my eyes as well as yours. He ought to be well paid, and to have good prospects of promotion. But in that case he must be available at all hours: he will be useless to you if he gets into the way of working only at certain hours, and amusing himself the rest of the day. And you will have to rebuke him for a tendency he shares with all Frenchmen to depreciate this country—all the more so as it is accompanied by melancholia. Frenchmen are never happy out of France.

Keep my household and stables in order, and make up all my accounts at least once a week; this is all the more necessary as they have no idea how to manage things here.

Hold a review at Milan every month.

Cultivate the young Italians, rather than the old; the latter are good for nothing. . . .

You have an important position, and will find it pretty hard work. Try to get to know the history of all the towns in my kingdom of Italy; visit the fortresses, and all the famous battlefields. It is likely enough that you will see fighting before you are thirty, and it is a tremendous asset to know the lie of the land.

One last word. Punish dishonesty ruthlessly. The exposure of a dishonest accountant is a victory for the government. And don't allow any smuggling in the French army.

[To Prince Eugène, 23 August 1810] I have received your letter of August 14. All the raw silk from the Kingdom of Italy goes to England, for there are no silk factories in Germany. It is therefore quite natural that I should wish to divert it from this route to the advantage of my French manufacturers: otherwise my silk factories, one of the chief supports of French commerce, would suffer substantial losses. I cannot agree with your observations. My principle is *France first*. You must never lose sight of the fact that, if English commerce is supreme on the high seas, it is due to her sea power: it is therefore to be expected that, as France is the strongest land power, she should claim commercial supremacy on the continent: it is indeed our only hope. And isn't it better for Italy to come to the help of France, in such an important matter as this, than to be covered with Customs Houses? For it would be short-sighted not to recognise that Italy owes her independence to France; that it was won by French blood and French victories; that it must not be misused; and that nothing could be more unreasonable than to start calculating what commercial advantages France gets out of it.

Piedmont and Parma produce silk too; and there also I have prohibited its export to any country except France. Why should Piedmont be treated in one way, and the Kingdom of Italy in another? If any discrimination were made, it should be in favour of Piedmont; for, whilst the Venetians fought against France, the Piedmontese came to her aid, taking sides against their own king. But never mind about all that. I understand Italian affairs better than anyone else. It is no use for Italy to make plans that leave French prosperity out of account; she must face the fact that the interests of the two countries hang together. Above all, she must be careful not to give France any reason for annexing her; for if it paid France to do this, who could stop her? So make this your motto too—*France first*.

If I were to lose a great battle, a million men—nay, two million men of my old France would flock to my banners, and every purse in the country would be opened for me; but my Kingdom of Italy would desert me. I find it odd, then, that there should be any unwillingness to help the French manufacturers in what is only another way of damaging the English. There is plenty of silk in the Three Legations, plenty in the district of Novara. What has Italy done to deserve these additions of 700,000 and 400,000 souls? How can she expect me to let these annexations result in opposition to my will? French commodities pay half dues on entering Italy; they ought not to pay anything at all . . .

On Nobility

[To Joseph Bonaparte,[3] King of Naples, 5 June 1806] The behaviour of the Roman Curia bears every mark of insanity. I wanted to show them at the start what they had to fear from me. Besides, I thought that under any circumstances the Benevento and Ponte-Corvo *enclaves* could only be a source of trouble to your Kingdom, so I turned them into two Duchies—that of Benevento for Talleyrand, and that of Ponte-Corvo for Bernadotte. I know that they are poor districts: but I will give grants in aid—or rather, I will do so in Bernadotte's case: Talleyrand is rich enough to do without. Occupy these districts, then, and do so with troops in the first instance. You will realise that, if I have given Bernadotte the titles of Duke and Prince, it is on your wife's account.[4] There are other generals in my army who have served me more faithfully, and on whose attachment I can better rely: but I thought it proper that the brother-in-law of the Queen of Naples should rank high at your court. As for the other six Duchies, I shall soon be in a position to appoint to them. Masséna and Jourdan would both be suitable men. Imperfections disappear in time, but titles that recall such victories as Fleurus or Zürich are immutable, and will be the first thought of those who see their children. When you are master of Sicily, found three more fiefs, one of them for Reynier—especially as I think you are putting him in command of the expedition; and this will be no small encouragement to him, if he has any doubts about my friendly feelings towards him.

Tell me what titles you would like attached to the Duchies in your Kingdom. They are titles, and no more: the essential thing is the money that goes with them: 200,000 livres a year will have to be set aside for this purpose. I have made it a further condition that each holder of a title shall keep up a house at Paris; for that is the centre of the whole system, and I want to have there 100 fortunes, which have all been built up alongside the throne, and which are the only estates of any size remaining in the country: for they are gifts by trust, whereas all others, under the working of the Civil Code,[5] gradually disappear.

Introduce the Civil Code at Naples, and at the end of a few years all the

3. Napoleon's brother, Joseph, was dispatched to southern Italy early in 1806 to drive out the Bourbon dynasty. He was proclaimed King of Naples in March of that year. In 1808 he became King of Spain.

4. Jean-Baptiste-Jules Bernadotte, one of Napoleon's generals, was married to Joseph Bonaparte's wife's sister. He was given the title of Prince and Duke of Ponte Corvo in 1806.

5. The Civil Code was the comprehensive, unified code of civil law initially promised by the Constitution of 1791, put into systematic preparation by the Convention, and finally promulgated by Napoleon in 1804. In 1807 it was officially designated as the Code Napoléon. The Napoleonic empire spread its influence throughout Europe.

fortunes not attached to you will be destroyed, and any that you wish to preserve will be consolidated. That is the great advantage of the Civil Code. If you don't like the idea of divorce at Naples, I see no objection to your deleting that article. I think it's useful, all the same. Why should the Pope denounce the granting of divorce on account of impotence, or some other compelling cause, which has no ecclesiastical bearing? However, if you think necessary, change it. And you can leave the registration of civil acts to the clergy. With these modifications you had better introduce the Civil Code. It consolidates your power, for by its means all wealth not in the form of gifts by trust disappears, and no great families remain except those you transform into fiefs. That is why I recommend a Civil Code, and why I established it. . . .

[To Louis Napoléon,[6] King of Holland, 30 March 1807] The news I hear is so extraordinary that I cannot believe it is true. They tell me that you have restored to the nobles in your states their titles and privileges. Is it possible that you are so short-sighted as not to see how fatal such a step would be to you, to your people, to France, and to myself? How could you, a French prince, have violated your simplest vow—to maintain equality among your subjects? [I refuse to believe it can be true.][7]

You are as good as renouncing the French throne: for a man who has broken his oath, a man who has robbed a nation of the fruit of fifteen years' fighting, toil, and endeavour, would be unworthy of such a position. I have, too, my own just grounds of complaint. For a long time past you have consistently acted against my advice. This cannot go on. My ambassador has instructions to inform you in so many words that, unless you revoke this measure, he is under orders to leave Holland, and I have done with you. You are an ungrateful brother, and the advisers under whose influence you have fallen are a pack of criminals. Further, I tell you this plainly, since you care nothing for good advice, that I will not have Frenchmen wearing your Order: so you can save yourself the trouble of conferring it on anyone. I have asked my ambassador for a copy of the act re-establishing nobility: if this measure is not rescinded, I shall look upon you as an inveterate foe. But perhaps I am making mountains out of mole-hills. The simple truth is, you have lost your head. Unless you retract this measure, look out for the consequences. You shall no longer be a French citizen, nor a prince of my blood. Haven't you sense enough to see that if your claim to the Dutch

6. Louis Bonaparte, Napoleon's brother, was proclaimed King of Holland in 1806. He was driven out in 1810, when Napoleon annexed that kingdom to the French empire.

7. When he revised this letter, Napoleon inserted this sentence and struck the entire paragraph that follows.

throne were to rest on noble birth, you would be at the bottom of the list? Is this all I am to expect of you? At the present rate, the next claim to a title will be to have fought against France, and to have sold ships to the English. Every local grandee will take up old claims to a title. Could nobody make you realise that you were alienating the people of Amsterdam—indeed, every Dutchman? An Order of nobility is bearable in a military country: in a commercial one it is intolerable. I think better of the humblest shop-keeper in Amsterdam than of the highest noble in Holland.

On the Church

[Address to the Clergy of Milan, 5 June 1800] It has been my wish to see you all assembled here so that I might have the satisfaction of informing you myself of my convictions on the subject of the Catholic, Apostolic and Roman religion. Persuaded that this is the only religion which can provide a well-ordered society with true happiness, and reinforce the foundations of a good government, I assure you that I shall make it my duty to defend it at all times and by every means. Ministers of that religion, which is cer-tainly also my own, I regard you as my dearest friends. I declare to you that I shall regard as a disturber of the public peace and enemy of the common good—and that I shall punish as such in the most rigorous and striking manner, even with death if necessary—anyone who commits the least offense against our common religion or dares to insult your sacred persons in the slightest manner.

It is my strict intention that the Christian, Catholic and Roman religion be preserved in its entirety, that it be publicly observed and that it enjoy this public observance with a freedom as full, extensive and inviolable as when I first came to these happy lands. All the changes which occurred then, particularly relating to discipline, did so contrary to my desire and my way of thinking. As the mere agent of a government without the least concern for the Catholic religion, I could not then prevent the disorders this govern-ment wished to incite at any cost in order to overthrow it. Now that I am armed with full power, I am determined to implement every means I be-lieve most fitting to uphold and protect this religion.

Modern philosophers have sought to persuade France that the Catholic religion is the implacable enemy of every democratic system and every re-publican form of government: hence this cruel persecution exercised by the French Republic against the religion and its ministers; hence all the horrors to which this unhappy people was condemned. The diversity of opinions on the subject of religion which reigned in France at the time of the Revo-lution was not among the least sources of these disorders. But experience has disabused the French, convincing them that of all religions none is as adaptable as the Catholic to different forms of government, and none is more favorable to republican democratic government in particular, better establishes the rights of that government or throws more light on its principles. I, too, am a philosopher, and I know that, whatever the society, no man can pass as virtuous and just unless he knows where he comes from and where he is going. Reason alone cannot enlighten us in this matter; without religion we always walk in darkness; and the Catholic religion is the only one which gives humanity certain and infallible knowledge regarding its first source and ultimate end. No society can exist without morality; there is no good morality without religion; thus religion alone gives the state a firm and enduring support. A society without religion is like a ship without a compass. A ship in that condition can neither ascertain its route nor hope to enter port. A society without religion, always disturbed, perpetually shaken by the clash of the most violent passions, experiences all the disorders of an internal warfare which casts it into an abyss of evils and, sooner or later, inevitably causes its ruin.

France, instructed by its misfortunes, has finally opened its eyes. It has recognized that the Catholic religion was like an anchor which alone could hold it fast in the midst of disturbances and save it from the blasts of the tempest. It has consequently recalled this religion to its bosom. I cannot deny that I have contributed much to this happy outcome. I assure you that the churches have been reopened in France, that the Catholic religion is regaining its former glory there, and that the people sees with respect those holy pastors returning, full of zeal, to the midst of their abandoned flocks.

Let the manner in which the late Pope was treated inspire no fear in you; Pius VI owed his misfortunes partly to the intrigues of those in whom he had placed his trust, and partly to the cruel policy of the Directory. When I am able to meet with the new Pope, I hope to have the happiness of removing all remaining obstacles to complete reconciliation between France and the head of the Church.[8] I am not unaware of what you have suffered, in your persons as in your property. Your persons will in future be once again inviolable and respected by all; as for your property, I shall take care to give the necessary orders for it to be restored to you at least in part, and for you to be assured forever of the means of living honorably.

That is what I wished to communicate to you on the subject of the Christian, Catholic and Roman religion. It is my wish that the expression of these convictions remain engraved on your minds, and that what I have just said be properly set down. I shall approve its printed publication, so

8. In 1801, Napoleon carried out these ideas by negotiating a Concordat with Pope Pius VII. The agreement brought to a close the breach opened by the Civil Constitution of the Clergy and restored the Catholic religion as the established religion of the state.

that my intentions may be known not only in Italy and in France, but also throughout the whole of Europe.

[To Pope Pius VII, 7 January 1806] Most Holy Father; I am in receipt of a letter from Your Holiness under date November 13. I cannot but be keenly affected by the fact that, when all the powers in English pay banded together to wage an unjust war against me, Your Holiness should lend your ear to ill advice, and write to me in such immoderate terms. Your Holiness is perfectly free either to keep my minister at Rome, or to dismiss him. The occupation of Ancona is an immediate and necessary consequence of the military incompetence of the Holy See.[9] It was better for Your Holiness to see that fortress in my hands than in those of the Turks or English. Your Holiness complains that, since your return from Paris, you have had nothing but disappointments. The reason is that all those who used to call themselves my friends, only because they feared my power, have since then taken heart from the strength of the coalition, and changed their tune: thus, since Your Holiness returned to Rome, I have met with nothing but refusal on your part, whatever the occasion; and this even in matters of the first importance for religion, as, for instance, the question of preventing a revival of Protestantism in France. I have always considered myself the protector of the Holy See; and it was in this capacity that I occupied Ancona. I have always considered myself, like my Valois and Bourbon predecessors, as the eldest son of the Church, and as the sole bearer of the sword with which to protect it, and to put it beyond danger of defilement by Greeks and Moslems. I shall continue to protect it, whatever the mistakes, ingratitude, and ill-will of the men whom these last three months have unmasked. They thought I was done for; but, by the success with which he favoured my arms, God has signally demonstrated his protection of my cause. So long as your Holiness consults the true friends of religion, and your own heart, I shall be your friend. . . . God knows, I have done more for religion than any other prince alive.

Hereby I pray God, Most Holy Father, to preserve you for many years in the rule and government of our Holy Mother Church.

Your devoted son,

Emperor of the French and King of Italy.

[To Cardinal Fesch, French Ambassador to the Papacy, 7 January 1806] The Pope has written to me, under date November 13th, a quite ridiculous and lunatic letter: these people thought I was dead. I occupied Ancona be-

9. French troops occupied the papal territory of Ancona in 1805. This response to the subsequent papal protest was written after the battle of Austerlitz (2 December 1805).

cause, in spite of your representations, nothing had been done to defend it; besides, things are so badly organised that, whatever had been done, it could never have been held against anyone. Make it clearly understood that I won't stand any more of this nonsense. . . . Tell Consalvi[10] . . . that I'm religious, but that I'm no bigot. Remind him that Constantine distinguished the civilian sphere from the military, and that I too can nominate a senator to command in my name in Rome. . . .

For the Pope's purposes, I am Charlemagne. Like Charlemagne, I join the crown of France with the crown of the Lombards. My empire, like Charlemagne's, marches with the East. I therefore expect the Pope to accommodate his conduct to my requirements. If he behaves well, I shall make no outward changes: if not, I shall reduce him to the status of bishop of Rome. . . .

An Emperor Returns

[Circular Letter to the Sovereigns of Europe, 4 April 1815]

Monsieur, My Brother,

You will have learnt, during the course of the last month, of my landing again in France, of my entry into Paris, and of the departure of the Bourbon family.[11] Your Majesty must by now be aware of the real nature of these events. They are the work of an irresistible power, of the unanimous will of a great nation conscious of its duties and of its rights. A dynasty forcibly reimposed upon the French people was no longer suitable for it: the Bourbons refused to associate themselves with the national feelings or the national customs; and France was forced to abandon them. The popular voice called for a liberator. The expectation which had decided me to make the supreme sacrifice was in vain. I returned; and from the place where my foot first touched the shore I was carried by the affection of my subjects into the bosom of my capital.

My first and heartfelt anxiety is to repay so much affection by the maintenance of an honourable peace. The re-establishment of the Imperial throne was necessary for the happiness of Frenchmen: my dearest hope is that it may also secure repose for the whole of Europe. Each national flag in turn has had its gleam of glory: often enough, by some turn of fortune,

10. Cardinal Consalvi was the papal secretary of state.

11. Defeated by an alliance of European powers, Napoleon was forced to abdicate in April 1814. However, he escaped from his exile on the island of Elba in February 1815 and returned to France, where the troops once again flocked to him and Louis xviii, the restored Bourbon monarch, fled. Napoleon's new reign, known as "The Hundred Days," came to an end with his defeat at the Battle of Waterloo in June 1815.

great victories have been followed by great defeats. To-day a finer arena offers itself to the sovereigns of Europe, and I am the first to descend into it. I have provided the world in the past with a programme of great contests: it will please me better in future to acknowledge no rivalry but that of the advocates of peace, and no combat but a crusade for the felicity of mankind. It is France's pleasure to make a frank avowal of this noble ideal. Jealous of her independence, she will always base her policy upon an unqualified respect for the independence of other peoples.

If Your Majesty's personal sentiments—as I confidently trust—are the same, there is assurance of a widespread and long continued repose; and justice, seated on the confines of the various states, will be competent to guard their frontiers. I eagerly embrace this opportunity to repeat the sentiments of sincere esteem and perfect friendship with which I remain,

> *Monsieur* my Brother,
> Your good Brother,
> Napoléon

5
Reflections on the French Revolution

49. Burke, *Reflections on the Revolution in France*

Edmund Burke (1729–97) was born in Dublin of a Catholic mother and a Protestant father. Educated at Trinity College, Dublin, he moved to London to study law, but abandoned his interest in that profession for a more precarious career as a man of letters. In 1765, he became private secretary to Lord Rockingham, the prime minister from 1765 to 1766, who secured his election to the House of Commons. Soon Burke was recognized as one of the great parliamentʌry orators of his age, and one of the most determined opponents of the policies of George III in regard to the American colonies.

A visit to France in 1773 left Burke distrustful of the philosophical tendencies he encountered there, and he watched the early events of the French Revolution (and observed expressions of enthusiasm for its principles in England) with growing alarm. His immensely influential *Reflections on the Revolution in France,* published in November 1790, articulated a conservative philosophy whose condemnation of revolutionary principles resounded throughout Europe.

You will observe, that from Magna Charta to the Declaration of Right, it has been the uniform policy of our constitution to claim and assert our liberties, as an *entailed inheritance* derived to us from our forefathers, and to be transmitted to our posterity; as an estate specially belonging to the

From Edmund Burke, *Reflections on the Revolution in France and on the Proceedings in Certain Societies in London Relative to that Event*, 3d edition (London: J. Dodsley, 1790), pp. 47–65, 85–92, 112–19.

people of this kingdom without any reference whatever to any other more general or prior right. By this means our constitution preserves an unity in so great a diversity of its parts. We have an inheritable crown; an inheritable peerage; and an house of commons and a people inheriting privileges, franchises, and liberties, from a long line of ancestors.

This policy appears to me to be the result of profound reflection; or rather the happy effect of following nature, which is wisdom without reflection, and above it. A spirit of innovation is generally the result of a selfish temper and confined views. People will not look forward to posterity, who never look backward to their ancestors. Besides, the people of England well know, that the idea of inheritance furnishes a sure principle of conservation, and a sure principle of transmission; without at all excluding a principle of improvement. It leaves acquisition free; but it secures what it acquires. Whatever advantages are obtained by a state proceeding on these maxims, are locked fast as in a sort of family settlement; grasped as in a kind of mortmain for ever. By a constitutional policy, working after the pattern of nature, we receive, we hold, we transmit our government and our privileges, in the same manner in which we enjoy and transmit our property and our lives. The institutions of policy, the goods of fortune, the gifts of Providence, are handed down, to us and from us, in the same course and order. Our political system is placed in a just correspondence and symmetry with the order of the world, and with the mode of existence decreed to a permanent body composed of transitory parts; wherein, by the disposition of a stupendous wisdom, moulding together the great mysterious incorporation of the human race, the whole, at one time, is never old, or middle-aged, or young, but in a condition of unchangeable constancy, moves on through the varied tenour of perpetual decay, fall, renovation, and progression. Thus, by preserving the method of nature in the conduct of the state, in what we improve we are never wholly new; in what we retain we are never wholly obsolete. By adhering in this manner and on those principles to our forefathers, we are guided not by the superstition of antiquarians, but by the spirit of philosophic analogy. In this choice of inheritance we have given to our frame of polity the image of a relation in blood; binding up the constitution of our country with our dearest domestic ties; adopting our fundamental laws into the bosom of our family affections; keeping warmth of all their combined and mutually reflected charities, our state, our hearths, our sepulchres, and our altars.

Through the same plan of a conformity to nature in our artificial institutions, and by calling in the aid of her unerring and powerful instincts, to fortify the fallible and feeble contrivances of our reason, we have derived several other, and those no small benefits, from considering our liberties in the light of an inheritance. Always acting as if in the presence of canonized forefathers, the spirit of freedom, leading in itself to misrule and excess, is tempered with an awful gravity. This idea of a liberal descent inspires us with a sense of habitual native dignity, which prevents that upstart insolence almost inevitably adhering to and disgracing those who are the first acquirers of any distinction. By this means our liberty becomes a noble freedom. It carries an imposing and majestic aspect. It has a pedigree and illustrious ancestors. It has its bearings and its ensigns armorial. It has its gallery of portraits; its monumental inscriptions; its records, evidences, and titles. We procure reverence to our civil institutions on the principle upon which nature teaches us to revere individual men; on account of their age; and on account of those from whom they are descended. All your sophisters cannot produce any thing better adapted to preserve a rational and manly freedom than the course that we have pursued, who have chosen our nature rather than our speculations, our breasts rather than our inventions, for the great conservatories and magazines of our rights and privileges.

You might, if you pleased, have profited of our example, and have given to your recovered freedom a correspondent dignity. Your privileges, though discontinued, were not lost to memory. Your constitution, it is true, whilst you were out of possession, suffered waste and dilapidation; but you possessed in some parts the walls, and in all the foundations of a noble and venerable castle. You might have repaired those walls; you might have built on those old foundations. Your constitution was suspended before it was perfected; but you had the elements of a constitution very nearly as good as could be wished. In your old states you possessed that variety of parts corresponding with the various descriptions of which your community was happily composed; you had all that combination, and all that opposition of interests, you had that action and counteraction which, in the natural and in the political world, from the reciprocal struggle of discordant powers, draws out the harmony of the universe. These opposed and conflicting interests, which you considered as so great a blemish in your old and in our present constitution, interpose a salutary check to all precipitate resolutions; They render deliberation a matter not of choice, but of necessity; they make all change a subject of *compromise,* which naturally begets moderation; they produce *temperaments,* preventing the sore evil of harsh, crude, unqualified reformations; and rendering all the headlong exertions of arbitrary power, in the few or in the many, for ever impracticable. Through that diversity of members and interests, general liberty had as many securities as there were separate views in the several orders; whilst by pressing down the whole by the weight of a real monarchy, the separate parts would have been prevented from warping and starting from their allotted places.

You had all these advantages in your ancient states; but you chose to act as if you had never been moulded into civil society, and had every thing to begin anew. You began ill, because you began by despising every thing that belonged to you. You set up your trade without a capital. If the last generations of your country appeared without much lustre in your eyes, you might have passed them by, and derived your claims from a more early race of ancestors. Under a pious predilection to those ancestors, your imaginations would have realized in them a standard of virtue and wisdom, beyond the vulgar practice of the hour: and you would have risen with the example to whose imitation you aspired. Respecting your forefathers, you would have been taught to respect yourselves. You would not have chosen to consider the French as a people of yesterday, as a nation of low-born servile wretches until the emancipating year of 1789. In order to furnish, at the expense of your honour, an excuse to your apologists here for several enormities of yours, you would not have been content to be represented as a gang of Maroon slaves, suddenly broke loose from the house of bondage, and therefore to be pardoned for your abuse of the liberty to which you were not accustomed and ill fitted. Would it not, my worthy friend, have been wiser to have you thought, what I, for one, always thought you, a generous and gallant nation, long misled to your disadvantage by your high and romantic sentiments of fidelity, honour, and loyalty; that events had been unfavourable to you, but that you were not enslaved through any illiberal or servile disposition; that in your most devoted submission, you were actuated by a principle of public spirit, and that it was your country you worshipped, in the person of your king? Had you made it to be understood, that in the delusion of this amiable error you had gone further than your wise ancestors; that you were resolved to resume your ancient privileges, whilst you preserved the spirit of your ancient and your recent loyalty and honour; or, if diffident of yourselves, and not clearly discerning the almost obliterated constitution of your ancestors, you had looked to your neighbours in this land, who had kept alive the ancient principles and models of the old common law of Europe meliorated and adapted to its present state—by following wise examples you would have given new examples of wisdom to the world. You would have rendered the cause of liberty venerable in the eyes of every worthy mind in every nation. You would have shamed despotism from the earth, by shewing that freedom was not only reconcilable, but as, when well disciplined it is, auxiliary to law. You would have had an unoppressive but a productive revenue. You would have had a flourishing commerce to feed it. You would have had a free constitution; a potent monarchy; a disciplined army; a reformed and venerated clergy; a mitigated but spirited nobility, to lead your virtue, not to overlay it; you would have had a liberal order of commons, to emulate and to recruit that nobility; you would have had a protected, satisfied, laborious, and obedient people, taught to seek and to recognize the happiness that is to be found by virtue in all conditions; in which consists the true moral equality of mankind, and not in that monstrous fiction, which, by inspiring false ideas and vain expectations into men destined to travel in the obscure walk of laborious life, serves only to aggravate and imbitter that real inequality, which it never can remove; and which the order of civil life establishes as much for the benefit of those whom it must leave in an humble state, as those whom it is able to exalt to a condition more splendid, but not more happy. You had a smooth and easy career of felicity and glory laid open to you, beyond any thing recorded in the history of the world; but you have shewn that difficulty is good for man.

Compute your gains: see what is got by those extravagant and presumptuous speculations which have taught your leaders to despise all their predecessors, and all their contemporaries, and even to despise themselves, until the moment in which they became truly despicable. By following those false lights, France has bought undisguised calamities at a higher price than any nation has purchased the most unequivocal blessings! France has bought poverty by crime! France has not sacrificed her virtue to her interest; but she has abandoned her interest, that she might prostitute her virtue. All other nations have begun the fabric of a new government, or the reformation of an old, by establishing originally, or by enforcing with greater exactness some rites or other of religion. All other people have laid the foundations of civil freedom in severer manners, and a system of a more austere and masculine morality. France, when she let loose the reins of regal authority, doubled the license, of a ferocious dissoluteness in manners, and of an insolent irreligion in opinions and practices; and has extended through all ranks of life, as if she were communicating some privilege, or laying open some secluded benefit, all the unhappy corruptions that usually were the disease of wealth and power. This is one of the new principles of equality in France.

France, by the perfidy of her leaders, has utterly disgraced the tone of lenient council in the cabinets of princes, and disarmed it of its most potent topics. She has sanctified the dark suspicious maxims of tyrannous distrust; and taught kings to tremble at (what will hereafter be called) the delusive plausibilities of moral politicians. Sovereigns will consider those who advise them to place an unlimited confidence in their people, as subverters of their thrones; as traitors who aim at their destruction, by leading their easy good-nature, under specious pretences, to admit combinations of bold and faithless men into a participation of their power. This alone (if there were nothing else) is an irreparable calamity to you and to mankind.

Remember that your parliament of Paris told your king, that in calling the
states together, he had nothing to fear but the prodigal excess of their zeal
in providing for the support of the throne. It is right that these men should
hide their heads. It is right that they should bear their part in the ruin which
their counsel has brought on their sovereign and their country. Such san-
guine declarations tend to lull authority asleep; to encourage it rashly to
engage in perilous adventures of untried policy; to neglect those provisions, preparations, and precautions, which distinguish benevolence from
imbecillity; and without which no man can answer for the salutary effect of
any abstract plan of government or of freedom. For want of these, they
have seen the medicine of the state corrupted into its poison. They have
seen the French rebel against a mild and lawful monarch, with more fury,
outrage, and insult, than ever any people has been known to rise against
the most illegal usurper, or the most sanguinary tyrant. Their resistance
was made to concession; their revolt was from protection; their blow was
aimed at an hand holding out graces, favours, and immunities.

This was unnatural. The rest is in order. They have found their punishment in their success. Laws overturned; tribunals subverted; industry without vigour; commerce expiring; the revenue unpaid, yet the people impoverished; a church pillaged, and a state not relieved; civil and military
anarchy made the constitution of the kingdom; everything human and divine sacrificed to the idol of public credit, and national bankruptcy the consequence; and to crown all, the paper securities of new, precarious, totter-
ing power, the discredited paper securities of impoverished fraud, and
beggared rapine, held out as a currency for the support of an empire, in
lieu of the two great recognized species that represent the lasting conven-
tional credit of mankind, which disappeared and hid themselves in the
earth from whence they came, when the principle of property, whose creatures and representatives they are, was systematically subverted.

Were all these dreadful things necessary? were they the inevitable results
of the desperate struggle of determined patriots, compelled to wade through
blood and tumult, to the quiet shore of a tranquil and prosperous liberty?
No! nothing like it. The fresh ruins of France, which shock our feelings
wherever we can turn our eyes, are not the devastation of civil war; they are
the sad but instructive monuments of rash and ignorant counsel in time of
profound peace. They are the display of inconsiderate and presumptuous,
because unresisted and irresistible, authority. The persons who have thus
squandered away the precious treasure of their crimes, the persons who
have made this prodigal and wild waste of public evils (the last stake reserved for the ultimate ransom of the state) have met in their progress with
little, or rather with no opposition at all. Their whole march was more like
a triumphal procession than the progress of a war. Their pioneers have gone

before them, and demolished and laid every thing level at their feet. Not one drop of *their* blood have they shed in the cause of the country they have ruined. They have made no sacrifices to their projects of greater consequence than their shoebuckles, whilst they were imprisoning their king, murdering their fellow citizens, and bathing in tears, and plunging in poverty and distress, thousands of worthy men and worthy families. Their cruelty has not even been the base result of fear. It has been the effect of their sense of perfect safety, in authorizing treasons, robberies, rapes, assassinations, slaughters, and burnings throughout their harrassed land. But the cause of all was plain from the beginning.

This unforced choice, this fond election of evil, would appear perfectly unaccountable, if we did not consider the composition of the National Assembly; I do not mean its formal constitution, which, as it now stands, is exceptionable enough, but the materials of which in a great measure it is composed, which is of ten thousand times greater consequence than all the formalities in the world. If we were to know nothing of this Assembly but by its title and function, no colours could paint to the imagination any thing more venerable. In that light the mind of an enquirer, subdued by such an awful image as that of the virtue and wisdom of a whole people collected into a focus, would pause and hesitate in condemning things even of the very worst aspect. Instead of blameable, they would appear only mysterious. But no name, no power, no function, no artificial institution whatsoever, can make the men of whom any system of authority is composed, any other than God, and nature, and education, and their habits of life have made them. Capacities beyond these the people have not to give. Virtue and wisdom may be the objects of their choice; but their choice confers neither the one nor the other on those upon whom they lay their ordaining hands. They have not the engagement of nature, they have not the promise of revelation for any such powers.

After I had read over the list of the persons and descriptions elected into the *Tiers Etat,* nothing which they afterwards did could appear astonishing. Among them, indeed, I saw some of known rank; some of shining talents; but of any practical experience in the state, not one man was to be found. The best were only men of theory. But whatever the distinguished few may have been, it is the substance and mass of the body which constitutes its character, and must finally determine its direction. In all bodies, those who will lead, must also, in a considerable degree, follow. They must conform their propositions to the taste, talent, and disposition of those whom they wish to conduct: therefore, if an Assembly is viciously or feebly composed in a very great part of it, nothing but such a supreme degree of virtue as very rarely appears in the world, and for that reason cannot enter into calculation, will prevent the men of talents disseminated through it from becoming only the expert instruments of absurd projects! If what is the more likely event, instead of that unusual degree of virtue, they should be actuated by sinister ambition and a lust of meretricious glory, then the feeble part of the Assembly, to whom at first they conform, becomes in its turn the dupe and instrument of their designs. In this political traffick the leaders will be obliged to bow to the ignorance of their followers, and the followers to become subservient to the worst designs of their leaders.

To secure any degree of sobriety in the propositions made by the leaders in any public assembly, they ought to respect, in some degree perhaps to fear, those whom they conduct. To be led any otherwise than blindly, the followers must be qualified, if not for actors, at least for judges; they must also be judges of natural weight and authority. Nothing can secure a steady and moderate conduct in such assemblies, but that the body of them should be respectably composed, in point of condition in life, of permanent property, of education, and of such habits as enlarge and liberalize the understanding.

In the calling of the states general of France, the first thing which struck me, was a great departure from the ancient course. I found the representation for the Third Estate composed of six hundred persons. They were equal in number to the representatives of both the other orders. If the orders were to act separately, the number would not, beyond the consideration of the expence, be of much moment. But when it became apparent that the three orders were to be melted down into one, the policy and necessary effect of this numerous representation became obvious. A very small desertion from either of the other two orders must throw the power of both into the hands of the third. In fact, the whole power of the state was soon resolved into that body. Its due composition became therefore of infinitely the greater importance.

Judge, Sir, of my surprize, when I found that a very great proportion of the Assembly (a majority, I believe, of the members who attended) was composed of practitioners in the law. It was composed not of distinguished magistrates, who had given pledges to their country of their science, prudence, and integrity; not of leading advocates, the glory of the bar; not of renowned professors in universities;—but for the far greater part, as it must in such a number, of the inferior, unlearned, mechanical, merely instrumental members of the profession. There were distinguished exceptions; but the general composition was of obscure provincial advocates, of stewards of petty local jurisdictions, country attornies, notaries, and the whole train of the ministers of municipal litigation, the fomentors and conductors of the petty war of village vexation. From the moment I read the list I saw distinctly, and very nearly as it has happened, all that was to follow.

The degree of estimation in which any profession is held becomes the standard of the estimation in which the professors hold themselves. Whatever the personal merits of many individual lawyers might have been, and in many it was undoubtedly very considerable, in that military kingdom, no part of the profession had been much regarded, except the highest of all, who often united to their professional offices great family splendour, and were invested with great power and authority. These certainly were highly respected, and even with no small degree of awe. The next rank was not much esteemed; the mechanical part was in a very low degree of repute.

Whenever the supreme authority is invested in a body so composed, it must evidently produce the consequences of supreme authority placed in the hands of men not taught habitually to respect themselves; who had no previous fortune in character at stake; who could not be expected to bear with moderation, or to conduct with discretion, a power which they themselves, more than any others, must be surprized to find in their hands. Who could flatter himself that these men, suddenly, and, as it were, by enchantment, snatched from the humblest rank of subordination, would not be intoxicated with their unprepared greatness? Who could conceive, that men who are habitually meddling, daring, subtle, active, of litigious dispositions and unquiet minds, would easily fall back into their old condition of obscure contention, and laborious, low, unprofitable chicane? Who could doubt but that, at any expence to the state, of which they understood nothing, they must pursue their private interests, which they understood but too well? It was not an event depending on chance or contingency. It was inevitable; it was necessary; it was planted in the nature of things. They must *join* (if their capacity did not permit them to *lead*) in any project which could procure to them a *litigious constitution;* which could lay open to them those innumerable lucrative jobs which follow in the train of all great convulsions and revolutions in the state, and particularly in all great and violent permutations of property. Was it to be expected that they would attend to the stability of property, whose existence had always depended upon whatever rendered property questionable, ambiguous, and insecure? Their objects would be enlarged with their elevation, but their disposition and habits, and mode of accomplishing their designs, must remain the same.

Well! but these men were to be tempered and restrained by other descriptions, of more sober minds, and more enlarged understandings. Were they then to be awed by the super-eminent authority and awful dignity of an handful of country clowns who have seats in that Assembly, some of whom are said not to be able to read and write? and by not a greater number of traders, who, though somewhat more instructed, and more conspicuous in the order of society, had never known any thing beyond their counting-house? No! both these descriptions were more formed to be overborne and swayed by the intrigues and artifices of lawyers, than to become their counterpoise. With such a dangerous disproportion, the whole must needs be governed by them. To the faculty of law was joined a pretty considerable proportion of the faculty of medicine. This faculty had not, any more than that of the law, possessed in France its just estimation. Its professors therefore must have the qualities of men not habituated to sentiments of dignity. But supposing they had ranked as they ought to do, and as with us they do actually, the sides of sick beds are not the academies for forming statesmen and legislators. Then came the dealers in stocks and funds, who must be eager, at any expence, to change their ideal paper wealth for the more solid substance of land. To these were joined men of other descriptions, from whom as little knowledge of or attention to the interests of a great state was to be expected, and as little regard to the stability of any institution; men formed to be instruments, not controls. Such in general was the composition of the *Tiers Etat* in the National Assembly; in which was scarcely to be perceived the slightest traces of what we call the natural landed interest of the country.

We know that the British house of commons, without shutting its doors to any merit in any class, is, by the sure operation of adequate causes, filled with every thing illustrious in rank, in descent, in hereditary and in acquired opulence, in cultivated talents, in military, civil, naval, and politic distinction, that the country can afford. But supposing, what hardly can be supposed as a case, that the house of commons should be composed in the same manner with the Tiers Etat in France, would this dominion of chicane be borne with patience, or even conceived without horror? God forbid I should insinuate any thing derogatory to that profession, which is another priesthood, administering the rites of sacred justice. But whilst I revere men in the functions which belong to them, and would do, as much as one man can do, to prevent their exclusion from any, I cannot, to flatter them, give the lye to nature. They are good and useful in the composition; they must be mischievous if they preponderate so as virtually to become the whole. Their very excellence in their peculiar functions may be far from a qualification for others. It cannot escape observation, that when men are too much confined to professional and faculty habits, and, as it were, inveterate in the recurrent employment of that narrow circle, they are rather disabled than qualified for whatever depends on the knowledge of mankind, on experience in mixed affairs, on a comprehensive connected view of the various complicated external and internal interests which go to the formation of that multifarious thing called a state. . . .

It is no wonder therefore, that with these ideas of every thing in their constitution and government at home, either in church or state, as illegitimate and usurped, or, at best as a vain mockery, they look abroad with an eager and passionate enthusiasm. Whilst they are possessed by these notions, it is vain to talk to them of the practice of their ancestors, the fundamental laws of their country, the fixed form of a constitution, whose merits are confirmed by the solid test of long experience, and an increasing public strength and national prosperity. They despise experience as the wisdom of unlettered men; and as for the rest, they have wrought under-ground a mine that will blow up at one grand explosion all examples of antiquity, all precedents, charters, and acts of parliament. They have "the rights of men." Against these there can be no prescription; against these no agreement is binding: these admit no temperament, and no compromise: any thing withheld from their full demand is so much of fraud and injustice. Against these their rights of men let no government look for security in the length of its continuance, or in the justice and lenity of its administration. The objections of these speculatists, if its forms do not quadrate with their theories, are as valid against such an old and beneficent government as against the most violent tyranny, or the greenest usurpation. They are always at issue with governments, not on a question of abuse, but a question of competence, and a question of title. I have nothing to say to the clumsy subtilty of their political metaphysics. Let them be their amusement in the schools. — *"Illa se jactet in aula—Æolus, et clauso ventorum carcere regnet."* —But let them not break prison to burst like a *Levanter,* to sweep the earth with their hurricane, and to break up the fountains of the great deep to overwhelm us.

Far am I from denying in theory; full as far is my heart from withholding in practice (if I were of power to give or to withhold) the *real* rights of men. In denying their false claims of right, I do not mean to injure those which are real, and are such as their pretended rights would totally destroy. If civil society be made for the advantage of man, all the advantages for which it is made become his right. It is an institution of beneficence; and law itself is only beneficence acting by a rule. Men have a right to live by that rule; they have a right to justice, as between their fellows, whether their fellows are in politic function or in ordinary occupation. They have a right to the fruits of their industry; and to the means of making their industry fruitful. They have a right to the acquisitions of their parents; to the nourishment and improvement of their offspring; to instruction in life, and to consolation in death. Whatever each man can separately do, without trespassing upon others, he has a right to do for himself; and he has a right to a fair portion of all which society, with all its combinations of skill and force, can do in his favour. In this partnership all men have equal rights; but not to equal things. He that has but five shillings in the partnership, has as good a right to it, as he that has five hundred has to his larger proportion. But he has not a right to an equal dividend in the product of the joint estate; and as to the share of power, authority, and direction which each individual ought to have in the management of the state, that I must deny to be amongst the direct original rights of man in civil society; for I have in my contemplation the civil social man, and no other. It is a thing to be settled by convention.

If civil society be the offspring of convention, that convention must be its law. That convention must limit and modify all the descriptions of constitution which are formed under it. Every sort of legislative, judicial, or executory power are its creatures. They can have no being in any other state of things; and how can any man claim, under the conventions of civil society, rights which do not so much as suppose its existence? Rights which are absolutely repugnant to it? One of the first motives to civil society, and which becomes one of its fundamental rules, is, *that no man should be judge in his own cause.* By this each person has at once divested himself of the first fundamental right of uncovenanted man, that is, to judge for himself, and to assert his own cause. He abdicates all right to be his own governor. He inclusively, in a great measure, abandons the right of self-defence, the first law of nature. Men cannot enjoy the rights of an uncivil and of a civil state together. That he may obtain justice he gives up his right of determining what it is in points the most essential to him. That he may secure some liberty, he makes a surrender in trust of the whole of it.

Government is not made in virtue of natural rights, which may and do exist in total independence of it; and exist in much greater clearness, and in a much greater degree of abstract perfection: but their abstract perfection is their practical defect. By having a right to every thing they want every thing. Government is a contrivance of human wisdom to provide for human *wants.* Men have a right that these wants should be provided for by this wisdom. Among these wants is to be reckoned the want, out of civil society, of a sufficient restraint upon their passions. Society requires not only that the passions of individuals should be subjected, but that even in the mass and body as well as in the individuals, the inclinations of men should frequently be thwarted, their will controlled, and their passions brought into subjection. This can only be done *by a power out of themselves;* and not, in exercise of its function, subject to that will and to those passions which it is its office to bridle and subdue. In this sense the restraints on men, as well as their liberties, are to be reckoned among their rights. But as the liberties and the restrictions vary with times and circumstances, and admit of infinite modifications, they cannot be settled upon any abstract rule; and nothing is so foolish as to discuss them upon that principle.

The moment you abate any thing from the full rights of men, each to govern himself, and suffer any artificial positive limitation upon those rights, from that moment the whole organization of government becomes a consideration of convenience. This it is which makes the constitution of a state, and the due distribution of its powers, a matter of the most delicate and complicated skill. It requires a deep knowledge of human nature and human necessities, and of the things which facilitate or obstruct the various ends which are to be pursued by the mechanism of civil institutions. The state is to have recruits to its strength, and remedies to its distempers. What is the use of discussing a man's abstract right to food or to medicine? The question is upon the method of procuring and administering them. In that deliberation I shall always advise to call in the aid of the farmer and the physician, rather than the professor of metaphysics.

The science of constructing a commonwealth, or renovating it, or re-forming it, is, like every other experimental science, not to be taught *à priori*. Nor is it a short experience that can instruct us in that practical science; because the real effects of moral causes are not always immediate; but that which in the first instance is prejudicial may be excellent in its remoter operation; and its excellence may arise even from the ill effects it produces in the beginning. The reverse also happens; and very plausible schemes, with very pleasing commencements, have often shameful and lamentable conclusions. In states there are often some obscure and almost latent causes, things which appear at first view of little moment, on which a very great part of its prosperity or adversity may most essentially depend. The science of government being therefore so practical in itself, and intended for such practical purposes, a matter which requires experience, and even more experience than any person can gain in his whole life, however sagacious and observing he may be, it is with infinite caution that any man ought to venture upon pulling down an edifice which has answered in any tolerable degree for ages the common purposes of society, or of building it up again, without having models and patterns of approved utility before his eyes.

These metaphysic rights entering into common life, like rays of light which pierce into a dense medium, are, by the laws of nature, refracted from their straight line. Indeed in the gross and complicated mass of human passions and concerns, the primitive rights of men undergo such a variety of refractions and reflections, that it becomes absurd to talk of them as if they continued in the simplicity of their original direction. The nature of man is intricate; the objects of society are of the greatest possible complexity; and therefore no simple disposition or direction of power can be suitable either to man's nature, or to the quality of his affairs. When I hear the simplicity of contrivance aimed at and boasted of in any new political constitutions, I am at no loss to decide that the artificers are grossly igno-

rant of their trade, or totally negligent of their duty. The simple governments are fundamentally defective, to say no worse of them. If you were to
contemplate society in but one point of view, all these simple modes of
policy are infinitely captivating. In effect each would answer its single end
much more perfectly than the more complex is able to attain all its complex
purposes. But it is better that the whole should be imperfectly and anoma-
lously answered, than that, while some parts are provided for with great
exactness, others might be totally neglected, or perhaps materially injured,
by the over-care of a favourite member.

The pretended rights of these theorists are all extremes; and in proportion as they are metaphysically true, they are morally and politically false.
The rights of men are in a sort of *middle,* incapable of definition, but not
impossible to be discerned. The rights of men in governments are their
advantages; and these are often in balances between differences of good; in
compromises sometimes between good and evil, and sometimes, between
evil and evil. Political reason is a computing principle; adding, subtracting,
multiplying, and dividing, morally and not metaphysically or mathematically, true moral denominations.

By these theorists the right of the people is almost always sophistically
confounded with their power. The body of the community, whenever it can
come to act, can meet with no effectual resistance; but till power and right
are the same, the whole body of them has no right inconsistent with virtue,
and the first of all virtues, prudence. Men have no right to what is not reasonable, and to what is not for their benefit; for though a pleasant writer
said, *Liceat perire poetis,* when one of them, in cold blood, is said to have
leaped into the flames of a volcanic revolution, *Ardentem frigidus Ætnam
insiluit,* I consider such a frolic rather as an unjustifiable poetic licence,
than as one of the franchises of Parnassus; and whether he were poet or
divine, or politician that chose to exercise this kind of right, I think that
more wise, because more charitable thoughts would urge me rather to save
the man, than to preserve his brazen slippers as the monuments of his
folly. . . .

It is now sixteen or seventeen years since I saw the queen of France,
then the dauphiness, at Versailles; and surely never lighted on this orb,
which she hardly seemed to touch, a more delightful vision. I saw her just
above the horizon, decorating and cheering the elevated sphere she just began to move in,—glittering like the morning-star, full of life, and splendor,
and joy. Oh! what a revolution! and what an heart must I have, to contemplate without emotion that elevation and that fall! Little did I dream, when
she added titles of veneration to those of enthusiastic, distant, respectful
love, that she should ever be obliged to carry the sharp antidote against

disgrace concealed in that bosom; little did I dream that I should have lived to see such disasters fallen upon her in a nation of gallant men, in a nation of men of honour and of cavaliers. I thought ten thousand swords must have leaped from their scabbards to avenge even a look that threatened her with insult.—But the age of chivalry is gone.—That of sophisters, œconomists, and calculators, has succeeded; and the glory of Europe is extinguished for ever. Never, never more, shall we behold that generous loyalty to rank and sex, that proud submission, that dignified obedience, that subordination of the heart, which kept alive, even in servitude itself, the spirit of an exalted freedom. The unbought grace of life, the cheap defence of nations, the nurse of manly sentiment and heroic enterprize is gone! It is gone, that sensibility of principle, that chastity of honour, which felt a stain like a wound, which inspired courage whilst it mitigated ferocity, which ennobled whatever it touched, and under which vice itself lost half its evil, by losing all its grossness.

This mixed system of opinion and sentiment had its origin in the ancient chivalry; and the principle, though varied in its appearance by the varying state of human affairs, subsisted and influenced through a long succession of generations, even to the time we live in. If it should ever be totally extinguished, the loss I fear will be great. It is this which has given its character to modern Europe. It is this which has distinguished it under all its forms of government, and distinguished it to its advantage, from the states of Asia, and possibly from those states which flourished in the most brilliant periods of the antique world. It was this, which, without confounding ranks, had produced a noble equality, and handed it down through all the gradations of social life. It was this opinion which mitigated kings into companions, and raised private men to be fellows with kings. Without force, or opposition, it subdued the fierceness of pride and power; it obliged sovereigns to submit to the soft collar of social esteem, compelled stern authority to submit to elegance, and gave a dominating vanquisher of laws to be subdued by manners.

But now all is to be changed. All the pleasing illusions, which made power gentle, and obedience liberal, which harmonized the different shades of life, and which, by a bland assimilation, incorporated into politics the sentiments which beautify and soften private society, are to be dissolved by this new conquering empire of light and reason. All the decent drapery of life is to be rudely torn off. All the superadded ideas, furnished from the wardrobe of a moral imagination, which the heart owns, and the understanding ratifies, as necessary to cover the defects of our naked shivering nature, and to raise it to dignity in our own estimation, are to be exploded as a ridiculous, absurd, and antiquated fashion.

On this scheme of things, a king is but a man; a queen is but a woman; a woman is but an animal; and an animal not of the highest order. All homage paid to the sex in general as such, and without distinct views, is to be regarded as romance and folly. Regicide, and parricide, and sacrilege, are but fictions of superstition, corrupting jurisprudence by destroying its simplicity. The murder of a king, or a queen, or a bishop, or a father, are only common homicide; and if the people are by any chance, or in any way gainers by it, a sort of homicide much the most pardonable, and into which we ought not to make too severe a scrutiny.

On the scheme of this barbarous philosophy, which is the offspring of cold hearts and muddy understandings, and which is as void of solid wisdom, as it is destitute of all taste and elegance, laws are to be supported only by their own terrors, and by the concern, which each individual may find in them, from his own private speculations, or can spare to them from his own private interests. In the groves of *their* academy, at the end of every vista, you see nothing but the gallows. Nothing is left which engages the affections on the part of the commonwealth. On the principles of this mechanic philosophy, our institutions can never be embodied, if I may use the expression, in persons; so as to create in us love, veneration, admiration, or attachment. But that sort of reason which banishes the affections is incapable of filling their place. These public affections, combined with manners, are required sometimes as supplements, sometimes as correctives, always as aids to law. The precept given by a wise man, as well as a great critic, for the construction of poems, is equally true as to states. *Non satis est pulchra esse poemata, dulcia sunto.* There ought to be a system of manners in every nation which a well-formed mind would be disposed to relish. To make us love our country, our country ought to be lovely.

But power, of some kind or other, will survive the shock in which manners and opinions perish; and it will find other and worse means for its support. The usurpation which, in order to subvert ancient institutions, has destroyed ancient principles, will hold power by arts similar to those by which it has acquired it. When the old feudal and chivalrous spirit of *Fealty,* which, by freeing kings from fear, freed both kings and subjects from the precautions of tyranny, shall be extinct in the minds of men, plots and assassinations will be anticipated by preventive murder and preventive confiscation, and that long roll of grim and bloody maxims, which form the political code of all power, not standing on its own honour, and the honour of those who are to obey it. Kings will be tyrants from policy when subjects are rebels from principle.

When ancient opinions and rules of life are taken away, the loss cannot possibly be estimated. From that moment we have no compass to govern us; nor can we know distinctly to what port we steer. Europe undoubtedly, taken in a mass, was in a flourishing condition the day on which your Revolution was compleated. How much of that prosperous state was owing to the spirit of our old manners and opinions is not easy to say; but as such causes cannot be indifferent in their operation, we must presume, that, on the whole, their operation was beneficial.

We are but too apt to consider things in the state in which we find them, without sufficiently adverting to the causes by which they have been produced, and possibly may be upheld. Nothing is more certain, than that our manners, our civilization, and all the good things which are connected with manners, and with civilization, have in this European world of ours, depended for ages upon two principles; and were indeed the result of both combined; I mean the spirit of a gentleman, and the spirit of religion. The nobility and the clergy, the one by profession, the other by patronage, kept learning in existence, even in the midst of arms and confusions, and whilst governments were rather in their causes than formed. Learning paid back what it received to nobility and to priesthood; and paid it with usury, by enlarging their ideas, and by furnishing their minds. Happy if they had all continued to know their indissoluble union, and their proper place! Happy if learning, not debauched by ambition, had been satisfied to continue the instructor; and not aspired to be the master! Along with its natural protectors and guardians, learning will be cast into the mire, and trodden down under the hoofs of a swinish multitude.

If, as I suspect, modern letters owe more than they are always willing to own to ancient manners, so do other interests which we value full as much as they are worth. Even commerce, and trade, and manufacture, the gods of our œconomical politicians, are themselves perhaps but creatures; are themselves but effects, which as first causes, we choose to worship. They certainly grew under the same shade in which learning flourished. They too may decay with their natural protecting principles. With you, for the present at least, they all threaten to disappear together. Where trade and manufactures are wanting to a people, and the spirit of nobility and religion remains, sentiment supplies, and not always ill supplies their place; but if commerce and the arts should be lost in an experiment to try how well a state may stand without these old fundamental principles, what sort of a thing must be a nation of gross, stupid, ferocious, and at the same time, poor and sordid barbarians, destitute of religion, honour, or manly pride, possessing nothing at present, and hoping for nothing hereafter?

I wish you may not be going fast, and by the shortest cut, to that horrible and disgustful situation. Already there appears a poverty of conception, a coarseness and vulgarity in all the proceedings of the assembly and of all their instructors. Their liberty is not liberal. Their science is presumptuous ignorance. Their humanity is savage and brutal.

It is not clear, whether in England we learned those grand and decorous principles, and manners, of which considerable traces yet remain, from you, or whether you took them from us. But to you, I think, we trace them best. You seem to me to be—*gentis incunabula nostrae*. France has always more or less influenced manners in England; and when your fountain is choaked up and polluted, the stream will not run long, or not run clear with us, or perhaps with any nation. This gives all Europe, in my opinion, but too close and connected a concern in what is done in France. Excuse me, therefore, if I have dwelt too long on the atrocious spectacle of the sixth of October 1789, or have given too much scope to the reflections which have arisen in my mind on occasion of the most important of all revolutions, which may be dated from that day, I mean a revolution in sentiments, manners, and moral opinions. As things now stand, with every thing respectable destroyed without us, and an attempt to destroy within us every principle of respect, one is almost forced to apologize for harbouring the common feelings of men.

50. Maistre, *Considerations on France*

Joseph de Maistre (1754–1821) was born in French-speaking Savoy, at the time of his birth still a part of the kingdom of Piedmont. Like his father, he entered the magistracy and adopted enlightened, reforming views. Although he was enthusiastic about the calling of the Estates General, he quickly condemned the revolutionary events of 1789 and welcomed the appearance of Burke's *Reflections on the French Revolution* a year later. Driven into exile by the French invasion of Savoy in 1792, he subsequently settled in Lausanne. There, he wrote his *Considerations on France*, one of the most profound and influential efforts of counterrevolutionary theorists to comprehend the radical novelty of the French Revolution as a political phenomenon. Published with a 1796 imprint, the work actually appeared in 1797.

More profoundly religious in his conservatism than Burke, Maistre represents a blending of Catholic faith and antirevolutionary conviction that remained powerful in France (and elsewhere) throughout the nineteenth century.

Of Revolutions

We are all attached to the throne of the Supreme Being by a supple chain that restrains us without enslaving us. Nothing is more admirable in the

From Joseph de Maistre, *Considerations on France*, translated by Richard A. Lebrun (Montreal: McGill-Queen's University Press, 1974), pp. 23–30, 79–81, 85–86, 91–97.

universal order of things than the action of free beings under the divine hand. Freely slaves, they act voluntarily and necessarily at the same time; they really do what they will, but without being able to disturb the general plans. Each of these beings occupies the centre of a sphere of activity whose diameter varies according to the will of the Eternal Geometer, who can extend, restrict, check, or direct the will without altering its nature.

In the works of man, everything is as wretched as their author; views are restricted, means rigid, motives inflexible, movements painful, and results monotonous. In divine works, the riches of infinity are openly displayed in the least part. Its power is exercised effortlessly; everything is supple in its hands, nothing resists it, and for it everything, even obstacles, are means; and the irregularities introduced by the operation of free agents fit into the general order.

If we imagine a watch all of whose springs vary continually in strength, weight, dimension, form, and position that nevertheless invariably keeps perfect time, we will form some idea of the action of free beings relative to the plans of the Creator.

In the political and moral world, as in the physical world, there is a usual order and there are exceptions to this order. Ordinarily, we see series of effects produced by the same causes; but in certain epochs, we see actions suspended, causes paralysed, and new effects.

A *miracle* is an effect produced by a divine or superhuman cause that suspends or contradicts an ordinary cause. If in the middle of winter, before a thousand witnesses, a man were to command that a tree be suddenly covered with leaves and fruit, and the tree obeyed, everyone would proclaim it a miracle and bow down before the wonder-worker. But the French Revolution and everything now happening in Europe is just as marvellous in its own way as the instantaneous fructification of a tree in the month of January. However, instead of being astonished, we look the other way or talk nonsense.

In the physical order, in which man does not play a role as a cause, he is quite willing to admire what he does not understand. But in the sphere of his own activity, where he feels that he is a free cause, man's pride easily leads him to see *disorder* wherever his action is suspended or disturbed. Certain measures that are in man's power regularly produce certain effects in the ordinary course of events; if he misses his mark, he knows why or believes he does. He knows the obstacles, he appreciates them, and nothing surprises him.

But in revolutionary periods, the chain that binds man is abruptly shortened; his action is diminished and his means deceive him. Then carried along by an unknown force, he frets against it, and instead of kissing the hand that clasps him, he disregards or insults it.

"I do not understand it at all" is the fashionable phrase. This is a sensible reaction if it leads to the first cause that is presently presenting so great a spectacle to men; it is stupidity if it expresses only vexation or sterile despondency. "How then," they cry on every side, "is it the guiltiest men in the universe who are winning? A hideous regicide succeeds as well as those who committed it could have hoped. All over Europe monarchy is benumbed. Its enemies find allies even on thrones! Everything succeeds for the wicked! The most gigantic projects are executed without difficulty on their side, while the good party fails ridiculously in everything it undertakes. Public opinion persecutes fidelity all over Europe! The foremost statesmen are invariably mistaken! The greatest generals are humiliated! etc."

Doubtless, for the first condition of an ordained revolution is that whatever could have prevented it does not exist and that nothing succeed for those who wish to prevent it. But never is order more visible, never is Providence more palpable, than when superior action is substituted for that of man and it acts all alone. This is what we are seeing at the present moment.

The most striking thing about the French Revolution is this overwhelming force that bends every obstacle. It is a whirlwind carrying along like light straw everything that human force has opposed to it; no one has hindered its course with impunity. Purity of motives has been able to make resistance honourable, but no more, and this jealous force, proceeding straight toward its goal, rejects equally Charette, Dumouriez, and Drouet.

It has been correctly pointed out that the French Revolution leads men more than men lead it. This observation is completely justified, and although it can be applied to all great revolutions more or less, it has never been more striking than it is in the present period.

The very rascals who appear to lead the Revolution are involved only as simple instruments, and as soon as they aspire to dominate it they fall ignobly. Those who established the Republic did it without wanting to and without knowing what they were doing. They were led to it by events; a prior design would not have succeeded.

Robespierre, Collot, or Barère never thought to establish the revolutionary government or the Reign of Terror; they were led to it imperceptibly by circumstances, and the like will never be seen again. These extremely mediocre men exercised over a guilty nation the most frightful despotism in history, and surely they were more surprised at their power than anyone else in the kingdom.

But the very moment these detestable tyrants completed the measure of crime necessary to that phase of the Revolution, a breath overthrew them. Their gigantic power, which had made France and Europe tremble, could not withstand the first attack; and as there could be nothing great, nothing august, in a completely criminal revolution, Providence willed that the first blow be struck by the Septembrists, in order that justice itself would be debased.

We are often astonished that the most mediocre men have been better judges of the French Revolution than men of first-rate talent, that they have believed in it completely while accomplished politicians have not believed in it at all. This is because this belief is one of the characteristics of the Revolution, because the Revolution could succeed only by the scope and power of the revolutionary spirit, or, if one may put it another way, by *faith* in the Revolution. Thus, untalented and ignorant men have very ably driven what they call the *revolutionary chariot*. They have dared everything without fear of counter-revolution; they have always gone ahead without looking back, and everything has succeeded for them because they were only the instruments of a force that knew more than they did. They made no mistakes in their revolutionary career for the same reason that Vaucanson's flutist never hit a false note.

The revolutionary torrent took successively different directions, and it was only by following the course of the moment that the most conspicuous men in the Revolution acquired the kind of power and celebrity they were able to achieve. As soon as they wanted to oppose it, or even to stand aside by isolating themselves or by working too much for themselves, they disappeared from the scene. . . .

In short, the more one examines the apparently most active personages in the Revolution, the more one finds in them something passive and mechanical. We cannot repeat too often that men do not lead the Revolution; it is the Revolution that uses men. They are right when they say *it goes all alone*. This phrase means that never has the Divinity shown itself so clearly in any human event. If the vilest instruments are employed, punishment is for the sake of regeneration.

The French Revolution Considered in Its Antireligious Character

Digression on Christianity

There is a satanic quality to the French Revolution that distinguishes it from everything we have ever seen or anything we are ever likely to see in the future. Recall the great assemblies, Robespierre's speech against the priesthood, the solemn apostasy of the clergy, the desecration of objects of worship, the installation of the goddess of reason, and that multitude of extraordinary actions by which the provinces sought to outdo Paris. All this goes beyond the ordinary circle of crime and seems to belong to another world.

Even now, when the Revolution has become less violent, and wanton excesses have disappeared, the principles remain. Have not the *legislators* (I use their term) passed the historically unique rule that the nation *will support no form of worship?* Some of our contemporaries, it seems to me, have at certain moments reached the point of hating the Divinity; but this frightful act of violence was not necessary to render the very greatest creative efforts useless. The mere omission (let alone contempt) of the great Being in any human endeavour brands it with an irrevocable anathema. Either every imaginable institution is founded on a religious concept or it is only a passing phenomenon. Institutions are strong and durable to the degree that they are, so to speak, *deified*. Not only is human reason, or what is ignorantly called *philosophy,* incapable of supplying these foundations, which with equal ignorance are called *superstitious,* but philosophy is, on the contrary, an essentially disruptive force. . . .

When we reflect on the attested facts of all history, when we understand that in the chain of human institutions, from those that have marked the great turning points in history down to the smallest social organization, from empires down to brotherhoods, all have a divine foundation, and that human power, whenever it isolates itself, can only give its works a false and passing existence, what are we to think of the new French structure and the power that produced it? For myself, I will never believe in the fecundity of nothingness.

It would be curious to examine our European institutions one by one and to show how they are all *Christianized,* how religion mingles in everything, animates and sustains everything. Human passions may pollute and even pervert primitive creations, but if the principle is divine, this is enough to give them a prodigious permanence. . . .

The present generation is witnessing one of the greatest spectacles ever beheld by human eyes; it is the fight to the death between Christianity and philosophism. The lists are open, the two enemies have come to grips, and the world looks on. As in Homer, *the father of gods and men* is holding the balance in which these two great causes are being weighed; one of the scales will soon descend.

To the prejudiced man, and especially to the one whose heart has convinced his head, events prove nothing; he having taken one side or the other irrevocably, observation and reasoning are equally useless. But all you men of good faith who may deny or doubt what I say, perhaps the great example of Christianity will settle your uncertainty. For eighteen centuries it has ruled a great part of the world, particularly the most enlightened portion of the globe. This religion even predates antiquity, for it is linked through its founder to another order of things, to an archetypal religion, that preceded it. The one cannot be true without the other being so; the one boasts of promising what the other boasts of having, so that this religion, by a chain that is a visible fact, goes back to the beginning of the world: *It was born the day the days were born.*

Such duration is without example, and even taking Christianity by itself, no institution in the world can match it. To compare it to other religions is mere wrangling; several striking characteristics exclude all comparison. This is not the place to list them; just a word will be enough. Who can show us one other religion founded on miracles and revealing incomprehensible dogmas, yet believed for eighteen centuries by the greater part of mankind and defended down through the ages by the greatest men of each era from Origen to Pascal, despite the utmost efforts of an enemy sect that, from Celsus to Condorcet, has never ceased its bellowing? . . .

On Divine Influence in Political Constitutions

Man can modify everything within the sphere of his activity, but he creates nothing: such is his law, in the physical world as in the moral world.

Undoubtedly a man may plant a seed, raise the tree, perfect it by grafting, and trim it a hundred different ways, but he would never imagine that he had the power to make a tree. How can he have imagined that he had the power to make a constitution? Would it be from experience? Let us see what experience teaches us.

All free constitutions known to men have been formed in one of two ways. Sometimes they have *germinated,* as it were, in an unconscious manner through the conjunction of a multitude of so-called fortuitous circumstances, and sometimes they have a single author, who appears like a sport of nature and enforces obedience. In either case, here are the signs by which God warns us of our weakness and of the rights that He has reserved to Himself in the formation of governments:

1. No constitution is the result of deliberation. The rights of the people are never written, or at any rate, constitutive acts or fundamental written laws are never more than declaratory statements of anterior rights about which nothing can be said except that they exist because they exist.

2. God, not having judged it appropriate to use supernatural means in this area, has at least so far circumscribed human action that in the formation of constitutions circumstances do everything and men are only part of the circumstances. Commonly enough, even in pursuing one goal they attain another, as we have seen in the English constitution.

3. The rights of the *people,* properly so called, often enough proceed from the concessions of sovereigns and in this case can be verified historically; but the rights of the monarch and the aristocracy, at least their essential rights, those which we may call constitutive and *basic,* have neither date nor author.

4. Even these concessions of the sovereign have always been preceded by a state of affairs that made them necessary and that did not depend on him.

5. Although written laws are merely declarations of anterior rights, it is far from true that everything can be written down; in fact there are always some things in every constitution that cannot be written and that must be allowed to remain in dark and reverent obscurity on pain of upsetting the state.

6. The more that is written, the weaker the institution becomes, and the reason for this is clear. Laws are only declarations of rights, and rights are declared only when they are attacked, so that a multiplicity of written constitutional laws proves only a multiplicity of conflicts and the danger of destruction.

This is why the most vigorous political system of secular antiquity was that of Sparta, in which nothing was written.

7. No nation can give itself liberty if it is not already free. When a nation begins to reflect on its existence, its laws are already made. Human influence does not extend beyond the development of rights already existing but disregarded or disputed. If imprudent men overstep these limits with reckless reforms, the nation will lose what rights it had without attaining those it hopes for. From this follows the necessity of innovating only rarely and always with moderation and trepidation.

8. When Providence decrees the more rapid formation of a political constitution, there appears a man invested with an indefinable power: he speaks and makes himself obeyed. But these marvellous men belong perhaps only to the world of antiquity and to the youth of nations. Whatever the case, the distinctive characteristic of these legislators par excellence is that they are kings or high nobles; there never has been nor can there ever be any exception to this.

This is why Solon's constitution was the most fragile of antiquity. Athens' days of glory, which were so ephemeral, were soon ended by conquest and tyranny, and Solon himself lived to see the Pisistratids.

9. Even these legislators, notwithstanding their extraordinary power, only combine preexisting elements in the customs and character of a people; and this gathering together, this rapid formation that resembles creation, is accomplished only in the name of the Divinity. The polity and the religion are founded together; the legislator is scarcely distinguishable from the priest, and his public institutions consist principally in *ceremonies and religious holidays.*

10. In one sense, liberty has always been the gift of kings, for all free nations were established by kings. This is the general rule, and the exceptions that may be mentioned would also fall under the rule if they were examined closely.

11. There has never been a free nation that did not have in its natural constitution seeds of liberty as old as itself, nor has any nation, by writing constitutional laws, ever succeeded in developing rights other than those in its natural constitution.

12. No mere assembly of men can form a nation, and the very attempt exceeds in folly the most absurd and extravagant things that all the Bedlams of the world might put forth.

To prove this proposition in detail, after what I said, would, it seems to me, be lacking in respect to the knowledgeable and paying too much honour to the ignorant.

13. I have spoken of one basic characteristic of true legislators. Another very remarkable feature, on which it would be easy to write a book, is that they are never what are called scholars: they do not write, they act on instinct and impulse more than on reasoning, and they have no other means of acting than a certain moral force that bends men's wills like grain before the wind. . . .

The Constitution of 1795, like its predecessors, was made for *man*. But there is no such thing as *man* in the world. In my lifetime I have seen Frenchmen, Italians, Russians, etc.; thanks to Montesquieu, I even know that *one can be Persian*. But as for *man,* I declare that I have never in my life met him; if he exists, he is unknown to me. . . .

What is a constitution? Is it not merely the solution of the following problem? *Given the population, the mores, the religion, the geographic situation, the political circumstances, the wealth, the good and the bad qualities of a particular nation, to find the laws that suit it.*

Now the Constitution of 1795, which treats only of man, does not grapple with this problem at all.

Thus every imaginable reason combines to prove that this work does not possess the divine seal. It is only a *school composition.*

Consequently, already at this moment, how many signs of decay!

51. Constant, *Ancient and Modern Liberty Compared*

Swiss by birth, Henri Benjamin Constant de Rebecque (1767–1830) was one of the most influential writers and political figures in France during

From Benjamin Constant, *De l'esprit de conquête et de l'usurpation dans leurs rapports avec la civilisation européenne* (1814), chaps. 6–8, in *De la liberté chez les modernes: écrits politiques,* edited by Marcel Gauchet (Paris: Librairie Générale Française, le Livre de Poche, 1980), pp. 182–95. Translated for this volume by Kent Wright and Keith Michael Baker.

the immediate postrevolutionary period. His education and early political views were shaped by travel to Belgium, England, Germany, and
Scotland. After serving in the court of the Duke of Brunswick for some
years, he moved to Paris in 1795, drawn there by his attraction to Mme
de Staël, daughter of the former French minister Necker, and an important writer and thinker in her own right. Constant's most fundamental
ideas took shape during the next ten years, which he spent in intimate
association with Mme de Staël. Moderate republicans under the Directory, both soon showed their opposition to Napoleon, who expelled Constant from the Tribunate in 1802, and forced Mme de Staël into exile in
1803.

Constant devoted the next few years to a treatise on politics in which
French liberalism took form as a reflection upon the purposes of government in modern society, the experience of the French Revolution, and the
nature of Napoleonic dictatorship. Though this manuscript was never
published in its entirety, Constant mined it for the arguments of his many
subsequent writings, including the work on *The Spirit of Conquest and
Usurpation* (1814) from which the following selection is taken. During
the Restoration, Constant became one of the most active advocates of
liberal constitutional principles in French politics.

On the Kind of Liberty Offered to Men at
the End of the Last Century

The liberty offered to men at the end of the last century was modeled on
that of the ancient republics. Now many of the circumstances . . . causing
the warlike disposition of the ancients also fostered their capacity for a
kind of liberty no longer possible for us.

This liberty consisted more in active participation in the collective exercise of power than in peaceful enjoyment of individual independence. Indeed, to assure such participation, it was even necessary for the citizens to
sacrifice the better part of this independence. But this sacrifice is absurd
to demand, and impossible to obtain, in the epoch humanity has now
reached.

The small size of the ancient republics ensured that each citizen enjoyed
a great personal importance in politics. Exercise of the rights of citizenship
constituted the occupation, even the amusement, of all. The whole people
participated in the making of laws, pronounced judgments, and decided on
war and peace. The individual's participation in the national sovereignty
was not, as it is now, an abstract supposition; the will of each citizen had a
real influence; the exercise of that will was a vivid and repeated pleasure.

As a result, the ancients were willing to sacrifice their private independence to preserve their political importance and their share in the administration of the state.

This sacrifice was necessary. In order that a people enjoy political rights to the fullest extent—in order that each citizen possess his share in the sovereignty—it is necessary to have institutions that maintain equality, prevent the growth of fortunes, prohibit distinctions, oppose the influence of wealth, talent and even virtue. And these institutions limit individual liberty and compromise individual security.

Thus what we call civil liberty was unknown among most ancient peoples. All the Greek republics, if we except Athens, subjected the individual to an almost unlimited social jurisdiction. The beautiful centuries of Rome were characterized by the same subjection. The citizen made himself a kind of slave of the nation to which he belonged; he abandoned himself wholly to the decisions of the sovereign, of the legislator; he recognized the right of the latter to watch over all his actions and to constrain his will. But he himself was, in turn, this legislator and this sovereign; he felt with pride all the value of his vote in a nation so small that each citizen was a power; and the knowledge of his own worth was for him an ample recompense.

Modern states are completely different: their size, far greater than that of the ancient republics, ensures that the mass of the inhabitants, whatever form of government they adopt, have no active role in government. At the most, they participate in the exercise of sovereignty only through representation, that is, in a fictive manner.

The advantage that liberty, as the ancients conceived it, brought to the people was to be counted among the number of those who governed: a real advantage, a pleasure both flattering and real. The advantage which modern liberty procures for the people is to be represented, and to participate in this representation through its choice. It is doubtless an advantage, since it is a guarantee; but the immediate pleasure is less vivid: it includes none of the satisfactions of power; it is a pleasure of reflection, while that of the ancients was a pleasure of action. Clearly the former is less attractive; one could hardly demand of men as many sacrifices to obtain and preserve it.

At the same time, these sacrifices would be much more painful. The progress of civilization, the commercial tendencies of the age, the communication between peoples, have infinitely multiplied and diversified the means of private happiness. In order to be happy, men need only to be left in complete independence in regard to everything relating to their occupations, their undertakings, their sphere of activity, their fantasies.

The ancients found more satisfaction in their public existence, and less in their private existence; consequently, when they sacrificed individual liberty for political liberty, they sacrificed less to obtain more. Almost all the satisfaction of modern peoples occurs in their private existence: the immense majority, ever excluded from power, necessarily shows but a fleeting interest in its public existence. By imitating the ancients, the moderns would thus sacrifice more to obtain less.

Social links are now more complicated, more extended than before; even classes which appear to be enemies are linked to one another by imperceptible yet indissoluble bonds. Property is more closely identified with human existence: any disruption it undergoes is more distressing.

We have lost in imagination what we have gained in knowledge; we are thus incapable of a lasting enthusiasm. The ancients lived in the youth of moral life; we are in its maturity, perhaps its old age; we always drag with us some sort of inhibition, born of experience, which defeats enthusiasm. The first condition of enthusiasm is not to observe oneself too closely. We are so fearful of being duped, and above all of appearing to be, that we watch ourselves constantly, even in our most violent experiences. The ancients had an absolute conviction about everything; there is scarcely nothing about which we have more than a feeble and irresolute conviction, the inadequacy of which we try vainly to ignore.

The word illusion is found in no ancient language, for the word was created only when the thing no longer existed.

Legislators must abandon any attempt to overturn customary habits, or to act forcefully against opinion. No more Lycurguses, no more Numas.

It would be easier today to turn an enslaved people into Spartans than to create Spartans through liberty. Formerly, wherever there was liberty, people could bear privation; now, wherever there is privation, there must be slavery for people to resign themselves to it.

In modern times, the people most attached to its liberty is also the people most attached to what it enjoys; it prizes its liberty above all else, because it is wise enough to see that it is the guarantee of its enjoyments.

On the Modern Imitators of the Ancient Republics

These truths were completely disregarded by the men who, at the end of the last century, believed themselves to be charged with the regeneration of the human race. I do not want to blame their intentions: their movement was noble, their goal generous. Which of us did not feel his heart beat with hope at the beginning of the course they seemed to open up? Woe to the person, even now, who does not feel the need to declare that to recognize these errors is not to abandon the principles that the friends of humanity have professed down through the ages. But these men took as their guides writers who never suspected that two thousand years might have wrought some changes in the dispositions and needs of people.

Perhaps in time I will examine the theory of the most famous of these writers, and I will demonstrate what is false and inapplicable in it. It will be seen, I think, that the subtle metaphysics of the *Social Contract* are, in our time, suitable only for furnishing weapons and pretexts for every kind of tyranny (whether it be that of one, many, or all), for oppression legally established, or exercised by the rule of the mob.*

Another philosopher, less eloquent than Rousseau but no less austere in his principles and even more exaggerated in their execution, had an almost equal influence on the reformers of France: the abbé de Mably. He can be regarded as the representative of that numerous class of demagogues, well- or ill-intentioned, who, from the height of the tribune, in the clubs and in the pamphlets, spoke of the sovereign nation so that the citizens were more completely subjected, and of the free people so that the individual was more completely enslaved.

The abbé de Mably,† like Rousseau and so many others, mistook au-

---

*I am far from counting myself among the detractors of Rousseau, who are very numerous at present. A crowd of minor writers, whose fleeting success consists of casting doubt on courageous truths, compete to tarnish his glory; all the more reason to be circumspect in blaming him. He was the first to popularize the sentiment of our rights: generous hearts and independent spirits awoke at his voice; but he was incapable of defining with precision what he felt so forcefully. Many chapters of the *Social Contract* are worthy of the scholastic writers of the fifteenth century. What is meant by rights which one enjoys all the more because one alienates them more completely? What sort of liberty is it, by virtue of which one is the more free because each individual does more completely that which is contrary to his own will? The supporters of despotism can take great comfort from the principles of Rousseau. I know one who, believing with Rousseau that unlimited authority resides in the whole society, supposed it transferred to the representative of that society, to a man whom he defined as the personification of its being, the individualization of its union. Just as Rousseau had said that the social body could harm neither the totality of its members, nor any one of them in particular, this man says that the possessor of power, the man constituting society cannot harm society because he would faithfully experience any harm he might do, inasmuch as he was society itself. Just as Rousseau says that the individual cannot resist society, because he has alienated all of his rights to it without reservation, this man claims that the authority of the possessor of power is absolute, because no member of society can resist the whole union; that the possessor of power cannot be held responsible, because no individual can demand a reckoning of the being of which he forms part, since the latter can answer him only by making him return to the order he never should have left. So that we should fear nothing from tyranny, he adds: "Now this is why his authority (that of the possessor of power) was not arbitrary: he was no longer a man, he was a people." What a marvelous guarantee is this change of wording! Is it not strange that this whole class of writers reproach Rousseau for losing himself in abstractions? When they speak to us of society individualized, of the sovereign who is no longer a man but a people, are they thereby avoiding abstractions? [Author's note.]

†Mably's work, *Of Legislation or the Principles of Law* is the most complete code of despotism imaginable. Combine these three principles: (1) legislative authority is unlimited: it must extend to everything, and everything must bend before it; (2) individual freedom is a bane: if you cannot destroy it, then restrain it as far as possible; (3) property is an evil: if you cannot abolish it, weaken its influence by all means. You will have, by this combination, the constitutions of Constantinople and Robespierre combined. [Author's note.]

thority for liberty and approved of any means of extending the action of authority over that recalcitrant part of human existence whose independence he deplored. Throughout his works he expresses regret that the law deals only with actions: he would have liked to extend it to thought, to the most fleeting impressions, so that it hunted man without respite, leaving him no sanctuary in which he could escape from its power. Hardly had he found a harsh measure among any people than he thought he had made a discovery and proposed it as a model; he hated individual liberty as a personal enemy; and whenever he found a nation that had been deprived of it (even if it had no political liberty) he could not help but admire it. He became ecstatic over the Egyptians, because, he said, everything among them was prescribed by law: from their diversions to their needs, everything yielded to the empire of the legislator; every moment of the day was taken up by some duty; even love was subject to these hallowed interventions; and the law, by turns, opened and closed the marriage bed.

Sparta, which combined republican forms with the same enslavement of the individual, aroused an even livelier enthusiasm in the mind of this philosopher. To him, this monastery for warriors seemed to be the ideal of a free republic; he had a profound contempt for Athens, and he would willingly have said of this first nation of Greece what a great lord and academician said of the Academy: *What appalling despotism! Everyone there does just as he wishes*.

When the tide of events had brought to the head of the state, during the French Revolution, men who had adopted philosophy as a prejudice and democracy as a fanaticism, these men were seized by a limitless admiration for Rousseau, Mably, and all the writers of the same school.

The subtleties of the first, the austerity of the second, his intolerance, his hatred of all human passions and his eagerness to subjugate them, his exaggerated principles of the competence of the law, the difference between what he recommended and what existed, his denunciations of wealth and even of property, all these things must have charmed men who were inflamed by a recent victory, and who, as conquerors of a power that was called the law, were more than pleased to extend this power over all matters. They found a precious authority in writers disinterested in the question and condemning the monarchy, who long before the overthrow of the throne had drawn up axiomatically all the maxims necessary to organize the most absolute despotism under the name of a republic.

Our reformers thus wanted to exercise the public force as their guides had taught them it had been exercised in the free states of antiquity; they believed that everything should yield again before the collective authority, and that all restrictions on individual rights would be compensated by participation in the social power. They tried to subject the French to a multitude of despotic laws, which grievously wounded them in all that was most precious to them; they proposed, to a people grown old in its enjoyments, the sacrifice of all that it enjoyed; they made into a duty what ought to have been voluntary; they even surrounded celebrations of liberty with constraint. They were astonished to find that the memory of many centuries did not immediately disappear before the decrees of a day. The law, being the expression of the general will, had in their eyes to overcome every other power, even that of memory and time. The slow and gradual effect of childhood experiences, the direction the imagination had received from a long succession of years, seemed to them to be acts of revolt. To habits they gave the name of ill-will. One would have thought that this ill will was a magic power which, by some kind of miracle, constantly forced the people to do the opposite of what they really willed. They attributed the misfortunes of the conflict to the fact that there was opposition, as if authority was always permitted to make changes that provoked such opposition, as if the difficulties that the changes encountered were not themselves the verdict upon their authors.

However, all these efforts constantly collapsed under the weight of their own extravagance. The smallest saint, in the most obscure hamlet, successfully resisted the whole national authority ranged in battle against him. The social power injured individual independence in every way, without destroying the need for it; the nation did not find an ideal part in an abstract sovereignty worth all that it was suffering. In vain were repeated to it the words of Rousseau: "The laws of liberty are a thousand times more austere than the yoke of tyrants is harsh." The result was that the nation did not want these austere laws; and since it knew of the yoke of tyrants only by hearsay, it believed that it preferred the yoke of tyrants.

On the Means Used to Give the Liberty of the Ancients to the Moderns

The errors of men who exercise power, by whatever title, can hardly be as innocent as those of individuals. Force is always behind these errors, ready to devote its terrible resources to them.

The partisans of ancient liberty became furious over the fact that the moderns did not want to be free according to their method. They redoubled their harassments, the people redoubled its resistance, and crimes succeeded errors.

"To have a tyranny," says Machiavelli, "it is necessary to change everything." It can also be said that to change everything, it is necessary to have a tyranny. Our legislators understood this, and they proclaimed that despotism was indispensable for the establishment of liberty.

There are axioms which seem clear because they are short. Clever men throw them to the crowd like fodder; fools take them up, because they save them the trouble of reflection, and they repeat them in order to give themselves an air of understanding them. Propositions whose absurdity astonishes us are thus lodged in a thousand heads and repeated by a thousand mouths, and one is continually reduced to demonstrating the obvious.

The axiom we just cited is of this number; for ten years it resounded from French tribunes: but what does it mean? Liberty is invaluable only because it brings soundness to our minds, strength to our characters, and elevation to our souls. But do not these benefits require that liberty exist? If, to introduce it, you have recourse to despotism, what do you establish?—empty forms. The substance will always escape you.

What needs to be said to a nation in order to imbue it with the advantages of liberty? You were oppressed by a privileged minority; the majority were sacrificed to the ambition of a few; unequal laws upheld the strong against the weak; all that you enjoyed was precarious, and arbitrariness threatened to take it from you at every moment; you contributed nothing to the making of laws, nor to the election of your magistrates; all these abuses will disappear, all your rights will be restored to you.

But those who claim to establish liberty by despotism, what can they say? No privilege will weigh on the citizens, but every day accused men will be struck down without being heard; virtue will be the first or the only distinction, but the greatest persecutors and most violent men will form a patriciate of tyranny, maintained by terror; the laws will protect property, but expropriation will be the lot of suspected individuals or classes; the people will elect its magistrates, but if it does not elect them in the manner prescribed in advance, its choices will be declared null; opinions will be free, but any opinion contradicting not only the general system but the slightest temporary measure will be punished as treason.

Such was the language, such was the practice, of the reformers of France for many years.

They won apparent victories, but these victories were contrary to the spirit of the institutions they wished to establish; and, since they did not persuade the defeated, they did not reassure the victorious. To form men for liberty, they surrounded them with the spectacle of torture. They brought back in yet more exaggerated form the attacks against thinking that the authority they destroyed had permitted itself, and the enslavement of thought became the distinctive mark of the new authority. They railed against tyrannical governments, and then organized the most tyrannical of all.

They postponed liberty, they said, until factions had subsided, but factions subside only when liberty is no longer postponed. Violent measures, adopted as a dictatorship in anticipation of the birth of public spirit, prevent it from being born. A vicious circle takes hold; the age envisaged is certainly beyond attainment, because the methods chosen to attain it prevent its appearance. Force renders force ever more necessary; anger is fed by anger; laws are forged like weapons; codes become declarations of war; and the blind friends of liberty, who have believed it possible to impose it through despotism, arouse all free souls against them and find support only among the vilest flatterers of power.

In the first rank of the enemies that our demagogues had to combat were the classes that had profited from the social organization which had been destroyed, those whose privileges, improper though they may have been, had nevertheless served as means of leisure, improvement and knowledge. A great independence of fortune is a guarantee against many kinds of baseness and vice. The certainty of seeing oneself respected is a preventive against that restless and stormy vanity which everywhere perceives insult or supposes scorn—an implacable passion, which avenges itself for the pain it experiences by the evil it does. The usage of pleasing forms and the habit of ingenious distinctions gives a delicate susceptibility to the soul, a quick flexibility to the mind.

These precious qualities should have been put to good use; the chivalric spirit should have been hedged in by barriers that it could not overleap, but left a noble momentum in the course that nature makes common to all. The Greeks spared captives who could recite verses of Euripides. The least knowledge, the least germ of thought, the least gentle sentiment, the least elegant form, ought to be carefully protected—they are so many elements indispensable to social happiness. It is necessary to save them from the storm, necessary both in the interests of justice and of liberty, for all these things lead to liberty by more or less direct routes.

Our fanatical reformers confused epochs in order to rekindle and foster hatreds. Just as some went back to the Franks and the Goths to sanction oppressive distinctions, they did so to find pretexts for oppression in an opposite sense. Vanity had sought its claims to honor in the archives and the chronicles; a more bitter and vindictive vanity drew out acts of accusation. The accusers wished neither to take the times into account, nor to make subtle distinctions, nor to reassure apprehensions, nor to pardon fleeting pretensions, nor to let vain protests die out, or puerile threats evaporate. . . . To the distinctions they wished to abolish they added a new one, persecution; and by carrying out that abolition with unjust severity they sustained the hope that these distinctions would reappear with justice itself.

In all the violent struggles, interests followed in the steps of exalted opinions, just as birds of prey follow armies ready to do battle. Hatred, vengeance, greed, ingratitude shamelessly parodied the noblest examples, because their imitation had been ineptly encouraged. The treacherous friend, the faithless debtor, the obscure informer, the corrupt judge, found their defense written in advance in the accepted language. Patriotism became the trite excuse for all wrongdoing. Great sacrifices, acts of devotion, victories won over natural inclinations by the austere republicanism of antiquity, served as pretexts for the unbridled fury of egotistical passions. Because unyielding but just fathers had formerly condemned their unworthy sons, their modern imitators delivered their innocent enemies to the executioner. The most obscure life, the quietest existence, the most unknown name, offered no protection. Inactivity appeared a crime, domestic affections a neglect of the *patrie,* happiness a suspect desire. The mob, corrupted both by danger and by example, repeated with trembling the slogan that was commanded, and terrified itself with the sound of its own voice. Each individual added to the number, and took fright at the number he had helped increase. Thus there spread over France that inexplicable delirium that we call the Reign of Terror. Who can be surprised that the people turned away from a goal toward which they were being led by a route such as this?

Not only do extremes meet, but they succeed one another. One exaggeration always produces the contrary exaggeration. Once certain ideas become associated with certain words, even when it has been demonstrated that this association is improper, their repetition long continues to recall the same ideas. In the name of liberty we have been given prisons, scaffolds, innumerable harassments; this name, the signal for a thousand odious and tyrannical measures, had to awaken hatred and fear.

But is it right to conclude that the moderns are disposed to resign themselves to despotism? What was the cause of their obstinate resistance to what was offered to them as liberty? It was their firm determination to sacrifice neither their peace, nor their habits, nor the satisfactions that they enjoyed. Now, if despotism is the most irreconcilable enemy of all peace and enjoyment, does it not follow that in believing that they loathe liberty, the moderns merely loathed despotism?

Index

Alembert, Jean Le Rond d', 4, 71
Aristotle, 21, 77
Artois, Charles-Philippe, comte de, 194, 197–98

Babeuf, François Noël (Gracchus), 12, 393–94, 403
Bailly, Jean Sylvain, 197, 273
Barère de Vieuzac, Bertrand, 351, 447
Barnave, Antoine Pierre Joseph Marie, 201
Barras, Paul François Jean Nicolas, 407
Barré, Marie-Rose, 236
Beauharnais, Eugene, 409, 417
Bernadotte, Jean Baptiste Jules, 421
Billaud-Varenne, Jacques Nicolas, 347, 349
Biron, Louis Antoine de Gontaut, duc de, 336
Bonald, Louis Gabriel Ambroise de, 2
Bonaparte, Joseph, 421
Bonaparte, Louis, 422
Bonaparte, Napoleon. *See* Napoleon I
Bossuet, Jacques Bénigne, 3, 31–32
Bouillé, François Claude Amour, marquis de, 269
Brienne, Loménie de. *See* Loménie de Brienne
Brissot, Jacques Pierre, 242, 324, 328, 339, 350–51
Brunswick, Karl Wilhelm Ferdinand, Duke, 291, 297, 453
Brutus, Marcus Junius, 306, 373
Buonarroti, Filippo Michele, 394
Burke, Edmund, 2, 428, 445

Caesar, Gaius Julius, 28, 317, 369, 376, 379

Calonne, Charles Alexandre de, 5, 124–26
Camus, Armand Gaston, 192
Capet, Hugh, 136–37
Catiline, 207, 307, 321, 323, 376
Cazalès, Jacques Antoine Marie de, 321
Chambers, Ephraim, 71
Chapelier, Isaac René Guy Le. *See* Le Chapelier, Isaac René Guy
Charlemagne, 70, 246, 426
Chaumette, Pierre Gaspard, 343, 346
Chilperic I, King, 37
Choderlos de Laclos, Pierre Ambroise François, 276
Clarke, Henri Jacques Guillaume, 404
Clodius, Publius, 317, 376
Collot d'Herbois, Jean Marie, 447
Comte, Auguste, 2
Condé, Louis Joseph de Boubon, prince de, 132
Condorcet, Marie Jean Antoine Nicolas de Caritat, marquis de, 2, 10, 242
Consalvi, Ercole, 426
Constant de Rebecque, Henri Benjamin, 2, 452–53
Cromwell, Oliver, 304, 369
Custine, Adam Philippe, comte de, 336

Danton, Georges Jacques, 298, 324, 347, 349, 368
David, King, 33–36, 39–40, 43
David, Jacques Louis, 384
Diderot, Denis, 4, 71
Ducos, Pierre Roger, 405, 409
Dumouriez, Charles François du Perier, 324, 336, 447
Dupont de Nemours, Pierre Samuel, 97

Eglantine, Philippe François Fabre d'. *See* Fabre
Eprémesnil, Jean Jacuqes Duval d', 148
Essars, Jean Louis Viefville des. *See* Viefville des Essars

Fabre (d'Eglantine), Philippe François, 362, 368
Fesch, Joseph, 425
Fleury, Joly de. *See* Joly de Fleury

Gensonné, Armand, 339, 350
Glain, Madelaine, 232
Gouges, Marie Olympe de, 7, 262

Hampden, John, 317
Hébert, Jacques René, 24, 368
Hegel, Georg Wilhelm Friedrich, 2
Henry IV, 133, 153

Joly de Fleury, Omer, 48

Laclos, Pierre Ambroise François Choderlos de, 276
Lafayette, Marie Joseph Paul Yves Roch Gilbert du Motier, marquis de, 197, 235, 242, 273, 328, 339
Launay, Bernard René Jourdan, marquis de, 196
Launey, marquis de. *See* Launay
Le Chapelier, Isaac René Guy, 201, 247–48, 278, 282–83
Le Pelletier de Saint-Fargeau, Louis Michel, 339
Lolme, Jean Louis de, 199
Loménie de Brienne, Etienne Charles de, 5, 125, 135, 143–46
Louis XI, 137, 159
Louis XIII, 133
Louis XIV, 31, 77, 159
Louis XV, 3, 47, 51
Louis XVI, 4–5, 7–10, 51, 90, 97, 145, 180, 231–32, 235, 249, 269, 272–77, 286, 294, 303, 305, 307–16, 318, 320, 322, 324
Louis Capet. *See* Louis XVI
Loyseau, Charles, 3, 13
Lycurgus, 373, 455

Mably, Gabriel Bonnot abbé de, 456–57
Machiavelli, Niccolo, 369, 458

Maillard, Stanislas Marie, 233–34
Maistre, Joseph Marie de, comte, 445
Malesherbes, Chrétien Guillaume de Lamoignon de, 51
Marat, Jean Paul, 324, 339–40
Marie Antoinette, Queen, 235, 339, 351
Martin, Jeanne, 233
Marx, Karl, 2
Maupeou, René Nicolas Charles Augustin de, 51
Maury, Jean Siffrein, 321
Mirabeau, Honoré Gabriel Victor Riqueti, comte de, 192, 206–8
Mirabeau, André Boniface Louis Riqueti, vicomte de, 234
Mounier, Jean Joseph, 201

Napoleon I, 12, 154, 404–5, 409, 416–17, 421–22, 424, 427, 453
Necker, Jacques, 5, 126, 145–51, 180, 186–87, 189, 192–93, 195, 197, 208–9, 217, 220, 453
Nemours, Pierre Samuel Dupont de. *See* Dupont de Nemours

Orléans, Louis Philippe Joseph duc d', 135, 147, 151, 191–92, 194, 197, 234, 276

Pasquier, Étienne, 28
Paul, Saint, 32–33, 37
Pelletier. *See* Le Pelletier
Pèthion. *See* Pètion de Villeneuve
Pètion de Villeneuve, Jérôme, 298–99
Philip IV (the Fair), 143, 164
Philip VI (of Valois), 137
Pius VI, Pope, 240, 424
Pius VII, Pope, 424–26
Provence, Louis Stanislas Xavier, comte de, 151

Rebecque, Henri Benjamin Constant de. *See* Constant de Rebecque
Reynier, Jean Louis Ebenezer, comte, 421
Richelieu, Armand Jean du Plesis, duc de, 159
Robespierre, Maximilien François Isidore de, 10–11, 282–83, 320, 343, 354, 368, 384, 386–87, 392, 394, 447
Roger-Ducos. *See* Ducos
Roland de La Platière, Jean Marie, 9, 290

Roland de La Platière, Marie Jeanne
  "Manon" Phlipon, 273
Romme, Charles Gilbert, 362
Rousseau, Jean Jacques, 179, 199, 403,
  456–58

Saint-Florentin, Louis Phelypeaux, comte
  de, 48
Saint-Just, Louis Antoine Léon de, 10–11,
  304, 354
Saint-Priest, François Emmanuel Guignard,
  comte de, 236–37
Sallier, Guy-Marie, 5–6, 145, 149, 151
Saul, King, 33, 39
Séguin (priest), 213
Sidney, Algernon, 317

Sieyès, Emmanuel Joseph, abbé, 6, 154,
  166–67, 170, 179, 200, 207, 405, 409
Socrates, 21, 317
Staël-Holstein, Anne Louise Germaine
  Necker, baronne de, 453
Staël, Mme de. See Staël-Holstein

Target, Guy Jean Baptiste, 201
Tocqueville, Alexis de, 2
Turgot, Anne Robert Jacques, baron de
  l'Aulne, 51, 89–90, 97, 118–19

Vergniaud, Pierre Victurnien, 10, 339, 350
Viefville des Essars, Jean Louis, 7, 243

Wimpffen, Louis Philippe, baron de, 336

DATE DUE